THE LAW
OF THE
MANOR

SECOND EDITION

THE LAW
OF THE
MANOR

SECOND EDITION

CHRISTOPHER JESSEL

Wildy, Simmonds & Hill Publishing

The Law of the Manor

British Library Cataloguing in Publication Data
A catalogue record for this book is available from the British Library

ISBN 978-0854901104

Typeset in Times New Roman and Optima LT Std by Cornubia Press Ltd
Printed and bound in the United Kingdom by Antony Rowe Ltd, Chippenham,
Wiltshire

First published in 2012 by
Wildy, Simmonds & Hill Publishing
58 Carey Street
London WC2A 2JF
England

Contents

PART II
LANDS

Preface to the Second Edition

Since the first edition was published in 1998 there have been major changes in the topics covered in this book. The most important is the Land Registration Act 2002. That will lead to the loss of manorial rights, particularly to minerals in former copyhold land and to some franchises, unless action is taken before that land is subject to first registration or to a disposition after 13 October 2013. I have therefore included a new section on the meaning of manorial rights, as well as extending the discussion of the various sorts of right a lord of the manor may have to minerals and sporting. Indeed, the Act not only prevents the registration of title to unregistered manors but also affects nearly all aspects of the manor from franchises to chancel repairs, and references to it will be found in most chapters.

Second to that are the Countryside and Rights of Way Act 2000 and the Commons Act 2006. Those Acts have between them revolutionised the law relating to common land. The law of town and village greens continues to develop and I have expanded the treatment of this as it affects the manor. With the spread of compulsory registration the issue of unclaimed common land will become more important than in the past.

There are many changes of detail. The House of Lords Act 1999 has excluded most hereditary peers from Parliament, and when this book was in preparation further changes were announced. The Hunting Act 2004 has affected sporting rights. The Legal Services Act 2007 has modified the rules about the conveyancing of manors. There have been changes in the way manors and the benefits from them are taxed. Even manors are not exempt from the need to take account of European law and of human rights.

I have also taken the opportunity of revising the treatment of several topics, in particular the early history and development of manors in the light of recent historical research. I have included a new section on rectorial manors which my experience since the first edition shows to be more widespread than I had then appreciated. I have enlarged the discussion of ownership of roadside verges, partly because of widespread misconceptions about the extent to which they can be manorial waste. I have also extended the discussion of escheat partly because this has come to be of growing importance in recent years now that trustees in bankruptcy and liquidators of companies no longer need the consent of the court to disclaim freeholds and partly because the issue has been raised by the Law Commission in its Report on Land Registration. The Report also indicated the need for reform of the law and I have therefore included some remarks on that in the final chapter.

I am grateful to North American correspondents for letting me know about the extension of manorial law across the Atlantic, especially in Maryland and Pennsylvania. This book is primarily about English law, but I have felt it right to include a brief reference to that topic. As much land in America was granted by the Crown to be held of the Manor of East Greenwich, as also was land in England sold by the Crown from the sixteenth century onwards, I have included some remarks on that manor and on the law of purprestures which is now invoked more in jurisdictions in the United States than in England.

The first edition was written as a general guide, on the basis that legal advisers would wish to pursue specific matters in more specialist textbooks. For this edition, while I have sought to keep the text accessible to those unfamiliar with the subject, I have included more detail on several topics and I have also referred to many more early decisions of the courts. I have also numbered the sections to make cross-reference clearer. Covering the law of the manor in the space available still means that the discussion can only be general. Practitioners will, I hope, find this book helpful as an introduction but they will need to follow up many details further elsewhere. I hope the book will remain of interest to those with no formal legal training who are interested in manors.

CRJ
August 2012

Introduction

This book aims to give an outline of so much of the law relating to manors and to related matters as still exists. That law has ancient roots and has developed over the centuries and now survives in fragments but it can still be important and can support valuable rights of property or give rise to disputes. It is necessary, as so often when describing legal ideas, to distinguish the meaning lawyers give to particular words from the way they are commonly used. In ordinary, as distinct from legal, usage the word 'manor' may refer to a large old house, rambling because bits of it have been built in different centuries in different styles, and been altered a good deal over those centuries. Parts of it are falling down, much has been demolished, and what remains is not in good repair, but it has its own homely attraction, and, like the stone of which it is built, it blends into the landscape of which it has formed part for hundreds of years. This book is not about houses, but about a legal idea, something that cannot be seen or touched, but which has been important, and is still significant. Even so, a house is not a bad image to have in mind, for two reasons.

First, the word 'manor' comes from the Latin *manerium*, which itself comes from *manere*, meaning 'to remain'.[1] *Manere* also led to *mansio*, which gave 'mansion'. The word 'manor' was introduced into England with the Norman Conquest of 1066. The manor was a house in Normandy. A system of estates called land had been developing among the Anglo-Saxons before the Conquest. The nearest equivalent Saxon word to *manerium* was *heal*, which was usually translated into Latin as *aula* and a mixture of *heal* and *aula* has given the modern word 'hall'. Manor houses are often called halls and the entrance hall to a modern house can be traced back to the great mediaeval halls that were the focal points of manors, where a resident lord would live, and where manorial courts were held. The Normans used *manerium* as their equivalent of *villa*, which was the usual word in the Roman Empire for a large country house. So, manor, mansion, hall and villa all originally meant much the same – a great

---

[1] FW Maitland, *Domesday Book and Beyond* (Cambridge University Press, 1987; first published 1897) 108; John Scriven, *A Treatise on the Law of Copyholds* (Butterworth & Co, 7th edn, 1896, by Archibald Brown) 1; Sir Edward Coke, *Complete Copyholder* (1630), s 31. Coke's derivation from '*mesner*' is not now accepted.

house dominating the local countryside – and then manor came to mean the legal institution by which the countryside was dominated.

The second reason is that the present state of the English law of the manor is reminiscent of a typical old manor house. The legal ideas were introduced at different times, fitted together in odd ways and many of them are worn out and obsolete. A great deal of the old law of the manor has been demolished (by Parliament) and what remains does not seem well suited to modern times. Too often it appears to be something to marvel at as a strange survival. But that is not the whole story because manorial law still involves important rights and duties.

The law of the manor brings together a variety of apparently unconnected fragments. Recent court cases have concerned the right to hold a market,[2] to charge house owners for driving cars across a roadside verge[3] or common land,[4] to fence and plough up areas of old rough grazing,[5] the ownership of a town centre market square[6] and whether a lord marcher in Wales owns a stretch of seabed.[7] Lawyers practicing manorial law have to advise on mineral rights, sporting and hunting, the ownership of old title deeds and the appointment of the vicar to a parish. These matters seem disparate but they have an old and intricate connection. They are like a collection of potsherds, stone and metal from which an archaeologist can reconstruct an ancient culture. There are, however, three important differences from the work of an archaeologist. First the rules of the manor are intangible and found in the mind. They can leave material traces, such as the shapes of fields, or the sites of houses, but they themselves are immaterial. Secondly, an archaeological find is a thing made at one time, while the legal ideas that comprise the manor developed over many centuries. Thirdly, there are guides, in the form of legal treatises written over the centuries, that tell us something (though never everything) about how the rules worked and what they were intended to achieve.

The purpose of this book is to describe the remaining fragments which comprise the law of the manor as it is now, not to reconstruct the history of an institution. It is a legal textbook, not primarily a book about history. Manorial law is very much part of modern law. However, in order to make sense of the modern law it

---

[2]   *Spook Erection Ltd v Secretary of State for the Environment and Cotswold District Council* [1988] 2 All ER 667.

[3]   *Crown Estate Commissioners v Dorset County Council* [1990] 1 Ch 297.

[4]   *Bakewell Management Limited v Brandwood* [2004] 2 AC 519.

[5]   *Hampshire County Council v Milburn* [1990] 2 WLR 1240.

[6]   *Gloucestershire County Council v Farrow* [1985] 1 WLR 741.

[7]   *Crown Estate Commissioners v Roberts* [2008] EWHC 1302 (Ch), [2008] All ER (D) 175 (Jun).

is necessary to have some understanding of how it has come to be. So there is in this book a good deal of what appears to be history.

It is only an appearance. The decisions of the courts in modern times have largely (but not entirely) been made by applying to the cases before them rules derived from decisions of judges in cases in earlier centuries and they in turn reached their decisions by applying the rules set out in the judgments of their own predecessors. Each generation understands its history differently, and before the nineteenth century our contemporary idea of history hardly existed, at least among lawyers. As a result, the modern law is based on what present day judges understand of how nineteenth- and eighteenth-century judges and textbook writers reached their views. Those in turn were based on seventeenth- and sixteenth-century cases and so on. If at any stage a new understanding of an old institution was introduced – and this happened from time to time, particularly around 1600 – that new view would be reflected, amplified and reinterpreted in later centuries. So when a modern lawyer speaks of custom as something which existed before 1189, or advises on mineral rights of the lord as preserved in 1926, what is being discussed is not what a person who lived eight centuries or even one century ago would have understood. There is a connection, but it is not the same.

The most important example of this is the nature of the manor itself. In modern times it is an incorporeal thing, but as recently as the eighteenth century it was thought to be tangible and physical or corporeal and this is clearer still in the middle ages. To a modern lawyer a manor is a set of concepts, removed from anything that can be experienced or depicted, but it has not always been so understood. The manor as an institution has a mixture of origins – economic, technical, social, military, even religious. In its day it was what might be called the dominant economic form. What the company was to the twentieth century and the trust was to the nineteenth, the manor was to the twelfth, the natural way of organising farms or a harbour or a mine.

The manor survived long after it had ceased to be an effective institution just because it was made up of a cluster of interrelated interests. No one sat down and devised it out of nothing. It developed from circumstances and mutual interests. It survived for the same reason. Any change, however much to the advantage of one person, would mean someone else would lose out. The loser would fight harder to keep what he had than the potential gainer would to get something which might not be worth having when he achieved it. In England the system was eroded over the centuries, but even here the structure of the manor was not dismantled until the Law of Property Act 1922 – passed in the reforming period after the First World War – came into force on 1 January 1926. In France it took a revolution in 1789 to destroy it. In Russia it survived until

1917, in Germany until 1918, and so in much of Europe. As this book shows, much still remains in England.

The main feature of the manor, the one that gave it such toughness, was the system of dual cultivation. In centuries when nearly everyone lived in villages, the right to take crops from land was divided between, on the one hand, a small class of lords – the king, the Church, aristocracy and knights – and, on the other, a large number of small farmers – bondsmen and freeholders. The land around most villages might belong to the lord or to the farmers but the smallholders, in addition to farming their own land, also cultivated the lands of the lord, and in return had privileges of grazing, taking wood and so on from common land. The lord had rights to minerals, timber and game in the smallholders' lands. There was also a class of officials – stewards, bailiffs, reeves and others – who mediated between the two, and a series of institutions usually known as courts (of which there was a great variety) which established the rules. It was this set of rights, institutions and offices and the mixture of different landholdings, the complex of vested rights, which gave the manor its stability.

There is no simple logical way to explain the manor, starting with basic ideas and developing from them, nor is there any clear outline that can be seen at a glance. The manor is not like a classical villa or a modern factory, but more like a mediaeval castle or cathedral, with towers and spires, passages and courts, buttresses and interlacing arches. Any one idea will depend on another, which depends on another, which depends on the first. For example, if anything is the most fundamental concept in the manor, it is custom. Custom was declared, preserved and interpreted in the manorial courts. The courts were composed of the landholders – freeholders in the court baron and copyholders in the customary court. These landholders held their land in return for services and payments. The terms of the services and the amounts of the payments were regulated by custom. Where does one begin? Furthermore, attendance at court was itself a service, and a copyholder could not take occupation of his land until he had been admitted in court. A manor was not a legal manor if there were less than two freeholders to attend the court baron. So it will happen that some institutions or rules described in earlier chapters only make sense in terms of ideas that are described later.

The first part of the book describes the general shape of the manor, what a typical manor might have looked like in the year 1189 (no such manor existed – all were untypical), the early development up to 1189, the decline since then and also treats of custom. Part II describes the lands of the manor, those of the occupiers and of the lord, as well as changes within the manor and changes to and the extinction of manors themselves. Part III, in the form of a commentary on the Law of Property Act 1925, s 62(3), describes rights, both of lords over the land of occupiers and the rights of tenants against their lord, and also considers the courts. Part IV looks at the legal aspect of the manor in its wider context – the village, the church, the town and the kingdom – and considers how manors were grouped together, and puts lords in their setting among greater dignitaries. Finally, Part V puts all that has gone before in a modern practical context and considers such matters as who owns manorial documents, how ownership of manors is transferred, and some special rules of taxation, but this part also looks at the theory and jurisprudence of the manor, what it is in legal terms, and how it can be defined. It concludes with suggestions for reform.

Finally, it is necessary to generalise, to say that lords had such and such rights or that copyholders could do something. Every generalisation in this book has exceptions. The one overriding, omnipresent feature of manors is that each is different, in geography, in history and, above all, in custom. It is not possible to say in every sentence that something was normally or usually the case in most manors or was unless there was a special custom to the contrary. The law develops by recognising and establishing general rules and the law of the manor is no exception. But in the end a manor that has identical rules to its neighbour ceases to be a separate manor, for the essential feature of a manor, before all else, is that it has its own unique customs. That should be borne in mind in considering everything in this book.

Table of Statutes and Other Laws

References to the Introduction are to page numbers.
References to the Appendix are to Appendix / Precedent numbers.
All other references are to paragraph numbers.

General Acts

Local and inclosure Acts

Church of England Measures

Royal laws

Other material

European legislation

United States of America laws

Table of Statutory Instruments

References to the Appendix are to Appendix / Precedent numbers.
All other references are to paragraph numbers.

Table of Cases

References to the Introduction are to page numbers.
All other references are to paragraph numbers.

PART I

ROOTS

Chapter 1

The Picture of the Manor

1.1   THE MANOR AS AN IDEA AND A PLACE

There is no formal legal definition of a manor and it will be simplest to leave the issue of definition to the end of this work in 27.7, once the detailed aspects of a manor have been discussed. Historically, the manor has operated partly as a social structure with degrees of status, partly as a system of control of land and other resources and partly as a form of ownership. Its main feature was originally social, administrative and economic. Later it became a piece of property producing an income and other benefits such as sporting privileges. Now it has become a luxury item.

Traditional accounts regard manors as part of the feudal system. As explained in 22.1, the notion of a special feudal legal structure is not part of English law and it is best to regard the rules about manors as distinct from those relevant to the hierarchy of tenures such as knight service and baronies which make up a feudal structure. In view of the fact that many judges, particularly in recent years, have used the word 'feudal' in their reported decisions it will also be used in this book, but the reader must be prepared to treat it with caution as many historians now consider feudalism to be an illusory concept.

The meaning of manor and its place in society has changed over the centuries and has often been different when used by lawyers from its use by others. From early times a manor was seen as an area of land, although its original function was not so much the land as the organisation of the people who worked on it – the freeholders and the villeins or copyholders. With time the land became more important so that the boundaries needed to be defined on the ground. By the seventeenth century John Donne could famously say in his meditation often called For Whom the Bell Tolls:[1] 'If a clod be washed away by the sea, Europe is the less, as well as if a promontory were, as well as if a manor of thy friend's or of thine own were.'

---

[1]   *Devotions upon Emergent Occasions* (1624) No 17.

The lawyers who over the centuries worked out and applied legal rules to the life and work of the manor did so by abstracting what they found in individual manors to a general standard or ideal. When a case came up for decision or when advice was wanted on a particular problem affecting individuals at a given date in a specific place the dispute or problem was resolved by the use of legal principles. Over the years these principles came to embody a typical or generalised manor. This hypothetical standard manor, which took shape around 1600 under the influence of Sir Edward Coke, did not correspond to any community that ever existed in any place or time.

Even so it was not dreamed up out of nothing. It was based on facts and institutions that had existed. As explained in 2.4 the traditional legal manor reached a classic form about a century after the Norman Conquest. Manors were very varied in structure but the typical manor so far as it existed and on which legal rules were based might have been found on the edge of the Midland plain on Sunday, 3 September 1189, the day on which Richard I was crowned.[2] That date has a special significance, as will be explained, but it is also a good moment to examine the English manor at its best, before it began the long disintegration.

This chapter therefore describes an imaginary standard manor of Middleton. Although it can be taken as a reference, it is indeed untypical. For simplicity the area of the manor corresponds to the ecclesiastical parish and both to the physical settlement, with one village without any dependent hamlets. There is a lord who lives in the manor house and a number of peasant farmers and dependent labourers and their families. The description includes the physical layout, beginning with the arable land, and then the village, and finally the woods and pastures. Then it considers the way the community worked – the basis of the agricultural economy – and finally the size of the units of area and the scale of activities.[3]

1.2   FARMLAND

The village lies in the middle of the manor surrounded by the lands on which crops are grown. These are of two kinds.[4] The first is familiar in the modern landscape and would have been familiar to farmers back to prehistoric times. It consists of a small area of ground surrounded by a boundary: a wall, fence or

---

[2]   Richard's father Henry II died on 6 July, but at the time a king's reign was not treated as beginning until the coronation

[3]   Bennett, HS, *Life on the English Manor 1150–1400* (Alan Sutton Publishing, 1937).

[4]   Taylor, C, *Fields in the Landscape* (Alan Sutton Publishing, 1987) ch 4 on this section generally.

hedge. In the Middle Ages such land was known as a close, from the Latin word *clausum*, meaning enclosed. If the land was also used for grazing the boundary was to keep beasts in it from escaping. When crops were grown the boundary was to keep out animals that might eat them.

In 1189 a field meant something different from that. It referred to the other type of cultivated land known as the field, or open field. It was very large, perhaps 200 acres. It was a vast expanse with no fences, hedges or trees. At first sight it comprised a mass of identical crops but closer examination shows more detail. A typical village in 1189 had three open fields, although there could be two or four. The great field was itself divided into smaller areas called furlongs and the furlong into yet smaller ones known as strips. The strips were, as the name suggests, long and narrow, perhaps 10 yards wide or a little more, and anything up to half a mile long. In theory they contained an area of an acre, although there is some suggestion that many were early divided (lengthways) into quarter acres.[5] They can sometimes be recognised by so-called 'ridge and furrow', the remains of which can still be found in many old field systems especially in the Midlands. These are long ridges, usually along the contours, with troughs between them. They are not quite the same as strips. The strip was the unit of cultivation and of legal rights, while ridge and furrow are physical features in the landscape, constructed for drainage, but the two often correspond.

Each strip was not quite straight but curved slightly at each end in an elongated reverse 'S' shape. The curve was to enable the oxen pulling the plough to approach the headland at an angle so that they could turn. The headland or balk was an uncultivated area at the end of a number of parallel strips that together made up the furlong. A furlong thus consisted of a group of strips of roughly the same length oriented in the same direction. Adjoining furlongs might be laid out in the same way but were more often at angles or right angles to get the best cultivation out of the lie of the land.

The variety of crops grown on the open fields was restricted and they tended to be the same throughout one field. This was not so much from legal compulsion as from practicalities. When the harvest was over, cattle were put out to graze in the field. The court leet would decide when that was. It might, for example, be Lammas Day. In many places that was originally 1 August, but when, in 1752, the calendar was rearranged to co-ordinate with the European mainland and the country nominally lost 11 days, Parliament provided that this should not affect the exercise of rights of common[6] so that it often takes effect as 12 August. In other villages it might be Michaelmas, that is 29 September. If anyone had a

---

[5] Maitland, FW, *Domesday Book and Beyond* (Cambridge University Press, 1987; first published 1897) 362.

[6] Calendar (New Style) Act 1750, s 5.

crop that was not grown and harvested by the due date, it would be eaten. So people tended to plant the same crops, the ones that experience had shown were best.

The cattle were left in the field throughout a fallow year. The three fields were cultivated on a systematic rotation, designed to get the best yield while resting the soil one year in three and allowing it to benefit from manuring by the grazing cattle or sheep.[7] Suppose there are three fields, Top Field, Bottom Field and Church Field. In spring of 1189 Top Field was ploughed and sown with barley which was reaped in August, when the cattle were put in. Top Field would lie fallow for a year and be ploughed again in the autumn of 1190 and sown with wheat. That would be reaped in the summer of 1191 and the cattle put in until it became too cold or the grass no longer grew. In the spring of 1192 the cycle began again. The other fields took up different parts of the round, so that in the early summer of 1189 the wheat in Bottom Field (sown in the autumn of 1188) was harvested, while Church Field lay fallow until the autumn of 1189 and by September was being ploughed. Thus of the three fields in any year one was under wheat, one under barley (or oats) and one fallow. Some other crops could be grown but only if they did not interfere with the grazing periods, and at all times there would be some land available for grazing somewhere on the manorial fields, even if there was no waste to graze. The task of ploughing was spread out through the year rather than concentrated at one time. Harvest was inevitably busy but even that was phased over as long a period as possible.

Individual farmers or families had land in all the fields and in strips scattered through any given field in as many different furlongs as possible (some furlongs were too small for everyone to have a strip). There was a fair share of strips on heavy clay and light sandy loam, on south- and north-facing slopes, on the valley floor and on the stony hillside, near the village and on the edge of the manor. So in good years and bad, wet years and dry, good and bad fortune was shared. The farmers lived close to subsistence and this distribution spread the risk.[8]

In some villages there is evidence of deliberate planning in this. Suppose there are three farmers, Edgar, Walter and John. The pattern might show that in each furlong throughout the fields their strips would adjoin so that Walter always had Edgar on one side and John on the other. This corresponded to the location of their cottages in the village. With time, with the effect of inheritances and sales and exchanges, this pattern became disrupted but traces of it survived into later

---

[7]   Bracton, Sir Henry, *De legibus et consuetudinibus angliae* (c 1257) f 228b.

[8]   Maitland, *op cit* 337; Langdon, J, *Horses, Oxen and Technological Innovation* (Cambridge University Press, 1986) 62, fn 95.

centuries.[9] Such an arrangement could only have come from deliberate planning when the houses were first built and the strips laid out.

1.3   VILLAGE AND SOCIETY

In the middle of the fields lay the village. In 1189 it was not very old – perhaps 100 years. People had lived in the area for thousands of years but on sites that shifted over the centuries. But about the time of the Norman Conquest many villages were laid out in a settled pattern. Middleton was grouped round a triangular village green, at a place where a side road from Weston meets the main highway. On the green were some geese and a few horses and donkeys.

The largest most prominent building was the church, itself built a little less than 100 years before. No doubt on this Sunday prayers had been said for the new king being crowned in London. The church was the only stone structure, having a square tower and a nave large enough to accommodate all the small population of the parish, which in the case of Middleton was also the manor. Round the church was the churchyard and burial ground for those people who were not important enough to be buried inside the church. Next to the churchyard was the priest's house, which, with its own farmyard, was indistinguishable from the farmhouses of the better-off villagers. There was also a nearby barn to take the tithes of crops and any other produce.

The other prominent building, second only to the church and near it, but set back in its own grounds, was the manor house or hall. This was large enough to contain two storeys, although inside there was only a first floor at one end, where the lady of the manor had her chamber. The main part of the hall was clear from floor to gabled soot-stained roof, built of massive timbers, large enough to accommodate all the landholders (the 'homage', from French *'hommes'*) assembled in their courts and all the lords servants. Around the hall were the lord's farm buildings, granaries and stabling.

The people who lived in the village did not regard themselves as equally important. This was long before modern democracy and no one believed that men (let alone women) were endowed by their creator with equal rights or indeed with any. The lord (if he lived in the village) was the most important person. Sometimes he might have some men of his own rank living with him, or his neighbours might send their sons to be trained in his hall in good manners. Second to him was the priest, the person or parson of the village. In a lesser rank there were a number of other freeholders who had their own land and, while

---

[9]   Beresford, MW, 'Mapping the Medieval Landscape, forty years in the field', in Woodell, SRJ (ed), *The English Landscape, Past, present and future* (Oxford, 1985) 124.

they had to attend the lord's court, they were independent. There might be one or two businessmen, a miller or a smith. Inferior still were several bondsmen. They could not leave the manor but they had their own standing. First among them were villeins, but there were others, such as cottars of yet lesser status. Finally, there might in 1189 still be a few slaves, although they were rare by then.

The houses of the villagers were of varied sizes and reflected their status. Some belonged to freeholders (although smaller than the manor hall) and still had yards and outbuildings. Others belonging to the more prosperous villeins were smaller yet, but they too had their buildings, although as often as not the beasts lived (in winter) in a part of the same structure as their owners. Some bondsmens' dwellings comprised little more than the toft, or immediate area of the cottage, and the croft or extended garden where apple trees and vegetables could grow. The humblest dwellings of all were occupied by cottars and, as the name suggests, comprised a cottage, no outbuildings and a small croft.

Middleton was unusual in being a nucleated single village with no outlying hamlets or scattered farmsteads, but even here there were some buildings away from the centre. On the uplands there were shepherds' huts. On the river was a mill. By the bridge there was a tollbooth, and a few years before, when the bridge had not been built, there had been a ferry, with a ferryman's house, which had crumbled to a mound of earth. In later centuries there would be a pesthouse for isolating people with contagious diseases, and a hermitage. In the deer park the lord employed a keeper who had a cottage, and by the warren was a warrener's house.

1.4   WASTE AND OUTLIERS

Around the manor lay lands which were open and uncultivated. Although called waste, they were not neglected and were used intensively. The largest areas were rough grazing mainly for oxen and sheep but also for horses and donkeys. By the river was meadow (not always reckoned as waste) where hay was grown for fodder in winter and where the beasts could be put out in early spring to revive their strength after the winter. By the river also was marsh where birds could be caught.

Woods were also managed. Some were harvested regularly as coppices for timber staves used in making everything from tools to fences. In the thicker woods grew large trees used for timber and among them the villagers put their pigs to forage. Part of the wood was set apart with a bank and ditch as the lord's deer park where he could get some gentle hunting, but the lord also kept deer for food. (Serious hunting was in the deep wood or, with royal permission, in the king's forest.) Where a stream ran down to the river it was diverted and embanked to make fish ponds. In later years mounds were constructed on the waste as rabbit warrens, again for food. Rabbits were at first valued as meat and for their skins and were not then a pest.

Through the village ran the highway. This was not a metalled road as we know it but a broad area, muddy in winter and dusty in summer, along which travellers made their way as best they could, detouring round potholes and rough patches over the adjoining land. Wandering pedlars sold their goods on the green and visiting showmen set up their booths there. The young folk met and the older ones gossiped in good weather and cottagers put out their geese to graze.

Finally there might be lands which legally formed part of the manor but were separated, perhaps by many miles. These included summer pasture, and perhaps isolated areas of arable land that by some historical accident formed part or 'parcel' of the manor. At the time of *Domesday Book*, and for some time after, many manors included a house in the county town or, if they were in the Home Counties, in London.

1.5   THE EIGHT-OX PLOUGH[10]

The physical layout described above was the consequence of one technological invention, and began to change when that became obsolete. Some important aspects of the manorial system – the dual ownership of land, the fundamental basis of custom, the need for a manorial court with two free suitors – could have arisen at any time. But the manor as an economic institution was the creature of the eight-ox plough.

From prehistoric times land had been cultivated with a small plough powered sometimes by humans, sometimes by oxen. It worked well enough in the light soils of the Mediterranean or the gravel of north European river valleys or the loess of the central European plain. But it was no use in the heavy clays that covered much of England and Western Europe. Until Roman times, much of these remained uncultivated woodland.

Historians are still arguing over the date the heavy wheeled plough came into general use. It combined several features. One was the iron ploughshare which

---

[10]   Langdon, J, *Horses, Oxen and Technological Innovation* (Cambridge University Press, 1986); Parain, C, 'The Evolution of Agricultural Technique', in Postan, MM (ed), *The Cambridge Economic History of Europe Vol 1* (Cambridge University Press, 2nd edn, 1966).

replaced the old wooden ones and which could cut through heavy soil. Another was the mouldboard which turned over the soil exposing it to weathering so as to break it into a fine tilth. Another was the addition of wheels so that the plough could be drawn over rough ground instead of having to be dragged or carried. The most important was a system of yoking eight oxen together to form a powerful team able to draw this heavy wheeled, iron-shod plough through clay soils. This technique was effective and, for its time, efficient, but it was not versatile and it dictated the shape of the village and its fields.

First, it was a massive system with great inertia, difficult to turn. So cultivation was best done in long narrow strips. At the end, as mentioned above, the strip curved to allow the team to approach the headland where it could be brought round to plough back again, but the headland itself had to be wide enough for the team to turn in and so could not itself be ploughed (so wasting good land) though it got trampled and muddy enough.

Secondly, it took time to get the team together and lead it out to the fields. Thus, wherever the beasts were kept – in byres in the village or on the open waste – the fairest system was one that allowed equal access to all parts of the arable land to everyone, hence another reason for the scattering of strips over the open field.

Thirdly, co-operation was essential. A few of the better-off farmers might own a complete team and plough. The lord might have several. But most farmers could only afford to own one or two beasts. They would share them with their neighbours on a reciprocal basis, like a modern machinery ring, and this meant co-ordinating ploughing times. It also encouraged a central village, and its associated institutions such as the courts and frankpledge.

Fourthly, oxen needed pasture. There had to be a basic minimum of grazing land which was not under crop. The oxen could be put onto the fields after harvest and even though stubble might not be as nutritious as grass there were still the headlands and the slight banks between adjoining strips. On the fallow field grass grew naturally. However, for bulk grazing in most settlements a large area of permanent pasture had to be maintained as grazing waste. Indeed, the oxen were put onto the fields not so much for their own benefit as for that of the farmers so that they would manure the fields to maintain fertility. Any other form of manure that was available, including human waste, was valued but cattle produced the best (better than horses) and could be left to wander over the fields doing their own thing. In some villages, especially on the sandy soils of East Anglia, the right of foldcourse was protected by the lords to ensure that the cattle of the whole manor grazed and so manured only on the lord's closes.

Cattle were the most valued form of wealth after the land itself. This has been true in many parts of the world over many thousands of years. But manorial law emphasised it. In English law property is one of two types. It may be real property, which includes land and a few other things such as franchises, or advowsons, which will be considered later. Everything else is a chattel, whether a tangible thing like a table or an intangible one like a debt. The word 'chattel' is related to cattle.

In time the eight-ox plough was replaced by the horse plough drawn by specially bred pairs of plough horses. Horses are more expensive than oxen and cannot so easily be exploited for their hides, and their flesh is not so edible (at least to English people). Nor do mares produce milk which is as good for butter or cheese. In the end, as commercial farming developed, horses were found to be more efficient. But for the best part of 1000 years the ox team was best, and with the ox went the manor.

1.6   SIZE

How large was a manor?[11] This is an impossible question. Manors varied enormously from great ones like Totnes, which included many villages, to the tiny ones of East Anglia, which comprised a house and a few acres, but there are some indications of the units involved. The basic unit was the acre. It remained so until European Council Directive 80/181/EEC 'On the Approximation of the Laws of the Member States Relating to Units of Measurement and on the Repeal of Directive 71/354' came into force on 1 January 1995, but this book will refer to acres since that was how people who formed the old laws referred to them. The modern acre is 4840 square yards (0.405 of a hectare) but the mediaeval acre was a functional unit like the foot. It was the area which could be ploughed in a day. That was not a full day's ploughing. Oxen had to be fetched, watered and allowed to graze so it might be five or six hours of ploughing. An acre on light gravel was larger than one on clay. An acre of hilly land was smaller than an acre on flat ground, and an acre of stony ground smaller than one of clear land. The modern acre is an average taken from the South Midlands.[12]

---

[11]   Maitland *op cit* 357, 388, 475; Hildebrandt, H, 'Systems of Agriculture in Central Europe up to the Tenth and Eleventh Centuries', in Hooke, D (ed), *Anglo-Saxon Settlements* (Basil Blackwell, 1988) 280; Harvey, SPJ, 'Taxation and the Ploughland in *Domesday Book*', in Sawyer, P (ed), *Domesday Book: A Reassessment* (Edward Arnold, 1985) 101.

[12]   Acre: Maitland *op cit* 368; but see Langdon *op cit* 160. Hide: Maitland *op cit* 388, 475; Loyn, HR, *Anglo-Saxon England and the Norman Conquest* (Longman, 2nd edn, 1991) 358; Harvey *op cit* 101; Hildebrandt *op cit* 280.

A number of arable acres, typically at one time 120, made a hide (about 50 hectares). This was becoming obsolete as a measure of land by the time of *Domesday Book* and became completely so thereafter. It originated as the land required for one free family in early Saxon times – presumably an extended family of grandparents and cousins, or perhaps a *familia* of master and slaves. It comprised not only those arable acres but also other land that went with it which was not ploughed but included grazing, wood and dwellings. The Saxon kings levied tax by reference to the hide and, inevitably, tax avoidance arrangements led to the taxable hide, as recorded in government records, becoming artificial and ever less like anything on the ground. The hide of *Domesday Book* bears little relationship to area and hardly more to productive capacity. A prosperous bondsman (or villein) typically held a virgate which was a quarter of a hide or 30 acres (about 12 hectares). In the thirteenth century, on good land where population was dense, half a virgate or 15 acres was reckoned enough for a family.

The acre itself was divided into four roods – possibly because landholdings of various sorts from hides to acres were often divided into quarters and this would be done using a measuring rod or rood. Strips originally of one acre in area were divided into four strips of the same length, each a rod wide, when the hide was divided into virgates. Roods were in turn each divided into 40 rods, poles or perches so that land sizes were estimated to a 160th part of an acre or about 30 square yards.[13] To complete this brief summary of areas, 10 hides made a tithing (19.4), the basic grouping for the view of frankpledge, and 100 hides made a hundred (19.2), which corresponded to modern local authority districts. A number of hundreds (10 to 40) made a shire or county (19.3).

A manor comprised several hides. Scholars working on *Domesday Book* have found that although manors are measured in all sorts of different sizes of hides, virgates and acres, if they are collated by settlement units where one settlement comprises several manors, the typical village had a precise multiple of five hides – say 20 or 25. This may be because the *Domesday* manor resulted from the subdivision and amalgamation of what had once been a functional unit.[14] Saxon laws of military service provided that it was compulsory for a man who had five hides to serve in the fyrd or national army.

---

[13]   Maitland *op cit* 369.

[14]   Round, JH, *Feudal England* (Longmans Green & Co, 1895); Blair, J, *Early Medieval Surrey: Landholding, Church and Settlement before 1300* (Surrey Archaeological Society, 1991) 21; Abels, RP, *Lordship and Military Obligation in Anglo-Saxon England* (University of California Press, 1988) 5.

A typical substantial manor of 20 hides[15] comprised 2400 arable acres and as much land again in waste – perhaps an area of seven-and-a-half square miles. A small manor might have five hides, or 600 acres of arable, or 1000 acres in total, the size of a substantial modern English farm. Today that might provide a livelihood for a farmer and one or two farm employees and their families. In 1189 it could support a lord, a priest, a dozen small farmers, some cottagers and the families of all of them. But the modern farm produces a surplus for the market and enough food for many city dwellers. The mediaeval manor was for subsistence. It produced a small surplus – enough to pay rents, tithes and taxes – but most of the produce was needed to feed the people who lived there.

---

[15] Blair *op cit* 21.

Chapter 2

Time Out of Mind

2.1   ROMAN

The manor came into being over a long time with different contributions made by different parts of Europe in different centuries. In England it took on a recognisable form after 1066 but its roots lie much deeper. While it cannot be said that manors existed in Roman times, the remoter origins, like those of the feudal system whose history is described in 22.2, can be traced far back. Some ways of controlling land in Roman Britain appear superficially similar to later manors but, more importantly, when mediaeval lawyers began to set down the rules about administration of land they were influenced by ides derived from Roman law. Although that influence was less in England than on the Continent, Roman concepts were still important here and they affected the way the law developed.

Across the Roman Empire there were, by the fourth century, three types of farming enterprise: first, the private estate or *fundus*; secondly, the smallholder or *tributarius*; and, thirdly, government land – the *fiscus*. The first was where a wealthy private landowner owned his estate. He might either farm the land in hand through his slaves and some hired labourers or he might let land on lease. Land could be hired out under a wholly commercial arrangement, called in Latin *locatio conductio*, with a tenant of means who also either ran his own business or in turn sublet. Alternatively, the landowner could hire (or his *conductor* could sublet) the land to cultivators, *coloni*, who were farmers on a small scale on a special type of *locatio conductio* under which the cultivator was bound to the land by the terms of his tenancy and by status (*adscriptus glebae*: 'inscribed to the clods'). These were not leases as we understand them and did not carry property rights or legal possession, but the arrangement conferred some protection, although in many ways *coloni* were hardly to be distinguished from the better-off slaves. Another approach was for a landowner to arrange for a slave of his to run a farm as a business on its own and to be entrusted with sufficient assets to do so. He was of course the property of his owner and therefore in principle he owned nothing but in practice masters found it better to give an incentive and such slaves could thereby build up their own capital known as *peculium*. Sometimes the slave could use his *peculium* to buy his own freedom and cultivate the land as *colonus*. The landowner was liable for taxes, not only from his own direct enterprise but also from his *coloni* and slaves and, as indicated below his *tributarii*.

The second type was the *ager*[1] or small farm run by what we would regard as a freeholder. The *tributarius* owned his land and was responsible for his own taxes or *tributum*. By the late empire the position of such men across the empire was depressed. Although nominally free, they (like *coloni*) were subject to laws that required sons to follow fathers on the farm[2] which they were not permitted to leave save in exceptional circumstances, for instance to become a soldier or priest. In many legal texts *tributarii* were often mentioned in the same phrase as *coloni* as if they were regarded as being similar.

The third type, the *fiscus*, comprised the imperial holdings. The estates were run in much the same way as the private estates but exploited under the control of agents of the emperor to secure the maximum revenue. It is thought that a large proportion of land in Britain was under imperial control, either directly administered through the emperor's agents or indirectly through management by the army.

Some of the private landowners were the descendants of former British aristocrats whose ancestors had been prominent before the Roman Conquest and who had come to terms with the Romans. Others were immigrants from across the empire or absentee investors. While the imperial estates probably comprised large blocks of land, it is likely that the private estates consisted of aggregations of farms, not necessarily continuous, although they would probably all be in the same area of the country. They might be intermixed with farms belonging to other landlords or with the small holdings of *tributarii*. In military areas, notably the west and north of the province, many farmers may have had to yield their surplus produce to the army.

The estate landowners had public duties as members of the council of the *civitas*. This was a unit of local government corresponding to the city state or *polis* as known around the Mediterranean but again adapted to British conditions. Certain substantial towns were not reckoned as being part of a *civitas* and it is likely that the same applied to imperial and military land; but apart from that the *civitas* was responsible for administration of justice, for repair of public facilities such as streets, roads and sea defences as well as

---

[1]   Percival, J, *The Roman Villa* (Batsford, P/b edn, 1988) 14.

[2]   Justinian, *Digest* 15.1.7.4; *Codex Theodosianus* 11.48.

markets and other public buildings. Men of substance were legally bound to be councillors, known as decurions. In the late empire their principal public duty was to collect taxes due from the *civitas*. If the collection fell short of the amount assessed the decurions were personally liable for any shortfall. In one sense this was fair in that they collectively controlled the wealth of the locality but it could be unfair if some landowner, perhaps a powerful one with good connections to the friends of the emperor, was able to avoid paying his share. The solution to this problem gives us the best insight into the structure of rural landholding in Britain and indicates a structure in some ways comparable to a manor.

This is contained in a law in a formal letter or rescript from the Emperor Constantine dated 20 November 319 to Pacatianus, the *vicarius* or senior governor of Britain.[3] It is found in the *Codex Theodosianus*, a collection of imperial laws issued in 437 after Britain had ceased to be part of the empire so it is not wholly clear if the enactment concerned Britain alone or if this is a general provision, but only the British copy has survived. In either case it must have applied here. When a later collection was issued by the Emperor Justinian in 533 the rescript does not appear. It is therefore likely that it only related to Britain although similar laws are known for other parts of the empire.

The rescript concerned the responsibility of decurions for taxes on land. Constantine said that they were only to be liable for the tax in respect of their own *coloni* and *tributarii* and not for that on other estates. This suggests that in Britain the *tributarii* were regarded as dependent on the greater landowners. It indicates that the lord's *fundus* in some sense included the land of free men, perhaps regarded as his clients, as well as tenants and dependent slaves. This may anticipate a similar structure found in the manor with different classes of tenant. It does not necessarily mean that there was continuity in Britain between the Roman institutions and those of the Middle Ages since similar economic conditions would produce similar arrangements but on the Continent we do know that there was much continuity.[4]

The word for owner was *dominus* and in classical Latin that means something more like owner or master. However, it also meant any superior – it was the usual word by which a soldier addressed an officer; in the later empire the word was used for the emperor and after the fall of the western empire it was applied to the kings who succeeded to his authority. After the break-up of the Carolingian Empire into small pieces (22.2) it came to refer to the counts and other lords who ruled until the possession of even a tiny fragment of authority

---

[3] *Codex Theodosianus* 11.7.2.

[4] Bois, G, *The transformation of the year one thousand* (French edn, 1989; Eng tr Jean Birrell) (Manchester University Press, 1992).

entitled a man to call himself *dominus*. Thus, in Mediaeval Latin it came to be the usual word for lord of the manor. Likewise, the term in Roman law for ownership of land was *dominium*. Strictly, that could only apply to land in Italy or possibly land treated as if it was, such as land in a privileged town known as a *colonia* which had a special status called *ius italicum*. It is possible that Colchester, Gloucester or Lincoln may have had such status but this is not certain. Roman lawyers would not have applied *dominium* to ownership of other land in the provinces which instead were said to be possessed or occupied. When continental lawyers came to accept concepts of Roman law in the thirteenth century they adopted the idea of *dominium* as ownership. By then English law had developed its own concepts, and *dominium* did not become applied to land, although it did apply to other rights such as a manor and the lands occupied by the lord were called demesne.

During the fourth century the practice in Britain was for the *dominus* to live in a villa on his estate. This had not been so earlier, nor was it usual around the Mediterranean where towns survived; but in Britain the towns declined. There were hundreds of villas in Britain.[5] They varied from comfortable farmhouses to palaces. Even a modest villa had mosaic floors, painted walls and heated bath houses and the great ones were luxurious. Historians do not know much about the system of management but there would probably have been a home farm with crops and livestock and a number of small dependent farms. We do not know the typical size but they would be small enough to be tilled with the simple equipment available.

In Britain the villas went with the collapse of the western empire, both as a result of economic decline and barbarian attacks. Many buildings were destroyed by fire and others fell into ruin. In Gaul there was more continuity and some villas were turned into churches. Many modern French villages have names derived from the Roman villa such as Antony, from *Fundus Antoniacum*.[6] It is likely that when the building became unsafe because there were no more professional builders to repair it or it was militarily indefensible, the owner moved elsewhere but retained his property rights. In Italy there was also much continuity. Something like the manorial system developed and declined early, becoming obsolete around 1050 before the northern manor had reached its prime,[7] while many towns in which the aristocracy lived continued to function. Continental experience may have influenced the way institutions developed or survived in England.

---

[5] Mattingly, D, *An Imperial Possession: Britain in the Roman Empire* (Penguin, 2006) 370.

[6] Percival *op cit* 31. See also Gelling, M, *Signposts to the Past* (2nd edn, Phillimore, 1988) 49.

[7] Jones, P, 'Medieval Society in its Prime: Italy', in Postan, MM (ed), *The Cambridge Economic History of Europe Vol 1* (Cambridge University Press, 2nd edn, 1965).

2.2 EARLY SAXON

In 410 Britain ceased to be part of the empire. A rescript of the Emperor Honorius instructed the *civitates* of Britain to see to their own defence.[8] By indicating that they were free from the monopoly of force exercised by the emperor and his army, this enacted that they were no longer within the governance of the empire and were therefore independent. In a similar way as happened when in the nineteenth and twentieth centuries the dominions of the British Empire became independent but kept their laws, so the rules of Roman law which were then in force would not cease to govern the lives of people but changes made by an emperor after that date would not apply in Britain.

It is thought that for some 50 years or so society continued much as before but there was increasing disorder as a result of attacks by Saxons and others from across the North Sea. Some historians believe that only a few Saxon war leaders took over the country and replaced the former Roman-British decurions. Others consider there was a large immigration with a general change in population. Probably there was a mixture as happened on the Continent.

It is not known whether or how long any landholding structures continued in Britain. Some historians have claimed to detect continuity between the boundaries of Roman and early Anglo Saxon estates but the evidence is hard to interpret. It is likely that there was some form of leadership, exercised more by military leaders than by men with inherited wealth, who would have needed followers to cultivate the land in order to give them the leisure to train for war. Possibly they took over the estates of former landholders.

In some places the old estate structure may have continued either under a descendant of the former proprietors or under a new Saxon one. In other places the original people were either killed or fled and immigrants took their place. In yet others the system collapsed and individual farmers went on cultivating their land as before but with no powerful estate to govern them. However, this could not have lasted long as the disorder meant that only by combining together under a strong leader could farmers protect their crops and livestock. Because the needs of a rural society remained there would have been a hierarchy with some farmers bound to the land, others who played a leading role in the local affairs having more secure arrangements, and a few powerful lords controlling the countryside.

---

[8]   Thompson, EA, Zosimus 6. 10. 2 and the Letters of Honorius, (1982) 32(2) *The Classical Quarterly* New Series, 445.

It seems that the kings, both of the regions which remained British – mostly in Wales and the West – and also in the new Saxon realms, took on much of the land which had comprised the imperial *fiscus*. They also appear to have had control of most of the land in their small kingdoms. The system of tax collection ceased but the kings obtained revenues from control of their own lands and from travelling around the countryside receiving renders in kind. As the Saxon kings were converted to Christianity many of the clergy came from Francia or further afield and introduced sophisticated ideas of government and law.

By the seventh century there seems to have developed an institution known as the multiple estate, although, like most features of the time, this is disputed. It may have been derived from Continental models or have been a local development. It involved a major landowner, such as the king, the Church, or a powerful noble controlling a large area divided into specialised units of production. The estate might have several farms, perhaps called Norton (the north farm), Sutton, Easton (or Aston) or Weston, or it might be Great Dale and Little Dale. It might include summer grazing several miles from the centre. There might be some localities where mining or smithing was carried on or where cattle were specifically raised for milk or leather. Each of these units would have been combined into a larger enterprise.[9]

These estates, like the Roman estates, were farmed by slaves, freemen or bondsmen who were intermediate in status. The word for a slave was *theow* but as time passed the word *weala*, which had once applied to free Britons or Welshmen, came also to mean slave. There are also references to subordinate holders of land called *geneat*, *gebur* and *cosetla*. Some of these were clearly unfree bondsmen as distinct both from freemen and slaves. The word for a free smallholder was *ceorl*, although it appears that the term *tributarius* is sometimes used in documents in Latin up to the end of the eighth century.[10]

There was little trade except for portable necessities such as salt and iron. The country became divided into small kingdoms of which the most powerful – Kent, Essex, Sussex and East Anglia – were the size of a modern county. Early Anglo-Saxon society was elaborately stratified with many degrees of rank, but on a tiny scale. Everyone from the king downwards lived in a village for there were no towns. The leaders were headmen elevated from among the peasants or aristocrats dependent on the king. In the villages children of all classes played in the river mud together: everyone knew everyone else, however great or humble.

---

[9]   Faith, R, *The English Peasantry and the Growth of Lordship* (1997) 11 and ch 2.

[10] Hutchinson, L, 'Roman and Anglo-Saxon Agrarian Conditions' (1983) 7(2) *The Quarterly Journal of Economics* 205.

The nobles, called ealdormen, held their land (on which the peasants worked) in one of two ways, as folkland or bookland. It was thought at one time that folkland was land of the folk, rather like African tribal land, but it is better to think of it as land of a lord held according to folk custom. Each locality or tithing was responsible for certain customs or dues to the king, either hospitality as he travelled round his petty realm or as tribute in corn, honey or wool sent to the royal hall.[11] It may have included service in wartime although that was more likely to be the personal duty of the king's warriors, some of whom would themselves be landholders. Bookland was an idea introduced by the Church from continental precedents and comprised a grant by charter (*bok* or book) to the Church when bishoprics and monasteries were founded and endowed. Later it was also used for grants to laymen. Land was specifically granted for a reason and the recipient became entitled to receive the folkland dues instead of the king and, in turn, owed to the king more restricted duties. Bookland was similar to ownership as known in Roman and modern law, for example it could be given away, but although it was in some ways like property it can better be seen as something that was to develop after 1066 into tenure.

Most settlements comprised in the folkland or bookland holdings were isolated communities, often of scattered farms, left very much to themselves and self-sufficient. They were not yet recognisable villages, but they had some identity and the inhabitants were not savages. After the conversion to Christianity most people were subject to the guidance, however slight and imperfect, of a Church whose leaders looked to Rome and knew Roman ideas of law, justice and formality. The rules that governed communities were not arbitrary taboos but social customs, worked out over the generations and handed down. Sometimes the customs were codified or even changed by laws issued by kings, but an English king acted on the advice of his witan, an assembly of experienced men, and no doubt the leaders of small settlements acted in a similar way. There were no police – although the king would deal with armed rebellion and dangerous brigands – and order was enforced through the forerunner of the frankpledge.

2.3   LATE SAXON

In the ninth century all Western Europe was afflicted by attacks from the south, the east and the north-west. For 200 years from 800 to 1000 people lived in a state of total war, always alert to the raids that threatened a civilization. In 875 the Vikings overran England and devastated the four kingdoms into which it was then divided. However in Wessex, Alfred the Great, his son Edward the Elder and Edward's son Athelstan were able to beat back the Danes and begin to

---

[11]   Laws of Ine c 70.

form what later became the kingdom of England. They did this by using all the resources of the country, by reorganising it on every scale, adapting the shire system of Wessex to the Midlands and the North, founding fortified shire towns or burghs, and organising local government in hundreds or wapentakes (weapon-takes). In an agricultural society, resources means agricultural surplus. The whole system of defence depended on securing as much as possible out of the farmers so it could be spent, in their interest as much as that of the rulers, in preventing invasion. The reorganisation affected, indeed was rooted in, the local settlements that became townships or villages.

The spread of the use of the heavy plough and the need for local co-operation encouraged people to gather into defined settlements. The needs of defence strengthened this. Isolated farms were vulnerable but villages could organise watchmen and evacuation and send for help when they were threatened. The strategy of Edward the Elder was to found strongpoints in *burhs*, later boroughs, mainly shire towns, and concentrate the local militia on them. Villages could send for help quickly to the *burh* which organised a response with armed men. These were not full-time professional soldiers but spent much of their time training for and practicing war. They needed transport (horses), weapons and armour, which could only be paid for by the surplus from agriculture. Landholders came to be expected to respect the *trinoda necessitas*[12] – the threefold conditions of service in the army, repair of burgh defences and repair of bridges.

Consequently, agriculture had to become efficient and the surplus was taken in two ways. One was taken directly, by giving all or part of a village to a king's theign to provide him with resources. The other was through a national tax known as Danegeld or geld assessed by reference to the hide, so that the king could either use the geld to pay the Danes to leave (which did not work very well because they came back for more) or he could take the tax yield to pay for his own army. While taxation was not the sole purpose of the Saxon estate, its organisation, which was beginning to resemble the manor, was adapted to simplify the collection of geld.

At around this time it became more common for the theign who controlled the estate – usually by then in bookland – to live in his own hall on his own lands, and useful to have his own priest to build him a church in which to preach and serve.[13] On a larger scale the countryside was organised in hundreds – the equivalent of modern districts – and minsters – the equivalent of modern deaneries.

---

[12]   Maitland, FW, *Domesday Book and Beyond* (Cambridge University Press, 1987; first published 1897) 271.

[13]   Abels, RP, *Lordship and Military Obligation in Anglo-Saxon England* (University of California Press, 1988) 46.

As society was militarised and the units of government included ever larger areas, up to the whole of England, orders of rank became more organised. Early Saxon England had an elaborate system of different orders and grades established on social grounds. Later Saxon England, like its continental counterparts, was organised by homage. Athelstan, in a famous law,[14] required every free man to have a lord, to whom he was accountable and who would be responsible for his behaviour. Slaves, of course, already had owners, but this law meant that within a village each free peasant had to accept the protection of a lord, perhaps a theign, who in turn had his own lord, possibly an earl, who was accountable to the king.

This contributed to the break-up of the multiple estates. As population increased there was less space to spread out a large enterprise and it was more vulnerable to disruption. Theigns wanted their own property to bring up their families. The kings therefore granted holdings to the theigns out of the areas under their control by units of about five hides. Several relatively small holdings or lands might have compact boundaries but if too many were taken out of a larger former estate the fragments that remained could have odd-looking boundaries. Consequently, many later manors and parishes have boundaries that would not have been deliberately planned, while the neighbouring parishes have sensible borders. The boundaries of many parishes to this day provide evidence of the way small estates were taken out, thereby leaving the original parish with a ragged boundary.

It is likely that the open field system began to develop in the ninth or tenth century. The countryside was ravaged by the Danes, and when people returned to their home districts they could accept a wholesale reorganisation of property in the interests of defence and under the new system of control. Even settlements that were not directly affected by Viking attacks could be rearranged as part of the general restructuring of the country. This restructuring was not done all at once, nor everywhere. Open fields continued to be created until at least the twelfth century. If this is compared with the period in the eighteenth and nineteenth centuries when the system was dismantled in the enclosure movement, it is evident that the process of rearranging landholdings on this scale must have required strong reasons and powerful and determined men to carry it out.

A text called the *Rectitudines Singularum Personarum*, 'the right things for different groups of people', possibly written or edited by Archbishop Wulfstan of York, sets out the description of what is said to be a typical village community around 1000. It describes all the groups of men, free tenants, serfs

---

[14]   Athelstan c 2; Stubbs, W, *Select Charters from the beginning to 1307* (Oxford University Press, 9th edn, 1913) 74.

and labourers. These types of status came not from any particular political or legal system but from the nature of the society and economics of the time. After describing the duties of typical members of society on a typical estate, the *Rectitudines* concludes that the laws and customs of estates are multiple and various and the description in the text is not to be taken as applying everywhere. This recognises that local customary rights varied from place to place, although even at that time it was possible to recognise some general customs across England.

2.4   NORMAN

The Norman Conquest is often represented as introducing a new system of land law into England and providing new arrangements for holding land. However, that does not appear to be how contemporaries saw it. William the Conqueror promised (as conquerors do) to respect established rights and laws. By the end of his reign all the former major lay landholders had been replaced by men with a Continental background; but many, perhaps most, smallholders and even the humblest of all remained in place, although the status of many was reduced from free to bond. Church lands of bishops and abbeys also remained although the holders of the offices were again largely from the Continent.

William had several problems. He had to hold his conquest against Saxon earls and the guerrilla activity of their followers. William also had to defend against foreign attack – there was an invasion scare from Denmark as late as 1086. He had to reward his followers. He wanted to reap the fruits of his venture and enjoy his power. The solutions lay in a complex of institutions. The frankpledge system was developed into a means of securing joint responsibility in the villages, so that if a 'frenchman', that is anyone from the Continent, whether Normandy, Anjou, Flanders or Brittany, was found dead, all the English inhabitants of the area were answerable without having to prove the guilt of any individual.[15]

For the rest, William adopted into England a legal structure that had evolved on the Continent. This is often referred to as the feudal system, to be examined further in 22.1. As explained there, historians nowadays do not regard this as an accurate term but it is still in use and, more importantly, when many of the rules discussed in this book were evolving it was regarded as a valid concept. Accordingly, whether or not there really was a feudal system, the idea has shaped the development of the law. This book will therefore use such terms, but it should be appreciated that they may not represent historical realities.

---

[15]   Bracton, Sir Henry, *De legibus et consuetudinibus angliae* (c 1257) (SE Thorne (ed)) (Belknap Press of Harvard University Press, 1977) f 133.

Although similar institutions had begun to emerge among the English they were not as developed as in France. Briefly the system involved granting large areas to tenants in chief, earls and barons, who undertook in return to supply a number of soldiers to the king's wars. They, in turn, subinfeudated land to their own followers on similar terms. The king and each lord owed a duty of protection to his feudatories and the tenant owed homage and services for his land. On the Continent, homage was owed only to a man's immediate superior, but in England, by the Oath of Salisbury (5.4), William ensured that all free men owed a duty direct to the king which overrode his duty to his lord.

The manor itself was not known in England before 1066.[16] Until then a system of estates (called in Old English *lands*) around a hall prevailed. Nor, strictly, was it known in Normandy, where *manerium* referred primarily to a house, not a landholding. By combining the English system of a legal complex, of a part of a village, or several villages, or parts of several villages, with the Norman concept of a man holding a defined area of land in return for services, the idea of the manor as a legal institution was evolved. The Normans believed, however, that there had been manors and they were simply taking over an existing system. The Saxon lands were sometimes reorganised but in many cases the rights of the new lords were derived from their predecessors or *antecessors* (22.3).

In 1086 William ordered the compiling of *Domesday Book*, a government survey of his realm of England.[17] This covered most of the country, except some northern counties and the cities of London and Winchester, which were not within manors. It was organised in shire units and within the shire by honour (see 22.4), namely the holdings of individual lords – first the king (starting with the shire town and then in order of hundreds), followed by the Church, the great lords, and finally the lesser estate owners. Throughout, the unit was the manor. All of England was divided into manors. The few cases where land was not in any manor were specifically noted.

Each manor was described in detail by the number of hides, virgates and acres. The inhabitants were counted, both free (socmen and radmen) and bond (villeins, geburs and cottars). The number of ploughs was given with an estimate of the number that could most efficiently be accommodated. All the other resources were reckoned up – the woods, the fisheries, the pigs, the churches and so on. A famous passage in the Anglo-Saxon Chronicle complains that:[18]

---

[16]   Loyn, HR, *Anglo-Saxon England and the Norman Conquest* (Longman, 2nd edn, 1991) 352.

[17]   Galbraith, VH, *The Making of Domesday Book* (Oxford University Press, 1961).

[18]   *Anglo-Saxon Chronicle* for 1085.

there was no single hide nor a yard of land, nor indeed (it is a shame to relate but it seemed no shame to him to do) one ox nor one cow nor one pig which was there left out, and not put down in his record.

Everything was organised by manor, not by settlement. In nearly every case the manor was treated as having existed in 1066 when it was held by a Saxon lord, or by the Church, which usually continued to hold the land in 1087. Some changes, for example when land was taken out of one manor and added to another, were noted. The division of settlements into premanorial units dates back to before the Conquest. The Norman, Flemish and Breton followers of William saw themselves as taking over an existing system, not imposing a new one. William himself was careful to proclaim that he was the lawful successor of Edward the Confessor,[19] confirming the old laws of the English. Nevertheless, within a few years after the Conquest there developed a general view that there had been a corresponding legal revolution in 1066.

In the century after *Domesday* manors developed into a small estates. A free lay tenant held his land from the king or some other lord in return for services which could be military, ecclesiastical or agricultural. At first, immediately after 1066, manors were not granted individually, but many manors together were granted as an honour to an earl or baron who retained them in his own hands. Subsequently, he made provision for his knights by way of a *feodum* or fee in the form of a grant of land, a manor house and sufficient revenues to support a mounted soldier. The knight's fee was not the same as a manor. Some manors could have supported several knights and one knight's fee may have included several manors. But there was a link, and where what had been a number of manors close together held by one knight who lived on one of them then, if the customs of the manors were sufficiently similar to be recognised by one court, instead of forming a small honour, they could merge to become one manor.

A knight's fee could be and frequently was divided. If a knight died leaving a widow or children it is possible that his fee reverted to his lord if he did not leave an heir old enough to fight. In practice the fee was inherited, even by a widow or an infant son, and the revenues of the fee went to pay for a substitute or were taken by the lord who kept the heir as his ward until he was of age. If the knight left daughters the fee was divided among their husbands. So there might be two holdings, each of half a fee. The knight's fee became a basis for a tax called scutage or shield money, from the Latin word *scutum* – a shield. Eventually the fee itself became a type of legal title to land. There were various different titles, including life estates and (after 1285) fees tail or entails and (later still) conditional fees. The Law of Property Act 1925 converted all types of fee except the most basic type – the fee simple – into equitable interests and

---

[19]   William 1 c 7; *Anglo-Saxon Chronicle* for 1066.

to this day, as explained in 5.7 and 22.7, anyone who owns freehold land holds a fee simple. By 1189 the manor had become a complex of various lands, institutions and rights not restricted to military service or to a specific village but a source of revenue and services. It could then be an efficient and effective system of exploiting the agricultural and other resources of the countryside.

Chapter 3

Decline of Years

3.1   DECLINE OF THE MANOR

From its dominant position in the twelfth century the English manor gradually dissolved until the procedures under the Law of Property Act 1922 were completed, mostly by 1936, although some elements survived until 1950. The manor disappeared, as it had appeared, by reason of changes in agriculture and society, in which the use of the horse and the growth of market towns were important. In particular, the existence of the manor, as a separate jurisdiction with its own local customary laws, was inconsistent with the emergence of a common law for the whole country.

If the manor owed its existence to the eight-ox plough, when that plough went out of use it was at risk. Two heavy plough-horses can draw better than eight oxen; they can turn in the short space of a close and so they do not need long strips in the open field or uncultivated headlands at the end. A man who owns two horses does not need to share plough beasts with his neighbours.[1] However, the horse is more expensive. It needs better care and cannot simply be put out on the rough waste or into the fallow field. In winter it needs a good supply of hay, and little of that was available until the technique of flooding water meadows was developed. In England people do not eat horsemeat, nor use mare's milk for butter or cheese, so the horse is less suitable in subsistence farming. The horse is faster than the ox but it uses more energy, and it was not until civilisation had energy to spare that horses became common on farms.

Where cattle were retained they were more specialised. By the seventeenth century, in Wiltshire, for example, cattle were raised in the lush low valleys to produce milk which was then made into cheese. In contrast to the 'cheese' lands of the valleys was the 'chalk' of the uplands,[2] where the soil was bare and more suited to crops. It needed fertiliser which was provided by great flocks of sheep.

---

[1] Langdon, J, *Horses, Oxen and Technological Innovation* (Cambridge University Press, 1986).

[2] Bettey, JH, *Wessex from AD 1000* (Longman, 1986) 126.

These were moved over a period of weeks or months over the open fields to fertilise them in turn, and this was regulated by a strong manorial discipline which, for that reason, survived on the chalky uplands long after the independent farmers who kept cows for their milk in their closes on the cheese lands had been able to secure their freedom. This discipline was exercised not so much by some tyrannical lord as by the homage putting pressure on their fellows for the common good. But even on the chalk the horse replaced the ox and sheep were needed to replace the manure produced by cattle. As explained below the open fields and common wastes came to be inclosed.

Arable farming changed, adapting to a market economy and producing food as a cash crop. In the thirteenth century old towns expanded and new ones were founded. Most villages in the lowlands were less than seven miles from a market town and it became worthwhile to sell produce there. New crops were introduced, old ones grown on a larger scale and the open field system became uneconomic. Some people continued to live by the old rules as long as possible but few could weave their own clothes, build their own cottages or provide their own utensils. Everyone, even the humblest, depended on earning an income. If they could not do so from farming they went on the road and drifted to the towns where there was a growing need for labour.

Lordship became ownership and ceased to involve control of peasants who worked the demesne. Landowners could either run their own lands in hand as a home farm or they could put it 'to farm' to a lessee, who paid a contractual rent as part of a commercial bargain. The former villein holdings became copyhold, also returning a money rent, and many copyholds were bought up by gentlemen. The manorial tenures were functionally obsolete by the seventeenth century but they lingered on until the twentieth and, as this book shows, fragments remain.

3.2   POPULATION PRESSURE AND THE BLACK DEATH

The picture of the manor in 1.1–1.5 was set in the year 1189 because after that date it was no longer possible to create new manors (4.1), although sub-manors could be created out of manors until 1290. This situation resulted from one or possibly two Acts of Parliament of that year. *Quia Emptores* is discussed in 7.3 and *Quo Warranto* in 4.3. *Quia Emptores*, by prohibiting subinfeudation, prevented both the grant of new manors and the grant of new common manorial freeholds within manors after 1290. *Quo Warranto* prevented the recognition of new customs or customary tenures since 1189. Until 1894 it remained possible to divide a manor where the holder left two or more daughters to inherit as co-parceners (8.3).

By 1290 the system was already under pressure because the population had expanded beyond safe limits. This was caused by, and itself contributed to, growing prosperity, trade and markets. People needed to eat, and the wealth meant that there was money to buy surplus food. There was a great demand for land but a limited supply. Lords, on the whole, did not sell, so rents soared, and the lords enjoyed wealth and power. Much waste land was converted to arable by the two approaches of approvement and assarting (7.11).

Woods were felled and marginal land that was not fit for arable was ploughed up. Old arable was overworked and exhausted. As the grazing waste was reduced there was less space to keep oxen and less manure for the larger areas of arable. Crop yields fell and famine threatened. In the early years of the fourteenth century there were several periods of disastrous weather (perhaps caused by a volcanic eruption) leading to crop failure. In 1348 the Black Death killed between a third and a half of the population.

The growing population led to a growing demand for land and growing power for the lords who controlled the land. They were able to exploit their power by extracting from the manor every possible advantage, but especially money by way of rents and other payments (14.2–14.6). The old ways had involved tenants, whether bond or free, providing services on or for the lord's demesne. These services were of unequal value. Suppose there were two holdings each of which owed a day's ploughing each week. One was held by a prosperous villein who could provide a full yoke of eight oxen or two plough horses, and a plough in good repair with a ploughman of 20 years' experience. The other belonged to a poor widow who could only send two broken-down beasts and an old plough with a blunted share guided by her teenage son who could barely steer a straight furrow. Where services were taken the lord could not know from one day to the next what services he might get, which is no way to run a farming business. As such, lords tended where possible to commute services for rents and pay their own farmhands from the proceeds (and there were plenty of landless men ready to be hired) or even cease farming the demesne altogether and put it to lease (and there were others ready to take leases). As commerce developed there were more uses for money. In much the same way as the lords preferred rents, so the king ceased to demand military services in kind, preferring to rely on professional soldiers who could be paid from the taxes and seigniorial dues collected from the lords which they, in turn, collected from their tenants. Likewise tenants preferred to pay a rent which they could predict and plan for, so that they could spend time on their own holdings.

After the Black Death (and the other plagues that followed it), fewer people but the same amount of land meant that there was less competition and less demand for farms. Marginal areas were abandoned and lords, instead of being able to pick the peasant with the highest bid, actively sought farmers who would pay any rent. Labourers were scarce and, despite government regulations, wages rose. Meanwhile, the need for cash did not diminish. The aristocracy were involved in the Hundred Years' War in France. At times the war was profitable, but more often taxes had to be levied to pay for it and all landholders paid tax. Lords looked for any man who would take a holding, no questions asked. He might be a bondsman illegally escaped from another manor but who was allowed to settle as a free man; indeed, to prevent their own villeins escaping, lords might instead free them. It was not possible to grant a customary tenancy after 1189 or a dependent manorial freehold after 1290, but leases became common. Many lords, who before the plague had farmed in hand with services of villeins administered by a bailiff, preferred to commute the services for a quitrent and put the land to farm to a tenant who was often the former bailiff.

In 1381 there was a widespread Peasants' Revolt. This was not directed primarily against manors but more against taxation, especially the poll tax. When the peasants rose the first thing they did in manor after manor was destroy the rolls and custumals[3] so that subsequently there was no written record – no evidence that could be produced in court – of the services they were bound to provide or even of their personal status.

3.3   COPYHOLDS AND ROYAL POWER

During the fifteenth century power, wealth and land concentrated in a few aristocratic families so that knights' fees and resident lords became fewer. Men who had made money in commerce and wanted to acquire land could, if they were not able to buy freeholds, at least purchase customary villein holdings, by then called copyholds. These purchasers were not bondsmen or even peasants, but investors who leased out their lands to farmers on annual contracts which were renewed from year to year. They were not content to rely on the manor courts to protect their rights. They could afford to litigate in the royal courts and they were accustomed to commercial procedures such as the action in trespass, rather than the old feudal writs going back to the time of Henry II known as the possessory assizes which could help freeholders but not manorial copyholders. For them the action of ejectment was developed as a relatively quick and cheap procedure in the royal courts which protected their rights. This new action, which originally protected leaseholders, was so effective that it was extended to

---

[3]   Brandon, P and Short, B, *The South-East from AD 1000* (Longman, 1990) 97.

allow copyholders to sue in the royal courts (thus further weakening the manor courts) and also became the way that titles to freeholds were tried.[4]

The result was that copyholders became as well protected as freeholders; and those who came to have full ownership of their copyholds were said to have a fee simple in the copyhold, just as the freeholder had a fee simple in his land (22.7). Sir Edward Coke, in a famous passage in his treatise on copyhold,[5] says:

> But now Copy-holders stand upon a sure ground, now they weigh not their Lords displeasure, they shake not at every sudden blast of wind, they eat, drink and sleep securely; onely having a special care of the main chance, (viz.) to perform carefully what Duties and Services soever their Tenure doth exact, and Custom doth require: then let Lord frown, the Copy-holder cares not, knowing himself safe, and not within any danger. ... Time hath dealt very favourably with Copy-holders in divers respects

Much of the power and wealth of the old aristocracy was destroyed by the Wars of the Roses. As the leading families became fewer they killed one another, or at least forfeited each other's land, and power concentrated in the hands of the Crown, first the House of Lancaster, then York and finally Tudor. Henry VII and Henry VIII between them executed most of the remaining powerful families and recruited new servants of their own to run the country. Government was expensive. Henry VII was able to make enough revenue from the royal estates to manage the government and reward his followers. Henry VIII did not have enough revenue. He therefore turned to the Church, both for cash and because the new royal servants wanted reward in the form of land.

The Church had been a great landowner since early Saxon times. At the time of *Domesday* it held a quarter of all manors. By the sixteenth century it held a third. Once land came into the hands of the Church – called in law 'mortmain' or 'the dead hand' because the Church, unlike laymen, did not die – it did not pass out again. In some periods the monasteries were forward-looking landowners, experimenting with new cropping systems or the building of watermills; but by the end of the Middle Ages they, like every other great landowner, were leasing out their demesne. In general monasteries were not subject to the same pressures as lay lords and Church lands were less advanced in organisation and less efficiently run.

---

[4] Gray, CM, *Copyhold, Equity, and the Common Law* (Harvard University Press, 1963); Simpson, AWB, *An Introduction to the History of the Land Law* (Oxford University Press, 1961) 152.

[5] Coke, Sir Edward, *Complete Copyholder* (E Flesher et al, 1673) s 9.

Henry VIII and his son Edward VI dissolved the monasteries and other religious institutions, and their estates were nationalised by various statutes. Some of the effects of dissolution were reversed under Queen Mary, notably by the Crown Lands Act 1557, but that, in turn, was reversed by Elizabeth I in the Religious Houses Act 1558. Many of the estates were sold (or occasionally given away) by the Crown, either as complete manors as formerly held by the monasteries or as severed areas of land. The new owners might be Crown servants or local gentry. Others were speculators who resold land or commuted services or rents at a profit. Often records were lost or confused, tending to weaken further the manorial system.

The new rich wanted dignities and, like nouveaux riches in any age, they fancied the title of lord of the manor. Notwithstanding *Quia Emptores*, many apparent manorial titles can be traced no further back than the mid-sixteenth century. In response, the laws on what was or was not a manor were tightened, not by Parliament but by the judges in the royal courts. Several cases from around the year 1600 clarified that a new manor could not by then be created, and defined what was a legal manor and what was a mere reputed manor, and how a manor could be destroyed or cease to be recognised (8.1).

At about this time bondage ceased. As late as the 1570s the status of bondsman was still said to survive at Leominster, Winslow and Helston in Cornwall.[6] The last reported case concerning a claimed bondsman was *Pigg v Caley*[7] in 1617. Caley took Pigg's horse. Pigg sued him. Caley said that Pigg was a villein in his manor and that all a bondsman's property was at the lord's disposal. The case went in favour of Pigg. Following this case bondage disappears from the record in England, although for some years formal grants of land containing general words (9.1) included rights over *nativi*. In *Somersett's Case*[8] in 1772 it was said that *Pigg v Caley* was the last case involving villeinage. *Somersett's Case* concerned an escaped slave, and the legal decision turned in part on the distinction between villeins appurtenant and villeins regardant or in gross (5.3).

One of the main motives for the dissolution of the monasteries was to boost royal revenues so that the king could be independent of taxes for which he needed the authority of Parliament. Another means of raising money was to exploit seigniorial dues, and James I and Charles I increasingly pursued this. A man was bound to make a payment on becoming a knight, but a man of sufficient wealth who declined a knighthood could be fined for refusing. Payments were due on inheriting a manor, on a young lord coming of age, on the knighting of the king's eldest son and on the marriage of his eldest daughter

---

[6]   Reed, M, *The Age of Exuberance 1550–1700* (Paladin Grafton Books, 1986) 19.

[7]   (1617) Noy R 27, 74 ER 997.

[8]   (1772) 20 ST 1. See 5.3.

(22.5). A major source of revenue was wardship, administered by the Court of Wards, whereby if a landholder died and his heir was under age his lord (usually by then the king) could run the land during the son's minority, notionally on the son's behalf but in practice for personal gain. Wardships were sold to bidders who simply exploited the land and might leave it a wreck. All sorts of archaic dues, founded in the old feudal law, were revived and enforced. These methods were resented by the gentry and nobility. The effect of *Quia Emptores* had been that mesne tenures tended to disappear and although within manors there were still some men who held freeholds of the lord, most land was now held, or thought to be held, in chief of the king.

The king's attempt to rely on non-Parliamentary revenues failed in the last years before the Civil War of 1642. Parliament and Oliver Cromwell won the war. By an Ordnance (in effect an Act) dated 24 February in the year which we would identify as 1646 but which, at the time (because the legal year lasted until the end of March), was formally dated 1645, Parliament (without the king) abolished the Court of Wards and all seigniorial dues and converted land held by knight service to free and common socage. Charles I was executed in 1649 but Cromwell's Commonwealth was likewise a failure and in 1660 Charles's son was restored as Charles II. All the laws made without the king's consent were regarded as nullities and most of the reforms of the Civil War and Commonwealth period were repealed and forgotten. However, the end of seigniorial revenues was not to be given up and the Tenures Abolition Act 1660, s 1 provided that all tenures by knight service or otherwise 'held either of the king or of any other person or persons bodyes pollitique or corporate are hereby enacted to be turned into free and common soccage', with effect from the passing of the Ordnance.

The Act contained exceptions for tenure by frankalmoign and by copy of court roll. It also preserved the honourable services of Grand Sergeanty, although the tenure itself was abolished. All remaining copyhold was converted to freehold in 1926 (14.8). Most frankalmoign was converted to socage either by the lands passing from an ecclesiastical person to a corporation or on the death of the holder after 1925, but some may remain (20.10). It also appears that tenure in ancient demesne (24.9) survived but as a form of socage.

In later years the most obvious way in which land passed out of the manor was by enfranchisement. This originally meant freeing a slave and, after slavery became unknown, giving a bondsman the status of a free man. Land held by a bondsman was called unfree land, while land held by a free man was freehold (5.3). By the thirteenth century status and landholding were separate so that villeins could hold free land and many free men held villein land. Enfranchisement thereby came to mean converting villein tenements – later copyhold land – to freehold. It retained that meaning until copyhold was abolished in 1926. Nowadays the word refers to long leaseholds being enlarged to freeholds under the Leasehold Reform Act 1967, the Leasehold Reform, Housing and Urban Development Act 1993 and the Commonhold and Leasehold Reform Act 2002. As land lost its unfree status it ceased to be linked to the manor (7.3) and transfers of the land were no longer made in the manorial court.

In the eighteenth century the main financial benefit to the lord from his manor was the revenue from copyholds, particularly quitrents, entry fines and court revenues (27.2). As indicated, copyholds became fully protected at law so that although still technically held at the will of the lord (and even that did not apply to customary freeholds), that will had to be exercised 'according to the custom of the manor' (5.5). Entry fines became restricted to a maximum of two years' annual value and were often less than that.[9] The main function of the manor court became as a register of title to copyhold land.

Even in the nineteenth century copyhold revenues were still worth having, but increasingly copyholders wished to enfranchise. At common law the way of doing this was for the copyholder to purchase the fee simple from the lord, which could involve long and therefore expensive investigation of the lord's title. If the lord was only entitled as tenant for life under a settlement he had no power to sell. In 1841 Parliament passed a Copyhold Act and by successive Acts the right of copyholders to enfranchise cheaply and easily was improved. Copyholds were increasingly seen as an antiquarian anomaly and the decision was taken to abolish them. On 1 January 1926 copyholds were converted to freeholds (with a few exceptions such as copyholds for years which became leaseholds) and the lord was compensated by a payment calculated according to rules laid down by Parliament (14.8). Indeed, the effect of the 1925 legislation was to transform property law, which means that today most lawyers no longer fully understand the old law. So complete was the effect of the 1925 legislation that many lords forgot their manorial titles and references to lordships disappeared from title deeds.

3.4   INCLOSURE

Inclosure[10] was the process by which common land or open fields became held in severalty – that is in separate private ownership as a close. It is linked to

---

9   Scriven, J, *A Treatise on the Law of Copyholds* (Butterworth & Co, 7th edn 1896, by Archibald Brown) 182.

10   On inclosure and enclosure see *Report of the Royal Commission on Common Land* (Cmnd 462 (1958) para 97.

enclosure, which refers to the physical process of putting a hedge, wall or fence around the land, but the two are not the same. Land may be inclosed but not enclosed. In arable areas uninterrupted expanses of crop may spread over miles without even roadside fences, but they comprise the separate fields of many farmers, each of whom cultivates only up to his own private (several) limits. Typically inspection of the fields will show small concrete blocks flush with the soil to indicate the points where boundaries turn a corner. Equally, land may be enclosed but not inclosed, such as a lot meadow shared by a number of participants, a fragment of an old open field or a small area of common land, subject to pasturage rights but hedged round.

With the decline in the manorial economy moves were made to inclose open fields and common waste. The legal details are discussed further in 7.11–7.12. After 1348 inclosure was carried out for commercial agriculture. Fewer people meant less demand for bread, and hence for crops. Instead, landowners turned to commercial farming, and in the late Middle Ages numbers of sheep were increasing, kept not for their dung but for their wool. Vast flocks were pastured especially in East Anglia and the Midlands, where now sheep are rarely seen. England became not only a wool producer but a cloth-making country. Arable farming was less profitable; sheep farming more so.

In earlier times lords had needed arable farmers to cultivate the demesne and pay rents. After 1400 it became profitable to clear villages and put the lands of whole parishes down to grass where sheep could graze in the old fields and village streets. At common law a bondsman had no protection if he held 'at the will of the lord', and even where local custom protected a tenant in theory, he had difficulty in enforcing his rights. Many sites of deserted mediaeval villages date from this time. Historians do not agree how widespread this was, but to contemporaries it became a scandal.[11]

Because local or common law enforcement was inadequate the government intervened though the jurisdiction of the Court of Star Chamber. Tudor and early Stuart governments publicised evictions and took steps to prosecute notorious inclosers in the Court of Star Chamber. Royal policy was opposed to inclosure until the Civil War. But the problem may have been exaggerated. England continued to produce enough bread to eat and it was too expensive to import staple food, so most land was still farmed for that purpose. It was because many villages had been so weakened by the agricultural crisis and the Black Death that they could not survive. The loss of manorial records both in the Peasants' Revolt and at the time of the dissolution of the monasteries 150 years later led to confusion about ancient customary rights so that they could not be proved or were forgotten.

---

[11]   A famous denunciation is in More, Sir Thomas, *Utopia* (1516) Book 1.

After 1600 sheep became less profitable, crops more, so but inclosure did not stop. Tenants became better protected by the procedure of ejectment so that inclosure came to be carried out by agreement, although strongly influenced by the will of a powerful landowner. As the number of small holdings declined and farm sizes grew it was easier to reach a consensus. If 20 farmers own strips scattered through the manor they are unlikely all to agree on the necessary exchanges to bring about inclosure. If there are only six it is much easier.

The greatest work of inclosure was done by Act of Parliament. Nearly 4000 inclosure Acts have been traced back to 1709. Provided a substantial majority (in value) of the proprietors in a manor, or part of one, or in a parish agreed, Parliament would allow them to override an objecting minority, redistribute the open fields and divide up the common waste. The principal periods of Inclosure Acts were first in the 1760s and 1770s and then during the French wars until 1815. However, later in the century people, particularly in towns, became conscious of the need to protect or, as we would say, conserve the countryside and the remaining commons came to be seen as a national resource. The Commons Act 1876 discouraged inclosure, which subsequently became virtually impossible under the Law of Property Act 1925, s 194.

3.5   THE TWENTIETH CENTURY

What we now know as the conservation movement (which goes back to the nineteenth century) became active in the 1960s, when there was concern that despite the end of formal inclosure, common land was still being lost. In 1965 Parliament passed the Commons Registration Act to set up a register of all common land, manorial waste and village greens. This led to disputes in the courts and, to protect their clients' interests, lawyers had to investigate manorial rights going back over centuries. In the 1970s the Law Commission became active in its attempts to clarify the law of England and abolish obsolete laws. One result was the passing in 1977 of s 23 of the Administration of Justice Act which deprived manorial courts of their power to hear and decide disputes. As discussed in 13.4 they were not actually abolished but the effect of the change may have been to convert any remaining legal manors to reputed manors.

In the 1980s many people who had spare money and looking for something unusual to spend it on found that they could purchase the title of lord of some rural manor for a few thousand pounds. The most famous lordship to be sold was Henley in Arden (which includes Stratford on Avon), which changed hands in 1988 for £87,000.[12] Even an obscure manor with no rights could, at the height

---

[12]   *The Times*, 10 December 1988, p 26.

of the boom, fetch £10,000. This was a pure status commodity and the market collapsed when the economy declined, but it left many people wondering about what manors were and what rights might be attached to them. More recently the market has stabilised. There is a steady demand from people who like the idea of being lord of a manor and a supply from owners who have died or lost interest. Titles to lordships are hardly a good investment but they are still an item of interest for those who have the spare cash.

Many such owners wished to secure their titles by registering them at the Land Registry. This caused considerable extra work for the Registry which is principally concerned with title to physical land. It also led to disputes (7.1) and the Land Registration Act 2002 prevented the registration of title to any further manors (25.7).

3.6   MANORS IN AMERICA

Although the manor declined in England after the high Middle Ages, there was a remarkable extension of the manorial system to lands across the Atlantic when, in the seventeenth century, people from England established colonies in what later became the United States. As far as possible the colonists took with them the ways of home. In particular they took the common law of England and adapted it to life in America. They also took specific institutions. In the settlement at Andover Massachusetts, incorporated in 1646, the colonists at first established an open field system, although this did not last beyond the 1680s.[13] This did not appear to involve a manorial structure as such, but there must have been arrangements, similar to those traditionally made in England, to operate the fields.

Landholdings throughout New England – some purchased from the local people, some simply taken by force – were legitimated by Crown grants expressed to be held of the King's Manor of East Greenwich,[14] although some in Pennsylvania and Maryland were held of the castle of Windsor and some in Georgia of the honour of Hampton Court. The reason for this was so that land could be bought, sold and leased according to the formalities of English law under which all land had to be held of a lord (24.5). Most remarkable of all was the wholesale importation of the manorial system into Maryland by Charles I when granting

---

[13]   Greven, PJ, Jr, 'Family Structure in Seventeenth-Century Andover, Massachusetts' (1966) 23(2) *The William and Mary Quarterly* 234.

[14]   Cheyney, EP, 'The Manor of East Greenwich in the County of Kent' (1905) 11(1) *American Historical Review*. McPherson, The Hon Judge BH, CBE, Judge of Appeal, Queensland, 'Revisiting the Manor of East Greenwich' (1988) 42(1) *American Journal of Legal History* 29–35.

Lord Baltimore extensive lands under a charter in 1636. Lord Baltimore was empowered to create manors and to hold a court baron and view of frankpledge with court leet.[15] William Penn did much the same in the adjacent colony of Pennsylvania.[16]

These exportations can be compared with the arrangements made in Ireland as illustrated by the Irish case of *Delacherois v Delachererois*[17] (7.5) where Charles I likewise granted a lordship with power to subinfeudate. This was not just antiquarianism. It was accepted that all land had to be held by tenure and it made sense to assimilate the way the king's subjects who occupied land in America held it. Although native Americans did occupy plots of land under their ancestral ways, this was not thought suitable and it was not practicable for the colonists to adopt a native approach which, in any case, varied from one people to another. Rules were required to ensure quiet enjoyment of farms and houses and to enable them to be sold or leased, and it was simplest to take over an established system of tenure. Even so, it was only thought necessary to adopt manors in a minority of colonies, not least because the manorial system had been in decline for so long in England.

At independence the system had to be dismantled. Thus, the Constitution of Virginia, adopted on 29 June 1776, enacts 'All escheats, penalties, and forfeitures, heretofore going to the King [George III], shall go to the Commonwealth [of Virginia], save only such as the Legislature may abolish, or otherwise provide for'. The Constitution of Maryland, dated 11 November 1776, provides in Section III 'That the inhabitants of Maryland are entitled to the common law of England' and goes on to say that 'the inhabitants of Maryland are also entitled to all property, derived to them, from or under the Charter, granted by his Majesty Charles I. to Cæcilius Calvert, Baron of Baltimore'.

In Pennsylvania an Act dated 27 November 1779 provided that the Commonwealth should be the source of tenure instead of the former lords who had been proprietaries. In *Wallace v Harmstad*[18] the court decided that Pennsylvania titles are allodial not feudal:

> We are then to regard the Revolution and these Acts of Assembly as emancipating every acre of soil of Pennsylvania from the grand characteristics of the feudal system. Even as to the lands held by the proprietaries (city of Philadelphia)

---

[15] Warman, HJ, 'Population of the Manor Counties of Maryland' (1949) 25(1) *Economic Geography* 23.

[16] Wheeler, G, 'Richard Penn's Manor of Andolhea' (1934) 58(3) *The Pennsylvania Magazine of History and Biography* 193–212.

[17] (1862) 11 HL Cas 62, 11 ER 1254.

[18] (1863) I 44 Pa 492.

themselves, they held them as other citizens held, under the Commonwealth, and that by a title purely allodial.

Similarly, while it is said that in New York the Dutch founders of the colony established military tenures, which may have survived when the colony passed to the English Crown in 1664, in 1787 the New York legislature converted all freeholds into a tenure in free and common socage; in 1830 this too was abolished and thereafter all lands in that state became held as allodial.

The effect of such provisions was that the lands in the former colonies were henceforward held without reference to the king. While land in some states may be owned allodially so that tenure has been abolished, and in others may be held by tenure in socage from the state, the practical consequences are much the same. Escheat (7.6–7.8) has therefore been given a wider meaning than in England. The treatment of abandoned property is a matter for each of the states to provide for, and there is a substantial practice in what is known as escheatment, although in the United States the term is not restricted to land and includes bank accounts and company shares whose owner is unknown.

A similar conclusion was reached in Canada on the construction of s 109 of the British North America Act 1867 where, in *Attorney-General of Ontario v Mercer*,[19] the Privy Council held that the expression 'Lands, Mines, Minerals, and Royalties' was sufficient to carry escheats and therefore the superior tenurial interest or *dominium directum* which thereby vested in the Provinces.

---

[19]   (1882–83) LR 8 App Cas 767.

Chapter 4

Custom and Variety

4.1   CUSTOM AND THE MANOR

The heart of the manor is custom. Custom, unique to each manor, distinguishes one from another, but it is more fundamental than that. Sir Edward Coke, Chief Justice from 1606 to 1616, was the most influential judge and legal writer in our history. In 1630 he wrote a book on the manor called the *Complete Copyholder* in which he said:[1]

> If the King at this day will grant a great quantity of Land to any Subject, injoyning him certain Duties and Services, and withall willeth that this should bear the name of a Manor; howsoever this may chance to gain the name of a Manor, yet it will not be a Manor in the estimation of the Law.

And further:[2]

> Hence it is that the King himself cannot create a perfect Manor at this day; for such things as receive their perfection by the continuance of time come not within the compass of a King's Prerogative: and therefore the King cannot grant Free-hold to hold by Copy, neither can the King create any new Custome, nor doe any thing that amounteth to the creation of a new Custome.

So what is custom?[3] In lay terms a custom is what people are accustomed to do, just as customers regularly go to the same shop and people tend to wear the same costume. Legal customs are law, just as much as the decision of a court or an Act of Parliament, but they are not made by the deliberate act of any central authority. They emerge by the acceptance of many people over a period of time

---

[1]   Coke, Sir Edward, *Complete Copyholder* (E Flesher et al, 1673) s 31.

[2]   Ibid s 31.

[3]   *Halsbury's Laws* Vol 12(1) (reissue) *Custom and Usage* (Butterworths Lexis Nexis, 4th edn) para 601; Bracton, Sir Henry, *De legibus et consuetudinibus angliae* (c 1257) (SE Thorne (ed)) (Belknap Press of Harvard University Press, 1977) f 1; Scriven, J, *A Treatise on the Law of Copyholds* (Butterworth & Co, 7th edn by Archibald Brown, 1896) 313.

in some particular locality and are recognised as complying with the standards expected of law. Customs can relate to a variety of matters, but in this context most concern services to be rendered, rules for the inheritance of copyhold land or practices carried out within a locality.

Custom can be understood in three ways. When the word is used, for instance in a judgment, it may be in any one of the following three senses, and the particular sense may not always be evident from the context. First, custom was the basis of the manor, which existed as a locality legally set apart from the country as a whole (although part of it) within which the rules of the common law are modified or displaced by custom. The manor was a separate jurisdiction and the customs of one manor could not be taken as evidence of those of another, at least unless one of them was a subinfeudation of the other.[4] That type of custom has long since ceased to exist and it was finally extinguished when s 23 of the Administration of Justice Act 1977 (13.4) abolished customary courts. Secondly, custom was the network of rules within the manor which governed the relationships between the lord and his tenants, between the tenants themselves, and between successive generations of them. Under the Law of Property Act 1922 most such rights were either abolished or converted to statutory rights, although there may be a few survivals, such as a custom to fence against a common.[5]

Thirdly, customs are specific rules and rights which could come into existence before 1189, which can disappear or which can be abolished by Parliament, but until that happens they are capable of surviving. There are few left, although some may survive, such as customary ways for freehold tenants of the manor (4.8)[6] or rights of fishermen (4.2). Until the Commons Registration Act 1965 customary rights of grazing could survive as commonable rights under the Law of Property Act 1922, Sch 12, para (4), but they have now become statutory rights of common (10.5). Customs of this third type may also relate to some other locality, but they are now rare.

The three meanings shade into one another and the way the word is used in one sense in one context can affect its meaning in another.

Any customary rights of the third type which still exist in registered land will be preserved as overriding interests under the Land Registration Act 2002, Sch 1 and 3, para 4 (25.9). It is possible that the customary rights of the second type constitute manorial rights (9.5) within Sch 1, para 11 and will not bind

---

[4]   *Lord Anglesey v Lord Hatherton* (1842) 10 M & W 218, 152 ER 448.

[5]   *Egerton v Harding* [1975] 1 QB 62, [1974] 3 All ER 689, 28 P&CR 369.

[6]   But see *Derry v Sanders* [1919] 1 KB 223: customary right of way did not survive enfranchisement.

registered land after the first registration or disposition of land after 12 October 2013 unless protected. However, a better view is that, although some of the rights preserved by Sch 12, paras (5) and (6) to the 1922 Act may have originated in custom, the effect of that provision was to convert them to statutory rights. The Land Registry view is that the reference to manorial rights is to those referred to in paras (5) and (6). If that is correct it would mean there is no overlap between paras 4 and 11 in the 2002 Act and consequently any other customary rights remain overriding.

To be binding customs must have four features: they must be local, ancient and continuous, reasonable and certain. Those are well established. The contents of customs may be taken as customs of services, of inheritance and disposition, and of enjoyment.

4.2　LOCAL

Customs must be local but they can be either general or special. A general custom is one that is found in many or most parts of the country, such as that the lord has the property in minerals while the copyholder had possession of them (11.7) or the lord cannot grant out part of the waste to the exclusion of commoners. Certain customs of services, such as week works, were general and two customs of inheritance, namely gavelkind and borough english, were also general. The significance of a general custom is that once established to subsist in a particular case the courts would take cognisance of it and not require it to be specially proved.

Some non-manorial customary practices, such as taking recreation on the village green, were general. This is a current topic of some importance since it affects new statutory greens as discussed in 19.6–19.8. Other practices could also be general, such as that established in *Mercer v Denne*[7] for the parish of Walmer in Kent for local fishermen to dry their nets on some shingle above high water mark, where the judge referred to several textbooks which mentioned the practice.

Special customs were specific to the locality. They might modify general customs, for instance allowing the copyholder to take minerals or the lord to grant waste with the consent of the homage. Others might replace them, as with the innumerable distinct inheritance customs in different manors. If someone claimed the benefit of a special custom he not only had to prove that the custom

---

[7]　[1904] 2 Ch 534, [1905] 2 Ch 538.

existed and applied to the particular locality in question but also had to bring evidence to show what the terms of the custom were.

Even though a custom was general in the sense that its terms were well known, it took force from being local. Its origin was local[8] even though its terms were the same as customs to the same effect found in other manors either in the same part of England or across the land, or in some cases across Europe. Coke points out that custom had to be local to a specific town (by which he refers to any locality) and adds that 'a custome cannot be alledged generally within the kingdome of England; for that is the common law'.[9] In *Veley v Burder*[10] Tindal CJ said 'Such a custom existing beyond the time of legal memory, and extending over the whole realm, is no other than the common law of England'. All types of custom are local in the sense that their authority derives from the locality, not the general law. In the case of *Hammerton v Honey*[11] (which concerned a claim to dance on Streatham Village Green) in 1876 the Master of the Rolls, Sir George Jessel, defined custom as a local law. In its locality and on the matter in question it takes the place of the common law.

Common law is a phrase which has many different meanings, usually in contrast to something else. Its standard meaning is the law laid down in the cases decided in the common law courts of Common Pleas, King's Bench and Exchequer which were held in Westminster Hall as distinct from the equity administered through the Chancery Court of the Lord Chancellor. In this sense common law deals with the nominal title to land as distinct from beneficial enjoyment. A second meaning combines both the foregoing as case law of the courts, whether in Westminster Hall or in Chancery, in contrast to statute law laid down in Acts of Parliament. The third meaning is the law (both statute and case law) derived from principles worked out in this country as distinct from those jurisdictions within England which used rules taken from Roman law, particularly Admiralty law concerning ships and deep waters and the canon law of the Church. The fourth meaning is all English law, and the law of those countries of the Commonwealth and the United States which adopted English law, as compared with civil law derived from Roman law which applies in Scotland, on the Continent and in Japan.

There is another meaning, relevant here, which contrasts custom that is local with the common law as the law common to the whole realm. Common law applies generally and in the absence of custom. Custom prevails locally over

---

[8]   Watkins, C, *A Treatise on Copyholds* (James Bullock, 4th cdn by Thomas Coventry, 1825) 2.41.

[9]   Coke, Sir Edward, *A commentary on Littleton being the first part of the Institutes of the Laws of England* (1628) 110b.

[10]   (1841) 12 Ad & E 265, 302.

[11]   (1876) 24 WR 603.

common law. The common law guides and corrects custom, so that a custom inconsistent with certain basic principles of common law will be held to be unreasonable and void, and in that sense common law prevails over custom. Furthermore, custom can always be restricted or abolished by statute.

Custom is local not only in the sense that it applies to one place rather than all places, but also in the sense that it applies to the locality rather than to persons or their property. An individual property may have the benefit of a specific right, such as a right of way, and may enjoy it by ancient prescription (that is to say by having had it before 1189) but that is a private right not a custom. Custom benefits the inhabitants of a locality, who will be a fluctuating class of people and undefined save by reference to the area.

The locality to which custom applies can vary. It may be a town, parish, hamlet, borough, hundred, shire or forest. Coke says that 'in special cases a custome may be alledged within a hamlet, a towne, a burgh, a city, a mannor, an honour, an hundred, and a county;' and that it might benefit a barony or an honour,[12] but the relevant cases are ancient and might now be followed only where the issue concerns a single locality. *Newton v Shafto*[13] in 1667 concerned an inheritance custom at Tynemouth which was both a manor and an honour. This book is primarily concerned with customs of the manor. A custom might benefit several manors[14] but it would seem that they must be a locality.

A final local requirement is that the custom of an English manor must be local to that manor. It was different on the Continent. In France and Germany, when new villages were founded they were often endowed with a set of customs taken from another settlement. The customs of Beaumont-en-Argonne and Lorris[15] were especially popular for that purpose. In new English towns it was also the practice to adopt customs from elsewhere in a block, especially during the expansive period of the thirteenth century, and the customs of Newcastle and Winchester[16] were given to several new towns. But this did not happen in English villages. This was because there were in any case very few completely new settlements in the long and densely settled countryside of England and those there were started as offshoots of existing villages in the form of hamlets

---

[12] Coke, *A Commentary on Littleton op cit* 110b. See also cases cited in *Halsbury's Laws op cit* para 616, fns 16 and 17.

[13] (1665–7) 1 Lev 172, 83 ER 354, 1 Sid 267 82 ER 1097, 84 ER 70, 2 Keb 111.

[14] *Fitzhardinge v Purcell* [1908] 2 Ch 139.

[15] Bloch, M, *Feudal Society* (English translation by LA Manyon) (Routledge Kegan Paul, 1961) 277.

[16] Stubbs, W, *Select Charters from the beginning to 1307* (Oxford University Press, 9th edn, 1913) 195.

which grew. There was no gap in the pattern of custom and no need to introduce new customs from outside.

In the twenty-first century the issue of locality has come before the courts in a new context. As discussed in 19.6 there has been much litigation about town and village greens arising from the possibility under s 22 of the Commons Registration Act 1965 of claiming as a green land which has been used by local people for 20 years. The original expression in the Act referred to 'inhabitants of any locality'. Because this statutory type of green was to some extent modelled on the ancient customary green, the judges interpreted the expression in the same way as they would have for a customary green[17] (19.7). However, many users of greens came from areas which were either less than a locality as so defined or an area which might straddle several. The expression was therefore amended in s 98 of the Countryside and Rights of Way Act 2000 to say 'inhabitants of any locality, or of any neighbourhood within a locality', but even that has given rise to problems of interpretation as to what is a neighbourhood and whether that can include several adjacent localities. In *Adamson v Paddico (267) Ltd*[18] the Court of Appeal held that a locality must, for this purpose, mean one recognised by law.

At common law, if those who used the land came from more than one locality that was fatal to the claim. In *Edwards v Jenkins*[19] there was a claim to carry on sports and pastimes on land in the parish of Beddington, in Surrey for all the inhabitants for the time being of that parish, and of the neighbouring parishes of Carshalton and Mitcham. The claim failed. In *New Windsor Corporation v Mellor*[20] Lord Denning said that that decision had gone too far. In *Oxfordshire County Council v Oxford City Council* Lord Hoffmann said[21] that there was 'no doubt that the locality rule was the pinch-point through which many claims to customary rights of recreation failed to pass'. Lord Hoffmann,[22] considering the meaning of what had been described in the Court of Appeal[23] as the 'new concept' of a 'neighbourhood within a locality' introduced by s 98 of the 2000 Act said:

> 'Any neighbourhood within a locality' is obviously drafted with a deliberate imprecision which contrasts with the insistence of the old law upon a locality defined by legally significant boundaries. I should say at this point that I cannot

---

[17]   See *Oxfordshire County Council v Oxford City Council* [2006] 2 AC 674.

[18]   [2012] EWCA Civ 262.

[19]   [1896] 1 Ch 308, per Kekewich J at 313.

[20]   [1975] Ch 380 at 387.

[21]   [2006] 2 AC 674 at [11].

[22]   Ibid at [27].

[23]   By Carnwath LJ: [2006] Ch 43 at [65].

agree with Sullivan J in *R (Cheltenham Builders Ltd) v South Gloucestershire District Council*[24] that the neighbourhood must be wholly within a single locality. That would introduce the kind of technicality which the amendment was clearly intended to abolish. The fact that the word 'locality' when it first appears in subsection (1A) must mean a single locality is no reason why the context of 'neighbourhood within a locality' should not lead to the conclusion that it means 'within a locality or localities'.

It is unfortunate that issues concerning modern public open spaces have become confused by ancient rules on the extent of customary rights.

4.3   ANCIENT AND CONTINUOUS

Customs must be ancient and continuous, that is they must have existed since the beginning of the reign of Richard I in 1189 and have been enjoyed ever since. In *Hammerton v Honey*[25] Jessel MR pointed out that the requirement of continuity simply brings out the legal status of custom: if it were not continually being practised, that is a strong indication that it is not a legal matter but one of permission or occasional activity with no legal standing.

Why 1189? The usual answer was given by Cockburn CJ in *Angus v Dalton*[26] in a case concerning easements. He explained it as analogous to a limitation period for the recovery of land. Under the Limitation Act 1980 if the titular owner of unregistered land is dispossessed for 12 years he cannot then evict a squatter – he has left it too late.[27] In the Middle Ages things were more leisurely. From time to time periods were fixed by reference not to a rolling number of years before a moving present but to a fixed date. The last time this was fixed was in 1275[28] when it was put at 1189. Parliament never got around to changing that until the modern system (initially with a period of 60 years) was adopted in the time of Henry VIII.[29] The logic is that the procedures for the recovery of land also applied to challenging easements. It is said that the judges applied the principle which Parliament had laid down for recovery of land to the recognition of customs.

That may be the correct reason, but another answer is possible. The year 1189 was relevant not just to limitation of actions but also to other rights, for instance

---

[24]   [2004] JPL 975.

[25]   (1876) 24 WR 603.

[26]   (1877) 3 QBD 85, confirmed by the House of Lords in *Dalton v Angus* (1881) 6 App Cas 740.

[27]   *JA Pye (Oxford) Ltd v Graham* [2003] 1 AC 419. Different rules apply to registered land.

[28]   3 Ed 1 c39.

[29]   32 Hen 8 c2.

putting rivers 'in defence' to create a several fishery (12.7). Not only did landowners dispossess other landowners (which only affected private landlords) but many people claimed royal rights or franchises (16.8) which affected the Crown. The Crown remedy was the writ of *Quo Warranto*. This was an order to the claimant to show 'by what warrant' he enjoyed the franchise. It might be addressed to the lord of a seaside manor who took the profits of wreck, an inland lord who held a market, or the burgesses of a town who claimed to be a corporation. If the claimant could not produce a written warrant from the king or his predecessor then the claim was disallowed unless he was prepared to purchase a formal charter granting the franchise. In 1290 (only 15 years after the period for possession of land was fixed) Parliament passed the statute of *Quo Warranto* which was a similar limitation Act applying to franchises. Just as under the Act of 1275 the occupier of land who had no ancient title deeds but could show that he and his predecessors had been there since 1189 could not be evicted, so under *Quo Warranto* 1290 the claimant to a franchise who could show exercise and enjoyment of the liberty since 1189 did not need to produce a warrant. That was only fair since some such rights went back to Anglo-Saxon times and if there ever had been a charter it had been lost.

Rights enjoyed by custom are more like franchises than the occupation of land. For example many claimed customs relate to the foreshore, such as the drying of nets as in *Mercer v Denne*[30] or the claim to take coals washed up on the shore as in *Beckett (Alfred F) Ltd v Lyons*[31] (where the custom was not established) and they are similar to the franchise of wreck, since the foreshore originally belonged to the Crown. Custom has to be claimed on behalf of a group of people living in a locality which is similar to the claim of a group of people to be a legal entity known as a corporation which is treated as a separate legal person, and the right to be a corporation is a franchise. However, other customs are more like private servitudes, which involve doing something like taking recreation or abstracting water on the land of another, which is a private right like the holding of land. For whatever reason 3 September 1189 became 'the time whereof the memory of man runneth not to the contrary'.

One point of curiosity is the position between 1189 (the last date a custom could arise) and 1275 or 1290 (when the rule became established that was so). One of the great books on English law, *De Legibus et Consuetudinibus Angliae* (*On the Laws and Customs of England*), was written at just that time. It is attributed to Henry de Bracton, a judge under Henry III, who died in 1268, but he was most likely the editor, although he added a good deal of material. Most of it was written before 1237 and it was published (long before printing) some time after

---

[30]   [1904] 2 Ch 534.

[31]   [1967] Ch 449, [1967] 1 All ER 833, 65 LGR 73.

1256.[32] Bracton (as it is convenient to call the book's author) was therefore writing at a time when new customs could not arise, but no one living at that time could have known that. What is his attitude to custom?

The most important type of custom (see 5.4) was customary landholding. Later called copyhold, in Bracton's time it was called land in villeinage. He distinguishes[33] between ancient villeinage or one newly created (*de antiquo villenagio vel de novo*). Speaking of villeinage land held by a man who is himself free and not a bondsman, Bracton also distinguishes[34] between such a man holding in pure villeinage and holding in villeinage which is not pure, granted under an agreement for certain specified services and customs. He seems to be distinguishing between ancient villein lands held purely by custom[35] and a newer type held at least in part by agreement. The later law was clear that copyholds could not (in general) come into existence after 1189. Bracton's text suggests that in practice at the material time they did not. This sets out the law as understood by later generations. What Bracton and his contemporaries thought is a matter for the historian not the lawyer.

Lay customs are distinct from ecclesiastical customs under the canon law which could continue to be created by unhindered practice for a period of 20 years. In England the rule about 1189 did not apply to them. Until the Reformation[36] Church law was separate from secular law. It was incorporated by the statute 35 Henry 8 c 16 (1543) and thereafter new Church customs could not come into existence. Thus the customs of parish churches can be younger than the customs of the laity[37] and this may be relevant for instance to the creation of churchways (20.6).

Once a custom is shown to have existed continuously for a long time the courts will presume that it existed in 1189 and it is then for the person opposing it to show that it could not have existed then. This is difficult. In theory it can be done on the basis that it was either physically or legally impossible. On both counts the courts have leant in favour of customs. Thus in *Mercer v Denne*[38] the drying of the nets could not have taken place on the foreshore in question in the case because the location had then been covered by the sea, but the court accepted that as the land accreted into the sea the custom was carried with it.

---

[32]   Bracton, Sir Henry (ed), *De legibus et consuetudinibus angliae* (c 1257) (S Thorne ed)) (Belknap Press of Harvard University Press, 1977) Introduction.

[33]   Ibid f 168.

[34]   Ibid f 208b.

[35]   Ibid f 199b.

[36]   Ecclesiastical Appeals Act 24 H8 c 12 1532/3.

[37]   See *Harthan v Harthan* [1949] P 115.

[38]   [1904] 2 Ch 534, [1905] 2 Ch 538.

The courts also recognised that customs of inheritance could include entails within the family even though entails were not introduced until an Act of 1285,[39] by assuming that there was common law or customary precedent. However, the argument on this point may be based on a misunderstanding (see 22.7). Nonetheless, if there is clear evidence that a custom must have originated later than 1189 the court will accept that evidence and disallow it.

To show that a custom is ancient it is not necessary to show how it originated. In most cases that is not possible, but theories of origin have affected the interpretation of rights. The traditional view, going back at least to the seventeenth century, is that all rights of the manor, including common rights, tenures such as copyhold and customs began with a grant by the lord who was once the unfettered owner. As late as 1960 in *Iveagh v Martin*,[40] which concerned certain rights claimed by Men of Bosham in Sussex, Paull J said: 'It is necessary before custom is proved to assume a lost grant to that effect in existence in AD 1189'. As discussed in 8.1 that is unhistorical. A better view was expressed in the House of Lords by Viscount Maugham in *Wolstanton Ltd and Attorney-General of the Duchy of Lancaster v Newcastle-under-Lyme Corporation*[41] where he said:

> The cases I have cited show that it is a mistake to suppose that we must assume that the lord in or previously to the year 1189 granted the copyholds to his tenants with a reservation of his rights in the terms of the alleged custom. ... Indeed the speeches in this House in *Salisbury (Marquis) -v- Gladstone*[42] proceed on the basis that it is not correct in the case of a custom to suppose that there has been a grant.

The origin of custom is relevant to its interpretation. If it was by grant then two rules apply: first, that if the terms of the grant are ambiguous the courts will find in favour of the person to whom it was made (or his successor); secondly, that the person who made the grant (or his successor) will be obliged to act in such a way that he does not derogate or diminish what he has granted. If custom is not a grant but simply an ancient arrangement then those rules will not apply and the matter will be decided on an even-handed basis.

---

[39]   Estates Tail Act (de Donis) 1285 (13 Edward I c1).

[40]   [1961] 1 QB 232, [1960] 2 All ER 668.

[41]   [1940] AC 850.

[42]   (1861) IX H L Cas 692, 11 ER 900.

4.4 REASONABLE

A custom must be reasonable in the sense that it must comply with minimum requirements of the common law. The law uses a test of reasonableness to lay down general standards, for instance in respect of behaviour in the context of crime or tort, often judged by reference to the conduct expected of the reasonable man or the man on the Clapham Omnibus[43] as he used to be called (no doubt on his way to take fresh air and exercise on Clapham Common). If a body such as a local council takes a decision that the law considers that no reasonable council could have taken, then the decision is ineffective. Likewise, the test that a custom must be reasonable means that the subject matter of the custom can be reviewed by the common law and be measured against the general standards laid down for the whole country. Reasonableness is not the same as common sense. Many customs, such as the widow's ram of Emborne described below, seem strange enough but were good in law. A custom will be unreasonable only if it violates legal standards.

The leading case, *Wolstanton Ltd and Attorney-General of the Duchy of Lancaster v Newcastle-under-Lyme Corporation*[44] in 1940, related to mineral rights in the manor of Newcastle-under-Lyme which belonged to the king as Duke of Lancaster. As explained in 11.7 there is a general custom that ownership of minerals in copyhold land is divided between the lord and the copyholder so that the lord owns the mineral rights but cannot work the minerals without the copyholder's consent. Some manors (of which Newcastle was one) have a special custom that the lord can work them without consent. This would usually be by deep underground workings that would not disturb the surface. The Duchy's licensee claimed to be able to work the minerals in such a way that it would cause subsidence and damage buildings on the surface of land which had once been copyhold but had been enfranchised in 1926 subject to the continuing mineral rights of the lord. The House of Lords found that such a custom was unreasonable and bad because, if exercised, it would destroy the surface and thus nullify the rights of the owner of that surface.

Other cases have held customs to be unreasonable because they were unfair by lumping together people with different interests. Some alleged customs are bad because they involve claims to rights that are unrelated to the needs of the holdings, particularly houses, within the manor to which they are claimed to be attached. Generally, reasonableness involves a sense of proportion. A custom

---

[43] The reference to the reasonable man being the man on the Clapham Omnibus has long been in legal circulation. It is sometimes attributed to Lord Bowen. For two much-cited examples, see *Director of Public Prosecutions v Smith* [1961] AC 290 at 331 in criminal law and *Bolam v Friern Hospital Management Committee* [1951] 1 WLR 582 at 586 in tort.

[44] [1940] AC 850.

will not be bad simply because it imposes a burden on a piece of land, or on the occupier of premises, but if it is an unduly heavy burden, or if it destroys the land or impoverishes the owner, it is unreasonable because it is unfair.

For that reason a profit cannot be a customary right.[45] A profit is the right to take something, such as grass, wood or stone from the land of another. Rights of common (10.3) are profits. A profit is liable to exhaust or deplete the resources of the land subject to it. In the case of a customary right, usually enjoyed by members of an undefined and fluctuating group of people, if there were a large number then the exercise of the right by them could destroy the land. It does not matter if more people than expected dance on the green or dry their nets on the shore, but it does matter if they take the soil and its produce such as turf, grass or wood. An apparent exception is the right to take water from a river. Although a river bed and the space through which the river flows are private property, the water is not; as such, abstracting it from the flow is not depriving anyone of anything. Such rights are now restricted by the Water Resources Act 1991 but there may still be customary rights for local people to take modest quantities of water under s 27 of that Act.

In general the law would not strike down an alleged custom as unreasonable if it simply affected the lord and tenant on the assumption that before 1189 their predecessors might have agreed anything.[46] If, however, it could affect third parties, such as a claim to deposit coals on the lands of other copyholders[47] or to take turf in unlimited quantities from the common,[48] it could be.

Rights of common and customary rights are similar in many ways, and in the context of the manor benefited the same people, but they were distinct. Rights of common may be governed by customary rules and regulated through customary courts but they could not be customs because they subsisted at common law. The rights of customary tenants were enjoyed by custom, not by common right, but where they were similar to rights of common they were called commonable (10.5) and would usually be subject to similar rules. On enfranchisement they were often enlarged into statutory rights of common and, if still exercised, they must have been registered and so became statutory rights.

---

[45] *Gateward's Case* (1607) 6 Co Rep 59b, 77 ER 344.

[46] *Salisbury (Marquis) v Gladstone* (1861) IX H L Cas (Clark's) 692, 11 ER 900.

[47] *Broadbent v Wilks* (1742) Willes 360, 125 ER 1214.

[48] *Wilson v Willes* (1806) 7 East 121, 103 ER 46.

4.5   CERTAIN

In *Hammerton v Honey*[49] Jessel MR observed that custom is law and all law must be certain. It is essential that a person knows what rights he can exercise or what others can do on his property. But certainty means more than that for, as the judge said, 'when we are told that custom must be certain, reasonable and continuous – that all relates to evidence of a custom. There is no such thing as law which is uncertain – the notion of law means a certain rule of some kind'.[50] If this were not so any vague practice, of unknown but ancient and undefined origin, practised by different people in different ages might be custom and hence law. Thus, a person who claims that some practice is a custom must show exactly what is claimed, where and when it can be exercised (it may be on a particular day, it may be at any time, but it must be known) and the class of people entitled to exercise it and, linking with the requirement of locality, the precise definition of where they come from.

Although a custom must be certain, the scope may vary within limits. Thus in *Fitch v Rawlings*[51] there was an established custom at Steeple Bumstead in Essex to play lawful games in a particular close. The question arose whether it was lawful to play cricket, which was unknown in 1189 and, if known, was made unlawful by an Act of 1477[52] (reversed by Henry VIII, since when cricket has been lawful) and therefore if it had existed it could not have been continuous. It was held that if the custom was to play lawful games then that meant such games as might be introduced and be lawful from time to time, so that cricket could be played. Similarly, the nature of customary services of bondsmen was uncertain, as distinct from the certain services of freemen. Yet, as explained in 5.2, provided that the fact and quantity of services was established the details could be left to be determined when the customary services were called for.

In the context of the manor, certainty as to persons depended on their being lord or tenants (either freehold or copyhold) of the manor and residing or holding land within its boundaries. Initially the nature of customs was ascertained by the evidence of free tenants or the homage in the manor court. From the thirteenth century many customs were recorded in writing in custumals (25.3).

---

[49]   (1876) 24 WR 603.

[50]   (1876) 24 WR 603 at 603.

[51]   (1795) 2 Hy Bl 394, 126 ER 614.

[52]   17 Ed 4 c 3.

4.6 SERVICES

Very few customary services now remain. Originally they were the most important feature of the manor but over the centuries nearly all have disappeared. The most straightforward were agricultural services. The manor was divided between the lord's demesne and the tenanted lands. The tenants worked their own lands and owed work services to the lord on his. As explained in 5.3 these services could be certain or uncertain in content and this affected the status of the tenant, but whether they were restricted to carting one load of hay at Michaelmas or involved three days' work every week of the year, they took up much of the tenant's time. Over the years most were commuted for quitrents, as mentioned in 14.6.

However, services did not just involve doing agricultural work. Just as manors might be held by a service that included, for instance, bridge repair, so a tenement within the manor could be similarly burdened, and such burdens have survived. The best known is fencing against the common. The leading modern case is *Egerton v Harding*[53] where Sprat's Cottage, owned by Miss Egerton, and Binswood Farm, owned by Mr and Mrs Harding, both adjoined Binswood Common at East Worldham, Hampshire. Cattle from the farm strayed into the cottage garden and caused damage. Miss Egerton claimed damages but lost because the court found that there was a custom that she was obliged to erect a fence against the common to keep cattle out and had failed to comply with her duty. Such fencing customs are found elsewhere. On Dartmoor they have been confirmed by s 9 of the Dartmoor Commons Act 1985 which declares 'for the avoidance of doubt' that the custom is to fence against the Commons. It is possible that, despite the declaratory wording, the effect has been to convert the service from a customary to a statutory obligation.

Another type of obligation arising from custom was found in *London and North-Western Railway Company v Fobbing Levels Sewer Commissioners*[54] where a railway company was found liable (either by custom or grant) to repair a sea wall. It does not here matter whether the origin is seen as an ancient grant of land in return for a service of repairing the wall or an ancient custom burdening the land. The result is the same. Such an obligation, as well as being a customary burden, is listed in the Land Registration Act 2002, Schs 1 and 3, para 13, and will be subject to the temporary provisions of the Act (see 25.9) so that if it is to continue to be enforceable it will need to be protected by registration or caution.

---

[53] [1975] 1 QB 62, [1974] All ER 689, 28 P&CR 369.

[54] (1897) 75 LT 629.

Other services include the former custom in the manor of Wimbledon[55] that the tenants (collectively) had to provide weights and scales, stocks and a whipping-post. Mill-service was once a general custom (see 17.3). In the manor of Sedgley[56] in Staffordshire an heir was bound to serve as beadle and reeve for one year after his father's death.

4.7   INHERITANCE AND DISPOSITION

The customs of inheritance and disposition are now all obsolete but until 1925 they were important and potentially governed the nature of thousands of customary estates throughout the country. Customs of disposition must originally have prevented villeins from selling their land, but by the sixteenth century such restraints were largely obsolete and the tenant could surrender his land and require a new tenant chosen by him to be admitted. Legal developments related chiefly to powers of leasing (see 5.6). Since a copyholder held in theory at the will of the lord but had the right to keep his land until harvest he was considered to have an interest from year to year. By general custom he could grant a lease for less than a year but no more.[57] In some manors it was recognised that he had a greater right to the land and by special custom he could grant long leases.

There were two general customs of inheritance. Gavelkind was usual in Kent though it existed elsewhere, for instance in the manor of Stepney and Hackney.[58] Instead of land descending to the eldest son it was divided equally among all the sons. In borough english, found in much of the country, the land passed to the youngest son. There were innumerable special customs of inheritance. For instance in the manors of Framfield[59] and Mayfield in Sussex[60] descent of assarted lands passed to the eldest son in the usual way but bond lands passed to the youngest son or daughter. The rules on inheritance by a widow of her late husband's holdings differed from manor to manor. A general custom was freebench under which a wife had a third (or sometimes a quarter) of her husband's lands during her life or so long as she remained unmarried and chaste. In the manors of East and West Emborne and Chadleworth in Berkshire[61] this was modified by a special custom that an unchaste widow, who

---

[55] Watkins *op cit* 2.554.

[56] Ibid 2.571.

[57] *Combes's Case* (1613) 9 Co Rep 75a, 77 ER 843.

[58] Watkins *op cit* 2.514.

[59] Ibid 2.493.

[60] Ibid 2.501.

[61] Scriven *op cit* 69.

repented and came into the manor court riding backwards on a black ram, confessed her offence and asked for restitution, would be allowed to have her freebench back. As explained in 7.10 it had been possible to leave copyhold land by will since 1815 (and in practice earlier by a surrender to the use of a will) so that in practice much copyhold land never passed by custom; but the rules applied on intestacy until abolition.

Under the Land Transfer Act 1897 freeholds vested in personal representatives, thereby abolishing any remaining customs of inheritance for them. However, s 1(4) provided that that did not apply to the legal estate in copyholds which, on intestacy, therefore vested in the customary heir in order to preserve the rights of the lord on admission, although an equitable interest in copyhold did so vest.[62] All customs of inheritance and disposition relating to copyholds were in law abolished in 1925.[63] In practice things may have been different. For instance in the Royal manor of Portland in Dorset descent was by gavelkind (or a similar special custom) and transfers of holdings were made by church-gift in the church of St George. Despite the 1925 legislation many islanders stuck to the old ways until at least the 1960s and some titles to land on Portland were accepted as passing in this way, although where lawyers became involved they supplemented the procedure by more orthodox methods.

4.8 ENJOYMENT

Examples of customs of enjoyment have been given in this chapter and others will appear in this book. While services were owed by tenants to the lord and inheritance regulated arrangements between tenants, enjoyment involved rights of tenants against the lord, such as doing things (dancing, drying nets, taking water) on his land. Sometimes they operate as special customs derogating from general ones. For instance the lord has by general custom the property in minerals (and until 1925 in timber) in copyhold land. In many manors special customs allowed the tenant to take minerals or timber from the tenant's own copyhold (11.7). Occasionally the tenant even had sporting rights. In the manor of Alrewas and Lapley[64] in Staffordshire the tenants seem to have owed a customary service of giving fish to the lord. Later that service was commuted for a quitrent but the tenants retained a customary right to catch fish.[65] In several other manors the tenants had fishing rights and the origin could be similar, although the courts may sometimes presume a different explanation, as in

---

[62] *Re Somerville and Turner's Contract* [1903] 2 Ch 583.

[63] Law of Property Act 1922, Sch 12, para (1)(d) applying to enfranchised land.

[64] Watkins *op cit* 2.558.

[65] Ibid 2.558.

Goodman v Mayor of Saltash[66] (21.5), which involved an oysterage in the River Tamar near Plymouth. The House of Lords explained the right as a profit being held in trust for the local inhabitants. The House may have considered that it could not be a customary right as it resembled a profit even though exercisable in tidal waters.

A particular custom of enjoyment was a customary way. Rights of way illustrate the distinction between common law, custom and prescriptive rights. A footpath may be used by many people but its legal nature depends on the nature of the use. First, it may be a highway, that is a public footpath open to use by anyone from anywhere. This may be so because of ancient use, or because the landowner has dedicated it, or because it was established under statute, such as a local inclosure act or the Highways Act 1980. Such a way is governed by common law in the sense that the rules both derive from ancient cases (although much altered by statute) and they are common to the whole of England. Highways are sometimes called common ways. Secondly, a footpath may be a private easement that benefits only a specific house. Again it might have been granted by the landowner to the house owner, or successive occupiers of the house may have used it long enough to have a prescriptive right. Thirdly, it may be a customary way, such as a churchway or a way to common fields which can only be used by inhabitants of the parish or the manor and not by the public at large.[67] *Brocklebank v Thompson*[68] concerned an issue whether a particular customary way was manorial or parochial. Simply by looking at the footpath it is impossible to discover its legal nature.

4.9   EXTINCTION OF CUSTOM

Customary rights cannot come to an end merely by disuse, although if a custom has not been legally established and is shown not to have been exercised for many years that may be taken as evidence that it never was a binding custom. It can be extinguished by statute or by loss of function. Where a right was annexed to a customary tenement the enfranchisement or permanent surrender (not just a surrender as part of admission of a new tenant) would extinguish that right by unity of seisin, as would an escheat where the lord retained and leased out the land.

---

[66]   (1882) 7 App Cas 633.

[67]   *Gatewards Case* (1606) 6 Co Rep 59b, 77 ER 344; *Poole v Huskisson* (1843) 11 M&W 827, 152 ER 1039; *Brocklebank v Thompson* [1903] 2 Ch 344; *Farquhar v Newbury Rural District Council* [1909] 1 Ch 12; *Loder v Gadden* (1999) 78 P&CR 223 at 228. Jessel C, 'Customary Ways' (2009) *Rights of Way Law Review* 11.9.

[68]   [1903] 2 Ch 344.

The Law of Property Act 1922, Sch 12, para (1)(d) provides that the enfranchised land 'shall not be subject to certain specified customs' or 'to any other custom whatsoever' but in the context this refers only to customs of inheritance. Customs of enjoyment at least as commonable rights held with copyhold land were continued under para (4). The status of customs of service is unclear.

A custom can also be extinguished if it benefits an estate or tenure which is itself extinguished. *Green v R*[69] concerned a customary practice of appointing churchwardens in the parish of Doddington in Lincolnshire. Some time prior to 1782 the custom was established by litigation. A private Act in 1847 reorganised the parish and the issue was whether the custom had survived the Act. Lord Cairns LC said:

> This custom was a custom connected with and attaching to the hamlet or chapelry of *March, quâ* hamlet or chapelry. The Act of Parliament does not continue the hamlet or chapelry of March. If it did, it might well be said that incidents of this kind were continued along with it. The Act of Parliament makes, ecclesiastically speaking, a *tabula rasa* of the whole of the ecclesiastically arrangements within the area of the old parish of *Doddington*, and, having made that *tabula rasa*, it proceeds to erect and to create three new well-known and clear ecclesiastically divisions, namely, parishes, or rectories, within the old area; and, creating these three new ecclesiastical divisions, it enacts that each of them is to be created after the pattern or example of the old and entire rectory, and that each new rectory is to have the incidents of the old one. My Lords, it therefore ceases to be a question as to whether a custom attaching to the old chapelry or hamlet of *March* is or is not taken away by express words. The hamlet itself as an ecclesiastical division disappears – the thing is gone – that to which the custom attached is no longer in existence, and therefore that has been done by the Act of Parliament which is much stronger than the abolition of a custom by express words; that is abolished upon which alone the custom could exist, and to which alone it could apply.

Extinction by statute is normally straightforward, although issues can arise as to construction of the Act.[70] A specific instance is failure to register a customary right to take recreation on a village green. At one time there was a theory that even if the green was not registered under the Commons Registration Act 1965 the right might continue to exist in some sense[71] but this view was rejected by the House of Lords in *Oxfordshire County Council v Oxford City Council*[72]

---

[69] (1875–76) LR 1 App Cas 513.

[70] *New Windsor Corporation v Taylor* [1899] AC 41; *Wyld v Silver* [1963] 1 QB 169, although either of those cases may have involved a franchise.

[71] *In re Turnworth Down, Dorset* [1978] Ch 251; *R v Suffolk County Council, Ex p Steed* (1996) 75 P&CR 102.

[72] [2006] 2 AC 674 at [17]–[19].

(19.7). All greens therefore now depend on registration, and the former customary rights must therefore have been converted to statutory rights. Thus, the logic in *Green v R* would apply for instance if a village green had, before 1970, been reached along a customary path and the green was not then registered. Even if it continued to be used for recreation and after 20 years it was registered as a new green, the customary way would have been extinguished and would not revive.

4.10 VARIETY

The effect of custom was that no two manors were alike. That both caused and reflected their diversity. Even considering England alone, apart from the rest of Britain or Europe, they were diverse enough. One elementary distinction, drawn more by geographers than lawyers, is between champion and woodland landscapes.[73] Champion country lies in the plains and in the Middle Ages comprised large open fields with few trees. The imaginary village of Middleton described in 1.1 is typical of such settlements. Woodland landscape by contrast had more closes, and such open fields as existed were smaller and irregular in shape. There were hedges with trees in them and great woods on the hillsides or in the valleys. Other things being equal, manorial control was stronger in the typical champion country of the lowland plain that extends across the middle of England, where discipline was needed to keep the open field system going, and where settlements were focussed in central or nuclear villages. In woodland manors habitations tended to be more scattered, with isolated farms whose holders valued their independence and took their own agricultural decisions free from interference by the manor court.

However, other things were rarely equal.[74] Another, sociological, distinction is between closed and open settlements. Closed manors were those where the lord held most of the land, normally in demesne, although some manors with copyhold could be closed to some degree, and most of the land was either leased or kept in hand. The lord controlled all aspects of life, appointed the vicar and the manorial officials, decided who lived where and prevented unwanted immigrants from settling. In an open village there was either no lord or many

---

[73] There is a considerable literature on this. The distinction seems to go back at least to the sixteenth century. See Williamson, T and Bellamy, L, *Property and Landscape* (George Philip, 1987) 16, map; Rackham, O, *The Illustrated History of the Countryside* (George Weidenfeld & Nicolson Ltd, 1994) 10; Rackham, O, 'Ancient Woodland and Hedges in England', in Woodell, SRJ (ed), *The English Landscape, Past, Present and Future* (Oxford, 1985) 68; Williamson, T, 'Explaining Regional Landscapes: Woodland and Champion in Southern and Eastern England' (1988) 10 *Landscape History* 5.

[74] Mills, DR, *Lord and Peasant in Nineteenth Century Britain* (Croom Helm Rowman & Littlefield, 1980).

small lords with none dominant, or, if there was only one or two lords, a strong element of freeholders and independent copyholders. Open villages tended to be spread out, often with cottages dotted over the waste. Any village organisation was done through the court leet or the church vestry rather than the manor courts. The inhabitants built their own houses in their own style and in places on their own land chosen by them.

Closed and open manors were found throughout the country. A closed manor could become open by loss of control, by sales of land by an impecunious lord or simply by tenants claiming and asserting customary rights over the centuries. Where they were not written down in custumals it was difficult to deny customs claimed by the inhabitants even if in fact they had emerged long after 1189. Conversely, an open parish could become closed by a wealthy lord buying up or engrossing the plots of independent holders, especially if they had been weakened by misfortune, famine or plague, or simply by the application of ruthless pressure backed by armed force.

Different parts of England had different styles of manor. Some were due to geology. Economic conditions on a Pennine hill manor or the moors of the South West gave rise to different customs from the lowlands of Bedfordshire or Hampshire. The rights of the lord in the mining districts of Cornwall or Derbyshire involved a form of control that was irrelevant in the fenlands of East Anglia, but in turn the sandy soils of Norfolk gave rise to practises such as foldcourse that were not needed on more fertile grasslands. Geography also affected rights. The lord of a manor on an established route or one that included a town would gain much of his wealth from the control of trade, market tolls and leases of shops. Manors on the coasts or on rivers, especially those with good anchorages, profited from a variety of harbour franchises. Likewise the customs of a manor on rich arable land differed from those that specialised in dairying or sheep pastures.

History had at least as much influence.[75] Kent was known for its peculiarities. As well as customs such as gavelkind, the very boundaries of the manor often included distant outliers of hill pasture. On the Welsh and Scottish borders manors long retained a military character.[76] Some land was held by the service of cornage – the duty to sound a horn when a raider was sighted. Much of East Anglia and the North East up to Yorkshire included small manors with many freeholders or socmen. Historians have derived this from the Danish invasion,

---

[75]   Loyn, HR, *Anglo-Saxon England and the Norman Conquest* (Longman, 2nd edn, 1991) 353; Blair, J, *Early Medieval Surrey: Landholding, Church and Settlement before 1300* (Surrey Archaeological Society, 1991) 75.

[76]   Scriven *op cit* 17, citing Lord Ellenborough in *Doe d Reay v Huntingdon* 4 East 271, 102 ER 834.

but it may be older and date back to the original Anglian settlement. By contrast the West and South West had (and still have) many large estates with dependent closed settlements which, some historians think, derive from the older pattern of Celtic and Roman control. However, much must depend on soil type, climate and the type of farming in the region.

Manors could be large like Leominster, which at the time of *Domesday* had 80 hides and 260 teams of oxen, or Taunton, which had 100 teams.[77] On the other hand, also in *Domesday*, there were manors of 30 acres or less (the size of a virgate) in Suffolk and Essex. In later years both extremes disappeared, the large ones by being broken up, the small ones by being recognised only as reputed manors (if at all) after the rule developed that every manor had to have at least two dependent freeholders. Manors could be compact within a single boundary line or scattered over miles of countryside in small and large pieces or with outliers beyond the core. Reputed manors could comprise only demesne land or have no demesne at all. They could be of any shape, size or make-up.

This diversity runs throughout the law of manors. This book deals largely with general customs and the common law of manors. These affected the rights of lords and tenants across England but they provide only a skeleton, a basic legal structure in which the full variety of manors could be worked out. This occurred partly in the customary courts and partly in the royal courts and in Parliament. In the royal courts the issues were mainly between lords and tenants, a constant struggle for their respective rights that continued through the centuries. The end result was that customs have been reduced to negligible importance and the rules of the common law and of statute have prevailed.

---

[77] Chibnall, M, *Anglo-Norman England 1066–1166* (Basil Blackwell, 1986) 136.

PART II

LANDS

Chapter 5

Freehold and Copyhold

5.1   SERVICE, TENURE AND JURISDICTION

To this day the former status of manorial land can affect the rights both of the lord and of the owner to minerals, sporting, old rents, grazing and other rights and burdens. Land within the manor which did not belong to the lord was freehold or copyhold and, of the two, copyhold was distinctive of the manor. This book is about the law of the manor, but if it had been written at any time between 1600 and 1925 it would have been called – as many such books were called – the law of copyhold. The earliest was *The Complete Copyholder; being a Learned Discourse of the Antiquity and Nature of Manors and Copyholds, with all things thereto Incident* by Sir Edward Coke. The two best known were by Watkins and Scriven.[1] *A Treatise on Copyholds* by Charles Watkins went through four editions between 1797 and 1825. *A Treatise on the Law of copyholds and of the other tenures (customary and freehold) of lands within Manors with the Law of Manors and of Manorial Customs generally and the rules of evidence applicable thereto including the Law of Commons or Waste Lands and also the jurisdiction of the various manorial courts* by John Scriven went through seven editions before the last (and most authoritative) in 1896. There were other books of less authority. This book relies much on Coke, Watkins and Scriven, but they contain a great deal of material that is now obsolete.

Since the enactment of the Law of Property Act 1925, s 1 there have been only two legal estates, a fee simple absolute in possession or freehold and a term of years absolute or leasehold.[2] Before 1926 copyhold was a third type of tenure. Copyhold can be described as an estate in land held by copy of court roll according to the custom of the manor. If it is simply so held it may also be

---

[1]   For the authority of Watkins and Scriven, see *Ecclesiastical Commissioners for England v Parr* [1894] 2 QB 420 at 428.

[2]   Commonhold is expressed to be a form of freehold by Commonhold and Leasehold Reform Act 2002, s 1.

known as customary freehold. If it is also held 'at the will of the lord' it is pure copyhold. Custom which 'is the very Soul and life of Copy-hold-estates'[3] according to Coke has already been considered in 4.3. Courts are examined in 13.1 and rolls in 25.2. This chapter considers how land was held and the will of the lord, and examines a few of the rules described so carefully and in such detail by Watkins and Scriven.

To say that land is held means that the holder has the right either to occupy it or to receive rents payable by or derived from an occupier. Land may be held by anyone from the king to the humblest peasant. In *Domesday Book* the king holds, Latin *tenet*, his land, and in later texts land that comes to him is said to come *in manibus nostris* into our hands. Likewise, the cottager held his cottage even if he could be evicted without notice. The word tenure, from Latin *tenere* or French *tenir*, suggests that all land is held from a lord except the royal demesne, but the way in which that result is reached needs some explanation. Freehold, leasehold and copyhold land are held by their respective tenures.

Tenure is one aspect of a threefold relationship, of which the other two are service and jurisdiction.[4] The law governs many sorts of relationships, such as family or contract law; this account relates to property law and the manor.

In modern law tenure, service and jurisdiction are distinct. Tenure concerns land, such as the home someone lives in or the farm on which he grows crops. Tenure is governed by land law, the law of real property for freehold land and the law of landlord and tenant for leaseholds. Jurisdiction, the law governing disputes and courts, is separate. Most present-day courts and public tribunals are provided or organised by the state, as under the Senior Courts Act (formerly the Supreme Court Act) 1981, the County Courts Act 1984 and the Tribunals Courts and Enforcement Act 2007. Private tribunals do exist, such as the City Panel on Takeovers or the disciplinary tribunal of the General Medical Council, but even if they are not regulated by Parliament they are subject to judicial review by the courts, which ensure that they operate fairly and without bias. There is also an active system of arbitration under the Arbitration Act 1996 which regulates arrangements for the private resolution of disputes but under ultimate court supervision. Courts were an important aspect of the manor and are considered further in Chapter 13.

Service or employment is different again. A contract for services, provided by an independent contractor, is distinct from a contract of service given by an employee. The contractor agrees to provide a specific result, normally works for

---

[3]   *Brown's Case* (1581) 4 Co Rep 21.

[4]   Maitland, FW, *Domesday Book and Beyond* (Cambridge University Press, 1987; first published 1897) 67.

a contractual fee, sets his own hours, bears his own expenses and organises the task himself. The employee is paid a wage, attends at hours specified by his employer and follows orders. These are generalisations and do not always apply so that it can sometimes be difficult to distinguish a contract for services from a contract of service in particular circumstances, but the idea of a difference exists and is important.

In Saxon times the three were also distinct. A man might hold his land from one lord (or be free to decide for himself which lord he held it from) while owing service (particularly military service) to another while again being commended to a third (whose court he attended, whose support he looked for in disputes and whose decisions he followed). Jurisdiction went by various names but the most common was *soc*. This could apply to individuals who had *soc* over others, or to districts, such as the Soke of Peterborough which was the area of jurisdiction of the Abbot of Peterborough.[5]

In 1066 the separation of landholding, service and *soc* ceased. The idea of divided lordship became unacceptable. For the Normans service, tenure and jurisdiction were three aspects of one thing. Land was held from a lord in return for services and one of those services was suit of court. The lord was bound to protect his men and to hold a court to resolve their disputes, including disputes about land. They, in turn, were bound to attend the court as suitors, and it was at the court they rendered service. Over the centuries since 1066 the three have again become separated, but it took a long time. The manor was one of the last places where the linkage persisted.

5.2   TENURE

All land (except allodial Crown Land – 24.3) is now freehold, and all freehold land (except some consecrated land – 20.6) is now held in fee simple. The tenure of all freehold land except land in ancient demesne (24.9) and possibly some land of ecclesiastical corporations (20.10) is free and common socage. The Law of Property Act 1925, s 1 provides that a legal estate in land can only be held in fee simple or as a leasehold, and leases can only be granted out of other leases, out of fees or out of Crown land. All land therefore must have a freeholder unless it is royal demesne. Since 1925 the freehold and the fee simple have been the same but this was not previously the case and the distinction still affects rights of and within manors. It is therefore necessary to look at older types of holding land. This chapter considers tenure as it used to exist and 7.3 discusses how tenure could change.

---

[5]   Ibid 47, 67; Sawyer, P, '1066–1086: A Tenurial Revolution?', in Sawyer, P (ed), *Domesday Book: A Reassessment* (Edward Arnold, 1985) 77.

The discussion relies a good deal on older writers of standing recognised in the law as authorities, that is textbooks by respected writers of past generations. An early book is *The Laws and Customs of England*. As mentioned in 4.3, it is attributed to Henry de Bracton who was a judge under Henry III, but modern scholars suggest that he was the editor and the last of several contributors. The book was not so much an impartial description of the law in its time as a combination of description and reforms of which the authors approved, some of which were taken up and some not. The best-known writer on tenures is Sir Thomas Littleton, a judge under Edward IV. Littleton's treatise, with a commentary by Sir Edward Coke published in 1628, is the leading work on the subject. Coke was no more than Bracton a detached analyst. As shown in 27.3, he was deeply involved in a dispute with the Crown in which he supported the authority of the common law with its immemorial antiquity against equity and, to a limited extent, even against Acts of Parliament. This explains why rules about the limit of legal memory in 1189 became important after his time. His book is known as *Coke upon Littleton* and it was the *First Part of the Institutes of the Laws of England*. Another respected authority is the *Commentaries on the Laws of England* by Sir William Blackstone, a judge and Professor of Law at Oxford, who included his own analysis of tenure.

It appears from these writers and others that tenure can be analysed in four ways, each of which is relevant to understanding the manor.[6] First, tenures could be honourable or base. Secondly, they could be certain or uncertain. Thirdly, as a consequence of the foregoing they could be free or unfree. Finally, as a further consequence they could be common or customary. Much of manorial law even today depends on the former status of land as copyhold, that is customary tenure.

Honourable tenures are those held by military and ecclesiastical services, soldiers and the Church. There were different varieties of both. Manors might be granted to knights to be held by knight service, including general military duties, or more specific ones such as castle-guard or grand sergeanty. They might be granted to bishops or to abbeys, again in various ways. Within manors land could be held by a foot-soldier or other servant in petty sergeanty or by the rector in frankalmoign or free alms.[7]

Base tenures were those of trade and production. In towns, houses were frequently held by burgage tenure (21.4). In the countryside, land was held for agricultural services. The principal free base tenure was socage, which Bracton derives from old French *soc* meaning a plough, but which more likely came

---

[6] Blackstone, Sir William, *Commentaries on the Laws of England* II-5-i.

[7] Simpson, AWB, *An Introduction to the History of the Land Law* (Oxford University Press, 1961) 1.

from the Anglo-Saxon *soc* or jurisdiction. A socman, or sokeman in *Domesday Book*, is a man who is free and holds land, usually from the lord of a manor, although manors could be held in socage if the lord did not owe military or spiritual services. Later, socage became more common and, since 1660, it has been universal. In *Domesday Book* socage is found mainly in the east of England. In other parts there were men of similar status such as radmen or ridingmen[8] whose duties may have been military (and honourable) or they may have been farmers who owned and rode horses, but their tenure was in the end replaced by socage.

Both honourable and base services could be certain or uncertain. Certain services were those clearly defined and known. Castle-guard, which involved the duty to hold and defend a particular castle, was certain. So was grand sergeanty, which comprised the performance of a specific duty for the king, often at his coronation service, as well as petty sergeanty, which involved certain services for the lord (18.4). Knight service, by contrast, was uncertain. It involved attending for 40 days in wartime and performing whatever military tasks were required – the knight on service could not know in advance what his duties would be.

Frankalmoign was uncertain in that it normally involved all the general duties of a priest – to pray, to administer the sacraments, to teach, to visit the sick and so on.[9] There could also be certain ecclesiastical services such as saying three masses a year for the patron and his wife on the anniversaries of their death or at particular feasts, but in early times these were rare and, by the time they became common in the late Middle Ages, the statute *Quia Emptores* had prevented the grant of new tenures (except by the king). As all land held by honourable services was free, the distinction between certain and uncertain services for honourable tenures was not important.

Agricultural services could be certain or uncertain and here the difference mattered. Certain services might, for instance, involve taking two loads of wheat to the local market town in the weeks before and after 29 September, clearing out a particular ditch on the manor or keeping a stretch of sea wall in repair. The landholder responsible for these services was like an independent contractor. He did the work in his own way, with his own equipment and, within reason, at his own time. Uncertain services included boon-days and work-weeks, the obligation to come (either by himself or with another and sometimes with such oxen as he had) to do, on a given number of days in the week or in the year,

---

[8]   Bracton, Sir Henry, *De legibus et consuetudinibus angliae* (c 1257) f 35b, 79b; Maitland *op cit* 57.

[9]   *AG v Dean and Canons of Windsor* (1860) 8 HL Cas 369, 11 ER 472.

whatever tasks the lord's bailiff allocated to him. A famous passage from Bracton[10] says:

> A pure villeinage is one that is so held that he who holds in villeinage, whether he is free or bond, will do from the villeinage whatever he is ordered, nor need he know at night what he is to do on the morrow. He will always be liable for uncertain services, may be tallaged at the will of his lord, high or low, and must give merchet for marrying his daughter. He will always be liable for uncertain services, whether he is free or bond, provided that if he is a free man he will do them in the name of the villeinage not because of his person, nor will he be liable de jure to give merchet because that does not fall on the person of a free man, only of a villein.

Tallage was an arbitrary payment to the lord. Merchet is discussed in 17.4. In contemporary terms a man who was liable to perform base uncertain services would be seen as an employee. In mediaeval terms he was reckoned as unfree, a bondsman or villein or, if he was free, his land was bound and, so long as he held it, he had to perform the services of an unfree man. This seems to have been decided in the Sussex case of *Bestnovere v Montacute*[11] in which John of Montacute claimed that Martin of Bestnovere was his villein because he did uncertain services for his land. Martin answered that he was a free man. The court accepted that as long as he held the land in villeinage he had to perform the uncertain services for it but that did not affect his personal free status.

5.3   FREE AND UNFREE TENURE

By around 1200 free men could hold unfree land and bondsmen could hold free land. That situation took time to develop. Whatever the position before 1066, it was Norman logic that assimilated status with tenure and concluded that if a man was unfree so was his land, and if the holder of land gave uncertain services, that affected his status.

Just as there were various classes of free men – nobles, knights, squires, franklins, clergy, burgesses, socmen – so also there were various types of bondsmen. Disregarding slaves, which seem to have disappeared soon after 1066, there were villeins, bordars, cottars, soscets, coliberts and other regional varieties. We tend to call them serfs but in mediaeval language they were rustics or in technical legal language, *nativi*, natives. They are usually referred to collectively as villeins because villeins were the most prosperous group. The affairs of others were unlikely to be relevant to the work of the royal courts.

---

[10]   Bracton *op cit* f 208b. See also f 26.

[11]   (1219), Bracton *op cit* f 199b.

In contrast to slaves, which were chattels, villeins were in some sense free men but they were also bound, usually to a manor (villeins appurtenant) or sometimes to a lord (villeins in gross or regardant).[12] Bracton propounds a theory[13] that villein status was only relative. As regards his lord he was unfree, but as regards the rest of the world he was free, with full legal personality. This does not seem to have corresponded to the law of Bracton's time, but something like it became established later. Bracton and his contemporaries were influenced by the status of a *colonus* under the Roman Empire, who was free but *adscriptus glebae*, bound by law to the land. However, that does not fully represent the thirteenth-century position.

If a villein escaped from the manor his lord could claim him back by a writ of naifty commanding anyone who had him to return him. If the villein could get to a town and stay there for a year and a day[14] he could not be recovered and became free. The writ could also be used to test status even where the man had not actually fled, but merely refused the expected services.

Unfree status was inherited, but the rules are unclear and probably varied in different parts of the country, perhaps from manor to manor. In an action of naifty the kin of the alleged villein were summoned to give evidence of their own, and the villein's, status. Status could be inherited from the father, or (as in the Roman law of slavery) from the mother, or from the place a person was born. Marriages often occurred between free folk and villeins, confusing the position, and enfranchisement complicated things further, because a child born before his father was given his freedom remained a serf, while a later child was born free.[15] Complex issues also arose as to how far the widows, widowers or children of mixed marriages could inherit land or how far personal status affected landholding. As late as 1391 a Bill was proposed in Parliament to prevent villeins holding free land, but Richard II refused his consent because by that time status and tenure had become distinct.

The personal status of villein was not formally abolished but seems to have disappeared by about 1600 (3.3). It became relevant in *Somersett's Case*[16] in 1772. That case concerned the status of a man claimed to be a slave and raised the issue as to whether it was possible in England. Lord Mansfield CJ[17] held that the Tenures Abolition Act 1660 abolished villeinage regardant to a manor (in

---

[12] Ibid II.6.iii.

[13] See Hyams, PR, *King, Lord and Peasants in Medieval England* (Oxford University Press, 1980).

[14] Bracton *op cit* f 7,198.

[15] Ibid f 5,168b, 193b, 194b.

[16] (1772) 20 ST 1.

[17] Ibid at 81.

gross) but not villeinage appurtenant. The decision appears to have been made on the basis that the Act specifically preserved the tenure of copyhold (along with socage and frankalmoign) but abolished all others. Copyhold could only relate to villeins appurtenant and not to villeins in gross, and slaves were considered to be in a similar position to them. As such, it would seem to follow that their status was also abolished. It must be admitted that neither the effect of an imperfectly drafted statute nor the reasoning in the case is clear.

Rights to land, however, retained relics of bondage until 1925. Pure copyhold land (as distinct from customary freehold) derived from unfree land, that was land originally held by an unfree man. Although in time all copyholds became held by what were in practice certain services (because they were fixed and predictable), in theory they remained uncertain. Thus, the Law of Property Act 1922, Sch 13, Part II, paras 1–4 deal with fines arbitrary, the payment to the lord on entry, but by then it had long since become established that a custom for a payment exceeding two years' value was unreasonable.[18] However, the distinctions between honourable and base, certain and uncertain, free and unfree had ceased to be important and the issue was whether the tenure was common or customary.

5.4 COMMON AND CUSTOMARY TENURE

Common socage was socage according to the common law rather than custom. The rights affecting common law tenures could be decided for the realm as a whole by the royal judges in the common law courts, while the terms of customary tenures could initially only be decided in local customary courts.

Because of the close connection between service and jurisdiction, if a man owed service to a lord, he could claim that lord's protection and the right to bring a case to defend his rights in that lord's court. If two freeholders holding under two different lords had a dispute, their respective lords were bound to take their part and the matter was referred to the lowest court not involved. If John holds his lands from Sir Ralph and Walter holds his lands from Sir Roger, in any dispute Sir Ralph is bound to support John and Sir Roger to support Walter however wrong they each think their follower to be. If both knights hold their manors from Earl Gilbert then the dispute between John and Walter will be held in Gilbert's honour court. Equally, if a man has a dispute with his own lord it will have to be referred to a higher court. Often the only court with jurisdiction will be the king's.

---

18 Scriven, J, *A Treatise on the Law of Copyholds* (Butterworth & Co, 7th edn, by Archibald Brown, 1896) 182. See Law of Property Act 1922, Sch 2, paras 1–4.

In England (in contrast to the Continent) it went further. In France and Germany domainal lordship involved a hierarchy with definite stages. A man owed homage to his own lord but not to that lord's lord. This applied to some extent in Anglo-Saxon England, but across the Channel it was more formalised. One relevant instance concerns William Duke of Normandy. In 1047, when he was a child, his subordinate counts rebelled but his own overlord, Henry I King of France, came to his aid. Six years later in 1053 when William was an adult, there was another rebellion by the counts but now King Henry supported the rebellion against William. Some counts were supported by their own subordinate viscounts, some were not. Normally a man was bound to follow his lord even if that lord was himself a rebel against his own overlord.

When William established his own kingdom in England where he was sovereign he determined that this should not happen in his new domain. In 1086 it is said that he summoned all free men to Salisbury[19] to swear an oath to him as king, known as an oath of allegiance (18.2). The result was that even if a knight held of a baron who held of an earl, if the earl rebelled the knight was bound to be loyal to the king whatever the baron did. The same applied to a socman who held of the knight either within or outside a manor. Of course, small as the population of England was, and fewer still the number of free men, it is inconceivable that all such did attend at Salisbury. Indeed, the contemporary accounts refer only to the 'landowning men of any account'. It may be that contemporaries took little note, but the oath of Salisbury became binding on all free men thereafter, whoever they were. This was strengthened by a law of William[20] that every freeman within England must bind himself to be faithful to the king.

This had two consequences. The first was formal. When a man was granted land he was enfeoffed by his lord and swore an oath of fealty, but that oath was always 'saving my duty to my lord the King'. The second was that because jurisdiction followed service, any free man, whoever he might be in dispute with over tenure, had the right to take his case to the king's court. Courts were a source of power and profit and lords did not like this. As late as Magna Carta 1215[21] the barons secured a clause that the king would not deprive any lord of his court. But it could not stand. From any free man having the right of access to the king's court there developed the rule that the holder of freehold land

---

[19] Stubbs, W, *Select Charters from the beginning to 1307* (Oxford University Press, 9th edn, 1913) 96; Chibnall, M, *Anglo-Norman England 1066–1166* (Basil Blackwell, 1986) 61; Clarke, HB, 'The Domesday Satellites', in Sawyer, P (ed), *Domesday Book: A Reassessment* (Edward Arnold, 1986) 56.

[20] Stephenson, C and Marcham, FG, *Sources of English Constitutional History* (Harper & Row, 1937) 36.

[21] C 34.

(whether or not he was personally free) had that right. Because the law administered by the king's court was the common law of England, not local custom, freehold land was held by common law rules and in fee.

The rule that holders of freehold land had the right to sue in the king's court had two modifications. The first was that the right could be claimed by some men who were not free and whose land was therefore not freehold. These were villeins whose own lord had originally been the king because they lived on royal manors held in ancient demesne (24.9). They, like all tenants, had the right to go to the court of their own lord, namely the royal court. They held their land by villein tenure. The law assumed that all who had access to the royal court were socmen holding in socage. So the villeins on manors or ancient demesne were known as privileged villeins (in contrast to pure villeins) or villein socmen.

The second was that some freehold land was not held according to the rules of the common law but according to the custom of the manor. The common law courts were unable to decide cases concerning such land because the relevant local customs could only be known and administered in the local manor court. This land was customary freehold. It was copyhold, and the fee simple was in the lord, not the freeholder; however, it was not held at the will of the lord, but according to the custom of the manor.[22]

5.5   THE WILL OF THE LORD

All land held by customary tenure, whether unfree villein land or customary freehold, became copyhold land. Because of the close association of tenure and jurisdiction, where the rules governing ownership of land were subject to the jurisdiction of the customary court, and because that court was held by the lord, the fee simple in that land was treated as held by the lord. There is a distinction here with fees simple of the manor. A free man could hold freehold land by socage tenure, which was a common law tenure recognised by the royal courts, even though he held it from the lord of the manor. In early days disputes over such land were decided in the court baron. That was not itself a common law court but the common law rules were applicable. In time, disputes were invariably referred to the royal courts and courts baron fell out of use. If a tenant held in common socage from the lord of the manor, he had a fee simple in the land while the lord had a fee simple in the manor.[23]

---

[22]   Scriven *op cit* 14.

[23]   See 22.7. See also Scriven *op cit* 44.

Where land was held by customary tenure, the royal courts recognised only the fee simple of the lord in the land itself and did not inquire further as to any subordinate rights. That was not their business. Clearly, that put the lord in a strong position against his tenants because he held the court where disputes were decided and tenants could not take disputes to the royal courts. During the sixteenth century the common law courts developed the procedure known as ejectment to simplify proceedings for establishing title to land. It worked by the fiction that the claimant to land granted a lease to an imaginary John Doe who, as leaseholder, could sue in trespass rather than having to use the ancient forms of writ such as novel disseisin. To use it the claimant had to be able to grant a lease and the courts came to recognise that there was a general custom that copyholders could lease their lands for a year.

By the eighteenth century the courts would allow a copyholder to demand a writ of mandamus to order the lord to hold a customary court. This was a late development, but even before then customary tenants still had rights. From the fifteenth century, when they were admitted into the possession of land that was recorded on the court roll, customary tenants became entitled to a copy of the extract dealing with their land as evidence of title. They were therefore known as copyholders. Once the common law courts came to recognise copyholds of inheritance they accepted that the copyholder had a fee simple interest in the copyhold even though he did not have a fee simple in the land itself (22.7). There were also lesser interests in copyholds such as copyholds for life or at will.[24]

As discussed, copyhold land could be either customary freehold (where, for instance, uncommon inheritance rights existed, such as gavelkind) or pure copyhold. Most pure copyhold had been (or was assumed to have been) villein land before 1189. Some, however, derived from a special custom which, as mentioned in 5.6, allowed the creation of new copyholds out of the waste. Copyholds were not limited to land. Other rights could be held by copy including a manor itself.[25] In addition, copyholders had rights over other land. The most important of these were similar to rights of common. Just as such rights belonging to a leasehold over the property of the landlord cannot, under current law, be rights of common, so, since the lord had the fee in both dominant and servient land, neither could the rights of copyholders. Such rights were known as commonable rights (10.5). There were other rights which would in the case of freehold land have amounted to easements or profits.

---

[24] Law of Property Act 1922, s 133.

[25] *Sir Henry Nevill's Case* (1613) 11 Co Rep 17a, 77 ER 1166.

Customary freeholds were held of the lord according to the custom of the manor. Copyhold land which had been unfree was held at the will of the lord according to the custom of the manor. When the law speaks of will it does not mean arbitrary unfettered discretion. Not every document of wishes left by a person who has died is a will, but only one drawn according to the Wills Act 1837, and it is interpreted according to many legal constraints. Where the courts acknowledge the will of Parliament as sovereign, it is only that will as expressed in special Acts passed according to a certain procedure which again are interpreted by special rules. Where a lease is held by a tenant at will, only the date of ending of the lease is in the control of the landlord: all other provisions, such as possession and fixtures, are governed by the normal rules of law.

Consequently, where copyhold land was held at the will of the lord, that will was constrained by law and the constraints grew tighter as the centuries passed. After the procedure of ejectment became available to copyholders, they had in practice as good a right to sue in the royal courts as any holder in fee simple (3.3). The courts would then order the lord to recognise the customary rights of the copyholder which, in the case of copyholds of inheritance, were as good (if not as valuable) as fees.

5.6   SURRENDER AND ADMISSION

Conveyancers, even in the current century, have had to consider titles to land which go back to copyhold origins, but that is now rare. Copyhold can arise in relation to land comprised in family trusts or on closure of a church school when questions are raised as to who is entitled to the site (20.7). It may also be relevant when examining titles on first registration where there has been no sale for many years. For instance, when in the 1990s the title to railway stations in London was being registered, many turned out to have been copyhold. Before 1926 the rules for transferring copyholds were important and pages of ancient learning on the subject fill Watkins and Scriven, to whom reference should be made for more detail. The subject is, however, worth a brief outline since it involves the important idea of a grant.

Conveyancing involves one person conferring on another the right either to go into occupation of land or to receive rents and services which come, directly or indirectly, from the occupier. It most often arises on a sale and purchase, but also to implement an inheritance, settlement or gift. Conveyancing can be carried out by grant or assurance, although those two words are used in a variety of senses and each can include the other.

A grant involves the creation of a new right. Originally, freehold land could be granted by a lord subinfeudating in fee to a tenant (22.4). Grants in fee simple were prohibited by *Quia Emptores* but grants of other fees, such as entails, conditional fees and the creation of freeholds for life, occurred until 1925. When the Crown conveys unregistered allodial land to become freehold it does so by grant and infeudation even now, although if the freehold already exists the fee will pass by assurance. New leases are invariably created either by grant or by an inside-out grant called a reservation of a term. Lesser rights, such as servitudes, arise from or, as the phrase is, lie in, grant, although in the context of rights of common discussed in 10.4 some rights are said to have been appendant and arose before 1189 from common right rather than from grant. Copyholds always lay in grant, but of a curious nature that was more like an assurance.

Assurances arise not by subinfeudation or grant but by substitution where the previous owner of the interest is substituted by the new one. Freeholds and existing leaseholds are transferred by assurance (nowadays a transfer, conveyance or assignment) but copyholds could normally not be so transferred. On an assurance the purchaser will need to be satisfied of the vendor's title, ie that the purchaser will be able to enjoy what he is buying without interference by a third party. There are two ways of showing this (25.1).

The first is by the vendor producing a summary of his title deeds known as an abstract and producing the originals on request. Under the old rules, going back to Norman times, where there was a dispute between two claimants to land, the one who could produce an unbroken chain of succession going back earlier would win; he was said to be 'higher in the right', on the basis that if his right (or the right of someone through whom he derived title) was earlier than the other then the other (or someone through whom he took his title) must have dispossessed him or his predecessor. As mentioned at 4.3, title could in theory go back to 1189. Indeed, it can go back further – sometimes titles derived from an Anglo-Saxon bishop can be in issue. In modern practice, however, title usually goes back little more than 15 years. The other method of showing or proving title is by producing an officially recognised document saying that the owner is the owner. In the case of registered land it is a Land Registry title guaranteed by the Government (25.6).

Title to copyhold land was shown more along the lines of the second method. A pure copyholder could not assure his land to a purchaser (although by special custom in many manors a customary freeholder could) but the copyholder and his purchaser went (in person or by proxy) to the customary court. The vendor then surrendered his copyhold to the lord. The surrender was often a long document and the law on it was complex. The lord was then obliged to grant the land to the purchaser, usually by a much shorter document called an admission.

All of this was recorded on the court roll (25.2) and the purchaser was given a copy which was his title deed – hence copyhold.

The copy was not necessarily conclusive of title. If the surrender was defective then the court roll could be disproved so that in practice it was necessary to investigate title. However, an unchallenged copy some years old was normally sufficient evidence, and better than many freehold deeds. One of the more useful functions of manor courts down to 1925 was that they made small-scale local conveyancing simpler than for a freehold, despite the formidable technicalities described in the textbooks.

Delivery of a copy might be accompanied by a ceremony. As Coke describes it:[26]

> In some manors, where a Copy-holder surrendreth his Copy-hold, he useth to hold a little Rod in his hand, which he delivereth to the Steward or Bailiff, according to the Custome of the Manor, to deliver it over to the party to whose use the Surrender was made in the name of Seisin; and from thence they are called Tenants by the Verge.

> In some Manors, in stead of a Wand a straw is used; and in other Manors a glove is used.

Although copyhold lay in grant,[27] new copyholds could not normally be granted. Copyhold was held by custom and new customs could not arise after 1189. It appears that there was a special custom in some manors under which part of the waste could, with the consent of the homage, be inclosed and held by copy. The matter was considered in various nineteenth-century cases, particularly *Curson v Lomax*[28] and *Paine v Rider*[29] and in some modern cases on the Commons Registration Act, *Re Yateley Common*[30] and *Re Broxhead Common*[31] and the position is unclear. This method was tried in the nineteenth century as a device to inclose common land and was effectively prohibited by s 6 of the Copyhold Act 1887 (subsequently s 81 of the Copyhold Act 1894).

Copyholds could, of course, be created by statute. When copyhold land fell within the terms of an Inclosure Act the award might provide that the new land allotted to the copyholder was also to be copyhold even though it had, before

---

[26]   Coke, Sir Edward, *Complete Copyholder* (E Flesher et al, 1673) s 39.

[27]   Bracton *op cit* f 26b.

[28]   (1803) 5 Esp 60, 170 ER 737.

[29]   (1857) 24 Beav 151, 53 ER 314.

[30]   [1977] 1 WLR 840, [1977] 1 All ER 505, (1976) 33 P&CR 388.

[31]   (1977) 33 P&CR 451.

inclosure, been freehold or waste. However, it was said in *Doe d Lowes v Davidson*[32] that that would need Parliament's authority.[33]

Ancient copyholds could only be granted exactly as they were without any amendment of any of the rents or services.[34] Thus, if a man had two holdings, one yielding a rent of five pence and one of three pence, it was not possible to surrender them and for his son or purchaser to take a single holding at eight pence. The development of quitrents (14.6) in commutation of services is an apparent exception to this but it is better seen as a substitute for the services which nominally were still due, although the law would not compel the tenant to perform such services as long as he paid the quitrent.

Thus, although copyholds formally lay in grant, in substance the surrender and admission could take effect as an assurance, but there was a distinction. If an existing copyhold was transferred, for example to a purchaser, the lord was obliged to accept a surrender and to admit the purchaser, and although the form was a grant for many purposes the law treated that as machinery for what in substance was an assurance. If the copyhold escheated or was forfeited the lord could (if he wished) regrant it (provided all the terms, including area, quitrents and services were identical) to anyone he chose, which amounted to a new grant of the existing copyhold.[35] However, if the lord took the copyhold into his own management by granting a lease he could not then later re-grant the land as copyhold.[36] Customary freeholds also passed by conveyance and not by surrender and admittance.

The rules of copyhold were not really satisfactory. The customs of inheritance on intestacy were peculiar, the transfer of land was made expensive by reason of various fees and fines and the land was subject to quitrents, heriots and other burdens. From time to time Parliament intervened, originally in a tentative way to allow copyholds to be left by will.[37] Copyholds tended to disappear by being enfranchised to freehold or converted to leasehold. The Copyhold Acts 1841 to 1894 encouraged the process until copyhold was abolished on 1 January 1926 by the Law of Property Act 1922.

---

[32] (1813) 2 M&S 175, 105 ER 348.

[33] Inclosure Act 1845, s 79.

[34] Scriven *op cit* 24, citing Blackstone *op cit* and Coke, *Copyholder, op cit* s 41.

[35] Scriven *op cit* 24.

[36] *French's Case* (1576) 4 Co Rep 31a.

[37] Preston's Act 1815, 55 George 3 c 192.

5.7   TENURES TODAY

It is often thought that the only tenures which still exist are leases and fees simple and that all fees are held of the Crown in free and common socage, but matters are a little more complex. This was explored recently by EG Nugee QC in an article in the *Law Quarterly Review* in 2008.[38] He suggested that superior freeholds and therefore mesne lordships might have survived more widely. He observed that the Law of Property Act 1922 reserved to the lord all mineral rights in former copyhold land and argued that therefore there had to be a superior estate of freehold to support such rights. He extended this argument to other cases such as enlarged long terms. Although he did not mention them, similar considerations might also apply to rights of re-entry.

There is nothing specific in the property legislation to restrict freeholds to one for each piece of land. Section 1(5) of the Law of Property Act 1925 permits legal estates to subsist concurrently as they did before the Act was passed. However, it would appear that any superior freehold must be equitable since although a lord holding a superior right would be seised he was said to be seised in service not in demesne (6.1). This corresponds to what in other jurisdictions is termed the distinction between the *dominium directum* of the lord and the *dominium utile* of the tenant. The distinction was developed on the Continent and introduced along with other mediaeval Roman law concepts into the law of Scotland, but the terms are rarely found in English law. Coke refers to it[39] at the beginning of his treatise as distinguishing the relationship of king and subject to land. It is sometimes applied to mesne lord and tenant. Here the concept is that a superior tenancy must exist before an inferior one and, as seisin goes with the highest in the right, that is the oldest interest. This is the theory underlying escheat (7.6) that if the later derivative fee is extinguished the earlier superior fee comes into possession. As it is not in possession before that happens it cannot, since 1926, be a legal estate and at most must subsist in equity.

Manorial tenures in socage could not be created after 1290 and where the tenant owed no duties to his lord the relationship tended to be lost to sight. A few cases involved heriots or other dues and were preserved[40] but in general the land came to be presumed to be held in chief of the Crown. As discussed in 7.7 this may be relevant to a possible claim to escheat. A mesne lord who wishes to establish his *dominium directum* may seek to do so in one of several ways:

---

[38]   Nugee, EG, 'The Feudal System and the Land Registration Acts' (2008) 124(4) *Law Quarterly Review* 586.

[39]   Coke, on *Littleton, op cit* 1a. See also 18a as to one fee simple absolute.

[40]   *Copestake v Hoper* [1908] 2 Ch 10.

- It may be shown that before 1290 the land was granted out of a sub-manor and the lord is the chief lord of the superior manor, or possibly honour.
- The land was glebe held formerly by the rector in an unappropriated manor (20.3).
- If the manor is ancient demesne it may be possible to show that the freeholder is a man of the manor (24.9) and therefore tenant.
- The land was formerly copyhold and was enfranchised by statute under the Copyhold Acts 1840 to 1894 between 1840 and 1925 where escheats were reserved[41] as that implies a continuing tenurial relationship.
- An instance of free tenure suggested by Nugee may be where a lord granted a long lease of demesne land or of surrendered copyhold land which was enlarged under the Law of Property Act 1925, s 153. As anyone could grant a long lease this is not restricted to manors.
- The lord may be entitled to receive a rent of assize or, before 1926, his predecessor was entitled to a heriot or quitrent out of common freehold land.
- If an inclosure act reserved seigniorial rights then it is possible that land which was formerly common manorial freehold might still be subject to a mesne lordship although it would be difficult to identify now. It would not normally apply where an allotment was made in respect of copyhold rights.[42]

In these cases superior tenure may still exist. The instances are not exhaustive and there may be other evidence.

Nugee also considers that the freehold of the lord still subsists for land enfranchised under the Law of Property Act 1922, at least where the lord still has the property in mineral rights. However, it may be considered that as Sch 12, para (1)(e) provides that the land 'shall not be subject to any estate, right, charge, or interest affecting the manor' this indicates that the lord's seigniory has been removed. The mineral rights can be explained in another way as the statutory preservation of a former customary right (9.5, 11.7) but the point remains to be decided.

By the Tenures Abolition Act 1660 all tenures were abolished except for free and common socage, frankalmoign and copyhold. The rights of grand sergeanty (18.4) were preserved but land held in grand sergeanty itself became held in socage. Copyhold was abolished by the Law of Property Act 1922. Frankalmoign (20.10) was abolished by the Administration of Estates Act 1925 save for the estates of those holding at the time and may still exist for an

---

[41] Copyhold Act 1894, s 21(1)(b).

[42] *Doe d Lowes v Davidson* (1813) 2 M&S 175, 105 ER 348 (5.6, 7.9).

ecclesiastical corporation. Land held in ancient demesne (24.9) is held in common socage (because the holder could enforce his rights in the courts of common law) but was not initially free. As explained in 24.3 there is still some Crown allodial land.

Section 128(3) of the Law of Property Act 1922 provides that 'all land ... shall be dealt with as land held in free and common socage'. This appears to relate only to the ways of dealing with land, such as the way it is transferred or leased, rather than abolishing other modes of tenure as such.

Chapter 6

The Lands of the Lord

6.1   DEMESNE AND OTHER LAND

Everything in the manor that could not be claimed by someone else belonged to the lord. The lands of the lord are classified as demesne and waste. That is something of an oversimplification. The old legal theory, which is, for most of the country, historically incorrect but which underlies much of the law, saw the lord as starting with an empty landscape which he then parcelled out.[1] First, the lord selected for himself the best land as his own demesne, then the free men chose freehold land and, finally, bondsmen were allocated their copyholds. What was left was the waste that no one wanted and which belonged to the lord for lack of any other owner, although it was used communally. Land can pass from one category to the other and the status of some areas, such as woodland, can be uncertain, but it is a starting point. In general, lords tended to have the best and the worst land, as demesne and as waste. They also might have the freehold in minerals beneath enfranchised copyhold or inclosed waste as discussed in 11.6–11.8.

The demesne was the land which was either retained in hand or leased. In champion country such land could comprise both strips and closes. The lord's strips in the open fields were indistinguishable from those of freeholders and copyholders, save that the lord had more of them and tended to have better land. Because he had more strips it was easier to consolidate and inclose. Elsewhere the lord had closes that had never been open fields, both arable and grazing. The demesne included buildings, namely the manor house itself, the home farm and its outbuildings, and houses and cottages in the settlement which were leased out or occupied by members of the lord's household. The demesne might include the mill, the bakery, the inn and other buildings used by the village, although they could be copyhold.

---

[1]   See *Henly v The Mayor and Burgesses of Lyme* (1828) 5 Bing N C 91 at 110, 130 ER 995, per Best CJ.

The demesne could include a deer park or chase. Only a few manors had them, but there were thousands around the country, comprising up to 4600 acres,[2] and surrounded by banks, ditches and deerleaps (so designed that wild deer could jump in but could not get out again). Deer parks tended to be wooded and were used partly for gentle hunting (being too small for serious pursuit) and partly as a ranch where deer could be raised and culled for venison. Associated rights are considered in 12.2. Over the centuries many deer parks became converted to farming as demand for good land increased. Others became parks in the eighteenth-century sense, an area of amenity land surrounding a great house, of the type landscaped by Capability Brown and Humphry Repton. Such parks could have come from many previous uses, including demesne farmland or inclosed waste, and many contain the sites of deserted villages or villages moved by the landowner so that his house could have a good setting free from disturbance. In Ireland the parkland surrounding a great house is still known as the demesne.

In the modern law since 1600 demesne has excluded villeinage or copyhold land, but that was not always so. Bracton[3] discusses this as if in his time it was doubtful and concludes that since the lord could revoke a grant of villeinage land at will it was part of the demesne. In the eyes of the common law that was true, but the fact that Bracton discusses it at all suggests that under customary law a holding of villeinage land could be protected. Coke[4] discusses Bracton's account and concludes that by his own time it was no longer correct to reckon copyhold land as demesne. Bracton[5] also distinguishes land in demesne from land in service. In this sense demesne is being used for possession (*dominium utile*) while land in lordship is like a reversion (*dominium directum*) (5.7). The lord does not have rights over the land itself but in the services reserved out of it. He merely has a bare lordship (*nudum dominium*).[6]

A person who is lord of a manor may often own other land in the vicinity, which may once have been common freehold of the manor or copyhold, or may never have been parcel of the manor but has passed with it for many years. In order to have the status of demesne the land must have been united with the manor at all times since 1290 or have accrued by act of law or possibly by statute. This is considered further in 7.4. As a result it can now be difficult to establish whether a particular piece of land is demesne. This is relevant to sales of manors. Formerly, it was clear law that a conveyance of a manor automatically included

---

[2] Fletcher, J, *Gardens of Earthly Delight: The History of Deer Parks* (Windgather Press, 2011) 2, 163.

[3] Bracton, Sir Henry, *De legibus et consuetudinibus angliae* (c 1257) f 263.

[4] Coke, Sir Henry, *Complete Copyholder* (E Flsher et al, 1630) ss 12–14.

[5] Bracton *op cit* f 263.

[6] Ibid f 264b.

any demesne land. In recent years many auction particulars and hence conveyances of manors have purported to exclude demesne land but either expressly or by implication they have incorporated the Law of Property Act 1925, s 62(3), which includes hereditaments reputed to appertain to the manor. Issues have therefore arisen as to whether land reputed to be parcel of the manor and therefore apparently covered has been included in a sale. This is considered further in 26.4.

6.2   MANAGEMENT AND LEASES

The demesne could be managed in one of two ways: in hand or by leasing. The farmland in the demesne was exploited for production on behalf of the lord, on which he grew crops to be consumed by his household or sold to provide an income. The tenants of the manor, both free and bond, performed services on that land as well as cultivating their own plots both for subsistence and, increasingly as time passed, to raise cash crops to sell for money to pay rents.

Patterns of running the demesne varied over the centuries. Sometimes it paid the lord to keep the land in hand, especially when grain prices were high, and to rely on services from the tenants to cultivate the land. However, as time went on this dual cultivation system became inefficient. Tenants were able to produce surpluses on their own lands, especially if they were freed from the need to work on the demesne, and could commute their services for quitrents. If the lord preferred to run the demesne in hand he did better to hire his own labourers but, particularly after the mid-fourteenth century, he more often entered into a commercial agreement with a cultivator under which he let the demesne or part of it for a money rent for a period of time. There was more certainty in an annual rent from the farmer, who had to pay in good times and bad, so that the lord did not have the expense of equipping the holding and running a business.

Such an arrangement is found in Anglo-Saxon times (as loanland) and under the Normans when it was called a farm, either from the Anglo-Saxon *feorm* meaning food or from the Latin *firma* meaning for a firm or fixed period. The period was also called a term, because it had a *terminus* or end date, and the cultivator was called a farmer (hence the modern word) or termor. This type of management became more usual as time passed. By 1900 nearly 90 per cent of agricultural land in England was in lease. Since then it has reduced as a result of the break-up of the great estates, the security given to farmers by the Agriculture Act 1947, the pattern of taxation and the effects of subsidies from the United Kingdom and under the Common Agricultural Policy. In modern law if the arrangement runs for more than three years it is called a lease and the occupier a lessee:[7] if for less, or if it is on a periodic renewable basis, such as yearly or monthly, it is more often known as a tenancy and the occupier a tenant, but it is better to avoid using that word in the context of the manor because tenant has other meanings as well.

Leases could be for any length. Some were for 99 years, some for 1000 years and many such granted in the sixteenth and seventeenth centuries are still running, with rents payable at the manor court (see 14.6). Leases could be for the lifetime of the lessee or for three lives, such as the lessee, his wife and son. These leases were for certain purposes, such as the Parliamentary franchise, reckoned as freeholds so that the lessee for life whose holding was worth more than 40 shillings a year had a vote before 1832. Leases for lives were of the in-between types of tenure that were converted in 1925 by s 149 of the Law of Property Act to leases for 90 years determinable on death.[8] There were also perpetually renewable leases, converted by s 145 of the Law of Property Act 1922 to terms of 2000 years.

Other leases were granted on an annual basis from one Ladyday (25 March) to the next or from one Michaelmas (29 September) to the next; in many parts of the country the dates are 6 April or 10 October because of the lost 11 days when this country converted from the Julian to the Gregorian calendar. Such annual leases run on until either side determines them by notice to quit, and those which were granted under the Agricultural Holdings Act 1986 are protected so that the landlord cannot evict the lessee during his lifetime (or in some cases his son and grandson), except on limited grounds.

Sometimes the manor was leased as a whole together with the services and other rights as a single unit including the right to hold the manor court. This was called putting the manor to farm. The freeholder was called the lord reversioner and the lessee, who stood in the place of the lord, was known as the lord farmer. Lords farmer were often found in early centuries as, in effect, a form of permitted subinfeudation. By the late nineteenth century they were rare, although still found on some Crown manors. Nowadays they are virtually unknown except in family arrangements where, for instance, the manor is held by family trustees who grant a lease to a member of the family not only of the lands but also of the lordship and any rights that go with it.

Another type of lease of the whole manor was to the tenants. There are examples going back to the eleventh century of the manor being put 'in farm to the homage'. This happened especially in the case of monastic lords who were bequeathed an isolated manor a long way from the monastery. They could not

---

7   Law of Property Act 1925, s 54(2).

8   See *Berrisford v Mexfield Housing Cooperative Limited* [2011] UKSC 52, [2011] 3 WLR 1091.

run it in hand, had no power to sell it, and it was not economic to put in a bailiff. So they offered it to let to the highest bidder. Any bidder would reckon what he would get from the tenants, deduct a profit for himself and bid the balance. The tenants or homage, provided they co-operated, could always outbid such a person because whatever they paid in rent would be less than the total of what they were already paying. Usually the lease was taken by nominees on behalf of the homage but sometimes, especially if the manor was a town, they were able to obtain a royal franchise to hold it as a corporation.

Leases could be granted by others beside the lord. Manorial freeholders, at least common sokemen, could grant leases without restriction. Copyholders could not do so, in the absence of special custom. The reason for this was that the lord was entitled to a fine when copyhold land changed hands. This could be fixed or arbitrary, that is, in theory, whatever the lord asked, although common law provided that a fine in excess of twice the annual value of the holding was void as being unreasonable. The annual value was the value at which the holding was or could be let. If the copyholder granted a long lease for a premium or a fine of his own, and then a peppercorn rent, and then sold, the lord would receive, instead of twice the full rent, only two peppercorns. In some manors either the lord's fine was fixed or was determined by what the full rent would have been, and often copyholders could grant leases. In Rowley Regis,[9] King's Sunford and Sedgley, copyholders could lease for 99 years, and in Lambeth,[10] they could lease for three years. In any manor general custom allowed leasing for one year, which was common. This general custom was confirmed in *Combe's Case*[11] in 1614. It was important because without it copyholders could not use the procedure known as ejectment (5.5) which allowed their rights to be protected in the royal court. From the fifteenth century copyholds were bought up by investors and rented out, often to the same men who were farming other land in the vicinity, so that the granting of leases of copyhold land had as much effect on the actual occupation of the countryside as the leasing of the demesne.

6.3 WASTE AND COMMONS REGISTRATION

The waste lands of the manor were a miscellaneous collection. The leading case on the definition of waste is *Attorney-General v Hanmer*.[12] In 1637 Charles I

---

[9] Rowley Regis: Watkins, C, *A Treatise on Copyholds* (James Bullock, 4th edn by Thomas Coventry, 1825) 2.557; King's Sunford: ibid 2.570; Sedgley: ibid 2.571.

[10] Lambeth: ibid 2.562.

[11] (1614) 9 Co Rep 75a, 77 ER 843, citing Bracton *op cit*. See also *Melwich v Luther* (1588) Cro Eliz 102, 78 ER 361, 4 Co Rep 26b, 76 ER 835.

[12] (1858) 31 LT 379, 4 de G & J 205, 45 ER 80. See also *Mills v Arun District Council* [2001] EWCA Civ 1601.

granted to Francis Braddock and Christopher Kingscote all the coal beneath the commons, waste lands and marsh grounds within the lordship of Englefield in the County of Flint. Englefield was a Crown manor both in 1637 and in 1856, by which time the right to the coal mines had passed to Sir John Hanmer. The case concerned the coal rights under part of the foreshore of the River Dee known as White Sands. White Sands were clearly not commons or marsh grounds but were they wastes? If they were then Sir John Hanmer had the right to work the coal: if not, the Crown had that right.

Normally foreshore is not part of a manor (24.4). The foreshore is the land around the coast between high and low water and belongs to the Crown as part of its general or prerogative rights. But in some cases the Crown has in the past granted foreshore to the lord of the adjoining manor and if that was before 1189 the foreshore may have become part of the manor. It was accepted in this case that in 1637 White Sands belonged to Charles I, not under his prerogative but as parcel of the manor of Englefield. Could it be described as waste? The judge, Baron Watson said:

> The true meaning of wastes, or waste lands, or waste grounds of the manor are the open, uncultivated, and unoccupied lands parcel of the manor, other than the demesne lands of the manor.

Those words were quoted by Lord Templeman in the 1990 decision of the House of Lords in *Hampshire County Council v Milburn*[13] (*'Milburn'*) which arose out of the Commons Registration Act 1965 and concerned the meaning of the word 'of'.

That Act was passed in the interests of conservation to protect the rural open spaces of England. The background (10.2) was that over the centuries most of the original open waste land had been inclosed. Although it became difficult to inclose more land after the Commons Act 1876 and especially after the coming into force of s 194 of the Law of Property Act 1925 there was very little practical, as distinct from legal, protection for commons and none for manorial waste which was not subject to rights of common. After the disappearance of manorial courts and changes in agricultural practice, so that many landowners who had common rights did not find it worthwhile to exercise them, open spaces were becoming overgrown, or were fenced in by farmers or by the owners of adjoining cottages extending their gardens. Many that were left had become tips for waste, in the sense of rubbish. The Royal Commission on Common Lands was appointed to look into the matter, and its report in 1958 led to the 1965 Act.

---

[13]   [1990] 2 WLR 1240.

The Act provided for the registration of common land and, separately, the registration of rights of common over it. Common land was defined in s 22(1) as meaning, first, land subject to rights of common and, secondly, 'waste land of a manor not subject to rights of common'. There seem to have been two reasons for the second definition. First, it allowed for the registration and protection of land which would have been common if the manorial system of grazing had continued but where, over the centuries, the rights had been forgotten or bought up by the lord. When land was enfranchised under the Law of Property Act 1922, the former commonable grazing rights of the copyholders continued either as such or as converted into common law rights of common. The value would be reflected in the compensation that copyholders paid to the lord. If they did not use their rights they might agree to give them up in return for a reduction in the compensation, so the lord took his waste free of the former copyhold rights. Secondly, the words 'of the manor' distinguished rural waste from urban derelict land which is subject to separate provisions such as the Derelict Land Act 1982.

The problem for those who had to operate the Act was, what is waste land of a manor? The point was very important. Open, uncultivated and unoccupied countryside which has no special status and could be converted to farmland (even rough grazing) had in 1965 a value of up to £1000 an acre. The Act itself did not impose restrictions on waste land but it was expected that such land would become subject to similar controls to those that applied to common land (such as the restriction on fencing, as happened when s 38 of the Commons Act 2006 replaced s 194 of the Law of Property Act 1925) or land opened to public access (as happened under the Countryside and Rights of Way Act 2000). Such land might be worth £10 an acre if indeed anyone could be found to buy it at all. The stretches of waste in issue in *Milburn* comprised 365 acres (and by the time the case was brought bare land values could exceed £2000 an acre) so it is evident that the potential sums involved were substantial, and why the case was worth fighting up to the House of Lords.

Sir Anthony Milburn had been lord of the manors of Hazell and Putham in Hampshire. The manor of Hazell included 338 acres of waste known as Hazeley Heath. Putham included 27 acres known as Mattingley Green. Both were rightly registered under the 1965 Act as common land. No rights of common were exercisable over them but they were clearly waste of the manor. In 1981 Sir Anthony sold the lordships of Hazell and Putham, so that he ceased to be lord, but he excepted out of the sales the ownership of Hazeley Heath and Mattingley Green. He then applied to Hampshire County Council to deregister the land because, he said, although still waste, they were no longer waste 'of' the manor and therefore their status had changed.

The House found in favour of the council. It considered a series of cases previously decided by the Commons Commissioners and the lower courts on the point. Two lines of cases pointed to opposite conclusions. The House looked at the purpose of the Act – to protect open spaces, irrespective of the identity of the owner of the freehold – and concluded that 'of' meant 'now or formerly of' and waste land 'of manorial origin'. It overruled the earlier case of *In re Box Hill Common*[14] where the land had ceased to be parcel of the manor in 1878. Consequently it is not clear how far back any inquiry must go into whether land was formerly of the manor. In *In re Chewton Common*[15] some manorial waste was sold and severed from the manor of Somerford in Dorset in 1804 but the buyer purchased the manor in 1809 and the two remained in common ownership thereafter. The court held that for the purposes of the 1965 Act the waste should be regarded as being still of the manor but this is an extreme instance of severance for only five years. At common law under the principle in *Sir Moyle Finch's Case*[16] the severance would be permanent; but for the purposes of the 1965 Act a different interpretation was taken. Clearly, it cannot go back to the Middle Ages, since when there has been a great deal of inclosure of waste; but the precise limits are not settled.

This may become clearer when cases come to be considered under para 4 of Sch 2 to the Commons Act 2006 to reinstate on the register land which was once entered as waste but which was removed. It is evident that before *Milburn* there was real doubt as to whether a lord who severed the waste from the manor could then have land deregistered on the basis that it was not 'of' the manor. It appears that many areas of former manorial waste were removed from the register either by agreement between the applicant for registration and the landowner or under an order by the Commons Commissioner. Once that happened it was too late, after *Milburn*, to restore the land. A good deal of that land has remained in its former condition – physically waste. There are a number of preconditions.

First, the land must be waste of the manor at the time para 4 comes into force in relation to the local authority area in question. The meaning of 'of the manor' must be the same as that given by *Milburn*, namely including land formerly of the manor back to some as yet unknown date. The meaning of waste means that it must still be reasonably described as waste, that is open, uncultivated and unoccupied at the time para 4 comes into force. The provisions are being brought into force for different parts of the country at different times. At the time of writing they are in force only for seven counties, known as the pilot areas. Secondly, the land must have been provisionally registered under the 1965 Act. Accordingly it is not possible to reopen the issue of land which has

---

[14] [1980] Ch 109.

[15] [1977] 1 WLR 1242,

[16] (1610) 6 Co Rep 63a, 77 ER 310; see 8.4.

never been registered. Thirdly, there must have been an objection (usually by the landowner) to the registration.

Fourthly, the registration must have been cancelled on one of three grounds. The first is that a Commons Commissioner cancelled it only because although it had once been waste of the manor it had subsequently been severed. The second is that the Commissioner simply decided that the land was not subject to rights of common, and did not go on to consider whether it was manorial waste. The third is that the person who applied for the land to be registered requested or agreed to the cancellation. The decisions of the Commons Commissioners are recorded and published so it is possible to know why they took a decision. If an applicant agreed to cancellation often there will be no record as to why. Most likely it was because he was advised that the claim would fail on the ground that it was either severed or not subject to rights of common. However, there might have been some other reason, for instance that it was not waste land, and in such a case the landowner will still be able to resist the application to amend the register if it is in fact still not waste.

In these circumstances the registration authority (usually the county council) is bound to register the land as common if an application is made before a specified date. A more difficult issue is if the landowner argues that it had not been part of a manor since the Middle Ages. Such an argument would probably fail. Schedule 2 gives no grounds for it and it would appear from *Corpus Christi College (Oxford) v Gloucestershire County Council*[17] that registration is conclusive even if the land was not and could not have been waste of a manor. As virtually all land must have been within a manor at some time since 1066 the logic of the House of Lords in *Millburn* would in principle apply without any limit of time.

There is provision in Sch 2, para 2 to the 2006 Act for registration of land not registered under the 1965 Act which is subject to a statutory designation as common land. This covers areas of land which ought to have been registered but were overlooked, sometimes because everyone who might have applied for registration thought that someone else was taking care of the matter. There is a corresponding provision in paras 6 and 7 for the deregistration of land registered by mistake. Paragraph 6 relates to buildings which were in existence at the time of provisional registration and are still in existence. Paragraph 7 deals with land which was never referred to a Commons Commissioner and became final often without the landowner's knowledge. Provided the land was not (at the time of registration) subject to rights of common and was not waste of a manor, a town or village green or land liable to be inclosed under the Inclosure Act 1845, s 11, then it may be deregistered. Again there are time limits which are already

---

[17]   [1983] QB 360.

running for the pilot areas. Normally this is 31 December 2020.[18] There is also provision in para 7 of Sch 2 to the 2006 Act for land wrongly registered as common to be deregistered. Many mistakes were made in registration including parts of people's gardens which under statute have had to be regarded as waste of a usually non-existent manor. This allows such errors to be corrected, again within the same time limits.

By definition, waste is unoccupied. The Occupiers Liability Acts 1957 and 1984 impose a duty of care on an occupier to his visitors that the land should not be in a dangerous condition. Some owners of waste were concerned that this duty might fall on them, and when a public right to roam was conferred by the Countryside and Rights of Way Act 2000 a special exemption was introduced to cover this (10.9). However, it is possible that commoners might be regarded as being occupiers. In *R v Watson*[19] Huntingdon Corporation was the owner of common land known as Mill Common and Pitts over which the burgesses had rights of common. Every year the corporation allocated the land to certain owners of animals who paid for the privilege. The court held that they were liable to the poor rate because they were occupiers of the land even though it was common because they were making profitable use of it. A person with a mere right of common is not an occupier within the Ground Game Acts[20] (12.8), but the fact that Parliament felt the need to make that provision suggests that, apart from this exception, such a person could be an occupier.

6.4   TYPES OF WASTE

Typical waste was rough grazing land. This was essential to the economy of the early villages, where they put out their cattle, ponies, sheep and goats. Most of what now remains as waste is poor quality, either moorland, heavy clay, undrainable bog or other land that centuries of ingenuity and inclosure have been unable to convert to productive closes. Much of this land is subject to common rights, although it includes many so-called commons, whether in the middle of towns like Clapham Common in London or on the edges of Welsh parishes where the rights have been lost over the years.

Village greens may often belong to the lord, particularly in a closed manor. These are discussed in 19.6. As a result of the legislation passed in the nineteenth century they are of little value in themselves. A variety of other, miscellaneous pieces of land may exist, such as village ponds or wells, pounds

---

18   Commons Registration (England) Regulations 2008 (SI 2008/1961), Sch 4, para 14(1).

19   (1804) 5 East 480, 102 ER 1154.

20   Ground Game Act 1880, s 1, proviso (2).

where straying beasts were confined after being rounded up, or pest houses where people with contagious diseases were sent to recover or die. The most important are roads, balks and rivers, discussed below.

Under the Countryside and Rights of Way Act 2000 there is now a public right to roam over all registered common land, as well as land mapped as mountain, moor, heath or down (10.9). This right is in the process of being extended to the foreshore (which, as in *Attorney-General v Hanmer*, would be regarded as waste) and coastal strips (which may be cultivated land) under the Marine and Coastal Access Act 2009. Open land and foreshore can be regarded as waste, but as they are not necessarily linked to a manor, separate provision has to be made for them.

Some woodlands may be classified as waste. Most are now managed but there may simply be areas where trees have grown. Lords may own belts of trees between farms if the landowners on either side do not have title. There has been discussion as to whether the public right to roam should be extended to woodlands not managed as a plantation, but in general it has been given only to managed Forestry Commission woodlands or to private woods which receive grants under the Farm Woodlands Scheme. Village ponds may also constitute waste and, in the absence of any other owner, may be regarded as belonging to the lord. Similarly, other, odd pieces of land may have no value and may indeed be a nuisance, where litter can accumulate or rubbish dumped, or where travellers park their caravans.

Certain types of waste may not belong to the lord even if they lie within a manor, but instead may be regarded as tenants' waste, for waste is a fact, a physical description. This question often arises in relation to the long, thin pieces of land that lie between defined areas. A road is, of course, important in itself as a means of communication, but there can be issues about who owns the soil over which the road passes, the verges along its side or the bed of a river.

6.5   ROADSIDE VERGES

One of the most frequent claims by lords of manors is to the ownership of roadside verges, that is the strip, usually of grass, between a field or house and the metalled carriageway. This is sometimes called the 'long acre'. Some lords have sought to charge owners of the field or house for the right to cross the verge or at least to construct a metalled access.[21] Many, perhaps most, such claims are unjustified, although there can be cases where the lord has title.[22]

The position in any particular case depends on several issues,[23] of which two are relevant here. The first issue is whether or not the verge is indeed part of the highway and subject to public rights of way. If it is not, the owner can usually (subject sometimes to planning consent) enclose it and treat it as private property. If it is, any obstruction of the highway is an offence. Occasionally, an enclosure is made and remains in place for many years but 'once a highway always a highway' – the obstruction remains unlawful.[24] The second issue is, whether or not a road is a highway, then who has title to it and to the subsoil.

Most often the verge will be part of the highway itself and therefore the surface will be vested in the highway authority, normally the county council. The Highways Act 1980, s 263 provides that 'Subject to the provisions of this section, every highway maintainable at the public expense, together with the materials and scrapings of it, vests in the authority who are for the time being the highway authority for the highway'.[25] In addition, s 130(1) provides that 'It is the duty of the highway authority to assert and protect the rights of the public to the use and enjoyment of any highway for which they are the highway authority, including any roadside waste which forms part of it'. The vesting only affects the surface and enough airspace to allow passage by vehicles and relates to use of the surface for highway purposes, principally going from one place to another.[26] The owner of the verge may therefore be able to charge for pipes and drains, overhead signs and structures such as telegraph poles. However, it is more usual for the verge to belong to the owner of the adjacent property.

The rule on vesting derives from the Public Health Act 1875, s 149, which vested certain streets within urban areas in the urban council. The Local Government Act 1888 created county councils and s 11(6) provided that 'A main road and the materials thereof, and all drains belonging thereto shall, except where the urban authority retain the powers and duties of maintaining and repairing such road, vest in the county council'. Further Acts vested other roads in borough or district councils.

---

[21] For cautions on verges, see 25.10 and, for a government view, see 29.1.

[22] *Case of Highways* (1690) 3 Salk 182, 91 ER 764.

[23] See Orlik, M, 'Roadside Waste and Manorial Waste', (2002) *Rights of Way Law Review*, 2.2.35.

[24] *R (Smith) v The Land Registry (Peterborough Office)* [2010] EWCA Civ 200.

[25] *Tithe Redemption Commissioners v Runcorn Urban District Council* [1954] Ch 383; but see *Sussex Investments Ltd v Cornell* (1993) *The Times*, 29 July, CA, considered in *Secretary of State for the Environment, Transport and the Regions v Baylis (Gloucester) Ltd* (2000) 80 P&CR 324 as to registered land.

[26] But see *DPP v Jones (Margaret)* [1999] 2 AC 240.

Previously, the surface of the highway was privately owned,[27] although subject to public rights. Mediaeval highways were not metalled, being simply routes across the countryside. Some have survived unsurfaced, as green lanes, winding between fields, over which the public may travel although since the Natural Environment and Rural Communities Act 2006, s 67 came into force they may not use mechanically propelled vehicles on green lanes. The great mediaeval highways have been turned into our modern A roads and are tarmacked. Tarmac is tough and does not become a muddy morass in the rain or raise clouds of dust in dry weather. Mediaeval roads could be unpleasant and travellers had to avoid the bogs and potholes by veering to one side or the other, so that highways were very broad and might comprise several more-or-less parallel routes spread laterally over several miles. Where a highway crossed waste land it may not have mattered how much of a diversion travellers took. Where the highway passed fields and closes the inhabitants at large had the duty to keep it in repair. However, this was difficult to enforce except where the local inhabitants had an interest in doing so (as in towns) and, if it were unusable, travellers would have trampled over the ploughsoil or the crops.

The broad width of a highway route, often 30 yards or more across, was a large expanse of land and some landowners, especially lords of the manor, were attracted to the idea of inclosing this waste. In the Middle Ages some landowners were allowed to do so on condition that they took responsibility for maintaining the narrower road that was left, so that the inhabitants at large were relieved of their duty. In theory there are still ancient public highways that are privately maintainable in this way, sometimes with the lord having the right to charge a toll for upkeep (15.2). In such a case the lord would be the owner of the whole width of the road. However, that was the exception. The general rule for publically maintainable highways is that the landowner adjoining the road owns up to the middle line – the *medium filum* or middle thread. If the same person owns the land on both sides he owns all the subsoil.

A much quoted authority is *Steel v Prickett*[28] in 1819. The case related to Haverstock Hill, the main road from London to Hampstead. A passer-by may notice that not only is the road itself very wide, but there is space to encroach on. Many of the houses are built back from the road and a few have extensions towards the pavement edge. Dame Jane Wilson was lady of the manor of Hampstead. The Dean and Chapter of Westminster Abbey claimed to be lords of the manor of Belsize, but the court found that there was no such manor; it was just a title assumed by the owners of Belsize Farm, which had once been within the manor of Hampstead until Henry VIII had granted the farm (and others) to them. The land fronted onto the highway. Both claimed the right to authorise

---

[27] *Goodtitle ex d Chester v Alker and Elmes* (1757) 1 Burr 133, 97 ER 231.

[28] (1819) 2 Stark 463, 171 ER 706.

house owners to build on the roadside verge, and to charge large sums of money for doing so. The question to decide was whether the roadside waste was waste of the manor, or whether the owner of the farm had the land up to the middle of the road. The parties were Mr Steel, a copyhold tenant of Lady Wilson, and Mr Prickett, a leaseholder or tenant from the Abbey, possibly so that the parties could use the ejectment procedure. The judge decided that this was not a question of legal principle, but a question of fact to be decided on the evidence. After considering the evidence the jury (which at that time still decided matters of fact in civil cases) found in favour of Mr Prickett and the Abbey as owners of the adjacent land, even though they were not lords of the manor.

This establishes that the issue of ownership of a verge is a question of fact to be decided on the evidence, not itself a matter of law. However, where there is no clear evidence the law has to give a guide. In *Doe d Pring v Pearsey*[29] the judge stated that the presumption is that where there is a strip of land between the highway and a close it belongs to the owner of the close. In *Commission for the New Towns v JJ Gallagher Ltd*[30] Neuberger J considered several cases on the *medium filum* presumption. He said:

> The highway presumption has been defined in the following terms:
>
>> 'Where a piece of land which adjoins a highway is conveyed by general words, the presumption of law is, that the soil of the highway *usque ad medium filum* passes by the conveyance, even though reference is made to a plan annexed, the measurement and colouring of which would exclude it.'[31]

However, in that case he concluded on the facts that the presumption was rebutted.

The issue may arise where a highway formerly crossed open country, typically waste, and the owner of the adjacent land, typically the lord or his lessee, has inclosed the waste and erected a fence. The fences on either side may be far apart and when, later, the highways authority has constructed a metalled surface down the middle, the broad verge looks tempting to enclose with a further fence. If the whole width between the fences was highway, that would be an unlawful obstruction.

---

[29]   (1827) 7 B&C 304.

[30]   [2003] 2 P&CR 3.

[31]   This quote is taken from the headnote in *Berridge v Ward* (1861) 10 CB NS 400, 142 ER 507, cited with approval by Waite LJ in *Pardoe v Pennington* (1996) 75 P&CR 264 at 269.

The general presumption is that the land between the fences is highway even where it has been enclosed from the waste.[32] In *East v Berkshire County Council*[33] cottages had been built in 1901 beside the Bath Road from Maidenhead to Reading. The county council surfaced the road and the lord of the manor claimed to prevent it from doing so. The judge found that the strip had been used as part of the highways and a dedication should be implied. However, this will not always be the case. In *Neeld v Hendon Urban District Council*[34] the lord had erected a fence on a strip of verge and the highway authority demolished it. People had picked flowers and walked over the land before enclosure and the fence had been allowed to remain for some time. The judge concluded on the facts that it was waste of the manor and not subject to highway rights. In *Friern Barnet Urban District Council v Richardson*[35] there was green sward between the Friern Lane which was part of the Great North Road, and a hedge, with a gravel path beside the hedge. There was evidence that the sward was treated as part of the waste of the manor and a tenant had been admitted on the rolls. The court found that the sward was not part of the highway.

Crown Estate Commissioners v Dorset County Council[36] concerned roadside verges in the Royal manor of Portland. Here it was not disputed that the Crown owned the verges but not the adjoining land. The verges had provisionally been registered at the request of the Commissioners under the Commons Registration Act 1965 as waste of the manor. The county council objected because under the Act of 1965 waste which is part of the highway should not be registered since highways have their own distinct rules. In 1977 the Commons Commissioner found in favour of the council. The Crown Estate then brought a case on the grounds that the verge was not in fact highway, but the court in 1989 found itself bound by the decision of the Commons Commissioner. The significance of this long dispute was that if the land was not highway the Crown could charge the adjoining landowners substantial sums for the right to construct and use an access driveway across the verge. If it was highway then anyone had the right to cross it. Although it is clear that the Portland verge was highway, the soil was still vested in the Crown which therefore, for instance, could charge for excavating a drain. It also owned the minerals beneath. Portland stone is the best in the country, used for many great buildings.

---

[32] *Harvey v Truro Rural District Council* [1903] 2 Ch 638: fence erected on former waste to separate it from highway.

[33] (1911) 106 LT 65.

[34] (1899) 81 LT 405. See also *Hale v Norfolk County Council* [2001] Ch 717.

[35] (1898) 62 JP 547.

[36] [1990] 1 Ch 297, (1989) 60 P&CR 1.

In some of these cases the title was ancient, but often the title to adjoining land is more recent and may derive from a sale by the lord. In a straightforward case it will simply be a matter of looking at the document that put the sale into effect. The conveyance may specifically state that it does not include the soil of a roadway, or this may be evident from the document, for example if a right of way is expressly granted. Frequently on modern housing estates the builder sells the house plots and enters into a separate arrangement with the local highway authority (typically the county council) to hand over the roadways. The sale may be of a field or house plot whose area is precisely stated, or the boundary is marked on a plan – although that by itself may not be conclusive. Thus, in *Simpson v Dendy*[37] the lord of the manor of Hendon in Middlesex sold a field in 1757. The land was described in detail in the sale catalogue with a schedule of areas. The case concerned a triangular strip of land between the field and the highway claimed by the owner of the field. The judge accepted that the lord owned the waste but considered that the strip was not part of the waste of the manor and found for the owner of the field.

In *Grose v West*[38] the plaintiff owned a farm called Penpont Barton in Cornwall and also a tract of land called Penpont Down. These were joined by a strip of land between the highway and a farm called the Tregildas Estate. Some years before the strip had been much larger as the highway curved round, but it had been reduced when the road was straightened by a new turnpike road. It was held that although there was indeed a presumption that such a strip and the soil of the highway belonged to the owner of the adjacent land, that presumption could be rebutted and was here, both because the strip connected two parts of the same farm and because the plaintiff could show acts of possession of the land. The judgment appears to indicate that the Down was common land but that was not essential to the decision. Gibbs CJ said: 'for if the narrow strip be contiguous to or communicate with open commons, or larger portions of land, the presumption is either done away, or considerably narrowed'.

6.6   OWNERSHIP OF ROADS

A problem arises in relation to the soil of roads, whether public highways or private ways, laid out under an inclosure award. The general rule was that if the lord shared in the allotment (which was the usual case) then the roadway would be regarded as belonging to the owners of the land to either side, who might include the lord but in many cases would not. In the less usual case where the lord of the manor did not receive an allotment, the soil of any ways laid out

---

[37]   (1860) CBNS 433; affd (1861) 7 Jur NS 1058.

[38]   (1816) 7 Taunt 39, 129 ER 16.

remained with him, whether use of them was private to the allottees or whether they were dedicated as public ways.[39]

Neaverson v Peterborough Urban District Council[40] related to land at Newborough, then in Northamptonshire, now in Cambridgeshire. An Act was passed in 1812, partly as an Inclosure Act and partly to drain the fens. It involved several manors, but it seems that Lord Exeter was lord of all of them. Part of the drainage system involved a large ditch called Moor Drain. Alongside Moor Drain ran Moor Road and on the other side of the road was a farm created by an allotment under the Act which, by 1900, belonged to Mr Neaverson. The Act provided that the roads should be maintained in an unusual way. The surveyor of the highways, a public official, should let out the grazing on the verge for healthy sheep. They would keep down the vegetation and prevent the growth of scrub, with the revenues to be applied in maintaining the roads. By 1900 the council had taken on responsibility for the roads. It let out the grazing, not only for sheep but also for cattle and horses. These bigger animals grazed so heavily that they broke down the peaty soil, eroded the banks of the drain and so caused an obstruction to the flow of water. They also broke down Mr Neaverson's hedge and ate his crops. The question arose to whom the soil of the roads laid out under the Act belonged. Was it to the allottees on either side, the lord, or the highway authority? The original judge, Cozens-Hardy J, considered that it might have belonged to the lord, but as the Lord Exeter in 1900 was not a party to the case he found in favour of the council that it had a right to graze whatever animals it wished. On appeal the Court of Appeal found for Neaverson. The court considered that the allottee of the land adjoining the road owned the soil, and in this case, as the other side was a ditch, he owned the whole width. He was therefore entitled to restrict the council to letting the grazing for sheep only.

The ownership of a road may go neither with the land on either side nor with the manor. *Curtis v Kesteven County Council*[41] concerned an argument between Charles Curtis (who was lord of the manor of Swinderby, though in the circumstances that was not relevant) and the county council as highway authority about who had the right to charge rent for allowing cattle to graze on the waste beside the road from Newark to Lincoln. In 1658 the 'common and usual lanes' in the Parish of Swinderby were assured to trustees for the poor of the parish. In 1876 the trustees sold the roadside waste to Thomas Curtis, the predecessor of Curtis. The county council claimed that under the Local Government Act 1888 'A main road and the materials thereof' belonged to it.

---

[39] *Poole v Huskinson* (1843) 11 M and W 827 per Parke B; cf *R v Inhabitants of the Tithing of East Mark* (1848) 11 QBR 877, 116 ER 701, 152 ER 1039.

[40] [1901] Ch 22, [1902] 1 Ch 551.

[41] (1890) 45 ChD 504.

The court held that the 'main road' did not extend to the roadside waste and found in favour of Curtis. The law was subsequently changed and the Highways Act 1980 refers to the 'highway', so that on similar facts Curtis would now fail.

Under modern law the highway authority owns the trees as well as the grass. This was established in *Law v Haddock Ltd*[42] where a house owner successfully claimed damages from the county council for harm done by the roots of trees on the highway. The court reached a similar decision in *Giles v County Building Construction (Hertford) Ltd.*[43] However, the house owner does own the subsoil.[44]

Another case where the lord of the manor claimed ownership of the highway but to little effect was *Gloucestershire County Council v Farrow.*[45] Mr Farrow was lord of the manor of Stow-on-the-Wold which has a market square. He did not own any of the houses around the square but (for the purposes of this action) it was assumed that he owned the soil of the square itself. He claimed the right to hold a market and did not succeed (21.2), However, no one suggested that it was impossible for him, as lord, to own the square itself.

It is convenient here to mention a development which for a short time gave lords of manors and owners of common land an income, but which ultimately led nowhere. In *Hanning v Top Deck Travel Group Limited*[46] heavy, long-distance buses used a private roadway across otherwise quiet common land at Horsell Common, Woking in Surrey. Trustees who owned the common obtained an injunction to stop this use. Generally, where someone has used a private road for 20 years he will have obtained a legal right of way, but the trustees argued that the use by the bus company was illegal because, under the Law of Property Act 1925, s 193, it is unlawful to drive across common land 'without lawful authority'. The trustees argued that only they could lawfully permit it. There was a similar provision in the Road Traffic Act 1930 (now the Road Traffic Act 1988, s 34). The *Hanning* case itself was uncontroversial but it opened a way for many lords to claim that house holders who had been using a route across a common for vehicular access had no right to do so and, if they wanted to continue, had to pay for it. If a house owner wished to sell his house and the buyer insisted on a lawful right to drive a car there, the owner had no choice but to meet whatever demands the common owner made. This naturally aroused resentment and, following pressure by several MPs, a provision was included in the Countryside and Rights of Way Act 2000, s 68 to provide in such cases that

---

[42]   [1985] EGLR 247.

[43]   (1971) 22 P&CR 978.

[44]   *Norman v Department of Transport* (1996) 72 P&CR 210.

[45]   [1982] 2 All ER 1031, (1984) 48 P&CR 85, [1985] 1 WLR 741.

[46]   (1993) 68 P&CR 14.

the house owner could insist on having a legal right of way at a price determined according to rules authorised by Parliament. The subsequent regulations provided for a payment equal to a percentage of the value of the house. However, in *Bakewell Management Limited v Brandwood*[47] the House of Lords held that *Hanning* was wrongly decided. If someone had used a way for 20 years then that itself constituted lawful authority. As a result, the need for ransom payments disappeared and s 68 was repealed by the Commons Act 2006.

Owners of commons may still be able to obtain payments, for instance where a way has not been used for the full 20 years or has been used only for one house and the owner sells for development involving many units, or where the use of the land served undergoes a major change, such as from residential to industrial. *Newbury District Council v Russell*[48] was decided before *Bakewell* when *Hanning* was still thought to be good law. The manor of Bucklebury had been held by ancestors of the defendant since at least 1540 and carried ownership of Bucklebury Common. In 1929 a scheme was made (with the consent of the family) under the Commons Act 1899 and management of the common was handed over to Bradfield Rural District Council, to whom Newbury succeeded in 1974. Some houses had been built next to the common and their only access was across it. The council claimed the right under the *Hanning* decision to make a charge for access and the family also claimed that right. The decision was in favour of the family. The judge accepted that the powers of management and the byelaws under it were for public purposes but that did not extend to granting a private right of way to the owner of a particular house

6.7 BALKS

Balks (or baulks, slades or meers) were strips of boundary ground in the middle of open fields. The traditional meaning was a narrow length, sometimes only a few inches wide, sometimes several feet across, which was left unploughed between adjoining strips to secure their boundaries. As they were by definition uncultivated they were waste by nature. Many cases in manorial courts or courts leet were concerned with people who unlawfully ploughed into or through these balks, either to get a few more square inches in which to sow their seed or to encroach onto their neighbour's land. The word can also refer to the headlands at the ends of the strips where the ploughteams turned.

---

[47]   [2004] 2 AC 519.

[48]   (1997) 95 LGR 705.

By the late eighteenth century public concern at the non-use of land taken up by balks led to the inclusion in ss 11–14 of the Inclosure Act 1773 of power to plough up balks provided the consent of the lord and of the majority of the people who had rights in the fields was obtained, and provided sufficient land was given by way of exchange for the grazing lost by the ploughing and boundary stones were set up to replace the ploughed-out balks.

Bracton[49] says that balks were held in common so that the owners of the strips on either side had each a half interest in the whole of the balk. Later the normal rule seems to have been that balks were waste of the manor but some balks between strips were divided lengthwise between the strips on either side or were allocated entirely to one side. On flat ground it hardly mattered unless they were wide enough for trees to become established and in any case timber in copyholds normally belonged to the lord (11.2). Headlands might also be waste of the manor but could be owned as an extension of the strip. They were more important, especially if there was inclosure by agreement.

Balks may be more extensive, especially on hillsides. On sloping ground the effect of ploughing is to loosen the soil, which, over the centuries, rolls downhill. Strips were usually arranged parallel to the contours rather than across them. The effect over time was that on the uphill side of the strip the plough dug into the subsoil and on the downhill side a thick deposit built up. The end result was what looks like a series of terraces on the hillside. The steps between these terraces (which on steep slopes can be six feet high and correspondingly wide) form the balks and are known as lynchets. Who owns the lynchet? Typical examples can be seen on the isle of Portland where, although the open field system is no longer managed in all its rigour, many strips still exist and are owned separately from their neighbours. The general rule derives from the fact that the ploughman of the lower land would go as far upslope as he could. The soil of the balk is formed from what has rolled downhill. Therefore the boundary is at the base of the lynchet.

A similar rule, known as the hedge and ditch rule, applies to closes. This rule was considered and confirmed by the House of Lords in *Alan Wibberley Building Ltd v Insley*.[50] It concerned what had once been the boundary between two farms in the village of Saverley Green in Staffordshire. The properties had been in separate ownership at least since the seventeenth century. There was a ditch and next to it a hedge on Mr Insley's side of the ditch. He demolished the hedge and erected a fence in its place. Wibberley complained that the hedge was its property. There was some indication from the title deeds that the boundary had been treated as the middle of the hedge. However, the House of Lords

---

[49]   Bracton *op cit* f 167, 180, 207.

[50]   [1999] 1 WLR 894, [1999] 2 All ER 897.

considered that while title deeds might be conclusive where a property originally in one ownership was divided so that the deeds indicated an agreement between the buyer and seller as to where a new boundary should be, it had no application to a case such as this. Instead it applied the hedge and ditch presumption. Lord Hoffmann said that the basis of this presumption was explained by Lawrence J in *Vowles v Miller* in 1810:[51]

> The rule about ditching is this: No man, making a ditch, can cut into his neighbour's soil, but usually he cuts it to the very extremity of his own land: he is of course bound to throw the soil which he digs out, upon his own land; and often, if he likes it, he plants a hedge on top of it ...

This appears to relate to the circumstances of inclosure typically of a group of strips in a former open field. The owner could make them into a close within a ditch and bank.

However, a hedge may itself belong to the lord even though the land on either side does not, for example where the closes have been won out of woodland and the hedge is the last fragment remaining of the ancient wood dividing two assarts. If the hedge is a broad one, especially if it has timber trees, it may be manorial waste.

6.8   RIVERS

The general rule, as for roads and balks, is that ownership of a river bed is divided, with the boundary line running down the middle. The leading case, *Duke of Roxburgh v Earl of Home*,[52] does not relate to manors but to the greatest boundary in the land, the Tweed between England and Scotland. Rivers are often the boundary between two manors, but where the river runs within a manor it may be owned separately from its banks, by the lord.

First, it has been common practice for the lord to sell the adjoining riparian land but retain the fishing rights and the bed of the river, or to sell the fishing but retain the dry land. Ownership of the river bed may include a narrow strip of land along the banks a few feet wide. In other cases there may only be a right to maintain the banks, cut weds and stand on the bank to fish. Secondly, the lord may have had the fishing as part of his general sporting rights (12.7). In that case it might be presumed that he also owned the bed, and that presumption is common in the case of several fisheries in tidal rivers.

---

[51]   (1810) 3 Taunt 137 at 138.

[52]   (1774) 2 Paton 358.

In *Ecroyd v Coulthard*[53] the lord of the manor of Cumwhitton in Cumbria had for many years enjoyed a private fishery in part of the River Eden. When the manor was inclosed one allotment comprised a holding on the bank. Evidence was produced to show that neither the stated area of the allotment nor the plan on the award included the river. It was held that the normal *medium filum* presumption was rebutted.

Thirdly, the lord had jurisdiction over mills and weirs. Here it need only be said that apart from the mill itself, there was usually a mill dam, holding back a mill pool which was fed by a mill leat or artificial channel which ran for anything between a few yards and several miles. Many survive, not all with running water, and the lord may still have title. Others have been filled in. Mills and leats are considered in 17.3. Disputes also occasionally arise over title to old mill ponds. These may have little value as they can be dangerous attractions to children or are protected as havens for wildlife. They may however be seen as benefits to converted mill houses whose owners may wish to control them. Again, often the lord retains ownership but there can be problems in persuading others of that.

Weirs are obstructions across rivers to preserve fishing. Manorial records may show that they were constructed either by or with the consent of the lord, or that a regular payment was made at the manor court for permission to retain them, and that can be evidence that the bed is manorial waste. Bracton[54] considers the problems where a weir has been unlawfully constructed and where the owner has only half the bed and has to use one remedy in trespass for his half and perhaps leave unpursued a different remedy in nuisance for the other.

As indicated above in *Attorney-General v Hanmer*[55] foreshore can be part of the manor although that is unusual. Most foreshore below high water mark around the coast belongs to the Crown. Sometimes where a lord was granted a franchise of wreck (16.6), since that was the most valuable perquisite of foreshore, it was often (but not invariably) presumed that the lord also had the foreshore. Although the owner of foreshore normally has it from mean high water to the lowest limit of tides, that is not invariable, as the case of *Baxendale v Instow Parish Council*[56] discussed at 7.4 shows.

Bridges are not usually relevant to title but the lord may have been responsible for repair; if so, the bridge and the underlying river may have been be treated as belonging to him. This is considered further at 15.3.

---

[53]   [1897] 2 Ch 554.

[54]   Bracton *op cit* f 234b.

[55]   (1858) 31 LT 379, 4 de G & J 205, 45 ER 80.

[56]   [1982] 1 Ch 14, [1981] 2 All ER 620.

6.9   UNCLAIMED LAND OF UNKNOWN LORDS

As indicated at 10.1 the ownership of much common land is unknown, but although this is a particular problem for commons and greens it can apply to any type of unoccupied land. It is unlikely to apply to occupied land because after a period of time[57] the occupier will obtain squatters' rights. Some land held on very long leases cannot be so acquired if the Law of Property Act 1925, s 153 does not apply. Where the rent is very low or even non-existent the landlord, usually a lord where the nominal rent was payable at the manor court (14.6), may have found that the cost of collecting it exceeded the amount, But, however long the time and even if the landlord is unknown that will not give rise to adverse possession. Waste is by definition unoccupied and therefore not susceptible to adverse possession.

In theory some unoccupied land might belong to the Crown. This could be because, like foreshore, it had never been comprised in a manor and had never been the subject of a grant by the Crown and, therefore, even if the Crown is not aware of it, it is part of the Crown Estate. This is unlikely, however, as virtually all land in England above high water mark has at some time been within a manor. If the land was within a manor which belonged to an abbey in the Middle Ages, and on the Dissolution if the Crown did not dispose of the manor as a whole but of its lands piecemeal, some waste might remain. If an individual died before 1926 intestate and without kin his land would escheat, and if he owned waste it might never come to the attention of the authorities.

If it is not Crown land then the fee simple must belong to someone, although it can be difficult to determine to whom. Assuming that the land was at one time vested in an individual or a corporation, how might the traces of ownership be lost?

The reason it may be difficult to establish ownership is because no one thought the land worth claiming or administering it. This is most likely where the rights of commoners took up the whole of the grazing and the land had no minerals or sporting value so that it was not worth taking the trouble to claim it. If the common land, as waste, belonged to the lord of some manor and the manor became a reputed manor and was sold before the Conveyancing and Law of Property Act 1881 the conveyance would not carry the waste (8.5) so the buyer would not take title. The existence of the manor itself may have been lost to sight if the demesne lands were sold, the copyholds enfranchised and the court ceased to be held.

---

[57]   Limitation Act 1980, s 15; Land Registration Act 2002, s 97 and Sch 6.

It is necessary to distinguish between the nominal title, vesting the legal estate, and beneficial or equitable ownership. If the manor belonged outright to an individual he would either hold it until his death or give it away in his life. If the owner died before 1540 owning the land it passed to his heir: if after that date it passed under his will, if he made one and the will covered it, the land passed to the designated beneficiary. If it did not, it still passed to the heir at law until the Land Transfer Act 1897 when it passed to his executors or administrator. Until 1925 it was common practice that the executors informally assented to the land vesting in a beneficiary, but it is possible that if it was not known that the deceased owned some waste land there might be no implied assent. In that case title might remain with the executors or administrator. If the land was settled and the legal estate was held by an individual then, before 1926, it passed automatically, for instance on the terms of an entail.

After 1925 title could only pass by a document, either a written assent, conveyance or court order (including a grant of probate). If the land became vested in executors or trustees and they did not dispose of it, legal title normally passed to the survivor and, if no replacements were appointed, legal title might vest in the executor of the last surviving executor or trustee. If title was vested in an administrator, on his death legal title vests in the President of the Family Division of the High Court.

The land may have belonged to a corporation such as a university college or the Church or a borough, which normally have good records of their holdings. It may have belonged to a company, either as having been purchased, perhaps along with other land as a commercial venture, or possibly have vested in the company, such as a bank, if it acted as trustee or executor. If the corporation still exists and has not disposed of the land it will still hold title. It may have been reconstructed, in which case unknown or valueless land may have been left out of the reconstruction. If the company is dissolved, its undisposed assets will have passed to the Crown as bona vacantia save for those held as trustee, where legal title may have escheated.

If the land was owned in undivided shares in 1925, for instance if common land belonged to those with grazing rights, the transitional provisions in Sch 1, Part IV, para 1 to the Law of Property Act provides for title to vest in up to four of the owners unless some shares were held in trust, in which case it vested in and remains with the Public Trustee. Where a majority in value of the beneficial owners are known they can together appoint a new trustee.

The Commons Registration Act 1965, s 8 directed that the parish council or sometimes another authority should be registered as owner of unclaimed town and village greens for the purposes of the Act (19.8). Under s 9 the local authority, usually the district council, was given powers to protect common land. Under the Commons Act 2006, s 45 the authority's powers extend also to a town or village green. However, these appear to be purely administrative provisions and are not intended to expropriate the true owner. So long as they subsist the green will be regarded as subject to the provisions of local government law relating to open spaces.[58] If someone is able to show a good beneficial title to the land then he should be able to obtain registration as proprietor.

Tracing the legal title, even if it can be done, will not affect the beneficial or equitable ownership. This may pass under a settlement, will or intestacy and have been divided among many descendants of a former owner or beneficiaries under a number of wills. Occasionally, if someone can be traced, perhaps by investigating a family tree and inspecting wills, he may be able to apply to the court for a vesting order.

If it is impossible to trace either legal or beneficial ownership the land remains in a legal limbo. The Crown will not assert any claim where there might be an owner; even where the land has escheated it may be reluctant to become involved. A local authority may be able and willing to make a compulsory purchase but only where circumstances justify it.[59] It is therefore likely that for some time to come much common land will have no identifiable owner.

As with any land, if someone is able to enter into possession and take control of the land that by itself will confer a title, however precarious, which may be asserted against anyone except someone with a better title. This can apply to waste land as much as to a close.[60]

---

[58] See Local Government Act 1972, ss 122, 123.

[59] See Compulsory Purchase Act 1965, Sch 2.

[60] See, generally on this section, *Walker v Burton* [2012] EWHC 978 (Ch); *Mellstrom v Badgworthy Land Co Ltd* (2010) LR Adj 2008/1498; 2009/0290; 2009/0953.

Chapter 7

Parcels

7.1 LIMITS OF THE MANOR

Manors were not fixed, geographical units. Before 1189 they could expand or contract. Since then they can only contract, save under special conditions such as inclosure Acts described below. The areas of land that make up the manor are known as parcels. This chapter describes how parcels became separated from the manor and the extent to which, if separated, they could again become part or parcel of it. As a manor is a unit of custom (4.1) which applies to particular pieces of land, once it became impossible to have a new custom after 1189 it was no longer possible for additional land to become comprised in a manor. Until *Quia Emptores* 1290 part of a manor could by subinfeudation become comprised in a sub-manor. Until 1897 a manor could be divided (8.3).

Some manors were defined on the ground as lying within a single continuous boundary which could be perambulated. The Anglo-Saxon predecessors were described in *boks* as so bounded. After the eleventh century this was unusual. The lands of one manor were intermixed with lands of others and with lands outside any manor. After 1290 this became increasingly frequent as lands were granted away from the manor. If there were two or more manors in a village the strips would be intermixed in the open field. Some lands might be distant from the manorial centre and not attached to other manorial lands.

In recent years some people who have bought a manor have sought to have a map drawn up. As explained in 25.7, when before 2003 lords were seeking to register titles to their manors the Land Registration Rules[1] required them to lodge a map of any demesne land. Many applicants misunderstood this as requiring a map of the historic limits of the manor. Quite apart from that lords have often sought to have a map of their manor even where they were aware that it had no legal significance. Others have sought to define the limits in the hope

---

[1] SR&O 1925/1093, r 51.

of being recognised as owner of roadside waste (6.5) or other miscellaneous pieces of land.

Boundaries may be relevant to the location of a court which has to be held within the manor (13.2). It may be important that someone is a man of the manor,[2] or that the owner of a particular house can use a customary way for the inhabitants of the manor, or that some other custom applies. It may relate to the extent of the lord's mineral or sporting rights or to whether a particular close is demesne land. The right to take water or fish or to have the benefit of a covenant[3] may be claimed by those living within the bounds.

Ancient boundaries could be arbitrary but tended to corresponded to natural features such as rivers or to obvious manmade features such as prehistoric banks or Roman roads. The limits of cultivated land were clear because each tenant acknowledged his own lord and attended his manor court. Where the boundary crossed the waste it might be less evident. Often it did not matter where on the waste the cattle were grazing as those of the tenants of adjacent manors were allowed to stray onto each other's waste under the rule known as vicinage (10.4). When mineral rights came to be exploited and when inclosure of waste was undertaken in the eighteenth century there could be serious boundary disputes. Section 39 of the Inclosure Act 1845 provided for boundaries to be resolved, suggesting that many were still uncertain as late as that. When in the 1970s ownership of common land had to be registered under the Commons Registration Act 1965 a number of these disputes, some involving 100 acres or more, came to light. Such disputes had rumbled on for centuries but had never been resolved because the value of the waste was not worth the costs of a law suit. If the rival claimants could not agree, the issue had to be determined by the Commons Commissioner, at least for the purposes of the 1965 Act, although that was not necessarily conclusive in other contexts such as land registration.

7.2   OUTLIERS AND DISTRIBUTED LANDS

The imaginary manor of Middleton described at 1.1 was a geographical unit, but few manors were like that. Most had a definite centre, around the manor house and where the court was held, but there were also detached parts that lay outside the main focus, known as outliers. These could have different origins.

The most ancient outliers were summer pastures. These can be found all over the country but are typical of certain areas such as Kent and Sussex where a

---

[2]   *Iveagh v Martin* [1961] 1 QB 232, [1960] 2 All ER 668.

[3]   *Re Mansfield District Council's Application* (1976) 33 P&CR 141, 241 EG 241.

manor in the coastal plain might include land in the Weald. The name 'Midsomer Norton' in Somerset suggests a similar arrangement and the practice is also found in Gloucestershire. Many such detached lands later developed into full manors in their own right. These arrangements may go back to prehistoric times when a community would go up with their flocks to the hills to seek pasture in summer and those pastures were part of the communal lands. Such arrangements have lasted until modern times in parts of southern Europe. In England the practice of summer grazing on pastures at some distance from the manor seems to have become unusual after the twelfth century, but the lords continued to claim jurisdiction over the separate lands.

A second outlier was the town house. *Domesday Book* does not include London in its description but many of the manors in the Home Counties, such as Walthamstow and Barking in Essex, are described as including houses within the City of London[4] and similar situations occur in other towns. Some of these may go back to the Anglo-Saxon system of burgh defence, part of the *trinoda necessitas*. This does not seem to have continued long after the eleventh century. Although in the eighteenth century many gentlemen had their town houses either in a county town or in London, these were in separate ownership and not part of any of their manors unless they also owned part of the town.

The third, and most common, type of outlier was the isolated parcel, perhaps a house and garden, perhaps a farm, many miles from the centre of the manor. Some of these derived from the Saxon system of *soc*, that certain socmen had the privilege of going with their land to whichever lord they chose, or deciding whose jurisdiction they would accept. After 1066 when jurisdiction and tenure were combined the land became part of the manor and stayed so even when the tenant changed. Many such isolated parts remained in the same manor until modern times. Even if it ceased to be part of the manor, the land might be a detached part of a parish originally based on a manor until the nineteenth century ecclesiastical and local government reorganisations.

Even within a settlement the manor was rarely a geographical unit within a ring-fence.[5] Most villages, especially in southern and eastern England, were made up of several manors. This seems to have been particularly so in Sussex where, in the early seventeenth century, the parish of Hailsham included land held of 14 different manors. In contrast, at the same time the manor of Robertsbridge extended into parts of 14 parishes and Allington into 22, comprising 6000 acres

---

[4]   Maitland, FW, *Domesday Book and Beyond* (Cambridge University Press, 1987; first published 1897) 114.

[5]   Bracton, Sir Henry, *De legibus et consuetudinibus angliae* (c 1257) f 434; cf Maitland *op cit* 136; Hilton, RH, *The English Peasantry in the Later Middle Ages* (Clarendon Press, 1975) 132.

in 1608.[6] In the adjoining county of Kent the manor of Wye was distributed among 20 modern parishes.[7]

The reason may derive from landholdings in the former kingdom of Sussex or it may relate to the way in which the Anglo-Saxon Church held rights in various properties which later came to be administered as separate manors. Others were the result of the break-up of the Anglo-Saxon multiple estates which had pieces carved out of them, leaving a scattered residue (2.3). In the rest of the country few villages were divided between more than three or four manors. That may have been because two originally adjacent but separate settlements merged; others arose when a single manor was divided, perhaps between co-heiresses (8.3).

7.3   SUBINFEUDATION AND *QUIA EMPTORES* 1290

Such unity as the manor possessed was further disrupted by the statute *Quia Emptores*. Wholly new manors could not be created after 1189 because new customs could not then arise (4.1). The result of *Quia Emptores* was that no new sub-manors could be created by an act of the parties after 1290 and manors could only be divided between co-parceners as described in 8.3. Within the manor demesne or waste land could not be granted by subinfeudation to be held of the lord[8] (in the absence of special custom) but the effect was that the land that was sold left the manor. Any copyhold land could only be enfranchised at common law by granting the freehold, so again it left the manor. However, if the copyhold was enfranchised by statute under the Copyhold Acts 1840 to 1894 it could remain within the manor (5.7).

Originally the fee, or fief, *feudum* or feu, was the reward granted in land for services rendered (22.5). Particularly in military tenures there was a close personal bond between the lord and his follower who became his tenant. By the end of the thirteenth century this personal bond had weakened and become commercialised, but the theory still governed the rules and had three consequences. First, assume Sir Hugh is the lord of land held by Ralph for which Ralph owes services. Ralph wishes to sell his land (or some of it) to Guy. If the result is that Guy will be the direct tenant of Sir Hugh, then his consent is needed and he needs to be satisfied that Guy will perform the services. Normally he will give his consent in return for a payment of money which he will fix at whatever the market will bear.

---

[6]   Brandon, P and Short, P, *The South-East from AD 1000* (Longman, 1990) 171.

[7]   Faith, R, *The English Peasantry and the Growth of Lordship* (Leicester University Press, 1997) 46.

[8]   Demesne: see *Re Holliday* [1922] 2 Ch 698 (see 8.1); waste exceptionally (see 5.6).

Secondly, if Ralph dies his eldest son (and therefore his heir) Robert will inherit his lands but Robert cannot take over the lands without paying Sir Hugh a sum of money called a relief. In the case of a knight's fee the relief became established at 100 shillings but there was a similar payment for succession to land held in socage which was normally set at about a year's income from the land.[9] There were similar rights of wardship (whereby the lord received the income of land if the heir, Robert, was a child) and marriage (whereby the lord had the right to arrange – or sell – the marriage of an unmarried tenant). All these rights of relief, wardship and marriage were over-exploited by James I and Charles I over their tenants in chief and were abolished for all freehold tenants, not just tenants in chief, by the Tenures Abolition Act 1660 (22.5).

Thirdly, if Ralph dies without heirs, or commits a serious crime, such as murder or theft of the type known as felony, his lands will come back or escheat to Sir Hugh as his lord. There were historically two types of escheat, both now abolished but there still exist others discussed below (7.6–7.8). While escheat was generally accepted in the thirteenth century as fair, or a fact of life, fines for sales and reliefs on inheritance were resented. The way round was subinfeudation.

This turns on the difference between grant and assurance described in 5.6. In the case of fees simple an assurance (by which the purchaser becomes the direct tenant of the vendor's lord) was called substitution. A grant involved the creation of a new subsidiary fee held of the seller and was called subinfeudation. This had three advantages over substitution. First, no consent was needed from the superior or chief lord. Ralph continued to be the tenant of Sir Hugh and Guy became Ralph's subtenant, which, in theory, did not affect Sir Hugh so no fine could be charged. Secondly, reliefs could be avoided. If Ralph held in socage he could grant his land to Robert in his lifetime reserving the service of a rose at midsummer, even though the value of the land was £100 a year. When Ralph died a relief was payable, but instead of £200 all Sir Hugh got was two roses. Thirdly, Ralph reserved the right to escheat if Guy died without heirs or committed felony, whereas if Ralph died without heirs, Sir Hugh would not recover the land but merely become Guy's lord.

One consequence of sales taking place by subinfeudation was that titles became very complex, as described in 22.6. There could easily be a chain of half a dozen lords and tenants in the same piece of land and, unlike modern leases (where the same can happen but which last for a limited time), the fees were perpetual and went on forever. It was difficult to discover who owned what. *Quia Emptores* was passed as part of a bargain, partly to remedy the

---

[9] Bracton *op cit* f 84–5; Simpson, AWB, *An Introduction to the History of the Land Law* (Oxford University Press, 1961) 17.

complications of title, but more to preserve seigniorial rights and allow the free sale of land. The Act states that it was passed because lords had lost their rights of escheat, marriage and lordship. This was true as someone in the position of Sir Hugh would know, but the greatest loser of all had been the Crown, and the Act was one of a long line of statutes passed to prevent the avoidance of death and other duties.

It provided that on any future grant of land in fee simple the effect would be substitution not subinfeudation, whatever the documents said. In return, lords lost their power to refuse (and therefore charge for) consent to sale. If only part of the land was sold then the services were apportioned. It did not apply to copyholds or to such interests as life estates and entails (which became equitable interests in 1925), nor did it or does it apply to leaseholds, which under the general law can be sublet, although the terms of the lease may prevent it. It did not bind the Crown, which still disposes of allodial land by infeudation. For some time the Crown also insisted on consenting to sales, although eventually that became obsolete.

The result of *Quia Emptores* was that no new freeholds could be granted in fee simple. In *Re Holliday*[10] in 1922 an attempt was made to argue that a lord who held his manor *ut de corona* (8.1) could still subinfeudate. In 1837 the lord of the manor of Brough in Westmoreland enfranchised Blackacre held by Mr Atkinson as customary tenant and granted it to him to be held of the manor in free and common socage. Brough was itself held of the Crown *ut de corona*. By 1910 Blackacre was held by Mr Holliday who died in that year intestate and without heirs. Both the Crown and the lord claimed escheat. The lord argued that *Quia Emptores* did not bind tenants in chief of the Crown. The judge, Astbury J, considered the cases, statutes and textbooks in detail and concluded that it did, or at any rate tenants in chief could not subinfeudate after an Act of 1361. Indeed, he discussed a series of statutes of Edward II and III from which he concluded that no subinfeudation by anyone was possible after 1290. It seems that by virtue of Chapter 32 of the reissue of Magna Carta of 1225 the rules that lords could not subinfeudate may also have applied to manors held by the Crown *ut de honore*.

As the existence of at least two free tenants is an essential feature of the manor this is sometimes given as the reason why there could be no new manors after 1290 apart from partition between co-parceners (8.3). Equally, no new common freeholds could be created within the manor after 1290. As no new customary holdings could be created after 1189 this meant that (leases or special custom apart) there could thereafter be no new tenancies within the manor.

---

[10]   [1922] 2 Ch 698.

7.4   RULE AGAINST ENLARGING MANOR

The general rule is that a manor cannot be enlarged, so that land which had never belonged to it cannot be attached to a manor. When manors were still taking shape, land could be added to them. There are many examples in *Domesday Book*. For example there was a hide of land formerly in the manor of Battersea in Surrey[11] which the reeve of the village took from the manor because of a feud and added to the manor of Chertsey. There are also examples of land previously outside any manor being put into one. On the Continent the process whereby the holder of allodial land could voluntarily submit to a lordship is known as commendation.

The present rule derives from *Quia Emptores* since, if land is sold and therefore becomes held from the chief lord, it follows that land formerly held of one lordship cannot subsequently be placed under another lordship. This has particular force where land is held of the Crown, as to place such land under another lord would be to deprive the king of his revenues; but it applies more generally.

Baxendale v Instow Parish Council[12] in 1981 arose under the Commons Registration Act 1965. It related to a coastal manor in Devon whose boundary went down to high water mark. In 1855 Mrs Clevland, the lady of the manor, purchased from the Crown a strip of foreshore between high and low water. Over the years the sea receded and this strip became dry land. It was registered under the 1965 Act as being waste of the manor. There is no doubt that the land was waste. The question was whether it was waste of the manor. Mr Baxendale was one of the trustees who, as successors to Mrs Clevland, held the strip, and who resisted the registration. The court held that the land could not have been added to the manor in this way. Counsel argued that it was held with the manor and by general repute was to be treated as part of it. For instance, in *Thinne v Thinne*[13] lands purchased by the lord and held by him, although not parcel of the manor, were reputed to be held with it and passed on its transfer. This rule is now statutory under s 62(3) of the Law of Property Act 1925. The court did not accept that that made it waste of the manor for the purposes of the 1965 Act.

To this general rule there are exceptions by statute. Certain statutory additions were introduced under the Copyhold Acts between 1841 and 1925 by virtue of ss 15(3) and 18 of the Copyhold Act 1894 under which compensation to the lord for enfranchisement of a copyhold could take the form not of cash but of land in

---

[11]   *Domesday Book*: Surrey 32b.

[12]   [1982] 1 Ch 14, [1981] 2 All ER 620.

[13]   (1660) 1 Lev 27, 83 ER 280.

exchange for the seigniorial rights. Such land had to be convenient to be held with the manor and if the manor was held in trust the land had to go with it on the same terms. The Act did not specifically make the land parcel of the manor but it could easily become so by repute.

Copyhold land could also be added to the manor under an inclosure Act or award where land was redistributed and a copyholder was allotted a new holding in return for his old one. The old land often became freehold or demesne, or left the manor altogether. Sometimes, instead of an allotment of new copyhold land, the tenant took a slightly smaller allotment as freehold and slightly more land was allotted to the lord to compensate for the loss of manorial incidents. If the Act provided for land to be allotted as copyhold which was not so before, it became parcel. Thus the Inclosure Act 1845, s 94 states that land allotted is to be of the same tenure as the former holding of the allottee and specifically that:

> the land taken in exchange or on partition or allotted in respect of copyhold or customary land shall be deemed copyhold or customary land, and shall be held of the lord of the same manor under the same rent, and by the same customs and services, as the copyhold or customary land in respect of which it may have been taken in exchange or on partition or allotted was or ought to have been held

It is also possible that the Crown has a prerogative power to add land to a manor as discussed in 24.10.

7.5   RULE AGAINST LAND COMING BACK TO MANOR

A related rule is that once land has been severed from a manor it cannot be reattached by act of parties although it can by act of law. This was established in *R v Duchess of Buccleugh*[14] in 1704. The report of the case does not give the facts and therefore it is a little difficult to understand it, but it seems as follows. The duchess was one of several owners of lands that had once been part of the demesne of the manor of Delamore in Hertfordshire. She was not lord of the manor – that was Sir John Bucknall – but she was presumably named as first defendant because she was the most important of the landowners. It was assumed for the purposes of argument that the manor carried with it the liability to repair a bridge used by the public. As it happened another case[15] decided that

---

[14]   (1704) 6 Mod 150, 87 ER 909, 1 Salk 358, 91 ER 312.

[15]   *R v Sir John Bucknall* (1702) 7 Mod 98, 87 ER 1091; See also 92 ER 29, (1702) 2 Ld Raym 792, 92 ER 37, (1702) 2 Ld Raym 804.

this liability could not be proved but it was not an unreasonable assumption because bridge repair was a recognised ancient burden of many manors.

At some stage parts of the demesne had been sold off and the question was whether the duchess and the other defendants as owners of former demesne were liable in addition to Sir John. The court held that she and they were, for 'a manor is an entire thing and not severable'. Each part of the former demesne remained subject to the liability. When he sells, the lord may well agree with the purchaser that he will continue to have full responsibility but that is a personal arrangement between them and does not affect the rights of third parties, such as highway authorities, to go against any owner of any part of the former demesne.[16] Furthermore, the purchaser holds from the chief lord (in this case the Crown because the manor had once belonged to the Duchy of Lancaster) by the same service as the lord holds – in this case knight service with a duty to repair the bridge. Although the report does not give the reasons of the court, this follows from the express words of *Quia Emptores*. Even though knight service became socage in 1660, the burdens were preserved. However, the court went on to say that once the land has been severed from the manor it can never again become legally parcel of it. It may do by reputation, so that for most practical purposes they go together, but not in law.

This point was further confirmed by the House of Lords in *Delacherois v Delacherois*[17] in 1862. This is an odd case in at least three ways. First, although always accepted as authority in English law, it relates to property in Ireland and the facts could never have occurred in England. Secondly, it was decided by the House against what seems to have been the unanimous advice of the judges. Thirdly, the actual decision was obsolete over 20 years before it was decided. Daniel Delacherois was lord of the manor of Donaghadee in County Down. He had no children and in 1836 made a will leaving all his lands to his sister Mary (who also had no children) for her life and after her death as she should appoint between their two nephews, sons of their dead brother Samuel, namely Nicholas the elder and David the younger. Daniel never changed his 1836 will and died in 1850. Mary favoured David. It is not clear why. She may have disliked Nicholas or he may have been a spendthrift or, as elder son of his father, he may have been provided for elsewhere. In any case she appointed that the lands held under Daniel's will should go to David. That clearly affected most of the manor and there was no problem about that. Mary died in 1854.

The dispute related to an estate called Ballyhayes. Nicholas claimed that it passed to him as his uncle's heir on intestacy. The ground of the claim was that under the law in force in 1836 when Daniel made his will it only covered

---

[16] The same rule applies to chancel repairs. See 20.8.
[17] (1862) HL Cas 62, 11 ER 1254.

property held at the date it was made. The very next year the law was changed by the Wills Act 1837, which provides that wills speak from death and cover all property owned at the date of death, but the Act did not cover wills made before it which were not subsequently changed. Ballyhayes had been purchased by Daniel from Mr Bradshaw in 1842 and, as the will was made before the Act, on the face of it the property would not have been covered by the will.

However, David claimed that the property was part of the manor of Donaghadee. It had originally been part of the manor, but in 1721 the then lord of Donaghadee, Hugh Montgomery Earl of Mount Alexander, granted Ballyhayes to Mr St Lawrence to be held in fee as a dependent freehold of the manor. In England he could not have done this following *Quia Emptores*, but that Act did not apply in Ireland and, indeed, when Charles I granted the manor to the earl's ancestor in 1626, he expressly authorised him to subinfeudate. So, at the time when Daniel Delacherois repurchased it in 1842, Ballyhayes was held of the manor of Donaghadee. Did it remain parcel or did the repurchase sever it from the manor? If the former it would be covered by the will and pass to David: if the latter it would not and passed to Nicholas.

The House of Lords, in accordance with a closely argued speech by Lord St Leonards, decided in favour of Nicholas. It was held that the grant in 1721 had made the land no longer demesne and although held of the manor it was not itself part of the manor but was severed. If the land had come back by operation of law (such as escheat if Bradshaw had died intestate without heirs) then indeed it would have merged again in the manor and become parcel of it. But Daniel purchased it by a voluntary act of parties (and the purchase deed was in the form of an assurance not a surrender) and so since he could not hold the land of himself he could only hold it of the chief lord, in this case the Crown, and following the repurchase it ceased to be held of the manor.

The importance of *Delacheriois v Delacherois* lies in more than the decision itself. Lord St Leonards, in his speech, accepted that the case was finely balanced – so finely that instead of following the usual practice of ordering the loser to pay the winner's costs he directed that each side bear their own. The case underlines the fragility of the law of the manor so that under the presumption against the manor the courts tend, given a choice, to favour a decision that disrupts the manorial system and frees land from its constraints. By the nineteenth century land was a commodity, like produce, manufactures or coal. The old system that saw land as the vital support of a social order based on knightly service was long gone.

Another instance of land coming back to a manor by operation of law has statutory authority. Under s 2 of the School Sites Act 1841 (20.7) where land is granted for use as a school and that use ceases it can revert to the manor out of which it formerly came. However, as suggested in *Delacherois* the principal instance is escheat.

7.6   OCCASIONS OF ESCHEAT

There were two traditional escheats which arose, one on the death of the tenant without heirs and the other on commission of a serious crime. Those two have been abolished but escheat can still arise on disclaimer of a freehold and other occasions mentioned below. The concept is that if the tenant's freehold ceases to exist then the rights of his chief lord come into effect including a better right to enter on the land than anyone else.

The first ancient occasion was escheat *propter defectum sanguinis*, when the blood of the tenant failed, namely when he died without heirs or kin close enough to inherit. In relation to freehold land the rules of the common law provided that the heir was primarily his oldest son (or the oldest son of an oldest son who had died before his father), then all his daughters together as co-heiresses or co-parceners, then his father, then his brothers in order of seniority and their sons and daughters, then his grandparents, uncles, aunts, cousins and so on. The class was wide but not inexhaustible. The heir could sometimes be deprived of his inheritance by a will. Leasehold land, being a chattel, could be left by will from early times and if the tenant died intestate it passed as such, and in default of family as bona vacantia usually to the Crown, so escheat never applied to leaseholds. Burgage land in towns (21.4) could also be left by will, and in default of heirs it passed to the chief lord, frequently the king.[18] The heir to copyhold land depended on the customs of the manor and these varied over the country. After 1540[19] it was possible to leave freehold land by will (in practice it could be managed earlier by means of a device called a use, but until then land as such could not be so left) and after 1815[20] copyhold land (again the use was employed before that where custom allowed). If there were no heirs (and after 1540 no will) then freehold land escheated to the lord. Copyhold land could escheat in a similar way, although inheritance customs varied between manors. Escheat *propter defectum sanguinis* was abolished by s 45(1)(d) of the Administration of Estates Act 1925.

The second occasion was escheat *propter delictum tenentis*, by reason of the fault of the tenant if, being tenant in fee, he committed felony, a serious crime,

---

[18]   Hemeon, M de W, *Burgage Tenure in Mediaeval England* (Harvard University Press, 1914) 24.

[19]   Statute of Wills 1540.

[20]   Preston's Act 1815, 55 Geo 3 c192.

such as murder, theft or rape, which was inconsistent with his standing as a freeholder. This did not apply to treason since in that case the traitor's land was forfeit to the Crown rather than escheating to the lord. Treasons tended to be committed by the greater lords who held *ut de corona* and therefore in practice there was little difference from escheat; but the rule applied to any traitor. Nor did it apply to copyholds which could forfeit to the lord for a wide variety of reasons including failure to attend the manor court or pay a fine, failure to keep a house in repair, taking the lord's minerals or timber, and many other faults. Escheat *propter delictum tenentis* and forfeiture to the Crown were both abolished by the Forfeiture Act 1870. Forfeiture of copyhold land to the lord was abolished by the Law of Property Act 1922.

Although these ancient varieties no longer exist, escheat still does, at least to the Crown.[21] In 2001 it was estimated that there were approximately 500 cases of escheat every year[22] and that number may have increased since. The most frequent modern types of escheat are by disclaimer by statute. Two of these arise under the Insolvency Act 1986, ss 178 and 315 when a liquidator of a company or a trustee in bankruptcy of an individual disclaims freehold land which is onerous. Escheat can also arise by statute by disclaimer of bona vacantia freehold land. If a company is dissolved its property passes to the Crown. For most of the country the responsible official is the Treasury Solicitor. If he does not wish to retain responsibility for land of a company he may disclaim freehold land under the Companies Act 2006, s 1013, in which case it will pass by escheat. In practice this is normally to another aspect of the Crown in the form of the Crown Estate Commissioners, although the royal Duchies may be involved in their counties and again disclaimer does not affect third parties.[23] The Duchies have a like power of disclaimer. Escheat also arises at common law where land belongs to a foreign corporation which is dissolved.[24]

Escheat can occur where the Crown exercises a right of re-entry. Where land has been granted, usually gratuitously for a good purpose, subject to reverter under the Crown Estate Act 1961, s 3(8) and the purpose fails, the Crown may re-enter and, if it does, then, at least where the original grant was out of allodial land, the estate determines.

---

[21]   *Scmlla Properties Ltd v Gesso Properties BVI Ltd* [1995] EG 52 (CS); (1995) 70 P&CR D1, [1995] BCC 793. See also Law of Property Act 1925, s 4(3).

[22]   Law Commission No 271, *Land Registration for the Twenty-First Century: a Conveyancing Revolution* para 11.22.

[23]   Companies Act 2006, s 1015.

[24]   *UBS Global Asset Management (UK) Ltd v Crown Estate Commissioners* [2011] EWHC 3368 (Ch), applying Law of Property Act 1925, s 181(1).

Where a private owner exercises a right of re-entry for condition broken[25] the estate survives. Before 1290 there was for practical purposes no distinction between a reverter and an escheat. *Quia Emptores* only affected fees simple so that until 1926 a lesser estate, notably a life estate (which was not a fee) or an estate tail, was held by tenure from the holder of the fee simple. The effect of the Settled Land Act 1925 was to vest the fee simple in the person who would otherwise have been tenant for life or in tail. Where, before 1926, a person alienated a fee simple by substitution but reserved a right of re-entry, that took effect by shifting the fee automatically. Since 1925 such rights can only subsist in equity, but the effect of re-entry under the Law of Property Act 1925, s 3(3)–(5) is to require the holder of the legal estate to vest it in the person entitled and, if he does not do so, the court may make a vesting order. The land revests in the person re-entering or to whom it reverts and there is no extinction of the estate.

Where certain settlements are created by statute the right of reverter, if the entail were to fail, is in the Crown. The best known instances are the Blenheim Estate settled on the Dukes of Marlborough and the Stratfield Saye Estate on the Dukes of Wellington. The Settled Land Act 1925, s 1(5) deems the potential interest of the Crown to be an interest comprised in the settlement, but that is only for the purposes of the Act. Accordingly, s 20(1) provides, for instance, that a tenant for life can exercise his power of sale and that overrides the Crown reverter. If these include manors then the reverter would cover them. It appears that the legal estate would vest in the Crown and not be determined, so it is not strictly an escheat but the effect is similar.

Escheat can also arise where freehold land belonged to an Industrial and Provident Society or a Friendly Society which has ceased to exist, or where a statutory company is dissolved, and in any of these cases provision has not been made to dispose of the land.

Finally, there may be an equivalent to a right of escheat if a commonhold is redeveloped under the Commonhold and Leasehold Reform Act 2002, s 49(3) where the commonhold association takes title to the freehold estate in each commonhold unit, although in that case the unit title continues to exist.

7.7   MESNE LORDS AND ESCHEAT

The logic of escheat is that where land is held in tenure and the interest of the tenant determines the superior interest comes into possession. In *Attorney-General of Ontario v Mercer*[26] the Earl of Selborne commented that 'when there

---

[25]   *Shiloh Spinners v Harding* [1973] AC 691.

[26]   (1883) 8 App Cas 767.

is no longer any tenant, the land returns, by reason of tenure, to the lord by whom, or by whose predecessors in title, the tenure was created'.

The first issue is whether the legal estate in the escheated land is extinguished or whether it passes to the Crown or chief lord. For the Crown, if the land was held in chief extinction would normally convert it to allodial but if *ut de honore* it may escheat to the manor or lordship of which it was held. As indicated at 24.5 much land sold or given by the Crown to subjects was granted to be held of the manor of East Greenwich or of some other manor or honour. This applies to most of the lands of monasteries and abbeys dissolved in the sixteenth century, amounting to perhaps one third of the land of England and probably also to much of the lands of families extinguished or disposed in the Wars of the Roses and to other ancient Crown lands. The Crown still holds East Greenwich, Hampton Court and other superiorities and therefore remains lord of the land granted in right of those interests rather than as Crown in chief. Escheat would therefore be to the freehold of that manor or honour rather than to the Crown allodium.

When land escheated to a mesne lord it did so as parcel of his manor, as contrasted with the situation where he purchased the land from his tenant.[27] The cases generally assume extinction and there is little in the way of an express statement, but one authority is *Pawlett v Attorney-General*[28] in which it was stated: 'And although by the escheat the tenure is extinguished ...'. That refers to tenure but it would seem to follow that the estate as such is extinguished.[29] In the parallel cases of re-entry on leasehold land forfeiture extinguishes the estate. Cases on forfeiture of copyholds by the lord of the manor are consistent with the extinction of copyhold estates on escheat.

In the *Case of the Dutchy of Lancaster*[30] it was said that:

> for the Crown, which receives any hereditaments by escheat (as it did these here) merges all jurisdictions, franchises, and liberties had and used in them, which were before derived from the Crown, for the greater extinguishes the lesser.

That case concerned the relation between the Duchy and the Crown because Edward IV argued that Henry VI had forfeited his estates and therefore the separate existence of the Duchy had to be confirmed again by a statute of Edward IV. The statement appears to distinguish jurisdictions and so on which

---

[27] *Delacherois v Delacherois* (1862) 11 HL Cas 62, 11 ER 1254.

[28] (1678) Hardres 465 at 469; 145 ER 550 at 553.

[29] *UBS Global Asset Management (UK) Ltd v Crown Estate Commissioners* [2011] EWHC 3368 (Ch) at [19].

[30] (1561) 1 Plow 212 at 219, 75 ER 325 at 336.

are extinguished, and hereditaments which are not expressly stated to be extinguished.

The Land Registration Act 2002, s 82 makes provision for escheat of a registered title. The practice is that on being notified of an escheat the Registry makes an entry to that effect on the title but keeps it open under r 173 of the Land Registration Rules 2003. If the Crown disposes of the land then the title is closed and a new one opened in the name of the transferee (strictly a grantee of a new estate).[31]

Although in theory a mesne lord might able to claim escheat, it would be difficult to prove and would not normally be worth doing. He must first be able to show that he is the tenurial superior of the holder of any escheated land and then establish that escheat to mesne lords still exists. As discussed in 5.7 there are a number of possible cases where a lord might be able to claim escheat because his superior interest still exists, including former copyhold enfranchised by statute under the Copyhold Acts 1841 to 1894 before 1926 (7.9), land formerly held of a sub-manor, land subject to a rent of assize (14.6) and former glebe land (20.4). The Administration of Estates Act 1925, s 45(1)(d), which abolished escheat for want of heirs, refers to the Crown and the Royal Duchies and to a mesne lord, apparently putting them on the same footing. The Law Commission has expressed the view[32] that:

> There is a strong presumption that a freeholder holds directly of the Crown and not of some mesne lord. See *Re Lowe's Will Trust*[33] ('the theoretical possibility of escheat to some mesne lord ... is one that is so remote that it may be wholly ignored': per Russell LJ). See too *Re Holliday*[34]. This has long been the case: see Real Property Commissioners, *Third Report on Real Property* (1832), p 3.

However, it did not refer to any specific provision abolishing escheat to mesne lords and, in the absence of such an enactment, it seems unlikely that it would be possible for a judge to conclude that it had gone under any common law doctrine.

The lord's interest in the manor itself and in any parcels such as waste are held for a legal estate in fee simple in possession. However, the tenurial superiority or *dominium directum* would not seem to give any right to possession within the meaning of the Law of Property Act 1925, s 1(3) and, if so, it could now subsist if at all only in equity. In the Land Registration Act 2002, s 131 the expression

---

[31] Land Registry Practice Guide 1 – First registrations, para 6.8.2.

[32] Law Commission 271 *op cit* para 11.5, fn 16.

[33] [1973] 1 WLR 882 at 886.

[34] [1922] 2 Ch 698 at 713.

'proprietor in possession' is widely defined so that land in the possession of a tenant is treated as being in the possession of his landlord, but it is likely that a court would restrict this to a tenant for years and not extend it to a tenant in fee simple. It may be better to regard a potential right to escheat as a *spes*, that is a possibility of occurrence, in which case it is possible that it would be regarded not as an interest but, if it exists, at most a mere equity.

However, if it is seen as analogous to a potential reverter it may survive. In *Bath and Wells Diocesan Board of Finance v Jenkinson*[35] it was held that a possibility of reverter under the School Sites Act 1841 (20.7) where, if the school were to be closed, the site might revert to a manor, was a sufficient interest capable of being devised by will, and it may be that escheat to a mesne lord would be regarded as similar; but the point is not decided. In that case it would be an equitable interest binding the land held of the manor. This does not apply to escheat to the Crown since the basis of Crown escheat is the radical title.[36]

A right of entry on reverter would be equitable. In *In re Mercer and Moore*[37] Jessel MR referred to the effect of disclaimer being a reverter. That was because s 23 of the Bankruptcy Act 1869, the predecessor of the Insolvency Act 1986, provided:

> When any property of the bankrupt acquired by the trustee under this Act consists of land of any tenure burdened with onerous covenants ... the trustee ... may... disclaim such property ... [after referring to various types of property not including freehold land] ... and if any other species of property it shall revert to the person entitled on the determination of the estate or interest of the bankrupt.

The judge said:

> As regards the words, if they are applicable to the Crown, I agree there must always be a person in existence as to the freehold estate as there is with a copyhold estate, because if there were no lords of the manor it would at once go back to the Crown.

It seems that the land in question in that case at Blackburn in Lancashire had been held in what the judge described as fee farm but subject to a rentcharge imposed in 1866 apparently to secure the performance of various onerous restrictive covenants, what would now be called an estate rentcharge. The result could evidently be a reverter to the lord of the manor but, as a grant in fee farm by a subject after 1290 operates by substitution, it would not do so in this case.

---

[35]   [2003] Ch 89.

[36]   See *Mabo v Queensland* (1992) 66 ALJR 408.

[37]   (1880) LR 14 Ch D 287.

The persons entitled to the rentcharge might of course be able to exercise their right of re-entry if they so wished. A similar conclusion comes from ss 180 and 319 of the 1986 Act which refer to land subject to a rentcharge which 'vests by operation of law in the Crown or any other person', and in the context of freehold land such other person would be a tenurial superior such as a lord of a manor. The sections do not seem to be referring to leaseholds subject to rentcharge as leases are covered by ss 179 and 317, although there might be a rentcharge imposed on assignment of part of a lease.

Even if a lord could claim, he is unlikely to wish to do so. By definition, escheats by disclaimer on insolvency must comprise onerous property. Where property of a dissolved company has passed to the Treasury Solicitor and has been disclaimed he will normally try to sell any property which has value, and therefore disclaimed land is likely to be worthless. The Insolvency Act defines onerous property in ss 178(3)(b) and 315(2)(b) as (in this context):

> any other property of the company [or comprised in the bankrupt's estate] which is unsaleable or not readily saleable or is such that it may give rise to a liability to pay money or perform any other onerous act.

Examples might be land subject to a heavy rentcharge or strict covenants or which was polluted, or a dangerous disused quarry. *Hackney London Borough Council v Crown Estate Commissioners*[38] concerned a heavily mortgaged listed building in disrepair and *In Re the Nottingham General Cemetery Co*[39] an insolvent burial ground. Likewise the Treasury Solicitor will normally wish to sell any saleable property passing as bona vacantia and will disclaim it if he cannot. Property of dissolved foreign companies will be rare and often some other party will have a claim. It is likely that any right to escheat would be interpreted as depending, like that of the Crown, on entry. It also appears that the Court has jurisdiction to reverse an escheat[40] and, where the justice required, that might be exercised in favour of at least a human bankrupt.

The question then arises whether a mesne lord would be liable for the property, for instance if it was contaminated, was a source of weeds or was a danger to visitors. Where land escheats to the Crown it is not liable for the land or anything on it unless it takes possession, but that depends on Crown immunity, now in the Crown Proceedings Act 1947, s 40(4). The same principle appears from *Attorney-General v Parsons*[41] although that involved forfeiture for mortmain and turned on construction of the Mortmain and Charitable Uses Act

---

[38] (1995) 72 P&CR 233.

[39] [1955] Ch 683.

[40] *Duncan v Official Receiver for Northern Ireland* [2008] NI Ch 20.

[41] [1956] AC 421.

1888, s 1(1). The position of a mesne lord is unclear. For example, the Environmental Protection Act 1990, s 78F(4) provides that in certain circumstances the 'owner' of contaminated land will be liable to pay the cost of remediation. 'Owner' is defined in s 78A(9) as (in effect) the person entitled to receive the rack rent if it were let. Until he has entered, and probably for registered land until the Land Registry has issued a title, the lord is not entitled to lease the land and probably therefore this excludes him. If the lord has taken no steps to enter he would not be an occupier for the purposes of the Occupiers Liability Acts 1957 and 1984.

The potential right to escheat would not rank as an overriding interest within the Land Registration Act 2002 nor, once it had occurred, would the right of entry. First, although these are rights belonging to the lord of the manor they would not be manorial rights within the Land Registration Act 2002, Schs 1 and 3, paras 11 since, if the Registry is correct as to the meaning of that expression, it is limited to rights in Sch 12, para (5) to the Law of Property Act 1922 (25.9). Secondly, an overriding interest binds the estate, not the land. The issue might be relevant to a dispute between the claimant lord and the Crown and how far the Crown is bound by the interest of the lord. There is no doubt that the Crown can be bound by equitable interests, particularly as most mesne tenants hold in chief. However, as neither the lord nor the Crown would be a purchaser for value and as neither is taking the legal estate which has been extinguished the competing equities are not relevant. In addition if escheat was to the radical[42] or allodial title then the normal rules that legal estates take precedence over equitable interests would not apply as the Crown right is not an estate. The situation might be different if the Crown claim was through the manor of East Greenwich or a similar interest.

The issue might arise if the land turned out to have some value[43] and there was a query as to whether the lord was able to make good title.[44] In order to do so he would have to show that the land was parcel of the manor. If escheat creates an equitable interest in the form of a right of entry it will do so at the moment it arises, that is on disclaimer or on dissolution of the foreign company or other event.

If someone else enters on the land any right to enter will be extinguished after the limitation period expires. If title to the land is unregistered the period is 12 years.[45] In the case of registered land under s 97 of and Sch 6 to the 2002 Act there is an initial period of 10 years and the squatter may then apply to be

---

[42]   See *Mabo v Queensland* (1992) 66 ALJR 408 and Ch 27.

[43]   See *Fenland District Council v Sheppard* [2011] EWHC 2829 (Ch).

[44]   Contrast *Mercer and Moore* (1880) LR 14 Ch D 287.

[45]   Limitation Act 1980, s 15(1).

substituted for the registered proprietor. The Registry serves notice on the registered proprietor who may ask for two years to establish his rights and evict the squatter. If title had been registered before escheat it is unclear if it should be regarded as still being so since the estate has ceased to exist. Under the Land Registration Rules 2003, r 173, as modified by r 79(3), the Registry keeps the title open until the land is sold, but that should not affect the principle that the registered estate has been extinguished. If so, it follows that the rules as to adverse possession of registered land will not apply and the Limitation Act 1980 will. The interests of the registered proprietor will have determined by the disclaimer so there is no point in serving notice on him or it. The Registry might serve notice on the Crown, in which case a squatter would have to show adverse possession for 30 years under the Limitation Act 1980, Sch 1, Part 2 as the land would not comprise a registered estate.[46] If a mesne lord was able to establish a right to escheat the 12-year period would apply.

While the Royal Duchies are considered to have freeholds in their lands their right to escheat applies throughout the county of Cornwall and the former county of Lancashire, but not in other parts of England where they have manors. Such jurisdictions within the two counties are more analogous to palatinates and, although they take the land as freehold, they do so by prerogative right. The Crown radical title by contrast is not a legal estate as such (just as an allodial right in possession, which is not a fee, is not an estate either), but nevertheless as the basis of any fee it subsists at common law. The Crown Estate Act 1961, s 8(3) provides that where land escheats to the Crown or the Royal Duchies 'then (without prejudice to the rights of other persons) the land shall vest accordingly and may be dealt with, and any proceedings may be taken in relation to it, without the title by escheat being found of record by inquisition or otherwise'.

7.8   ESCHEAT AND APPURTENANT RIGHTS

It is clear that rights binding the property survive escheat.[47] In *Attorney-General of Ontario v Mercer*[48] the Earl of Selborne said that on escheat '[t]he tenant's estate (subject to any charges upon it which he may have created) has come to an end, and the lord is in by his own right'. However, the position of third parties is in fact less clear than that statement suggests. The Insolvency Act 1986, ss 178(4)(b) and 315(3) both state that the disclaimer 'does not, except so

---

[46]   *Hill v Transport for London* [2005] Ch 379.

[47]   *Scmlla Properties Ltd v Gesso Properties BVI Ltd* [1995] EG 52 (CS), (1995) 70 P&CR D1, [1995] BCC 793; *UBS Global Asset Management (UK) Ltd v Crown Estate Commissioners*, [2011] EWHC 3368 (Ch). See also *Hindcastle Ltd v Barbara Attenborough Associates Ltd* [1997] AC 70.

[48]   (1883) 8 App Cas 767.

far as is necessary for the purpose of releasing the [company or the bankrupt's estate and the trustee] from any liability, affect the rights or liabilities of any other person' and the Companies Act 2006, s 1015(2) says the same.

It is not so clear that rights appurtenant to an escheated estate survive because it is straining language to say that an easement such as a right of way is a liability of another person, although it might be said that he is liable to allow the dominant owner to cross his land.[49] The Insolvency Act 1986, s 181(3) allows for the disclaimed property to be vested in a person, and it appears from s 436 that property is widely defined to include an interest incidental to property, so presumably it also includes an easement. Otherwise the reference in the Insolvency Act, s 178(4)(a) suggests that a right might be regarded as a right of the company (and similar for the Companies Act, s 1015), in which case it could determine. The result may turn on the distinction between rights *in rem* and *in personam*.[50]

On escheat the Crown required land to be rendered with its appurtenances[51] so that it would be able to get the benefit of appurtenant rights. It appears from the cases[52] that the Crown is entitled to rents, so presumably it is also entitled to easements. Presumably also what escheats is a bundle of rights. It is possible that when a freehold escheated the Crown would claim any easements benefiting the escheated land, but the point does not seem to have been decided, possibly because it was thought to be obvious. In *Proctor v Hodgson*[53] it was held that a claimed right of way by necessity did not survive escheat, but that was on the grounds that a way of necessity did not lie in grant. The case seems to have been lost on a pleading point that the lord ought to have claimed his own necessity rather than that of the deceased (because he might have had other means of access over other manorial lands) and it seems to have been assumed that if there had been a grant then the way could have survived. In *Ross and Morrices's Case*[54] there is a reference to an advowson appendant escheating along with a manor. In *Gilbert's Case*[55] it was indicated that subordinate rights are not affected and presumably, therefore, neither are benefiting rights. On balance it appears that such rights do survive and are capable of being granted out again. When registered land escheats and the Crown disposes of it so that a

49   Law Commission No 327, *Making Land Work: Easements Covenants and Profits à Prendre* para 6.184.

50   *Scmlla* at 795.

51   See writ cited in *Scmlla* at 799.

52   Discussed at *Scmlla* at 807.

53   (1855) 10 Exch 824; see *Nickerson v Barraclough* [1981] Ch 426.

54   (1587) 2 Leo 23, 74 ER 326.

55   (1538) 1 Dy 44a, 73 ER 96.

new title is opened, Land Registry practice is that any subsisting entries such as easements and leases are copied on to it.

7.9   ESCHEAT AND COPYHOLD ENFRANCHISEMENT

Although *Quia Emptores* did not apply to the transmission of copyholds which, indeed, could only be granted (save that some customary freeholds could be assured), it did apply if the copyhold was enfranchised. Until the Copyhold Act 1841, enfranchisement could only be done at common law by conveying or releasing the fee simple to the copyholder. This caused *Quia Emptores* to apply so that the former copyholder now held not of his former lord but of the chief lord. The same generally applied where waste was inclosed. *Doe d Lowes v Davidson*[56] concerned the Ridley (Northumberland) Inclosure Act 1751. The Act reserved seigniorial rights to the lord of Ridley. An allotment of part of the waste was made to the tenant of a customary freehold in respect of his commonable rights. Mr Lowes, a later owner of the allotment, died, leaving it by will to Mr Davidson. At the time copyhold land could not pass under a will. Lowes' brother would have been heir according to the custom of the manor and he argued that the effect of the reservation was that the allotment was copyhold held from the lord. The court, applying *Townley v Gibson*,[57] held that copyholds could only be created specifically by Act of Parliament and therefore the allotment was freehold and passed under the will.

Under s 4 of the Copyhold Act 1887, re-enacted in s 21(1)(b) of the Copyhold Act 1894, in the case of statutory enfranchisement the lord could not only reserve the sporting, minerals and timber (which could be done at common law) but also escheat. It is not unusual in titles to land enfranchised under the Copyhold Acts to find that the holder of the land died without heirs before 1926 and the land escheated to the lord.

As mentioned above, escheat *propter delictum tenentis* was abolished by s 1 of the Forfeiture Act 1870 and escheat *propter defectum sanguinis* by s 45(1)(d) of the Administration of Estates Act 1925. That Act did not mention any other form of escheat in relation to freeholds. However, in the case of copyhold land, Sch 12, para (1)(c) to the Law of Property Act 1922 applies. It provides that in place of the lord's right to escheat, the Crown (or Royal Duchies) may become entitled to the land as bona vacantia under Part VIII.[58] There is no restriction on the types of escheat. The opening words of para (1) refer to 'the enfranchised

---

[56]   (1813) 2 M&S 175,105 ER 348.

[57]   (1788) 2 TR 701, 100 ER 377.

[58]   Replaced by the Administration of Estates Act 1925.

land', that is the land enfranchised under the 1922 Act, not under earlier Copyhold Acts. Read literally, that would apply if land enfranchised in 1926 were at any time thereafter to be disclaimed by a trustee in bankruptcy, in which case it would fall to be administered by the Treasury Solicitor, not by the Crown Estate. However, as the Crown is regarded in law as one and indivisible[59] the distinction would only involve internal Crown administrative arrangements and should not affect third parties. In practice it is now difficult to distinguish between land enfranchised under the 1922 Act and any other land, including land enfranchised under earlier Acts, and the Crown Estate administers escheats.

Land enfranchised at common law ceased to be parcel of the manor as a result of *Quia Emptores*. Land enfranchised under the Copyhold Acts between 1841 and 1925 probably remained parcel of the manor and was (and still is) held of the lord because escheat was reserved and land can only escheat to the lord. Copyhold land remaining in 1925 and enfranchised under the 1922 Act ceased to be parcel of the manor at common law and became held of the Crown. It would follow that the lord thereby lost his tenurial superiority over land enfranchised under the 1922 Act.[60] It is possible that for some purposes in equity it remained parcel of the manor at least in relation to the benefit of restrictive covenants.[61]

Where a sub-manor was held by subinfeudation before 1290 (or a manor was held from an honour) the effect of either a freehold disposal or an enfranchisement would in principle simply make the land parcel of the higher one (or honour). However, as discussed in 22.4, although an honour or barony was formerly an interest superior to a manor the current meaning refers to an association of manors which devolve together rather than a superior lordship. It is therefore possible that land would not now pass to the holder of such a right. It appears that although an honour is held in fee simple it is not itself a right to land and is no longer to be regarded as superior in such a way as to be capable of holding escheated land.[62]

7.10   ACQUISITION OF COPYHOLD BY LORD

If the lord acquired copyhold land it remained parcel of the manor and simply became demesne free from customary tenure. The theory was that the lord had

---

[59]   *Town Investments Ltd v Department of the Environment* [1978] AC 359.

[60]   But see Nugee, EG, 'The Feudal System and the Land Registration Acts' (2009) 124(4) *Law Quarterly Review* 586 discussed in 5.7.

[61]   *Re Mansfield District Council's Application* (1976) 36 P&CR 141, 241 EG 241; see 17.6.

[62]   A comparable issue was considered in the context of Marcher lordships (see 22.4) in Wales in *Crown Estate Commissioners v Roberts* [2008] EWHC 1302 (Ch), [2008] All ER (D) 175 (Jun).

originally granted copyhold land (as he always granted pure copyhold by admission if a new tenant bought or inherited) and so it could always be surrendered (as on a sale) and then simply not be regranted as copyhold. Likewise if the copyhold escheated or was forfeited it became demesne unless the lord granted it out again as copyhold.

The land could be forfeit on various grounds. Examples are: if the copyholder died and his heir failed to claim the land; if the copyholder committed waste (such as pulling down his cottage, ploughing up a meadow, working a mine or cutting timber); if he altered the boundaries of his land (especially his strip, and even if he held the adjoining one); if he transferred his land to someone else; if he failed to do his services (particularly suit of court); or if he committed felony or treason.

If the copyhold came into the lord's hands he had a choice. He could hold it in hand, for example as part of the home farm. If he wished to put in an occupier he could do one of two things. He could put in a copyholder subject to precisely the same customs as the previous copyhold down to the last penny of the quitrent. Alternatively, he could put the land to lease, but if he did so it lost forever its character as copyhold and could not again be granted as such.[63]

Land was often converted from copyhold to leasehold by agreement between lord and tenant. This was especially frequent in the seventeenth century. The lease would be long, perhaps 99 years or three lives, or perhaps 1000 years. The advantage to the lord was that when the lease ran out, his heirs would inherit the land free of the lease, while by that time copyhold land was protected forever. While the lease ran the lord would have a landlord's remedies rather than the less effective remedies of a lord. Some lords therefore sought to pressure their copyholders to take a lease instead.

There were indeed advantages to the tenant. The first was that until Preston's Act 1815 copyholds could not be left directly by will. There was a cumbersome process of surrendering the land to the use of the tenant's will, but this had to be done publicly in the manor court, and every time the will was changed the process had to be repeated. In default of that the customs of the manor dictated who would inherit copyhold. Those customs did not apply to a lease which, being a chattel, could be left by will without publicity. Secondly, if the lease was for life rather than for years the tenant was treated for some purposes as a freeholder – for example if the holding was worth 40 shillings a year he could vote in Parliamentary elections. Thirdly, if the lease was for a term the tenant knew that his successor would have a definite interest and the rent was fixed

---

[63] Coke, Sir Edward, *Complete Copyholder* (E Flesher et al, 1630) s 62. *French's Case* (1576) 4 Co Rep 31a, 77 ER 960.

during the term. His successor would not have to pay an entry fine (the copyhold equivalent of a relief) unless it was expressly reserved, although in practice fines were often reserved on succession.[64] In this way many copyholds were converted and eventually, after the term ran out or the life holder died, the lord took the land back. If the term was for many centuries it may still be running, although often it is capable of enlargement under the Law of Property Act 1925, s 153 (14.6).

7.11   INCLOSURE AT COMMON LAW

Enfranchisement, conversion and substitution involved changes in the ownership of land, or interests in the land, but did not bring about changes in the layout of the fields or waste. This was effected by inclosure, which is the conversion of common or commonable land to land held in severalty, that is as a close in the exclusive occupation of one proprietor or group of proprietors. It was usually accompanied by enclosure, that is the division of the land by fences, hedges, walls, banks or ditches, although this was not essential. It applied principally to the open fields and to the waste of the manor; the nature of land liable to be inclosed is discussed in 10.1. There were three principal ways of inclosing land. The first was unilateral. The second was by agreement, which might be accompanied by a court order. The third was by inclosure Act.

The unilateral conversion of waste land from waste to arable took two forms with the same effect: approvement and assarts. While in the eleventh and twelfth centuries conversion involved new or expanded open fields, as time passed conversions were mostly forms of inclosure. Approvement was the conversion by the lord (or others with his authority) from waste to tillage. Where the tenants had rights of grazing over the waste inclosure could not be done without their consent, until the Commons Act 1236[65] provided that the lord could do so if sufficient grazing was left for the tenants. To begin with this Act was effective but subsequently it fell out of use, first, because the onus was on the lord to prove that there was sufficient grazing (and this could be difficult to establish) and, secondly, approvement only extinguished common of pasture, not other rights such as turbary. Approvement was finally abolished by the Commons Act 2006, s 47.

---

[64]   See Reed, M, *The Age of Exuberance* 1550–1700 (Paladin Grafton Books, 1986) 53. See also Law of Property Act 1925, s 144 and exclusion of it.

[65]   Known as c 4 of the Statute of Merton. Even though there was at the time no Parliament in the modern statute sense, because no House of Commons, the Commons Act 1236 is treated as an Act.

Assarting was more frequent. It tended to start as squatting by unauthorised occupiers who put up a cottage and ploughed the land. In some parts of Wales there was said to be a custom that if a house could be erected on waste land between sunset and sunrise (in one night: *ty un nos*) the squatter had a right to stay, but that was never a legal rule in England. However, in practice if the squatter did not take much land the villagers would not disturb him and by the time the lord's bailiff found out it would cause too much fuss to evict him. It was easier and more profitable to allow the squatter to stay in return for a payment. Originally, this was a fine or amerciament in the manor court, but it would quickly harden into a regular rent. Indeed, lords frequently granted licences to assart before it happened. There was little legal distinction between the approvement of waste by one farmer who paid rent to the lord for a lease and assarting by another who paid a regular sum in court as a fine. The effect of both was to reduce the common land. Assarting was prevented for land subject to rights of common by the Law of Property Act 1925, s 194, and for other waste by the Commons Act 2006, s 38.

Approvement and assarting could inclose the waste but they were not suitable for the open fields and, after about the sixteenth century, as rights over the waste became more defined, they ceased to be useful. In particular, as landowners were able to establish rights of common they could not be extinguished by assart and there were always uncertainties on the extent of the right to approve. In addition, the former dominant position of lords was weakened by the development of individual rights of property. It became necessary to obtain the agreement of those whose rights over the land to be inclosed would be extinguished.

Open fields could be inclosed gradually by consolidation, often following exchange. This is in theory a simple process whereby the owner of one piece of land swaps it for another. It was used to aggregate areas so that the holders of individual strips scattered about the fields could build up compact farms. As they did this the whole geography of the manor changed; what remained of the open fields was eroded into scattered patches and control of the court leet over cropping and pasturage ceased to be enforced. Inclosure could be carried out in commonable fields (10.5) by the incloser accepting that he lost the right to pasture his beasts in the rest of the field. In common fields inclosure could only be done with the consent of all persons having rights of common. Where these persons were the other farmers, this might be straightforward, especially if there were only a few. If there were others, for instance in Lammas lands near towns, the burgesses might refuse to give up their grazing rights, which is why many Lammas lands have survived.

In general, where a small number of right holders were absolutely entitled to those rights, inclosure could be brought about by agreement. Even if they were not so entitled, it might be possible to obtain the necessary consents. However, someone might refuse to agree or seek to obtain an excessive benefit in return. Agreement between more than six people was problematic, although a persistent incloser might be able over the years to get the agreement of each right holder. The rights were many and varied. A copyholder could not exchange his land for another piece of copyhold or freehold without the consent of the lord, and not at all if it would have involved freehold becoming copyhold. There could be rights of common, easements, tithes and public highways. There could be leases, tenancies and mortgages. It was more of a problem if the right holder was not able to agree. He might lack mental capacity, or be an infant, or in some cases a married woman could not agree without her husband's consent. The holder might be absent or unknown and the incloser did not want to take the risk of someone appearing years later to claim his grazing rights over the inclosed land. Increasingly after 1660 much land was in settlement, with vested or contingent remainders or reversions to various members of the settlor's family, some of whom might be unborn or unascertained. The current tenant for life or in tail could not bind his successors. On any exchange there were problems of value because the two pieces were unlikely to be worth precisely the same. Despite this, much land was inclosed by agreement. Sometimes the ownership of rights was clear and simple. In other cases the landowner took the risk of subsequent claims by third parties, often with good reason as the intention of inclosure was to give those taking part more valuable properties than before.

Some of the problems could be overcome by obtaining a court order. Owners would take a friendly action and the decree would record their respective entitlements to the land as inclosed. Two procedures were used: one by a collusive action of covenant known as levying a fine, which could be used to overcome some entails, the other by a chancery procedure which involved an agreement, an alleged violation and a decree affirming it. However, a court order can in general only bind those before the court and their successors and there was always a risk of third parties appearing subsequently who were not before the court. Such an order or decree also could not override public rights such as diverting a highway, and although procedures existed to overcome this problem, they were not consistent. Finally, there were considerable delays and expense in getting an order or decree.

7.12   STATUTORY INCLOSURE

In view of the uncertainties, delays, costs and complications of inclosure by agreement and the difficulty of overcoming third party rights, those wishing to inclose, particularly if the plans involved large areas of land, sought an alternative. The solution was in an inclosure Act as the power of Parliament can override any obstacles.

It seems that from an early date statutes could authorise better management of land, for instance in reclaiming fens which involved a form of inclosure. The Tudor and Early Stuart governments and indeed the Protectorate were in general opposed to inclosure, which was believed to harm the free yeomen and lead to dispossession, unemployment and destitution. After 1660 the climate slowly changed. The first inclosure is said to have occurred in 1709 in relation to Ropley Commons in Hampshire.[66] In 1719 an Act was passed to inclose Baltonsbury Common in Somerset.[67] Eight private inclosure Acts were passed between 1724 and 1799. Thereafter, numbers steadily increased, and some 4000 Acts in all were passed.

Local inclosure Acts were privately drawn, although after a while they tended to follow common patterns and adopted similar wording. Acts were drafted by specialist counsel who developed considerable experience. Nevertheless, the contents of the bill were a matter for the promoters and many curious provisions were allowed to be included. The final form of the bill was for the Parliamentary committee which examined it to approve, but in practice it would normally not require changes unless an objector raised an issue.

From 1756 onwards, Parliament passed a number of general Inclosure Acts which governed various aspects, including one in 1773 dealing with fencing and boundaries. The Inclosure Act 1836 permitted inclosure without the need to obtain a specific Act if enough persons interested agreed. That freedom was restricted by s 12 of the Inclosure Act 1845 and reversed by s 1 of the Inclosure Act 1852, which required Parliamentary authority for any inclosure, although this may have been by order without a full Act. The Act of 1845 prescribed standard clauses and parts of that legislation are still on the statute book. By then the great age of inclosure was over. The term 'Inclosure Acts 1845 to 1882' includes an almost annual series of successors from 1846 to 1859 and some later legislation up to 1882.

However, the climate of opinion changed. Only about 200 statutory inclosures post-date 1845. The Commons, Open Spaces and Footpaths Preservation Society was founded in 1865. In 1876 Parliament passed a Commons Act which provided that inclosures would only be approved if they were for the benefit of the neighbourhood. This effectively put an end to inclosures. After 1876 only

---

[66] 8 Ann c16; *Encyclopaedia Britannica* (Cambridge University Press, 11th edn, 1911), Commons; Thompson, EP, *Customs in Common* (1991) 109.

[67] 6 Geo I c5.

about 30 applications for inclosures were made, of which the last was in 1914.[68] By s 194 of the Law of Property Act 1925 it became unlawful to enclose any land subject to rights of common, and the Commons Act 2006, s 38 extended this to all registered common land (including waste not so subject) without the consent of the Minister (now the Secretary of State), a consent which is rarely given and usually only after a public enquiry. Section 13(3) of the 2006 Act has also effectively prevented inclosure (10.4). Much of the general inclosure legislation has been repealed, most recently in the Statute Law (Repeals) Act 1998.[69]

Statutory inclosure changed the face of England. The amount of land is variously estimated but was of the order of seven million acres. Many titles to land and rights of way, boundaries, minerals and recreation depend on Inclosure Acts and the awards made under them are frequently relevant to property disputes. The precise procedure could vary from one Act to another and the following account is a general account from which there could be substantial variations. The Inclosure Act 1845 laid down a standard procedure, but that was after the great age of inclosures was over.

The procedure was for a sufficient majority in value of the land proposed to be affected, sometimes as many as two thirds, of the landholders to petition Parliament for a private bill or, later, to apply to the Inclosure Commissioners. At one time four fifths in value had to concur.[70] Under s 25 of the 1845 Act there had to be at least one third in value. This was confirmed by the Commons Act 1876, but the consent of the Inclosure Commissioners was also required and they had only limited powers to give it. Rights were assessed by value not by number. A large number of smallholders could be outvoted by a few substantial landowners. If waste was to be inclosed the consent of the lord of the manor was required under s 29 of the 1845 Act and, under s 1 of the 1847 Act, if the title to the manor was in dispute, all claimants had to consent.

Land liable to be inclosed is widely defined in s 11 of the 1845 Act (10.1). Under s 86 of the Act owners in severalty of land which was not itself common could bring it into the distribution, for example where there had been earlier voluntary piecemeal inclosure which had left oddly shaped or scattered pieces in

---

[68]   According to *Hampshire County Council v Milburn* [1991] AC 235, [1990] 2 All ER 257, (1990) 61 P&CR 135 there were 29. According to Law Commission, *16th Statute Law (Repeals) Report* (20 May 1998) there were 36.

[69]   Following research by Roger Maitland of the Law Commission: see *16th Statute Law (Repeals) Report* (20 May 1998) Part 6, paras 39–45.

[70]   Yelling, JA, *Common Field and Enclosure in England 1450–1850* (MacMillan Press Ltd, 1977) 8, citing Homer, HS, *An Essay on the Nature and Method of Ascertaining the Specific Shares of Proprietors upon the Inclosure of Common Fields* (1766).

several ownership; but in that case all several owners affected had to agree and there was no place for an overriding majority.

The commissioners nominated by the private act or later the Inclosure Commissioners appointed a surveyor, who was the most important single individual in the process. A handful of professional surveyors in the late eighteenth century changed the appearance of England. The surveyor took all the land to be inclosed into his survey. He mapped it (often the first map ever made of some parishes) and valued all the interests to be taken into account. In some cases this was straightforward – the market value of a strip in the open field might be well known. Other cases were more difficult, such as the value of the right to collect tithes. This would be calculated by comparing the income with that yielded by government bonds. The most contentious valuations related to waste, where each commoner who had a legal right to put out stock or take turf or timber was entitled to have his interest valued and the lord who owned the soil had that valued. If the waste was fully stocked the soil might have no value, but the value of the right to put out one cow was small. If someone put out, say, a goose on the common by general permission but without any legal right that was disregarded.

Mineral or sporting rights were often preserved, as were the rights of lords over copyholds such as the right to quitrents, entry fines and escheats and any services that still existed, but it was possible to include them in the division. The surveyor put all the various proprietary customary and common rights into a pot and could then total the former value of all the interests. The pot itself was the land and the land as a whole was more valuable than the sum of the interests in it because of the right to deal with the land without interference from someone having a right of common or other interest. Inclosure was designed to release this marriage value. The surveyor then allotted the land between the participants in proportion to the value they had put in. Even a cottager who had the legal right to put out one beast on the common would be allocated some land. In practice this might cause him hardship because he could not raise the animal on the area allotted, so forcing him to sell his land and move to the town. The lord and the larger farmers tended to gain. Land was not only allotted to individuals. Inclosure involved rerouting highways, and if their repair had been a parish responsibility, land could be allotted either as a quarry for roadstone or be let with the rents applied to the cost of maintenance. Sometimes land was allotted to trustees to use the rents to support the poor of the parish.

The landscape was laid out by the surveyor on rational lines, free from historical complications. Typical inclosure landscapes have straight boundaries, straight roads and rectangular fields. They look as if they were laid out with rulers on a map, as indeed they were. The allottees of land were obliged to enclose it (quite an expense, especially for a smallholder) and the duty to maintain boundaries often continues to this day and may be enforceable by a neighbour. Farms were allotted in compact units where new farmhouses could be built in the centre. Sometimes smallholders were allotted small fields far from the village, but most surveyors were humane and tried to make sensible, workable allocations. Provision was made in s 82 of the 1845 Act:

> That the Valuer, in making the several Allotments hereby directed, shall have due Regard as well to the Situation of the respective Houses or Homesteads of the Persons interested in the Land to be inclosed as to the Quantity and Quality of the Land to be allotted to them respectively, so far as may be consistent with the general Convenience of such Persons, and that such Valuer in making the said Allotments shall have particular Regard to the Convenience of the Persons interested in respect of the smallest Estates in the Land subject to be inclosed under this Act.

A former freeholder received freehold land in return, while a leaseholder was given a lease of his new land on the same terms. If land was held only for life or within a settlement, the land allotted was held on the same terms. If a man had both leasehold and copyhold land their replacements might be allotted together so that he received a compact allotment of different tenures.[71] In legal theory, therefore, there was little change, merely the substitution for one set of acres and rights of another set of acres. In practice, the end of common rights over the waste and of such open fields as still existed meant that the system of the manor had no further use, and in many inclosed manors the manor itself disappeared.

The effect of statutory inclosure was to diminish the manor. This applied to the physical area owned by the lord, as the freehold in large areas of waste passed to former commoners and others as compensation for the loss of rights. It also applied to intangible rights. Although there was power to allot to a copyholder in return for his strip in the open field or, more rarely, a close included in the redistribution, subject to the same customary burdens as before, it might be preferred to allot to the copyholder a slightly smaller area as freehold, reflecting the end of quitrents and entry fines. Sometimes lords sought to retain some benefits even after allotment. In relation to waste, many Acts and awards reserved seigniorial rights but the courts tended to interpret them restrictively (9.5). Seigniories were preserved under the Inclosure Act 1845, s 96, so that former common manorial freeholds might still be held of the lord, but such instances would be difficult to identify. It was possible by the use of apt wording for the lord to have mineral or sporting rights in the allotments (11.6, 12.5), but these were more likely to be construed as an exception of mineral strata, usually with rights of working rather than copyhold type rights, and as a

---

[71]   Yelling *op cit* 139.

reservation of a profit of sporting rather than a customary sporting right. In principle as the award operated as a conveyance of title in the absence of provision to the contrary any freehold land would, under *Quia Emptores*, be regarded as taken out of the manor.

7.13   HEDGES IN INCLOSURE ACTS

Inclosure Acts and awards not only allotted lands; they also provided for the construction of boundaries between the new neighbours. Often this was done by providing that an allottee had to erect and maintain a hedge. Thousands of miles of hedge, often of hawthorn, still border fields across the Midlands. In recent years people have tried to use these provisions for various purposes, sometimes far removed from their original function. In *Seymour v Flamborough Parish Council*[72] an award under the Flamborough Inclosure Act 1765 provided that a hedge along the highways from Flamborough to Bempton should be maintained, and Mr Seymour and the Flamborough Wildlife Trust used it to compel the parish council to maintain the hedge. By contrast, in *Marlton v Turner*[73] an inclosure Act of 1808 required the owners of land at Field Dalling in Norfolk to keep a hedge against the highways in good repair. The judge interpreted this statutory obligation in the same way as a positive covenant in a conveyance and held that it could not be enforced against a successor to the original allottee even though it was in a statute which imposed the obligation on his heirs, which the judge interpreted as successors in title. In *Meddick v Shiplake Parish Council*[74] an award made in 1867 under the Inclosure Act 1845 required the owners of certain plots of land to make and maintain fences. Planning consent was granted for the development of part of the land and, in order to give access to the highway, it was necessary to make an opening in the fence. The court held that 'owner' meant 'owner for the time being'; however, as the intention was not to remove the fence entirely but only enough to make an access, that would not be a breach of the terms of the award. The judge also considered that the complainant, Mr Meddick, did not have sufficient standing to bring proceedings as his legal rights were not affected by the works.

In *R v Solihull Borough Council, Ex p Berkswell Parish Council*[75] the borough council wished to construct a road and roundabouts to bypass Balsall Common. This involved removing hedges planted under the provisions of the Berkswell Inclosure Act 1802. The borough carried out a careful assessment of the

---

[72]   *Farm Law*, 1 February 1997; noted also in *Smith v Muller* [2008] EWCA Civ 1425 at [39].

[73]   [1998] 3 EGLR 185.

[74]   Unreported, December 1999.

[75]   (1999) 77 P&CR 312.

ecological value of the hedges, obtained planning consent and then demolished
the hedges. The parish council could not show that any of its private law rights
had been infringed, but argued that the Act provided criminal penalties for
removing the hedge and therefore it was unlawful. It asked for an order that the
hedge be replanted. The judge held that even if the planning consent was in
contravention of the Inclosure Act (which was not established) it was not void.
The road had been the subject of public debate and was a longstanding
improvement scheme. In any case, once a 200-year old hedge was removed,
planting a modern one would be valueless.

In *Smith v Muller*[76] a claim was made to a private right of way over a route
which was crossed by a fence line which, under an award made in December
1804 under the Messingham Inclosure Act 1798, provided for a permanent
fence. The defendant argued that the statutory provision made it illegal to make
a way through the fence. The Court of Appeal, distinguishing *Seymour v
Flamborough Parish Council*, held that the existence of the fencing obligation
was itself no bar to the creation of private rights.

In general, therefore, the courts have not been sympathetic to attempts to revive
ancient obligations, at least to interfere with modern rights. It might be different
if the duty still had its original context. If an award provided for a fence to be
maintained between two farms then, even if such an obligation would not now
be enforceable if contained in a deed,[77] it might still be possible for one farmer
to use it to compel his neighbour to make repairs. However, a more effective
sanction is in the Hedgerow Regulations 1997[78] made under the Environment
Act 1995, s 97, which require someone proposing to remove substantial hedges
to obtain consent before doing so.

---

[76]   [2008] EWCA Civ 1425.

[77]   *Rhone v Stevens* [1994] 2 AC 310.

[78]   SI 1997/1160.

Chapter 8

Legal and Reputed

8.1 CREATION OF MANORS

The manor was a complex of lands, tenures, jurisdictions and services. Some of these could be separated from the manor without prejudicing the continued existence of the whole, but if too much was taken away the manor itself ceased to exist. Even if the manor was regarded by laymen as continuing, the law considered that it continued by reputation only. Rights could still belong to a reputed manor, but they were more fragile than the full rights of a legal manor. Manors cannot now be created and most (perhaps all) former legal manors have become reputed manors. To understand how this happened it is necessary to consider how manors first came into existence, what their vital features are, and how, by losing those features, they dissolve. This chapter discusses history back to Anglo-Saxon times but, as pointed out in the Introduction, this may bear little connection to what people then thought; it is a later interpretation with later ideas of what from that perspective was seen to have happened.

One key legal concept is the distinction between allodial land and land held by tenure. Some historians consider this was not particularly important in the eleventh century and only became so on the Continent later[1] (22.2), but the effect of legal hindsight is that it became a necessary part of the way land was considered to be held. It is relevant to the English manor even though, since the eleventh century, the only allodial land in England has been Crown land (24.3).

Allodial land is land held outright and absolutely. A holder may, of course, have owed duties as a citizen. He had to pay taxes, perhaps serve in the army, and may have been responsible for local administration, for the repair of roads, bridges and so on, but the land was conceived as being his and that of his family after him. Land held by tenure, by contrast, is granted by a superior on specific terms (5.1). The terms may be similar, such as to serve as knight or repair town walls, but these were seen not so much as duties of a citizen as consequences of

---

[1] Reynolds, S, *Fiefs and Vassals* (Oxford University Press, 1994).

a bargain which, if broken, meant that the superior, often the king but sometimes a mesne lord, could take the land back. The relationship between lord and vassal was initially seen to be personal so that the holder, the tenant, may not have been able to pass the land on to his son, or only with consent, or subject to making a payment to the lord and offering homage.

It is not clear whether land in the early Anglo-Saxon kingdoms was held allodially or by tenure, and contemporaries may not have seen a distinction. The kingdoms were small, about the size of a shire, and relationships were personal. It seems that most land, at least that of the more prominent holders, was initially *folcland*, that is land held by folk custom. The holder was bound to render to the king certain services, either in person, such as fighting in the army, or in kind, such as providing corn, or beer or honey. Later, kings granted – first to the Church and then to lay lords – the right to receive customary dues and, in return, the lords rendered to him the *trinoda necessitas* of service in the fyrd or army, burgh defence and bridge repair. The grant was made by a written charter or *bok* and is known as bookland (2.2). Titles guaranteed by a written document were safer than traditional titles based on custom and therefore holders tended to ask for a charter. As the *bok* was issued by the king or under his authority it seems to have become accepted that all land was in some, possibly undefined, sense, derived from the king. Sometimes whole hundreds were granted in this way (19.2), but more often, especially in later times, grants were smaller and resembled what became manors,[2] often carved out of what had formerly been large estates. It is thought that folkland was allodial and bookland was tenurial, but that is probably anachronistic.

In theory land could become held in one of three ways. First, the king could grant to a lord the right to receive the services of a group of cultivators, or a lord's predecessors may have had such rights since earlier times. Secondly, the king could grant a lord vacant land or waste, which the lord could then allow a farmer to occupy as tenant. Thirdly, an allodial landholder could voluntarily (or otherwise) accept the protection of a lord by a process known on the Continent as 'commendation'. King Athelstan, who was the first effective king of all England, made a law[3] that all free men must have a lord. Until 1066 certain landholders retained the right to choose and change the lord of their land or to go with their land to whoever they wished, but after the Norman Conquest that power ceased.

---

[2]   Maitland, FW, *Domesday Book and Beyond* (Cambridge University Press, 1987; first published 1897) 244.

[3]   2 Athelstan c 2 (c 930) s 1-2; Abels, RP, *Lordship and Military Obligation in Anglo-Saxon England* (University of California Press, 1988) 87, n 44; Stubbs, W, *Select Charters from the beginning to 1307* (Oxford University Press, 9th edn, 1913) 74.

In practice, the first of these ways of holding land was how most arrangements worked or were understood to work. There can have been little vacant land suitable for a wholly new settlement. While something like commendation no doubt existed, in practice it would be a bold landholder who would say to an existing lord 'I do not want you as my lord any longer and I am going to another'. To the extent that he could, and still retain the land, it might be seen as allodial. There are several references in *Domesday Book* to *alodiarii* but these are regarded as still holding from a lord and the expression may refer to some feature of tenure such as inheritance rights.[4]

English law did not develop in total isolation from the Continent but it appears that, after the Conquest, ideas were at least clarified and a new terminology, in French or Latin, brought with it new ideas. By the end of William the Conqueror's reign all land not part of the royal demesne ceased to be allodial (if it had been) and was held in fee by tenure. Manors could be held directly of the Crown, as part of an honour or as sub-manors of a greater manor. Indeed, a sub-manor could be held by copyhold[5] (22.7) as there is no reason why a manor should not be held by non-feudal tenure.

At the time of *Domesday Book* in 1086 nearly all land was in a manor and most manors were grouped in honours (22.4). This assumes a similar state of affairs before 1066 since it describes the situation in the time of King Edward the Confessor in the same terms as its own account of the position in 1086. There was some non-manorial land, held by the occupier direct from the king, in which case it was said to be held *ut de corona*, as from the Crown; but even then where possible *Domesday* assumed a manor even of only a few acres. Within a manor or honour, land which belonged to or was occupied by a tenant was held from the lord. If the manor or honour was itself held in demesne by the king (and perhaps as much as a quarter of England was so held) then the land was said to be held from the Crown *ut de honore*, as from an honour, which here includes a manor, although the expression *ut de manerio* was sometimes used. If the king then granted that honour (or part of it) to a subject, all those who had held their land *ut de honore* held from the new lord. That did not apply to land held *ut de corona*, which could only come into a manor if added to it or if a new manor was created (so long as that was possible). Such land was said to be held *in capite*, that is in chief. The distinction became important in relation to the seigniorial dues which could be taken by the Crown on the death of a tenant (24.5).

---

4   Maitland *op cit* 153–4.

5   *Sir Henry Nevill's Case* (1613) 11 Co Rep 17a, 77 ER 1166; but see *R v Stafferton* (1610) 1 Bulst 54, 80 ER 756: ref Aylesham Norfolk.

A manor or honour could itself be held from a mesne lord or from the Crown and, if the latter, it was held either *ut de corona* or *ut de honore*. The greatest honours were held by the leading men of the country – lay nobles or churchmen – as tenants in chief *ut de corona* and this entitled them to advise the king in his council or later to receive a writ to attend the House of Lords. The expression 'chief lord' refers to any superior lord, so that where a tenant held from the lord of a sub manor, the lord of the head manor was chief lord; but the expression 'tenant in chief' applies only to barons and other great lords.

In theory, new manors could still arise after 1066 in one of two ways. One undoubted way was out of an existing manor either by grant by subinfeudation of a sub-manor of which it was then held or by division of a manor. The sub-lord or lord of part received the benefit of the services of some of the tenants, part of the demesne and waste and the right to hold a court. A new manor could also arise where a lord granted land, possibly former waste, to occupiers to hold either in fee or at the will of the lord. That, by itself, did not create a manor but if, over the years, the tenants accepted the burden of customary services (and before 1189 customs could typically arise after 20 years' practice), the group of holdings would develop into a manor. This type of creation corresponds to circumstances in parts of the Continent, especially in eastern Germany[6] (where there was a good deal of colonisation with the deliberate introduction of a set of customs); but if it did happen in England it was probably rare after 1066 as virtually all productive land was already comprised in manors. This must be distinguished from the formation of a new vill or village, which was common up to 1300 but which did not normally involve a new manor.

After 1189 no new customs could exist even though people may not have realised that at the time (4.3). In *Sir Moyle Finch's Case*[7] (below) Coke CJ said that no manor could arise after 1189 because it had to exist from time 'whereof the memory of man runneth not to the contrary'. It was still possible to create a sub-manor until 1290 when *Quia Emptores* forbade subinfeudation, although its customs would be the same as those of the chief manor from which it was taken. In *Morris v Smith and Paget*[8] the Court of Common Pleas held that 'a manor can not be created at this day, neither by a common person nor by the Queen'. This arose in the context where a single manor had extended into several townships and the lord sold off the properties in one of them. The issue was whether the buyer could establish a new court for the tenants of that town.

---

[6]   Hildebrandt, H, 'Systems of Agriculture in Central Europe up to the Tenth and Eleventh Centuries', in Hooke D (ed), *Anglo-Saxon Settlements* (Basil Blackwell, 1988).

[7]   (1610) 6 Co Rep 63a, 77 ER 310.

[8]   (1582) Cro Eliz 38, 78 ER 303; see also *R v Stafferton* (1610) 1 Bulst 54, 80 ER 756.

Although the rule did not apply to the allodial land of the Crown, it follows from the passage from Coke's *Copyhold* quoted in 4.1 that since the king could not create a custom, wholly new manors could not be created even out of Crown land after 1189 (24.10). Thus, no manor could come into existence after 1290 by voluntary action, although it could still arise from division between co-heiresses.

8.2   PROVING THE MANOR

If the existence of a manor was disputed it was necessary to prove it. A dispute might involve a claim by a person to hold a court, or that wastes belonged to one lord rather than another, but most often the issue arose, and can still arise, where a manor was or is being sold and bought. The best form of proof is if the manor is mentioned in *Domesday Book* or in a royal grant, such as happened when Crown lands were sold, especially after the Dissolution. Many institutions, such as the Church Commissioners and Oxford and Cambridge colleges, have records of their holdings. Where manors were comprised in a landed estate belonging to a wealthy or noble family their wills and title deeds often list them. If manorial documents have survived (25.2–25.3) a list of these and where they are deposited is held by the National Archives. A manor may have been involved in a reported legal case or be mentioned in some government document such as the Pipe Rolls. An inclosure Act or municipal Act may refer to a manor. Another normally reliable source is the Victoria County History which, if it covered the parish in question, will have investigated the history of the manor to a high standard of scholarship.

A further source suggesting the existence of a manor, often relied on in the twentieth century by firms which specialised in selling manors, is nineteenth-century directories of towns and villages which refer to local prominent families and their possessions. However, these must be used with caution since, to a considerable extent, they were originally compiled from details provided by local people, such as the clergy, who may have only guessed at what a family owned.

On occasion courts have had to consider what evidence of the existence of a manor is acceptable. In general, courts have adopted a broad approach. The best evidence is the court rolls, but these are not always available. In *Doe d Beck v Heakin*[9] a cottage was built on some land which was claimed to be waste of Mr Beck's manor of Hope in Shropshire. His father had died some years before and there was some indication that he had held courts, but no rolls could be

---

[9]   (1837) 6 Ad and El 495, 112 ER 189.

produced. The father's will left the manor to the plaintiff. There was also evidence that the plaintiff had appointed a gamekeeper.

In *Merttens v Hill*[10] the plaintiff claimed to be lord of the manor of Rothley in Leicestershire. The manor was referred to in *Domesday Book* and in the Middle Ages had belonged to the Knights Templar and later to the Knights Hospitaller. On the Dissolution it passed to the Crown. In 1543 Henry VIII granted to Mr Cartwright 'all that the site of our manor of Rothley' but not the manor, nor all the demesnes. Further Crown grants were made by Edward VI and Elizabeth I but not grant of the manor itself. However, the plaintiff was able to show that his predecessors had held courts since at least 1576 and one was referred to as lord in an Inclosure Act of 1765. The judge held that the title had been established and said that, if necessary, a lost Crown grant must be implied. In *Steel v Prickett*[11] (6.5) the Dean and Chapter of Westminster Abbey claimed roadside waste as lords of the manor of Belsize. The court found that there was no compelling evidence of the existence of such a manor.[12]

Where a manor is shown to have existed but the present holder is unknown title may be proved in the same way as title to land (6.9).

8.3   DIVISION BY OPERATION OF LAW

Before 1290 a new manor could come into existence by the division of an old manor. Bracton includes a precedent of a writ of partition.[13] A sale of part could be made by subinfeudation creating a sub-manor. After 1290 subinfeudation was no longer possible and a manor could not be divided by voluntary action such as sale or gift, it could still be divided between co-parceners by substitution. Where the holder of freehold land died without sons (and after 1540 intestate) his daughters took his property as co-heiresses known as co-parceners. The share of an unmarried daughter passed on her death to her sisters as joint tenants. If two or more daughters were married, their husbands could insist on the manor being divided, including the demesnes, wastes, tenants, services and courts. In this way new manors came into existence.[14] In *Heath v Deane*[15] there was a suggestion that 'In modern times (in fact, since the year

---

[10]   [1901] 1 Ch 842.

[11]   (1819) 2 Stark 463, 171 ER 706.

[12]   See also *Walker v Burton* [2012] EWHC 978 (Ch).

[13]   Bracton, Sir Henry (ed), *De legibus et consuetudinibus angliae* (c 1257) (SE Thorne (ed)) (Belknap Press of Harvard University Press, 1977) f 72b, vol 2, 214.

[14]   *Beverly's Case* (1627) Latch 224, 82 ER 357. See also Coke, *op cit* s 41; but cf Bracton *op cit* f 349 on advowsons.

[15]   [1905] 2 Ch 86.

1700) the ancient manor of Norton has in some way been divided or partitioned, it is said, between co-parceners'. However, it is not clear whether the judge in that case, Joyce J, thought that this was a legal division. Such a division would normally be on tenurial rather than geographical lines. The lands and services of a tenant (whether free or bond) would be allocated to his new lord. His lands were scattered in strips and closes throughout the old manor and that scattering was repeated in the new manor. However, the land of his neighbour, previously in the same manor, was now in a different one. Waste would also have to be divided, although for that a geographical division was simpler.

Partition between co-parceners arose by act of law and there could be no legal division by act of parties. In *Melwich v Luther*[16] the court held that if the lord sold the freehold of a number of copyhold tenements the new freeholder could hold court for surrender and admission for the copyholders, thus creating a customary manor or quasi-manor, but not a legal manor. Likewise, this did not arise where the manor belonged to tenants in common who agreed to partition. Under the general rules of the law, where any property, particularly land, was held by joint owners each could require a division of the property under an Act of 1540[17] that extended to manors.[18] However, it appears from *Hanbury v Hussey*[19] that this would not authorise the division of a manor into two. The court held that the benefit would be divided but this did not involve actually splitting the manor itself. As with an advowson, which could be exercised alternately, or a mill, where the revenues might be divided, so the benefits of a manor could be shared. As established in *R v Duchess of Buccleugh*[20] a manor is an entire thing and cannot be severed. Division could be made by allowing the lords to hold the court alternately, or the greater part of the land could be allotted to one lord, with a smaller part together with the court and services to another, but the lordship itself could not be divided so as to create new manors.

Even division between co-parceners ceased under the Land Transfer Act 1897, which provided that on the death of a holder of real property it passed to his executors or administrators and not direct to his heir. Heirs ceased to have rights under the 1925 legislation, specifically the Administration of Estates Act 1925, s 45. Under s 1(6) of the Law of Property Act 1925 the interest of a joint tenant or tenant in common was converted to an interest in the notional proceeds of sale of the land so that the partition rules ceased to be relevant. Although there

---

[16] (1587) Cro Eliz 102, 78 ER 361, (1588) 4 Co Rep 26b, 76 ER 935; see also *Morris v Smith and Paget* (1582) Cro Eliz 38, 78 ER 303; *R v Stafferton* (1610) 1 Bulst 54, 80 ER 756.

[17] 32 Henry 8 c 32 Joint Tenants 1540.

[18] *Sparrow v Fiend* (1761) Dick 348, 21 ER 303.

[19] (1851) Ch Cas 152, 14 Beav 152, 51 ER 244.

[20] (1704) 6 Mod 150, 87 ER 909, 1 Salk 358, 91 ER 312. See also *Sir Moyle Finch's Case* (1610) 6 Co Rep 63a, 77 ER 310; Bracton *op cit* f 266.

was a power of partition under s 28(3) of the Law of Property Act 1925, that was consequential on a division of the notional cash into which the land had been converted. The Trusts of Land and Appointment of Trustees Act 1996 has reconverted that interest to one in the land itself and, accordingly, s 7 of the Act reintroduces provision for the trustees to partition the land. The Act provides in s 23 that expressions used in it have the same meaning as in the 1925 Act 'unless the context otherwise requires'. Land is defined in s 205 of the 1925 Act as including a manor (27.6) and therefore, on the face of it, the 1996 Act would allow a manor to be partitioned. However, the court would probably apply *Hanbury v Hussey* and hold that in such circumstances the context does require otherwise. Thus, it is not now possible for a manor to be divided.

8.4   DISSOLUTION – LOSS OF LORDSHIP, TENANTS OR SERVICES

A manor ceases to be a legal manor if it is dissolved. For this purpose a manor comprises lordship, tenants and services. If any of these elements ceases to exist or becomes separated from the others dissolution follows. Demesnes are not an essential feature of the manor in the same way, so that their severance, whereby they cease to be parcel of the manor, will not by itself destroy it; a legal manor could exist as such without any demesne land, known as a manor or seigniory in gross.[21]

Loss of lordship occurs where the tenants acquire the rights of the lord. This normally happens in one of two ways, one relating to sub-manors and the other to the homage. In *Hutton v Gifford*[22] the lord of a sub-manor purchased the superior manor. He could not be his own lord and in consequence the inferior manor was extinguished by being merged in the chief manor out of which it had originally been granted. This principle applies all the way up the honorial ladder. It is unusual for a tenant in chief to acquire the Crown but on a change of dynasty this can happen. In 1399 Henry Bolingbroke, Duke of Lancaster, ejected Richard II and became Henry IV. He had previously been the holder of the extensive honour of the Duchy but Richard had forfeited the Lancaster estates. When Henry became king he resumed them, but as king, not duke. The normal result would have been that his honour of the Duchy of Lancaster would have dissolved and simply become a collection of honours and manors held *ut de corona*. To prevent this, Parliament enacted a charter which gave the Duchy

---

[21]   Scriven, J, *A Treatise on the Law of Copyholds* (Butterworth & Co, 7th edn by Archibald Brown, 1896) 3.

[22]   (1582) Sav 21, 123 ER 989.

a special character, which it has retained to this day.[23] By contrast if the lord of a superior interest acquires an inferior one it does not merge, but under the rule in *Delacherois v Delacherois*[24] is thenceforward held of the chief lord. Where the Crown acquires a manor the manor is retained as a separate entity and land which is parcel of the manor is held of the Crown *ut de honore* as lord of that manor.

The second type of loss of lordship is if the homage acquire the manor. As described in 6.2 in the eleventh century many manors were put to farm to the homage.[25] In the troubled times of King Stephen many leaseholders ceased to pay their rents to distant landlords and the lords lost their rights. If the leaseholder was an individual he would assume the manor but if it was farmed to the homage they became their own lord and the manor dissolved. In later times the homage would acquire the freehold of the manor. Sometimes they retained it intact in the names of trustees, just as nowadays many leaseholders in blocks of flats purchase the freehold of the block collectively. In the eighteenth century the manor of Shilton[26] in Leicestershire was held by lords as trustees for the copyholders. Similarly, the copyholders purchased the manor of Paris Gardens in Southwark in 1578.[27] The reason seems to have been that they wanted to continue to have the advantage of relatively simplified conveyancing by using the copy of court roll instead of the complex procedures of freehold sales. For all practical purposes the manor had disappeared. There were probably many cases where the homage purchased the manor to free themselves from services and then dispensed with it.[28]

Although escheat extinguishes a tenure (7.7) it does not extinguish a manor and many manors have escheated to the Crown and been granted out again. A more difficult but common issue is where all trace of the title to the manor has been lost. In principle a manor no more ceases to exist where the owner cannot be traced than a freehold does, but the physical land comprising the freehold will still exist, whereas a manor is incorporeal. In theory at least the manor may still exist and someone may be able to claim it later (6.9). If all the land within the boundaries of a manor is destroyed by erosion and the land becomes the foreshore or seabed and thereby passes to the Crown, the manor will be treated as destroyed as there can be no tenants or services.

---

[23] Charter of Duchy of Lancaster 1399. See *Case of the Dutchy of Lancaster* (1561) 1 Plowd 212, 75 ER 325.

[24] (1862) HL Cas 62, 11 ER 1254; see Ch 7.

[25] In Germany this practice was known as meiergut.

[26] Watkins, C, *A Treatise on Copyholds* (James Bullock, 4th edn by Thomas Coventry, 1825) 2.551.

[27] Paris Gardens: Watkins *op cit* 2.566.

[28] See also Maitland *op cit* 141 for lordless villages in 1066.

Loss of tenants has a similar effect. One essential feature of a manor is the
manorial court, which is in two parts (13.1). The court baron is the court of the
free tenants; if there are insufficient tenants the court and the manor cannot
function. For some centuries there was doubt about the number of tenants
required,[29] but it was finally established that the minimum number was two –
one to be suitor to the court and the other to constitute the court itself. In
Baxendale v Instow Parish Council[30] Megarry J said:

> For centuries there has been a category of manors known as 'reputed manors.' If
> there ceased to be at least two free tenants of a manor, the manor became a 'reputed
> manor'; for the freeholders were the judges of the court baron, and at least two
> were needed so that an only freeholder would not be his own judge[[31]] ... As Lord
> Denman C.J. said, speaking for the Court of Queens' Bench in *Doe d. Molesworth
> v. Sleeman*[[32]], 'a reputed manor is that which has been a manor, though from some
> supervening defects it has ceased to be so.' With the decay of the manorial system,
> more and more manors became reputed manors.

Free tenants could be lost either by oversight or acquisition of the holdings by
the lord. Oversight was more common. New free common tenancies could not
be granted after 1290 and, since the land was conveyed by assurance between
parties without reference to the manor court and the terms of sale did not
distinguish between socage within a manor and outside, there was no reason for
the tenant to have any connection to the manor. Sometimes a tenant may have
owed a rent of assize or heriot, or enjoyed common rights, but in most cases it
did not matter whether or not he held of the manor and so the fact of his tenure
was forgotten. In some manors customary freehold could also pass by assurance
and even though title might in theory be by copy of court roll it was possible for
this formality to be overlooked.

Alternatively, a wealthy lord, especially in a closed manor, might buy up the
freehold of all the land in the vicinity until there were no free tenants left. It
seems that a manor could disappear by loss of copyholders, but this is not clear.
If all customary holdings were either enfranchised or converted to demesne[33]
there would be no more custom of the manor. Other local customs could exist in
the parish but this was not the same. The court customary would cease to

---

[29] See *Long v Heminge* (1587) Cro Eliz 209, 78 ER 466, where one tenant was considered
sufficient.

[30] [1982] 1 Ch 14, [1981] 2 All ER 620. See also Scriven *op cit* 3 and cases there cited; *Tonkin v
Croker* (1703) 2 Ld Raym 860, 92 ER 74 for two tenants.

[31] See *Chetwode v Crew* (1746) Willes 614, 125 ER 1348; Scriven *op cit* 3; *Bradshaw v Lawson*
(1791) 4 Term Rep 443, 100 ER 1109.

[32] (1846) 9 QB 298 at 301.

[33] This no doubt happened where a lord forcibly and unlawfully dispossessed the tenants in order
to inclose.

function and so would the manor. That at least seems the position, but there were many claimed legal manors with no copyholders and the point does not seem to have been decided.[34] There would be no practical point in litigating since all land would be the lord's freehold. Thus, a former manor which comprised only demesne land would become a reputed manor. If it had waste then that would of course remain physically waste land but it could not be subject to the commonable rights of tenants although it might be subject to common rights of others. However, as mentioned below, for the purposes of the Commons Registration Act 1965 it was held in *Re Box Hill Common*[35] that waste of a reputed manor was waste of the manor within the Act. That must be the case since it is likely that all manors are now reputed manors.

A manor is also destroyed if the court and services are separated from the demesne. This was decided in *Sir Moyle Finch's Case (Avery v Crat*[36]) which was the first case in which Coke sat as Chief Justice. The case related to the manor of Beamston in Kent and to a dispute between Sir Moyle Finch and Heneage Finch, the latter being described in the report as the brother of the former, although he was probably his son. Beamston had belonged to Sir Thomas Moyle who was Speaker of the House of Commons in 1542, and a loyal supporter of Henry VIII and of Queen Mary. He died in 1560 at his manor of Eastwell, also in Kent. Under his will his Kentish manors, including Eastwell and Beamston, were left to his widow, Catherine (Lady Moyle), during her life and after her death to her daughter, also Catherine, the wife of Sir Thomas Finch. He was a soldier who served Henry VIII and died in a shipwreck in the Channel in 1563 on a campaign near Le Havre and was buried at Eastwell leaving his own widow (Lady Finch) and a son called Moyle Finch, after his grandfather.[37]

Lady Finch remarried Nicholas St Leger but in the report she is referred to as Lady Finch. In various matters she joined with her second husband, but for the sake of simplicity he need not be mentioned. In 1568 she wished to grant a lease of the demesne lands of Beamston for 50 years, and to do that it was necessary to rearrange the family settlement. The rearrangement did not affect Lady Moyle's rights so that as the lease was subject to her life estate it would only come into possession on her death. The reversion in the demesne was taken out of the settlement under the will of Sir Thomas Moyle (by a method known as levying a fine) and put into a new settlement for Lady Finch for life and then as she should appoint. The courts and services were not affected by this

---

[34]   See *Warrick v Queen's College, Oxford* (1870–71) LR 6 Ch App 716 at 722.

[35]   [1980] Ch 109, [1979] All ER 113, (1978) 37 P&CR 181.

[36]   (1610) 6 Co Rep 63a, 77 ER 310.

[37]   *Dictionary of National Biography.*

rearrangement and remained subject to the terms of Sir Thomas Moyle's will. Lady Finch then granted the lease.

In 1574 the other terms of Sir Thomas Moyle's will were reorganised by another fine and became held (still subject to Lady Moyle's life estate) for Lady Finch for life and were then entailed for Moyle Finch. This fine referred to all Lady Finch's lands in Kent except 'the manor of Beamston'. In 1584 the arrangements for Beamston under the 1568 fine were reorganised on the assumption that it was a manor. In 1584 Lady Moyle died. Lady Finch then became lady of the manor of Eastwell and it was presumed of Beamston as well. She also held all Sir Thomas Moyle's lands in Kent. The 1568 lease of the Beamston demesne took effect in possession and rent was paid. In 1585 Lady Finch appointed that Beamston, on her death, should pass direct to her grandson, Heneage, son of Moyle (now Sir Moyle) by his wife Elizabeth, daughter of Sir Thomas Heneage. Lady Finch died the same year. Following her death Beamston passed to Heneage but there may have been few practical consequences because of the lease. The demesne lands passed by virtue of the fine of 1568 and the services and court by virtue of the fine of 1581. All the rest of the Kentish estates passed to Sir Moyle.

In 1589 the lessee of the Beamston demesne stopped paying rent. In 1602 Heneage's bailiff, Mr Crat, demanded the rent. It was then that Sir Moyle claimed that Beamston belonged to him. This was despite the fact that the fine of 1574 specifically excluded the manor of Beamston. His counsel argued that the fine of 1574 caught all of Lady Finch's lands in Kent and only excluded the manor of Beamston. But, he said, Beamston was no longer a manor in 1574. The effect of the fine of 1568 was to sever the demesnes from the court and services and that severance destroyed the manor. The express exclusion of a non-existent manor in 1574 was meaningless. The demesne lands were lands, they were in Kent, and therefore, counsel argued, they passed to Sir Moyle Finch. Heneage's counsel argued, first, that the manor of Beamston had not been destroyed in 1568 but, secondly, even if it had, it had been resurrected because it was referred to and treated as a manor, and, thirdly, even if that was not so the parties had made it clear in 1574 what they intended even if the 1574 documents were technically defective. He lost on the first two points and won on the third and, with it, won the case.

The court held that even though in 1568 Lady Moyle was lady of the manor and remained so until her death in 1584, and even though the separation of the demesne from the services only affected the terms of the settlements (so that Lady Finch was still entitled to both) the separation was sufficient to destroy the manor and to do so forever, even though the rights were rejoined in 1581 or 1585. As the separation was by act of parties (not, like co-parceners, by act of law) the severance was final. On the second point the court held that a manor cannot be created (or recreated) by only a few years or indeed at all because it had to have existed continually since the beginning of legal memory. However, neither of those two points decided the case. The documents made it clear that in 1574 Lady Finch did not intend to include Beamston and it still had the reputation of being a manor even though it was not a legal manor. The court took the meaning the parties intended and found in favour of Heneage.

8.5   REPUTED MANORS

Under the rules set out in this chapter virtually all manors must now be reputed manors: there can be few, if any, legal manors left. In *Crown Estate Commissioners v Roberts*[38] Lewison J said that most manors today are reputed manors. Some may still have free tenants in common socage (granted either before 1290 or under the Copyhold Acts) but since 1925 there are no customary tenants. Save for the exceptions in Sch 4 to the Administration of Justice Act 1977 (13.4), the manorial courts have no legal jurisdiction and most have ceased to sit. There can be very few subsisting manorial services. Nearly all land is now held *ut de corona*.

In practice this has few consequences today. In *Doe d Clayton v Williams*[39] the court considered that a conveyance of a reputed manor did not carry with it the wastes. This has been altered by what is now s 62(3) of the Law of Property Act 1925 (9.1) which provides that a conveyance of a manor carries the waste; s 205(1)(ix) defines manor to include a reputed manor. If s 62 is only concerned with incorporeal rights not with land (9.2) the point might still be important. In *Re Box Hill Common*[40] the court held that 'manor' for the purposes of the Commons Registration Act 1965 included a reputed manor and that was confirmed by *Hampshire County Council v Milburn*.[41] If unregistered[42] land is reputed to belong to a manor (whether a legal or reputed manor) then it will pass with the manor on a sale even though not truly part of it. The distinction between reputed parcels and parcels of reputed manors was discussed and accepted in *Baxendale v Instow Parish Council*[43] where it was held that land was not regarded as waste of the manor for the purposes of the 1965 Act where

---

[38]   [2008] EWHC 1302 (Ch) at [137].

[39]   (1843) 11 M&W 803.

[40]   [1980] Ch 109, [1979] All ER 113, (1978) 37 P&CR 181.

[41]   [1990] 2 WLR 1240, [1990] 2 All ER 257, (1990) 61 P&CR 135.

[42]   Registered land can only pass by transfer under the Land Registration Act 2002: see 25.6.

[43]   [1982] 1 Ch 14, [1981] 2 All ER 620. See also *Thetford v Thetford* (1589) 1 Leon 204, 74 ER 187.

it was only reputed to belong to the manor (whether the manor itself was legal or reputed).

It is evident that a legal manor is a fragile thing, easily destroyed, but the destruction seems now to have few practical consequences. Once a legal manor has become a reputed manor it cannot be reconstituted and, indeed, manors cannot be created since 1189.[44] Land cannot be added to a manor[45] and, if separated, cannot be re-annexed by act of parties.[46] Copyhold land, if converted to freehold, cannot be reconverted.[47] If it escheated or was surrendered to the lord and not granted out again with exactly the same incidents, or if it was leased out before re-grant, it ceased to be copyhold. If rights were held with a manor the court would not easily accept that they were annexed to it,[48] or if they were annexed they could easily be detached.[49] Where an inclosure Act awarded mineral or sporting rights to the lord the courts interpreted it restrictively.[50] The courts seem to have assembled a mass of detailed rules which, taken together, worked against the manorial system.

This was not a conscious policy. Many judges were themselves lords of manors and before they became judges had, as barristers, appeared for lords. They respected property and established rights. Two reasons guided the logic of the law, one explicit and the other in the nature of the common law. The first reason was proclaimed in strong terms by Best CJ in *Garland v Jekyll*[51] when speaking of the emancipation of villeins, who became copyholders:

> Whatever the situation of copyholders might have been in the early part of our history, custom has now confirmed their interest as tenants, and this same custom has confirmed and established the rights of the lord. This alteration has been brought about by no statute; the statutes to which we refer with so much satisfaction have only secured the rights of men already free. It is to lawyers in Westminster Hall, and I speak it with pride, that slaves, for such was the state of men in pure villeinage, are indebted for the permancy of their property, and for that weight in society which permancy in property has conferred upon them; it is by the establishment of the customs referable to copyholds as established in courts of

---

[44]   *Sir Moyle Finch's Case* (1610) 6 Co Rep 63a, 77 ER 310.

[45]   *Baxendale v Instow Parish Council* [1982] 1 Ch 14, [1981] 2 All ER 620.

[46]   *R v Duchess of Buccleugh* (1704) 6 Mod 150, 87 ER 909, 1 Salk 358; *Delacherois v Delacherois* (1862) 11 HL Cas 62, 11 ER 1254: see 7.5.

[47]   *French's Case* (1576) 4 Co Rep 31a, 77 ER 960: see 5.6; 7.10.

[48]   *Morris v Dimes* (1834) 1 Ad & E 654, 110 ER 1357: see 12.3; *Staffordshire and Worcestershire Canal Navigation v Bradley* [1910] 1 Ch 91: see 12.7.

[49]   *Attorney General v Ewelme Hospital* (1853) 17 Beav 366, 51 ER 1075: see 17.5.

[50]   *Townley v Gibson* (1788) 2 TR 701, 100 ER 377: see 9.5.

[51]   (1824) 2 Bing at 292, 130 ER 311.

justice, that this permanent interest has placed copyholders in the happy situation in which they are now found.

That case concerned the right of the lord of the manor of Weeks Park Hall in Essex to heriots. Heriots themselves, as discussed in 14.3, illustrate that 'lawyers in Westminster Hall' had played a double part in the process. But the point that Best CJ was making was that over the years the common law had worked to ensure the freedom of peasants from manorial control. Some historians claim to detect a *favor libertatis* or presumption of freedom as early as the writings of Bracton, that unless a lord could prove a man to be his villein the man went free.[52] That may be an exaggeration for that time although the presumption must have existed by 1600; and in *Somersett's Case*[53] in 1771, in which Mansfield CJ held that any slave who stepped on English soil was thereby freed, it became the undoubted law.

The other reason for the way the law developed relates to the very nature of the manor and the common law. The manor was a separate local legal system, governed by its lord, with its own courts, customs and local officers. Inevitably such systems clashed with the law common to all England administered from the royal courts. The inconsistency is as old as Magna Carta 1215, in which c 34 preserved the right of a lord to hold his own court. Over the years the courts in Westminster Hall took priority, they claimed jurisdiction over customs to review whether they were reasonable, and the local customary law disappeared. Neither king, royal judges nor Parliament could, in the long run, tolerate the separate local peculiarities that made up the manor and, whatever the judges as individuals may have consciously intended, the effect of centuries of growing central government was to destroy the manor.

Thereby, legal manors became reputed manors. Once that had occurred it was enough. The underlying threat to the nation had gone and what was left was a bundle of rights to, over and in land. That was no threat, rather the reverse, for the growing common law was built on and enforced respect for property and indeed it has been turned, as *Hampshire County Council v Milburn*[54] shows, to the interests of conservation. It was as a piece of property that the manor survived.

---

[52] Hyams, PR, *King, Lord and Peasants in Medieval England* (1980).

[53] (1772) 20 ST 1.

[54] [1991] AC 235, [1990] 2 All ER 257, (1990) 61 P&CR 135: see 6.3.

PART III

RIGHTS

Chapter 9

General Words

9.1   RIGHTS AND THE MANOR

The manor was not only, indeed not principally, land, but also a bundle of rights. There were rights of the lord against the tenants (such as rents and minerals) and of the tenants against the lord (such as commons and being admitted to a copyhold). There were rights of the lord against the Crown (particularly franchises) and of the government against the lord (such as highways). All these rights needed to be clarified and defined. Some were rights in the strict sense of the word, corresponding to a duty on someone else, for example to receive and pay a rent. Some were what are called privileges, such as holding a court, or immunities, such as allowing cattle to stray, or powers, such as approving regulations.[1]

The question of what rights go with a manor usually arises when the manor is sold. When one person ceases to hold it and another takes it, what does the former retain? For example in *Doe d Clayton v Williams*[2] (9.2) the question arose whether a conveyance of a reputed manor included the waste; the court held it did not. The conveyance did include the name of the manor – as that was part of the reputation – the demesnes and services and even the right to appoint a gamekeeper, but not the wastes. So when drafting documents conveyancers took care to state what they were including. Often they did not know whether or not a particular right belonged to the manor and so, out of caution, they added words to cover the possibility. Over time these 'general words' hardened into standard formulae, long outlasting changes in the law.

The style of drafting is old. A charter of Charles King of the Franks (who later became the Emperor Charlemagne) in 775 granted two villas, one at Luzarches near Paris, the other at Messy near Meaux:

---

[1]   Hohfeld, WN, *Fundamental Legal Conceptions as appplied in judicial reasoning* (Yale University Press, 1919).

[2]   (1843) 11 M&W 803, 12 LJ EX 429, 152 ER 1029.

with their lands, houses and other buildings, their tenants, slaves, vineyards, woods, meadows, pastures, waters and watercourses, flour mills and other movable and immovable belongings.[3]

By the eleventh century a standard alliterative Anglo-Saxon formula developed in England when land was granted with 'sac and soc, toll and team, infanthief, bloodwite and weardwite, hamsoc, forestal, grythbrice and mundbrice and all the rights which belong'[4] or with other words such as 'in tide and out of tide, binnan *burh* and butan *burh*, on street and off street'.[5]

A typical seventeenth-century conveyance of a manor might use words such as the following:

all and singular the said manor, messuages, lands, tenements, meadows, pasture, common pasture, demesne lands, waste land, furze and heath, moors, marshes, woods, woodlands and trees, rents, reversions and services, courts leet, views of frankpledge, perquisites and profits of courts and leets, and all which to courts leet and views of frankpledge doth belong, goods and chattels of felons and all other rights, jurisdictions, franchises, liberties, privileges, profits, commodities, advantages, emoluments, and hereditaments whatsoever ... chattels, abandoned goods, impounded strays, chattels of felons, fugitives and suicides, deodands, ... male and female free and unfree and villeins with their families, estovers and common estovers, fairs, markets, tolls, customary tolls and all other rights ...[6]

As a result conveyances became lengthy and full of words that were largely irrelevant to the particular manor. In s 6(3) of the Conveyancing and Law of Property Act 1881 Parliament enacted that certain general words would automatically be included in a conveyance of a manor (and s 1(4) defined a manor as including a reputed manor) so that it was no longer necessary to repeat them in full. That provision was re-enacted in s 62(3) of the Law of Property Act 1925 (with the same definition in s 205(1)(ix)) as follows:

A conveyance of a manor shall be deemed to include and shall by virtue of this Act operate to convey, with the manor, all pastures, feedings, wastes, warrens, commons, mines, minerals, quarries, furzes, trees, woods, underwoods, coppices, and the ground and soil thereof, fishings, fisheries, fowlings, courts leet, courts, baron, and other courts, view of frankpledge and all that to view of frankpledge doth belong, mills, mulctures, customs, tolls, duties, reliefs, heriots, fines, sums of money, amerciaments,

---

[3]   McKitterick, R, *The Frankish Kingdoms under the Carolingians* (Longman, 1983) 82.

[4]   Edward the Confessor's grant of Islip to Westminster Abbey.

[5]   Maitland, FW, *Domesday Book and Beyond* (Cambridge University Press, 1987; first published 1897) 266.

[6]   Taken from a confirmatory grant by James I to Sir Warwick Hele dated 6 June 1615 of the Manor of Kenton in Devon. I am grateful to the Earl of Devon (formerly Lord Courtenay) the lord of the manor for his kind permission to quote from the letters patent.

> waifs estrays, chief-rents, quitrents, rentscharge, rents seck, rents of assize, fee farm rents, services, royalties, jurisdictions, franchises, liberties, privileges, easements, profits, advantages, rights, emoluments and hereditaments whatsoever, to the manor appertaining or reputed to appertain, or at the time of conveyance, demised, occupied, or enjoyed with the same, or reputed or known as part, parcel, or member thereof

At first sight this looks like an unruly jumble of properties and rights in no particular order. Closer examination shows it to be carefully drafted.

9.2   CORPOREAL AND INCORPOREAL

The first distinction to note is between the words up to 'and the ground and soil thereof' and those after. The first group refers to rights over land that can be seen and touched – wastes, warrens, commons, quarries, trees and coppices – and then refers to the ground and soil of the land affected by such rights. The rest of the subsection is primarily concerned with rights of various sorts (although it does include mills, which are tangible, for a reason that will appear). The distinction is one that used to be important between corporeal and incorporeal hereditaments.

A hereditament is property that, on the death of its owner, passed to his heir, as distinct from a chattel, which passed to his family. Originally chattels could be left by will but hereditaments could not. Before the sixteenth century a way round this was found by conveying land to feoffees to the use of the owner's will, but this was a complex procedure employed by those wealthy enough to have access to legal advice. By the Statute of Wills 1540 most freehold land could be left by will. If the landowner did not leave a will his hereditaments still went to his heir (either directly or, after the Land Transfer Act 1897, through his administrators) but since s 45 of the Administration of Estates Act 1925 came into force there has been no difference in the way that hereditaments and chattels pass on death.

Both hereditaments and chattels can be corporeal (or tangible) or incorporeal (or intangible). Tangible chattels include cattle, tractors, furniture and jewellery. Intangible chattels include debts and copyrights.[7] Corporeal hereditaments are primarily land, although in English law land as such cannot be owned and the corporeal hereditament is an abstraction, a legal estate in land (22.7). A manor was originally thought of as corporeal since, as explained below, it passed by livery. In *Tyrringham's Case*[8] in 1584 the court specifically said that a manor

---

[7]   Bracton, Sir Henry, *De legibus et consuetudinibus angliae* (SE Thorne (ed)) (Belknap Press of Harvard University Press, 1977) (c 1257) f 7b.

[8]   (1584) 6 Co Rep 36b, 76 ER 973.

was a corporate thing. Sir William Blackstone,[9] writing in around 1760, gives a list of incorporeal hereditaments and does not include manors. This issue is discussed further in 27.6. It appears that manors have now become incorporeal not only by statute but also at common law, but a conveyance of an incorporeality may be able to carry corporeal property with it. Things in or on land are part of it and so buildings, fixed stones, walls, minerals, trees and growing crops are also corporeal hereditaments. Water flowing in a stream or percolating through the soil is not part of the land. Water held in a pond may be part of the land, although it may be better understood as a tangible chattel. Tame animals are, of course, chattels (the word means cattle). Wild animals cannot be owned and therefore cannot be either hereditaments or chattels, but the right to catch or kill them may be an incorporeal hereditament (12.1).

Incorporeal hereditaments are generally ideas. Blackstone lists several types, most of which are considered in other chapters: advowsons (20.2); tithes (20.9); commons (10.3); ways (4.8, 15.2); offices and dignities (23.1); franchises (16.1); and corodies, annuities and rents (14.5–14.6). Others, not listed by Blackstone, could include seigniories (such as a manor), profits, and future interests such as reversions and remainders.

Ways are a type of easement, and easements include rights to light and water. Profits include rights of common and some mineral and sporting rights. Corodies are an ancient form of customary render of goods, usually to churches. Annuities would not normally be hereditaments at all but would be intangible chattels, but in the Middle Ages fees were sometimes granted in money instead of in land, and later some family annuities were hereditaments, especially if charged on land. Offices are not nowadays regarded as property but in earlier times official positions, such as an army commission or a position in government administration, could be bought and sold. If any of the obligations and rights to take part in the Coronation under Grand Sergeanty (18.4) have become separated from land and are now held in gross they might be regarded as hereditaments taking effect as offices.

The distinction between corporeal and incorporeal hereditaments was that the first were said to lie in livery and the second to lie in grant. Livery was a form of land transfer that did not involve a written document and usually applied to subinfeudation. The parties would come together on the land and the tenant knelt before his lord in the ceremony of fealty (18.1). In token of the grant the lord handed the tenant a clod of earth. In the case of copyholds the steward frequently handed the tenant a rod. After *Quia Emptores* the same ceremony could in theory be used to assure by substitution. In practice it was obsolete and although some transfers were effected by feoffment until the eighteenth century,

---

[9]   Blackstone, Sir William, *Commentaries on the Laws of England* II.3.i.

the feoffments themselves were written documents and, if livery took place, it was between lawyers handing over symbolic boxes of earth.

Incorporeal hereditaments could not be transferred in the same way and so livery could not be used. In practice if land had the benefit of, for example, a right of way, then livery of the land would include the easement[10] but a new easement could not be granted on its own by livery. Similarly, it is likely that in the eleventh century an assurance of an advowson could be transferred by livery of the church building although if the transfer was to a bishop or abbey the recipient would almost certainly request a written confirmation. Otherwise incorporeal hereditaments had to be granted and usually transferred by deed.

Leases of land could originally be granted orally or by informal writing which did not amount to a solemn legal deed. This led to abuses, and the Statute of Frauds 1677 provided that a lease for more than three years or which was not at the best rent or did not take effect in immediate possession had to be by deed. That provision is now in s 54 of the Law of Property Act 1925. However, even before 1677 leases of incorporeal hereditaments had to be by deed since they could not pass by livery alone. Thus, a lease of sporting rights, a right of way or a right of common must be by deed even if only for a year or from year to year. This is not affected by the fact that the rights created by the lease itself constitute a chattel, not a hereditament, since it is the subject matter of the lease that matters here, not the grant.[11] The application of this rule to manors as such is considered in 27.6.

Although originally manors could pass by feoffment with livery of seisin, that became obsolete before the end of the Middle Ages and ceased to be possible under the Real Property Act 1845. Section 51 of the Law of Property Act 1925 now provides that:

> All lands and all interests therein lie in grant and are incapable of being conveyed by livery or livery and seisin, or by feoffment, or by bargain and sale; and a conveyance of an interest in land may operate to pass the possession or right to possession thereof, without actual entry, but subject to all prior rights thereto.

Land is defined in s 205(1)(ix) as including a manor so that title to a manor can now only pass by a deed. As a manor is regarded as incorporeal a deed is required even for a lease not exceeding three years at the best rent and taking effect in possession. Occasionally a manor may pass by operation of law; for example, on the bankruptcy of the owner it will pass to his trustee in bankruptcy under the Insolvency Act 1986, s 306. On death it passes to his personal

---

[10] Bracton *op cit* f 222–3.

[11] *Wood v Leadbitter* (1845) 13 M&W 838, 153 ER 351.

representatives under the Administration of Estates Act 1925, s 1, who may then pass it on to a beneficiary by an assent (which does not have to be a deed but must be in writing) to give effect to directions under a will or to an entitlement under intestacy. Land may pass in other ways, as by vesting declaration under the Compulsory Purchase (Vesting Declarations) Act 1981. The compulsory powers will not extend to the manor itself, but they can apply to demesne land and it is common to find waste passing in this way where the lord is unknown. A manor can, like land, escheat (7.6) and the disclaimer does not have to be by deed.

Section 62 is primarily concerned with incorporeal rather than corporeal hereditaments. In *Commission for the New Towns v JJ Gallagher Ltd*[12] Neuberger J considered that s 62(1) was concerned with incorporeal rights. He accepted that that included 'a mixture of physical things and incorporeal hereditaments' but said:

> The first question is potentially wide-ranging: is s.62 apt to include other physical land, not referred to in the conveyance, with the land expressly to be conveyed? In my view, while, in very exceptional circumstances, it might be possible (a point which I leave open), it would not be a permissible result in a normal case.

Neuberger J was focussing on s 62(1), but similar considerations apply to s 62(3). 'Pastures' will normally mean a right of pasture rather than any pasture land, which would normally be demesne. 'Minerals' may refer to the property in minerals in former copyhold land which, by general custom, will not carry possession, although where mineral rights were excepted on enfranchisement they will be included, as discussed in 11.8. As common land is usually waste the reference in s 62(3) of the 1925 Act to commons is to rights of common which normally have to be appurtenant to land. Most of the other corporealities mentioned in s 62(3) occur on waste, which will normally be included in a conveyance of a manor. The wording specifically includes 'the ground and soil thereof'. Although, strictly, a conveyance cannot include land as such but only an estate or interest in land, the intention of the section is clear and it appears that the original wording was taken from forms of conveyance in general use.

As a general rule s 62 covers rights which either already exist as separate interests or which, because they have been exercised by people in separate occupation, such as by one tenant of a common landlord against another, are regarded as quasi-rights. If a right or quasi-right already exists it will be included, but the section will not create something wholly new. Although corporealities will be included where not specifically mentioned this will depend on older rules of construction. Thus, at common law wastes will be

---

[12]   [2003] 2 P&CR 3.

included on a conveyance of a legal manor but not on conveyance of a reputed manor. In *Doe d Clayton v Williams*[13] there was a settlement in 1785 of the manor of Great Marlow with all buildings, outhouses, wastes and waste ground belonging to the manor. Brick kilns had been built on former waste but as they were in use the land was waste no longer. The court held that as there were no freeholders or copyholders it was not a legal but a reputed manor and therefore in law there was no manor for the kilns to belong to. As indicated above that decision was reversed by the provision in the Conveyancing and Law of Property Act 1881, now in s 62.

Where it was uncertain whether or not wastes belonged to a manor the inclusion of the word 'wastes' was sufficient to pass them. In *Cator v The Croydon Canal Company*[14] Lord Spencer, who was lord of the manor of Battersea which included land at Penge, in 1773 conveyed to Mr Smithson various lands including wastes, but the conveyance did not expressly refer to Penge. Mr Cator was Smithson's successor in title. The company built a canal and was due to pay compensation to the landowner and the issue was whether Mr Cator had title. The court held that as it appeared that Lord Spencer had been entitled to the wastes including Penge Common the conveyance included it.

General words often have to be construed restrictively. In *Rooke v Lord Kensington*[15] Lord Kensington intended to convey some lands in London defined by what was, at the time, in a mortgage. He was entitled to the manor of Earls Court in the Parish of Kensington which was then in Middlesex. The manor had formerly been subject to the mortgage but had been released before the conveyance. The words of the conveyance referred to the mortgage and then added 'and all other the lands, tenements and hereditaments (if any) in the county of Middlesex aforesaid, whereof or whereto the said Lord Kensington is seised or entitled for any estate of inheritance'. Although a manor is a hereditament the court held that the general words were not intended to, and in the context did not, include the manor.[16]

---

[13] (1843) 11 M and W 803, 152 ER 1029.

[14] (1841) 4 Y and C 405, 160 ER 1064.

[15] (1856) 2 K and J 753, 69 ER 986.

[16] Contra in a settlement *Norris v Le Neve* (1744) 3 Atk 82, 26 ER 850: see *Walker v Burton* [2012] EWHC 978 (Ch).

9.3   PROPERTY AND POSSESSION, SUBSTANCE AND REVENUE

A second distinction relates to the group of rights in s 62(3) of the Law of Property Act 1925, from 'mines' to 'fowlings', that bridges the gap between corporeal and incorporeal hereditaments. This group relates in part to rights in demesne or waste land and in part to rights in copyhold land. In the latter case there is a distinction between the proprietary right of the lord (which he could not exercise without the copyholder's consent) and the possessory right of the copyholder (which is of no value without the lord's consent) which is in practice most relevant to mineral rights and which will therefore be considered in 11.7. It used to apply also to timber although timber rights were abolished by the Law of Property Act 1922.[17] It may have applied to the exercise of sporting rights since although there is no property in wild animals while alive the issue may have been relevant to whether the lord could enter on to a copyholder's close to shoot game or recover fallen birds.

The distinction between property and possession is, apart from the above, generally of little importance in English law although there may be a distinction between seisin and possession. The reason for this is that remedies for recovering land and associated rights developed out of various writs, of which the best known were the possessory assizes, instituted in the reign of Henry II which protected seisin. Initially 'seisin' meant merely possession, and was contrasted with right, which was protected by what appears to be an older procedure, the writ of right. This has two forms: the *Breve de recto tenendo* for a case to be heard by a mesne lord and the *Praecipe quod reddat* for a case to be heard by a royal judge. Right protected a more basic title albeit one demonstrated by proving a seisin earlier than that of any rival claimant. In practice the writ of right was complex and cumbersome to use and became rarely invoked for genuine disputes, although in the form of the collusive common recovery it did play an important part in barring entails. In time the possessory assizes and other remedies protecting seisin themselves became antiquated, not least because the term 'seisin' itself came to acquire a complex and artificial meaning. After the fifteenth century claims to land were decided by the procedure in ejectment which was a form of trespass protecting possession not seisin. The writ of right and the possessory assizes were abolished by the Real Property Limitation Act 1833 and English law now only protects possession.[18] However, seisin still exists at common law and in an unregistered conveyance (including a conveyance of a manor) it is usual to

---

[17]   Section 138 and Sch 13, Part 2, para 12.

[18]   See *JA Pye (Oxford) Ltd v Graham* [2003] 1 AC 419 at [32]–[35].

recite that the seller is seised of the property conveyed for a legal estate in fee simple.

There is no doubt that the lord had seisin of the freehold of the manor including the villein or customary land. However, the general principle of English property law since the development of ejectment is that rights now depend on possession. As a general rule someone in possession does not need to show title. In *Alan Wibberley Building Ltd v Insley*[19] Lord Hoffmann said that 'Possession is in itself a good title against anyone who cannot show a prior and therefore better right to possession'.[20] That does not necessarily mean actual physical control[21] and, with particular reference to mineral rights, a landowner is deemed to have possession of the subsoil.

Villeins may not have had possession. A serf was not apparently regarded as having possession of his holding.[22] He could not use novel disseisin but that was in part because he did not hold a free tenement. His free successors were regarded as seised of their copyholds, in contrast to a leaseholder who was possessed of his land. However, when copyholders were given the action of ejectment, they were also assumed to have, or at least be able to grant, possession so that their lessees could sue in trespass. On the Continent, under systems derived from Roman law, the distinction between property and possession became more important and was the subject of much debate.

Possession should be distinguished from occupation, although the two generally go together. This is relevant to liability for rates and under the Occupiers Liability Acts 1957 and 1984. This is considered in the context of common land in 6.3. Someone may be occupying land as licensee while someone else is in legal possession as freeholder or under a lease.

A third distinction in s 62 relates to matters listed as far as 'mills' and those from 'mulctures' to 'royalties'. The first group are rights to the enjoyment of a thing – a right to pasture, fish or hold a court. The second are financial, namely the right to receive money, considered in 14.3–14.6 and as annual or accidental services in 27.2. Mills and mulctures go together because a mulcture is the right to payment for use of a mill. As indicated in 9.5 references to manorial rights were often to the income derived by way of rents, court payments and accidental services.

---

[19] [1999] 1 WLR 894.

[20] *Asher v Whitlock* (1865) LR 1 QB 1.

[21] *Bocardo SA v Star Energy UK Onshore Ltd* [2011] 1 AC 380.

[22] This may have followed the Roman law that a *colonus* did not have possession.

9.4   INCIDENTS, APPURTENANCES AND OTHER RIGHTS

Another type of distinction can be applied to rights held with a manor. These distinctions are not on the whole formal technical terms and usage is not consistent so that a given right may be described in different ways while the same word can be used for different types of right, but they can be used to explain why the courts have decided a case in a particular way. Many rights held with a manor are described as manorial incidents. Thus, the Law of Property Act 1922, s 128(2) refers to quitrents, fines, heriots, forfeitures and timber rights in the context of their intended abolition under s 138. Incidents are rights incidental to the manor.

There are rights, sometimes called adjuncts, which (if the lord has them at all) are automatically part of the manor. They are so integral to the manor that the law treats them as not being distinct. For a legal manor they would include the manor house, demesne land, services and manorial courts. They also include waste (not for a reputed manor) and mineral rights in copyhold land which belong to the manor by general custom. Section 62(3) (and its predecessor, the Conveyancing and Law of Property Act 1881) therefore did not need to apply to adjuncts, which passed with a manor automatically.

Appurtenances are rights which pertain to the manor (Latin *pertinens*), separate from it but which benefit it and often belong to it. They include advowsons appurtenant[23] (now abolished by the Patronage (Benefices) Measure 1986) (20.2), franchises and courts leet. Again s 62(3) would apply.

Annexures are rights which do not usually belong to the manor but which may be attached to it. They include such things as the statutory right of appointment of the type discussed in 17.5. Where land is sold or inclosed and the minerals are excepted they may remain annexed to the manor rather than be held as separate property. The same may be true of reserved sporting rights, which can pass with the manor or be held as separate property in gross.

Annexures are fragile. First, the courts may not recognise that something the owner considers to have been annexed has been. *Morris v Dimes*[24] (12.3) is a case where sporting rights were held with a manor under a separate right in gross and not as an appurtenance. In *Staffordshire and Worcestershire Canal Navigation v Bradley*[25] (12.7) fishing rights were granted by Parliament to the

---

[23]   Bracton *op cit* f 243b.

[24]   (1834) 1 Ad & E 654, 110 ER 1357.

[25]   [1910] 1 Ch 91.

lords of manors and owners of lands but the court held that they were not annexed and were held separately. In *Attorney-General v Ewelme Hospital*[26] (17.5) a right of appointing the head of a hospital was an annexure but it was held to be easily detached from the manor. The courts do not encourage the annexation of rights to the manorial system. It follows that s 62(3) will normally not apply.

Appendances or rights appendant are rare. The term is most often found in relation to certain rights of common (10.4) where it refers to a right more like an adjunct to land, something automatically held with a tenement when it first came into existence. As a result of the Commons Registration Act 1965 such rights have merged with other registered rights. In the context of the manor the term can refer to an advowson appendant (20.2) which used to pass automatically with a manor without being mentioned[27] but, like advowsons appurtenant, no longer exists.

9.5   MANORIAL OR SEIGNIORIAL RIGHTS

The expression 'manorial rights' seems to have been used initially to refer to the services or revenues of the manor (27.2) and as such was used when manors were offered for sale to describe rights which went with them. It later came to be used in private inclosure Acts to refer to rights other than surface land intended to be retained by the lord. Judges had to interpret the term whether used in private documents or in legislation and had to give it a precise meaning. It is therefore a common law term but applied to and used in statutes.

The expression has been used widely with differing meanings in numerous cases, including estrays,[28] minerals,[29] admittance fines and other financial benefits[30] and fishing rights.[31] It may have included courts, suit of mill and timber rights. Often a manor was said to have been purchased with or without the manorial rights – usually financial benefits – which could typically be valued, or the rights had to be valued separately, which referred to the financial dues.[32] The same expression appears in the Copyhold Act 1887, s 11 which says 'The valuers appointed under the provisions of the Copyhold Acts shall

---

[26] (1853) 17 Beav 366, 51 ER 1075.

[27] *Long v Heminge* (1587) Cro Eliz 209, 78 ER 466.

[28] *Nicholson v Chapman* (1793) 2 Bl H 254, 126 ER 536.

[29] *Hilton v The Earl of Granville* 41 ER 498, (1841) Cr & Ph 283.

[30] *Bruce v Helliwell* (1860) 5 H & N 609, 157 ER 1323.

[31] *Neill v Duke of Devonshire* (1882–83) LR 8 App Cas 135.

[32] For example, *Borell v Dann* (1843) 2 Hare 440, 67 ER 181. See also 27.2 as to annual services.

determine the value of the manorial and other rights and incidents, such value to be a gross sum of money'.[33] The corresponding provision in s 6 of the Copyhold Act 1894 refers to 'the facilities for improvements, customs of the manor, fines, heriots, reliefs, quitrents, chief rents, forfeitures and all other incidents whatsoever'.

A number of cases concerned the use of the expression in inclosure Acts affecting the waste. The allotment to former commoners and others was usually in fee simple but it was frequent practice to provide that the lord should retain seigniorial rights either in general or specifically of minerals or sporting. Thus, the Inclosure Act 1845, s 96 saved 'all seigniories, royalties, franchises, and manorial jurisdictions whatsoever in or upon the land to be inclosed' unless the award provided otherwise. A frequent question was whether the lord therefore retained mineral and sporting rights in the former waste, which after inclosure became either cultivated land or was built on. Much depended on the specific words used, but in general the courts held that these were not manorial rights because they did not exist before the inclosure and allotment. It is not possible to have such existing rights in a person's own land as they are part of the freehold and therefore there was no distinct right to preserve.

This was established in *Townley v Gibson*[34] in 1788. Mrs Gibson, the lady of the manor of Yealand, had granted a lease of minerals under waste land. An inclosure award allotted the land as freehold to Mr Townley and others, but the award did not affect the lease and specifically reserved all seigniories to the lady and all rents, services 'and all other royalties and manerial jurisdictions whatsoever'. Kenyon CJ held that the effect of the award was that people who became freeholders also became entitled to the property in the underlying minerals and they, and not the lady, were entitled to the rents and royalties from working the minerals.

The consequence is that in order to qualify as a manorial right the right must have existed anciently, in most cases since legal memory. In *Duke of Devonshire v O'Connor*[35] Fry LJ commented on a provision in an inclosure Act (which the Court of Appeal considered to be badly drafted) and said:

> Under this declaratory part of the clause the earl is to enjoy 'all rents, services, courts, perquisites and profits of court and mills (except for the grinding and grist of malt), piscaries, fishing, hunting, hawking, and fowling, goods and chattels of felons and fugitives, felons of themselves, and put in exigent, deodands, waifs,

---

[33]   See *R v Land Commissioners for England, Ex p Vigers* (1889) LR 23 QBD 59.

[34]   (1788) 2 TR 701, 100 ER 377.

[35]   [1890] LR 24 QBD 468. See also *Ewart v Graham* (1859) VII HL Cas 331, 11 ER 132; *Sowerby v Smith* (1873–74) LR 9 CP 524.

estrays, forfeitures, escheats'; I pause there because the next part of the clause is separate. Now all those are either manorial rights, or they are franchises or rights in the nature of a franchise; they are either rights which are incident to the manor as a common law manor, or which are vested in the lord by grant from the Crown; many of them have no particular reference to waste lands, and would, so far as I can see, be wholly unaffected by the inclosure of the wastes; they appear to be put in simply ex abundanti cautelâ.

'Manorial rights' also seem to have included rights of market and fair[36] even though, as franchises, they would not normally have been regarded as customary. It may be that, as the benefit of such rights was in the tolls, they were seen primarily as revenues in the same context as fines and other payments and therefore capable of valuation.

The meaning of the expression is now important for the purposes of land registration. The Land Registry Act 1862, s 27(2) provided that certain rights remained enforceable even though not mentioned on the register of title and these included 'manorial rights'. This concept was carried into the Land Registration Act 1925, s 70(1), which described such rights as overriding interests. Paragraph (j) comprised 'Rights of fishing and sporting, seigniorial and manorial rights of all descriptions (until extinguished) and franchises'. This has now been replaced by the Land Registration Act 2002 in which paras 11 of Schs 1 and 3 simply refer to 'a manorial right'. This term is not defined.

The Land Registry view,[37] considered in 25.9, is that this refers to those rights preserved from enfranchisement by Sch 12, paras (5) and (6) of the Law of Property Act 1922. Those paragraphs state that enfranchisement 'shall not affect' any right of the lord to rights described at some length, but in effect minerals, markets and sporting rights nor any liability (presumably of any person) for certain works considered below. However, s 70(1)(j) of the 1925 Act included the words '(until extinguished)'. The 1922 and 1925 Acts were part of a single code. This suggests that the reference there is to the rights temporarily preserved by s 128(2) of the 1922 Act, namely such things as quitrents, fines, heriots, forfeitures and timber rights which were to be the subject of compensation and therefore the owner of the enfranchised land was bound to continue to respect the lord's rights until either compensation was paid or the time limit for payment ran out.

---

[36] *Manchester Corporation v Lyons* (1883) LR 22 Ch D 287; *Gloucestershire County Council v Farrow* [1985] 1 WLR 741; *Manchester City Council v Walsh* (1985) 50 P&CR 409.

[37] Land Registry Practice Guide 66, *Overriding interests losing automatic protection in 2013* para 4.6.3.2.

The meaning in the 2002 Act therefore depends on the former meaning developed in the cases. The expression refers to ancient rights arising from custom and in that context would include customary mineral and sporting rights in former copyhold land but not those reserved out of inclosure of the waste as these did not exist as separate rights before inclosure. It is possible that the expression may include ancient payments such as rents of assize or fee farm rents as discussed in 14.6.

There remains the question what 'shall not affect' means in the Law of Property Act 1922, Sch 12. Paragraph (1)(a) states that 'The [enfranchised] land shall be freehold land'. The lord's former rights to minerals and probably any rights to sporting derived in part from his being seised of the fee simple in the copyhold and were matters of custom. The lord had the property while the tenant had the possession. Once the freehold was vested in the tenant the lord's fee simple rights were gone and any rights had to depend on custom. Some rights, as Fry LJ indicated in the earlier context, were franchises. These would include market rights and rights of chase and warren but not other sporting rights or minerals. Franchises can exist as independent rights (16.1). The reference to markets and fairs is anomalous but appears established.

The lord might have agreed an exception of minerals on enfranchisement but as a newly created right that stands on its own without needing to refer to para (5) (see 11.8). Where he had a customary right to enter and work the minerals without the tenant's consent the retained manorial right may have taken effect as a profit (11.9). In the absence of an exception or a power of entry it seems that what para (5) preserved was the customary rights. The right may either be seen as remaining customary, even though its retention is authorised by statute, or as having become statutory, but based on its customary origin. It appears not to be a legal estate since possession is in the freeholder (successor of the copyholder). It may be a right in or over land, or a privilege within the Law of Property Act 1925, s 1(2)(a). Privilege means private law and would correspond to the former local (if general) customary law. In that case it would subsist as a legal interest.

One possible interpretation is that as the lord had a fee simple in the copyhold land before 1926 then that fee simple is not affected and the lord still holds it. As he did not have possession it could not be a legal estate within the Law of Property Act 1925, s 1(1) and would be an equitable fee simple. However the Land Registration Act 2002, s 131 provides that land in the physical possession of one person may in certain relationships be treated as being in the possession of another. One such relationship is that of landlord and tenant. If 'landlord' can be interpreted as including 'lord' then the lord will be treated as having possession and therefore as having a legal estate in the minerals but it is unlikely that a court would construe the section in that way.

The Land Registry view is that manorial right also refers to para (6) of Sch 12, which provides that:

> An enfranchisement by virtue of this Act shall not affect any liability subsisting at the commencement of this Act (whether arising by virtue of a court leet regulation or otherwise) for the construction maintenance cleansing or repair of any dykes, ditches, canals, sea or river walls, piles, bridges, levels, ways and other works required for the protection or general benefit of any land within a manor or for abating nuisances therein

This could include a liability of a tenant to carry out works on his holding or a liability of the lord to do works for the benefit of tenants. If the liability subsists under a regulation of a court leet it will only remain enforceable to the extent it is preserved by the Administration of Justice Act 1977 (13.4). It could arise otherwise, notably by custom (4.6). In the Middle Ages a burden of cleansing or repairing ditches was a frequent customary obligation and, as it was certain, it could attach to freehold land. The current law of flood defences is confused and while there are some statutory duties on public bodies, private obligations have not been extinguished.[38] However, the Land Registration Act 2002, Schs 1 and 3, para 11 refer to a manorial right, and Sch 12, para (6) to the 1922 Act refers to a manorial liability. One person's liability may correspond to another's right but it would not be usual to refer to such obligations as rights.

Manorial rights can cease to be enforceable if not protected by the first registration or disposition of land after 12 October 2013 (25.9) but, where they are protected (and protection may be in general terms), the sums at stake, particularly if minerals can be worked, may lead to the matter being litigated.

---

[38] Pitt Review, *Lessons learned from the 2007 floods* s 3, Ch 8.

Chapter 10

Common and Pasture

pastures, feedings, wastes, warrens, commons

10.1   COMMON LAND

Across England there are thousands of acres of open land of rough grass which do not form part of any farm and which are subject to a variety of rights enjoyed by people other than the owner. These are the commons of England. They are valued now for conservation and public access but most are still important for the agriculture of nearby farms. Many still belong to the lord of the manor. In times past nearly all did.[1]

The word 'common' is often used in non-legal contexts to refer to common land that is land subject to rights of common; but in many of the older cases, and in the Law of Property Act 1925, s 62(3), 'a common' means a right of common, an incorporeal hereditament. The right had to subsist at common law. Rights of common are rights of freehold tenants or other freeholders against the lord, or of one lord against another. Similar rights appurtenant to copyhold land and therefore exercised over the lord's freehold by virtue of custom were customary rights not common and were called commonable. 'Feedings' has a wide meaning but can include certain rights of a lord against his tenants. 'Warrens' in this context are the right of the lord to construct and maintain a warren, usually for rabbits, but now they have become a naturalised pest and the right is obsolete. A different, more important meaning of 'warren' is considered in 12.3.

There is no single statutory definition of common land but the Inclosure Act 1845, s 11 sets out lands liable to be inclosed:

---

[1]   For the material in this chapter, see Gadsden, GD, *The Law of Commons* (Sweet & Maxwell, 1988), described by Lord Templeman in *Hampshire County Council v Milburn* as 'the excellent book'. See also *Report of the Royal Commission on Common Land*, Cmnd 462 (1958). Although the law of Wales is broadly the same as that of England the rules stated here apply with modifications in the Principality.

All such lands as are herein-after mentioned, (that is to say,) all lands subject to any rights of common whatsoever, and whether such rights may be exercised or enjoyed at all times, or may be exercised or enjoyed only during limited times, seasons, or periods, or be subject to any suspension or restriction whatsoever in respect of the time of the enjoyment thereof; all gated and stinted pastures in which the property of the soil or of some part thereof is in the owners of the cattle gates or other gates or stints, or any of them; and also all gated and stinted pastures in which no part of the property of the soil is in the owners of the cattle gates or other gates or stints, or any of them; all land held, occupied, or used in common, either at all times or during any time or season, or periodically, and either for all purposes or for any limited purpose, and whether the separate parcels of the several owners of the soil shall or shall not be known by metes or bounds or otherwise distinguishable; all land in which the property or right of or to the vesture or herbage, or any part thereof, during the whole or any part of the year, or the property or right of or to the wood or underwood growing and to grow thereon, is separated from the property of the soil; and all lot meadows and other lands the occupation or enjoyment of the separate lots or parcels of which is subject to interchange among the respective owners in any known course of rotation or otherwise, shall be land subject to be inclosed under this Act.

While rights of common can subsist over any land, in practice they related primarily to waste of the manor and secondarily to a minority of open fields. Typically the freehold in waste belonged to the lord. The freehold in strips in open fields might belong to him or to some other person and other neighbouring landowners had either a right or an accepted practice of grazing their beasts on the land.

For most contemporary purposes 'common land' can be taken to have the meaning in the Commons Registration Act 1965, s 22, that is land subject to rights of common and waste land of a manor not so subject (see 6.3). It follows that there can be land comprised in the s 11 of the 1845 Act definition which is not within the 1965 Act. Once land had been registered under the 1965 Act its definition did not need to be repeated and, accordingly, the Commons Act 2006 refers to registered common land as existing, although it includes provisions for additional registration and deregistration. However, para 7 of Sch 2 to the Commons Act 2006, which provides that land wrongly registered, of which there was a great deal, may be removed from the register, states in para 7(2)(d)(iv) that land cannot be removed if it was land of a description specified in s 11 of the 1845 Act. It follows that even if it was not subject to rights of common or waste of a manor (nor a town or village green), for example if it was a lot meadow or subject to sole herbage, if registered it will remain on the register.

Under the Localism Act 2011, Chapter 3, Part 5 a local authority has to prepare a list of land of community value which, under s 88, 'furthers the social wellbeing or social interests of the local community' and under s 90 land may also be nominated by a local person or body. If land is on the list then (subject to numerous exceptions, mostly but not exclusively referring to the land being inherited or kept within a family) the owner may not dispose of the land without giving local groups an opportunity to bid for it. Some common land and waste will be regarded as land of community value.

Much common land has no known owner. The possible identity of the current owner is considered in 6.9. In 2002 the Department for the Environment, Food and Rural Affairs estimated that some 1900 commons totalling some 4000 hectares (10,000 acres) in England had no known owners and in Wales 500 commons totalling 21,000 hectares (50,000 acres).[2] The Commons Act 2006, s 45 provides that where the owner cannot be identified a local authority may take the same steps to protect the land that an owner could take.

Registration under the 1965 and 2006 Acts differs from that under the Land Registration Act 2002 and its predecessor, the Land Registration Act 1925 (25.8). The 1965 Act included a provision[3] making registration under the 1925 Act compulsory on sale of land registered under the 1965 Act, even though waste of the manor was not compulsorily registrable even on sale in compulsory areas[4] but, because all land is now registrable on sale, there is no longer any exemption for waste of the manor. The 1965 Act also provided in s 1(1) that rights of common registered under its provisions should not be registrable under the 1925 Act. In case there were rights of common already entered on a registered title s 1(2)(b) provided that 'no rights of common shall be exercisable over any [land in England or Wales which is common land or a town or village green[5]] unless they are registered either under this Act or under the Land Registration Acts 1925 and 1936'. The effect is that such rights would remain enforceable even if not registered under the 1965 Act but that rights not registered under the 1965 Act over land not registered under the 1925 and 1936 Act would be extinguished. As profits were overriding interests, and as in 1965 most common land fell outside areas of compulsory first registration on sale, few may in fact have been been registered under the 1925 Act. The Commons Act 2006 provides in s 3(7) that 'No right of common over land to which this Part applies is to be registered in the register of title', that is the register under the 2002 Act, but it does not specifically state that rights registered before 1965 should be removed; and, if there are such rights, they still subsist.

---

[2] Department of the Environment, Food and Rural Affairs, *Common Land Policy Statement* (July 2002).

[3] Commons Registration Act 1965, s 12.

[4] Land Registration Act 1925, s 120(1).

[5] Taken in from s 1(1)(a).

The 2002 Act, s 27(2)(d) provides that while a grant of new profits must be registered against the title to the burdened land that does not apply to a new right of common. Such new grants will be rare but s 6 of the 2006 Act permits this. Correspondingly, s 33(d) of the 2002 Act provides that no notice of a right of common may be entered on the register of title. In Sch, 3 para 3 (which differs from the corresponding provision in Sch 1 in this case) it is provided that a legal profit is not overriding if it is not known, obvious or recently exercised but this does not apply to a profit registered under the 2006 Act. This means that a buyer of common land cannot exclude a registered commoner on such a ground.

10.2   BACKGROUND TO THE CURRENT LEGISLATION

The law of commons has been the subject of major changes in the twenty-first century. These changes were preceded by the Commons Registration Act 1965 which itself did not directly alter the law, but its implications were brought out by two statutes. First, public access to commons has now become as important as the grazing rights. In the Countryside and Rights of Way Act 2000 ('the CROW Act') Parliament conferred a public right to roam over common land. It is therefore worth outlining the preceding law on this and the principal issues in this chapter. Secondly, the Commons Act 2006 has both revised the registration procedures and created a new system of management for commons.

The effect of inclosure (3.4, 7.11–7.12), particularly by Act, was to convert most former common land to severalty and, by the late nineteenth century, only fragments remained, although they were still extensive. In the last quarter of that century a number of Acts were designed to protect and regulate commons. After 1876 large-scale inclosure virtually ceased. However in most parts of the country common lands were protected only by private rights. If commoners surrendered or abandoned their rights or were not prepared to defend them in court, land could still be enclosed and became in practice inclosed. Perhaps as serious were many piecemeal encroachments which eroded commons. Such public protection as there was depended largely on municipalities, some of which obtained local legislation to protect common land as an amenity, but they were exceptions. The Law of Property Act 1925, s 194 prohibited erection of a building or fence on land subject to rights of common. However erection was not an offence and if this did happen the status of the enclosed land was uncertain. Furthermore the prohibition did not apply to waste land not subject to rights of common.

By the mid-twentieth century it became apparent that the physical condition of many commons was unsatisfactory and this reflected defects in the law. Rights of common had developed to suit agricultural practices which were by then obsolete in much, although by no means all, of the country. In part this was the consequence of inclosure. There were also limited rights of public access for metropolitan commons, for commons in urban districts and for certain other commons where the landowner was willing to permit it. There was no general public right of access although, as it was unlawful under the Law of Property Act 1925, s 194 to fence a common, in practice access was difficult to prevent and there was widespread so-called de facto access. In addition, there was a movement (10.9) towards public access for fresh air and exercise.

Meanwhile many rights of common were being abandoned or lost. Although rights of common are still valuable to some farmers who could not survive without them, especially in the uplands, for many others the right served no purpose. As explained in 10.5 on enfranchisement some former copyholders surrendered their former commonable rights. In other cases, both freehold and former copyhold, those entitled to rights simply lost sight of them. Often they were not recorded on title deeds, particularly where land had been in a family for many generations and the original deeds were either lost or may not have mentioned them. If the rights were not exercised then no one might know about them.

The surrender of former rights and the lack of use by those who still had them were compounded by problems on the ground. Some commons were abandoned to scrub and encroaching woodland. Others, particularly near towns, became dumping grounds for rubbish. Where there were no enforced rights a landowner could simply enclose the land and convert it to farmland or building and, unless local opponents could prove it was common and were prepared to spare the time and energy to do so, nothing could stop him.

In 1955 the Government appointed a Royal Commission on Common Land which reported in 1958.[6] Although its recommendations were not accepted in full, the report led to a two-stage process. The first was to assess what common land remained in England and Wales and this was done by the Commons Registration Act 1965. The Act provided that all common land should be registered by (as it turned out) 1970. If that was not done then the land ceased to be common. If land was registered by mistake then its status was conclusive even if it was part of a garden or a housing estate. The Act also dealt with town and village greens as discussed in 19.7. In relation to commons the Act required to be registered both land subject to rights of common and waste of the manor not subject to such rights. The Act was not well drafted and gave rise to a great deal of litigation.

---

[6]   *Report of the Royal Commission on Common Land*, Cmnd 462 (1958).

As the first stage of a larger process, the 1965 Act was not by itself intended to alter rights, nor to create public rights, but merely to make a record of the then current situation; but its effect was to do so. If land was not registered as common it lost that status. If rights were not registered they were extinguished. If land was registered then people came to assume that even if it was not already subject to some sort of public rights it would be at some stage. In view of the confusion over the meaning of waste of the manor, discussed in 6.3, some land which ought to have been registered either was not, or was removed from the register perhaps on the basis that the lord had (prior to *Hampshire County Council v Milburn*[7]) severed the commons from the manor. The status of common land is rarely a priority for governments and it took a long time for the second stage to be put in place. However, by the end of the century public pressure had grown sufficiently for Parliament to confer a right to roam by Part 1 of the CROW Act in 2000 and for a further Commons Act in 2006.

The Act of 2006 has made substantial change to the law of commons. It provides procedures to deal with the mistaken registration of land as well as land mistakenly taken off the register. More importantly it introduces new procedures for the creation of rights of common and imposed restrictions on extinction. Part 2 of the Act introduces a new system of regulating common rights. Most of the Act is being brought into force in stages. Part 1 came into force on 1 October 2008 for seven counties, known as the pilot areas, in order to gain experience of how the new rules would work before they are extended to the country as a whole. There is a transitional period for the correction of the register which will expire in those pilot areas on 31 December 2020.[8] It appears likely that there will be an extension to further pilot areas in April 2013 but there is no timetable for the rest of the country.[9]

10.3   RIGHTS OF COMMON

There are six types of right of common: pasture, piscary, pannage, estovers, turbary and rights in the soil. Piscary is similar to sporting rights considered in 12.7. Pannage and estovers relate to woods and rights in the soil to minerals and are considered in 11.3–11.4. Turbary – the right to take turf – relates to the same sort of land as pasture but, since the rules which govern it are similar to estovers, it will be examined with them.

---

[7]   [1991] AC 235.

[8]   Commons Act 2006 (Commencement No 4 and Savings) (England) Order 2008 (SI 2008/1960), Sch 4, para 14(1).

[9]   *Hansard*, Commons Written Answers, col 654W (28 November 2011).

That leaves pasture – the right to take grass through the mouths of cattle, sheep and horses. Pasture is by far the most important right of common and many farms could not be made to pay without it. Most of the law of commons concerns pasture and it is the essential type of right of common. It is sometimes argued that the word 'pastures' in s 62(3) of the Law of Property Act 1925 carries the physical land with it. That may sometimes be so,[10] but in the context it is more likely to be an incorporeal right of pasture over the land of another person. As discussed in 9.2, s 62 is primarily concerned with incorporeal rights.

In this context the word 'common' has three separate meanings, all of which affect the law, and which overlap. It can be difficult with some writers to know in which sense they are using it and this confusion has affected the development of the law. The first meaning is as in common law, mentioned in 4.2, namely various types of right under English law as contrasted with other types and systems. Within this initial meaning there are three distinctions. The first is contrasted with custom for, as explained in 4.4, a right of common cannot be enjoyed as a customary right since it is a profit and a customary profit, enjoyed by an undefined and fluctuating class of people, would be unreasonable and bad. However, before 1926 a commonable right (10.5) could subsist by custom as it benefited a defined piece of land. The second distinction is contrasted with equity, for certain rights in land which could exist as common law rights before 1925 can now only subsist as equitable rights or interests under a trust. Such rights, although similar to rights of common, cannot be such at law. The rights of joint owners under the third meaning below are now equitable. The third distinction under common law is between rights enjoyed 'of common right', such as common appendant, and rights enjoyed by grant or prescription, such as common appurtenant (10.4).

The second meaning of common is as in community. Thus, a common innkeeper is one who is obliged (providing he has a spare room) to take in any member of the public who asks to stay at his inn and can pay. A common scold abuses everyone in the village, not just her own family. The House of Commons is the House whose members are elected to represent the communities throughout the country, as distinct from the House of Lords, whose members are summoned in their own right. Therefore, common land is sometimes seen as a communal resource, not simply a private matter. This underlies much legislation, from the Metropolitan Commons Act 1866 to the CROW Act.

---

[10]   See Coke, Sir Edward, *A commentary on Littleton being the first part of the Institutes of the Laws of England* (1628) 5b.

The third meaning is a right enjoyed in common.[11] If two or more people own land, whether a flat, house, farm or regulated pasture, they will hold the nominal titular ownership as trustees, so that if one dies the title will remain with the survivors. This is known as the legal estate or common law ownership. But the beneficial interests may be different. They can pass to the survivors, known as joint tenants in equity. Alternatively, each owner can retain his own share, give it away, sell it or leave it on his death as an interest separate from the rights of the others. This is known as a tenancy in common. Before 1926 there could be tenancies in common known as undivided shares at common law but that is no longer possible.[12] Of particular relevance to rights of common are regulated pastures and similar lands where those entitled to the grazing are also the owners of the land sharing occupation so that their beasts roam over the land. However, this is not strictly a profit, as a right of common, but simply the consequence of holding the land in undivided shares. Under the transitional provisions of the Law of Property Act 1925, Sch 1, para 1 legal title to the land is usually vested in four of the holders or sometimes in the Public Trustee. Even where the land was once within the bounds of a manor and appears to be waste the lord will in such a case have no rights, at least over the surface. In many cases graziers have assumed ownership where title can be shown to be vested in the lord, even though the freehold has no apparent value.

Brackenbank Lodge Ltd v Peart[13] concerned whether the soil of Burnhope Moor in County Durham comprising 3151 acres belonged to the lord of the manor of Stanhope or to the stint holders on the moor. There was no doubt that the stint holders had the grazing rights, but whoever owned the soil also had the right to shoot (and charge sportsmen for shooting) grouse on the moor. The case finally turned on an earlier decision of the Court of Queen's Bench in 1867, which itself turned on the interpretation of an award of 1815 under an Inclosure Act of 1799 and the title of the Bishop of Durham as lord of the manor at that time. The House examined the words of the Act and concluded that the lord still had the soil and the shooting rights.

Although by definition rights of common are enjoyed in common with others, they still subsist at common law as profits à prendre. A profit is the right to take something – such as grass, timber or sand – from the land of another. Grazing rights over the waste are typically enjoyed by several people who have similar rights over the same land in common. It is also possible for one person to own the soil but another to have exclusive freehold grazing rights, known as sole

---

[11] Bracton, Sir Henry, *De legibus et consuetudinibus angliae* (SE Thorne (ed)) (Belknap Press of Harvard University Press, 1977) (c 1257) f 222.

[12] Law of Property Act 1925, s 1(6). See also the Trusts of Land and Appointment of Trustees Act 1996.

[13] [1996] EG 134 CS.

vesture or sole herbage. Common rights of pasture are found throughout the country, although more usual in the West and especially the South West and Wales. Rights of common must be common law rights and a right of common is a freehold interest only, although leaseholders can either enjoy the benefit of a right appurtenant to a freehold[14] or have a right granted in the lease to graze in common with others over the landlord's waste as part of the landlord's surplus (10.7).

10.4 CLASSIFICATION OF RIGHTS OF COMMON

The rights are said to be of four kinds: appendant, appurtenant, in gross and pur cause de vicinage. These distinctions are now of limited relevance, however. Rights appendant and appurtenant have merged in a class of registered rights, whatever their origin. Rights in gross still exist although they cannot now be created.[15] The status of vicinage rights is obscure since straying rights may no longer be regarded as common rights in the full sense.[16]

Common appendant had to subsist before 1290 and possibly before 1189. When the lord granted by subinfeudation a new manorial arable freehold (which could not happen after 1290) it automatically carried with it a right to put out to pasture on the waste of the manor animals engaged in the arable work, namely oxen and horses to pull the plough and cattle and sheep to dung the land. Common appendant could not subsist for the benefit of meadows, or a house, although the conversion of a holding to such a use did not destroy the right. Common appendant subsisted automatically by common right as a consequence of the first grant and was limited to tenants of manors over manorial waste.[17] When, as explained in 1.6, originally land was measured in hides, which were areas of arable land, and wastes were in addition to the arable,[18] rights over the waste may automatically have been included with a grant of arable. Because this is of the very nature of a manor it may have had to subsist before 1189. Bracton, writing in the mid-thirteenth century, seems to suggest[19] that it could be granted in his time, but he uses the words *cum pertinentiis* usually (but not invariably) translated as appurtenant. However, he does distinguish[20] between common enjoyed by long use or the nature of holding in villeinage from rights of

---

14   *Hall v Moore* [2009] EWCA Civ 201.

15   Commons Act 2006, s 9.

16   But see *Dance v Savery* [2011] EWCA Civ 1250.

17   Bracton *op cit* f 230.

18   Maitland, FW, *Domesday Book and Beyond* (Cambridge University Press, 1987; first published 1897) 389.

19   Bracton *op cit* f 222b.

20   Ibid f 228b.

common created by express grant. The view of the Court of King's Bench in *Tyrringham's Case*[21] was that common appendant had to go back to 1189.

That case concerned the distinction between common appendant and common appurtenant. Common appurtenant lay in prescription or grant and did not arise automatically of common right. Grant was considered in 5.6. Prescription is a process whereby if a benefit is enjoyed for long enough it becomes a legal right. Originally it had to have been enjoyed since before 1189 but, by use of the fiction of lost modern grant, the law came to recognize shorter periods and, under the Prescription Act 1832, s 1, a right of common could formerly be acquired by unchallenged exercise for 30 years (or in some cases 60). However, prescription is no longer possible under s 6(1) of the Commons Act 2006 and the rest of s 6 lays down restrictive conditions for the express grant of new rights. Initially these apply only to the pilot areas.

The rules for common appurtenant and appendant were similar and the mediaeval writers used the same Latin word, *pertinens*, for both. However, the distinction became clear by the sixteenth century. The main difference was that if the holder of land to which a right was appurtenant acquired part of the waste over which the right was exercised then the right was completely destroyed. In the case of common appendant it continued to exist over the rest of the waste he did not own. For example, the owner of Blackacre Farm had the right to graze 20 cattle on West Down, which comprised 100 acres. He then bought the freehold of 25 acres of West Down. If his right was appurtenant, he could not graze any cattle over the remaining 75 acres. If it was appendant, he could graze 15 cattle there.

The rule may originate in the time of assarting in the thirteenth century. If a local farmer inclosed part of the common, that might be taken as satisfaction of his right just as, under the eighteenth century inclosure Acts, land was allotted for common rights. The principles are the same as for commonable rights in the sense of mutual arrangements. The rules for common appendant are much older and go back to a time when there was much more open land and less pressure on it. In *White v Taylor*[22] Buckley J considered that the explanation was that since rights appurtenant derived from a grant, or presumed prescriptive grant, they could not be apportioned because either the person entitled had what he was granted or he had nothing. He could not have something different from the grant. The same does not apply to common appendant, which is in common right not in grant.

---

[21]   (1584) 6 Co Rep 36b, 76 ER 973.

[22]   [1969] 1 Ch 150, [1967] 3 All ER 349.

In *Tyrringham's Case*[23] in 1584 Thomas Tyrringham was freeholder of a house, meadow, pasture and 44 acres of arable land at Titchmersh in Northamptonshire. He had rights of common over 30 acres of land belonging to John Pickering and over 40 acres belonging to Boniface Pickering. Boniface then purchased Tyrringham's 44 acres and other land and let them to Mr Pheasant. (The lease may have been a procedural device to use the action of ejectment.) Pheasant put two cows on the land of John but John's lessee, Mr Salmon, with a small dog, *leviter et molliter*, lightly and gently (thus doing no harm to the cows) drove them off. Pheasant sued Salmon though really it seems to have been a dispute between Tyrringham and the Pickering brothers. The court held that common appendant could only relate to arable land, and indeed to land anciently arable, and not to meadow or pasture or a house. In this case the right was claimed to benefit the house, pasture and meadow and so it could only be appurtenant. (There could be common appendant to a manor because the demesnes were presumed to be arable.) Consequently, as Boniface was the freeholder both of the 40 acres and of the 44 acres that had previously belonged to Tyrringham, that unity destroyed the right of common appurtenant not only over his 40 acres but also over John's 30 acres.

The law remained the same at least until 1967. In *White v Taylor*[24] in 1967 Mr White and a number of others sued Mr Taylor in an action relating to common land at Fordingbridge in Hampshire. White, who had held a right appurtenant over the common land, had purchased part of it and the court held that the consequence was to destroy his common right. However, the effect of registration under the Commons Registration Act 1965 was to abolish the distinction. If a right of common was registered for the benefit of any land and the registration became final, it now subsists by virtue of being on the register, irrespective of its origin. The register is final and conclusive evidence of the rights of the person registered although it may be possible to challenge the extent of the rights. Although s 18(5) of the 2006 Act provides that there may be constraints on the exercise of a right of common which is not mentioned in the register,[25] complete extinction is rules out by s 13(3) which prevents extinction of registered rights at common law.

Paragraph 97 of the explanatory notes to the Commons Bill when it was introduced into Parliament said of what is now s 18:

> Subsection (5) preserves what is believed to be the present position under the 1965 Act, which is that, where a right of common is subject to any customary constraint not mentioned in the register (for example, that the rights may be exercised only at

---

[23] (1584) 6 Co Rep 36b, 76 ER 973.

[24] [1969] 1 Ch 150, [1967] 3 All ER 349.

[25] See *Dance v Savery* [2011] EWCA Civ 1250 at [68].

certain times of the year, that stock should be hefted in accordance with local custom, or that the times at which stock may be turned out are to be determined by a manorial or other ancient court), those constraints are preserved notwithstanding that they are not mentioned in the commons registers.

The third type of right of common is a right in gross which, unlike rights appendant or appurtenant, is not attached to land. While, before registration under the Act of 1965 rights attached to land could be for an uncertain number of beasts (provided the land to which the rights belonged was defined), it was essential that the number of beasts which could be pastured under a right in gross be specified otherwise the person having the right could, by increasing the numbers, consume all the grass on the subject land. Under s 15 of the 1965 Act holders of all rights had to state the number of their animals and the effect of registration was that they could graze no more than a maximum of that number.

One issue was whether this change also affected rights determined by levancy and couchancy. Before 1965 many grazing rights were determined by the capacity of the dominant farm and the farmer could only put out on the common in the spring such a number of beasts as his farm could support in the winter either standing up (*levant*) or lying down (*couchant*). The number of beasts was therefore undefined or *sans nombre*. If the effect of the quantification was to convert rights *sans nombre* into ascertained rights then the established law was that they could be severed from the land and converted to rights in gross. In subsequent years many rights formerly attached to land were sold off to owners of herds who wished to build up their stocking rights on common land.

This was confirmed by the House of Lords decision in *Bettison v Langton*.[26] In that case Mrs Langton was the owner of Sina Farm on the edge of Bodmin Moor in Cornwall with rights of grazing, originally determined by levancy and couchancy over the moor. In 1987 she sold her grazing rights to Mr and Mrs Bettison but retained ownership of the farm. In 1988 she mortgaged the farm to a bank and in 1994 the bank sold the farm to Mr and Mrs Penter. They claimed the grazing rights on the ground that it was not legally possible to sever levancy and couchancy rights from the land. The House of Lords held that the effect of the 1965 Act, by requiring all rights of common to be quantified, was to convert them from rights without number into ascertained rights and therefore they could be severed and sold as a separate right to been enjoyed in gross. Around Dartmoor this had already been a serious problem and it was prohibited by the Dartmoor Commons Act 1985. The Commons Act 2006, s 9 has now extended this to the whole country and, with limited exceptions, the most important of which is that a freeholder can grant the grazing rights temporarily by lease,[27]

---

[26]   [2002] 1 AC 27.

[27]   Commons (Severance of Rights) Order 2006 (SI 2006/2145).

rights can no longer be severed. Any rights now subsisting in gross will remain as such but they can be attached to land, in which case they cannot thereafter be severed.

The final type of right of common is not really a right at all but an immunity. A right pur cause de vicinage means that if cattle can lawfully be put on the common of one manor[28] and stray onto another they cannot be turned off. This is a practical matter since open lands are not enclosed and there is no barrier to straying; indeed, it would now be unlawful to erect one. The rights are mutual so that if the tenants of the manor of Easton have vicinage over North Down belonging to Norton, the tenants of Norton will have a corresponding right over East Down belonging to Easton. Many vicinage rights may have derived from a time when what was a single manor, with its wastes, was divided (either before 1290 or between co-parceners) but the cattle continued to wander where they had always been. It was not a true right in the sense of corresponding to a duty and the owner of the subject land could exclude it. If the tenants of Norton agreed to inclose North Down (when it could still be done) the tenants of Easton could not stop them (which they could if they had a true right) although it would be up to the owners of the inclosed pieces of North Down to put up fences to stop the straying. Some vicinage rights appear to have been registered as straying rights and have been interpreted as rights to graze on the second common beasts which had lawful rights on the first. Such rights have been upheld as substantive but not independent rights.[29]

10.5 COMMONABLE RIGHTS

Certain rights falling short of rights of common were known as commonable. These are now largely obsolete. The word has several meanings. Sometimes it is incorrectly used, even in legal writings, as a synonym for common. There are two principal usages.

One was the customary right of a copyholder to graze or enjoy other rights on the lord's waste. As the freehold of both the waste and the copyhold were vested in the lord and a person could not have a right over his own land this could not be a right of common; but since the law recognised that it was a right it was called commonable. Under the Law of Property Act 1922, Sch 12, para (4) and its predecessors any such right was preserved on enfranchisement. That paragraph does not actually convert it to a right of common but said that it should continue (presumably as a commonable right) attached to the

---

[28] Bracton *op cit* f 230.

[29] *Dance v Savery* [2011] EWCA Civ 1250.

enfranchised land. In practice, after 1925 many lords and former copyholders often agreed under s 138(12) that the grazing rights of the tenant were no longer required and they were released as part of the terms of extinction of manorial incidents. This contributed to the loss of rights over manorial waste which led to the Royal Commission on Common land and the 1965 Act. Where the rights continued to be exercised they should have been registered under the 1965 Act and have become conclusive as freehold rights of common. The effect of s 1(2)(b) of the 1965 Act is to extinguish unregistered rights of common.[30] The section does not state that it also extinguishes commonable rights but it would probably be construed to do so.[31]

The other principal meaning of commonable concerned open fields where there was a mutual practice of letting beasts graze across the whole field made up of strips. Commonable rights or intercommoning in this sense was similar to vicinage. In open fields without hedges it was impracticable to prevent beasts straying over the common (communal) fields. These contained strips belonging not only to several common freehold proprietors but also to different manors and their customary tenants. This was unlike the waste which belonged to, and was used by the tenants of, one manor. Accordingly, grazing in the common fields was under the jurisdiction of the court leet, which served the community, not the manor courts. This intercommoning was by mutual tolerance and subsisted as a practice, not by right. Consequently, if one tenant consolidated a number of strips and enclosed them within a fence he was entitled to exclude his neighbours' beasts, but in return his beasts could not graze the strips of others.[32] The principles are similar to common appurtenant on waste.

It was possible to have a true right of common over common fields. The equivalent rights in France were known as *vaine pâture* and in Germany as *Feldgraswirtschaft*, and on the Continent these were widespread legal rights.[33] Their usual absence in England meant that inclosure of the open fields was easier and took place earlier. There were two types of right of common in open fields in England. One was shack, often seen as similar to a vicinage right,[34] where the class of commoners was the same as the class of owners of the strips in the field, and is not often found outside Norfolk. The other concerned Lammas lands which are fields in which other persons have the right to graze

---

[30] *Oxfordshire County Council v Oxford City Council* [2006] 2 AC 674 at [18]. This was a case on greens, but the same logic applies to rights of common.

[31] See *ADM Milling Ltd v Tewkesbury Town Council* [2011] EWHC 595 (Ch) at [64].

[32] Note to *Cheesman v Hardham* (1818) 1 B & A 706 at 712, 106 ER 260 at 262.

[33] See Jones, P, 'Medieval Society in its Prime: Italy' in Postan, MM (ed), *The Cambridge Economic History of Europe Vol 1* (Cambridge University Press, 2nd edn, 1965) 368.

[34] *Sir Miles Corbet's Case* (1584) 7 Co Rep 5a, 77 ER 417.

their cattle after Lammas Day, 1 August, until Lady Day, 25 March next following. Lammas rights are also sometimes referred to as commonable.

It follows that the open fields could either be common or commonable. The expression 'open field' was widely used in legal texts, including in many judgments,[35] but it does not seem to have become a term of art. It was also used in various statutes, mainly inclosure but also public statutes.[36] The meaning of commonable seems also to have varied according to the context.[37]

The word also applies to commonable animals which are those, typically sheep, cattle and horses (but sometimes also goats, pigs or geese) which can lawfully be put out to graze. Rights can exist in relation to other beasts such as goats and geese but not for exotic animals such as alpacas. Pigs were normally not commonable in the context of the right of pasture as they had a separate right of pannage. This can vary from place to place so that it is said that in the New Forest commonable animals comprise ponies, cattle, donkeys and mules and only rarely sheep, with pigs having a separate right of mast.

10.6   LOT MEADOWS AND REGULATED PASTURES

A special type of movable freehold resembles a common right and indeed, in the Inclosure Act 1845, s 11, this is defined as 'lot meadows and other lands the occupation or enjoyment of the separate lots or parcels of which is subject to interchange among the respective owners in any known course of rotation'. For many purposes this is equated with common land but legally it is distinct. It is also sometimes called commonable. Meadows were a special type of land, irrigated either by a natural watercourse or artificially. The grass was of good quality and meadows were a valuable asset. One of the ways they were shared out was by dividing up the ownership annually. Every year (or sometimes every few years) the portions of the meadow would be reallocated between the right holders, usually by drawing lots to decide who would have which piece. They were therefore known generally as lot meadows although there were many local terms such as beast leazes in Somerset. In *Welden v Bridgewater*[38] Mr Welden was lord of the manor of Paunchborn. The manor included a meadow called Wide Meadow comprising 80 acres. There was a long-standing practice of

---

[35]   *The Company of Proprietors of the Grand Union Canal v Ashby* (1861) 6 Hurl & Norm 394, 158 ER 162; *Cheesman v Hardham* (1818) 1 B & A 706, 106 ER 260.

[36]   For example 6 & 7 Will 4 c 115 Inclosure of Open and Arable Fields in England and Wales Act 1836.

[37]   *ADM Milling Ltd v Tewkesbury Town Council* [2011] EWHC 595 (Ch): land subject to sole vesture or sole herbage.

[38]   (1591) Cro, Eliz 421, 78 ER 662. See also Coke on *Littleton op cit* 4a, 48b.

allotting the meadow in portions of 18 acres to the various lot holders and Welden apparently shared in the process, presumably along with other holders. Mr Bridgewater took some of the grass. It is possible that Welden was chosen to represent the lot holders because he was also lord. He sued for trespass and the defendant argued that the right he had was only that of a profit à prendre not a freehold. The court held that he did indeed have a freehold right although one that moved every time the lot was held.

Similarly, many pastures were owned collectively by the graziers, sometimes known as gated or stinted pastures. The expression can refer either to pure rights of common or to a situation where the rights also carry the freehold. As the grazing usually accounted for the whole value of the land, many lords regarded their residual interest in the freehold as negligible and effectively abandoned it to the right holders. However, sometimes new values appeared, such as mineral rights or sporting (as in *Brakenbank Lodge Ltd v Peart*[39]). It can often be a fine point whether the freehold is vested in the right holders. Under the Commons Registration Act 1965 not only did rights of common have to be registered but so also did the freehold where the owner was known.

There remain many varieties of communal ownership of pasture. The Commons Registration Act 1965 treats as common land many such cases even though not common in the sense of being subject to rights of common over land owned by another. Some land, known as beastgates, cattlegates, leaze land or regulated pastures under the inclosure Acts, are within the 1965 Act even though in those cases, like shack lands, the group of graziers is the same as the owners of the freehold. The freehold was held by them as tenants in common at common law before 1926 and subsequently by trustees (10.4). In addition, different types of land are held by churchwardens or other trustees on public trusts for the use of all or some of the local inhabitants. Such land may derive from a purchase of the manorial rights or the waste from the lord by the homage acting collectively through trustees.

10.7   RIGHTS OF THE LORD

The foregoing sections have concentrated on rights of the tenants against the lord because the waste belonged to him. He would share in commonable rights in the common fields if he still had strips, but often the lord's strips were the first to be inclosed.

---

[39]   [1966] NPC 124.

He might have rights known as foldcourse or foldage. Foldage was the right, once found on the sandy lands of East Anglia and now long obsolete, for the lord to require the tenants to pasture their sheep on his land to manure it. It was generally resented as a harsh privilege.[40] Foldcourse is the right to feed sheep on the land of another and is sometimes called sheepwalk. In practice it is now no different from a normal profit or right of common, save that it has no reference to arable land and the rules of levancy and couchancy do not apply.

In modern times the lord is not necessarily the owner of the waste but many older laws assume that he is, and interpretation can be difficult if he is not. The owner of the soil, whether or not the lord, may wish to take the grass either for his own beasts or to sell to another grazier. Important issues can arise as to whether this is possible. The law has become complicated by two factors. First, there is the theory (which does not correspond to historic facts) that all manorial tenancies were originally granted by the lord and accordingly that the rules against derogating from that grant apply. Thus, there may be a presumption that commoners have first call on the grass and the lord comes in only after they are satisfied. This idea does not work well in practice and can be unfair. Secondly, this has to some extent been overcome by the modern rules on registration.

On some wastes the lord was excluded altogether even if his right to the soil was not challenged. The grazing might be stinted or shared out exclusively in some way between tenants of the manor or independent freeholders who could dispose of all the grass. Assuming that that did not apply, the position, at least before the 1965 Act, was as follows. The first call was for freeholders who had rights of common. Their rights might be defined by number, which was necessarily so if they were in gross and could be so even if they were appurtenant.[41] Alternatively, they might be variable, specifically if they were by levancy and couchancy.

After or perhaps equally with them were commonable rights formerly attributable to copyholds and which were preserved on enfranchisement. Before 1926 the fee in the copyhold was held by or in the lord and so the right of the copyholder could not be a legal right at common law but could only be enjoyed as attached to the customary holding. On a voluntary enfranchisement those rights were extinguished unless the lord expressly granted them in fee to the tenant, in which case they would in theory be new rights and so postponed to the rights of the existing commoners so that if there was not enough grass the enfranchised tenant would lose out. On a statutory enfranchisement s 22 of the

---

40 Maitland *op cit* 76.

41 *Bettison v Langton* [2002] 1 AC 27.

Copyhold Act 1894 or para (4) of Sch 12 to the Law of Property Act 1922 expressly preserved the commonable rights. If on enfranchisement the copyholders and the lord agreed to exclude the rights in order to reduce the compensation, and if there were no freehold commoners, the lord then had an unencumbered right to the waste, which he could enclose. If preserved and still exercised commonable rights had by 1965 become indistinguishable from freehold rights.

After allowing for these independent rights, there were and indeed still are leasehold grazing rights of farm tenants of the lord. *Owen v Blathwayt*[42] concerned a private piece of land called Porlock Common which was not registered as common and indeed had been inclosed in 1878. It had then been grazed by four adjacent farms. One of the farms was sold in 1954 to Mr Owen's parents together with a right to graze on the land in common with the other three farms. At the time of the case the farms were still owned by Mr Blathwayt and each was subject to a farm tenancy. In 1992 English Nature imposed restrictions on the amount of stock that could be grazed and the issue was whether Owen, as having a separate freehold right, could put out the full number of sheep under the terms of the 1954 sale or whether his rights abated in proportion to those of the tenant farmers. Neuberger J held that the grazing should abate proportionately because the rights were in common. While the facts of the case were special it is likely that the same principles would apply to common land.

There are then rights which were once independent but had subsequently been acquired by the lord. He might have purchased a freehold with common rights or have taken a surrender of copyhold land with commonable rights, or the rights could have come in by escheat. It is likely that such rights would be treated as having merged with the fee simple and extinguished. The lord might also have put out beasts to graze from his own in hand demesne farms. Finally, there could be a surplus, available after all the commoners had been satisfied. In law it seems that all of these were regarded as being postponed to the rights of others. The lord took the benefit of any surplus after independent rights were satisfied and therefore took the risk that they might exhaust the capacity of the common. In practice things may have been different since, where a lord made regular use of the common, it would be difficult to penalise him if the weather was bad and the grass did not grow.

Sometimes the matter has been resolved by the 1965 Act as in many parts of the country farm tenants of an estate, which also included the common, registered rights over their landlord's waste. Strictly they have no better right than the lord

---

[42]   [2002] 1 P&CR 444.

because a person cannot have a right over his own land, and the farmers' grazing rights derived from their landlord. In addition, the lord may have registered rights for the benefit of his own home farm. Many such registrations were not opposed and therefore became final even though strictly they were not rights of common. There are indeed some commons whose only registered rights are those of leaseholders and the owner. The land is correctly registered but as waste land of the manor not as land subject to rights of common. Where there are independent commoners it is probable (although the point has not been decided) that the registered rights of the lord and his leaseholders would rank along with them as the register is, by statute, conclusive.

There remains the true surplus which is not enjoyed with any farm and which the lord could use in any way he wished. Often he did so by letting the agistment, granting a shepherd or cowherd the right to put on the common any beasts of other owners for hire. Rights attached to farms whether appendant or appurtenant could not be let separately from the holding and could only be used for beasts kept on it, but lords could authorise anyone to have the agistment of the common and take the surplus grazing which would vary from year to year. If the only right of common was pasture of tenants of the manor then, under the Commons Act 1236 (often called the Statute of Merton), the lord could approve the surplus by inclosing part of the common provided he left enough pasture for the needs of the commoners. However, this right was always of very limited scope and subject to many restrictions. Bracton states[43] that this was so from the beginning. Approvement was abolished by s 47 of the Commons Act 2006. In September 2008 the Department for the Environment, Farming and Rural Affairs consulted on a number of issues affecting common rights and question 5 concerned the treatment of the landowner's surplus. The conclusion issued in February 2010 was that the surplus should only be subject to management by the commoners council with the landowner's consent.

10.8   REGULATION

The main function of common land remains the feeding of livestock. Where farmers have valuable rights to use a shared asset there is always a possibility of abuse by someone seeking to gain more than his share or being careless about putting diseased or vicious animals on the common. Regulation is required to prevent overgrazing, to control indiscriminate breeding by entire (uncastrated) male animals, to regulate the burning of bracken and other growths and to

---

[43]   Bracton *op cit* f 227b-8.

prevent unlawful inclosure. In modern times new controls have been introduced, for example to ensure that only cattle that are accredited as free of brucellosis are pastured, or (in the New Forest and on Dartmoor) to preserve the native stock of ponies from interbreeding with other lines. An important issue is also the availability of grants and subsidies for environmental controls. On private land these are paid to the farmer but on commons the law has had to develop sophisticated ways to divide up the payments between the lord or owner of the common and the commoners.

The principal control in the past has been on overgrazing, by farmers tempted to put out more animals than the grass can feed. Traditionally, two approaches were used. One was by stinting, which attributes to a defined (usually small) number of commoners the right to graze a specific number of beasts. Stinting tends to lead to one of two results. Either it becomes a right in gross which can be sold apart from the land to which it was originally appurtenant and often such rights accumulate in a few hands; alternatively, the soil of the common becomes treated as belonging to the owners of the stints, to the exclusion of the lord. Such commons are known as gated and stinted.

The other control was formerly by the rule of levancy and couchancy. During the registration period under the 1965 Act some graziers registered far greater numbers than their holdings could support (even with modern feedstuffs) and many such registrations, being unchallenged, have become final. As mentioned above it appears from *Bettison v Langton* that the rules of levancy and couchancy have disappeared. This is of course relevant to the amount of the lord's surplus.

Regulation was originally carried out by the manor court for manorial commons and by the court leet for commonable lands and, to this day, it is the main function of some of those few courts that survive. However, most such courts have long ceased to operate and even where they are preserved they can no longer exercise a legal jurisdiction so they cannot fine offenders or re-order them to remove animals (13.4). Although rights of common subsist at common law the regulation of those rights can be made by custom and supervised by the customary court.[44] In practice many commons are now regulated by more-or-less informal arrangements between a small group of professional farmers, but such arrangements are not legally binding. In *Hall v Moore*[45] a commoners committee had agreed that the commoners at Luckwards Hill, Powick, Worcestershire would not exercise certain rights. The Court of Appeal held that

---

44   *Follet v Troake* (1705) 2 Ld Raym 1186, 92 ER 284.

45   [2009] EWCA Civ 201, [2009] All ER (D) 235.

such a commitment by an informal body was not binding on someone who had a legal right of common. The extent of the committee's abilities was to make voluntary arrangements for the proper running of the common but it had no power to override private rights.

Powers are available under the Commons Act 1876 for holders of the majority in value of the rights in regulated pastures to make byelaws, but under s 15 the consent of the lord of the manor is required, apparently even if he does not own the surface of the common. On other commons the graziers generally can make regulations in relation to entire animals under the Commons Act 1908 without such consent. Any remaining common fields can be regulated under the Inclosure Act 1773 and parts of the Act (for example turning out of rams) also apply to wastes. However, all of these powers are limited either in scope or by geography. Various provisions can also be found in local acts and a comprehensive regulation system is in force for Dartmoor under the Dartmoor Commons Act 1985.

Until recently, there was no national system for regulating commons. Accordingly, Part 2 of the Commons Act 2006 contains detailed provisions to establish commons councils with statutory powers of management. They are based on the experience of Dartmoor. Councils will be responsible under s 31 of the 2006 Act for management of agricultural activities, vegetation and rights of common. The Act gives councils powers to establish and maintain boundaries and remove unlawful ones. There are also powers to limit or impose conditions on the exercise not only of rights of common but also the exercise of rights of surplus. A standard constitution is laid down in regulations.[46] However, s 33 provides in effect that a council will need the consent of the owner of the common to do anything other than those things which might already by law be done by commoners without consent. Thus, councils will not be able to plant tree breaks or put up even temporary fencing without permission. The procedure is to serve formal notice on the owner (if known) and, if he does not object, he is treated as consenting. If he is not known then the notice must be posted on the common.

10.9   PUBLIC ACCESS AND CONSERVATION

It will be evident that common lands, in the sense of lands subject to rights of common, are not common in the sense of belonging in any way to the community. They are private lands, typically belonging to the lord, subject to

---

[46]   Commons Councils (Standard Constitution) (England) Regulations 2010 (SI 2010/1204).

rights of tenants of the manor and their successors. Nevertheless, in modern times common land has been seen as a communal asset and it is this that underlay the vision in the Report of the Royal Commission on Common Lands that led to the Commons Registration Act 1965 and, more recently, the CROW Act. Communal access has a long history. This applies not only to common land and open country but also to town and village greens (19.6).

Where there are no fences it is impractical to prevent people from going on to land. One early distinction between closes and open fields was that the close was regarded as private and indeed had its own remedy in the action of trespass *quare clausum fregit*, 'because he has broken into the close', although in time this remedy was also extended to disputes over strips in fields. For many centuries anyone had access to open fields or waste without hindrance, although in practice that meant local people. However, by the late nineteenth century several factors combined to put this on to a formal footing. One was the loss of such lands by inclosure. Another was the desire of town-dwellers to get out to the country for air and exercise coupled with the freedom to do so quickly and easily on the railways. Another was what we would call a conservation movement which wished to preserve open spaces for public amenity.

As London grew the nearby ancient commons came to be used in the same way as village greens – for recreation rather than livestock. Well-known commons such as those of Clapham, Tooting Bec and Wimbledon as well as Hampstead Heath became places for public enjoyment. In 1866 Parliament passed the Metropolitan Commons Act which allowed local authorities to make schemes to manage those commons within the Metropolitan Police District (which is slightly larger than Greater London), to preserve order and prevent nuisances. Bylaws regulated matters such as playing golf and making speeches. Although the lord of the manor could promote a scheme, he had no veto. In theory a scheme could not affect his rights, but in practice the existence of a scheme meant that the main value – of being able to buy out a limited number of commoners and then use the land for building – was gone.

The 1866 Act did not apply to the rest of England. Around the country many municipalities followed suit with their own local schemes. Some acquired areas of land either as parks or as areas of common and obtained local acts of Parliament which conferred a right of access on inhabitants of the borough, although in practice it could be enjoyed by anyone.

In 1876 Parliament passed the Commons Act which applied to all common land throughout the country. It allowed schemes for regulation which could, among other things, secure that there should be free public access to any particular points of view, or that remains of historical interest were to be preserved, or reserving a privilege of playing games, perhaps for the local golf club. However, applications for orders could only be made by people whose interests totalled at least one third in value of the interests in the common and in particular, where the interest of the lord was likely to be affected, he was entitled to compensation. Furthermore, under s 12(5) the lord's consent was needed if the land belonged to the manor (but not, apparently, if it merely happened to be held by the same person who was also lord if it had become severed from the manor). The Commons Act 1899 gives district councils power to make regulations within former urban districts, but either the lord of the manor (or owner of the soil) or one third of the persons interested in the common can veto it. As a result while this Act was used in some cases it did not affect the bulk of common land across the country.

Section 193 of the Law of Property Act 1925 conferred on members of the public a right of access for taking air and exercise to any common land which, before local government reorganisation in 1974, was within a borough or urban district, subject to similar regulation powers as under earlier Acts. The lord of the manor or owner of the soil of other common land could confer a public right of access anywhere in the country even if the commoners objected.

The commons of the North Country were seen as a valuable means of recreation for those who lived in industrial towns. Many landowners resented this, either as infringing their privacy or as damaging grouse moors and disturbing game. The conflict between sporting rights and recreation came to a head in the famous mass trespass at Kinder Scout on 24 April 1932 by some 400 members of the Lancashire Branch of the British Workers Sports Federation. The trespassers were opposed by landowners and their gamekeepers and the trespass led to imprisonment for some of the leaders. The event raised emotions and it became a political imperative to demand a right to roam over open country.[47] The first response of Parliament was the Access to Mountains Act 1939 which provided a mechanism whereby a minister, on application, could make an order for a public right of access during the daytime to mountain, moor, heath, down or cliff. The owner did not have a veto as such but in practice the Act was a dead letter because s 3(5)(c) provided that if the minister considered that the order would cause material depreciation of the value of the land or material loss or damage to the owner or occupier and it was not practicable to prevent it then he must not make the order. As any public access reduces the privacy of the land and affects its value any objection was fatal. However, the Act did produce a form of words which have influenced subsequent legislation.

---

[47] Hey, D, 'Kinder Scout and the legend of the Mass Trespass' (2011) 59(2) *Agricultural History Review* 199.

In 1949 the Labour Government passed the National Parks and Access to the Countryside Act which was intended to allow for public access to open country as mountain, moor, heath and down. The Act authorised the owner of open land (whether or not subject to common rights or waste of the manor) to make an access agreement with the county council, but very few were made.[48] A backup provision for compulsory access orders was little used because landowners were entitled to compensation. It is said that only two compulsory access orders have ever been made under the 1949 Act, one relating to a private beach at Seaton in south Cornwall and the other covering moorland at Wolf Fell in Lancashire.[49] In addition, in the light of the then perceived need to protect agriculture, as any public access might disturb grazing sheep, access rights were limited. Although, therefore, the Act had some impact in encouraging attitudes to access, it did not meet the needs which had been so strongly expressed in 1932. When the CROW Act came into force these corresponding provisions of the 1949 Act were not repealed and remain in force. This may be because the few agreements and orders that remain need a framework to govern them. It might have simplified the law to rescind them but as it is there are two parallel systems, albeit one of them is little used.

There were other arrangements for access. The Dartmoor Commons Act 1985 conferred a public right over Dartmoor. The Act specifically preserved the rights of lords of manors (of which there are many – and active – around the edges of the moor) but such rights are now of little value. Many amenity bodies own common land or waste. Some, such as the National Trust, have powers to make byelaws governing access. Local authorities have acquired much common land. There are also innumerable small local trusts, established both for public enjoyment and for conservation, which encourage or permit access.

The CROW Act provided for a public right of access over land mapped as mountain, moor, heath and down. Of more relevance to manors the right also extends to any land registered as common land (not village greens) under the 1965 Act. Originally this applied to all land registered at the date of the Act but, as the Commons Act 2006 amended the rules to make deregistration more difficult, this was also changed so that it applies only to land registered for the time being.

The provisions are detailed and are fully discussed in specialist books. This account needs only to refer to issues relevant to manors. The legislation provides that any member of the public who comes on to access land for

---

[48] 'Very few access agreements were made under the 1949 Act': Select Committee on Environment, Food and Rural Affairs Ninth Report, 14 July 2008, para 8.

[49] Shoard, M, *A Right to Roam: Should We Open Up Britain's Countryside* (Oxford University Press, 1999); but see Hey *op cit* 215.

recreation will not be regarded as a trespasser so long as he observes certain simple conditions such as not damaging the land. There is, as indicated, a mass of detail to protect the environment and safeguard private activities.

The general rule is that access exists over all registered common land, but there are exceptions. First, the right does not apply where there is already a right of public access under some other provision set out in s 15. This refers to s 193, schemes under the Commons Act 1899 and local Acts (but s 15(2) enlarges the right of local inhabitants to one for the public generally), access agreements or orders under the 1949 Act, and access to ancient monuments under the Ancient Monuments and Archaeological Areas Act 1979.

Secondly, the right does not apply to certain types of land described in Sch 1 known as excepted land. This includes land under cultivation, land used as a park or garden, quarries, golf courses, and a number of other heads. Little common land is now cultivated but many quarries have been dug in common or waste land and several golf courses have been created on commons. Thirdly, the landowner may exclude public access for certain limited times under s 22 for limited periods of up to 28 days in any year but not on most weekends in the summer. This may be relevant for instance if the landowner wishes to have a shoot over a grouse moor. Other exclusions apply to land management, nature conservation, in case of emergency and so on.

Initially, many landowners were opposed to the idea of compulsory access over open country but this opposition has largely died down and the right has become accepted. In part this is because most of the land involved is of little use or value; often it was already crossed by public footpaths and indeed there had been so-called de facto access for many years. Landowners had therefore been vulnerable to a claim for damages under the Occupiers Liability Acts 1957 and 1984 if someone was injured by the condition of the land. It is not clear who is the occupier of waste (6.3) but in the absence of any other occupier there was risk that the owner might be regarded as being in occupation. Section 13 therefore largely excludes this risk. It still remains, however, for land already subject to access under s 15. If for example a lord owns common land where a predecessor had voluntarily conferred a right of access under the Law of Property Act 1925, s 193, that will remain in force and there is no provision in s 193 corresponding to s 13 of the CROW Act. It would therefore be prudent to revoke the voluntary access right and rely instead on the CROW Act right.

The right of access is being extended, with modifications, to a coastal strip under Part 9 of the Marine and Coastal Access Act 2009. This will generally involve private land, but it includes foreshore, much of which belongs to lords of coastal manors. The provisions are not automatic and each stretch of coast is being separately considered by Natural England the responsible agency and it is likely to take many years before rights are in place around the whole of the coast.

Since common land is not intensively farmed or treated with sprays or fertilisers it tends to retain ecological value, for instance as having unusual types of grass or insects. Where it comprises stretches of open country, especially in hill or mountain districts, it can also have landscape value. Much of the land in National Parks is common. These aspects are now recognised as important in their own right and have attracted their own statutory protection. The relevant provisions are extensive and do not directly affect the manor but they can materially restrict any changes the owner of common land might wish to make.

Chapter 11

Minerals and Timber

mines, minerals, quarries, furzes, trees, woods, underwoods, coppices

11.1   NATURE OF RIGHTS TO WOOD AND MINERALS

Trees and minerals in the ground are part of the land and therefore automatically pass with the surface on sale or inheritance unless there are specific provisions to separate the legal ownership. Both may be physically severed by felling the timber (or cutting branches) or digging the minerals, in which case a new piece of property in the wood, coal, ore or stone arises. Such property will be regarded as being owned as a chattel by the first person to take it – normally the woodsman, miner or their employer. Such rights are valuable and, in the context of the manor, developed special rules.

In former times minerals and timber were seen as similar and in many respects the rights attached to them are comparable. Both were seen to be products of the soil. A tree will grow larger over the centuries and minerals will become workable or new types of mineral may become valuable. The felling of trees and working of minerals both constituted waste that is a material change in land. This could work to the detriment of a future owner. The doctrine of waste applies to other changes such as erecting or demolishing a building and is often encountered in the context of settlements. Where land was held by a tenant for life with the remainder vested in some other person such as a son or cousin the remainderman had the power to prevent the tenant for life from committing waste. This could be a source of tension in families.

When a lease was granted it was often implied that it did not carry the right to work minerals or fell timber as that would be waste. Occasionally it could go further and imply an exception to the landlord, although that is not so under the modern law. Likewise clear rules applied to copyholds. Thus, in *Eardley v*

Granville[1] (discussed in 11.7) Sir George Jessel MR, in considering the respective rights of lord and tenant in copyhold land, held that the estate of a copyholder includes all the soil except timber-trees and minerals:

> As regards the trees and minerals, the property remains in the lord, but, in the absence of custom, he cannot get either the one or the other, so that the minerals must remain unworked, and the trees must remain uncut. The possession is in the copyholder; the property is in the lord ... The same rule applies to minerals as to trees. If you once cut down the tree, the lord cannot compel the copyholder to plant another. The latter has a right to the soil of the copyhold where the tree stood, including the stratum of air which is now left vacant by reason of the removal of the tree.

Rights to minerals were the most contentious and litigated aspect of manorial law because substantial values were at stake. Some disputes concerned the rights of copyholders and commoners to minerals in the lord's waste. Others involved the lord's rights to minerals in copyhold land and that is reflected in current issues. Under the transitional provisions of the Land Registration Act 2002 many of these rights could be at risk unless protected before the first registration or disposition of land after 12 October 2013. This chapter therefore sets out the issues in some detail. It needs to be read with the discussion of the nature of manorial rights in 9.3 and with the analysis of the 2002 Act in 25.9–25.10 and some of the same issues apply as to sporting rights in 12.4.

Copyholders had a general duty to the lord not to commit waste. The origin lies in the nature of unfree land. Villeins, the predecessors of pure copyholders, had both a duty and a right to remain on and cultivate their holdings, to live in their homes and to keep them in good order. Their purpose and needs were agricultural and they were concerned with crops and animals. Other things were not their business and, like everything in the manor that was not specifically appropriated, these belonged to the lord. Therefore, the lord had the property in the minerals that lay under the land and in the trees that grew on it. However, the copyholder had possession[2] of the land. He could refuse access to anyone, even (in the absence of special custom) the lord, and anyone who tried to burrow under his copyhold or move among the trees above it was a trespasser.

The lord, as owner, had the right to minerals and timber on his own property both demesne and waste, although on the waste he could not exercise his rights so as to interfere with rights of common. The inclosure legislation contains a good deal of material about the lord's rights but much of that is now obsolete because opening a new quarry[3] or establishing a new plantation will involve

---

[1]   (1876) 3 Ch D 826.

[2]   Scriven, J, *A Treatise on the Law of Copyholds* (Butterworth & Co, 7th edn by Archibald Brown, 1896) 194.

[3]   Mines and Quarries Act 1954, s 151.

fencing off the land and that can only be done with the consent of the Secretary of State under the Commons Act 2006, s 38 (formerly the Law of Property Act 1925, s 194). The general rule apart from that is that the lord can (subject to planning consent) take minerals by underground workings, and small quarries or coppices are usually tolerated by the commoners provided their interests are not harmed. Indeed, a cluster of trees may give shelter to grazing animals.

11.2 TREES

The lord's customary right of property in timber on copyhold land was abolished by the Law of Property Act 1922.[4] Under Sch 13, Part II, para 12 to the Act compensation was equal to the full value where there was a special custom for the lord to enter the land and take the timber; otherwise compensation was one half of that value. Timber means trees fit for building and repairing houses. Oak, ash and elm are timber by common law or general custom throughout the country provided they are at least six inches in diameter or two feet in circumference and at least 20 years old. In some parts of the country special rules apply in relation to trees such as birch in Yorkshire and willows in Hampshire. In some localities horse-chestnut, lime, beech, asp, walnut and even cherry can be timber, although fruit trees are not usually included.[5]

The effect of the old custom of timber was unfortunate. It was said that 'the oak scorns to grow but on free land', not from any special freedom-loving quality of oaks but because where an acorn began to sprout or a sapling to grow on unfree land it was against the interests of the copyholder. He would be excluded from an ever-expanding area of this land as the girth of the tree increased, perhaps for centuries, with no power to cut or remove it. Thus saplings tended to disappear before they could grow any larger. The lord, on the other hand, had no power to enter and plant trees. As a result, vast areas, particularly of the champion manors, were denuded of trees for hundreds of years and, as old ones died, they were not replaced. Trees began to reappear only after the inclosures of the eighteenth century and it is many of those, now over-mature, that have fallen to storms in our own times. This rule was always subject to special custom and many custumals note that tenants could cut timber on their own copyholds, although usually only for their own use.

Woodland as such belonged to the lord, but is included in the Law of Property Act 1925, s 62(3) because it can be hard to classify either as demesne or waste. Although not arable, woodland was cultivated and coppices were carefully tended. Coppice

---

4   Law of Property Act 1922, s 128(2)(d), s 138, Sch 13, Part II, para 12.

5   *Stroud's Judicial Dictionary of Words and Phrases* (Sweet & Maxwell, 5th edn by John S James, 1986): Timber.

trees[6] were trunks from which young shoots were harvested every few years for poles, fencing, plough shafts and other needs. Coppices are similar to underwood, although underwood may have a wider meaning and extends, for example, to fir trees. In *R v Inhabitants of Ferrybridge*[7] in 1823 it was held that immature fir plantations did not come within the meaning of 'saleable underwoods'.

Woods in England were not the same as forests. Forests are lands formerly subject to forest law which related to sporting rights, and are discussed in 12.2. The position may be different on the Continent where forests were *foris* or beyond the areas of settlement. In eastern Germany and parts of France areas, mainly covered with trees, remained as wilderness until late in the Middle Ages, but in England there was very little wildwood left after the Stone Age. Woodlands were intensively managed for timber, underwood fodder and sport. Indeed, some areas covered with trees may have been left to nature to a greater extent since the fellings of the First World War than for hundreds of years before, with the decline of the great estates and management for sporting.

11.3   ESTOVERS, BOTES, FURZE AND TURBARY

Estovers is the right to take wood and other growing things for building, fencing or fuel. It can extend to gorse, heather, fern and bracken for animal litter or the right to cut and take grass for fodder. The precise extent of estovers varies from place to place and even within a manor there may have been different rights for different holdings. In the New Forest estovers are called fuelwood. Estovers for building are restricted to certain ancient houses. If a house decays, or is destroyed and rebuilt, the right can still be claimed, but only for a replacement of the same size. Similarly, if an ancient house is extended the right does not apply to wood used in the extension.

Estovers and botes are sometimes considered to be the same thing. Botes were various forms of right to take wood from the commons. They derived from the duty of the villein to keep his holding, in particular his cottage, in repair, and failure to do so was waste; as such, the villein had to be provided with the means to perform this duty. Four botes in particular were well-known, namely: house-bote, to take timber to repair houses; fire-bote, to take lops and tops, underboughs and windfalls for fuel; plough-bote, to take wood to repair agricultural equipment; and hedge-bote, to take wood to repair fences and gates. Fire-bote was normally subject to the restriction that the tenant could take only such as he could get 'by hook or by crook and no more'. So far as these are rights of common they have now been lost unless registered.

---

6   See Rackham, O, *Trees and Woodlands in the British Landscape* (JM Ltd, 1990) Ch 1.

7   (1823) 1 B&C 375, 107 ER 139.

Furze, otherwise known as gorse or whin, grows over most of England and used to be valued both as fuel and as fodder for beasts. It is now recognised principally for its bright yellow flowers. The right to take it could be an estover if it was used for fuel but if for fodder it would be similar to a right of pasture. Bracton considers it to be an estover.[8]

One possible right that does not feature in legal sources is the right to edible fruits such as blackberries, rosehips, sloes, mushrooms and similar things. This was probably because the only people interested in such rights were cottagers who could not have afforded to fight a case in the royal courts. The Theft Act 1968, s 4(3) now provides:

> A person who picks mushrooms growing wild on any land, or who picks flowers, fruit or foliage from a plant growing wild on any land, does not (although not in possession of the land) steal what he picks, unless he does it for reward or for sale or other commercial purpose.

Acorns, however, were important as feed for pigs. The right to acorns is known as a right of common of pannage, which is a separate form of pasture.[9] Great herds of pigs were put out in the autumn in mediaeval woods, so this right was valuable. Not only did this practice feed a useful source of meat, it also discouraged the growth of oak trees and kept much of the woodland clear. In the New Forest pannage is called mast.

The common or commonable right of turbary is the right to dig turf or peat for fuel. It belongs to a house, although if the extent of the right is fixed it can become a profit in gross. It applies only to use by the person cutting, who cannot sell the turf or peat for cash or use it to remake his lawn. Bracton states that the extent of the right must be reasonable having regard to the needs both of the house having the benefit and the resources of the land from which it is taken.[10]

These types of rights of common are rare nowadays although some, especially turbary, were registered and confirmed under the Commons Registration Act 1965. The existence of such rights makes the land in which they subsist common land. Estovers apply to woodland or rough land where gorse and bracken grow. Turbary often applies to normal grassland where beasts are pasturing.

---

[8] Bracton, Sir Henry, *De legibus et consuetudinibus angliae* (c 1257) f 231.

[9] Bracton *op cit* f 226b; but see 222b.

[10] Ibid f 231.

11.4   TENANTS' MINERAL RIGHTS IN THE WASTE

Tenants sometimes had rights of common in the waste relating to minerals. In *Heath v Deane*[11] it was held that a custom for both freehold and copyhold tenants of the manor to take stone from a quarry was reasonable provided it was for use on a holding within the manor and not for sale outside.

Rights of common in the soil include digging for sand, stone, coal and other minerals, and often relate to specific quarries. Stone would be for use in the commoner's house; sand or limestone for marl for improving the soil of his arable land; and coal for fuel in his house. In the New Forest marl is a distinct right. The right can extend to brick earth, again for the house. Bracton states that the right can extend to gold, silver[12] and tin,[13] but that is unlikely today and may not even have been correct in his own time.[14] Gold and silver are royal prerogative rights and do not belong to private persons (11.5). There are ancient tin rights in Cornwall called tin bounding which are said to apply in a number of manors in eastern Cornwall,[15] but those are not rights of common and may only be exercised by a person recognised as a privileged tinner, that is as engaged in the mining business.

Custumals note that tenants had special mineral rights on the common. In the manor of Stepney and Hackney[16] tenants could dig gravel, sand, clay and lome (loam) from the waste provided they filled up the holes. In Woking in Surrey[17] the manorial court entreated the lord to allow the tenants to take loam, gravel, clay and ragstone from the waste. These rights are best understood as a form of right of common (or commonable right) in the soil and would be subject to the normal restriction that they were for use on the tenant's holding only and not for commercial exploitation. In the manor of St Mary Abbotts in Kensington[18] the tenants had similar rights. There the wastes included the well-known Notting Hill gravel pits and it is said that much of West London was built from the deposits.

---

[11]   [1905] 2 Ch 86.

[12]   Bracton *op cit* f 222b.

[13]   Ibid f 231b.

[14]   *Attorney-General for Duchy of Lancaster v GE Overton (Farms) Ltd* [1981] Ch 333, [1982] Ch 277, [1982] 1 All ER 524.

[15]   *R v Crease* (1840) 11 Ad & E 677, 113 ER 571; *Rogers v Brenton* (1847) 10 QB 26, 116 ER 10.

[16]   Stepney and Hackney: Watkins, C, *A Treatise on Copyholds* (James Bullock, 4th edn by Thomas Coventry, 1825) 2.527.

[17]   Woking: ibid 2.559.

[18]   St Mary Abbot's: ibid 2.546.

A similar customary right to take sand from the sea shore for the purpose of fertilising land was confirmed by the Sea Sand (Devon and Cornwall) Act 1609. This applies to all farmers in the two counties whether or not the foreshore is part of the waste of a manor.

11.5   MINERAL SUBSTANCES

One issue relating to mineral claims, particularly in copyhold land, concerned what was at stake. The word 'minerals' needs to be interpreted and applied to particular circumstances. There have been many cases on the meaning of mines and minerals in a particular document or Act of Parliament but they are not of much help in the manorial context. There is little difference in meaning between mines and minerals although the former refers to shafts and galleries and the latter to the substances extracted. Quarries are open mines as distinct from underground mines. Usually a document, such as a grant, will be interpreted in the light of the particular circumstances, for example the experience of commercial men involved with minerals at the time the document was made and in the place to which it relates.[19] Similarly, a statute which provides, for example, that on a compulsory purchase minerals either are or are not to be taken will be interpreted in view of its purpose. In particular it is sometimes said that the natural rock of the countryside cannot be a mineral.

However, the lord's rights in copyhold land derive from custom, not from a document or statute, and must predate 1189. Much of the modern law derives from decisions about copyhold minerals in the nineteenth century which involved deep-mined coal. The technology to extract coal did not exist in the early Middle Ages and so, although coal was worked from surface pits, deep coal would not then have been thought of as a valuable right for the lord. Many such cases arose because deposits of coal were found in the champion manors of the Midlands where copyhold tenure was widespread.

The nature of minerals in this context relates to the purpose of the copyhold. The villein cultivated the soil. Therefore the topsoil and things in it are not minerals, but everything else which occurs naturally is, including not only deep minerals and metallic ores, but also brickearth, limestone, sand, gravel and clay. In *Dearden v Evans*[20] stones had fallen from a cliff many years before onto copyhold land and become embedded in the soil. They became valuable because they could be sold to make sleepers for a railway. It was held that the

---

[19]   See the discussion in *Earl of Lonsdale v Attorney-General* [1982] 1 WLR 887, [1982] 3 All ER 579, (1983) 45 P&CR 1.

[20]   (1839) 5 M&W 11, 151 ER 5.

copyholder could not remove them since they had become part of the land and therefore the property of the lord.[21]

Schedule 12, para (5) to the Law of Property Act 1922 contains a full description of the manorial rights of the lord in relation to minerals:

> An enfranchisement by virtue of this Act of any land (including any mines and minerals hereinafter mentioned) shall not affect any right of the lord or tenant in or to any mines, minerals, limestone, lime, clay, stone, gravel, pits, or quarries, whether in or under the enfranchised land or not, or any right of entry, right of way and search, or other easement or privilege of the lord or tenant in, on, through, over, or under any land, or any powers which in respect of property in the soil might but for the enfranchisement have been exercised for the purpose of enabling the lord or tenant, their or his agents, workmen, or assigns, more effectually to search for, win, and work any mines, minerals, pits, or quarries, or to remove and carry away any minerals, limestone, lime, stones, clay, gravel, or other substances had or gotten therefrom, [the rest of the paragraph refers to rights relating to fairs and markets and sporting].

The lord did not and does not have all mineral rights. The Crown has the right to all mines of gold and silver. Often these are found in conjunction with other minerals and initially the Crown claimed that where any royal minerals subsisted, even if they were minimal in comparison with others, it was entitled to work the mine. However, the Royal Mines Act 1688[22] provided that no mine of tin, copper, iron or lead should thereafter be taken to be a royal mine, even though gold or silver might be extracted from it. To preserve the right to royal minerals s 2 of the Royal Mines Act 1693 provided that where a mine of other mineral contained royal mineral (such as tin mines where silver often occurs in small quantities) the Crown had a right of pre-emption at a fixed price determined by the nature of the principal mineral, but this was repealed by the Statute Law (Repeals) Act 1969. *Attorney-General v Morgan*[23] concerned a mine near Dolgelly in North Wales, which was primarily a gold mine and worked as such. There were traces of copper, iron and lead but they were of insufficient quantities to be worked independently. It was stated that where a mine is mainly for gold it cannot be worked by a subject, even on his own land, without a licence from the Crown.

Oil and gas were also nationalised under the Petroleum (Production) Act 1934 (now the Petroleum Act 1998) and coal under the Coal Act 1938 (11.7). In general where there are legal difficulties in obtaining rights to work minerals in any land the Secretary of State can authorise the working under the Mines

---

[21]   See, by analogy, *Waverley Borough Council v Fletcher* [1996] QB 334.

[22]   1 Wm & M (c 30).

[23]   [1891] 1 Ch 463.

(Working Facilities and Support) Act 1966, and thereby override any veto of a lord or tenant.

11.6 LORD'S MINERALS – DEMESNE AND INCLOSED WASTE

Apart from the special rules applying to enfranchised copyholds the owner of land is presumed to own the minerals under it. In the context of manors the lord owns the mineral rights in the demesne land and in waste. However, mineral rights may be separated from ownership of the surface. For freehold land this is frequent on a sale or lease and may arise occasionally on other dealings, such as inheritance or partition. The surface may be sold or leased and the minerals excepted, or the minerals may be conveyed or leased and the surface retained. The minerals, or rather a volume of the earth beneath the surface, thereby become a separate piece of property.[24] This may be defined by reference to a depth, such as minerals below 200 fathoms, or by reference to the type of mineral, such as coal or tin or limestone, or by reference to a specified seam, most often of coal. By use of clear words it can extend to the natural rock of the country, such as an exception of all mines, minerals, stone and substrata. Such mineral freeholds or leaseholds thereby have their own title and may be bought, sold or leased, or rights (such as wayleaves) may be granted through them as pieces of land separate from the surface.

In such cases issues can arise as to the relationship between the minerals and the surface. In particular a mineral operator may wish to open a shaft or work the minerals by a quarry, thus destroying all or part of the surface. He may wish to deposit spoil on the surface or construct roads or tramways, or divert streams. Particularly in relation to deep seams of coal, he may not need any direct access but as the material is excavated from the workings the surface itself may subside, causing damage to buildings or the whole surface to fall away. Experience has led lawyers to draft detailed provisions to cover such eventualities in conveyances and leases but in the context of the manor that has not always been done or indeed been possible and the courts have had to resolve the resulting disputes. Many disputes relate to inclosures of the waste.

The lord could not work minerals in open waste if that would materially interfere with the rights of commoners There was however much litigation over mineral rights in inclosed waste. On inclosure parts of the waste were allotted as freehold to commoners and others in return for their releasing their rights of

---

[24] *Batten Pooll v Kennedy* [1907] 1 Ch 256; relying on the Scottish House of Lords case of *Duke of Hamilton v Graham* (1871) LR 2 Sc & Div 166.

common over the parts allotted to the lord. If waste was allotted to a participant in the inclosure then, in the absence of any provision to the contrary, the new owner had full rights, including minerals.

Often the lord wished to retain mineral rights (as well as sporting: see 12.5) and an inclosure Act or award sought to provide for this. The first issue was whether the rights were reserved at all. In early inclosure Acts lords attempted to use a reservation of seigniorial or manorial rights (see 9.5) on the basis that since such rights subsisted in copyhold land (below) they therefore also existed in the waste. However, the courts consistently held[25] that, since the rights did not exist before inclosure as separate from the freehold in the waste, words purporting to reserve them were ineffective.

In consequence later inclosure Acts created new exceptions and reservations of rights and used more specific language in relation to minerals. The wording of individual Acts could vary but was usually effective to sever the minerals from the surface, leaving no doubt that the lord still had the minerals. A late wording is contained in ss 76 and 98 of the Inclosure Act 1845.

A further issue is whether the lord can only get minerals by underground workings and whether and how far he is able to cause subsidence or what compensation he has to pay. The general law is clear. A surface owner has a natural right to the support of his land by the mineral owner and, if subsidence results, he is entitled to damages. This may be modified by agreement between the parties, typically at the time of initial severance, and any future owner of the surface will be bound; however, clear words are vital, and in general the courts lean against a right to damage the surface. In addition, even if a right of support for bare land is effectively excluded on the severance, and a building is later erected and remains for 20 years, it may acquire an easement of support by prescription.

Many inclosure Acts included provisions purporting to exclude or restrict the right of support or prescribing a level of compensation which could be nominal or inadequate. In general the courts found that such provisions did not protect the lord or his licensee from claims and upheld the surface owner's right of support. This was established by the House of Lords in *Love v Bell*[26] which was followed by the more famous decision in *Butterknowle Colliery Co v Bishop Auckland Industrial Co-operative Co*[27] where the numerous earlier cases were reviewed. The whole issue was discussed in detail in *Wakefield v Duke of*

---

[25]   *Townley v Gibson* (1788) 2 TR 701, 100 ER 377.

[26]   (1883–84) LR 9 App Cas 286.

[27]   [1906] AC 305.

Buccleugh[28] where, exceptionally, there were held to be clear and wide words permitting subsidence although subject to payment of compensation. There are occasions where the terms of an Act override even this. An instance is *Consett Waterworks Co v Ritson*[29] where the Bishop of Durham was entitled to let down the surface and not pay compensation, but the cases indicate that this is very much an exception. The same wording was considered further by the Court of Appeal in *Consett Industrial and Provident Society Ltd v Consett Iron Co Ltd*[30] where the court upheld the earlier decision in *Ritson*, principally on the grounds that although *Butterknowle* had disapproved of *Ritson*, it had not actually overruled it and Younger LJ indicated that in any case he considered it correctly decided on the wording of the Act.

Minerals can also be appurtenances or annexures (9.4). Mineral appurtenances are found in the metallic mining areas of the South West where mineral rights in land are often held in common. The surface may belong to a farmer but the minerals may have been severed centuries ago and may belong in various shares to lords of nearby manors. On a division of a manor, either before 1290 or between co-parceners, the minerals were sometimes not physically partitioned but remained held in undivided shares and those shares passed with the successor manors. What passed might not be the full property in minerals but a right known as dish or toll of tin which is a right to one-fifteenth of the mineral value. Tin was mined underground and the ore was loaded into baskets which were then brought to the surface, and the lord's bailiff had the right to select one basket in 15. This right could simply subsist as a normal royalty of one-fifteenth of the proceeds of sale.

Mineral annexures are less common, but there were instances as late as the 1950s where a lord sold the surface of some demesne land but reserved the mineral rights to himself in right of his manor. The reason for such steps may have been that where the surface of land has been sold it is easy for people dealing subsequently with the property of a former owner to forget about the minerals. Once the conveyance has been handed over to the purchaser of the surface a copy may not be kept with the lord's title deeds. If the rights are specifically annexed to the manor then title will pass with it so that there will always be someone who can deal with the mineral rights. If the minerals are a separate asset on their own and the title to them is not passed on, problems may arise later.

---

[28] (1867) LR 4 Eq 613; on appeal LR 4 HL 377 at 382.

[29] (1889) 22 QBD 318 at 702.

[30] [1922] 2 Ch 135.

11.7   LORD'S MINERALS IN COPYHOLD LAND

As explained in 9.3, by general custom the copyholder had possession of the minerals and could prevent the lord from having access, but, correspondingly, the lord, who had the property in the minerals, could stop the copyholder working them. In such circumstances, joint action was needed to exercise rights of ownership. This was always subject to special custom. Sometimes the tenant could work the mineral without the lord's consent. In the manor of Framfield in Sussex[31] every tenant was permitted to dig for mines in his own land and in Hindringham[32] in Norfolk tenants had coal-bote on their own holding. In *Marquis of Salisbury v Gladstone*[33] a custom for copyholders to dig and sell clay from their holdings was considered good although if the tenant had also claimed to sell the soil as well as the bare clay that would have been excessive. It follows that a lord cannot necessarily prevent working of minerals although the presumption will be that he can, and it is then up to the tenant to prove a special custom for that manor.

Likewise by special custom the lord could work the minerals without the tenant's consent. As discussed in 11.9 this may take effect as a profit. The best known instance is *Eardley v Granville*[34] in 1876 which related to the Duchy of Lancaster manor of Newcastle-under-Lyme. In that manor the lord had by special custom the right to enter copyholds and work minerals. The Duchy granted to Lord Granville the right to work mines by a pit known as the Deep Pit which was within the manor. He acquired the right to work mines in some freehold land outside the manor belonging to Mr Sneyd. Mr Eardley's copyhold lay between the Deep Pit and Sneyd's land. Previously, the coal under Eardley's land had been worked out leaving a void. Lord Granville wanted to construct an underground mine railway between the Deep Pit and Sneyd's land and the only way to do it was through the void under Eardley's land.

It was well settled[35] that there could exist a special custom for the lord (and his mining lessees) to mine under copyhold land in order to work minerals within the bounds of a manor where the custom applied. This case established that the lord had no such right to do so in order to work minerals outside the manor. In the passage quoted in 11.1 Sir George Jessel MR distinguished between the property in mineral substances, which belonged to the lord, and the possession in the land, which was the tenant's. It followed that when the minerals were dug

---

[31]   Framfield: Watkins *op cit* 2.493.

[32]   Hindringham: ibid 2.495.

[33]   (1861) 9 HL Cas 692, 11 ER 900.

[34]   (1876) 3 Ch D 826.

[35]   *Bowser v Maclean* (1860) de Gex, Fish & J 415, 45 ER 682.

out the copyholder had the right to the space where they had previously lain. In this the position is different from a separation of the minerals from the surface by grant or reservation where what is granted is a volume of the earth, so that when the mineral is removed the space in that volume still belongs to the grantee. Of course Eardley was probably not interested in the space itself, but more likely in the fact that if Lord Granville needed his permission to cross it he would have to pay for the wayleave.

As with minerals in inclosed waste, subsidence was a major issue for copyhold minerals. Where the general custom applied so that the copyholder could prevent the minerals being worked at all this was not a problem since, when giving consent, the copyholder could impose terms as to any subsidence which might occur. Where, however, as in many manors in mining districts, the lord had a right to work the minerals without the copyholder's consent then, if subsidence did occur, disputes could arise. The lord did not have the right to deprive the surface of support. This was established in relation to Newcastle by the case of *Hilton v Granville*[36] (the same defendant as in *Eardley*) in 1844 and that decision was itself subsequently confirmed by the leading case of *Wolstanton Ltd and Attorney-General of the Duchy of Lancaster v Newcastle-under-Lyme Corporation*[37] mentioned in 4.4 on the subject of reasonableness in custom. The House of Lords held that an alleged custom for the lord to withdraw support from the surface was unreasonable and bad.

Where the lord still has property in minerals in former copyhold land then, unless there is a special custom (as in Newcastle) allowing him to enter and work them, all he has in practice is a right of veto, as the landowner also has. In theory either veto can be overridden by a procedure under the Mines (Working Facilities and Support) Acts 1923 to 1974[38] which allows a prospective mineral operator to apply to the Secretary of State and the court for compulsory powers to work the minerals; but the procedure is cumbersome and complex and rarely used in practice. The usual division of royalties between lord and landowner is half and half, as used to be the case for timber (11.2).

When coal was nationalised in the Coal Act 1938 coal rights in copyhold land were classed as retained interests under s 5(6), that is the right to work them was not nationalised. This was corrected by the Coal Industry Act 1975, s 3, now the Coal Industry Act 1994, ss 49, 50 and Sch 7, which confer full rights of working subject to a notice procedure.

---

[36] (1844) 5 QB 701, 114 ER 1414, 5 Ad & El NS 701; 5 Beav 263, 49 ER 579, Cr & Ph 283, 41 ER 498, d & Mer 614, 10 LJ Ch 398.

[37] [1940] AC 850.

[38] See *Star Energy Weald Basin Limited v Bocardo SA* [2010] UKSC 35, [2011] 1 AC 380.

As the lord's right in copyhold land is a part of the property of the manor then, strictly speaking, the general words under the Law of Property Act 1925, s 62(3) are not needed to pass title in minerals in copyhold land because it will pass automatically. At common law it would have passed with the manorial fee simple in the land.

11.8   EXCEPTIONS ON ENFRANCHISEMENT

The position under custom as recognised by the common law has been materially altered by the enfranchisement of copyholds. Enfranchisement could be carried out at common law, or by statute, either compulsorily or voluntarily under the Copyhold Acts 1841 to 1894 or automatically under the Law of Property Act 1922. In any of these cases standard provisions could apply or could be modified by agreement. Each of these might lead to different consequences.

At common law enfranchisement took effect as a conveyance (or release) of the fee simple to the copyholder. As such it included all the rights the lord was able to convey in the freehold and the land ceased (as a result of *Quia Emptores*) to be parcel of the manor but came to be held of the chief lord (usually the Crown). The parties could incorporate any special terms in the deal. If the lord expressly excepted the minerals, that created a separate corporeal freehold as the lord's property. This was so whether or not the lord also reserved the power to enter and work the minerals. The lord might also, instead of using specific words, except minerals by reference to the statutory provisions. Provided the enfranchisement itself took effect at common law then the use or incorporation of a statutory formula did not affect the position and the rights were governed by common law.

A release of the freehold by the lord by itself would mean that the copyholder still retained possession of the minerals. However, if the intention of the arrangement was that the lord had the same rights as he would have had under an exception out of a sale of waste or demesne then it would follow that the copyholder had released his possession in the minerals to the lord. In contrast to a conveyance of a legal estate there were no special formalities for delivering up possession but, as enfranchisement at common law had to be by deed, the effect of a release by the tenant of possession of mineral rights was to transfer it to the lord.

Compulsory enfranchisement under the 1894 Act was by a statutory procedure by award under the seal of the Board of Agriculture under s 10. Voluntary enfranchisement was by agreement between the parties under s 14, in which case it was effected by deed under s 16 and the consideration could be partly a conveyance of mines or minerals. Thus the tenant could pay for the enfranchisement partly in cash and partly by releasing his possessory right to the minerals. Under s 23 an enfranchisement under the Act (either voluntary or statutory) 'shall not without the express consent in writing of the lord or tenant respectively affect the estate or right of the lord or tenant in or to any mines, minerals, limestone, lime clay, stone, gravel, pits or quarries'.[39] The meaning of 'not affect' has been considered in 9.5. The effect is a statutory preservation of the customary rights of the lord notwithstanding that the fee simple passed to the tenant. On a voluntary statutory enfranchisement it was possible for the parties to agree to modify this. Even where the enfranchisement was compulsory the parties could nevertheless agree to except the mineral rights, although if they had to have recourse to the Board it was less likely that they could agree about minerals.

Schedule 12, para (5) to the Law of Property Act 1922 is in similar terms to s 23 of the 1894 Act but simply says that enfranchisement does not affect the right of the lord or the tenant 'in or to' the mineral rights, and there is no reference to consent in writing. However, s 138(12) of the 1922 Act provides for agreements between lord and tenant. It allows the grant to the lord as compensation for the extinguishment of manorial incidents of any estate or right of the tenant or other right for winning and carrying away any mines or mineral under the land. There is then a proviso to the section as follows:

> Provided that, where any such agreement relates to mines or minerals, the consideration for the estate or right shall be determined by agreement and not otherwise, and any such agreement for the extinguishment of the right of the lord in or to any mines and minerals shall, subject to the provisions of the agreement, operate as a conveyance to the tenant of such right notwithstanding that the agreement may not be under seal.

The proviso states that an extinguishment of the lord's right of property need not be under seal and will have the same effect as if it was. There is no corresponding provision for a release of the tenant's right to possession. The reason is that the lord's right was held in fee simple and that, statute apart, required a deed to transfer it. The tenant's right was to possession and possession could be given up informally by a simple agreement. Where that happened the lord was fully entitled to the minerals in the same way as if there had been a normal sale subject to an exception and he could apply for registration of the minerals with their own title. Although under s 128(1) and Sch 12, para (1)(a) the fee simple vested in the tenant from 1 January 1926 while an agreement might take several years, the provisions of the Act should be

---

[39] There was formerly a similar provision in Copyhold Act 1852, s 48.

read together so that the arrangement as finally reached should be read into the initial enfranchisement.

In contrast to unaffected customary rights, where minerals were expressly excepted to the lord on enfranchisement the effect was to give him the freehold in a volume beneath the surface so that once the minerals were removed the lord would still own the void. This is of course subject to other rules so that, for instance, under the Coal Act 1938 the National Coal Board took over all coal mines and responsibility for claims arising from subsidence as a result of coal working. It is, however, possible that a lord may still have responsibility for a void left by other workings which is still his property. Where a void is suitable for the deposit of commercial or domestic waste it may have a value of its own. This applies in particular to worked-out quarries. In other cases it may be a danger and a source of possible accidents or pollution.

Where copyhold strips in an open field or copyhold ancient enclosures were included in an inclosure award as freehold land (to a former copyholder who thus might have bought out quitrents and similar dues or to a new freeholder) the boundaries were changed so that the old property limits were no longer recognisable. If an inclosure Act provided for the lord to retain seigniorial or manorial rights then, in principle, the lord would retain customary rights to the property in minerals within the bounds of the former copyhold tenement and such rights would pass to a successor. In practice it would now be difficult to identify the land where this right subsisted as it would comprise parts of wholly different modern fields. Sometimes lands subject to manorial incidents were intermixed with other land so that it was difficult to identify it. The 1922 Act provided in s 139(1)(vi) for the land to be identified by the minister by reference to the Ordnance Survey map. That section has now been repealed and the power is probably no longer available. A court has a general power to determine any dispute and, if necessary, that jurisdiction would have to be invoked.

11.9   LAND REGISTRATION

Land registration is discussed in 25.6–25.11 where it is explained that on first registration or disposition after 13 October 2013 a lord's manorial rights lose overriding status. In practice mineral rights in former copyholds are the most important of these. The Land Registry has issued guidance in Practice Guide 65: Registration of mines and minerals, but this is not necessarily the final word. Not all rights of the lord of the manor are manorial rights for this purpose (9.5). A lord must protect his rights to those which are by lodging either a caution or a notice, preferably before 13 October 2013. However, cautions and notices are not by themselves evidence of title but simply demonstrate a claim to a right.

The issue arises whether the lord needs to take action and whether he can substantively protect his rights by registration of the minerals with their own title either as land or as a profit. This may turn on the origin of the right.

The rules on mineral exceptions to the lord are similar to those affecting exceptions to other landowners who do not have lordships. It is worth setting out the rules under the Land Registration Act 2002 as they are relevant to the distinction between excepted and manorial minerals. The starting point is that at common law there is a presumption that the owner of an estate in the surface also has the minerals. The Act primarily deals with registration of title to an estate in land, and 'land' is defined in s 132(1) as including mines and minerals whether or not held with the surface. On the face of it therefore where a person is registered as proprietor of land that registration will also carry the minerals.

The basis of land registration is a government guarantee of title which operates by reference to an indemnity given by the registrar to any person who suffers loss as a result of a mistake in the register. As mineral severance is so frequent, the Land Registration Act 2002 provides in Sch 8, para 2 that no indemnity is payable in respect of any mines or minerals unless there is a note on the register that they are included in the title to the registered estate, normally of the surface. In the vast majority of cases there is no such note and therefore there is no guarantee that the title includes minerals. This is supported by the Land Registration Rules 2003. Rule 5(b)(i) provides that, where appropriate, details of the inclusion or exclusion of minerals must be contained in the property register, and this is reinforced by r 32 which provides that where the registrar is satisfied that the title includes or excludes the minerals he must make a note of it on the register. Rules 70 and 71 were both substituted by the 2008 amending Rules and provide that the registrar may make an entry that negatives any implication as to whether the minerals are included, but if an applicant provides satisfactory evidence that they are included then the registrar must make a note to that effect.

As indicated above, where a landowner excepts minerals out of a sale of a freehold of the surface, that excepts a volume of the earth. That volume subsists as land in its own right and is capable of being registered with its own title. While the Land Registration Act 2002, s 4(9) provides that registration of such minerals is not compulsory, it is voluntary and the lord is able to apply for a separate title to them. The extent of the title may be defined by depth or simply as being the mineral strata, but it is capable of definition as a specific part of the physical land. Rule 25 requires an applicant for first registration of minerals to provide details which define the rights.

If the minerals were excepted out of a sale of demesne land then in principle no problem arises. If the surface owner was unaware of the severance of minerals when he acquired his land then, unless there is a note incorrectly saying that they are included, he cannot claim compensation for not having the minerals in his registered estate. Correspondingly, the mineral owner's rights are not affected and he can make a voluntary application for his mineral title to be registered. If they were excepted under an inclosure Act or award (of former waste or open fields) then, provided adequate words were used, the lord could apply for voluntary registration. The wording may be unclear, and several forms of word in common use in inclosure Acts have been the subject of judicial interpretation (11.6). One potential problem is whether, if the minerals were excepted to the lord, they may have become an annexure and therefore may be seen as a manorial right within Schs 1 and 3, para 11 to the Land Registration Act 2002. The better view is that the expression 'manorial right' has a specific meaning (9.5) which applies to rights in enfranchised copyholds and would not extend to other mineral rights belonging to the lord.

The lord's right to minerals in former copyhold land may subsist in one of three ways. First, it may be a legal estate in a mineral stratum under the surface by virtue of an exception on enfranchisement, in which case it will constitute a freehold interest in a volume of subsoil separate from the surface and will be land. It follows that the lord can apply for voluntary registration. Such a freehold would seem not to be a manorial right within the Act and although there might have been some doubt in view of the wording of r 5(b) mentioned below it is evident that the 2002 Act cannot operate so as to transfer the lord's freehold in the mineral stratum to the tenant. If it were to be regarded as a manorial right it would be vulnerable after the first registration or disposition of land after 12 October 2013 if not protected. Practice Guide 65 considers the position where the parties dealt with minerals by agreement in either a common law or statutory enfranchisement.[40] The Registry accepts that it is possible for the minerals to be excepted to the lord and in that case the lord may be able to establish a separate registrable title to the mineral stratum as indicated above. Similarly, where on inclosure the lord retained title to the minerals, that could give rise to registration with its own title.[41]

Secondly, the right may subsist as a profit of minerals. In principle it would be possible for the lord on enfranchisement to have reserved an incorporeal freehold mineral profit à prendre, that is the right to dig and take minerals without retaining any corporeal freehold in the land itself. More likely that would have arisen by operation of law. It is the view of the Land Registry[42] that where the lord had not only the property in minerals (therefore falling short of a legal estate) but also (as in Newcastle) a right by special custom to enter to work

---

[40] *Practice Guide 65* paras 4.2, 12.3.

[41] Ibid para 12.2.

[42] Ibid para 2.

the minerals, that is equivalent in modern terms to a profit. On that analysis the effect of enfranchisement was to convert (by use of the words 'shall not affect') what had been a customary right into a legal interest by reservation to the lord out of the statutory conveyance of the fee simple to the tenant, thus preserving to the lord the right to work what became the tenant's minerals. This is capable of being a manorial right.

A profit may be noted against a registered title; where it is not it will need to qualify as an overriding interest. On first registration under Sch 1, para 3 any legal profit qualifies. Following a subsequent disposition it will qualify under Sch 3, para 3 only if it satisfies the statutory conditions. These are that the right must be known to the owner of the registered estate or reasonably obvious on inspection (for instance a quarry in operation) or have been exercised within a year before a disposition (for instance by underground working). In many cases a mineral profit will not satisfy these conditions. Alternatively, a profit in gross is voluntarily registrable under the Land Registration Act 2002, s 3(1)(d) with its own title. Assuming it to be a manorial right it also needs to be protected by caution or notice.

Rule 5(b) (as amended) provides that the register of a registered estate must contain where appropriate details of 'all exceptions [or reservations] arising on enfranchisement of formerly copyhold land'. The words in square brackets were added by the Land Registration Rules 2008. When the rule refers to enfranchisement, it clearly includes statutory enfranchisement, whether compulsory or (before 1926) voluntary. It is not clear if it also includes common law enfranchisement which took effect as a conveyance of the fee simple to the tenant. Although the rule states that such details must be on the register, the consequence of not being on the register is unclear. An exception creates a separate property and therefore failure to note it will not affect the lord's ownership of the minerals. A reservation is not separate and is probably vulnerable to not being noted.

Thirdly, the lord may be entitled to former general customary rights (that is property without possession or power of entry) which, under the Law of Property Act 1922, Sch 12, para (5) and its predecessors, are not affected on enfranchisement. These cannot be exceptions since the lord does not have a legal estate in the minerals, possession of which is vested in the tenant. Strictly speaking they are not reservations either since Sch 12, para (5) simply says that the Act does not affect the lord's rights – it does not create a new reservation. However, as the effect of enfranchisement was a statutory conveyance of the fee simple to the former tenant, it may be that the courts would interpret para (5) as a statutory reservation. In any event such mineral rights are almost certainly manorial.

The Practice Guide considers[43] that the lord's rights, which it refers to as reserved on (even though the Acts say are not affected by) enfranchisement are not estates in land but are easements, rights or privileges within the Law of Property Act 1925, s 1(2)(a). As discussed in 9.5 the right may be a privilege. Therefore, in this case the lord has no legal estate or profit in the minerals under the enfranchised land which is capable of substantive registration but some other interest which can be protected by notice on the register (or caution in the case of unregistered land). As explained in 25.10 the lord may need to take steps before the first registration or disposition of land after 12 October 2013 or such manorial rights may be at risk.

That view is probably correct although it is not beyond question because, before 1926, the lord had a fee simple in the whole of the land, even though subject to the copyholder's customary rights. The meaning of 'shall not affect' in Sch 12, para (5) to the 1922 Act cannot mean that the lord's fee simple in the minerals is not affected because the Act passed the fee simple in the land to the tenant. The fee simple comprised everything in the tenant's possession, including the minerals. Accordingly, it seems that now the former copyholder has the legal fee instead of the lord it is the lord's rights that depend on statutory continuation of a customary right, albeit derived from a pre-1926 legal estate in fee simple. Although s 131(2) of the 2002 Act provides that where land is treated as being in the possession of one person (a tenant) it is also treated as being in the possession of another (the landlord) it is unlikely that the courts would so interpret this as extending to lord and successor to copyholder so that the lord would not be treated for this purpose as being in possession of the mineral interest. The lord may have an equitable fee simple – see 9.5.

To summarise a set of rules whose application is far from clear and may need to be resolved by the courts, the position appears to be as follows. First, if the terms of enfranchisement resulted in the lord having, usually by exception, a freehold in the mineral strata then that is a separate property and in principle the lord does not need to take any action. The same applies if the terms of an inclosure Act or award excepted the mineral out of the former waste. Therefore, in order to determine the position it is necessary to examine the enfranchisement deed if there was one, the receipt for compensation or the agreement, and in the case of inclosure to inspect the Act and the award. Excepted minerals do not subsist as an overriding interest – they are not included in the proprietor's title at all. At most there may be a boundary issue, such as the depth to which the surface title extends. Secondly, if the lord has a right of entry to work minerals then that may take effect as a profit. Thirdly, if neither applies then the lord's rights in former copyhold land will be manorial. In the third case it is necessary to lodge a caution or notice. In the second it is necessary, unless the conditions

---

[43]   Ibid para 2.

for a profit to be overriding under Sch 3, para 3 apply, and, assuming the right is manorial, it may be necessary even the conditions do apply. In the first case it is probably not necessary but the matter is not beyond argument.

The practical course for lords seeking to protect their mineral rights is, where possible, to apply for substantive registration of the minerals or, where only a profit is claimed, of that right. In addition it will be sensible to seek a notice on the register of the surface title or lodge a caution where it is unregistered. This is good practice in any case and is essential where the rights subsist as manorial rights preserved on enfranchisement. In view of the doubts about the meaning of manorial right, where the rights belong to and devolve with the manor, even if they arise from inclosure or from an agreement on enfranchisement, they should also be so protected. Indeed, even where there is no doubt as to the status of the mineral rights it would be sensible to do so in order that the surface owner cannot claim ignorance. The position where a surface owner is registered with no reference to exclusion of the minerals is unsatisfactory. A notice will attract a fee for each surface title affected (save for one lodged before 13 October 2013 to protect manorial rights) and if the area of mineral ownership is extensive and there are many surface owners the cost may be uneconomic. It should be noted that even if title to the (incorporeal) manor itself was registered before 13 October 2003 that is not sufficient protection of the mineral rights, which need to be noted against the title to each piece of land affected.

References to 'lord' may of course include a successor who is himself not the lord. Where a lord has sold off the bare title of lord but has excepted manorial minerals they still remain a manorial right following the logic in *Hampshire County Council v Milburn*[44] (6.3) and so a caution or notice should be registered.

Although evidence is not required for registration of a caution or unilateral notice or for an agreed notice if the proprietor consents, it is necessary for any substantive registration of title to the minerals as a freehold title or for an agreed notice if the proprietor does not consent. If a caution or notice is disputed, evidence will need to be produced to the adjudicator. Where it is required the evidence should relate both to the lord's title and to the status of the land. The lord should be able to produce a chain of deeds in the normal way showing that the title has passed to him. Where the chain is incomplete, for instance because there was an implied assent before 1926 or there is a chain of executors, this may involve further research. If the lord has a registered title to the manor that may be sufficient but the Registry may ask for confirmation that the mineral rights have not been separated from the manor.

---

[44]   [1991] AC 235, [1990] 2 All ER 257, (1990) 61 P&CR 135.

Proving that the land was copyhold or establishing its boundaries may be more difficult, especially if the lord has no access to the surface owner's deeds or they have been lost or destroyed. Even where they survive the deeds frequently do not include any plans. Some traditional estates will have map records of copyhold land within their manors. Where the estate still functions the estate office may have the records. Otherwise they may have been deposited at the local record office or in the National Archives. The manorial documents, particularly the rolls, should refer to the land, but again they may simply name a holding without defining its boundaries. Other evidence may exist, such as the papers of a lawsuit or even a narrative such as memoirs or a local history. In coal bearing areas the information obtained on nationalisation should indicate copyhold rights and, while coal itself cannot belong to the lord, he may have other minerals.

Where minerals were excepted on inclosure there will normally have been a good quality inclosure map and such maps as survive are often held at the county record office or in the National Archives and some (such as those for Berkshire) are available on the internet. Where the minerals were excepted on enfranchisement the evidence will comprise the enfranchisement document. Often, however, the evidence will be difficult to locate or interpret and expert help may be needed from an archivist or a historian.

Chapter 12

Hunting, Shooting and Fishing

warrens ... fishings, fisheries, fowlings

12.1   SPORTING AND WILD ANIMALS

Many manors carry with them sporting rights not only over the demesne, but also over the waste and other land. Throughout history, hunting and taking game have been major sports. In the eighteenth century sporting was so significant in general speech that in Jane Austen's novels, when a character referred to 'the manor', he meant the shooting rights. The Hunting Act 2004 has now rendered some hunting unlawful. Controversy surrounding the subject has delayed reforms of other aspects of the law on sporting which are long overdue. Furthermore, the existence of rights to shoot over common land used as grouse moors was one of the main reasons why some landowners opposed reforms of the law, because they anticipated that unlimited public access would interfere with the shooting. As a consequence much of the general law on this topic is complex and inconsistent. This account is primarily about the law so far as it affects manors, which is particularly confused, but it is also necessary to look at related topics in the general law of sporting.[1]

Wild animals roam freely in the countryside (zoos and menageries raise different issues) and do not respect property boundaries. In relation to fishing rights, no single owner controls a whole river from source to mouth. Therefore, unlike domestic animals which are chattels, wild animals are not treated as being owned until they are dead.[2] Ownership is meaningless in this context. In *Blades v Higgs*[3] Lord Westbury LC referred to:

---

[1]   For sporting franchises generally, see Chitty, J, *A Treatise on the Law of the Prerogatives of the Crown and the Relative Rights and Duties of the Subject* (1820) 133 ff.

[2]   Bracton, Sir Henry, *De legibus et consuetudinibus angliae* (c 1257) f 8, 8b.

[3]   (1865) 20 CBR (NS) 214, 144 ER 1087 also at 11 HL Cas 621, 11 ER 1474 where the speech is reported in different words.

a qualified or special right of property in game, that is in animals ferae naturae which are fit for the food of man, whilst they continue in their wild state, I apprehend that the word 'property' can mean no more than the exclusive right to catch, kill and appropriate such animals which is sometimes called by the law a reduction of them into possession ... Property ratione soli is the common law right which every owner of land has to kill and take all such animals ferae naturae as may from time to time be found on his land, and as soon as this right is exercised the animal so killed or caught becomes the absolute property of the owner of the soil.

Some animals which are considered wild by nature can be treated as owned if they adopt the habit of coming back to the same place (*animus revertendi*) and some beasts of warren, especially rabbits in rabbit warrens and deer in parks, can be confined, but even then they are not owned in the sense of being chattels. It follows that rights to land, whether an estate of thousands of acres, a strip in an open field, a close of the tenant or the boundaries of a manor, do not automatically carry ownership of wild animals in them. The rights may include an exclusive or shared right to kill, but that is not the same.

A traditional distinction, although of little current relevance, divides animals and birds into three categories – beasts of forest, beasts of chase or park, and beasts of warren. These are not mutually exclusive and some animals fall into more than one. Beasts of forest are hart, hind, hare, boar and wolf. Wild boar and wolf are now extinct in England. (Some farmers are now raising wild boar for food and wolves are kept in zoos but neither is relevant for the purposes of this discussion.) Hares are also beasts of warren. Beasts of chase or park are buck, doe, fox, marten and roe. Foxes are also vermin. Buck and doe with roe and hart and hind are deer. As explained below the distinction between beasts of forest and beasts of chase is artificial since one derives from the other.

Beasts and fowls of warren include rabbits, hares, pheasants, partridges, roe, quail, rail, woodcock, herne and mallard, but not grouse. They probably include fox, wildcat (now only found in Scotland), badger, marten, otter and squirrel (possibly the red squirrel not the grey). In *Lord Fitzhardinge v Purcell*[4] the court considered that wild duck were probably birds of warren. That case related (among other things) to a claimed customary right to shoot duck on part of the River Severn which lay within Lord Fitzhardinge's manors of Slimbridge, Hinton and Ham but the decision was that the right claimed would amount to a profit and for the reasons set out in 4.4 could not be exercised by custom.

The principal meaning of 'game' was found in the Game Acts, discussed below, but the word is also used in conveyances, transfers and leases. The meaning, as with any word used in a deed, depends on the context. In *Inglewood Investment*

---

[4]   [1908] 2 Ch 139.

Co Ltd v Forestry Commissioners[5] the Court of Appeal held that a reservation of 'game' in a lease did not include deer.

12.2 FOREST, CHASE AND PARK

Forests in law were not areas of woodland but regions in which the Forest Laws applied. They were *foris* or beyond the scope of the normal laws. The Forest Laws and the status of forest were abolished by the Wild Creatures and Forest Laws Act 1971 but some of the old law still affects manorial rights.

Before 1066 Anglo-Saxon kings and the greater lords had wide rights of hunting. The Norman kings were particularly keen on hunting and William I and his successors designated large areas of the country as royal forests where special rules applied. The most famous (which still exist as forests in the modern sense of large wooded expanses) are the New Forest in Hampshire, which was largely created by William I, and the Forest of Dean, but there were many forests throughout the country. At its greatest the forest law applied to nearly a third of England. Hunting rights were restricted to the king and those he authorised, and special rules governed occupation of land, trees and undergrowth, and any other matter relevant to hunting. The soil of a forest was normally Crown land although it might fall within a manor held by a subject. Forests were distinguished by being under the jurisdiction of the special forest court, to the exclusion both of the manorial courts and of the regular courts of the land such as hundred and county courts. Royal courts had jurisdiction but upheld the royal forest law. These royal rights were much resented not just by the ordinary folk but also by the more powerful who saw them as an encroachment on their power over their own land. Controls were imposed on King John in Magna Carta 1215 and, after his death, in the Charter of the Forests of 1217, the guardians of his young son Henry III accepted that no new forests would be created. Over the centuries much land was disaforested. Thereafter Crown powers gradually declined, albeit slowly. Charles I enforced such forest laws as he could to raise revenue. Some forest laws were still enforced in the eighteenth century but by then they were largely seen as anachronistic.

The king could grant a forest to a lord but it would only stay as a forest if it was granted with the right to hold the forest court, which and this was rare. If it was granted without that right it became a chase. The king could also disaforest land while retaining it as part of the royal lands and, under political pressure, this

---

[5]   [1988] 1 WLR 1278.

happened increasingly over the centuries. Many chases were held by subjects, often as parcel of a manor.

The king could also, as mentioned in 6.1, grant to a lord the right to enclose land within a paling to make a park. Within the park the lord had specific sporting rights. Even though the park was enclosed and the paling was so designed that wild animals could not get out they were not thereby made the subject of ownership but remained wild. If the park ceased to hold deer it lost its status as a park 'for a park consisteth of vert, and venison, and enclosure: and if it be determined in any of them it is a total disparking'.[6]

12.3   WARREN

Apart from forests, chases and parks, which were special areas of land, the king also had certain sporting rights to kill beasts of warren by virtue of his prerogative. These were concurrent, that is the right of the king to kill, for example, partridge, anywhere in the country did not affect the right of the lord to do so on his own manor. Of course, if the king in person wished to hunt on his land the lord would take that as a sign of favour and would not wish or presume to interfere with the royal pleasure. However, he might not approve of someone else, perhaps a rival, being authorised by the king to hunt on his land. Accordingly lords often sought a grant of franchise of free warren, that is the exclusive right to take beasts of warren over their own land. Normally this related to the demesne but it could extend to copyhold.[7] Franchises included various types of sporting rights (16.6). The grant was free, not (like freehold land) because it was to a free man but because it was held free of the right of the king. It could be expensive to purchase.

The nature of free warren is important because of the effect of the 1971 Act which abolished it. Blackstone[8] considered that the origin of the royal right was in the nature of a reservation by the king when the lands were originally granted in or after 1066. Historically, that is unlikely. It is more probable that it arose from a general mediaeval theory of rights that attached to kingship, coupled with the fact that wild beasts could not be confined and roamed freely over many manors. However, the reservation theory is important even though unhistorical. The effect of a grant of free warren therefore was to release the reservation over demesne land so that it was extinguished. Warren could in theory subsist over freehold land or even the manor of another lord. It appears

---

[6]   *Sir Charles Howard's Case* (1626) Cro Car 59, 79 ER 655, Jones W 266, 82 ER 139, Hutton 86, 123 ER 1119.

[7]   See *Morris v Dimes* (1834) 1 Ad & E 654, 110 ER 1357.

[8]   Blackstone, Sir William, *Commentaries on the Laws of England* II.25.ii, II.27.

that the right was only granted by the Crown over a third party's land with his consent.[9] Such rights of warren must have existed but as the landowner consented they may be seen as profits as well as franchises.

The Act of 1971 was mainly concerned with royal forests and the Forest Laws that had for most purposes been obsolete since the seventeenth century. However, it expressly abolished the franchises of forest, free chase, park and free warren and thus thereby abolished what in theory were valuable rights. The result therefore was that where lords had not in previous centuries acquired rights of warren over their own lands, or where forest rights still existed over land within manors, those rights of the Crown were extinguished and the freeholder of the land now holds it free of those royal rights. No private forest courts now exist or existed in 1971 so that there cannot have been a subject who enjoyed forest rights over the land of another subject. The Court of Verderers of the New Forest is not a forest court in the sense of the forest laws.

The position may have been different where a lord had rights of chase or warren over the land of another person, although there was a presumption that a Crown grant of land would extinguish pre-existing rights of warren of a third party.[10] Since franchises of free warren were only rarely granted over land other than of the grantee, the most likely occasion was over copyhold which was subsequently enfranchised. Rights in copyhold generally are considered in 12.4.

Morris v Dimes[11] concerned such a grant. In 1628 Charles I granted free warren, fowling and hunting over the demesnes and copyhold land of the Manor of Rickmansworth, Hertfordshire to the Duke of Portland. It seems likely that at the same time, or immediately before, and in a separate deed, he had granted the manor itself to the duke. The manor and warren devolved together for many years. Mr Morris was the freeholder of certain closes at Rickmansworth known as Great Wood Field. This had once been copyhold but it was enfranchised at some date between 1628 and 1818. In 1818 there was a conveyance of the manor together with (using general words) all rights of fishing, fowling, hawking, hunting and shooting and all franchises. Warren was not specifically mentioned and for the purposes of the case it was assumed that there was no separate transfer of warren. The court did not consider that the general words operated in that way. In 1834 Mr Dimes, the lord of the manor who derived title through the conveyance of 1818, exercised sporting rights in Great Wood Field. Morris sued Dimes and the court found in favour of Morris. The warren had originally been granted by separate deed and had not become an appurtenance of

---

[9]   Chitty *op cit* 140–1. The discussion is of chases but it is implied that the rules for warren were the same.

[10]   *Anon (Gray v Fortescue)* (1572) 3 Dyer 326b, 73 ER 738.

[11]   (1834) 1 Ad & E 654, 110 ER 1357.

the manor. It was therefore held in gross as a separate property from the manor and Dimes could not use the general words in the conveyance of 1818 to prove title.

What is the position of the holder of a right of warren after the Act of 1971? Suppose that someone could prove that he had succeeded to the right over Great Wood Field? One possibility is that the court would apply a general presumption that an Act such as that of 1971, which is intended to tidy up the law and remove obsolete material, should not be interpreted so as to destroy private rights without compensation. The other possibility is that whatever the general principles may be, they do not apply to franchises, which are not so much basic rights of property as special grants. What the Crown has granted, the Crown (in Parliament) can remove (16.8). Rights of warren over land of another person must always have been rare. Possibly, over the centuries, what originated as a royal grant changed in nature to being more like a profit, and after the 1971 Act it has continued in existence as such. If someone had regularly exercised sporting rights as of right over land since 1971 he will probably have acquired a profit in gross under the Prescription Act 1832, s 1 after 30 years (or possibly after 20 years as a lost modern grant).

If a proprietor is able to show that he has a right derived either from a franchise of warren or from continuous exercise he may need to protect it under the Land Registration Act 2002. If he relies on prescription he can have the right noted against the title to the land like any other profit and can apply to register the profit with its own title. Alternatively, the proper analysis is that the right may in some way have retained some legal status as a franchise or former franchise, in which case, unless it is noted against the title to the land (or a caution is lodged if the land is unregistered) before the first registration or disposition of land after 12 October 2013, it is vulnerable to extinction under the transitional provisions discussed in 16.9. This is less likely as the 1971 Act specifically abolished the franchise. As a profit it will only take effect as an overriding interest having priority over the rights of a proprietor taking under a disposition for value if it satisfies the conditions in the Land Registration Act 2002, Sch 3, para 3 – specifically that it must be known to the disponee, or obvious, or have been exercised within a year before the disposition. It will therefore be prudent for a claimant to have the right noted on the servient title or protected by caution.

Warrens, as distinct from warren, are referred to in the early part of s 62(3) among commons and pasture. This refers to rabbit warrens, which fall into the group of rights where the lord has the ground and soil thereof. Warrens were usually constructed on or adjacent to waste so that there was plenty of grass available and if the rabbits escaped they would not eat up the crops on the arable land. Rabbits are not native to England and were introduced after the Norman Conquest. They were valued because they produced both meat and fur. They were kept in an artificial mound – the warren – looked after by a warrener. Rabbits were beasts of warren and presumably, in theory, a warren could include any physical structure designed to contain any other such beast; but in practice the word was limited to rabbit warrens. Later, rabbits became naturalised and are now found as wild or feral beasts throughout the country, and are considered as pests. The Ground Game Act 1880 and the Ground Game (Amendment) Act 1906 provide that any occupier of land has the right to kill rabbits even though other sporting rights are reserved to his landlord. A few warrens survive and some have become protected ancient monuments.

12.4   SPORTING IN COPYHOLD LAND

For the same reasons that a copyholder had no right to mines or timber, so also he might be expected to have no sporting rights. Copyhold land was originally arable so that rights to kill wild mammals would not have been worth much, but cultivators may have wished to have the right to kill birds. Where the copyhold was in strips in open fields there was unlikely to be much sporting value. As with minerals and timber, it might be expected that the lord's right would be to property, not possession, so that, in the absence of special custom, he would have no right to enter the copyhold to take game and, correspondingly, the copyholder would have no right to kill game on his copyhold. There seems to be little authority on the point. In practice, customary sporting rights of the lord in copyhold land were rare, and where they may have existed were hardly worth the cost of litigating. In *Pickering v Noyes*[12] Bayley J said, 'We all know that a very mistaken notion long prevailed that the lord of a manor had a right to go not only over his own lands, but over the lands of others within his manor'. That is because sporting rights of any value for beasts of forest, chase, park and warren would have been franchises and depended on a royal grant. The only sporting rights which were not so covered were for humble beasts, birds and fish or for vermin such as foxes. No new customary sporting rights in copyhold land could come into existence after 1189. Even where sporting rights might have subsisted in copyholds, special customs could vary between manors as to whether the lord had a right of entry, at what season and to take what game.

Section 23 of the Copyhold Act 1894 (re-enacting earlier provisions) and Sch 12, para (5) to the Law of Property Act 1922 provided that enfranchisement did not affect the right of the lord to any rights of chase or warren, piscaries or other rights of hunting, shooting, fishing, fowling or otherwise taking game, fish

---

[12]   (1825) 4 Barn & Cress 639, 107 ER 1198.

or fowl. The reference to 'any right' did not mean that such rights actually existed in any given case. The Land Registry view (considered in 25.9) is that all the rights listed in para (5) are manorial; the nature of manorial rights is considered in 9.5. From the cases[13] it appears that sporting franchises (presumably of chase and warren) in enfranchised land could be so regarded. For Land Registry purposes this is irrelevant since whether the rights arise from being manorial or franchises they are both at risk if not protected by notice or caution before the first registration or disposition of land after 12 October 2013, when they cease to be overriding interests.

Where the enfranchisement was at common law or by agreement under statute, sporting rights could be reserved as a profit out of the conveyance. Similar issues applied as to the exception of minerals (11.7).

12.5   SPORTING RESERVATIONS ON WASTE OR SOLD DEMESNE

The lord has the normal rights of sporting over his own waste, whether or not it is subject to rights of common.[14] Common rights of taking wild animals may exist but, apart from piscary (the right of common to take fish), they are rare. They would have to be of a type that would serve the land to which they are attached or, if they were in gross, would have to be limited by number. Any such rights that might have existed may have been lost under the Game Laws. Section 10 of the Game Act 1831 confirmed and may have extended the rights of lords of the manor to game on their own wastes and commons although, any extension of existing rights was probably not intended.

When waste was inclosed lords often wished to reserve sporting in much the same way as they excepted mineral rights. The issues are different as the right to the mineral strata was corporeal land, while sporting could only be an incorporeal profit. As with minerals a reference to seigniorial rights was ineffective since the lord did not have any such existing rights over his own waste distinct from ownership. An inclosure award could specifically entitle the lord to sporting rights. In *Musgrave v Forster*[15] Knaresdale Common in the manor of Knaresdale was inclosed under an award of 1853. The Inclosure Commissioners severed the sporting rights from the freehold in the soil and awarded the sporting to the lord of the manor. The court held that this was

---

[13]   See *Sowerby v Smith* (1873–4) LR9 CP 524, *Neill v Duke of Devonshire* (1882–3) LR8 App Cas 135, *Eckroyd v Coulthard* [1898] 2 Ch 358.

[14]   See *Brackenbank Lodge v Peart* [1996] EG 134 (CS) where the commoners had exclusive grazing rights but the lords were entitled to the grouse shooting.

[15]   (1870–71) LR 6 QB 590. See also *Ewart v Graham* (1859) VII HL Cas 331, 11 ER 132.

within their powers and was effective. Much depends on the precise wording of the inclosure Act in question. In *Greathead v Morley*[16] there was a reservation in an inclosure Act[17] for Marrick in Yorkshire to the lord of a list of manorial rights including hunting, hawking, fishing and fowling. The Court of Common Pleas held that the intention was simply to reserve manorial rights and as the claimed right of sporting had not existed before the Act since the lord had no separate right in his own waste, the purported reservation was ineffective. However, a similar provision was considered by the House of Lords in *Ewart v Graham*,[18] which concerned the interpretation of the Bailey Hope Inclosure Act.[19] Sir James Graham was lord of the manor of Nicholforest, in the county of Northumberland. On inclosure of the wastes and allotment of part of them to other persons there was a proviso to protect any seigniories belonging to the manor and the exclusive right of hunting and shooting over the allotments. The manor did not have a right of free warren. The House of Lords held that the sporting was not a seigniorial right but Sir James was nevertheless entitled to it as a profit à prendre created by the Act.[20] The Lords distinguished *Greathead v Morley* but did not overrule it.[21]

One type of sporting right looks like a residue of copyhold but is in fact a modern device. This is a reservation which specifically excludes any power of entering on the land subject to it for exercising sporting rights. At first sight this seems odd, for what use is a right of killing game if the person having the right cannot enjoy it? The answer is that in recent years many landowners have organised shoots, purchased their own pheasants and employed keepers to rear them, all of which is expensive. Where old farmhouses or cottages were sold from the middle of an estate, the owners found that in some cases the buyers (often people of some means buying a country home) would put out a bowl of corn, seize an unwary pheasant and wring its neck. Even though the bird (or perhaps its parents) had been purchased, it was still wild and therefore not owned, so the owner of the cottage could not be accused of theft. Accordingly it is common nowadays for landowners to instruct solicitors when selling surplus farm cottages to reserve the sporting but with no right of entry.

---

[16] (1841) 3 Man & G 139, 133 ER 1090.

[17] 52 Geo 3 (c cxxvi).

[18] (1859) 7 HL Cas 331, 11 ER 132.

[19] 51 Geo 3 (c x).

[20] See also *The Overseers of the Townships of Hilton and Walkerfield v The Overseers of the Township of Bowes* (1865–66) LR 1 QB 359, per Lush J.

[21] See also *Duke of Devonshire v O'Connor* [1890] LR 24 QBD 468 and *Sowerby v Smith* (1873–4) LR 9 CP 524, following *Greathead v Morley* (1841) 3 Man & G 139, 133 ER 1090; but cf *Lord Leconfield v Dixon* (1867–68) 3 Ex 30, following *Ewart v Graham* (1859) 7 HL Cas 331, 11 ER 132.

It is also common practice, when estates are being broken up and the farms sold, to reserve sporting rights with full powers of entry and rights to rear game, and these are then sold separately. Such rights often exist as profits created by deed either reserved on the sale of land[22] or granted by a landowner who retains ownership. Although sporting rights are often reserved on sales of former demesne land from a large estate where the owner is also lord, the rules here are not special to manorial law.

A sporting right, whether arising under inclosure, created between parties or created by agreement on enfranchisement, is a profit and will subsist as a legal interest. As a profit it is capable of registration with its own title. If not mentioned on the register of the servient title it will only be enforceable as an overriding interest under the Land Registration Act 2002 so long as it satisfies the conditions in Sch 3, para 3. As it is not a manorial right, if it does not so satisfy it may already have ceased to take priority against a person taking under a disposition for value after 12 October 2003.

12.6   HUNTING

Hunting has long been an important part of rural life, enjoyed by many lords and landowners. Lords had the right to hunt over their own demesne and waste and to permit others to do so. Access by those without a legal right was a trespass. It may also have been a criminal offence under the Game Laws (12.8) but, because of the importance of hunting, s 35 of the Game Act 1831 formerly provided that the provisions in the Act against trespassers did not apply to persons 'hunting or coursing upon any lands with hounds or greyhounds, and being in fresh pursuit of any deer, hare, or fox already started upon any other land'. Those words were repealed by the Hunting Act 2004.

When landowners sold their land they often reserved hunting rights, especially if they continued to live in the area. Hunting can subsist as a separate right from other forms of sporting,[23] although in practice many reservations of sporting rights include hunting along with shooting or hawking. The same applied to inclosure of the waste, where similar issues arose as to other forms of sporting mentioned above, although a large concourse of huntsmen and dogs would be capable of causing more damage to fences and crops than entry for shooting.

Hunting has in recent years been the subject of much political debate, which culminated in the Hunting Act 2004. Section 1 prohibits hunting a wild mammal

---

[22]   See eg *Well Barn Shoot Ltd v Shackleton* [2003] EWCA Civ 2.

[23]   *Moore v Earl of Plymouth* (1820) 7 Taunt 614, 129 ER 245.

with a dog subject to numerous exceptions set out in Schedule 1. It therefore does not apply to hunting without dogs, nor does it apply to hunting animals which are not wild mammals. Although it was expected that the Act would destroy a long-established activity, the practical effect has been limited as people have instead turned to drag hunting and similar variations. The provisions are so complicated and difficult to interpret that in some parts of the country the police have decided that enforcing the Act has to take a low priority as compared with other law enforcement.

In addition to the penalties on huntsmen themselves, an offence is also committed under s 3 if a person 'knowingly permits land which belongs to him to be entered or used in the course of the commission of an offence under section 1'. By s 11(3) land is treated as belonging to a person if he owns an interest in it or manages or controls it, or occupies it. A right of hunting would be a profit and therefore an interest in land. However, the Act does not extinguish such rights and to make exercise in particular ways unlawful does not by itself abolish them. It is therefore possible that lords may still have rights of this nature, particularly over inclosed waste.

12.7 FISHING

Different rules apply to fishing in tidal waters and fishing in non-tidal waters. For inland manors many of the same rules that apply to mammals and birds apply also to fish. Fish can be owned if they are confined in a fishpond.[24] Such ponds were common in the Middle Ages when they were a good source of food in winter and could be eaten in Lent when meat was forbidden. Many manors, especially those held by monasteries, had ponds, and the remains are found all over England. Fish in the river are wild and belong only to the person who catches them. Fish weirs were often built across streams and small rivers, sometimes by the lord and sometimes by his permission given through the manor court.

Modern fishing in inland rivers is mainly done for sport. Ownership of the bed of a river was considered in 6.8. Fishing rights belong to the owner of the bed, the owner of the bank or the owner of the incorporeal fishery, and these may be different persons. If the river is the boundary between two properties then, strictly speaking, fish can only be caught by the owner of one side up to the middle line,[25] but fish cannot be expected to observe property limits and, in practice, the usual rule is that someone standing on the bank can catch as far as

---

[24] Carty, P, 'The ownership of fish', *Water Law*, July–August 1995.

[25] Bracton *op cit* f 208b.

he can cast, and someone in a boat can also take any fish within reach. The rules vary and incorporeal rights of fishing over river beds of other owners also exist.

Barton v Church Commissioners for England[26] concerned a dispute over a private fishery in a stretch of the River Wye at Hereford. Morgan J described many of the basic rules applicable to inland fisheries:

[28] There is a distinction between a corporeal fishery and an incorporeal fishery. Fisheries are profits, in the sense of being an advantage, of the soil over which the water flows. The title to a fishery can arise from title to this soil. A fishery may be severed from the soil and it then becomes a *profit à prendre in alieno solo* and as such is an incorporeal hereditament. The term 'corporeal fishery' is used to describe a corporeal hereditament such as, in non-tidal waters, the soil coupled with the right of fishing over it. A corporeal fishery may be owned by one who owns no land adjacent to it. The term 'incorporeal fishery' is used to describe an incorporeal hereditament, that is, a right to take fish or a specified class of fish in a defined stretch of water without interference with the soil. An incorporeal fishery may be held freehold, or for a term of years absolute. An incorporeal fishery may be appurtenant to, or a parcel of, a manor.

...

[30] A private fishery may be either a several fishery or a common of fishery. A several fishery is an exclusive right of fishing in a given place, either with or without the property in the soil. By 'exclusive' is meant that no other person has a co-extensive right with the owner of the several fishery. The fact that some other person has a right to a particular class of fish in the fishery or has a right to fish in common with the owner of the several fishery does not destroy the severalty of the fishery. A common of fishery or a common of piscary is a liberty of fishing in another man's waters in common with certain other persons who might be the owners of the soil or other persons enjoying the same right. It may be held as appurtenant to land, or in gross. If the common of fisheries is appurtenant to land, it may not be 'without stint' i.e. unlimited. An incorporeal fishery may be held in gross or appurtenant to, or parcel of, a manor or appurtenant to land. An incorporeal fishery in gross is a *profit à prendre*. Under the Land Registration Act 2002, section 3(1), a *profit à prendre* in gross, when the subject of an absolute grant or for a lease of more than seven years is capable of registration at the Land Registry. An incorporeal fishery can be only transferred by deed. A lease of an incorporeal fishery must be by deed.

[31] There is a general presumption of law that the owner of land abutting on a non-tidal river is entitled to the soil of the river *usque ad medium filum aquae*. In the absence of any express reference, this presumption applies to all grants and leases of land described as bounded by a river, when the grant or lease is made by a

---

[26] [2008] EWHC 3091 (Ch).

person who is in a position to part with the soil of the river. There is a presumption that the owner of the soil of a river is the owner of the fishery over it. There is a presumption that the owner of a fishery is the owner of the soil of the river. This presumption will prevail over the presumption in favour of a riparian owner, in the event of a conflict as to the title to the soil which arises between the owner of a fishery and the owner of riparian land.

In some manors the lord's right to fishing extended to copyhold lands. The bed might be waste and retained by the lord (6.8) but otherwise, if the copyhold was on the bank, it could include half the bed. Thus, in *Tilbury v Silva*[27] the lord of the manor of Chilbolton had the right to fish from a copyhold before it was enfranchised. On enfranchisement in 1845 the enfranchisement deed released the right of fishery. The court, in a judgment by Cotton LJ, construed this to extend not only to the interest of the enfranchised copyholder but to extinguish the lord's fishing rights permanently.

Piscary, the right of common to take fish, is well established, although rarely found in practice. It is subject to the same general rules as other common rights, so that, if appurtenant, it can only be used for the needs of the householder of the property that benefits or, if in gross, it must be limited by a specific number of fish.

It appears that there is a customary right to take fish. This is an anomaly since taking something is normally a profit and there cannot be a customary profit because exercise by an undefined and fluctuating class of persons is liable to exhaust the subject matter[28] (4.8). *Mills v Colchester Corporation*[29] concerned a claim that certain inhabitants of Colchester had the right, on payment of a licence fee, to take oysters. In the event the custom was not upheld because taking oysters had been by permission of the corporation but the court considered that in principle there could be such a customary right. Fish may be special since, unlike taking minerals or grass, there is a constant flow, so the objection that the subject matter will become exhausted may not apply.

There can also exist corporate rights of ancient origin. Their nature was considered in *Goodman v Mayor of Saltash*[30] (21.5) and *Gann v Free Fishers of Whitstable*[31] (15.5) and they usually exist through some form of corporate or trust holding of or on behalf of the tenants. Such rights seem to exist for

---

[27] (1890) 45 Ch D 98.

[28] *Lloyd v Jones* (1848) 6 CB 81 at 89, per Wilde CJ.

[29] (1866–67) LR 2 CP 476. The contrary view in *Bland v Lipscome* (unreported) (1854), cited in *Race v Ward* (1855) 4 Ell & Black 702, 119 ER 259, was explained as *obiter*.

[30] (1882) 7 App Cas 633.

[31] (1864/5) 11 HLC 192, 11 ER 1305.

commercial exploitation rather than the usual form of enjoyment by tenants for domestic purposes and are probably best understood as an early form of fishermens' co-operative.

In tidal rivers special rules apply. The presumption is that the bed of tidal waters belongs to the Crown unless it has been granted to a subject. Originally, the bed alone was of little value and the fishing rights were more important. In Saxon times tidal rivers were often included in bookland as part of an estate, and the Norman kings also granted such fisheries to the lord of the adjoining manor. This was known as putting the river in defence. Many such rights have been exercised continually down the centuries and still exist. Grants of several fisheries were resented since they removed the right of members of the public to fish in Crown waters. Even if the Crown took back a manor which included a several fishery, that did not destroy the franchise, which continued in existence (16.7) as it had not been part of the prerogative right before grant.

Putting tidal rivers in defence was among the grievances that led to Magna Carta 1215, which revoked all such grants made in John's reign since 1199. John died in 1216 and in 1217 the guardians of his young son, Henry III, issued a new edition of the Charter, which confirmed the prohibition on putting waters in defence and the rescission of grants made in John's time. The Great Charter was reissued by Henry III's son, Edward I, and this provision was ultimately enacted as c 16 of the Statute of Magna Carta in 1297, which is the basis of the modern law. This legislates by reference to the charter of Henry III, but c 16, instead of referring to the start of John's reign, revokes grants made after the time of Henry II, that is 1189. In *Malcolmson v O'Dea*[32] in 1863 it was held that new several fisheries could not have been created after 1189.

It is not unusual for coastal manors to claim several fisheries in suitable estuaries. Where there was industrial development upstream the river often became so polluted as to make the fishery worthless, but as rivers became cleaner under modern environmental laws fish have returned. Where rights have been exercised without interruption the fishery may be recognised and unchallenged, but where it has not been exploited for one or two centuries it may now be difficult to establish a claim.

Under statute, fishing rights can be held with a manor but this may be difficult to prove. An example was *Staffordshire and Worcestershire Canal Navigation v Bradley*.[33] The plaintiffs were a canal company set up under an Act of 1766. Mr

---

[32]   (1863) 10 HLCas 618, 11 ER 1155. The case concerned a claimed fishery in the River Shannon in County Limerick. Because Henry III was also Lord of Ireland, Magna Carta was incorporated into Irish law very early.

[33]   [1910] 1 Ch 91.

Bradley was a member of the Stoke-on-Trent Angling Society and claimed the right to fish under a lease granted in 1910 by the Earl of Shrewsbury to the society. The canal company did not recognise that right. Section 74 of the Act provided that:

> the lord or lords, or owner or owners, of all and every manor and manors through which the said intended cut or canal shall be made, shall have and be entitled to the sole, several and exclusive right of fishery

in so much of the canal as was made through the common waste or other land of the manor. Part of the canal was cut through the manor of Tixall which belonged to the Hon Thomas Clifford. In 1845 the manor was put into a settlement under which, eventually, Lord Shrewsbury was the beneficiary. The 1845 deed did not refer specifically to the fishery in the canal, but did contain general words including 'fisheries'.

The court held that s 74 created a right of fishery in gross because it was without limit and not related in any way to the use of the land or the manor of Tixall. As there had been no express assignment in 1845 it had not passed into the settlement or to the earl. Accordingly, he had no right which he could grant to the angling society. The decision in this case is similar to *Morris v Dimes*[34] in that there seems to be a presumption against sporting rights being annexed to manors.

Statutory sporting rights on canals are so widespread that no one knows how many there are. In 1991 the British Waterways Board wished to abolish them as being a nuisance to the proper management of canals. It introduced a Bill into Parliament which proposed, *inter alia*, abolishing any provision in any private Act that conferred on lords of manors 'fishing or sporting rights over, or rights to use pleasure boats without payment' on any inland waterway. This provision aroused a great deal of opposition and when the Act was finally passed in January 1995 the clause was omitted.

It is possible to establish several fisheries for shellfish by statute, now governed by the Sea Fisheries (Shellfish) Act 1967, as amended by the Marine and Coastal Access Act 2009, Part 7, Chapter 2. This provides a procedure to confer private rights in tidal waters whether they belong to the Crown or to any other landowner. Where local fishermen consider that there is a good prospect of establishing a fishery they may apply for an order under the Act conferring rights for up to 60 years. Under s 1(5):

---

[34]   (1834) 1 Ad & E 654, 110 ER 1357.

> No order under this section shall take away or abridge any right of several fishery
> or any right on, to or over any portion of the sea shore, being a right enjoyed by any
> person under any local or special Act of Parliament or any Royal charter, letters
> patent, prescription, or immemorial usage, except with the consent of that person.

Apart from that the owner of the river bed has a right to be heard at a public
inquiry into the Order but has no veto.

12.8   THE GAME LAWS

The Game Laws are a collection of Acts ranging from the Night Poaching Act
1828 to the Ground Game (Amendment) Act 1906, of which the most important
is the Game Act 1831. They are still in force but comprise a confusing and
illogical set of rules, and among the curiosities is the place they give to the lord
of the manor.

The purpose of the Game Laws was to control poaching. It follows from the rule
that living wild animals cannot be owned that they cannot be stolen for there is
no owner from whom to steal. That rule is confirmed in s 4(4) of the Theft Act
1968 (although under s 32 there can be theft of fish). However landowners, in
the early nineteenth century, and before, considered that poaching was similar to
stealing. It was only between 1823 and 1832 that stealing ceased to be a capital
offence, but even some Regency landowners hesitated before hanging a
poacher. Previous Game Laws in 1389 and 1673[35] had limited the right to kill
game to people of a certain social standing or income but this was
unsatisfactory.[36] The Game Laws provide a variety of rules, prohibiting the
taking of game on certain days and at certain times of the year, which vary for
different parts of the country, with exceptions for certain people. Other
provisions required a licence for anyone (with exceptions) to kill game. Others
make it a crime to trespass in pursuit of game or with certain equipment such as
a 'gun, net, engine or other instrument'.[37] Normally trespass is a civil wrong, not
a crime, but it would do landowners little good to sue the typical poacher for
damages. Poaching was therefore made a crime triable in the magistrates' court
and in the early nineteenth century the magistrates were the local landowners.

It would be out of all proportion to include here a detailed account of the Game
Laws and all their ramifications. This account is limited to the law as it
specifically affects lords of manors. At first sight it is odd to include them at all.

---

[35]   13 Ric 2 (c 13); Keeping of Dogs to Hunt 1389, 22 & 23 Cha 2 (c 25); Game 1670.

[36]   Skyrme, Sir Thomas, *History of the Justices of the Peace* (1994) 549–562 concludes that the
       eighteenth-century Game Laws were not operated harshly.

[37]   Night Poaching Act 1828, s 1.

In the case of statutes concerning commons their inclusion makes sense in that until recent times common land was largely waste of the manor; but, even so, the statutes usually refer to 'the lord of the manor or other owner'.

Poaching occurs on any moorland or in any wood where there is game, whether or not the land belongs to the lord. The explanation for this is that in 1831 in practice game rights were still largely held by lords even though by that time much of the country had long been taken out of manors.

There is no established or universal meaning of 'game' at common law.[38] In the Game Laws it is defined variously. The principal definition in the Night Poaching Act 1828 includes hares, bustards, pheasants, partridges, grouse, heath or moor game and black game and some provisions extend to rabbits. In the Game Act 1831 the same definition occurs excluding bustards. The Poaching Prevention Act 1862 also omits bustards and adds rabbits, woodcock, snipe and the eggs of pheasants, partridges, grouse and black or moor game. The Game Licences Act 1860 includes deer, rabbits, woodcock and snipe. Ground game for the purposes of the Ground Game Act 1880 means hares and rabbits.

Under s 2 of the Night Poaching Act 1828, where a poacher by night takes game or rabbits in any land then either the owner of the land or the occupier or the lord of the manor wherein the land is situate and the gamekeeper of any of them can seize the offender, and can pursue him onto other land, but he must be handed over to a peace officer (now a policeman) and taken before the magistrates. Presumably, in addition to waste and demesne, this also applies to ancient manorial freeholds and also probably to former copyhold land.[39]

Under the Game Act 1831, s 13 the lord of a manor can appoint a gamekeeper to preserve or kill game within the limits of the manor and can authorise the gamekeeper to seize all 'dogs, nets, and other engines and instruments for the killing or taking of game' as are used by poachers. Of course, anyone can appoint a gamekeeper, but only keepers appointed by lords have that power. Under s 14 the lord may appoint his gamekeeper to be gamekeeper for other people but the gamekeeper's special powers apply only when he is acting on behalf of the lord. The same limits to the area of the manor presumably apply. The appointment of a gamekeeper under s 13 must, under s 16, be registered with the clerk of the peace who, as a result of the Courts Act 1971, s 56, is the clerk of the local authority.

The Game Act 1831, s 35 stated that its provisions against trespassers did not apply to any person exercising a right of free warren or free chase, but those

---

[38] *Inglewood Investment Co Ltd v Forestry Commissioners* [1988] 1 WLR 1278.

[39] *Re Mansfield District Council's Application* (1976) 33 P&CR 141, 241 EG 241.

words were repealed by the Wild Creatures and Forest Laws Act 1971. The 1831 Act still provides that it does not apply to 'to any lord or any steward of the crown of any manor, lordship, or royalty, or reputed manor, lordship, or royalty, nor to any gamekeeper lawfully appointed by such lord or steward within the limits of such manor, lordship, or royalty, or reputed manor, lordship, or royalty'.

If demesne land has been sold it will cease to be part of the manor and the special rules in s 2 of the 1828 Act and s 13 of the 1831 Act will not operate for the benefit of that land. It may be arguable that if waste land is separated from the lordship the powers will still apply following the reasoning in *Hampshire County Council v Milburn*,[40] but if the matter ever came to be tested in court it is unlikely the court would extend that reasoning to the Game Laws.

12.9   STATUTORY PROTECTION OF WILDLIFE

The Ground Game Act 1880 gives occupiers of land a right (which cannot be taken away) to kill hares and rabbits on the land they occupy. This is concurrent with anyone else who has sporting rights and is subject to certain rules. It was introduced as a measure of pest control to protect crops. The Wild Mammals (Protection) Act 1996 makes it an offence to mutilate or injure in certain defined ways any wild mammal with intent to inflict unnecessary suffering. There is a defence if the animal is taken in the course of lawful shooting or hunting and the killing is swift and humane or if the injury is authorised by enactment. However, this does involve further controls on the killing of wild animals.

Certain Acts, such as the Deer Act 1991 and the Protection of Badgers Act 1992, regulate the killing of particular species. There is a wide measure of control under the Wildlife and Countryside Act 1981 in which a large number of animals and birds are listed and their killing prohibited or controlled. Under the National Parks and Access to the Countryside Act 1949, s 20(2)(b) and (c), where land is comprised in a nature reserve, byelaws may be made to prohibit or restrict killing living creatures or shooting birds in adjacent areas. Under the Wildlife and Countryside Act 1981, s 28, areas may be notified as sites of special scientific interest and if the notification specifies fauna then it is an offence to carry out specified operations which may include killing the animals referred to under ss 28E and 28P. This is binding on the owner and occupier of the land and 'owner' is defined by reference to s 114 of the National Parks and Access to the Countryside Act 1949, which does not directly include someone with sporting rights. However, an offence may also be committed by a person,

---

[40]   [1991] AC 235, [1990] 2 All ER 257, (1990) 61 P&CR 135.

which extends to cover people other than owners. There is also relevant European Union legislation. Under the Birds Directive on the conservation of wild birds of 30 November 2009[41] and the Habitats Directive[42] of 21 May 1992 on the conservation of natural habitats and of wild fauna and flora (both incorporated into English Law by the Conservation (Natural Habitats Etc.) Regulations 1994[43]) wild birds and animals are protected against being killed in certain defined areas. Thus, even if the lord still retains sporting rights he may not be able to exercise them.

---

[41] Originally Directive 79/409/EEC now consolidated in 2009/147/EC of the European Parliament and of the Council of 30 November 2009.

[42] Directive 92/43/EEC.

[43] SI 1994/2716; see also the Wildlife and Countryside Act 1981 (England and Wales) (Amendment) Regulations (SI 2004/1487).

Chapter 13

Courts

13.1   COURTS BARON, CUSTOMARY AND LEET

The manor court was the essential feature of the manor: a necessary adjunct.[1] It was inseparable from the lordship, which could not exist without it. Thousands of manor courts still exist, although they have been deprived of nearly all their legal functions and any lord who can locate two free tenants may hold a court even though he can no longer compel tenants to pay suit.

The word 'court' (Latin *curia*) comes from *curtis*, meaning 'an enclosed place, typically a courtyard'. Many large paved areas surrounded by buildings are called courts, as in Cambridge colleges. When kings or great men gathered their close followers for advice or information the meetings were held in such places because buildings were too small and courts were sheltered from the wind. The assembly itself took its name from the meeting place. Nowadays, different types of court exist. There is the court of the monarch, attended by courtiers wearing court dress and behaving (one hopes) with courtesy, and by ladies making curtseys. There is the High Court of Parliament which is the assembly of selected people to advise the sovereign on making law and to discuss matters of general concern. There are courts of justice where professional judges perform on behalf of the Queen the duty of deciding disputes and interpreting law.

These great courts have a long history. In the Middle Ages they were mirrored at a local level but in humble fashion and without the distinction between executive, legislature and judicial functions that subsists between Whitehall, Westminster and the Strand. There was a system of shire court, hundred court

---

[1]   Watkins, C, *A Treatise on Copyholds* (James Bullock, 4th edn by Thomas Coventry, 1825) 1.8; Scriven, J, *A Treatise on the Law of Copyholds* (Butterworth & Co, 7th edn by Archibald Brown, 1896) 422; *see R v Stafferton* (1610) 1 Bulstrode 54, 80 ER 756.

and court leet (discussed in 19.2–19.5). In the towns there were borough courts and courts of pie-powder (considered in 21.1). There were also Church courts as explained in 20.1. The manor courts were general bodies, able to deal with any matter that arose. Until 1925 these were a source of profit to the lord and his steward. In many places they are still a convenient gathering to consider what Sch 4 to the Administration of Justice Act 1977 calls 'matters of local concern'. The manor courts could be judicial, for settling disputes, but that jurisdiction has long been obsolete and was formally abolished (save in two cases) by the 1977 Act. Their main function was much wider.

Courts of the lord are of two types: courts baron and courts leet. A court leet with view of frankpledge was a franchise (16.3) and was not a function of the manor. Charles Watkins in the preface to Volume 2 of his book on Copyholds, says:[2]

> It has even been intimated to him that the law relative to COURTS-LEET was expected; but he must beg leave to say once more, that he was writing on the law of COPYHOLDS; and surely the law of courts-leet formed no part of that law. He might as well have a dissertation upon thunder, or upon the seat of the soul.

It will be necessary to look briefly at courts leet since they cannot be separated from courts baron, but they will be considered more fully in 19.5.

The court leet was a court of record,[3] that is a court whose records of its own proceedings had automatic legal standing and were recognised by other courts of record, notably the royal courts, without having to be specially proved in evidence. The manorial courts were private courts and were not courts of record, but in practice it was not difficult to produce the court rolls with an official to state that they were a true record of proceedings. The Law of Property Act 1922, s 144 now provides that:

> Court Rolls shall (whether before or after the manorial incidents have been extinguished), for the purposes of section fourteen of the Evidence Act, 1851, be deemed to be documents of such a public nature as to be admissible in evidence on their mere production from the proper custody.

There has been a good deal of discussion as to whether there were one or two manor courts and different writers express different views, but the best view is that there was a single manor court which, from at least the sixteenth century, had two aspects.

---

[2]   Watkins *op cit* 2.v. See also *Delacherois v Delacherois* (1862) HL Cas 62 at 79, 11 ER 1254.

[3]   Blackstone, Sir William, *Commentaries on the Laws of England* IV.19.i; see also III.3.i; *Griesley's Case* (1587) 8 Co Rep 38a, 77 ER 530.

The first was the court baron (or common law court baron). Baron here does not mean a peer but refers to the legal standing of any free man who could be referred to as a baron. The barons of the court baron were the common freeholders or socmen of the manor. They were usually referred to as suitors because they owed suit of court – the obligation to attend the court when summoned. The suitors themselves comprised the court and although the lord's steward was essential to the working of the court baron, he was not a president or judge but simply an officer. Suitors sat as the court and had a legal right to have the lord summon a court if he failed to do so, a right enforceable by writ of mandamus from the royal court.[4] As the suitors were an integral part of the court, there had to be at least two in the manor: one to bring his case and the other to act as judge. Thus, if there were less than two freeholders of the manor, it could not have a properly constituted court baron and became a reputed manor (8.4).[5] However, it seems that if a single remaining freehold of the manor was divided, as by sale of part, so that the buyer, as well as the seller, held of the lord, that might reconstitute the manor. That view may be inconsistent with *Sir Moyle Finch's Case*[6] but the point seems undecided.

The other aspect of the manor court was the customary court (or customary court baron), that is the court where the customs of the manor were applied and therefore in which matters relating to customary or copyhold land were dealt with. This court was presided over by the lord's steward who acted as judge and was responsible for the records. The customary tenants, called the homage, were obliged to be present. They were said to owe suit of court but were not called suitors. The homage simply meant the men of the manor and had only an indirect relationship with homage as a duty owed along with services. Homage here was a collective word for *hommes*. Their function was like a jury and in particular they would decide whether or not a practice was a custom of the manor.

In the late Middle Ages the court baron appears to have been the more important of the two courts. However, as no new common manorial freeholds could be created after *Quia Emptores* 1290 save by statute, all trace of existing manorial freeholders tended to become lost and, as the services owed by socmen became obsolete or forgotten or (if they were in money) eroded by inflation, so the number of manorial freeholders diminished and courts baron ceased to sit. It is possible that the effect of the Copyhold Acts 1841 to 1894 was to create more such freeholders but by that time it was too late to revive courts baron even if there had been any point in doing so. Meanwhile, as the rights of copyholders

---

[4] Scriven *op cit* 96, 142; Adkin, BW, *Copyhold and other Land Tenures of England* (Sweet & Maxwell, 3rd edn, 1919) 128.

[5] See *Baxendale v Instow Parish Council* [1982] 1 Ch 14, [1981] 2 All ER 620; Scriven *op cit* 424.

[6] (1610) 6 Co Rep 63a, 77 ER 310.

received greater protection and copyhold itself became a valuable property, so the customary court became important. In many manors it took over the name of court baron.

Courts leet, particularly where the manor corresponded to the settlement or vill, were held at the same time as the manorial court and in the same place. Often the proceedings of the court baron, the customary court and the court leet were recorded on the same roll and the two (or three) bodies were fused into one. This was particularly so when the villagers were considering matters of local organisation. In theory the making and enforcement of byelaws to control animals on the manorial waste was a matter for the manor court, while byelaws to control animals grazing on the fallow in the open fields were for the court leet.

By the nineteenth century in many villages both the manorial courts and the courts leet were moribund and responsibility for local administration, until the local government reforms (which themselves took from 1832 to 1894), fell partly to justices of the peace and partly to churchwardens acting through the vestry. The theoretical mediaeval division of functions between manor, community and Church disintegrated in the centuries after 1500 and it was a matter of chance which of the three picked up the pieces. By 1925 the principal function of most manor courts had for long been the surrenders and admissions involved in the sale of copyhold land with the entry fines and heriots due on inheritance. A few had other functions, particularly in relation to common land, which some still retain.

The lord had a duty to hold the court. In *Henly v Lyme Corporation*[7] Best CJ said:

> Lords of manors hold courts, which courts they are obliged to hold, as one of the considerations on which the lands have been granted to them. If a lord of the manor were to refuse or neglect to hold a court, by which a copyholder should be prevented from having admission to his copyhold, does any man doubt an action could be maintained against such lord?

13.2   TIME AND PLACE

Originally 15 days' notice was usual for the holding of courts baron, including three Sundays because the suitors and homage were obliged to attend and had to be given good warning and notice (like banns of mariage) could be given at church. A special court could be held without notice and, if it affected only one or two tenants, such as transferring land, it often was so held. The court was

---

[7]   (1828) 5 Bing NC 91, 130 ER 995.

originally held every three weeks,[8] but by the eighteenth century the lord could not compel suitors to attend more often than once a year and by general custom the court was held at Michaelmas (29 September). Courts baron could be held at night and it might be convenient to hold them after the working day. In the manor of Kingshill in Rochford, Essex a court was held on the Wednesday following Michaelmas in each year at cockcrow known as the Lawless Court.[9] Courts leet also required 15 days' notice and were bound to be held at least twice a year within a month after Easter and Michaelmas.[10] As explained, they were often held together with the manor court.

The usual place[11] for the court to meet was the lord's hall, if there was one. If all the tenants of a manor in 1189 were to be present then the hall or the church were the only places large enough to hold them. Watkins[12] mentions a manor in Shropshire where the court was held 'under a very aged ash-tree where the steward called over the copyholders and formed a jury, and then adjourned the court to a neighbouring inn for dispatch of business'. He says that he had personal knowledge of other such manors. No doubt the adjournment proceedings would be speedy if it was raining. In the eighteenth century courts often met in inns. By then the homage was much smaller and perhaps only half a dozen people, including tenants and steward, might be present. Indeed, in emergency the court could be held elsewhere, such as in the home of a copyholder on his deathbed, who was too ill to be moved but who wished to pass his land on to his family during his lifetime to avoid inheritance customs.[13]

By the nineteenth century the steward was usually a local solicitor dealing with the main business of transferring copyholds. Originally, the court had to be held somewhere in the manor, save that if it was parcel of an honour, custom might authorise one court for several manors. The Copyhold Act 1841, s 87 allowed grants and admittances to be made out of the manor and without holding a court. It further provided that a customary court could be held even though no copyholders were present. Thereafter, most admittances tended to be made over the desk of the steward in his office, usually in a nearby market town. However, it still seems to be the law that if a court is held it must be within the manor.

---

[8]   *Tonkin v Croker* (1703) 2 Ld Raym 860, 92 ER 74.

[9]   Kingshill: Watkins *op cit* 2.14.

[10]   Ibid 2.11.

[11]   Coke, Sir Edward, *Complete Copyholder* (E Flesher et al, 1630) s 31.

[12]   Watkins *op cit* 2.9.

[13]   Bettey, JH, 'Manorial Custom and Widows' Estate', in Archives XX No 88, October 1992.

The right to hold a court was not lost by disuse. In *R v The Steward and Suitors of the Manor of Havering Atte Bower*[14] a manor court had, by royal charter, a civil jurisdiction. It had not been held for that purpose for some 50 years, although there had been other court proceedings in that time. The judges held that where the court was established for the public benefit mere failure to hold it did not deprive it of jurisdiction.

13.3   PROCEDURE[15]

To those used to attending meetings of contemporary local government, companies or clubs some aspects of the procedure may seem familiar. This is no coincidence. When English people began to hold meetings for such purposes they naturally adopted old familiar ways and almost everything, from apologies for absence and reading the minutes of the last meeting onwards, has an ancient origin.

When the steward, suitors and homage met, the steward first entered on the roll the time and place, his own name as presiding, and the nature of the meeting. Courts baron were styled 'the Court Baron (or Customary Court) of AB Esq. lord of the Manor of X'. The court leet was either 'the Court Leet of AB Esq.' or 'of Our Lord the King'. The bailiff then made a first proclamation calling on the suitors and tenants to appear and do suit and service. Only one proclamation on the court day was needed for a court baron (although more could be made), but three on that day were necessary for a court leet.

The suitors were then called over by name. A second proclamation was made. Then the steward said, 'If anyone will be assoigned, or enter plaint, let him come in'. As suitors were bound to attend they could be fined or amerced if they did not. An essoin was an excuse for absence such as being abroad, being away on the lord's business or being ill.[16] As long as courts baron could hear civil actions these were taken next. That jurisdiction has now been removed. The third proclamation was then made and the jury (of the court leet) and homage (of the customary court) were sworn, the foreman first:[17]

> You shall inquire and true presentment make of all such matters and things as shall be given to you in charge,

---

[14]   (1822) 5 B and Ald 691, 106 ER 1343.

[15]   Watkins *op cit* 2.382.

[16]   Bracton *op cit* f 336–364.

[17]   Watkins *op cit* 2.387–8.

> The King's council, your own and your fellows, you shall well and truly keep; you shall present nothing out of hatred or malice, nor shall conceal anything out of fear, favour or affection, but in all things you shall well and truly present, so as the same shall come to your knowledge
>
> So help you God.

The general business of the court then followed; the presentment of the deaths of tenants since the last court and their heirs, and the presentment of suitors who were absent without leave or good cause. The court then turned to forfeitures such as cutting timber or committing felony, and then to withholding of services, trespasses on the demesne, and overstocking of the common. Further, any nuisances or offences within the manor were presented. Byelaws could also be made at this stage. The steward minuted all of these matters and entered most of them on the roll. The next step was to appoint, swear and admit officers. Quitrents and other rents were then paid, together with any leasehold rents payable at the manor court. Where an offence had been committed the fine was then payable. Sometimes the jury or the homage had to fix the amount of the payment; sometimes it was fixed by custom (14.2). Subsequently, new tenants, including heirs, were admitted to their holdings and the steward would hand them a rod as token of admission.

Finally, the steward read over the heads of entries in his minute book and wrote underneath 'We present this as our verdict', which first the foreman and then the other members of the jury in order of seniority signed or made their mark. The beadle then adjourned the court if necessary or else discharged it altogether with the words:[18]

> O Yes (or Oyez), All manner of persons that have appeared at this (customary) court of AB Esq have leave to depart home, keeping their day and hour on a new summons

13.4   ADMINISTRATION OF JUSTICE ACT 1977

Section 23 of the Administration of Justice Act 1977 was passed on the initiative of the Law Commission[19] which was concerned that various ancient courts (including manorial courts) might be revived unexpectedly and be required to meet and take legal steps. Most had been moribund since at least the 1930s and some for centuries. Nevertheless, as a matter of law, a court does not lose jurisdiction simply because it has not met for a long time.

---

[18]   Watkins *op cit* 2.385.

[19]   Law Commission No 72, *Jurisdiction of Certain Ancient Courts*.

Much of the legal jurisdiction as a court of justice had long since gone. Actions relating to real property (principally land) were abolished by s 36 of the Real Property Limitation Act 1833, and personal actions by s 28 of the County Courts Act 1867. Any jurisdiction which remained in 1925 was, under s 188(6) of the Law of Property Act 1922 (a definition section), transferred to the High Court (later under the Courts Act 1971 to the county court). Criminal jurisdiction had been obsolete long before and any probate jurisdiction was abolished by s 3 of the Court of Probate Act 1857.

If anything remained, s 23 of the 1977 Act provided that courts of certain specified descriptions, including courts baron, customary courts of the manor, courts leet and views of frankpledge (19.5), should cease to have any jurisdiction to hear and determine legal proceedings. There are two exceptions: one the Estray Court for the lordship of Denbigh and the other the court leet for the manor of Laxton.

The Act did not abolish courts. It specifically provided that any courts could sit and transact 'such other business, if any, as was customary for it' immediately before the Act came into force. The word 'customary' here probably means according to legal custom as described in 4.1, but it may have the wider meaning of 'usual' or 'often done'. The Act helpfully has a list in Part III of Sch 4 of the business that is treated as having been customary for certain specified courts, apart from the appointment of officers. Thirty-two courts are listed. The Law Commission's Report also mentions the court leet for the manor of Staines, but because the lord and the commoners disagreed on the nature of its business it was not included in Sch 4 to the Act.

Of the 32 courts listed, two (the City of London Court of Hustings and the Norwich Court of Mayoralty) are not manorial at all. Of the 30 remaining, six (Bideford, Bucklebury, Cricklade, Dunstone, East Horndon and Heaton in Bradford) appear to be courts baron only. Seven (Fyling, Portland, Southampton, Southwark, Wareham, Warwick and Whitby) appear to be courts leet only. The remaining 17 appear to be both manorial and leet. The business recorded varies, some courts dealing with several types of business. Nineteen courts are concerned generally with matters of local concern, 18 with the administration of the commons. Thirteen appoint officers and two receive audited accounts. One (Heaton in Bradford) perambulates boundaries (occasionally), one (Southwark) receives an address from the High Steward and one (Bromsgrove) proclaims a charter and observes a Midsummer Fair.

The list of these courts and their business is not exclusive but it may be difficult to establish any other. Any doubt as to the scheduled courts will be resolved by the Act. Anyone who claims that another court should operate will have to prove his case that, immediately before 17 October 1977, when s 23 came into force, it was customary for the court to sit and conduct particular business. If the lord or his steward refuses to call the court the matter will need to be resolved by judicial review. This has replaced the former remedy of mandamus which used to be invoked to require a court to be called. It is hard to say what 'immediately' means. In normal language it means a few hours or days. In the context of an institution which has been developing over 1000 years the word may mean more like 20 or 30 years.

Recently, some lords who have bought manorial titles and take an interest in the affairs of the locality have summoned manorial courts and local people have been prepared to go along. Such courts can be colourful affairs with ceremonial proceedings. They may even in principle be legal courts, but they have no standing to determine legal rights or to conduct other business.

13.5   OFFICERS

The principal matter for which courts still meet is the appointment of officers. Officers include a reeve, a portreeve, a people's warden, a waywarden, a foreman, a tithingman, a bailiff, a hayward, byelawmen, a pasture master, a sergeant and a constable. Others are a pindar and a swine-ringer. No doubt there were many more.

To begin with the most important, the steward was appointed by the lord, and may have had a deputy. He represented the lord and was an officer of the common court baron. He also presided over and was the judge in the customary court. Detailed law governed how and when a steward could be appointed and dismissed[20] and especially what fees he could charge. Compensation to stewards for loss of fees was a feature of enfranchisement. Most of those rules are no longer of importance. It is worth noting that in the case of Crown manors the steward may still be significant and is still mentioned in Sch 1 to the Crown Estate Act 1961. Appointment to the stewardship of the Chiltern Hundreds or of the manor of Northstead is one of the ways of resigning from the House of Commons (24.8). Crown manors are different in certain ways because where the lord was the king the lord's court was a royal court (24.9).

The reeve was an Anglo-Saxon official originally (it seems) elected by the community. In many manors he came to be appointed by the lord. The tithing-man also had an Anglo-Saxon origin with the tithing. He, and the sheriff or

---

[20]   Coke, *Copyholder op cit* s 45; Scriven *op cit* 426.

shire-reeve, who was a local official appointed by the king to be responsible for the shire, related to the institutions described in 19.3–19.4.

The bailiff[21] was appointed by the steward to carry out his orders. Court bailiffs still play an important part in carrying out the orders of operating courts, and certificated bailiffs in levying distress for unpaid rent (14.5). The hayward was responsible for hedges. The swine-ringer looked after the pigs and some manors had common herdsmen and shepherds. The pindar looked after the village pound where straying animals were kept. The constable did much as modern constables do and kept the peace. The constable was appointed by the court leet. In *R v Wakeford*[22] in 1714 the court leet of Lymington, in accordance with its usual practice, appointed a constable. The justices of the peace who, by that date, were generally responsible for public order, appointed their own nominee. The royal court upheld the leet appointment, holding that the justices could not appoint if there was an established and observed custom for the leet to do so.

---

[21] Scriven *op cit* 433.

[22] (1714) Sess 98, 93 ER 100.

Chapter 14

Rents and Revenues

customs ... duties, reliefs, heriots, fines, sums of money, amerciaments, ... chief-rents, quit-rents, rentscharge, rents seck, rents of assize, fee farm rents, services, royalties

14.1 NATURE OF MANORIAL REVENUES

Some lords are still entitled to small sums of money, usually a few pence a year, payable at the manor court by freeholders and leaseholders. They are of little value, now normally worth less than the stamp on the letter that demands or pays them, and they are viewed as a curiosity. Formerly the manorial revenues were, next to the demesne, the most valued interest.[1] *Domesday Book* valued manors, and while no doubt much of the value turned on the profits from exploiting the demesne, a significant part reflected the payments by tenants. By the seventeenth century annual revenues were the essential features of the manor (27.2). Money features most prominently in those provisions of the Law of Property Act 1922 which abolished copyhold tenure.

The number of words used to describe payments shows how important they once were. Some words, such as custom, duty, fine, service and royalty have several meanings, which confuses understanding. Most, but not all, derive from the trinity of service, tenure and jurisdiction discussed in 5.1 and, as those three overlap, so do the nature of the payments.

Payments can be classified in several ways. The basic classification is between manorial or seigniorial dues or incidents (9.4–9.5), arising from custom and in theory either dating from or derived from the period before legal memory, on the one hand, and on the other conventional payments arising from agreements. The distinction can be blurred: in particular quitrents are regarded as customary even though the obligation to pay them derived from the commutation of services requiring work on the land. A custom (in this sense) can be a customary

---

[1] See Blackstone, Sir William, *Commentaries on the Laws of England* II.3.x.

payment and the Latin word *consuetudo* seems to have been used from Anglo-Saxon times for regular and ancient dues.

This should be distinguished from the modern usage of customs duty, which is a tax voted by Parliament for the Crown to collect payments from people importing items into the country. Internal customs in England disappeared long ago, if they ever existed. In France, internal customs existed until the Revolution and in Germany until the Zollverein was established in the years after 1819. Throughout Continental Europe many small lords could charge customs. Much of the law of customs is now governed by European law. Importation payments were claimed by the Crown as dues the king was accustomed to have but they were not customary in the sense discussed in 4.1. The issue was litigated under James I[2] and after 1660 it was established that Parliamentary authority was needed – indeed most of the Tenures Abolition Act 1660 concerns the customs duties granted to Charles II in return for surrendering feudal dues.

Customary payments strictly so-called, which were simply a matter between the lord and an individual tenant, such as rents, should be distinguished from payments which were decided by the local court often as a mark of communal disapproval, such as an amerciament. A further distinction is between rentservices and rentcharges (14.5–14.6). There were also general payments such as tolls and duties which could be owed by anyone and only incidentally belonged to the manor. A duty is anything that is due. Tolls are related to charges for markets and other commercial activities and are considered in 15.1–15.5.

14.2   COURT PAYMENTS

Fines (in one sense – see 14.4) and amerciaments are payments in the manor court. Fines are still payable in modern courts. They are sums of money either determined by the general law or fixed (within predetermined limits) by the judge or magistrate to put an end (latin *finis*) to the offence for which someone is charged.

Amerciaments are not so fixed. Although a manor court might charge a fine, an amerciament was more usual.[3] If a tenant did something wrong he was 'in mercy'. (The phrase is still used in the High Court, for example where someone has committed contempt and the penalty is decided by the court not under the general law.) Strictly speaking an amerciament is a variable penalty fixed not by

---

2   *Bates's Case* (1606) Lane 22, 145 ER 267.

3   See *Griesley's Case* (1587) 8 Co Rep 38a, 77 ER 530.

the judge or steward but by the jury or homage (in modern civil courts there is usually no jury). A suitor or tenant who did not attend court when he should, or who sold his holding without leave, or failed to repair his house or put up an unauthorised building, was in mercy. If he overstocked the common with his beasts, enclosed part of the waste, allowed weeds to grow on his strip, failed to clear a ditch or pond for which he was responsible, put up a dovecote without consent, cut the lord's timber, or dug the lord's minerals, he was in mercy. Some of these matters might also give rise to a forfeiture of his land but the usual procedure was less drastic. The matter was presented to the manor court and the homage (which consisted of his neighbours) fixed a suitable amerciament. Some became settled by custom, some were charged so often that they appear more like a licence fee than a penalty, for example for assarting the waste. Collecting amerciaments was a problem – many court records show unpaid sums carried forward from sitting to sitting and, of course, if a tenant failed to pay, he was again in mercy.

The money, if and when paid, belonged to the lord, and in well-controlled manors in the Middle Ages was a good source of income. Later it was less important, but as long as the manor court functioned the power to amerce was a source of social control. Often manorial discipline was exercised through amerciaments by the homage since a tenant's neighbours were the ones who suffered from straying cattle, uncleared ditches and strips covered with thistles. Any jurisdiction of the manor court to fine or amerce which still remained was abolished by s 23 of the Administration of Justice Act 1977 since fixing a penalty is determining a legal proceeding. It is therefore now obsolete.

14.3   RELIEFS AND HERIOTS

Reliefs and heriots were death duties within the manor. Reliefs payable to the king by tenants in chief are considered in 7.3. Reliefs were sometimes payable for land held in knight service, but when the Tenures Abolition Act 1660, s 3 converted such tenure to socage such payments ceased. Section 5 of the Act specifically preserved reliefs where they already existed on the death of a tenant in socage. Such payments seem to have been rare but where lords were entitled to reliefs from free tenants they could continue to collect them from the incoming heir who succeeded on death. Scriven[4] describes them as still existing in his time. The effect of the Land Transfer Act 1897, which provided that land passed on intestacy to the administrator not to the heir, may have had the effect of abolishing reliefs but, if not, they were covered by the Law of Property Act 1922, s 138(1).

---

[4]   Scriven, J, *A Treatise on the Law of Copyholds* (Butterworth & Co, 7th edn by Archibald Brown, 1896) 243.

Reliefs could also refer to payments from copyholders. The Copyhold Act 1894, s 94 defines rent as including reliefs and so they could be redeemed under that Act in the same way as freehold heriots. The Law of Property Act 1922, s 188, on the other hand, does not define rent as including reliefs possibly because they were covered by s 128(2)(b).

Heriots were more important.[5] Most heriots were due from the estate of a dead copyholder but a very few freeholds were also subject to heriot. As explained below both copyhold and freehold heriots were abolished under the 1922 Act. Freehold heriots were rare, but they existed in the Devon manor of South Tawton (or Itton) and occurred in some parts of Surrey and Sussex, of which the case of *Copestake v Hoper*[6] is an example.

Heriots were of two types, heriot custom and heriot service, and seem to have had two different origins. The word comes from Anglo-Saxon *here* (army) and *geat* (provision). It is said that Saxon lords provided war gear for their followers and on the death of the warrior his arms and armour had to be returned to the one who had given it. This could only be owed by free men capable of fighting. After the Norman Conquest the status of the surviving Saxon landowners declined until they were peasants and the descendants of many became bondsmen. The Saxon word became applied to the liability not to give up arms (because the tenant had none) but his best beast. This was heriot service relating to land held by service.

On the other hand true bondsmen who held their land by custom could not have property of their own, either land or chattels. Everything they had belonged to their lord. However, by custom they were allowed to keep, and pass to their heirs or family, such possessions as they had, and by heriot custom the lord who, in theory, could take anything at any time, was restricted to the right to take the best beast on death.

Heriot custom (like any other custom) was due as a result of immemorial usage. Heriot service was in theory a reservation by the lord when the holding was originally granted and was in the nature of a rent. There were practical distinctions but these are not now important. Heriots could also be reserved under a lease when copyhold was converted to leasehold. Thus a relief is a payment due by the incoming tenant for the right to succeed and is strictly a succession duty. A heriot is due from the estate of a deceased tenant and is a death duty. In practice there is little difference. A relief was fixed in money while a heriot was the best beast or its value.

---

[5]   *Damerell v Protheroe* (1847) 10 QB 20, 116 ER 8; Scriven *op cit* 263.

[6]   [1907] 1 Ch 366, [1908] 2 Ch 10.

In *Copestake v Hoper*[7] Richard Hoper was the owner in common socage of an ancient freehold tenement known as Capons held of Sampson Copestake, lord of the manor of Ewhurst in Sussex. The land was subject to fealty, suit of court, a quitrent of £1-0-10d per year, a relief of one year's rent on death or disposal and a heriot of his best beast on his death. In 1887 Hoper granted a mortgage to Mr Browell, who may have been a friend. Before 1926 mortgages of freeholds were made by transferring title to the lender so that Browell became the nominal owner of Capons but Hoper remained in occupation and to all outward appearance was the owner of Capons. In 1905 Hoper died. Copestake claimed Hoper's best beast – described as a bay gelding called Captain, which may have been a racehorse and was certainly valuable.[8] The Court of Appeal found that the tenant in law was not Hoper who really owned the land, but Browell as mortgagee. As he was still alive, the heriot was not due.

14.4   TRANSMISSION FINES AND ROYALTIES

A second sense of fine has nothing to do with a penalty but is a payment due to the lord by an incomer on admittance. Such fines arose on the sale of a copyhold or on death when the heir entered. Fines in this sense could (and can) apply to leasehold land but copyhold fines were abolished under the 1922 Act. These could either be a fixed sum (which lost value with inflation) or arbitrary which, until the sixteenth century, meant they were whatever the lord asked but later had to be reasonable (like any other custom), and the courts consistently held that they could not exceed a sum equal to two years' rent for the land. In some manors, fines were determined by the homage but that was an unusual special custom.

Fines do not appear to have been payable by freeholders, presumably because of *Quia Emptores*. Section 6 of the Tenures Abolition Act 1660 preserves fines for alienation due 'by perticular customes of perticular mannours and places other then fines for alienations of lands or tenements holden immediately of the King in capite'. It appears therefore that if manorial freehold fines existed in 1660, except in royal manors, they were preserved, but it is probable that s 138 of the 1922 Act extinguished them. The matter is unlikely to be of practical importance.

Fines could and can be charged on the grant or assignment of leaseholds. On the grant they are usually called premiums and are common. Section 144 of the Law of Property Act 1925 prohibits the landlord from charging a fine when the

---

[7]   Ibid.

[8]   Between £2000 and £3000 according to *Encyclopaedia Britannica* (1911), 'Copyhold', assuming the reference is to this case.

tenant assigns unless the lease has expressly provided for it, and although rare this does sometimes happen. If therefore there was an ancient manorial lease of the type described below which reserves the right to a fine on death or assignment, it may still be due and payable in the manorial court but such cases must be very rare.[9]

The original meaning of 'royalty' was similar to franchise, which is considered (16.5). A common royalty was a Crown grant to take minerals[10] and the word came to mean a payment which varied according to receipts so that the more minerals the grantee extracted (or the more they were sold for) the more he paid. This contrasted with rent which, until the development of rent review clauses in the 1960s, was generally fixed. The word has been extended further to copyrights and patents where again the payment varies with volume or value.

In the context of the manor, royalty normally relates to minerals. It does not appear different in principle from a contractual royalty, although some royalties, such as toll of tin in certain Cornish manors,[11] may derive from custom (11.6). In Cornwall, tinners have a right, known as tin bounding, which probably derives from a custom of the shire. This involves the right under the Stannary Laws to mine tin whether or not the lord, as owner of the property in the minerals, or the surface owner, gives permission. The person exercising the right must make a payment determined by custom.

14.5   RENTCHARGES AND RENTS SECK

A rent is the recompense[12] for the exclusive possession of a corporeal hereditament. It is usually (but does not have to be) in money and if in money it must be a sum which is either certain or which can be determined with certainty (for instance by a mathematical calculation or the decision of an independent valuer with clear instructions). It is payable by the holder for the time being of land. Rents are of two kinds: rentcharges and rentservices.

Rentcharges originally had little to do with the manor which operated by tenure and service; but later they became common in that context. A charge, such as a mortgage, is a sum of money due to somebody who does not have an interest in the land tenurially superior to that of the payer. When a landlord grants a lease he usually reserves a rent as rentservice. If the rent is not paid he has four

---

[9]   See also Landlord and Tenant Act 1927, s 19 as amended by the Landlord and Tenant (Covenants) Act 1995.

[10] For example *Attorney-General v Hanmer* (1858) 31 LT 379, 4 de G&J 205, 45 ER 80.

[11] Pennington, RR, *Stannary Law* (MW Books, 1973).

[12] See Blackstone *op cit* II.3.x.

remedies. First, he can sue for it as a debt in the courts. Secondly, he can forfeit the lessee's interest: if the lease was granted on condition that the lessee paid a rent and he does not do so then the deal can be undone and the lessee loses his rights in the property. Thirdly, if the lease contains the necessary provision, the landlord may re-enter the land, that is to say take it back in hand and either collect rents from it or sell it. Fourthly, he may distrain, that is he may go on the land and take any chattels he finds there, sell them and recompense himself.

All of these rights are subject to restrictions in the modern law[13] which in principle are available for rentservices where there is tenure. These restrictions could apply to the rights of a superior lord of freehold land or the lord of a copyhold.

The owner of a rentcharge cannot use forfeiture because there is no tenure. Before 1290 land was sold by subinfeudation, but after *Quia Emptores* if a seller wished to reserve a rent it had to be done by charge. An action for the debt has always been available. Distraint and re-entry could originally only be used if they were specifically provided for, and a rentcharge without a power of distress was known as a rent seck or bare rent. By s 5 of the Landlord and Tenant Act 1730 a right of distraint was given to anyone entitled to a rent seck (and a rent of assize and chief rent described below) and for practical purposes rents seck ceased to exist. This was confirmed by s 121 of the Law of Property Act 1925 (replacing s 44 of the Conveyancing and Law of Property Act 1881) which also gives a right of re-entry.

A rentcharge is a type of charge. The most familiar charges nowadays are mortgages when money is borrowed, as from a bank or building society, and the borrower's land is used as security for the debt and the interest on it. Mortgages have only generally been charges since 1926. Land may be charged for other reasons. The owner may wish to make a gift of money or an annuity, often to charity, but may not have any cash, in which case he can charge his land with the sum due. He may wish to leave his land in his will to his eldest son but require that son to make payments to other members of the family, which can be charged on the land. In the nineteenth century when builders of housing estates wanted to pass on the land to an occupier but keep an income they frequently reserved rentcharges instead of selling for a lump sum, and lords of manors made arrangements with builders whereby the builder was paid out in cash by the occupier of the house built on former demesne land, but the lord continued to receive a rentcharge. These arrangements are especially common in the north of England (21.4).

---

[13] Law Commission No 194, *Landlord and Tenant: Distress for Rent.* Distraint is prospectively abolished by Tribunals, Courts and Enforcement Act 2007, s 71, but that section is not yet in force.

Under s 5 of the Inclosure Act 1846, where a lord would otherwise be entitled to an allotment of land, he could instead receive a rentcharge. Under ss 15 and 16 of the Copyhold Act 1894 the compensation to the lord on enfranchisement could be a rentcharge and if it was more than £1 it could be an annual sum which varied with the price of corn. Likewise under ss 138 and 139 of the Law of Property Act 1922 compensation could also be a rentcharge, either terminable for 20 years, or, if the parties agreed, perpetual.

Many manorial rentcharges still exist, although they are usually for small sums. Under the Rentcharges Act 1977 no new rentcharges can be created (with limited exceptions) and existing rentcharges will be extinguished in the year 2037. However, the Act does not extinguish those created under any Act of Parliament providing for the creation of rentcharges in connection with the execution of works on land (whether by way of improvements, repairs or otherwise) or the commutation of any obligation to do any such work. As explained below, quitrents are precisely that, so that rentcharges under the Copyhold Act or the 1922 Act may continue to run even after 2037. The Copyhold Act 1894 was repealed by the Statute Law (Repeals) Act 1969, but s 2 of that Act preserves the effect of rentcharges under the 1894 Act.

Furthermore, the Rentcharges Act can only be used to extinguish rentcharges that fall within its terms. Section 1 provides that rentcharge does not there include rents reserved by a lease or tenancy. Tenancy here cannot have the usual modern meaning of a lease for less than three years because no one would suggest that a rent under such an arrangement was a rentcharge. Tenancy must therefore mean a tenancy other than a lease, namely a freehold tenancy subsisting since before 1290, and therefore rents of assize and other tenurial freehold rents cannot be redeemed under the Act. That is borne out by the regulations under the Act which expressly require an applicant for redemption to produce the document creating the rent.[14] For rents payable since before 1290 this is likely to present problems. If the draftsman of the Rentcharges Act had intended to limit the expression 'tenancy' to a term of years he would have said so and therefore it must be assumed that the term includes a freehold tenancy.[15]

Under the Land Registration Acts 1925 and 2002 rentcharges are not treated as overriding interests because normally a reference must appear on title deeds. Where the deeds are lost the Land Registry practice in areas where rentcharges are common is to put a reference to the possibility that the land may be subject to a rentcharge. Often manorial rentcharges are not referred to in deeds and may apply in any part of country. However, they are generally very small in

---

[14] Rentcharges Regulations 1978 (SI 1978/16).

[15] For a different view see Law Commission No 271, *Land Registration for the Twenty-First Century: a Conveyancing Revolution* fn 158.

quantum. It is possible to register the title to receive a rentcharge, although for manorial ones this is unlikely to be economic.

14.6   RENTSERVICES – CHIEF, ASSIZE, QUIT AND FEE FARM

The most common type of rent is rentservice, namely rent payable as service to a superior in tenure. Most leases reserve a rentservice and some manorial revenues come from this source. Besides leases, rents could be payable for freeholds and, until 1926, copyholds. As copyholds could not (with rare exceptions) be created after 1189 and freeholds not after 1290 such rents must either themselves be ancient or replace other ancient rights.

In the years around 1600 it was frequent practice (often on the conversion of copyholds to leaseholds) for the lord to grant a lease of 1000 or 2000 years at a fixed rent payable at the manor court (7.10). Under s 153 of the Law of Property Act 1925 where the term was for not less than 300 years and has at least 200 years still to run, the rent is £1 or less and has not been collected for 20 years, and the lease does not contain a right of re-entry, then the lessee can enlarge the lease into a freehold. In many cases this has never been done because the lease itself has been lost and it is unclear whether or not it qualifies. If the lord can prove his rights he can demand the rent but as that is usually only a few pence it is hardly worth doing. There may however be other rights of a landlord, such as minerals or timber, which are worth claiming.

Fee farm rents were similar to lease rents. As explained in 6.2 a farm previously meant a lease. Fee is explained in 22.1. A fee farm was an inferior freehold that was like a lease in that it reserved not just a nominal rent but a substantial rent of between half and a quarter of the full annual value of the land. The Law of Property Act 1925, s 146(5)(a) defines lease for the purposes of the section as including a grant at a fee farm rent, indicating that the expressions can be used flexibly. A chief rent is a rent payable by a freeholder, and in areas where rentcharges are common the term is often used to refer to these, but its likely origin is a rent payable to a chief lord, or superior lord of the freehold. Private landowners could only make such grants before 1290.

If rents are still payable under any such grants they will continue in force. If they are payable out of registered freehold land to a lord of a manor and are not noted on the title it is possible that they will cease to be enforceable after the first registration or disposition of land after 12 October 2013 under the Land Registration Act 2002, as discussed in 25.9. This is because such rents may be regarded as being manorial rights (9.5). It is likely that they would have been included in the expression 'manorial rights' in the nineteenth century. If the Land Registry view that the expression refers only to rights mentioned in Sch 12, para (5) to the Law of Property Act 1922 is correct, they are not caught, but the point is open.

Crown rents are referred to in Schs 1 and 3, para 12 to the Land Registration Act 2002 as rights which are temporarily overriding until the first registration or disposition of land after 12 October 2013. They probably arise from sales by the Crown at rents and could be made after 1290. Several Crown grants were made in the nineteenth century.[16] In theory this still can still be done although it is not modern practice. The Crown Estate Commissioners may administer some Crown rents but there may also be others due to manors sold by the Crown in the past; if a lord is in receipt of such payments he will need to protect them.

A rent of assize is also payable by a freeholder. The origin of the phrase is unclear. It may mean that a previously uncertain payment has been assised (assessed) or made certain. More likely it is a rent payable at an assize, or sitting, of a manor court. There were two types of rents of assize. The first was black rent payable in pepper cumins. This may date to the time when spices were rare and valuable, or may be like the peppercorn often reserved as a nominal rent under modern leases. The second was white rent payable in silver. Section 5 of the Landlord and Tenant Act 1730 extends to chief rents and rents of assize as it does to rentcharges.

Quitrents were only rarely reserved out of freeholds but were usual, indeed almost universal, for copyholds. Quitrents were a payment to the lord to be quit of other services and it appears that they arose by a two-stage process. As explained in 5.2 tenants (whether free or bond) held their land in the manor in return for services to the lord – ploughing, sowing, harvesting, ditching, carrying and so forth. Over the years it suited both the lord and the tenant to commute those services for annual money payments. Sometimes one type of service would be commuted while others continued, but over time most services came to be represented by money. The logical second step was to combine all the various payments into a single composite sum by the payment of which the tenant was quit of other dues (save for suit of court, fealty, reliefs and heriots). All quitrents were extinguished under the 1922 Act as explained below.

---

[16] Law Commission 271 *op cit* para 8.43.

14.7   WAYLEAVES

One source of revenue for lords to this day is represented by wayleaves. Many service providers such as British Telecom and electricity companies erect poles and lay cables across the countryside. Where these cross fields or gardens the companies make a small payment known as a wayleave for permission to erect and retain their plant. Most have compulsory powers to do this, for instance under the Telecommunications Code or the Electricity Supply Acts, but prefer to resolve matters by agreement. Many such features run along roadside verges. Although the surfaces of some verges are vested in the highway authority as part of the highway, plant needs to be dug into the subsoil or erected into the airspace above the public right of way; service providers therefore need legal authority. There is power to do this under Part III of the New Roads and Street Works Act 1991, but companies often prefer to have an agreement with the owner of the adjacent land who is also in many cases the owner of the verge (6.5). However, some lords have been able to claim ownership of the verge and secure the wayleave payment from the companies. The returns are usually modest but £1 per pole or a few pence per metre if extended over several miles can produce a worthwhile income. Other installations may run across common land where the lord has the freehold.[17]

14.8   EXTINCTION OF MANORIAL INCIDENTS

The variety and number of payments with which it was burdened was the most resented feature of copyhold land. In this, England was not unique. In eighteenth century France the burden of manorial dues, of the *cens*, *lods et ventes*, *terrage*, *champart*, *agrier*, *tasque*, *bordelage*, *marciage* and others were among the causes of the Revolution.[18] English burdens were not so heavy but with the passing of time they were seen as increasingly unjustifiable. Naturally, the lords wished to continue to receive fines, heriots, quitrents and other dues, and the stewards who ran their courts wished to continue to receive the fees they earned on manorial matters, but in a sceptical age, manorial incidents could not survive simply because they were ancient.

The Copyhold Acts 1841 to 1894 were passed with the intention of securing the gradual elimination of copyhold with its various manorial incidents, sometimes by agreement, sometimes on the initiative of one party or the other. However, they did not achieve their object of voluntary extinction of incidents, and in

---

[17]   See *Mellstrom v Badgworthy Land Co Ltd* (2010) LR Adj 2008/1498; 2009/0290; 2009/0953.

[18]   de Tocqueville, A, *Ancien Regime* (English translation by J Bonner (JM Dent & Sons Ltd, 1998), 1856): note on feudal rights.

1913 the Lord Chancellor, Lord Haldane, introduced a Real Property Bill to abolish copyholds and special tenures and extinguish manorial incidents, as well as making other changes to the law of property. The reform was delayed by the First World War, but in 1922 another Bill was passed. Most of the provisions of the Law of Property Act 1922 were repealed, amended and re-enacted in the series of Acts passed between 1922 and 1925 but the provisions for manors remained under the 1922 Act. All the legislation came into force on 1 January 1926.

Most copyholds were converted to freehold under Part V although some, particularly copyholds for years, became leaseholds under s 133 and copyholds for life required separate treatment. Certain incidents were temporarily saved by s 128, namely (a) quitrents, chief rents and similar payments, (b) fines, reliefs, heriots and dues, (c) some forfeitures and (d) timber rights. Part VI and s 138 then provided for these incidents to be extinguished and compensation paid to the lord and steward. This applied not only to those affecting copyhold land, enfranchised under Part V of the Act but also, under s 138, 'to all manorial incidents of a like nature affecting any other land'. Therefore heriots, quitrent and the like affecting common freeholds but due to the lord of a manor were abolished.

The parties could agree on extinction and the tenant could at any time require the lord to accept extinction of the incidents. After five years (that is from 1931) the lord could require the tenant to extinguish them. If a trigger for payment (such as death of a tenant or entry of a new tenant) arose before the incidents had been dealt with, a payment (such as a relief) under the pre-1926 rules might be due. If no agreement was made or notice served within 10 years compensation was treated as due on the expiry of the 10 years even if not then ascertained. If notice had been served but the process of resolving any dispute, for instance on the amount of compensation payment, s 138(4) provided that, if there was no agreement by the end of the specified period, then the procedures set out in the Copyhold Act 1894 would apply. These provided for a valuer, appointed (in default of agreement) by the Board of Agriculture – by 1922 the Ministry of Agriculture – to determine compensation, and the extinction was suspended until the issue was resolved. In any case no further payments would accrue after 1936, for instance if the owner (former copyholder) died later but before any compensation was paid.[19]

The effect of the legislation was that either party could trigger the procedure but it would not operate automatically if neither did so because no one else had any incentive to get involved. If nothing had occurred by 1936 then, under s 140(a), there was a further five years until 31 December 1940 during which either party

---

[19]   See generally the Manorial Incidents (Extinguishment) Rules 1925 (SR&O 1925/810).

could apply to the minister to determine the amount of compensation (but no interest was due on any sums due between 1936 and the date of application so there was a financial incentive on lords to act promptly). Under s 140(c) if no agreement or application was made by the end of 15 years (ie 31 December 1940 for manors other than the special exceptions mentioned below) then the legislation originally provided that no compensation would be payable and the former copyholder would hold his now freehold land free of any obligation to the former lord. In 1939 the time limit was extended by the Postponement of Enactments (Miscellaneous Provisions) Act 1939. By the Postponement of Enactments (Miscellaneous Provisions) Act 1939 (Manorial Incidents Extinguishment) Order 1949[20] the period was finally ended on 1 November 1950.

Further, s 138(1)(ii) provided that if there were more than 1000 tenants on any manor, the minister could extend the period of 10 years In three cases the time was extended, namely for the honour of Clitheroe in Lancashire (which comprised several manors) until 1 January 1940, the manor of Wakefield in Yorkshire until 1 January 1939, and the manor and lordship of Newcastle-under-Lyme in Staffordshire also until 1 January 1939.[21] The time limit for Clitheroe ran into the Second World War and was extended by s 3 of the Postponement of Enactments (Miscellaneous Provisions) Act 1939, but by the 1949 Order its period was also finally made to expire on 1 November 1950. Since that date no payments in relation to manorial incidents have been due except in the rare cases where the lord and former tenant agreed on a permanent rentcharge.

The 1922 Act laid down a detailed procedure and scale of redemption payments. The parties were encouraged to agree against the background of the statutory provisions and in practice most did so. The variety of payments, methods of calculation, occasions, times and circumstances of incidents made the enactment of general rules almost impossible. No doubt there were irreconcilable disputes which had to be resolved under the Act but these must have been rare or the system would have been unworkable, certainly in the mere 10 years allowed.

The final step was the payment by the former tenant to the steward, who issued a formal receipt. Some of these survive in deed packets. Some manors produced good quality documents, but most receipts were small pieces of printed paper supplied by law stationers with blanks for details which were completed in barely legible handwriting and faded ink. They are not impressive documents as witnesses to the end of 1000 years of manorial relations: the grievances that led the French to storm the Bastille left England with 100,000 scrappy forms.

---

[20] SI 1949/836.

[21] *London Gazette*: Newcastle, 8 November 1935; Wakefield, 29 November 1935; Clitheroe, 31 December 1935.

Chapter 15

Tolls

tolls

15.1 TOLLS AND WAYS

One of the sources of income for manors depended on exploiting their geographical position. The right to charge for the use of roads, taking boats on rivers and estuaries and anchoring them, and crossing rivers by ferries and bridges can be described as a toll. Most ancient tolls are long gone but enough traces remain to call for an explanation. Tolls are franchises, discussed in 16.6, or are attached to franchises such as toll of market discussed in 21.2. As such, at common law they must be authorised by royal charter, although if they predate 1189 (or have been collected for many years and there is no evidence to contradict a pre-1189 origin) this will be presumed.

Other tolls were created by statute, for example under eighteenth-century turnpike Acts for the building and repair of roads.[1] Others were for the maintenance of bridges. Modern tolls can be authorised under the New Roads and Street Works Act 1991 for new private roads.

In England tolls were relatively rare, in contrast with the Continent. Until the nineteenth century one of the great obstacles to travel and commerce throughout Germany, France and Italy was the innumerable tolls charged by every graf, count or bishop at every possible point. Navigation up the Rhine was for centuries hindered by the number of barriers erected to mulct traders. Although tolls did exist in England one of the main sources of law concerns not charging but exemption – the privilege of tenants of manors of ancient demesne (24.9) to be free of tolls throughout the realm. In Anglo-Saxon times there were many

---

[1] Law Commission, Statute Law Repeals: Consultation Paper, *Repeal of Turnpike Laws* (February 2010).

import or market tolls. Since Norman times the general picture in England has been of free trade which has encouraged prosperity.

Tolls had a function beyond simply earning money for their proprietor, for example to defray the expenses of operating markets and harbours, and for the repair of roads, bridges and town walls. The owner would expect to make a profit, but that was not the main object. To the extent that tolls are franchises they may need protection under the Land Registration Act 2002 (25.9).

15.2   ROAD TOLLS

Road tolls were rare. Public roads are the Queen's highway and it would not be right for a subject to charge toll over them without clear legal authority. However, some tolls still exist, known as toll thorough and toll traverse.[2] Toll thorough is a charge for passage over a highway such as a road, ferry or bridge supported by a service performed by the person entitled to receive toll. If for example a lord holds his manor by service which includes the obligation to repair a highway this may entitle him to charge toll to cover the cost. Toll traverse occurs where a highway has been dedicated by the landowner subject to toll.

Apart from very ancient highways such as Roman roads and Saxon *herepaths* (military roads), roads can become highways in one of two ways. One is positive action by government (either central or local) which acquires land for a highway under statutory powers. The other is dedication usually accompanied by adoption. A landowner may give up or dedicate land to public use as a highway. This often happens on building estates. At common law dedication may be implied by long use by the public. Under the Highways Act 1980, s 31 if members of the public use a way without interference for over 20 years as of right without permission, force or secrecy, dedication can be presumed, although a landowner may take steps to ensure that tolerating public use is not treated as dedication. Presumed dedication is unlikely to involve any toll.

A highway can be deliberately dedicated subject to conditions. One common condition relating to footpaths that cross fields is that the path can be ploughed up to enable crops to be planted in the field. The Rights of Way Act 1990 was passed to regulate this practice. So likewise a lord may have dedicated a highway subject to his right to charge toll, either as a fixed sum for each passer by or a variable one.

Toll traverse should be distinguished from the private right to charge people for using private tracks. For example the owner of land between a public road and a

---

[2]   *R v Marquess of Salisbury* (1838) 8 Ad & E 716, 112 ER 1009.

beach may make a road across his private land and charge the public for using it. That is no different from any other charge for coming onto private property. The route may be a public footpath which anyone can use on foot without charge, but if it is not a public road the owner can still charge for vehicles. This is often called a toll, but in law it is not. Similarly, there may be a private easement of way subject to the dominant owner contributing to maintenance and leasehold rights of way subject to payment of a rent.

There were many different names given to road tolls. Passage (or peage or payage) was a sum paid for the right to pass along a road. Cheminage is similar, the word derives from the French *chemin*. Pedage may mean the same but may be limited to walking. Pavage was linked to payment to the person responsible for paving or surfacing the road. Carriage was a general word for a fee for carrying goods through a territory. All of these tended to belong to the lord of the manor, if only because, as shown in 6.6, he often owned the soil of the highway or because he had secured the necessary franchise.

15.3   BRIDGES AND FERRIES

Bridge tolls or pontage used to be more common than road tolls although most that now exist are authorised by statute, such as the Whitchurch Bridge Act 1792 and the Severn Bridge toll authorised by the Severn Bridges Act 1992. The ancient tolls arose because bridges need to be maintained and tolls were the means of raising money. Private responsibility for the repair of bridges is ancient. Bridge repair was one of the three *trinoda necessitas* under which land was held in Saxon times; throughout the Middle Ages many bridges were maintained by the lord of the manor.

By around 1700 commerce was fast increasing throughout England. The cost of bridge repair and improvement to accommodate growing traffic was enormous. In general it then fell on the county (that is the justices of the peace meeting at quarter sessions) or parish or borough to raise the money. Wherever possible counties and boroughs tended to pass costs on to private people, notably lords of the manor. Although a duty to repair did not itself permit a lord to charge a toll to recover his costs, this was often the case.

The issue of repair appears to have come to a head in relation to the manor of Delamere in Hertfordshire. The lord of the manor was Sir John Bucknall but in previous years parts of the manorial lands had been sold off and had become owned by a variety of other owners. In *R v Duchess of Buccleugh*[3] (discussed in 7.5) it was assumed for the purposes of argument that the lord of the manor was

---

[3]   (1704) 6 Mod 150, 87 ER 909, 1 Salk 358, 91 ER 312.

liable to repair the bridge and the question for decision was whether the cost should be shared among the various owners of the lands. In *R v Sir John Bucknall*[4] the issue was whether the lord was liable at all. The court held that while in theory it was possible for a lord to be liable, it was difficult to prove. If, before 1660, the manor was held by knight service, and if that service included bridge repair, then the duty continued despite the Tenures Abolition Act. The court held that the burden of proof was on to the people claiming that the lord was liable to prove their case and in that particular matter they were unable to produce the necessary evidence.

In *R v Inhabitants of Bedfordshire*[5] the inhabitants sought to resist a claim to repair Harrolds Bridge, which comprised six arches over the Great Ouse, on the basis that Crewe Alston ought to repair the first arch by reason of his tenure of the manor of Odell, Earl De Grey ought to repair the second arch by reason of his tenure of the manor of Harrold, and Mary Trevor, Elizabeth Trevor and Catherine Trevor ought to repair the third arch by reason of their tenure of the manor of Chellyton. The case turned on whether certain evidence should be admitted and it appears the case was proved. The county council took over responsibility in 1930.

Another instance where the liability was established was the Crown manor of Newark in Nottinghamshire. In 1837 part of the manor was sold and the buyer required, as a condition of his purchase, that an Act of Parliament[6] be passed to make it clear that he had no responsibility for the repair of the Trent Bridge or the Markham Bridge. As the Great North Road (now the A1) then crossed the Trent at Newark this would have been a heavy burden. The opportunity was taken in the Newark Bridge Act to relieve the whole manor of the liability in return for a single payment.

Nearly all road bridges which are highways are now the responsibility of the relevant county or unitary council and the lord has no duty to repair and no corresponding right to charge pontage. There may still be a few footbridges over streams where the old rules apply. The Highways Act 1980, s 49 (re-enacting the Statute of Bridges 1530[7]) provides, 'Where a person is liable to maintain the approaches to a bridge by reason of the fact that he is liable to maintain the bridge by reason of tenure or prescription, his liability to maintain the approaches extends to 100 yards from each end of the bridge'.[8]

---

[4]   (1707) 7 Mod 98, 87 ER 1091.

[5]   (1855) 4 El and Bl 535, 119 ER 196.

[6]   7 Will IV (c 15).

[7]   22 Hen 8 (c 5).

[8]   See *Hertfordshire County Council v New River Co* [1904] 2 Ch 513.

Where, by virtue of a charter or a special Act, someone has the right to take tolls in respect of the use of a highway or owns a bridge, then highway authorities, typically county councils and unitary authorities, have powers to take over the tolls under the Highways Act 1980, s 271. This may be done by agreement with the owner or by compulsory purchase. The transfer will include the property in the highway and all other property, rights and obligations relating to the highway under the charter or special Act, which will then vest in the authority. Occasionally lords of manors have such rights by virtue of charter but most instances would have predated legal memory rather than deriving from charter or local Act.

Before bridges, many rivers were crossed by ferry. There are still many private ferries operated for public use although these tend to be established by statute or at least governed by it. Thus, the Sandbanks Ferry across the mouth of Poole Harbour operates under the Bournemouth and Swanage Motor Road and Ferry Act 1923. Others, such as the Maker Ferry across Plymouth Sound, used to belong to the lord of the manor of Maker but was sold to the council after the Second World War. If there is no monopoly then anyone can charge for allowing members of the public to be carried in his boat. However, a franchise of ferry is a monopoly and charges can only be levied under the terms of the franchise or by statute. Where a franchise exists the franchisee is bound to operate it sufficiently to meet the public need and his charges must be reasonable. Ferries were often held by lords of manors but most have become uneconomic or have been replaced by bridges.

A bridge may exist as a freehold or leasehold separate from the underlying river, and if it is a highway it will be a public right of way. Private bridges may subsist as easements. Likewise a ferry can exist as an incorporeal hereditament of franchise separate from the river bed.

15.4 PORTS AND HARBOURS

A port is a place of trade (and strictly does not have to be near water, such as an airport), while a harbour is a place for boats to shelter; but in practice the two have historically gone together. They can be purely natural, but in ancient ports quays, piers, wharves, warehouses, embankments and docks were built over the centuries. These were expensive to construct and maintain. Therefore, the lord of the harbour was entitled to various tolls to recover the cost. Because of the difficulty of determining whether any particular user of the harbour gets a benefit, harbour dues are payable by all vessels using it and it follows that (space permitting) anyone has the right to use the facilities on payment. This is connected to the public right of navigation which applies to all tidal waters.

In theory the rights exist by franchise, but in practice the number of sites for harbours is so limited that they have been in use since long before legal memory. Nowadays most functioning ports are governed by schemes under statute, either a private Act or an order under the Harbours Docks and Piers Clauses Act 1847, with other powers under later legislation such as the Harbours Act 1964. These harbours are no longer under the control of the lord of the manor but he may still be involved for historical reasons or as owner of the fundus or seabed. A few unregulated harbours may still exist where ancient rights apply.

Tolls are many and various, and the following are only the more common. Anchorage is the most important, as discussed below. Bushellage is a payment for each bushell of corn landed. Loadage is a charge for all items loaded onto the vessel. Ballastage (or ballatage, lastage or lestage) is a charge for taking on ballast, which would be a local material such as sand or stone taken from the waste. Keyage (or quayage) is a fee for use of a quay, and wharfage for a wharf. Pilotage is charged for the service of a pilot and, so far as it relates to modern harbours, is regulated by the Pilotage Act 1987. Some tolls are not restricted to ports, but are commonly found there, namely portage, which is a fee for items carried over an area, and porterage, for employment of a porter, presumably a common porter. Metage is a fee for items measured and weighage for things weighed, similar to tronage. Most ancient ports had some of these tolls.

15.5   ANCHORAGE AND MOORING

An important feature of modern waterways is the mooring of pleasure boats, yachts and motor boats. The construction and running of marinas is big business. It is not surprising that legal disputes have arisen about mooring rights, but the law is reasonably clear as a result of a number of decisions.

The basic rules were laid down in two nineteenth-century cases involving the Free Fishers of Whitstable in Kent. There had been oyster fishermen in Whitstable since before legal memory in 1189. The cases ostensibly concerned the right of the company of the Free Fishers to charge a fee of one shilling for each boat putting down an anchor in Whitstable Harbour. Even in the 1860s when the cases were fought, a shilling had little value so that the dispute was really about deeper issues. It was accepted that the Free Fishers held the freehold of the seabed.

The manor of Whitstable had a typical history. Once it was called Northwood and was a subinfeudation of the Barony of Chilham which, under William I, was held by Odo Bishop of Bayeux. Under Edward I a *Quo Warranto* was issued against the then lord, Alexander de Baliol, who claimed toll with merchandise in the manor and established his claim. Later the manor escheated to the Crown, was granted out by Edward II, was forfeited, and then granted to the Earl of Athol. Later it passed to the college of Plecy in Essex and on the Dissolution came back to the Crown. Henry VIII granted it to John Gates, who was attainted under Mary and his lands escheated. Elizabeth I granted it to T Heneage, Moyle Finch and M Heneage (the same family as in *Sir Moyle Finch's Case*[9] in 8.4) and it was then resold. In 1791 the manor was bought by Mr Foad who seems to have been a nominee for the oyster fishermen. In 1792 they obtained a private Act which incorporated them as the Free Fishers of Whitstable and enabled them to buy the manor, which they did in 1795.

In *Gann v Free Fishers of Whitstable*[10] they claimed a customary due for all vessels putting down anchor on their property. Mr Gann anchored his vessel Amoret on one of their oyster beds and refused to pay his shilling. The case was fought up to the House of Lords which held that a mere customary right, however ancient, for the owner of the seabed to claim a fee could not be supported unless the area was within a harbour and the Free Fishers had not proved that in their case. Lord Chelmsford (who sat in both cases) said that whenever possible the court would uphold an ancient practice, but in this case it could not be established on the evidence produced.

The Free Fishers licked their wounds, did some more research and tried again in a second case against Mr Foreman,[11] owner of the vessel Sancho Panza, The case reached the House of Lords in 1869. This time the Free Fishers produced some evidence, though scanty, suggesting that in the time of Alexander de Baliol and again when it was held by the Heneage Finch family the lords of the manor had exercised port rights. This was enough for the House of Lords. It held that the holder of the port franchise could charge an anchorage fee for vessels which came into the port.

There is a general public right of navigation in navigable waters which includes the right to put down an anchor. The owner of the soil as such cannot charge for that, but within the limits of a franchise the lord of the port can charge even for anchorage if he has toll of anchorage. This remains true even if the owner of the soil and the lord of the port are different people.

A hundred years later in 1960 came the case of *Iveagh v Martin*.[12] Lord Iveagh was lord of the manor of Bosham in Sussex which adjoined the Port of

---

[9] (1610) 6 Co Rep 63a, 77 ER 310.

[10] (1864/5) 11 HLC 192, 11 ER 1305.

[11] *Foreman v Free Fishers of Whitstable* (1869) LR 4 HL 266.

[12] [1961] 1 QB 232, [1960] 2 All ER 668.

Chichester. The manor included foreshore on which a quay had been built. Mr Martin had a boat-repairing business and claimed the right to use the quay without payment for that purpose. His claim was based on two points: first, that he was a Man of Bosham and as such had special rights in the port; secondly, that he had a general right to use the quay.

It is clear that Men of Bosham had existed since at least the time of Elizabeth I. When the Chichester Corporation Act 1938 was passed, a special provision was included for their protection, but that only extended to fishermen, which Martin was not. The judge, Paull J, found that Martin was indeed a Man of Bosham quite apart from the 1938 Act. He was born at Bosham, although outside the limits of the manor and so could not qualify by birth. But by the time of the case he had a lease from Lord Iveagh of Canute House, Fishbourne, on the manor. The judge considered that although he could not be considered a tenant of Bosham (because since 1925 tenancy was restricted to tenants in fee and did not include leaseholders) the phrase 'Man of Bosham' had a wider meaning and included inhabitants.

However, the rights of Men of Bosham related to fishing and navigation. They may have had the right to pass over the quay free of toll, especially if its construction had interfered with their use of the foreshore, but no ancient right could authorise Martin to carry on a boat-repairing business on Lord Iveagh's quay. Lord Iveagh was not claiming keyage, but the normal right of the owner of land and a structure on that land to prevent other people using the structure.

The leading modern case on moorings is *Fowley Marine (Emsworth) Ltd v Gafford*.[13] The case related to Fowley Rythe, another part of Chichester Harbour. This had once been parcel of the manor of Emsworth and Warblington and, although there was some doubt as to how the company had come to be the owner, it was accepted as such by the court. Mr Gafford claimed the right to put down a permanent mooring on the bed of Fowley Rythe as incident to the public right of navigation. The court found there was no such right. Navigation involves movement. There may be a right to put down an anchor overnight, or in emergency, or while waiting for a storm to blow over, or for other good reason, but that was not the same as permanently taking a mooring. That was a trespass against the owner of the soil who could have the mooring removed or charge a fee.

In *Ipswich Borough Council v Moore*[14] the council had once had a port franchise granted by a charter of Henry VIII in 1518. Under various Acts since 1805 administration of the port and the associated franchises passed to a body now

---

[13]   [1968] 2 QB 618, [1968] 1 All ER 979.

[14]   [2001] EWCA Civ 1273.

known as the Ipswich Port Authority, but the council remained owner of the river bed. The 1805 Act and a later Act of 1837 expressly reserved to the council the tolls of anchorage and groundage but the tolls were abolished in 1863. In 1950 the Ipswich Dock Act expressly conferred on the predecessor of the authority the right to charge for moorings. The Court of Appeal[15] held that the effect of these legislative changes was to deprive the council of its right to charge for moorings and confer it on the port authority.

The present position therefore involves a clear distinction between the port authority, whether under a private Act or order, the Harbours, Docks and Piers Clauses Act 1847, the Ports Act 1991, or under an ancient franchise of port, on the one hand, and the owner of the soil, on the other. The soil owner cannot prevent or charge for anchorage in the course of navigation. The port operator can (if he has the right) charge anchorage toll and may be able to control the right. On the other hand only the owner of the bed can authorise a long-term mooring of a pleasure vessel or a commercial boat (unless there is a local custom for fishermen to have a mooring) and the port authority cannot charge a profit rent for the use of another person's seabed. In the past the owner of the bed and the franchise were normally the same person – the lord. Now that is usually not the case. A port authority may be set up specially or may be the local council. The lord of the manor will often still own the seabed. Both need to co-operate in the control of moorings.

---

[15] Citing the statement of Bowen LJ in *The Mayor and Citizens of the City of Manchester v Lyons* (1882) 22 Ch D 287 at 310, quoted in 16.8.

Chapter 16

Franchises and Liberties

waifs, estrays ... jurisdictions, franchises, liberties

16.1   NATURE OF FRANCHISES

Many manors have franchises annexed to them. These are a miscellaneous group of rights[1] defined as a portion of the royal prerogative in the hands of a subject; they can be seen as a privatised governmental function. In the Middle Ages kings who were responsible for government had common law powers to carry it out. These powers long predated the existence of Parliament and were exercised simply by virtue of royal authority. They included defence, administration and justice, and matters relating to the currency and to commerce. Some were granted out to subjects. Some rights are held by the Crown by virtue of the Royal Prerogative, which includes the Government's conduct of foreign policy, power to pardon convicted prisoners and do certain other public matters. Over the centuries much of the Prerogative has been taken over by Parliament and conferred on the Government by statute on specific terms.[2] Other franchises, such as wreck or treasure trove, were grants of a portion of the Crown's rights, analogous to a disposal of Crown lands.

In addition, the Crown had power to create and grant certain new rights to subjects. Some were in the form of monopolies such as markets and ferries, that is the right to prevent others doing what they would otherwise be able to do. Others could involve special privileges associated with defence or

---

[1]   See generally Bracton, Sir Henry, *De legibus et consuetudinibus angliae* (c 1257) (SE Thorne (ed)) (Belknap Press of Harvard University Press, 1977) f 55b, 120, 123b; Chitty, J, *A Treatise on the Law of the Prerogatives of the Crown and the Relative Rights and Duties of the Subject* (1820) 119; Hale, Sir Matthew, *The Prerogatives of the King* (c 1660) (Selden Society, 1976) Ch 19.

[2]   See Ministry of Justice, *The Governance of Britain: Review of the Executive Royal Prerogative Powers*: Final Report (October 2009); Maer L and Gay, O, *The Royal Prerogative* (House of Commons Library SN/PC/03861, 2009).

administration. Grants of this type are in general no longer made under charter although some can be granted by statute. However, certain franchises, especially of corporate status such as that of a new university or a professional institution, are still issued by the Privy Council.

Such rights have become private property and therefore any change made by Parliament for constitutional purposes has to be exercised in such a way as not to affect private rights. The following account describes the main types of franchise, looks at certain rules that apply to them, and considers other similar rights. It includes a suggested classification under modern headings which does not correspond to any established analysis, but many of the rules apply to different franchises in ways that are not wholly logical.

The word 'franchise' is now used in different senses. One is a purely private arrangement where the owner of a right licences others to exercise it, for example by running a restaurant along the lines worked out by the franchise owner. It has also been adopted by government to refer to the grant of certain rights. For example, the Railways Act 1993, s 23(3) sets out terms for arrangements known as franchise agreements, but the right to carry passengers by rail is not a franchise in the sense here discussed.

Franchises such as courts leet, waifs, strays and free warren were attached to most manors. Others, such as wreck, were widely but not generally found. Yet others, such as treasure trove, were rare. Markets and fairs came to be regarded as manorial rights. Thus, a discussion of franchises in the manor is far from straightforward.

Where a franchise carries the right to a chattel, it can usually be exercised only where the true owner is unknown. Thus, if an item which would otherwise be treasure is found to be someone's property, he can claim it.[3] Likewise if items come ashore from a sunken ship the owner of the cargo has rights prior to the owner of rights to wreck.

The prerogative rule for waifs (16.3) appeared to be different in that if the king's representative obtained custody of stolen goods first his claim prevailed over that of the owner of goods, but if the owner obtained the goods first his right prevailed.[4] It seems this was done to encourage swift pursuit of the thief. It is not clear if this applies where a lord has the franchise and seizes the stolen items.

A franchise, which may affect a defined area, therefore needs to be distinguished from the location of any such objects. A thing capable of being

---

[3]   See *Re Sulzbacher's coins*, 18 April 2011, Coroner for Inner North London.

[4]   Chitty *op cit* 147; *Foxley's Case* (1600) 5 Co Rep 109a, 77 ER 224.

treasure is probably best regarded as part of the land while it is buried (so that it will pass with the land unless an owner of the chattel can show a better right) and the franchise right arises when the object is dug up and severed and it is then a chattel.[5] The status of wrecked items which may remain on the shore and get buried in the sand is less clear. They may retain their status as wreck indefinitely or accrete to become part of the foreshore.

16.2   DEFENCE

In one sense the whole feudal system, described in 22.1, was a privatisation of defence. Land and castles were granted in return for military service. In England this never went as far as on the Continent and English kings were careful to retain ultimate control over military matters. However, where frontier defence was needed, on the Marches of Wales and on the Scottish Borders, local lords were granted very wide powers. Chester and Durham were counties palatine, which involved the grant of substantial powers of defence to a lord holding wide lands. Wherever possible the king ensured that the Earldom of Chester was under his control. Since 1254 it has (with a temporary exception) been held by the heir to the throne and since 1399 by the Prince of Wales. Durham was held by the bishop (sometimes called the prince-bishop) who could only be appointed with royal consent. Lancaster, the third county palatine, was held by the Crown after Henry Bolingbroke Duke of Lancaster became Henry IV. Other so-called palatines were Pembrokeshire, and Hexhamshire in Northumberland. For some purposes the Cinque Ports were so reckoned presumably because of the special jurisdiction involved in defences against France. So was Ely apparently by virtue of a charter of King Edgar although the bishop was more a marsh lord than a march lord.[6]

The Percy Earls (later Dukes) of Northumberland enjoyed substantial privileges as Wardens of the Scottish Marches. In Wales there was a more far-reaching system of Lords Marcher. These were principally jurisdictions held by the lords who, with the consent of the King of England, conquered the country and established themselves there. The bishop of St Davids had the status of Lord Marcher even though episcopal rights went back long before the Conquest. A number of the rights created by Marcher Lordships fell to be considered in *Crown Estate Commissioners v Roberts*.[7] The judge concluded that the status of Lord Marcher could only be held by direct grant from the Crown and could not be bought or sold.

---

[5] *Waverley Borough Council v Fletcher* [1996] QB 334.

[6] See Hale *op cit* Ch 19.

[7] [2008] EWHC 1302 (Ch), [2008] 4 All ER 828, [2008] P&CR 255.

On a more local level the franchise of murage allowed a baron (or occasionally a knight) to erect defensive walls. Murage rights were also granted to corporations and the toll charged to cover the cost of repairs was also known as murage.[8] After the chaotic times of King Stephen, castles and defended manor houses could only be built under a royal licence to castellate. In the fifteenth century many moated manor houses were built, but if defended they needed a franchise. These rights of defence are now obsolete. Anyone who wishes to erect a castle nowadays would need planning consent, but since the use of gunpowder became widespread such fortresses have had little military value.

16.3   LOCAL ADMINISTRATION AND JURISDICTION

The counties palatine of Chester, Durham and Lancaster, the royal franchise of Ely and the Cinque Ports of the south-east coast all existed by royal grant. They were not themselves manors but could be honours. As well as the defence functions of the palatinates all of these included powers of jurisdiction over local people.

In villages, courts leet existed by franchise although it was so common for a lord to hold one that the grant was widely assumed to have been made into private hands. Hundreds (19.2) could also be privately held, again by the theory of a royal grant. In practice any private hundreds go back beyond legal memory. There are traces of grants relating to the three hundreds of Oswaldslaw in Worcestershire which were said to have been the subject of an express grant by King Edgar to Bishop Oswald of Worcester in 964. The surviving evidence of the grant may be a forgery, but the grant itself could be genuine.[9] William II granted the hundred court of Normancross in Huntingdonshire to Thorney Abbey at a fee farm rent of 100 shillings.

Liberties were areas within a county that were exempt from the jurisdiction of the sheriff. The most famous was the Liberty of the Fleet at the western edge of the City of London which, in the eighteenth century, was a notorious no-go area. Another was the liberty of St Albans in Hertfordshire whose origins lay in Saxon times and had some of the features of a palatinate. At the Dissolution of the monasteries it was placed under the Borough of St Albans and was finally abolished in 1874. The principal liberty now surviving is the Inner and Middle Temple which, although geographically within the City of London, does not form part of it. The word 'liberty' is often used to describe a privately owned

---

[8]   *Truro Corporation v Reynalds* (1832) 8 Bing 275, 131 ER 407.

[9]   Maitland, FW, *Domesday Book and Beyond* (Cambridge University Press, 1987; first published 1897) 267–8. See also Stubbs, W, *Select Charters from the beginning to 1307* (Oxford University Press, 9th edn, 1913) 12.

hundred or an honour or any other area of land within the control of one person, although it is rare to find a manor so described.

Waifs were stolen goods dropped or waived by a thief in flight. The Crown claimed them even where the true owner was known. This was an inducement to bring the thief to justice because on conviction the owner could reclaim them. Waifs were generally granted to lords of the manor and are now obsolete.

Deodands were animals or inanimate things, such as carts, that caused the death of a person. If a horse and cart killed someone the whole thing, including any luggage in it, was forfeit to the king or the owner of the franchise. This law was applied to railway trains which ran people down so the engine and carriages were forfeit[10] and to steamboats whose engines exploded causing death.[11] This was unacceptable in an industrial country and so deodands were abolished by an admirably succinct Act of 1846

It appears that some lords were entitled to the goods of people who killed themselves.[12] Suicide was a felony and such entitlement probably ceased to exist when forfeiture for felony was abolished by the Forfeiture Act 1870. Nowadays the goods of a suicide pass under his will or intestacy unless he was abetted by the heir, in which case that person will forfeit his inheritance, although there is jurisdiction to grant relief under the Forfeiture Act 1982.

16.4 LEGAL PERSONALITY

A corporation is an individual or collection of individuals or corporations united in one body which is itself treated as a legal person and which has perpetual succession, that is to say that it does not die, although it may be dissolved. The collection of individuals usually involves many people alive at the same time and their successors often for centuries, known as corporations aggregate, but there can be corporations sole of which the best known examples are rectors and vicars (20.2) and various public officials such as the Public Trustee or the Treasury Solicitor.

There is an enormous variety of corporations aggregate. The older ones were usually described as the head of an institution and his colleagues, such as the

---

[10] *R v The Eastern Counties Railway Company* (1842) 10 M & W 58, 152 ER 380; *R v Great Western Railway Co* (1842) 3 QB 333, 114 ER 533.

[11] *R v Brownlow* (1839) 11 A&E 119, 113 ER 358; but see *R v Polwart* (1841) 1 QB 818, 113 ER 1345.

[12] Scriven, J, *A Treatise on the Law of Copyholds* (Butterworth & Co, 7th edn by Archibald Brown, 1896) 264.

abbot and chapter of a monastery, the dean and canons of a cathedral, the master and fellows of a college or the mayor and burgesses of a borough. From the seventeenth century, chartered corporations such as the Bank of England, the East India Company, the College of Surgeons and others came into existence. Nowadays most corporations are created not by franchise but under the Companies Acts. However, the Privy Council Office is still concerned with chartered corporations and some, such as new universities, can still be created by franchise.

Apart from the incumbent of the parish,[13] few corporations directly affect the manor but many corporations held manors. Vast numbers of manors belonged to abbeys until the Dissolution of the Monasteries. Oxford and Cambridge colleges and other old schools still hold many manors. When a town became a borough (21.1) one of the things that many mayors and commonalties tried to do was to acquire the lordship of the manor that comprised the borough. When the Administration of Justice Bill was going through Parliament in 1977 there was a move to give local authorities a right of first refusal to acquire any lordships which came up for sale affecting their area, but the Government did not accept the proposal.

In rare cases the homage or men of a manor might be recognised as a corporation and could sue and be sued collectively. Otherwise, like the Free Fishers of Whitstable discussed in 15.5, some might be incorporated by statute. In *Goodman v Saltash Corporation*[14] the inhabitants of certain ancient tenements within the borough of Saltash claimed the right to take oysters from the River Tamar from Candlemas to Easter. They claimed that their predecessors had done so since at least the time of Henry II. The claim was opposed by Saltash Corporation which was itself established by several royal charters of Richard II, Henry VIII, Elizabeth I, Charles II and George III and claimed to have a several fishery in the oysterage of the river. The House of Lords held that the grant of the fishery to the borough was subject to a condition in favour of the inhabitants of the tenements that they had the right to take oysters as claimed. The right was regarded as being in the nature of a trust and the House held that it should be presumed that it lay in a royal grant preceding the grant to the corporation.

---

[13]   Bracton *op cit* f 226b.

[14]   (1881–82) LR 7 App Cas 633.

16.5   CURRENCY

In the Middle Ages money meant gold and silver. Abstractions, such as the level of credit authorised by banks, were not treated as money. In Anglo-Saxon times kings used private moneyers who established mints in many towns, but it is unclear to what extent they were under royal supervision and how far they were businessmen literally making money on their own account. After the Norman Conquest money came under firm royal control but the rights to the silver and gold to make it could be granted out. Royal mines are mines of gold and silver and these substances belong to the Crown even if the landowner or lord of the manor has other mineral rights (11.5).

Treasure trove was formerly an item of gold or silver deliberately hidden whose owner was unknown. Many items from prehistoric and later times have been found to be treasure trove by coroners' juries. However, its origins are not archaeological but fiscal. The law assumed that anyone who hid precious items did so to avoid royal revenues. Treasure trove could be granted as a franchise. In *Attorney-General v Trustees of the British Museum*[15] discussed below an unsuccessful attempt was made to claim a franchise of treasure trove.

Grants of or including treasure trove were made during the Middle Ages, especially in the fifteenth century before 1485. In general, palatinates had this right along with other regalities. Grants were also made to abbeys (which reverted to the Crown at the Dissolution) and great lords, most of whose estates were forfeited during the Wars of the Roses or under the Tudors. Grants were also made to town corporations such as London and (it is said) to Bristol and Rochester, and to educational foundations such as King's College, Cambridge and Eton College. Since 1485 very few grants have been made. A grant may have been made to Newark-upon-Trent in 1672. The standard textbook[16] says there was a confirmation of the franchise to the Barony of Wark in Northumberland in an Act of 1793 but recent research has found no trace of the right to treasure trove.[17] In *Duke of Somerset v Cookson*[18] the duke claimed to be the owner of an altar piece as treasure trove in right of his manor of Corbridge in Northumberland. That manor, like Wark, appears to have been part of the former Percy estate and the claims to treasure trove may be linked to the privileges of the wardens of the Scottish Marches. The most recent grant is said

---

[15]   [1903] 2 Ch 598.

[16]   Hill, Sir George, *Treasure Trove in Law and Practice from the Earliest Time to the Present Day* (Oxford University Press, 1936) Note A.

[17]   See *Duke of Northumberland v Pattison*; discussed in Fenwick, J, *Treasure Trove in Northumberland* (1851) 46. I am grateful to Christopher Garrison for drawing my attention to this.

[18]   (1735) 3 P Wms 390, 24 ER 1114.

to have been a Crown grant on the sale of the Hundred of Wirral to John Williams in 1820, although it is unclear whether he or his successors actually claimed treasure trove. Many, perhaps most, of these alleged grants appear to be unsupported by evidence or are no longer claimed. Even if there was once a grant, unless the franchise had been specifically assigned (16.8) it may have been lost.

Treasure trove has now become treasure. For many years the Crown used the law of treasure trove as a basis to claim finds of gold or silver of archaeological interest. In theory it had to be shown that they had been hidden with a view to recovery, not abandoned. This caused problems with gold cups placed in Bronze Age graves intended for the everlasting use of the deceased, but the point was often stretched. With the invention of metal detectors valuable objects were discovered and sites were looted. The shortcomings of the law were illustrated in *Attorney-General for the Duchy of Lancaster v G. E. Overton (Farms) Limited,*[19] discussed in 27.4. The objects found were late Roman coins with an insignificant silver content and although of archaeological interest were held not to be treasure trove.

Those who wished to protect the heritage pressed for change and the Treasure Act 1996 was passed as a private member's bill (with government support). It converted both the prerogative right and the franchise into a new greater right of treasure which includes everything that used to be treasure trove and a good deal more. Treasure includes many antiquities, items associated with valuable finds and other things designated by the Secretary of State. As a Crown right this now rests on statute rather than the royal prerogative. Any former holder of treasure trove was given a new statutory franchise of treasure in exchange.

If an object which may be treasure is discovered the coroner has a duty to hold an inquest to determine whether it is treasure. When the Coroners and Justice Act 2009 is in force this will be the Coroner for Treasure, a new office created by Ch 4 of and Sch 4 to the Act. Under s 29(2) a franchisee may notify the Coroner that he has disclaimed the object, in an inquest will not to be held. The object will then vest either in the landowner or in the finder depending on the circumstances.[20]

The prerogative right of treasure belongs to the Crown. Within their jurisdictions the Royal Duchies have that right. This is not a franchise as the Duchies also hold prerogative rights, but under the Treasure Act 1996, s 5(2) they are treated as if they were franchisees for the purposes of the Act. The Department for Culture, Media and Sport accepts that the City of London has a

---

[19]   [1982] Ch 277.

[20]   See *Waverley Borough Council v Fletcher* [1996] 2QB 334: 'the Farnham Jewel case'.

franchise although it is more cautious about the City of Bristol, simply saying that it 'may' hold a franchise.[21] No others appear currently to be recognised but the legislation makes allowance for the possibility.

As indicated above, the Treasure Act 1996 involved a substitution of a new wider statutory right for the old franchise. It is not clear if the current right is to be regarded as a franchise in the strict sense. The effect of s 4 is to abolish the old franchise of treasure trove. The new right of treasure is then vested by ss 4 and 5 in the person who, immediately before the Act came into force, was the franchisee of the Crown for the place where the treasure was found.[22] The result appears to be that the holder of the old franchise now has a new and wider statutory right in place of his old common law right but is still referred to as franchisee. As the only franchise at present fully recognised is that of the City of London it may have been considered that the extension of rights was justified in the public interest, but if a lord was able to establish a former right to treasure trove he would have the new greater right. In practice it may be difficult to do this. Under the rule in *Morris v Dimes*[23] a person claiming a franchise in gross needs to show that it has been specifically assigned and the use of general words is not sufficient. It will be rare for the right to treasure trove to have been mentioned in a conveyance.

Where a lord can show title, the question arises whether it is exercisable where an object has been discovered in registered land after 12 October 2013 (or the first disposition after that date) if the franchise has not been noted on the title (25.9). In practice the object, under the code of practice (which has statutory force under s 11 of the Treasure Act 1996) will have been delivered to the coroner or an institution such as the British Museum. The lord's claim to the item will in the first instance therefore not be to an interest in land against the owner of the place it was found but to a chattel against the museum. A Crown disclaimer under s 6 will of course be ineffective if treasure is vested in a subject. The effect of the rules on overriding interests is not to extinguish the right but to govern priority between the registered proprietor and the franchise owner and does not affect third parties. If the museum, without knowledge of the claim by the franchise owner, delivers the item to the landowner then the effect of the Land Registration Act 2002 may be to defeat the franchisee's claim, but otherwise he should be able to pursue it.

---

[21] Department for Culture, Media and Sport, *The Treasure Act 1996 Code of Practice* (2nd Revision 2007) para 20.

[22] See also Coroners and Justice Act 2009, s 29(5).

[23] (1834) 1 Add & E 654, 110 ER 1357.

16.6   COMMERCE AND ANIMALS

There are many commercial franchises such as tolls of anchorage, passage, ferry and pontage considered in some detail in 15.1–15.5 and markets and fairs in 21.2.

'Wreck' is a slightly different form of commercial franchise. There are four varieties of wreck. 'Flotsam' is where a ship is split and the goods being carried float onto the foreshore. 'Jetsam' is where a ship is in danger of sinking and the goods are thrown into the sea to lighten it. 'Ligan', 'lagan' or 'ligam' is where goods are deliberately thrown into the sea with a buoy marking the spot, so they are not abandoned, but if the owner does not come and claim them (if, for instance, he went down with the ship) then they are wreck. 'Derelict' is where a ship itself comes to land or sinks. Franchises of wreck normally comprised only jetsam, flotsam and ligan but the jurisdiction of the Receiver of Wreck under the Merchant Shipping Act 1894 extends to derelict, and, in practice, particularly where a ship broke up, the tenants of a coastal manor would often take and keep the timbers for themselves.

Wreck was often granted to lords of coastal manors. By itself it did not necessarily include title to the foreshore but it was often implied or presumed that the lord having the franchise was also to have (or perhaps already had) the foreshore. This was certainly not always so. In *Crown Estate Commissioners v Roberts*[24] Mr Roberts had purchased the manor of Dewisland in Pembrokeshire which had once belonged to the bishops of St David's. It was established that over the centuries the bishops had been entitled to half the proceeds of wreck. In the case Roberts was claiming to own the foreshore and part of the seabed. That claim was specifically not established and the judge found that the foreshore was under the management of the Commissioners on behalf of the Crown. However, that did not affect the right to half the proceeds of wreck which had therefore passed to Roberts.

The Merchant Shipping Act 1894 made express provision for the rights of a lord who claimed a right of wreck; under s 524 a notice of the finding of wreck had to be given to the lord and under ss 525 and 526 he had an opportunity to claim wreck. The law was amended under the Merchant Shipping (Registration etc) Act 1993. The 1894 Act was replaced by the Merchant Shipping Act 1995. The legislation no longer refers expressly to lords of the manor but their rights are not affected. However, nowadays wreck is more often a nuisance to be cleared up than a profitable advantage, and local authorities who want unsightly rubbish

---

[24]   [2008] EWHC 1302 (Ch), [2008] All ER (D) 175 (Jun).

removed from a beach may try to pin the responsibility onto a lord who has wreck.

Franchises of wild animals, namely chases, parks, warrens and fisheries, are discussed in 12.2–12.3. The royal right to swans is shared with the Worshipful Company of Vintners and the Worshipful Company of Dyers, who were granted franchises in the fifteenth century. In theory royal fish (whales, sturgeon and grampuses) might have been granted as franchises but was not.

Estrays are valuable tame animals found wandering whose owner is unknown. Most lords had this franchise and the Crown rarely reserved it. The finding of an estray must be proclaimed in the church of the parish and in the two nearest market towns and if the true owner does not claim the animal within a year and a day the holder of the franchise can keep it. In practice nowadays unclaimed property, including tame animals, is normally handed over to the police.

16.7   MERGER IN CROWN RIGHTS

It is evident from what has been said that franchises are a mixed collection of rights. They can be classified into two groups: flower franchises and others. *Attorney-General v Trustees of the British Museum*[25] involved gold treasure including a collar, model boat, bowl, necklace and chain found in 1896 near Lough Foyle in the north of Ireland. The British Museum bought them from the person who claimed them under seventeenth-century charters of James I and Charles II, which included the word franchise. The Crown claimed the items from the Museum as treasure trove. It seems that the modern practice that the Crown automatically awards treasure trove to the British Museum or another museum did not then exist.

The court applied the definition of franchise as being a grant out of the royal prerogative, and divided the items into two classes. One class, following the *Case of the Abbot of Strata Mercella*,[26] was described as flowers of the Crown. That is, they already existed as, and were exercised as, royal rights when granted. They would include, in addition to treasure trove, wreck, waifs, estrays and deodands. Thus, when the Crown grants such a franchise, royal rights are diminished. If the lord of a manor has wreck or waifs the Crown cannot at the same time exercise that right where previously it could. The other class is not specified in the case but, since it includes (amongst other rights) rural markets,

---

[25]   [1903] 2 Ch 598.

[26]   (1591) 9 Co Rep 24a, 77 ER 765.

franchises of this type may be termed 'produce franchises'. This relates to those which did not exist before the grant, such as fairs, parks and ferries.

The distinction is relevant in circumstances where the manor with which the franchise is held comes into the hands of the Crown. Flower franchises cease to exist and merge in the Prerogative. The *Strata Mercella* case concerned waifs. The manor of Tallerthege in Montgomeryshire had belonged to the abbey and passed to the Crown on the Dissolution. In 1546 the manor was granted to Sir Arthur Darcy. It was held that the grant did not carry with it the right to waifs formerly held by the abbey. Produce franchises by contrast remain in existence. Suppose Sir Hugh as lord of the manor of Middleton obtains a grant of market appurtenant to the manor and subsequently the manor comes back to the Crown. If the Crown then grants it out again to Mr Brown with all franchises, then he will be entitled to hold a market.

In *Heddy v Wheelhouse*[27] the court held that:

> such liberties which a common person hath by prescription or grant, and which, if the common person had not, the King himself should have throughout England, as Ways, Estray, Wreck, &c., there, if the common person hath them by grant, or prescription, and they come to the King by forfeiture or otherwise they are extinguished in the Crown, and the Queen will have such liberties by her prerogative, and they cannot afterwards be granted, but by a new creation. But such liberties, which a common person hath by grant, or prescription, which the King (if such prescription had not been) could not have by his prerogative, as warren, park, fayr, market with toll, &c., if these come to the Crown, &c., they remain in esse, and are not extinct; for, if the King should not have them by this means, they would be lost.

This restrictive interpretation applies generally. In the British Museum case, even though the charter of Charles II through which the claim was made included the word 'franchises', the judge held that it was limited to franchises appurtenant to the manor and the right to treasure trove remained with the Crown. In *Morris v Dimes*[28] (discussed in 12.3) the same applied to an assurances between subjects even where, as in that case, general words had been used.

Once granted, franchises become separate private property and do not keep their royal nature. *Spook Erection Ltd v Secretary of State for the Environment and Cotswold District Council*[29] related to a market held in Moreton-in-Marsh in

---

[27]   (1596) Cro Eliz 591, 78 ER 834; see *Duke of Newcastle v Worksop Urban District Council*. [1902] 2 Ch 145.

[28]   (1834) 1 Add & E 654, 110 ER 1357.

[29]   [1988] 2 All ER 667.

Gloucestershire. The high street of Moreton is broad and consists of two metalled highways. Between them is a long strip of unsurfaced land. Market rights were held by the lord of Moreton under letters patent of Charles I and from 1638 until 1923 the market was held in the high street. In 1923 the owner of the manorial rights sold the market rights to a local cattle dealer who moved the market to another part of town where it was held as a cattle market until 1955. In 1976 Mr Maby purchased the market rights and revived the weekly market through his company, Spook Erections Ltd. He held it on the long strip of land which had been manorial waste, but by 1976 or thereabouts the land became owned by the local council. The council did not claim in trespass but under the Town and Country Planning Act 1971 for breach of planning control. Although the use of land for any purpose in 1948 (when planning was introduced) was protected, as the market was then being held elsewhere, planning permission was needed to hold it in the high street. Spook applied for consent, which was given, but on conditions it did not like.

The Crown was at the time not legally bound by the planning laws even though it did in fact voluntarily submit to a similar procedure. Spook claimed that as the market was a franchise, namely a grant out of the royal prerogative, it could claim the benefit of the Crown exemption. The Court of Appeal did not agree. Once the grant has been made the franchise becomes a private right. The holder can treat it as his property. It is therefore subject to normal rules which apply to private rights.

16.8   CREATION AND EXTINCTION

As franchises are by definition Crown grants there must have been a grant. As they are incorporeal hereditaments there must be a document such as a charter. As explained above modern franchises are granted by charter out of the Privy Council Office. *Nyali Ltd v Attorney-General*[30] concerned a right of pontage in the Protectorate of Kenya in a territory under the sovereignty of the Sultan of Zanzibar but administered by Britain. It was accepted that English law applied. In that case Denning LJ said:

> There are no modern instances of a Crown grant of franchise, but it is one of the prerogatives of the Crown; and in order to be valid it must be made by matter of record, that is to say, by Royal Charter or by Letters Patent under the Great Seal.

He went on to say that in the special circumstances of the Kenya Protectorate a charter or letters patent were not needed. However, it remains true that they are needed in England. In 1955 when the case was heard new universities had not

---

[30]   [1956] 1 QB 1.

been set up for some time and other chartered corporations were rare, but there have been many such grants for those purposes since then.

It has been the case since at least the statute *Quo Warranto* 1290 and probably many years before that a person claiming a franchise had to produce the warrant or charter on which he based his claim. *Quo Warranto* proceedings were frequently used by the Crown to challenge the powers and the very existence of corporations such as town councils and colleges, as well as claims to franchises by lords. As mentioned in 4.3 the statute itself contained an exception for rights that could be shown to have existed in 1189, so that some of the oldest corporations, as well as the holders of ancient rights of wreck, several fisheries and many other franchises cannot produce a documented origin. Some rights which would have been created as franchises after 1189 are almost universal. Most courts leet were held by a lord long before that date and a franchise must be presumed. Likewise a rector of a parish was a corporation sole and again that status must, under the later law, have been a franchise, but ancient rectories predated 1189.

Most modern equivalent rights to franchises are now established under Acts of Parliament including corporate status (as under the Local Government Act 1972 and the Companies Act 2006), several fisheries (under the Marine and Coastal Access Act 2009) and markets (under the Food Act 1984, Part 7). It is unlikely now that a lord of the manor as such would wish to establish a new franchise annexed to his manor and it is equally unlikely that the Crown would grant it.

Franchises can cease to exist in different ways. Some may be lost by failure to exercise them. Many manors formerly had franchise of ferry, which is a monopoly of the right to carry passengers across a short stretch of water. Because it is essential to commerce, the owner of a ferry who does not keep boats ready and available risks forfeiture for non-use.[31] Likewise, if a deer park ceases to hold deer the area is disparked and if the owner wanted the privilege revived he would need a new royal grant (12.2). The right to hold a court leet might be lost by disuse.[32]

Other franchises are not lost by non-use. Many markets, for example, were granted to lords to hold in their manors in the thirteenth century (16.2). Some flourished and formed the basis of market towns which still have markets to this day, but many were speculative and failed. Nevertheless, the right still exists and even though no market has been held for over 600 years it can be revived and the holder can prevent a rival market. However, *Gloucestershire County*

---

[31] *Attorney-General v Colchester Corpn* [1955] 2 QB 207 at 215, [1955] 2 All ER 124 at 127.

[32] *Darell v Bridge* (1749) 1 Bl Wm 46, 96 ER 25, although in that case there was some doubt as to title.

Council v Farrow[33] shows that a market may in practice be lost. In that case Mr Farrow, as lord of the manor of Stow, claimed the right to hold a market on the town square. The whole area of the square had become public highway and therefore the erection of market stalls would have been an unlawful obstruction. Although the market still existed in theory, in practice it could not be held, at least in the traditional place.

A flower franchise will be lost by merger if the manor comes into the hands of the Crown, but that does not apply to produce franchises. Franchises can also be lost by Act of Parliament. The Deodands Act 1846 and the Wild Creatures and Forest Laws Act 1971 are examples. In those cases no compensation was paid to lords whose property was taken away. This may have been because it was felt that what the Crown has granted, the Crown (in Parliament) can take away. However, it may also have been because no loss arose, particularly if the sporting rights abolished in 1971 were converted into profits. Corporate status is often abolished by Parliament, as on local government or educational reorganisation, but that is usually thought to be in the public interest and individuals rarely suffer financial loss in such cases. Franchises, as a grant of public authority, are vulnerable when new public policies come into play.

The principle was stated by Bowen LJ in *The Mayor and Citizens of the City of Manchester v Lyons*:[34]

> Where there is a franchise created by charter, and the legislature afterwards operates upon it, it is obvious that the legislature can do exactly what it pleases. It can either leave the old franchise standing, and place a new parliamentary right beside it, or it may leave the old franchise standing and incorporate certain statutory incidents into the old franchise, provided it makes its intention clear; or it may extinguish the old franchise, either expressly or by implication, and substitute in its place not a franchise properly so called, but parliamentary rights and obligations as distinct from a franchise. We must therefore in each case look at the statute itself to see what the legislature has chosen to do.

In the case of treasure the old franchise of treasure trove has been substituted by a statutory right conferred on the holder of the franchise, who is still called a franchisee.

Franchises can also be forfeited by the Crown although in rare circumstances. The Land Registration Rules 2003, r 196B[35] makes it clear that where a

---

[33]   [1985] 1 WLR 741, [1982] 2 All ER 1031, (1984) 48 P&CR 85.

[34]   (1882) 22 Ch D 287 at 310.

[35]   Inserted by the Land Registration (Amendment) Rules 2008.

franchise is registered the registration is without prejudice to any right of the
Crown to forfeit the franchise.

In addition, the effect of *Morris v Dimes*[36] is that a franchise in gross can be lost
by failure to assign it. The franchise itself may in theory still exist but it will be
difficult to determine who is entitled to it. If it is possible to identify the
beneficiaries in equity then it may be possible to establish legal title either by an
appointment of new trustees by the court under the Trustee Act 1925, s 41 or,
possibly, by a grant *de bonis non administratis* to the estate of the last known
legal holder.

16.9   LAND REGISTRATION

The Land Registration Act 2002 allowed the owner of a franchise to apply for a
registered title. Registration in general is discussed in 25.8. Specific rules apply
to franchises and the Act has introduced a new classification.

Although the general principle is contained in the Act it did not go into details.
The preceding Law Commission Report concluded that franchises were valuable
pieces of property and it was right to give their proprietor the ability to buy and
sell them using the procedures of registration. However, the Act simply provides
that the details will be set out in rules. These are in the Land Registration Rules
2003. In applying the principles to franchises an immediate problem appeared.
The register is primarily one for land as corporeal property and the subject
matter of registration is defined by reference to an official plan. That is not
practicable for most franchises although some can affect a specific area of land.

Rule 217(1) therefore distinguishes between an 'affecting franchise', which
means 'a franchise which relates to a defined area of land and is an adverse right
affecting, or capable of affecting, the title to an estate or charge', and a 'relating
franchise', which means 'a franchise which is not an affecting franchise'.
Rule 5(a) provides that the property register of a title to an affecting franchise
must refer to a title plan.

The Land Registry points out in the context of franchises that 'Most franchises
are considered to be relating franchises and are not overriding interests because
they do not affect land. They cannot, therefore, be the subject of an application
for a notice'.[37] Corporate status is intangible, and while a borough or a
university may be situated within a specific town or on a defined campus, it is

---

[36]   (1834) 1 Add & E 654, 110 ER 1357.

[37]   Land Registry Practice Guide 66, *Overriding interests losing automatic protection in 2013*
        para 4.6.3

not the location. The same is true of jurisdictions, notably a court leet which may have physical boundaries to its jurisdiction, but which, at least since the Administration of Justice Act 1977, is not capable of affecting the title to an estate. Waifs and estrays may relate to a defined area but to goods or animals, not to land. The view of the Registry is that markets likewise do not normally so relate (21.2).[38]

Treasure can relate to a particular area. Treasure of the City Corporation relates to the City of London. However, this may best be seen as concerning a jurisdiction and in this context the courts would probably give a restricted meaning to the expression 'defined area of land'. It is possible that if a lord were able to establish a franchise of treasure within the limits of a manor that could be affecting, but equally it may be that the effect of the Treasure Act 1996 would be to convert what had been a franchise into a statutory right (even though called a franchise in the Act). Other rights can concern a defined area of land and be affecting. Wreck will apply to a specific stretch of foreshore. It entitles the owner of the right to go there to take his wreck although the jurisdiction of the receiver will be paramount. Ancient tolls such as anchorage will likewise affect a defined location, such as a port.

Rule 7 says that '[Where practicable, the] property register of a registered estate in a ... franchise ... must, if the estate was created by an instrument, also contain sufficient particulars of the instrument to enable it to be identified'. The words in square brackets were substituted by Sch 1, para 3 to the Land Registration (Amendment) Rules 2008 with effect from 10 November 2008, since if a franchise was (or can be presumed to have been) in existence before 3 September 1189 there may be no instrument – specifically a royal charter. Even if the franchise was granted later it may have been lost.

As discussed in 25.9, under the Land Registration Act 2002, Schs 1 and 3, para 10, affecting franchises may lose their status as overriding interests after the first registration or disposition of land after 12 October 2013. Unless they have been noted against a registered title or a caution has been lodged against unregistered land by that date they are at risk of ceasing to be enforceable against certain proprietors who take after that date for value. This is separate from the registration of the franchise with its own title. It is not clear what happens if a franchise affects a piece of land, is not noted or cautioned before that time and the owner of the franchise applies to register it substantively later. Probably the court would prefer the right of someone who had paid for the land not knowing about the franchise, but this remains to be decided.

---

[38] Land Registry Practice Guide 18, *Franchises* para 5.2.

Chapter 17

Mills and Maidens

mills, mulctures, ... privileges, easements, profits, advantages, rights, emoluments

17.1   MISCELLANEOUS RIGHTS

This chapter deals with several miscellaneous rights of the lord, most of which are now obsolete or of little importance, but some have left traces in the modern law. They fall into two categories. The first is rights which benefit land or rights which may belong to any landowner and are not specific to manors. Thus, demesne land may benefit from an easement, such as a right of way or a right of drainage. Waste land does not usually benefit from easements, but if it is isolated from a highway a means of access may be necessary. Such rights go with the land under s 62(1) rather than s 62(3). It is now rare for a common law easement to be recognised as having existed since before 1189 but in the context of the manor it may be possible, for instance, for water rights. A manorial customary way must predate 1189. Manorial lands may also be subject to easements. Manorial lands may also be subject to easements.

Profits are an important feature of the manor. These include rights of common (10.3), some mineral rights (11.1) and sporting and fishing rights (12.4). As s 62 is concerned with implications in a conveyance it may be relevant when part of the manorial lands is sold. In *Duke of Devonshire v Pattinson*[1] the duke held the manor of the Socage of the Castle of Carlisle which included fishing rights in the River Eden. In 1667 and 1846 the then owners of the manor sold fields abutting the river to Carlisle Corporation. The corporation claimed that the sales impliedly included the bed of the river and the fishing rights. The Court of Appeal affirmed the decision of the judge that the river and fishing rights in this case were a separate property and any implication was excluded. A manor may also benefit from common law profits such as sporting or mineral rights dating from before 1189, and manorial lands may be subject to similar freehold rights.

---

[1]   (1888) LR 20 QBD 263.

Privilege literally means private law. The basis of the manor was its customs, which created a special jurisdiction, but in this context it is more likely that privilege refers to some exemption from the general law. Privilege is used in the context, for instance, of legal privilege, in that lawyers are not liable to disclose things their clients have communicated in confidence, as well as public matters, such as in defamation where certain remarks are privileged. Members of Parliament also enjoy certain privileges in the public interest. The lord of the manor does not have any special privilege of that sort. However, it is possible that, as mentioned in 9.5, the term 'manorial rights' with the specific meaning given in various statutes, including the Land Registration Act 2002, may constitute a privilege for the purposes of the Law of Property Act 1925, s 1(2)(a). A liberty (16.3) can be a privilege.

Similarly, rights and advantages are used in a general sense. An advantage might be the power of the lord to join in the use of the common even when the rights of commoners have not been satisfied. Other rights are considered below.

17.2   BANALITIES

'Banalities' is not an English term but has been taken from French and German law to represent a group of English rights.[2] The most important relates to mills which can still be a valuable asset. Old mills, millponds and leats can still produce problems. The 'ban' was the name given to the group of great lords who followed the Emperor Charlemagne and his successors and who also followed the kings of Germany and France when the empire broke up. The same word was used for the assembly of those followers and for the decrees of the assembly. As the empire and kingdoms weakened the decrees became merely negative. (The word 'ban' in English now means to prohibit something.) For example, in 1521 the Diet of Worms was convoked to consider putting Martin Luther under the Ban of the Empire, although he escaped before it could be put into force. The assembly could also banish someone from the empire. There is a slightly different meaning when a marriage is announced and anyone who knows a good reason why it should not take place, or be banned, is asked to appear when the banns are read.

With the disintegration of government on the Continent, royal power was taken over by lesser lords. The word *dominus*, which once meant emperor, came to refer to any local seigneur. Those seigneurs likewise claimed the right to a ban

---

[2]   See Ganshof, FL and Verhulst, A, 'Medieval Agrarian Society in its Prime, France, the Low Countries and Western Germany', in Postan, M (ed), *The Cambridge Economic History of Europe Vol 1* (Cambridge University Press, 2nd edn, 1966) 334; Poly, J-P and Bournazel, E, *The Feudal Transformation 900–1200* (Holmes and Meier, 1991) 25; *Encyclopaedia Britannica* (1911) Ban.

within their jurisdiction. The most common were the *ban de moulin* for mills, the *ban de four* for ovens (furnaces) and the *ban de vin* for the production of wine. All were seigniorial monopolies and were forbidden to others within the seignury. In *L'Ancien Regime*[3] Alexis de Toqueville refers to other banalities existing in France before the French Revolution, including cloth-presses, wine-presses, butcheries and the keeping of bulls, but these were rare. The Ban of the Vintage was common and in Burgundy the seigneur could gather his crop of grapes one day before any other wine-grower. In France to this day there is a formal *ban de vendage*, so that if a grower wishes to harvest grapes before a set date he needs special permission.

Banalities did not exist as such in England which was not part of the empire where the ban could be enforced but similar rights were found. As vines did not grow well the *banvin* was not known but the lord had certain rights in relation to the brewing of ale and indeed a jurisdiction known as the assize of bread and ale was exercised through borough courts in many towns for a long time, although in practice more to control its quality than to assert the lord's monopoly.[4]

Oven rights disappeared at an early date. They made sense at a time when houses of wood and straw were close together and fires could spread disastrously but, of course, they were exercised to give the lord a monopoly of baking and to make a charge. Blackstone[5] discusses rights to bakehouse, kiln and malthouse under the same heading, along with mills.

17.3 MILLS

Suit of mill is more common, last longer and the mills themselves can still be important. Originally, suit of mill applied only to watermills, although in some manors the rules seem to have been transferred to windmills when they became widespread. A custom that all the inhabitants of a manor (whether bond or free) must have their corn ground at the manor mill was held to be good in many mediaeval cases although it was unpopular, resented and breached as often as possible. The reason for the custom lay in the expense of constructing and maintaining the mill. In *Harbin v Green*[6] in 1617 such a custom was held to be unreasonable, void and unenforceable. It was still claimed as late as 1797 in *Attorney-General of Duchy of Lancaster (Ord) ex rel Neville v Buck*[7] which

---

[3]   de Tocqueville, A, *L'Ancien Regime* (English translation by J Bonner, 1856) (JM Dent & Sons Ltd, 1998): note on feudal rights.

[4]   See Thompson, EP, *Customs in Common* (Merlin Press, 1991) Ch 4 for later developments.

[5]   Blackstone, Sir William, *Commentaries on the Laws of England* 3152.

[6]   (1617) Moore (KB) 887, 72 ER 975.

[7]   (1797) 8 Bro PC 106, 3 ER 473.

involved the custom as found in Leeds in Yorkshire. In that case the custom was admitted but an attempt to extend it was defeated. In *Richardson v Walker*[8] in 1824 the court held that although the custom that residents must grind the corn they grew at the manor mill was good, they could nevertheless buy corn already ground elsewhere – and in an urban and industrial age that signalled the end.[9]

A watermill worked by releasing the gravitational energy released by water as it fell from a higher to a lower level. This was used to turn a mill wheel to which was attached a shaft which turned the grindstones which converted wheat to flour. In hill country the streams fell steeply and needed little alteration to make a gradient for the water to pour over. In flat champion country where the typical manor of open fields was found, major works were needed. If the river fell, say, 10 feet over two miles, a channel, known as a leat, was connected at the upper part of the river and made to run as flat as possible, often cut through the slopes at the edge of the river valley or banked up artificially.

Sometimes the soil of the leat is separately owned, perhaps along with the mill, while the land on either side belongs to a tenant. Often, however, there is simply an easement of the right to a flow of water along it. This can lead to problems if the mill becomes disused, the leat is filled in, and later the mill is acquired by an enthusiast who wishes to restart the operation. It is not unknown for such people to take direct action to assert their rights and dig up the leat even if it passes through a field where cattle are grazing. The matter may turn on whether the easement has been abandoned. It may be possible to resolve the dispute by allowing water to flow along a buried pipe.

The leat wound across country with a very gentle fall to a point by which the river had flowed down so that the level in the leat was eight or nine feet higher. The water ran into an artificial mill pond (6.8) separated from the river by a mill dam on or beside which was the mill. The flow over the dam into the river powered the mill wheel. All of these works were expensive but were worth constructing and keeping in repair if the only alternative was grinding the grain by hand or by animal power. Later, windmills were introduced which did not need the elaborate system of leat, pool and dam.

The expense was met by a multure or mulcture. This was originally a proportion of the flour. For free tenants it was one cup in 20 or 24. For villeins it was one in 13 or 15. Later, the mulcture was often commuted for a cash payment which later still merged in the quitrent. Whether in cash or kind it was resented,

---

8   (1824) 2 B&C 827, 107 ER 590.

9   Blackstone *op cit* 315ii; Bennett, HS, *Life on the English Manor 1150–1400* (Alan Sutton, 1937) 129; Watkins, C, *A Treatise on Copyholds* (James Bullock, 4th edn by Thomas Coventry, 1825) 2.497 (Littlecott); Scriven, J, *A Treatise on the Law of Copyholds* (Butterworth & Co, 7th edn by Archibald Brown, 1896) 318; Thompson *op cit* Ch 4.

particularly as yields improved, farms grew bigger, and the miller took a large return for little value, even if he was honest.

Mulctures became obsolete long ago, but as the lord usually owned the mill (the miller might be a copyholder but more usually was a lessee), the building and all that went with it belonged to him. Until recently many landed estates included old mills or their site. Claims to leats are more rare because when they became disused they were often treated as belonging to the owner of the land through which they ran. In principle, however, a lord might have had title to a potentially valuable strip comprising a muddy ditch or old embankment, which controlled access to a building site or cross a potential quarry. Occasionally, the owner of a mill sought to assert rights to a disused leat, giving rise to disagreements with neighbours.

Emolument does not have the modern meaning of an employee's remuneration but derives from Mediaeval Latin *emolumentum*, which originally meant a payment to a miller for grinding corn, from emolere, meaning to grind up.

17.4   MAIDEN RIGHT

The one thing that everyone knows about the manor is that the lord enjoyed the *droit du seigneur*, the right to sleep with the village maiden on her wedding night. Like so many commonly held beliefs, this is not true, and never was. But the idea is at least as old as the eighteenth century and is based on an older custom that was widely observed, known as merchet.[10] Merchet applied to bondsmen and their daughters. When the daughter of a villein was to be married to a man of another manor her father needed the consent of his lord. The reason was that if she had stayed in the manor her children would, like her, have been serfs of the lord and, by marrying out of the manor, she was depriving the lord of their services. The custom varied and in some manors merchet was claimed, at a lower rate, for marriage within the manor as well. Consent was always given, but it had to be paid for.

Most manors had a standard fee. In Wednesbury[11] in Staffordshire in 1310 the lord claimed two shillings for merchet within the manor and three shillings out of it. This appears to be a reasonable level of charge because by the 1350s at

---

[10] Bracton, Sir Henry (ed), *De legibus et consuetudinibus angliae* (c 1257) (SE Thorne (ed)) (Belknap Press of Harvard University Press, 1977) f 195; Miller E and Hatcher, J, *Medieval England: Rural Society and Economic Change 1086–1348* (Longman, 1978) 117; Rowlands, MB, *The West Midlands from AD 1000* (Longman, 1978) 29.

[11] Hilton, RH, *The English Peasantry in the Later Middle Ages* (Clarendon Press, 1975) 238: Wednesbury.

Pattingham,[12] also in Staffordshire, merchet varied between five and ten shillings. This was at a time when a daily wage was fourpence, so that merchet was between a week's and a month's wages. The general level around the country settled at about five shillings or a crown. No doubt there were instances where the tenant could not afford the fee. In such a case if the lord was vigorous and the girl was pretty consent might have been given on other terms, but the Church would never have tolerated a legal custom which, in its view, amounted to immorality.

Merchet became obsolete when villeinage disappeared but the nominal right remained and was not forgotten either in England or on the Continent, where it was known as formarriage. By the eighteenth century it had become a standard joke. One of the best known is in the Marriage of Figaro, originally a play by Beaumarchais then an opera by Mozart. The plot develops because Count Alma Viva, an enlightened eighteenth-century aristocrat, has renounced his feudal rights in this respect and then, when his wife's maid Susanna is to marry his own valet Figaro, he regrets his decision and decides to win by guile what he cannot now claim in law. Of course it is absurd. Beaumarchais, Mozart and their audiences knew well that if the *droit du seigneur* had ever existed it would have applied only to simple village girls, not a sophisticated urban lady's maid like Susanna.

The idea is also mentioned by Blackstone.[13] It appears in a passage on the inheritance customs of copyhold where he is discussing borough english. Blackstone considers the reason for the strange rule in some manors whereby land descends to the youngest son, not the eldest. Why should this be? Because, says Blackstone, in earlier centuries a villein could not be certain who was the father of his wife's eldest child but he could be surer about the youngest. Although this might look as if Blackstone was trying to introduce into a dry part of his lectures a learned note of light relief as a slightly risqué if obscure joke, there may be more to it.

Borough english and merchet do go together. Watkins, in his survey of custumals, mentions several cases of marriage claims. He was writing in 1797, but most of the custumals were much older. Although many customs had long been obsolete when he wrote they had never been formally abolished. Thus, he says of Gissing[14] in Norfolk: 'the bondmen to fine for their marriage at the lord's will'. There can have been no bondmen there for 200 years or more. At Dinevor[15] in Camarthenshire he says that every tenant at the marriage of his

---

[12]   Ibid 58: Pattingham.

[13]   Blackstone *op cit* II6ii.

[14]   Watkins *op cit* 2.558: Gissing.

[15]   Ibid 2.486: Dinevor.

daughter paid 10 shillings. Of Hackford Hall[16] (later Herling Thorp) in Norfolk he reports from a custumal of 1364 that copyhold descended to the youngest son and that every copyholder that married gave the lord a bolster, sheet and pillow (except for tenants called Mol men). From a survey of Balshall,[17] Warwickshire of 1657 he again finds that lands of copyholders descended to the youngest son and that every female heir needed the lord's licence to marry for which the fee was five shillings. The best contemporary attitude he reports is from Builth in Radnorshire where he says, 'In this manor the maiden rent prevails but the lord is said to prefer tapping a hogshead of cyder to exercising his custom of Marcheta'.[18]

17.5   APPOINTMENTS

The lord of a manor may have the right to appoint people to certain positions. Court and community officials have been considered in 13.5. The lord appoints the steward and sometimes the bailiff. In theory others are appointed or elected by a court. In practice if a court is not active and a job needs to be done the appointment will have to be made by the lord or his steward. If the tenants did such services for the lord it may put him to expense. In Dymock[19] in Gloucestershire any tenants serving on the homage when the two-yearly courts were held and any manorial officials in office that day were entitled 'to have there dinners at th'onlie cost and chargs of the lorde of the manor for the tyme beyng'.

In *Jones v Waters*[20] the manor of Llywell in the county of Brecknock belonged to the burgesses of the borough of Brecon and the manor was vested in the bailiff. He appointed a town crier or bellman and the case was a claim against a rival bellman. The court held that the custom of appointing a town crier was good.

A second principal type of appointment relates to Church matters considered in 20.2. The lord often appointed a rector or vicar (20.2). In *Soane v Ireland*[21] in 1808 the lord of the manor of Froome Selwood had the right to appoint a sexton. Mr Soane was appointed to that post by the lord, Mr TS Champneys. The vicar,

---

[16]   Ibid 2.564: Hackford Hall.

[17]   Ibid 2.575: Balshall.

[18]   Ibid 2.481: Builth.

[19]   Ibid 2.490: Dymock.

[20]   (1835) 1 Crom Mees & Ros 713, 149 ER 1267.

[21]   (1808) 10 East 259, 103 ER 773.

Mr Ireland, claimed that as the manor was not a legal one but a reputed manor the appointment was invalid. The court found in favour of Soane.

The leading case is *Attorney-General v Ewelme Hospital*[22] in 1853. In 1437 William de la Pole, Duke of Suffolk, lord of the manor of Ewelme, founded and endowed Ewelme Hospital. The terms included the right of the lord of the manor to nominate the master of the hospital and also to nominate almsmen to benefit from the hospital charity. The Dukes of Suffolk were involved in high politics and at some date before 1513 the manor was forfeit to the Crown. In 1618 James I granted the office of master of the hospital to Oxford University so that it should automatically be held by the Regius Professor of Medicine. In 1818 the Commissioners of Woods, who by that time managed Crown lands, sold the manor of Ewelme to Jacob Bosanquet and the conveyance included the general words. Bosanquet resold it to the Earl of Macclesfield. In 1826 Sir Robert Peel, the Home Secretary, recognised that the earl, as lord of the manor, was entitled to nominate almsmen. In 1851 the Regius Professor of Medicine died and the earl claimed to appoint the Rev AH Napier as master. The Queen appointed Dr Ogle to be Regius Professor and the university claimed to appoint him as master. Was Mr Napier or Dr Ogle the master of Ewelme Hospital?

The court held that when the manor forfeited to the Crown the right to appoint a master was not extinguished (as a flower franchise might have been) but remained as a separate right in the Crown. Although the nomination right could pass with the manor it was not inevitably annexed forever (as the right to appoint the steward of the manorial court would be) but could be separated. If the right had still been vested in the Crown in 1818 it would have passed to Mr Bosanquet even though neither he nor the Commissioners of Woods intended it. But in this case the right was severed from the manor in 1618. The king had the power to do so (and presumably a private lord would have had the same right) and so the right was not included in the sale of the manor.

Rights of appointment may be annexed under statute. In the eighteenth and nineteenth centuries many of the works that are now called infrastructure were carried out by bodies of commissioners or special companies set up by private Acts of Parliament. The members of the board could be self-appointed, or elected by investors, or by people in the locality and nominated by local landowners and lords of manors. This often happened with harbours where, as explained in 15.4, the lord had ancient rights of anchorage or bushellage which he transferred to the commissioners in return for a say in their affairs. Otherwise he may simply have been invited to appoint a commissioner as he was an important landowner in the neighbourhood.

---

[22]   (1853) 17 Beav 366, 51 ER 1075.

A recent example (replacing earlier enactments) is the Padstow Harbour Revision Order 1987 which provides for 10 commissioners, three elected by each of the three local parishes and the tenth appointed by the lord of the manor of Padstow. Padstow is an ancient port and may have held manorial harbour rights.

17.6 COVENANTS

It appears that a manor can benefit from a restrictive covenant which limits the use of a piece of land. The use of covenants in building estates is discussed in 21.4. If a restrictive covenant no longer serves a useful purpose the Lands Tribunal has power under the Law of Property Act 1925, s 84 to release it. Covenants may be positive or restrictive and may either be personal or may bind the owner of land for the time being, but in general, restrictive covenants can only exist for the benefit of land. In *Re Mansfield District Council's Application*[23] Douglas Franks QC in the Lands Tribunal upheld a covenant apparently for the benefit of a manor.

The Duke of Portland had been lord of the manor of Mansfield and as such had a franchise of fairs and markets. He also owned the land on which the market was held. After his death in 1876 his trustees sold the fairs, market rights and the site of the cattle market to the Mansfield Improvement Commissioners and imposed a covenant for the benefit of the manor that the land could only be used as a market. In 1975 it was still a thriving local market for the sale of cattle, sheep and pigs. The council (as successor to the commissioners) waned to build a leisure centre and close the market. The successors of the trustees objected. The Lands Tribunal considered that the market still benefited the manor. Despite the 1925 legislation the manor still existed. The owners of the demesne land of the manor, as well as the owners of what had previously been copyhold land, still benefited from the fact that animals raised on their farms could be sold at the market. Accordingly, the covenant remained useful and was upheld.

The case suggests that owners of former copyhold land were entitled to the benefit of a covenant taken for the manor. If so, it would follow that, even if all the demesne land has been sold, such covenants may still be enforceable, whether or not the covenant benefits the demesne. The decision stands alone and a court might not necessarily follow it.

---

[23] (1976) 33 P&CR 141, 241 EG 241.

17.7   CEREMONIAL RENDERS

In the past many lords were entitled to a variety of rights. Gloves and spurs feature frequently in mediaeval sources as renders for freehold land but most cannot have been collected for centuries and will now be obsolete. A few ceremonial rights survive specifically those associated with the Royal Family. Thus, when in 1973 the Prince of Wales as Duke of Cornwall made a formal visit to his Duchy he was greeted by the Mayor of Lostwithiel who handed him 100 silver shillings and a pound of peppercorns as a quitrent. The town of Truro rendered a bow. These appear to relate to duties owned by the burgesses of towns and may be classified as Crown rents, but there were also seigniorial dues from Duchy manors. The manor of Stoke Climsland or Clymeslond provided a salmon spear and a load of firewood, the manor of Trevelga a pair of white gloves and the manor of Lanihorne and Elerky in Veryan a pair of greyhounds.[24]

A private example is said to be that the lord of the manor of Spreyton in Devon is entitled to a pair of gloves as rent for two freehold farms in the manor. A more public occasion involved the Shaftesbury Byzant – a gilded ornament which was presented every Sunday after Holy Rood day in May by the mayor to the lord of the manor of Gillingham, apparently for the right of the townsfolk to draw water from a spring. The mayor then bought back the Byzant with a pair of white gloves, two wheaten loaves, a calf's head and a gallon of ale and the townsfolk retained it until the following year. The ceremony was accompanied with much dancing and feasting. It ceased in 1830 save for a single revival in 1972.

Such renders are best seen as rents payable by reason of tenure. They do not appear to be manorial rights for the purposes of the Land Registration Act 2002, Schs 1 and 3, para 11 and so would not need to be protected by notice or caution (25.9).

---

[24]   Burnett, D, *A Royal Duchy* (Dovecot Press, 1996) 21.

Chapter 18

Fealty and Protection

services

18.1   HOMAGE AND FEALTY

Before the manor came to be seen as land or other property it comprised a set of relationships. The most basic relation, possibly going back before the conversion to Christianity, is homage.[1] In its simplest form the man (Latin *homo*, French *homme*) knelt in front of the one he would follow. He put his own hands between his lord's and promised to serve him. The lord then kissed him on the lips. Homage always remained a simple ceremony. The classic description in English law is in Bracton:[2]

> He who has to do homage ... ought to go to his lord anywhere he can find him within the realm or even elsewhere if he can conveniently get there; for the lord is not bound to seek out his tenant. And he ought to do his homage thus. The tenant ought to put both of his hands between the hands of his lord, by which is signified on the lord's side protection, defence and warranty, and on the tenant's side, reverence and subjection. And he ought to say these words: I become your man for the tenement which I hold of you, and I will bear you faith in life and member and earthly honour against all men, saving the faith due to the lord King.

---

[1] The principal account is Coke, Sir Edward, *A commentary on Littleton being the first part of the Institutes of the Laws of England* (1628) 64a ff. Discussions of homage and fealty most often occur in the context of feudalism: see 22.1. See also Bloch, M, *Feudal Society* (English translation by LA Manyon) (Routledge Kegan Paul, 1961); Poly, J-P and Bournazel, E, *The Feudal Transformation 900–1200* (Holmes and Meier, 1991); Chibnall, M, *Anglo-Norman England 1066–1166* (Basil Blackwell, 1986) 61; Hilton, RH, *The English Peasantry in the Later Middle Ages* (Clarendon Press, 1975) 132; Stubbs, W, *Select Charters from the beginning to 1307* (Oxford University Press, 9th edn, 1913) 193; also see Britton, *Containing the Ancient Pleas of the Crown* (c 1290) Bk 3, Ch 4.

[2] Bracton, Sir Henry (ed), *De legibus et consuetudinibus angliae* (c 1257) (SE Thorne (ed)) (Belknap Press of Harvard University Press, 1977) f 78–84, esp 80.

Homage as such was basic and did not imply any relation with land. It was strictly personal. If the man died his son was not bound by his father's homage and had to make his own. If the lord died his men were not bound to his son and the first thing an heir had to do, whether he was a new king or the heir to a manor, was to assemble his father's followers and ask them to do homage. If they did not then they were not bound to him.

Peers have done homage at coronations, although since that of Edward VII this has been shortened. It may be further altered at the next coronation bearing in mind the altered status of hereditary peers (23.2).

The unfree peasantry did not need to perform homage. If the lord inherited land he automatically inherited the people bound to the land. When a child was born into a villein family it was automatically a serf. These people did not voluntarily become bound by homage, they were bound by law, and so they were the homage without needing a ceremony. After the end of villeinage the body of copyholders continued to be called the homage in the customary court.

On the Continent the clergy did not do homage.[3] The reason stated was that it was not proper for a priest who had to handle the consecrated elements of the eucharist to place his hands between the hands of a lord who, however virtuous, had shed blood in war or in punishing malefactors. The true reason may have been related to the controversy over investiture, that the Church claimed to hold its lands free from the need to acknowledge services due to a secular king or leader. Accordingly, the Church encouraged, alongside homage and performed at the same time, the development of an oath of fealty[4] or faithfulness. Unlike homage this was a Christian ceremony and was part of a bargain usually related to tenure. The lord granted the fee: the tenant swore fealty. The Continental priest could swear an oath whose terms were clear, as distinct from the ancient, implied and vague obligations of homage.

In England homage for secular estates of freehold was abolished by s 2 of the Tenures Abolition Act 1660. That Act, by s 7, did not extend to copyhold (for which homage was not due in any case) nor to land held in frankalmoign which did not owe fealty. Bishops still do homage to the sovereign on appointment. A form of oath was set out in the Act of Supremacy 1558. The Promissory Oaths Act 1868, s 14(3) provides that nothing in it shall affect the oath of homage taken by archbishops and bishops in the presence of Her Majesty. The present form is as follows:

---

[3]   Britton *op cit* Bk 3, Ch 4, s 9.

[4]   For fealty, see Bracton *op cit* f 80, 84, 207; *Hill and Redman's Law of Landlord and Tenant* (Butterworth Lexis Nexis, looseleaf) A2181; Hilton *op cit* 63; Bloch *op cit* 146; Adkin, BW, *Copyhold and other Land Tenures of England* (Sweet & Maxwell, 3rd edn, 1919) 34, 44.

I A.B. having been elected, confirmed and consecrated Bishop of C. do hereby declare that Your Majesty is the only supreme governor of this your realm in spiritual and ecclesiastical things as well as in temporal and that no foreign prelate or potentate has any jurisdiction within this realm and I acknowledge that I hold the said bishopric as well the spiritualities as the temporalities thereof only of Your Majesty and for the same temporalities I do my homage presently to Your Majesty so help me God.

God save Queen Elizabeth

Now that episcopal lands have been vested in the Church Commissioners there is no call for episcopal homage for lands and frankalmoign itself has now been abolished under Sch 2 to the Administration of Estates Act 1925, with the possible exception of ecclesiastical corporations aggregate (20.10). A corporation can not do homage.[5] It was held in *Anthony Lowe's Case*[6] that when land formerly held in frankalmoign has passed to a lay tenant it is converted to socage. Bishops do still hold advowsons (20.2) which for this purpose may be regarded as temporalities. They are held of Her Majesty since if the bishop does not exercise the appointment within a given period it reverts to the Crown.

All other landholders were treated as owing fealty[7] and within the manor it was due from socagers and copyholders alike. The copyholder did fealty on admittance. The form of fealty could vary. One version for freeholders given in Bracton is:[8]

Hearest thou this, my Lord N that I will bear faith to you of life and member, body and goods, and of earthly honour, so help me God and his Holy Evangelists.

Another form for copyholders is given by Watkins:[9]

You shall swear to become a true tenant to the honourable W.A.Esq. lord of this manor, for the estate to which you are now admitted tenant; you shall from time to time bear, pay, perform, and discharge all such rents, duties, services and customs therefor due, and of right accustomed; you shall from time to time be ordered and justified in all things at the lord's courts to be holden in and for the manor of B. as other the tenants of the said manor for their respective estates are, shall, or ought to be; and you shall in all things demean yourself as a faithful tenant ought to do.

So help you God

---

[5]   Coke on *Littleton op cit* 66b.

[6]   (1610) 9 Co Rep 122b, 77 ER 909.

[7]   Coke on *Littleton op cit* 67b.

[8]   Bracton *op cit* f 80.

[9]   Watkins, C, *A Treatise on Copyholds* (James Bullock, 4th edn by Thomas Coventry, 1825) 2.413.

Fealty is still in theory due from freehold tenants but as mesne lordships are rare it is never in practice given. Fealty by copyholders was abolished by s 128 of and Sch 12, para (1)(b) to, the Law of Property Act 1922 but would have gone on enfranchisement in any case.

There was a form of tenure called homage auncestrel where a tenant and his ancestors had held of the same lord and his ancestors since time immemorial;[10] but Coke thought it probably obsolete by his day. Its importance was mainly procedural in that the lord was bound to warrant the title of his tenant (18.3).

18.2   ALLEGIANCE

There is a special form of duty derived from homage which survived and is still of great importance. It is not directly relevant to the manor but relates to the leet. This is what once was called liege homage and is now allegiance and it is due only to the Queen or (in other countries) to the state.[11] Homage was originally done by one man to one lord but when a man (whether a great aristocrat or a humble farmer) began to hold land from several lords, by grant for services, inheritance or purchase, he did fealty for each holding and therefore did homage as well. If a dispute arose between two lords, whose man was he? Each lord could claim his duty. Several rules were suggested – that he follow the earliest or the greatest lord – but the solution was that one lord demanded liege homage or paramount service.

In France and Germany this was associated with another problem. The issue of divided loyalties applied not only where a man held land directly of several lords but also where he held of a lesser lord in a chain and that lord was rebelling against a superior. If a knight held of a count who held of a duke who held of the king, and the count rebelled against the duke or the duke against the king, whom should the knight follow? In England as shown in 5.4, William the Conqueror imposed a solution. The Oath of Salisbury[12] bound all free holders to the king, and the oath to any other lord, as set out above, always included the proviso 'saving the faith [ie fealty] due to the lord king'. The laws of Henry I[13] provided that if a man had several lords, his primary duty (after that to the king)

---

[10] Coke on *Littleton op cit* 100b.

[11] Bloch *op cit* 214; Maitland, FW, *Domesday Book and Beyond* (Cambridge University Press, 1987; first published 1897) 295.

[12] Clarke, HB, 'The Domesday Satellites', in Sawyer, P (ed), *Domesday Book A Reassessment* (Edward Arnold, 1986) 56; Chibnall *op cit* 61; Stubbs *op cit* 96.

[13] Stephenson C and Marcham, FG, *Sources of English Constitutional History* (Harper & Row, 1937) 56.

was to the lord whose liegeman he was. However, allegiance to lords other than the king eventually disappeared.

The nature of liege homage was considered by the court in *Calvin's Case*[14] in 1609. There are four types of allegiance, of which the fourth is legal ligeance done on oath at the torn of the leet. The court leet, even when owned by the lord of the manor, who could keep its revenues, was still the court leet of Our Lord the King and accordingly homage sworn in the leet was sworn to the king. It was not necessary for every subject to do it. The other three types of ligeance mentioned in the case applied automatically by birth, by presence in the country or by acquisition. But the fourth type was especially binding as it was a voluntary oath. Like other forms of homage it could only be sworn once by one subject to one king and it then remained binding as long as subject and sovereign both lived.

Allegiance is now the subject of much international law, which is beyond the scope of this book. The modern form of oath is set out in s 2 of the Promissory Oaths Act 1868 with a version for new lieges on naturalisation in Sch 5 to the British Nationality Act 1981. As swearing ligeance does not involve hearing or determining any legal proceeding, there seems to be no reason in principle why it could not be sworn in any surviving court leet, although in practice this would never occur.

The current form of oath and pledge in the 1981 Act (as substituted by the Nationality, Immigration and Asylum Act 2002, Sch 1, para 2) is:

Oath [affirmation] of allegiance

I (name) swear by Almighty God [or do solemnly, sincerely and truly declare and affirm] that on becoming a British citizen, I will be faithful and bear true allegiance to Her Majesty Queen Elizabeth the Second, her Heirs and Successors, according to law.

Pledge

I will give my loyalty to the United Kingdom and respect its rights and freedoms. I will uphold its democratic values. I will observe its laws faithfully and fulfil my duties and obligations as a British citizen.

---

[14] (1609) 7 Co Rep 2a, 77 ER 377.

18.3   WARRANTY

Homage, fealty and allegiance were given by a follower to a lord, but with that
went a corresponding duty on the part of the lord of protection or warranty.[15] At
one time this was of great practical and legal importance, and underlay the
whole basis of the feudal system. The lord had a duty to protect his followers.
Indeed, when free men voluntarily commended themselves to a lord they did so
precisely because they needed protection.

When the title to the ownership of land became more settled the lord had a duty
to warrant or guarantee the title of his man to the land he held of him. If the
tenant's title was challenged, the lord could be vouched to warranty. If the
dispute was between two tenants of the same lord then the lord had a duty to
hold a court to determine the argument. If the dispute was between tenants of
two lords then those lords had the duty to protect and further their tenants'
claims in the court of the lord from whom both held or, if none, the king. If the
tenant lost the lands the lord had guaranteed to him then the lord was bound to
replace them with land of equal value.

The principal legacy is in title guarantee. After *Quia Emptores*, when assurances
of freeholds replaced grants, this obligation passed to vendors. Over the years
this became hardened into a set formula of covenants for title. There were four
principal covenants, set out in verbose form in the Law of Property Act 1925,
Sch 2, which applied where the seller conveyed as beneficial owner. They were
(in brief): (1) that the seller had full power to convey the property; (2) that the
buyer would have quiet enjoyment of it; (3) that it was free from incumbrances
other than those disclosed to the buyer and the buyer would have an indemnity
against claims; and (4) that if the conveyance turned out to be incomplete the
seller would make any necessary further assurance. Some of these were also
implied where different forms of word were used. Following a report by the
Law Commission[16] this system was changed in the Law of Property
(Miscellaneous Provisions) Act 1994 under which a seller would transfer with
full title guarantee or limited title guarantee or none. This may be important on
the sale of a manor (26.4).

Although the obligation in its tenurial form disappeared in relation to freeholds,
it still has relics in the law of leases. Most leases contain a qualified covenant
for quiet enjoyment, which appears to be a voluntary warranty by the landlord
but which in fact is a legal device to limit, not extend, the landlord's duties. In
the absence of such a form of words the lessor would have an unqualified

---

[15]   Bracton *op cit* f 37, 384–399; Simpson, AWB, *An Introduction to the History of the Land Law*
       (Oxford University Press, 1961) 109.

[16]   Law Commission No 199, *Transfer of land: Implied covenants for title.*

warranty that the tenant would hold the lease free from any interference. The qualified covenant in common use excludes disturbance of the lessee by a title paramount to that of the lessor. Separately lessees have a corresponding implied obligation not to dispute the landlord's right to grant the lease. If they do dispute it, they may forfeit the leasehold.[17]

18.4 GRAND AND PETTY SERGEANTY

Sergeanty means service. Many mesne lords granted land in petit or petty sergeanty for services, such as being a butler or a messenger, as well as to those soldiers to whom the term sergeant is still applied. It came to be regarded as a form of socage tenure.

Grand sergeanty was a special form of military tenure from the Crown. The services were owed to the king by great lords. They included leading the army, serving in the Exchequer and, in one case, supporting the king's head when he crossed the sea to Normandy. The best known, and those that have survived, are connected to coronations.[18] One is the office of King's Champion held by the Dymoke family for many centuries originally in right of the manor of Scrivelsby although it may now have become hereditary in gross in the family. Other services are to be Great Chamberlain (also now hereditary in gross), Chief Butler, assistant to the Chief Butler (now claimed by the Lord Mayor and Corporation of London), Almoner (carrying a bason or alms bowl and distributing the alms) and to carry the Coronation Sword before the sovereign.

On 6 July 1994 the manor of Worksop was sold for £40,000 at auction to a local resident. The price was so high because of grand sergeanty rights attached to the manor. These were said to be to support the sovereign's right arm during the coronation or, in another version, to present an embroidered glove for the sovereign's right hand.[19]

Originally, a manor in tenure in grand sergeanty was held conditionally on the holder being ready to perform the service. As with any service, the king did not have to call for it but, if he did, and the lord failed to serve, then the manor could be forfeited. If this ever applied it ceased in 1660. The Tenures Abolition Act abolished tenures in grand sergeanty along with all other free tenures in knight service, but s 7 specifically preserved the honourable services, which are

---

[17] *Warner v Sampson* [1959] 1 QB 297, [1959] 1 All ER 120; *Abidogun v Frolan Health Care Ltd* [2001] EWCA Civ 1821, [2002] L&TR 16.

[18] Simpson *op cit* 9; *Halsbury's Laws* Vol 12(1) (reissue), *Crown and Royal Family* (Butterworths, 4th edn) para 22.

[19] Simpson *op cit* 9, n 2; *The Times*, 23 June 1994, 7 July 1994.

now owed out of land held in socage. As such, the manor could probably not now be forfeited if the lord failed, on request, to serve at the coronation but of course it is seen as a privilege not an obligation.

It is said that the tenant has to perform the services in his proper person and cannot do so by deputy unless the nature or terms of the grant authorise it. It is also said that the services cannot be performed by any person below the degree of knight, nor by a child or a woman but that in those cases a deputy can be appointed. But if that ever was the rule it may have changed. Under Sch 6, para 3 to the Equality Act 2010 any dignity or honour conferred by the Crown is not a personal or public office so as to attract the non-discrimination rules, but even so it would appear to be open to the Crown to waive any such restriction. In some cases a substitute is essential. The office of Lord Great Chamberlain (which is now hereditary in gross and not held by tenure of land) includes the obligation to carry to the king his clothes on the morning of the coronation. If the sovereign is a queen that duty must be performed by a woman.

The services cannot be performed by a limited company, even through a director, and it is reported that a company that tried to claim the right in 1952 was not permitted. It is however separately reported that in 1953 the lord of Worksop was out of the country and he was permitted to present the glove embroidered with the arms of Worksop through the Royal College of Needlework as his deputy. If there is a dispute or doubt as to the right to perform the services or the qualification of a claimant at the time of the coronation then it is referred to the Court of Claims held before commissioners appointed for the occasion by the sovereign.

The Law of Property Act 1922, s 136 saved the services incident to grand and petty sergeanty and deemed them not to be manorial incidents. Tenure in grand sergeanty had of course been abolished in 1660 but the services were retained. Part V of the Act deals with copyholds, but s 138 in Part VI relates to incidents, and without such a provision it might have been argued that the duties under grand sergeanty had been covered. It is not clear if any duties in petty sergeanty have survived.

PART IV

SETTING

Chapter 19

Village and Hundred

19.1   MANOR AND VILLAGE

Manors existed in and around villages, but the two are not the same. A village or vill or township can include several manors or parts of manors and a manor can include all or part of many villages. The two are however connected and their relationship is important. They both developed at much the same time in the eleventh century.[1]

In some parts of the country, especially the west of England, manors tend to correspond to one settlement but often the dwellings are so spread out, especially in the woodland districts, as not to be a single village. In the East, especially in the champion districts, villages may be divided between several small manors. In the North manors can include several townships. In the South patterns are much more complex and villages include parts of manors, themselves including parcels and outliers in several settlements. Within a single manor there might be several settlements. One reason for this could have been that they were grouped in an estate or a knight's fee to provide sufficient income to support the purpose for which the manor was created. Another reason could be that an initially dominant village had several dependent hamlets which developed into villages themselves. Correspondingly, a single village containing several manors could arise after division between co-heiresses or on sale of part. There might have been two nearby villages which grew until there was a single settlement.

The manor was primarily concerned with title to land, with services and with waste. Where a village included lands of several manors the waste was divided between them although with vicinage rights. The village, where people lived,

---

[1]   See, eg Hoskins, WG, *The Making of the English Landscape* (Penguin Books, 1970); Rowley, T, *Villages in the Landscape* (JM Dent & Sons Ltd, 1978); Muir, R, *The Lost Villages of Britain* (Michael Joseph Ltd, 1982); Taylor, C, *Village and Farmstead* (George Philip, 1983); Roberts, BK, *The Making of the English Village* (Longmans, 1987).

was concerned with the common fields, with ordinary disputes and neighbourly matters and with taxes levied by central government. Over the years the public functions of both manor and vill fell into abeyance as the jurisdiction of justices of the peace was extended. Until the nineteenth century matters of local importance were often run by officials of another system, the churchwardens.

In the eleventh century in many parts of England people came to live in centralised or nuclear villages, laid out along a street or around a green. Many were associated with the adoption of new systems of farming in the open field system. While villages are to be found all across England, the classic nucleated village is a product of the champion country. Some villages may have formed in Saxon times and a few could be earlier. Many will have been deliberately planned and archaeologists are finding evidence that they were laid out presumably by the decision of a lord of what was becoming a manor. In some cases, however, the village may have formed from local people deciding to live together. Many manors, especially in the North and West or in woodland areas, did not relate to a concentrated village and were based instead on groups of farmers over an area.

It follows that while any typical village will have one manor this cannot be assumed. Two or more claimants may claim to be lord of a manor corresponding to the name of a village and it may transpire that there are two manors in existence. Usually there will be historic evidence of this and the manors may have slightly different names. Further, the name of a manor will frequently not correspond to that of the village. This may be because one or the other has changed over the centuries. Sometimes the manor is known by a Latin version of the village name.

19.2   HUNDREDS

Before villages the important unit was the hundred, which still exists although it now has no legal significance. The title 'lord of the hundred' is common, and hundreds and manors are nowadays sometimes sold at the same auction. The hundred, with the village and the shire, formed a system of government distinct from the manor and honour and were part of a different hierarchy, but both were headed by the Crown and interacted.

The hundred is an ancient institution whose origins are unknown. Some historians think it derives from Germany, where Tacitus[2] mentions an

---

[2]   Cornelius Tacitus: *De origine et situ Germanorum* (c 98), in *Tacitus on Britain and Germany* (Penguin Books, 1948) 6; Blackstone, Sir William, *Commentaries on the Laws of England* I.int.4.

arrangement of a similar nature, and were brought over by Saxon immigrants. Others observe that the meeting places of hundreds were often at prehistoric sites such as a standing stone, a tumulus or a hillfort, and suggest that they are older. However, this does not necessarily mean that their origins are prehistoric because the Saxons may have used ancient sites. More often, hundreds met under great trees. Others again compare them with the *Centena*, a similar institution in the Frankish kingdoms of France and Germany.[3]

The name 'hundred' simply refers to 100 hides. The hide (1.6) was about 120 acres of arable land plus the waste that went with it and was the land needed to support a substantial free family with its dependants. In some parts of the country a hundred is called a wapentake, or weapon-take, and may have been a local militia unit. The men of the hundred gathered in regular meetings and together formed the hundred court. The area of a hundred was something like a modern district and it had a similar function to a district council, where most business of local relevance was done; but it also handled law cases including some criminal matters. Local groupings of this nature may have developed in different localities at different times but it seems to have become established throughout England by late Anglo-Saxon times.

By the eleventh century many hundreds had become privately owned by abbeys or lay lords. The owner or his deputy presided at the hundred meeting and kept the proceeds of any fines levied in the court. Although grants of hundreds have survived (for example William II granted the hundred of Normancros in Huntingdonshire to the abbey of Thorney, and Stephen granted Stowe to the church of St Edmund[4]), the hundred itself does not seem to have been involved in the system of tenure.

Hundreds were still important after the Norman Conquest but gradually lost their place to shires (with the shire court under the sheriff) and villages (with their courts leet). The court jurisdiction, obsolete in practice, continued in theory for centuries. One late manifestation was on the introduction of the Poor Law Amendment Act 1834 under which many poor law unions were established by reference to hundreds. Section 28 of the County Courts Act 1867 virtually abolished the jurisdiction of the hundred court and by s 23 of the Administration of Justice Act 1977 they were, like manor courts, deprived of any power to determine matters of law. Hundreds themselves have not formally been abolished. They were so inactive that when rural and urban districts were set up

---

[3] Abels, RP, *Lordship and Military Obligation in Anglo-Saxon England* (University of California Press, 1988) 21.

[4] Stubbs, W, *Select Charters from the beginning to 1307* (Oxford University Press, 9th edn, 1913) 122.

under the Local Government Act 1894 it was not thought necessary to abolish any residual local government function of hundreds.

The title 'lord of the hundred' may still be held by the successors of the lords who originally acquired the jurisdiction as a franchise from the Crown but the hundred is even more intangible than the manor. It does not carry demesne land, services, sporting or mineral rights or any other matters of value.

19.3 SHIRES

Several hundreds, perhaps 12 or 20, were grouped in a shire or county, but the number could vary from the six hundreds of Lancashire and the seven of Cheshire to over 60 each in Kent and Sussex that had once been kingdoms on their own. Shire is a Saxon word and means share. Like hundreds, the origins of shires are obscure although a little more is known. They seem to have started in the kingdom of Wessex, south of the Thames. For instance the territory around Williton was called Wilt-shire, and the land behind Southhampton, or Hamwic, was Hamp-shire. Later Wessex came to dominate the old kingdoms of Sussex, Kent and Essex. All of these, and others, became shires with their own assemblies or shire-courts, under a shire-reeve, or sheriff appointed by the king. After the devastation of the Viking invasions Wessex became the core of the new kingdom of England and the idea of shires spread to the Midlands. Certain towns were selected as strong-points for militias to rally in the event of an attack and were surrounded by areas on whose resources, especially armed men, they could draw. Thus, Worcester had Worcester-shire, Oxford had Oxford-shire and so on.

Towards the end of the Saxon period and in early Norman times powerful men tried to appropriate the office of sheriff to their families as hereditary property but the kings were always strong enough to prevent this. The shires became the focus of local government. The court of the shire or county was busy and not only as a court of justice. In the thirteenth century the knights of the shire, as county members of Parliament, were chosen there. Justices of the peace were organised on a county basis with quarter sessions taking the place of the old shire court.[5] The shire courts were reorganised in the County Courts Act 1846 so that modern county courts are barely recognisable as being derived from their Saxon forerunners.

Shires became called counties by a misnomer. The Normans translated sheriff by *vicecomes* or viscount. Counts and viscounts were continental officials

---

[5] See Skyrme, Sir Thomas, *History of the Justices of the Peace* (Barry Rose Publishers, 1994).

unknown in England but counts corresponded roughly to earls. The county should therefore have strictly been the viscounty, the area of jurisdiction of the *vicecomes*. To confuse matters further earls were often given titles corresponding to a shire name; and much later the title of viscount was introduced without any territorial jurisdiction (23.2).

Once the sheriff had great powers. He presided over the administration of justice (as he still does in Scotland) and the pursuit of criminals (as he still does in the United States). In England his powers were reduced over the centuries and since the Sheriffs Act 1887 his duties have been ceremonial. One of his most important duties was visitation of local courts in the villages under the sheriff's tourn which led to the view of frankpledge and court leet.

19.4   TITHING AND FRANKPLEDGE

The institutions of shire, hundred and vill operated through bodies called courts. As explained in 13.1 'court' originally had a wide meaning and referred to any assembly which had governing functions. The men of the village assembled as and when needed to take decisions about managing their affairs. They were organised and guided by the leading men of the village and others would defer to them, but in most cases someone who had something sensible to say would get a hearing. They decided disputes, sorted out arrangements for the open fields and made byelaws to regulate their affairs. Likewise there were less frequent meetings of the men of the hundred or wapentake and occasional meetings for the men of the shire. These last would be more formal and were chaired by the sheriff or an earl. As time went on assemblies became more regulated and tended to develop formal procedures. The knights of the shire who represented the counties in Parliament were elected at meetings of the shire, but otherwise these bodies became courts of law.

A vill or village (or tun, in the North often called 'township') is not essentially a legal term but a factual description, although for some legal purposes it was necessary to describe land as lying within a certain vill.[6] Let us suppose that Oldvill is surrounded by fields within that vill. Some houses are put up on one of the fields and become known as Newvill. The new houses may, with equal legal accuracy, be described as being within one or other or both.[7]

However, a village often corresponded to a tithing. A tithing is a tenth part of a hundred, comprising 10 holders of hides. Later a tithing was reckoned to have

---

[6]   Bracton, Sir Henry, *De legibus et consuetudinibus angliae* (c 1257) (SE Thorne (ed)) (Belknap Press of Harvard University Press, 1977) f 211.

[7]   Bracton *op cit* f 211.

12 men and that is part of the origin of the jury. They normally comprised groups of neighbours within the vill or tun.[8]

In 1895 in his account of Feudal England[9] the historian JH Round analysed *Domesday Book*, in which the areas of manors were shown as all sorts of multiples and fractions of hides. Frequently, manors shared land in the same vill. Round discovered that if he added together all the land of various manors within one vill the total often added up to five, 10 or 15 hides. There is also some evidence from Anglo-Saxon laws that a lord of five hides was reckoned wealthy enough to be a theign and to serve as such in the army. This system of shires, divided into hundreds, each of 10 tithings, in turn divided into units of five hides seems, and is, artificial. The government of Anglo-Saxon England was not really so organised, but it indicates how local administration was supposed to work.

The members of the tithing were responsible for each others' behaviour and collectively responsible for peace-keeping in their area. They were by definition free (frank) men with a common pledge. After the Conquest the Normans took this idea of the frankpledge and made it the basis of local law. They combined it with the presentment of englishry, a system of collective responsibility designed for the period immediately after 1066 when England was an occupied country. If a follower of King William (a Frenchman, whether Norman, Breton or Fleming) was found dead in an area and his killer was not known the whole tithing was held accountable. Thus, the frankpledge was extended from free men to all Englishmen. Most Saxon landholders lost status and those who did not become villeins were socmen, so that frankpledge applied to bond and free alike.

When the sheriff asserted the king's authority he did so by making a survey of his shire, village by village, known as the sheriff's tourn. This took place at meetings of the hundred twice a year when the sheriff held a view of frankpledge. The purpose of this was originally to check that all men were inrolled in a frankpledge and so members of a mutually accountable group. The frankpledge itself also operated more locally within the tithing or vill and formed a village court and is usually identified with the court leet. Thus leet, frankpledge, tithing and tourn had overlapping meanings.

---

8   Blackstone *op cit* I.4.

9   Round, JH, *Feudal England* (Longmans Green & Co, 1895).

19.5   COURT LEET

The court leet was the village court. It was a royal court in the sense that it was public and part of a system under royal supervision, unlike the manor court which was the private court of a landholder. The court leet had a general jurisdiction including petty crimes and disputes between neighbours. Where the vill included more than one manor the court leet could deal with general disputes such as trespassing between strips. It was responsible for byelaws. It also regulated the common field system, such as the date on which they were opened to cattle or the clearing out of common drains. Communal officers such as haywards (for hedges) and shepherds could also be appointed in the court leet (13.5).

As a royal court, the Court Leet of our Lord the King, it was a court of record so that the official summary of business transacted was accepted by the king's judges without having to be proved in evidence. Allegiance to the king could be sworn in the leet (18.2).[10] Initially and in theory it was under the supervision of the sheriff through his tourn, but in practice most lords were able to secure a liberty whereby the sheriff had no power to intervene. In theory this was a franchise but it is rare to find an express grant and it is likely that most courts leet had become private before 1189. This was especially likely where the vill was all within one manor. The lord took the profits of the court including keeping fines paid by wrongdoers. The leet was therefore sometimes referred to as the court leet of the lord in question. As discussed in 13.1–13.4 it was often held with the manor courts. It nevertheless remained a royal court of record.

Where the lord had the leet the view of frankpledge went with it.[11] This meant not only that the lord could exclude the sheriff but that he had the right to deal with breaches of the peace for which the frankpledge was responsible and again keep fines or amerciaments levied. When the Sheriffs Act 1887 revised and largely removed the duties of sheriffs, s 18(4) abolished the sheriff's tourn but s 40 expressly preserved the existing jurisdiction of 'every court leet, court baron, law day, view of frankpledge, or other like court'. Finally, s 23 of the Administration of Justice Act 1977 (13.4) removed the jurisdiction of all courts leet and views of frankpledge, with the exception of the court leet for the manor of Laxton. Of the courts permitted to continue to transact business, 24 were courts leet (some also being courts baron) which suggests that this ancient institution still has some value.

---

[10]   *Calvin's Case* (1608) 7 Co Rep 1a, 77 ER 377.

[11]   Bracton *op cit* f 124b.

19.6   VILLAGE GREENS

Town and village greens have been the subject of a great deal of recent litigation. Here it will be sufficient to summarise the law (which is still developing) so far as it is relevant to the topics discussed in this book.

The green was under the jurisdiction of the court leet. Many greens are subject to rights of common but they were not used just for grazing. Their modern function as described in the Commons Registration Act 1965 discussed below is for recreation by local people. Typically cricket is played on the green, and in the past it was where the butts were set up for archery practice. Some greens were the sites of fairs, although markets had a more permanent place.

The origins of greens seem to lie in the initial layout of villages. Some were planned with a space in the middle. Others may have formed where houses aggregated in an unplanned manner but left a space where activities could take place. The people of the locality had rights of access for lawful sports and pastimes.[12] Since the rights were enjoyed by a fluctuating group of people, before the Commons Registration Act 1965 they can only have been enjoyed under custom, in which case they must have been capable of existing in 1189. In practice if the land had been used as a green for many years then the courts would assume that such use predated 1189 unless there was evidence that it could not have been so used continuously after that date.

Other greens have been created by statute such as inclosure Acts. Some early inclosure Acts included greens, but more often they were not inclosed and indeed land might have been allotted for local recreation, even where there was no existing green, to replace access to the open fields. The Inclosure Act 1845, s 15 provided that village greens could not be inclosed under its provisions but any existing green could be allotted for the purpose of exercise and recreation and, in addition, other land could be allotted for the same purpose.

19.7   REGISTRATION OF GREENS

The current stream of cases has concerned a new type of green created by use by local people for 20 years on any land which is not necessarily related to a manor. They are therefore more a type of modern, semi-public open space than a traditional feature. Many of the cases concern land on which the owner intends to build, and local opponents of development seek to use the status of green to

---

[12]   *Abbot v Weekly* (1664) 1 Lev 176, 83 ER 357 – dancing on the green; *Hall v Nottingham* (1875–6) LR 1 Ex D 1 – erecting a maypole.

preserve an open space. Because a great deal of money is at stake, the cases have been hard fought, often up to the House of Lords or Supreme Court, and the law has developed some fine distinctions. As a result it has become complex, not to say obscure, and for a full account reference should be made to specialist works.[13]

The Commons Registration Act 1965 Act provided for the registration of town and village greens. The procedure was the same as for common land. Anyone could apply to the county council to register the land and if there was no objection the registration became final. If there was objection the matter was referred to a Commons Commissioner. In the 1970s there were fewer disputed green registrations than disputes concerning common land, perhaps because most were recognised as such, they were small in area and often the owner was unknown.

The disputes emerged after 1990 and focussed on the definition in s 22, which referred to three classes of green. The Act does not subdivide these but the courts have found it necessary to do so[14] and the terminology has become widespread. Class (a) greens comprise land allotted under a local Act, principally an inclosure Act but it could also be a municipal Act. Class (b) greens are the traditional greens which subsisted by virtue of ancient custom and therefore in theory had to have existed since 1189.

It is the third type of class (c) green which has given rise to the recent litigation. The 1965 Act provided that this was land 'on which the inhabitants of any locality have indulged in lawful sports and pastimes as of right for not less than twenty years'. An example of the way this was initially applied is *Re Bittacy Green in the London Borough of Barnet*[15] where there was evidence that the claimed green had in fact been agricultural in 1796 and therefore could not have been a customary green since 1189. It was acquired by the local authority in 1952 as a public open space and therefore had been used for recreation from then until 1970 but the issue was whether it was also to be registered as a green. This was because the council in 1970 took much of it for building houses. While part remained used as an open space there were concerns that the remaining piece might be built on later. The Commissioner found evidence that at least since the 1940s and possibly back at least to 1910 there had been an annual bonfire on the land and drew the conclusion that it had been done as of right since otherwise the landowner would have interfered. He therefore confirmed the registration.

---

[13] Various textbooks cover the topic but it the law is changing too rapidly for them to keep up. There is, however, regular cover of recent cases in the *Rights of Way Law Review*.

[14] *R v Oxfordshire County Council, Ex p Sunningwell Parish Council* [2000] 1 AC 335.

[15] Commons Commissioners decisions Greater London 59/D/20: 24 May 1976.

The last date for registration of village greens which then existed was 2 January 1970. Any land which ought to have been registered by that date and was not ceased to be a green. At one time there was a theory that if a traditional green was not registered it remained in limbo and could be registered later;[16] but in *Oxfordshire County Council v Oxford City Council* ('the *Oxfordshire Case*')[17] the House of Lords refuted this view. Thus the effect of non-registration was to extinguish the customary rights of local inhabitants.

In 1990 20 years had passed from the closing date in 1970 and several successful applications were made to register new areas of land on the basis of modern use as class (c) greens.[18] This has now become a major industry. In the *Oxfordshire Case* the House considered the extent to which rights in such greens were related to traditional customary rights. It concluded that the same rules and controls applied. It therefore appears that, since the status of land comprised in a green is now governed by statute, rights which had once been customary have, by virtue of registration, become statutory. Class (a) and (c) greens are undoubtedly so. The origin of class (b) greens is customary but as any right to recreation on an unregistered green must have ceased in 1970, it follows that the right to recreation on a registered green can only subsist by virtue of statute.

The litigation has related to several aspects of class (c) greens but, as they can subsist on any land and have no necessary connection with manor, this book is not the place to describe the complications of the subject. Two main issues have dominated. One is the extent to which use by the local inhabitants must be 'as of right' and what that means. In broad terms it is now clear that there is an objective standard so that if to an outside observer it appeared that people were taking recreation on land openly and freely without any obvious consent for 20 years that will be sufficient.

The other issue is the extent to which use must be by inhabitants of a locality and what that means. The problems arise from a much-quoted statement of Jessel MR in *Hammerton v Honey*[19] that:

> if you allege a custom for certain persons to dance on a green, and you prove in support of that allegation, not only that some people danced, but that everybody else in the world who chose danced and played cricket, you have got beyond your custom.

---

[16]   In *In re Turnworth Down, Dorset* [1978] Ch 251 and *R v Suffolk County Council, Ex p Steed* (1996) 75 P&CR 102.

[17]   [2006] 2 AC 674 at [17]–[19].

[18]   *R v Oxfordshire County Council, Ex p Sunningwell Parish Council* [2000] 1 AC 335.

[19]   (1876) 24 WR 603.

That, as discussed in 4.2, is a requirement of custom that it must be local. It was taken into the Commons Registration Act 1965 on the basis that class (c) greens were like traditional greens. The problem is that there is clear authority that 'local' means a defined locality known to the law, such as a parish or manor. Modern users of vacant land, particularly when the land is in a built-up area, do not correspond to residents of traditional localities. At the date of writing this issue has not been resolved but it has been partly sidestepped. In amendments to the 1965 Act made in the Countryside and Rights of Way Act 2000, s 98 and the Commons Act 2006, s 15, Parliament has extended the qualification for users for 20 years to come from a neighbourhood within a locality. In *Leeds Group plc v Leeds City Council*[20] the Court of Appeal gave this a wide meaning so that 'neighbourhood' included neighbourhoods.[21]

Before the Commons Act 2006, while a so-called green could be created by the owner dedicating it to public use, because it existed neither by custom nor by statute, it would be like any other open space, and it could not become a class (c) green. In particular the statutory provisions for the protection of village greens would not apply to informally created spaces. Section 15(9) of the 2006 Act expressly authorised a landowner to apply to dedicate land as a green but this can only be done with the consent of the registration authority, usually the county council. The same applied if the local people used it by right (for instance under the Housing Act 1936, s 80) and not as of right.[22]

As explained in 25.9, under the Land Registration Act 2002 in general a landowner has to respect rights over his land only if they are entered on the register of title, and few if any greens are so entered. This does not apply to overriding interests. The lists of such interests in Schs 1 and 3 to the Act do not mention town and village greens. Although they do refer to persons in occupation under para 2, local inhabitants are not regarded as occupying a green.[23] They also refer to customary rights in para 4 and to public rights under para 5. As indicated, even class (b) greens are now statutory.[24] In any case neither class (a) nor class (c) greens would be customary. Even if class (b) greens do derive from custom, a customary way is regarded as a private right[25] not a public one, and the same could apply to a green. However, in charity law a trust for the benefit of the residents of an area such as a parish has long been

---

20 [2010] EWCA Civ 1438.

21 See also *Adamson v Paddico (267) Ltd* [2012] EWCA Civ 262; *R (Oxfordshire and Buckinghamshire Mental Health NHS Foundation Trust) v Oxfordshire County Council* [2010] EWHC 530 (Admin).

22 *R (Barkas) v North Yorkshire County Council* [2011] EWHC 3653 (Admin).

23 *Epsom Borough Council v Nicholls* (1998) 78 P&CR 348.

24 See *Oxfordshire County Council v Oxford City Council* [2006] 2 AC 674 at [53].

25 *Brocklebank v Thompson* [1903] 2 Ch 344.

held capable of being charitable and therefore satisfying the public benefit test. It appears that the rights of the inhabitants generally would be regarded as public for this purpose even though they are not enjoyed by all members of the public but only by local inhabitants.[26]

19.8   MANAGEMENT OF GREENS

Greens existed by general custom which was presumed to permit any lawful recreation. In *Fitch v Rawling*[27] (see 4.5) there was a claim to play cricket on what was described as a close at Steeple Bumpstead in Essex. The owner of the land resisted this on the basis that an Act of Edward IV[28] would have made it illegal and it was not reversed until the reign of Henry VIII. He argued, therefore, that it could not be said that this had been continually done since 1189. The court held that the true nature of the custom was to play such games as might be lawful from time to time. While special customs may govern the use of particular greens, they are rare. It follows that the use of most ancient greens must be governed by general custom.

This is relevant to the new class (c) greens. In the *Oxfordshire Case* there was some discussion in the House of Lords speeches as to the type of activity which could be carried on. The *Bittacy Green* case was discussed on the basis that the Guy Fawkes bonfire had only occurred once a year. That may in fact be a misunderstanding of the case as the Commissioner was satisfied that the green had been used for recreation but based his decision on the bonfire as an instance. The matter was referred to again in the Supreme Court in *R (Lewis) v Redcar and Cleveland Borough Council*[29] where Lord Walker indicated that the reference to *Bittacy Green* should be treated with caution. In the *Oxfordshire Case* the House considered what activities might lawfully take place on class (c) greens and concluded that they were the same type as class (b) greens. Once land is registered as a green its origin is no longer relevant save that it may not always apply to class (a) greens if the local Act lays out particular conditions or authorises byelaws.

---

[26]   See *Overseas Investment Services Limited v Simcobuild Construction Limited and Swansea City Council* (1995) 70 P&CR 322. In *Fortune v Wilts County Council* [2012] EWCA Civ 334 at [13] the Court of Appeal applied *Fairey v Southampton County Council* [1956] 2 QB 439 at 457. See also *Oxfordshire County Council v Oxford City Council* [2004] Ch 253 at [100], per Lightman J.

[27]   (1795) 2 Hy Bl 394, 126 ER 614.

[28]   17 Edw 4 (c 3): Unlawful Games.

[29]   [2010] UKSC 11, [2010] 2 WLR 653, [2010] 2 All ER 613.

Village greens are protected under two nineteenth-century statutes. Section 12 of the Inclosure Act 1857 makes it a criminal offence to damage fences, lay any manure, soil, ashes, rubbish or other material or do any other act (such as digging turf) which causes damage, or to take any cattle or other animals onto a green without lawful authority (many greens are also subject to grazing rights) or indeed to do any act which interrupts the use or enjoyment of a green as a place of exercise and recreation. Section 29 of the Commons Act 1876 makes it a public nuisance to encroach on a green or inclose a green or erect any structure other than for the purpose of the better enjoyment of the green or disturb, occupy or interfere with the soil of the green other than for the purpose of the better enjoyment of that green.

Where a green is common land it will also be subject to other controls. These are contained in the Commons Act 2006, s 38 which replaced the Law of Property Act 1925, s 194. In *Rabett v Poole*[30] Mr Rabett was lord of the manor of Depden near Bury St Edmunds in Suffolk and owner of Depden Green. Miss Poole had a right of common to graze two horses. She put out her horses on the green (to which there was no objection). However, she also erected a movable electric fence which she repositioned from time to time. She said that the purpose was to protect the horses from people. Section 194 was in force at the time and she applied to the Secretary of State for consent to enclose, but no decision was issued before the court hearing. The county court judge held that even if the Secretary of State gave consent that would not override the private law right of Rabett as landowner to prevent someone putting up a fence on his property as otherwise Poole would have been able to exclude not just the public but also the owner from his land.

Even though greens are not part of the manorial system, but relate more to the village structure, the freehold will often belong to the lord. Where there was one manor or a dominant manor in a village the green was usually seen as waste. Where there were several manors involved with a village it might be a matter of chance to which manor the green belonged, or ownership might be divided. The Commons Registration Act 1965, s 8(5)[31] provided that if no owner could be found then the green would be treated as held by the parish council and many greens are now so regarded. However, this is to protect the green, so that if a lord or other owner were able to establish title that would take precedence over any title of the council (6.9).

Ownership can carry potential risks. In *Cole v Davies-Gilbert*[32] a woman was injured by catching her leg in a hole on a village green at East Dean in Sussex.

---

[30]   [2003] 3 EGLR 143.

[31]   Substituted by Local Government Act 1972, s 189. See now Commons Act 2006, s 45.

[32]   [2007] EWCA Civ 396.

The hole had probably been dug to insert a maypole for a village fete and had not been filled in adequately after the fete. She claimed against the owners of the estate which owned the freehold of the green, against the parish council and against the British Legion which had organised the fete. The claim did not succeed and the judge took the opportunity to comment:

> If the law were to set a higher standard of care than that which is reasonable in cases such as the present, the consequences would quickly become inhibited. There would be no fêtes, no maypole dancing and none of the activities that have come to be associated with the English village green for fear of what might conceivably go wrong.

The decision is some comfort to owners of greens but the risk of a claim cannot be ruled out completely.

Chapter 20

Parish and Church

20.1 MANOR AND PARISH

Many lords have rights and duties affecting the parish church.[1] The lord may appoint the vicar and may be responsible for the repair of part of the church building. Just as the manor does not necessarily correspond to the village, so it may not coincide with the parish.[2] The imaginary manor of Middleton in 1.1 did so for the sake of simplicity, but that is unusual. All three institutions developed at the same time in the eleventh century and their concurrent jurisdiction affected the way each developed.

Parishes are parts of dioceses, the sphere of responsibility of a bishop. When the Anglo-Saxons were converted to Christianity each kingdom became a separate diocese. Several have now been split up but English dioceses were – and are – large by continental standards. At an early date they were divided into parts each called a *parochia* which was organised from a regional church called a minster from which a group of clergy ministered to the local people. *Parochiae* were the religious counterparts of hundreds and in some parts of the country had the same boundaries, so that most people lived within walking distance of their minster church.[3]

As private estates developed within hundreds the theigns who administered them employed their own clergy. This was partly because a priest was educated and could read and write. More importantly, he could preach and administer the sacraments, which was necessary for the wellbeing of the souls of the theign and his family. The theign built the priest a church next to, or even as part of, his hall. To this the people of the estate came and as time passed the priest was expected to look after the moral and spiritual wellbeing of the villagers, thus

---

[1]   See generally *Halsbury's Laws* Vol 34, *Ecclesiastical Law* (Butterworths, 5th edn).

[2]   Blackstone, Sir William, *Commentaries on the Laws of England* I.4.

[3]   Blair, J, *Early Medieval Surrey: Landholding, Church and Settlement before 1300* (Surrey Archaeological Society, 1991) 104, 119, 153.

gradually taking over this duty from the minster clergy. The area became known as a parish, derived from *parochia*, although only a part of it. If one village included several estates – or, after 1066, manors – it was likely that the church belonged to the principal estate.

It is common to find several manors within one parish but rare to find several parishes wholly within one manor. In the north of England, where manors could be very large, townships, which often had their own chapels, were made into parishes after the Middle Ages. This also occurred in growing towns where the Victorians often organised new parishes. Thus, the boundaries of the parish of Kensington in London at one time corresponded to the manor of that name but in the mid-nineteenth century the parish was divided. Modern town parishes may be smaller than the remains of a manor. Likewise the result of parish reorganisation in the twentieth century often involved combining a number of parishes which were once distinct and whose boundaries once corresponded to those of a manor.

A few villages had several churches and parishes, especially in East Anglia. The best known is Swaffham Prior where the church of St Mary is only a few feet away from the church of St Gyriac and St Julia. East Anglia had many small manors and independent freeholders and some of this duplication may have come from groups of freeholders who built their own church (often dedicated to St Mary) to be free of the lord who was hardly more powerful than themselves.[4] By contrast some churches were physically divided, perhaps following the division of the manor, with the rectors in the same building. Bracton[5] gives an example of this in the case of *de Huwelle v Richard rector of Claypole*.[6]

When parishes were carved out of *parochiae* the minster church remained responsible for what was left. A few minsters, such as York, rose in standing to become the equal of cathedrals. Others became little more than parish churches with a few special privileges such as the right to demand that parishioners of another church (once part of the *parochia*) be buried in the minster churchyard. Parts of the old *parochia* which were some distance from the church and were cut off when parishes were carved out of the *parochia* remained as extra-parochial areas until the reorganisation of the nineteenth century. Part of the

---

[4]   Warner, P, 'Shared churches, freemen church builders and the development of parishes in eleventh century East Anglia', in *Landscape History* Vol 8 (1986) 39; Rowley, T, *Villages in the Landscape* (1978) plate VII; Rowley, T, *The High Middle Ages* (1988) 88; Williamson, T and Bellamy, L, *Property and Landscape* (George Philip, 1987) 34.

[5]   Bracton, Sir H, *De legibus et consuetudinibus angliae* (c 1257) (SE Thorne (ed)) (Belknap Press of Harvard University Press, 1977) f 286.

[6]   Ibid f 286.

income needed to support the rector of the parish came from tithes and part from glebe land, both discussed below.

Until the Reformation the law of the Church was separate from the secular law administered through the royal courts and those of shire, hundred and leet. There was a hierarchy of church courts from that of the archdeacon to the bishop, eventually up to that of the pope of Rome. The rules of canon law owed much more to the civil law derived from Roman law than to principles of English law. Church courts were responsible for administering wills and dealing with the inheritance of chattels. The Church also had a wide jurisdiction over family law matters including marriage, separation and legitimacy. As a result there were numerous conflicts of jurisdiction, the best known of which ended in the death of Archbishop Thomas à Becket. At the Reformation the system of church courts was brought into domestic law, although it still exists. It no longer has a wide general jurisdiction but it deals with many matters relating to the property of the Church of England, the behaviour of clergy and other issues of domestic significance.

20.2   ADVOWSONS

An advowson is the right to present a clergyman to a benefice, the living of a church, so that he becomes the parish priest or parson as rector or vicar. When Anglo-Saxon lords built churches for their own house or estate priest they naturally had the right to appoint whoever they wished, provided he had been ordained. Where there was originally no estate church the right to appoint clergy belonged to the bishop or the king and many advowsons still belong to the diocese or the Crown for that reason; but private appointments were more usual. Where several manors were held together in honours the lord was usually no longer resident. By that time, the law of the Church required that there should be at least one clergyman for every parish. The parish priest became the most important person – or parson – in the locality. He was also known as the ruler – Latin *rector* – of the parish.

Advowsons were highly valued property. As explained below, most parishes had substantial endowments for the clergy and the patron decided who could have that income. In the Middle Ages the pulpit was the main place from which people learnt news or received ideas and control over that meant control over peoples' minds. In the seventeenth century much of the struggle between Puritans and High Churchmen, and hence between Parliament and the King, was influenced by who had the advowson and appointed the preacher. In the eighteenth century financial influences were more to the fore. The plot of Jane Austen's novel *Mansfield Park* depends on what happened when Sir Thomas

Bertram ran into financial difficulties and had to accept money for the appointment of a wealthy sophisticated urban cleric whose family introduced unsettling ideas, rather than keep the living for his younger son for whom it had been intended.

In the nineteenth century advowsons were bought for large sums by supporters of both High and Low Church ideas, which was considered scandalous. Under a number of statutes, including the Sale of Advowsons Act 1856, the Benefices Act 1898 and the Benefices Measure 1933, advowsons could not be sold except in conjunction with a landed estate. Section 3 of the Patronage (Benefices) Measure 1986 provides that they cannot be sold at all. Some advowsons have always been exercised in turn[7] with one patron making the appointment only on every second or third vacancy. This may originally have derived from disputed rights or manors divided among co-heiresses. In the twentieth century it became common practice as parish churches were closed and parishes amalgamated.

Formerly, most advowsons were attached to manors.[8] The first to be detached were on royal grants. The statute, *De Prerogativa Regis* 1324[9] provided that if the Crown granted a manor to a subject and an advowson had previously been enjoyed with it, the grant did not include the advowson unless it was expressly mentioned. The advowson was treated as similar to a flower franchise. In *Attorney-General v Sitwell*[10] Sir George Sitwell agreed to purchase from the Crown the manor of Eckington in Derbyshire and the contract contained general words including appurtenances. Sitwell claimed that this included the advowson of the parish church which he said was either appurtenant or appendant. The court, relying on the statute, held that while such words would have carried the advowson if it had been between subjects, the effect of the Act was that it was excluded.

Advowsons could, however, be appendant to a manor and passed with it without having to be mentioned in the conveyance.[11] Advowsons are not included in s 62(3) of the Law of Property Act 1925 and were not previously included in general words. Under ss 3 and 32 of the Patronage (Benefices) Measure 1986 all advowsons have been severed and are now in gross. Only advowsons appendant are mentioned in s 32 but it presumably includes advowsons appurtenant. If the purchaser of a landed estate or manor wishes to have the advowson of the church it might be possible to transfer it at the same time, but a contract to give away an advowson would be unenforceable. The only way to get round this is

---

[7]   Ibid f 245

[8]   Ibid f 243b–244.

[9]   17 Ed 2, stat 1 (c 15).

[10] (1835) 1 Y & C Ex 559, 160 ER 228.

[11] Bracton *op cit* f 433; Blackstone *op cit* II.3.i.

for the completion of the purchase to be conditional on the purchaser first being registered as patron. In any event the Parochial Church Council must be consulted on any transfer of an advowson and in many cases the bishop will take into account the council's views in considering whether to consent. Although the bishop must act reasonably, and any decision is potentially subject to judicial review, he would be justified in refusing consent if the purpose of the transfer was in effect to sell the right of presentation.

Patrons used to have rights in addition to presenting the incumbent to a living. If the glebe land was to be sold the patron had a right of first refusal but that was abolished by s 34 of the 1986 Measure. If a parson wished to make alterations to the parsonage house (the vicarage) he had to ask the patron's permission. Section 34 has also removed that requirement although the parson must still inform the patron of his intention and consult with him. Most clergymen now live in small modern houses but if a historic rectory, often of architectural interest, is still in use that could be important.

Under r 50 of the Land Registration Rules 1925 it was possible to register title to advowsons. The 1986 Measure, s 6 provided that advowsons should cease to be interests in land and amended the definition of land in s 3 of the 1925 Act, and also provided them to be removed from the register. It is therefore no longer possible to register advowsons at the Land Registry. Instead, the registrar of each diocese keeps a formal register.

20.3   APPROPRIATE AND IMPROPRIATE RECTORIES

The patronage of many advowsons belongs to laymen. Others are exercisable by the Crown, by bishops and by ecclesiastical societies. Until the Reformation many belonged to abbeys, the legacy of which still produces problems today that affect the manor. In addition to parishes established on the estates of theigns, many monasteries and bishops had estates in Saxon times and were often slow to appoint a priest. They had no need of an educated ordained man themselves and although some were aware of the need to care for the souls of the peasants, not all abbots felt the need to have a local resident priest. There was a feeling that the minster church was good enough.

More importantly, in the centuries after the Norman Conquest pious laymen gave, or more often bequeathed, lands to a monastery or nunnery they or their family had founded. Sometimes they did it as rich people today establish a charity or a foundation, because they see the need. Sometimes they did it to fulfil a vow made in a time of crisis, such as battle or shipwreck, that if they were spared they would give land to God. Often they did it in the hope of securing favourable treatment in the next world. Whatever the reason, vast areas of land were given to Church institutions. Although abbeys were the most prominent recipients there were others such as Oxford and Cambridge colleges. Such bodies never died, rarely became insolvent and could not give their property away. The land, usually including a manor, but sometimes a rectory on its own, passed into the control of the institution. It would include the tithes, the glebe land and the advowson.

When an abbey acquired a manor to which an advowson was appendant it would appoint one of the monks, such as the abbot, as rector. The abbey then appropriated to itself the glebe land, the tithes and any other income of the living. The rector appointed a substitute, his *vicarius* or vicar, to preach and administer the sacraments. The vicar was poorly paid and little better off than his parishioners while the benefit of the endowments of the parish church went to the abbey. Acts passed by the Parliaments of Richard II and Henry IV tried to curtail this abuse and ensure that vicars had a proper income but they were of little effect and easily avoided. The glebe land, which had formerly been held by the priest by tenure from the lord, became merged with the manorial demesne and records of the distinct holdings were lost.

Between 1536 and 1540 Henry VIII dissolved the monasteries and confiscated their lands. Over the next 70 years most were sold off and became the private property of laymen. The Crown, however, retained some and others continued to belong to dioceses or colleges. On their sale, *Prerogativa Regis* was not applied and the manor and the advowson were sold together, along with the former appropriated rectory which, now that it passed into the hands of a layman, was called 'impropriate'. Alternatively the rectorial rights (including tithes) might be sold separately from the manor. Where an advowson was retained by a bishop, college or other institution it continued to be termed appropriated.

The lay rector of a parish could not preach or administer sacraments and had to appoint a vicar, but he normally retained the income of the rectory as the abbey had before him. He kept the glebe land (which by that time had usually become indistinguishable from demesne) and the tithes. Vicarages were expected to have some endowment (often by gift over the years after appropriation) although the amount varied a great deal from one parish to another. The vicar's income was supplemented by fees and collections and in more recent times by grants from Queen Anne's Bounty, now the estates of the Church Commissioners. In modern times the Church of England has made great efforts to secure proper incomes for its clergy. That is beyond the scope of this book save that similar efforts in the dioceses to equalise incomes led to the centralised management of glebe land. Impropriate and appropriated rectories have the responsibility for chancel repairs (20.8).

20.4   GLEBE

Certain properties pass or used to pass to the incumbent, namely the church building, and, unless the patron was also lay rector, the churchyard. Until 1976 the glebe land, which was often held from the manor by tenure in frankalmoign, also passed. When a clergyman is appointed to a living he is put in charge by two separate gifts although both are usually performed at the same service of institution. The spiritualities, namely the right to preach, to administer the sacraments and generally to run the ecclesiastical matters of the parish, are granted by the bishop. The clergyman has to receive (or be invested with) the temporalities from the archdeacon, which is known as induction.

The incumbent, whether rector or vicar, was a corporation sole who, as such, never died or resigned.[12] The individual changed but the lands belonged to the office. Technically, the status of corporation sole is a franchise dependent on royal grant (16.4) but as all ancient livings existed before 1189 their status could not be questioned under *Quo Warranto*. Thus the induction of the temporalities by the archdeacon is neither a grant nor an assurance of land. Nor did the incumbent do homage or fealty[13] (as bishops do to the sovereign) but there is merely a recognition that as the incumbent has been validly presented by the patron and instituted by the bishop he is entitled to have the temporalities. Indeed, the patron and lord need not be the same person, or the lands might be held from different lords, but that does not affect the right of the incumbent to have them.

The most important temporality was glebe land, but the Endowments and Glebe Measure 1976 changed its nature and management. In Latin, *gleba* meant clod or lump of earth and hence soil or land. It now refers only to the unconsecrated church land of a parish. When the theign originally established his chapel the priest was part of his household, eating at the theign's table, clothed by his gift. As lords became increasingly non-resident, the parson needed an income. In part this came from tithes but he was also granted land. This can be seen as similar to a clerical demesne on which crops and vegetables could be grown for the priest's own consumption. Sometimes, especially where the rector came from the same level of society as the humbler freemen, it was seen as his proper share

---

[12]   Bracton *op cit* f 226b–227.

[13]   Coke, Sir Edward, *A commentary on Littleton being the first part of the Institutes of the Laws of England* (1628) 95b–96a.

of village resources. Some glebes were a hide or more; others were like the peasant holding of a virgate or half virgate, say 15 to 30 acres.

After the Conquest the glebe was incorporated into the manorial system. A more substantial glebe might constitute a sub-manor with its own customary tenants who owed services and rents. Glebes could only be freeholds since a priest had to be a free man: bondsmen were ineligible. Some glebes may have been held as customary freeholds but as the incumbent was a corporation sole who never died, so that there was no need for surrender and admission, it would have been difficult to distinguish them from common freeholds. By reason of their origin, glebes (and other clerical lands such as the church and churchyard) remained parcel of the manor held from the lord.

Although tenure of glebe was by frankalmoign,[14] as explained below, this converted to socage when the holder died after 1925. By the time of the 1976 Measure there were few (if any) glebe lands where the holder was still the same individual as before 1926. The 1976 Measure, by transferring all glebe land to diocesan boards of finance, completed the conversion. However, the land remained held from the lord by tenure so that, if the board of finance were to sell the land, say to a builder, the builder went into liquidation and the liquidator disclaimed, then the land could escheat to the lord rather than the Crown.

The rules that applied to freehold land belonging to the benefice should not be confused with the so-called parson's freehold. That has nothing to do with land but relates to the office of incumbent which, in past centuries, was like an incorporeal hereditament. The phrase refers to the right of the parson, once presented, instituted and inducted to remain in the living for the rest of his life should he wish to do so. It has been weakened in recent years by the introduction of a compulsory retiring age and by provisions for removal for misconduct or incompatibility with the parish, but it remains important. Parish priests who have been instituted and inducted and behave properly cannot be removed or relocated at the will of the bishop. If this freehold were to go, as some wish, it would weaken the right of a patron to exercise his advowson because any person appointed could then be removed. In practice many bishops suspend livings in the interests of pastoral reorganisation, but once a parson is in place he still has his freehold.

---

[14]   Coke on *Littleton op cit* 93b ff.

20.5   RECTORIAL MANORS

Some manors are described as rectorial. The expression is not a term of art although it has been used in argument by counsel.[15] Legal references should be to 'the manor and rectory' or 'manor of the rectory' of Dale in the County of Barset. It is used in two inconsistent senses: one to a manor combined with a rectory and the other to glebe which constituted a manor. The first is to an appropriated or impropriate rectory where the rectory has stayed with the manor. This could be because it became attached as appropriated to a bishopric and remained so, in which case it has now passed to the Church Commissioners (under the Ecclesiastical Commission Act 1868 and subsequent legislation) who hold many such manors. Alternatively it could refer to an impropriate rectory where the lay rectorship has remained owned by the same person as the manor. Such manors can be owned by laymen.

The other sense applies conversely where the rectory was not merged with the manor. A large glebe might have been sufficiently extensive to have become a manor or sub-manor with its own free and copyhold tenants. It would usually be a sub-manor held from the chief manor belonging to a layman and out of which the endowment was initially made, for example where an abbey acquired the rectory with its lands but not the principal manor. More often it describes a situation where the rectory and its glebe remained with an independent rector throughout the Middle Ages and afterwards.

Such a manor must have been constituted before 1290 and usually before 1189. *Monck v Huskisson*[16] concerned the manor of Barking in Essex. Some of the copyholds were of the manor, some subject to tithe and others which claimed to be exempt from the tithe of corn and hay. The claim was on the basis that before the Dissolution the manor had been held by the Abbess of Barking and the lands in question were then free of tithe. It was clear that any freehold demesne land of a manor where the lord was rector would be free of tithe since the tithe payer and recipient would be the same person. In general copyhold land was considered to be subject to tithe, even if the lord was rector. The issue turned on when the copyhold was granted, bearing in mind that by general custom new copyholds could not be created after 1189. If the copyhold existed as a separate holding before the rectory and manor were united then tithe was payable and due. If the land had originally been demesne, and the abbey acquired the manor and then first granted the copyhold out of the demesne land after the union (but of course before 1189) then the land would be exempt because of the former demesne status. As there was evidence that the copyholds in question were

---

[15]   *Halsey v Grant* (1806) 13 Vesey Jun 73, 33 ER 222.

[16]   (1827) 1 Sim 280, 57 ER 582.

exempt, the vice chancellor was prepared to assume in this case that the union had been made and the copyholds subsequently granted all before 1189.

Many rectorial manors had no dependent tenants and so would be regarded as reputed manors. They could be small, extending to the parsonage house itself, a garden and perhaps a field or two, but they might be accorded the dignity of manorial status. *Halsey v Grant*[17] concerned a copyhold held of the manor and rectory of Woking in Surrey which comprised the parsonage house and some 79 acres.

20.6   CONSECRATED LAND AND CHURCHWAYS

In relation to the church and churchyard there is a distinction between the freehold and the fee simple. The general rule in relation to ancient consecrated land is that where the incumbent is also the rector then the freehold in the land is vested in him. Where there is a distinction, ie the incumbent is a vicar, the position is uncertain but the better view is that it remains vested in the rector, even if a layman.[18] It therefore appears that a lay rector can claim such benefit of the land (eg timber) as is not inconsistent with the consecrated purpose of the churchyard. Where the freehold is vested in the incumbent as rector he only has a limited interest and the fee simple is said to be in abeyance.[19] This is sometimes compared to a life interest although as the rector is a corporation sole it is better seen as belonging to the corporation of which the rector is only the temporary representative. Where land is acquired in modern times for consecrated purposes it is conveyed to the Church Commissioners and is vested in the incumbent, whether rector or vicar, under the New Parishes Measure 1943. Where the land is clearly vested in some person in fee simple then the fact that it is consecrated does not by itself divest the proprietor.[20]

Many of the same rules for glebe also applied to the church and churchyard but with the difference that glebe could be (and usually was) leased and rights could be granted over it, while holy ground was consecrated to the service of God and the use of the parishioners both alive and dead. Unlike glebe, which could be dealt with and ultimately sold, churches and churchyards could not be sold, leased or subjected to rights of way or other easements without following

---

[17]   (1806) 13 Vesey Jun 73, 33 ER 222.

[18]   *Greenslade v Darby* (1867–68) LR 3 QB 421; *Winstanley v North Manchester Overseers* [1910] AC 7. See the discussion in *Halsbury's Laws op cit* para 847, n 2.

[19]   *Rector of St Gabriel's Fenchurch Street v City of London Real Property Company* (1896) Trist 95.

[20]   *Re Tonbridge School Chapel* [1993] Fam 281, [1993] 1 WLR 1138, [1993] 2 All ER 338.

special procedures. Bracton[21] makes the point that consecrated land cannot be a free tenement. He was discussing this in the context of whether an action could be brought to recover such land, but the same principle applies to selling it. Churches and churchyards can only be sold under the Pastoral Measure 1983 if they are redundant to church use and so declared by a formal scheme made by Her Majesty in Council.

Consecrated land is subject to the faculty jurisdiction of the Church exercised by the chancellor of the diocese or the archdeacon acting on his behalf.[22] Most of the rules relate to ecclesiastical law but a few are relevant to the manor. Thus, the incumbent had the right to let the grazing in the churchyard, which could be valuable to a smallholder. Many churchyards and the naves of churches were used for local gatherings. If there was no village green the churchyard might be the only open space where people could relax, although some decorum was expected. The Statute of Winchester 1285 prohibited the holding of fairs and markets in churchyards and although the Act has been repealed the law did not change back.

Leading families owned or had rights in their own burial vaults and a resident lord was normally buried in or near the church. Many parish churches are adorned with memorial brasses, tombs and monuments to former lords, often with long inscriptions and fine sculptures. Such works can no longer be constructed without a faculty, which is only rarely granted. A part of the church was sometimes set aside for the use of the occupiers of the manor house or some other mansion. This may simply have been a pew, which could be owned in perpetuity or rented by the year. Occasionally, a sizeable part of a church, such as an aisle or an attached chapel, might be private to the squire. The freehold did not vest in him but he was responsible for the repair of the part set aside. The right was not an appurtenance or annexure of the manor but, like an easement, went with the right to occupy a specific house.

Although many churches adjoined the public highway this was not invariable and access might have to be gained over private land. The church was not private property so there could be no private easement. Likewise access was required only by parishioners, not the public generally, so it could not be a highway. The law therefore recognised a special type of access known as a churchway. Since this was for a fluctuating and undefined body – the inhabitants of the parish – it could only subsist by custom; but in this case the

---

[21] Bracton *op cit* f 180b.

[22] Newsom, GH and Newsom, GL, *Faculty Jurisdiction of the Church of England* (Sweet & Maxwell, 2nd edn, 1993).

custom did not have to predate 1189. Ecclesiastical customs could be created until the Reformation.[23]

In *Brocklebank v Thompson*[24] there was a way leading to Irton Parish Church in Cumberland. The plaintiff was lord of the manor of Irton and the defendant was the owner of land within the adjoining manor of Santon but also within the ecclesiastical parish of Irton. Although there was some indication that a few local people believed the way to be a public highway, the evidence was against that and both parties accepted that it was a customary way – the dispute being whether those who could benefit were the tenants of Irton Manor or the parishioners of Irton Parish. The judge found that it was a parochial churchway. He held that a customary way was not a highway and was to be regarded as a private way.

Farquhar v Newbury Rural District Council[25] concerned a claimed new customary way. Before 1743 there had been a way to the church at Shaw at Newbury in Berkshire. The church was near Shaw House and the way passed through a farmyard. In 1841 the church was pulled down and rebuilt and in 1842 the owner of Shaw House made a new road along a different route. Thereafter people used the new road to get to the church. Mrs Farquhar, who owned Shaw House at the time of the case, admitted that parishioners had the right to go along the road but denied that it was a public highway and locked two gates. The council removed the locks. The court found evidence of general public use since 1842 so that a public highway was deemed to have been dedicated. It held that it was not possible to create a new customary churchway at common law even if it was by way of substitution and diversion of an old one. The court relied on *Poole v Huskisson*.[26] In that case a private carriage road at East Bridgeford in Nottinghamshire had been set out under an inclosure Act. Local parishioners claimed that it had become a churchway but not a public highway. Parke B said: 'There may be a dedication to the public for a limited purpose, as for a footway, horse-way, or drift-way; but there cannot be a dedication to a limited part of the public.'

In *Batten v Gedye*[27] the rector and churchwardens of Barwick in Somerset removed certain ancient steps leading from the churchyard up to the highway. Some parishioners claimed a mandatory injunction for the steps to be restored. The court found that the steps were not a public highway but constituted an ancient churchway and therefore the matter fell within the jurisdiction of the

---

[23]   *Harthan v Harthan* [1949] P 115.

[24]   [1903] 2 Ch 344.

[25]   [1909] 1 Ch 12.

[26]   (1843) 11 M&W 827, 152 ER 1039.

[27]   (1889) LR 41 Ch D 507.

Ecclesiastical Court (which had power to grant a faculty to remove the steps) and was not a matter for the High Court.

20.7   SCHOOLS

In the nineteenth century, as industry developed and democracy was introduced, Parliament accepted the need to educate people who could not afford to pay for schooling. Universal education was not brought in until 1870 but before that many schools were founded around the country especially by the Church. In 1841 the School Sites Act encouraged landowners to give sites on which Church schools could be built. Many of these survived for over a century, but with the changing patterns of rural population and the educational reform in the 1970s some of the schools closed.

In order to encourage gifts of land the 1841 Act provided that if a school was closed the land would come back to the donor, with any building erected on it, even though that would often have been paid for by public subscription. Section 2 says:

> Any person, being seised in fee simple, fee tail, or for life, of and in any manor or lands of freehold, copyhold, or customary tenure, and having the beneficial interest therein ... may grant, convey, or enfranchise ... land, as a site for a school ... Provided also, that upon the said land so granted as aforesaid, or any part thereof, ceasing to be used for the purposes in this Act mentioned, the same shall thereupon immediately revert to and become a portion of the said estate held in fee simple or otherwise, or of any manor, or land as aforesaid, as fully to all intents and purposes as if this Act had not been passed,

After 100 years of social changes the meaning of this reverter clause has become difficult to apply. Usually it is taken to mean that the land comes back to the donor's heir. If he owned the land outright, this will be the people inheriting under his will and the wills of his heirs. If the land was in a trust, it will be the people who now benefit from that trust or a successor.[28]

The point came up for decision in *Marchant v Onslow*[29] in 1994. In 1848 under the 1841 Act Elizabeth Foley and her nephew Richard Onslow gave land at Picklenash in the Parish of Newent to the vicar and churchwardens for the site of a school. Elizabeth Foley is described as lady of the manor, but there was no evidence whether the land granted was manorial land or other land that happened to be owned by her. In 1984 the school closed. The vicar, Canon

---

[28]   *Bath and Wells Diocesan Board of Finance v Jenkinson* [2003] Ch 89.

[29]   (1994) 13 EG 114.

William Marchant, and the churchwardens claimed a declaration that they could retain the proceeds of the school which had been sold. Susan Margaret Onslow was the heir of Elizabeth Foley. She was not lady of the manor and indeed all trace of the manor had been lost in the intervening 136 years. She claimed the proceeds as heir. The vicar claimed that the site reverted to the lord of the manor and, as he could not be traced, the church had a better title than anyone else. The court held that there was no evidence to show that the site was specifically granted out of a particular estate or manor and in that case it reverted to Miss Onslow as general heir to the original grantor. The judge found it difficult to give a clear interpretation of the section but he considered that in some circumstances land might revert to a landed estate. In *Fraser v Canterbury Diocesan Board of Finance*[30] the Court of Appeal considered that that view was wrong: 'The reverter is of that estate held on that tenure to the original grantor of the site and not to the land out of which the site granted was carved and conveyed.' The court saw no reason why someone who had bought the land next to the school should benefit from its closure. The reference to estate was to a legal not a landed estate (22.7–22.8).

This raises the problem that, if the site had been parcel of a manor and the family of the original donor still owned the lordship then, on the wording of the section, it would seem to accrue to that manor. Under the rule in *Delacherois v Delacherois*[31] the land will have ceased to be within the manor when it was given, but Parliament can make an exception to the rule. Occasionally, the issue may now arise in practice. In the nineteenth century some schools were built on copyhold land which the school trustees bought at full value but the lord was prepared to donate his fee simple under the 1841 Act. If such a school now closes, the purchased interest would not revert since the trustees had given value and in any case it came from the former copyholder not the lord. Copyholds were converted to freeholds in 1926 and it is now too late to claim compensation for manorial incidents (14.8). What, if anything, reverts? Probably the lord again becomes entitled to any rights which would otherwise have been preserved under the Law of Property Act 1922, Sch 12, para (5).

Where the donor did provide the land (in the case of a lord out of demesne or waste) then, under the Reverter of Sites Act 1977, the claim is now normally to the proceeds of sale of the land rather than to the land itself. However, if he can establish his rights in time the claimant can require the land itself to be handed over to him.

---

[30]   [2001] Ch 669 at [44].

[31]   (1862) HL Cas 62, 11 ER 1254.

20.8   CHANCEL REPAIRS

In the Middle Ages the general custom of parishes was that the congregation were responsible for repair and maintenance of the nave of the church, and the rector for the chancel. Both are now normally looked after by the Parochial Church Council. To this there is an important exception. In appropriated parishes the liability of the rector became that of the institution. If the parish is still held by the same body, such as a college, then it retains that liability to this day. If the rectory became impropriate then the liability passed to the lay rector and can still exist. While sometimes it was the responsibility of the owner of the tithes, normally it attached to land. In theory this would be to the glebe but that has long since ceased to be separately identifiable, so that in such cases the liability for chancel repairs attaches to the whole of the demesne (including glebe), typically as it existed at the Dissolution.

If part of the demesne is sold off it may be agreed between the selling lord and the buyer either that the liability is apportioned, so that the purchaser of one per cent of the demesne will take on one per cent of the cost of chancel repairs, or the lord will indemnify the buyer and retain the whole liability, which is a private arrangement between landowners. Since this does not affect the church, the Parochial Church Council is legally entitled to sue the landowner of any part of the former demesne (however small) for the whole cost of the repairs. The landowner may, however, be able to recover a contribution from the other landowners.

This issue came to the fore in the case of *Parochial Church Council of the Parish of Aston Cantlow and Wilmcote with Billesley, Warwickshire v Wallbank*.[32] Mr and Mrs Wallbank were the owners of Glebe Farm, Aston Cantlow. Part of the farm included land previously known as Clanacre. Clanacre was comprised in an award in 1743 under an inclosure Act of 1742 and was allotted to Lord Brooke who was the lay impropriator and owner of tithes and glebe land at Aston Cantlow. The award extinguished his tithes and, in substitution, allotted Clanacre, which thereby became rectorial property and subject to the liability to repair the chancel. The liability was recorded in the title deeds and when Mrs Wallbank's parents bought the farm in 1970 the purchase deed referred to it. The Wallbanks therefore knew of the potential claim. The procedure for recovering a contribution is now set out in the Chancel Repairs Act 1932. In 1994 and 1996 the Parochial Church Council served notice on the Wallbanks requiring them to put the chancel into repair. The cost was then estimated at approximately £95,000. The Wallbanks disputed liability on the grounds that the council was a public body subject to the Human Rights Act

---

[32]   [2003] UKHL 37, [2004] 1 AC 546.

1998 and the claim was an unfair tax. The judge upheld the claim, the Court of
Appeal disallowed it and the House of Lords agreed with the judge. It
concluded, on the basis of certain cases previously decided in the European
Court of Human Rights, that the council could not be a public authority for this
purpose, that the liability simply attached to the land at Clanacre, and that the
Walllbanks knew about it and were therefore liable to pay.

This caused public concern, principally because although in this particular case
the liability was mentioned in the title deeds, in many cases it is not and some
people may be potentially liable to pay for something they know nothing about.
It has consequently become the practice for conveyancers to make enquiries as
to whether such a liability exists, but there are no conclusive records and even in
parishes where there is known to be a liability there is no definite way of
discovering if the liability attaches to a particular piece of land. Many buyers
take out insurance against what, in the vast majority of cases, is a remote risk.

Liability for chancel repairs was covered by the Land Registration Act 1925,
s 70(1)(c) and was an overriding interest which bound the land irrespective of
whether it was mentioned on the register of title. When the Land Registration
Bill, which became the Act of 2002, was going through Parliament the law was
as decided by the Court of Appeal and therefore at that time chancel repairs
were not a liability. The decision of the House of Lords in overruling the Court
of Appeal changed the law and revived the liability. Accordingly, by the Land
Registration Act 2002 (Transitional Provisions) (No 2) Order 2003[33] chancel
repair liability was added to the list of temporary liabilities in Schs 1 and 3,
para 16 until 2013 (discussed in 25.9). It follows that anyone buying land after
2013 will only be subject to this liability if either it has been registered by
caution against unregistered land or, if the title is registered, there is a notice on
the register. As a result many church councils that wish to protect their right to
claim the cost of repair of the chancel in future are carrying out research to
discover the extent of land subject to this liability.

20.9   TITHE

Virtually all English legal tithe is now abolished; and although once it was an
important matter, little need be said about it here. The concept of tithe is ancient
and is said to have biblical origins. Broadly, it was a church tax of 10 per cent of
all produce, but many different types of tithe existed in relation to how they
were calculated and who paid. The payment was always difficult to collect.
Mediaeval priests were often, for lack of a better remedy, driven to

---

[33]   SI 2003/1953.

excommunicate non-payers; and Chaucer in his *Prologue to the Canterbury Tales* remarks approvingly of the parson that he did not curse for his tithes but that instead he gave money out of his own pocket to his destitute parishioners.

The Tithe Act 1836 converted most of the old tithes to a variable rentcharge whose amount depended on the price of corn. Tithe rentcharges were in principle registrable under the Land Registration Rules 1925, r 50. In 1936 tithe was taken over by the Government (which compensated the Church and other tithe owners such as lay rectors) and by the Tithe Act 1936 it was converted into a fixed redeemable rentcharge. Section 56 of the Finance Act 1977 abolished tithe rentcharge and it is no longer payable.

The Church was not the only owner of tithes. In the Middle Ages and especially in Saxon times lords could grant up to two thirds of the tithe of their estate to an abbey. Otherwise they were paid to the rector. Sometimes individuals became entitled to a portion of the tithe. On the Dissolution various people could acquire the right to tithe although the most usual was the impropriate rector.

Along with tithes were two other similar payments. One was modus, which had to be created before 1189 as a fixed commutation of the previously variable tithe. The other was corn rents,[34] which were continuing monetary payments. These were fixed according to the local price of grain (wheat, oats and barley). The Tithe Amendment Act 1860 enabled pre-1836 corn rents to be converted into tithe rentcharges. Few survive and most that do are of negligible value. In practice a few small payments of both and a very few small tithe payments were not caught, probably because they were not worth the cost of converting to the new system, and have continued to be payable to the present time. Such payments rarely exceed a few pence, are often collected purely for historical reasons, and generally get forgotten when they have not been paid for a few years. Most are payable to the Church Commissioners, but some are payable to landowners, tithe owners or their successors and were not covered by the provisions for redemption. Such payments are included in Land Registration Act 2002, Schs 1 and 3, para 14 as interests which will cease to have overriding status after 2013 (25.9). If still payable they must be protected either by notice on a registered title or by caution against an unregistered title before first registration or disposition after 12 October 2013 or they will not be enforceable.

Annuity payments or rentcharges were also payable to churches[35] by reason of tenure. These may derive from cases where, before 1290, Church land was

---

[34] See Law Commission No 254, *Land Registration for the twenty-first century: a consultative document* para 5.40.

[35] Bracton *op cit* f 286b.

alienated by subinfeudation at a rent. They are rare and will be subject to the same rules as other rentcharges (14.5).

20.10   FRANKALMOIGN AND EPISCOPAL PROPERTY

Just as barons and knights held their land by knight service, so bishops, abbots and indeed any spiritual person including a parson were considered to hold their lands for services. These may have been knight service, especially where land became assured by substitution to the Church. Otherwise land and manors could be held by frankalmoign or free alms and the service was the service of prayer. Frankalmoign involved the *trinoda necessitas*[36] although military service was performed through subtenants, but it was free in the sense that it was free from the king's right to demand service from the holder in person. Where land was granted to a monastery or other institution it could be granted specifically for services of prayer. To this day most Oxford and Cambridge colleges still offer regular prayers for their benefactors, although not for tenurial reasons.

Frankalmoign tenure was saved by the Tenures Abolition Act 1660, s 7. The relevant part of s 7 was repealed by s 56 of and Sch 2 to the Administration of Estates Act 1925 so far as it applied to deaths after 31 December 1925. The effect is that where any holder in that tenure died after that date the tenure would convert to become socage. On the face of it this would not apply to a corporation sole although it may be possible to interpret it in the sense that the incumbent died. Equally, it would not appear to apply where the incumbent resigned and his successor took on the land. A transfer of frankalmoign land from a clergyman to a layman would by itself have effected a conversion to socage tenure even before 1660.[37]

It seems that where the holder was an ecclesiastical corporation aggregate,[38] possibly only under a royal grant,[39] it cannot have died so there will have been no transmission. An instance is *Attorney-General v Dean and Canons of Windsor*[40] where land at Windsor was granted by Edward VI. The House of Lords held the grant to be in frankalmoign. Presumably it is still so held. Lord Campbell LC referred to the special nature saying, 'this tenure, although consistent with a beneficial interest in the grantees, is likewise consistent with a charitable trust, beyond making orisons, prayers, and other divine services for

---

[36]   Blackstone *op cit* II.6.v.

[37]   *Sir Anthony Lowe's Case* (1610) 9 Co Rep 122b, 77 ER 909; Coke on *Littleton op cit* 98a–b.

[38]   Coke on *Littleton op cit* 94.

[39]   Ibid 98a.

[40]   (1860) 8 HL Cas 369, 11 ER 472.

the souls of the departed donors, and for the prosperity and good life and good health of their heirs who are alive'.[41] It is possible that diocesan boards of finance or the Church Commissioners might be regarded as spiritual corporations and therefore the episcopal and glebe lands which have passed to them may still be held in frankalmoign. There would seem now to be no practical consequences of holding in this tenure rather than socage.

Bishops had the status of barons and as such may still attend the House of Lords, although there are proposals to reduce their numbers.[42] It followed that a bishop's estates, to the extent that they consisted of manors, comprised an honour (22.4). The Ecclesiastical Commissioners Act 1860 made new arrangements as to the ownership of property belonging to a bishopric. Section 2 of the 1860 Act provided that upon the first avoidance of the see of any bishop in England after the passing of the 1860 Act, the lands, hereditaments and emoluments of or belonging to the see were to vest absolutely in the Ecclesiastical Commissioners for England. Section 3 of the 1860 Act provided for the possibility, after such vesting had occurred, of an arrangement being made, assigning to the bishop of the relevant see and his successors, such lands and hereditaments as were appropriate to form an endowment for the see.[43] Finally the Episcopal Endowments and Stipends Measure 1943 provided for the transfer of the endowments and property of any see to the Ecclesiastical Commissioners. As a result their successors the Church Commissioners now hold numerous manors.

---

[41] Ibid at 399.

[42] See House of Lords Reform Bill, Part 4 in 2012 session.

[43] See *Barton v Church Commissioners for England* [2008] EWHC 3091 (Ch).

Chapter 21

Towns and Trade

21.1   TOWNS AND BOROUGHS

The lord of a manor may also be lord of a borough. He may have market rights and own the town square or parts of nineteenth-century housing estates. The mayor and burgesses may themselves have acquired the manor in which their borough is situated and the title may belong to the corporation or to an official as nominee.

Manors are usually associated with country villages, and most of this book has been concerned with these. However, they could not exist without trade or the towns that trade created. If the manor depended on the heavy plough drawn by eight oxen, where did the peasant get his iron ploughshare? A few villages were located near outcrops of iron ore and many had a village blacksmith, but ploughs and harnesses were traded over long distances. To pay the quitrent or merchet the peasant had to find the cash by selling something he had produced in the local market town.

Several towns date back to Anglo-Saxon times and are described as such in *Domesday Book*. They were sometimes regarded as entities separate from lordships and holding direct from the king. In other cases they were comprised within manors or a lordship might include as an outlier property within a town. It appears that some great towns, notably London, may have been seen as having some form of corporate status.

In the early Middle Ages many towns were founded to exploit their commercial potential. An abbot or great lord might petition the king and pay a substantial sum for the franchise of a market with right of toll within his manor. He might then lay out a market square on some demesne land or land taken from an open field with a number of building plots around it. The boundaries of some of those plots (which may exist to this day) often have slightly curving sides reflecting their origin in enclosed strips. Other towns may have developed by expansion of villages although the lord must have been involved in some way. Some of these ventures did not work out and the project had to be abandoned although there may be relics such as an unusual layout for a village and perhaps an unexercised right of market. In such cases the lord continued to own any land which was not held by someone else.

In order to run their affairs towns developed a variety of local courts. As described in 13.1 courts originally had a general function although it appears that in many towns courts were judicial from the beginning. There was always a need to provide an impartial forum for townsmen to resolve their disputes, collect debts and enforce contracts. That was particularly important where traders from far away might come to a fair or a regular market as if there was a risk they would not get justice that might deter them from coming. Most boroughs had borough courts, which might have a variety of local names. The mayor was a magistrate and would sit, as a justice of the peace, to hear criminal cases. However, as contract law became more complex these magistrates would tend to leave hearing commercial cases to professional lawyers. Other courts included pie-powder (21.2), which determined disputes in markets. Where the town was comprised within a manor some of these courts may have belonged to the lord although if the town obtained a borough charter it would often seek to acquire the courts and the manor.

If the town flourished its inhabitants developed a sense of identity as a community and sought independence from any controlling lord. If they did not have corporate status (16.4) they might apply for a charter to grant them the franchise so that they could operate as a body, typically the mayor and burgesses, but there were many variations in name, with perpetual succession, a common seal and other rights such as power to make byelaws. Later the corporation might seek to acquire either the manor itself or, if not, the manorial rights, specifically including market rights or tolls. In addition to their involvement in trade and commerce, many burgesses remained farmers, at least part time, and some, such as butchers, depended on agricultural products. As a result burgesses often retained or acquired rights in the surrounding countryside, specifically grazing rights over nearby waste or open fields comprising Lammas lands. These rights might belong to the freemen collectively rather than to specific tenements in the town, and the benefit might be shared out among them or sold to the highest bidder with the proceeds applied to the town funds.

At the Dissolution urban manors that belonged to abbeys passed to the Crown and many were sold so that the new lord acquired the rights formerly held by the abbey.

In the nineteenth century many towns expanded through sales and leases from local landowners, often including the lords of adjoining manors. They might also become involved with canals and railways. In 1894 local government was reorganised and many boroughs became urban districts while still retaining their borough status.[1] A further reorganisation took place in 1974 and while boroughs were entitled to continue to call themselves such, many became demoted to little better than parish councils.[2]

21.2   MARKETS

A market is a franchise conferring a monopoly right to hold (and prevent other people holding) a gathering of buyers and sellers in a common place.[3] In the absence of market rights anyone can allow traders on his property but the effect of the franchise is that the holder has the power to stop any rivals. The monopoly typically extends to six and two-thirds miles, or one third of a day's journey of 20 miles[4] so that people attending the market spent no more than a third of the day coming, a third at the market and a third going home. Market towns tend therefore to be spaced about 14 miles apart. That is the general rule which will apply where the franchise predates 1189 and there is no charter. Where there is one the limits of the franchise will be defined in it by reference to other bounds. Fairs are occasional markets, often held once a year, which aim to attract business from afar, as distinct from a market which is more local.

Market franchises were usually granted to lords of manors who could exercise control through their courts and landholdings, but markets could be given to anyone such as the burgesses of a town. A market can be held anywhere within the market area unless (unusually) it is restricted to a specific place. Thus, in *Gloucestershire County Council v Farrow*[5] (16.8) the judge commented that although Mr Farrow could not hold his market in the old market place because that had become a highway, he was still free to hold it elsewhere. Similarly, in *Spook Erection Ltd v Secretary of State for the Environment*[6] (16.7) the market which had once been held in the high street had moved in 1923 to another site and the problem arose because of Spook's wish to move it back.

---

[1]   Local Government Act 1894.

[2]   Local Government Act 1972.

[3]   See generally Pease, JG and Chity, H, *Law of Markets and Fairs* (Butterworths Lexis Nexis, 1984 edn by Edward F Cousins and Robert Anthony).

[4]   Bracton, Sir Henry, *De legibus et consuetudinibus angliae* (c 1257) (SE Thorne (ed)) (Belknap Press of Harvard University Press, 1977) f 235b.

[5]   [1985] 1 WLR 741, [1982] 2 All ER 1031, (1984) 48 P&CR 85.

[6]   [1988] 2 All ER 667, (1988) 86 LGR 736.

A franchise of market on its own is of limited value. Other rights make it more profitable, particularly toll and stallage. Tolls are discussed in 15.1. Market toll is the right to charge either buyers or (more usually) sellers for attending the market. It is not automatically implied in a market franchise and must be specifically mentioned in the grant. There are many toll-free markets. A variant on simple market toll is where the owner has the right of tronage to make a charge according to the weight of goods sold – a sort of turnover rent. Stallage is the right to charge for having a stall, similar to a rent. Stallage often goes with piccage – the right to charge for making holes in the ground to insert posts to support a stall – and pennage – the right to charge for the erection of pens for animals.

In the past, markets needed a court to deal with disturbances and resolve disputes between traders. Disturbances were within the criminal jurisdiction of the sheriff's tourn and therefore the lord of the manor (assuming he had view of frankpledge) could supervise the market. He might also have an assize of bread and ale to regulate consumables and those who sold them. Commercial disputes were dealt with at a court of pie-powder (from *pied-poudre* or dusty-feet) which was incident to the franchise. Such courts lost jurisdiction under s 23 of the Administration of Justice Act 1977.

If an over-optimistic lord of a manor obtained a franchise of market but the venture was not successful the franchise right did not disappear. In modern conditions, with new settlements or the growth of car boot sales, the time may be ripe for a lord to revive the market and this could be a valuable opportunity. Although mere disuse may lead to the extinction of some franchises such as a right of ferry, that does not appear to be the case with markets although presumably if the owner was not holding one regularly he would not get an injunction to prevent a rival. The Crown may take action to forfeit a market if it is not held.[7] In present times many market franchises are owned by local authorities, which will authorise a local firm of auctioneers to hold the market and give them a lease of the cattle market.

In rare cases a market can only be held on a defined area of land. Where in such a case the franchise holder is not the same person as the landowner of the market place the market will be an affecting franchise (16.9) governed by Schs 1 and 3, para 9 to the Land Registration Act 2002. The right should be protected before the first registration or disposition of land after 13 October 2013 by noting on the register of title or by caution as discussed in 25.9. If, as is more usual, the market can be held anywhere in the franchise area, many

---

[7]   The point does not seem to have been decided. In *Manchester Corporation v Peverley* (1876) 22 Ch D 294, reported in a note to *Manchester Corporation v Lyons* (1883) LR 22 Ch D 287, Little V-C indicated *obiter* that this was the case.

potential sites will belong to different owners. The Land Registry view is that where the market place is not fixed, it will be a relating franchise, so the issue will not arise. It says:[8]

> there is strong authority for the view that a market franchise will be a relating franchise. Even if the market franchise relates to an area that can still be defined, it does not appear to give the franchise-holder the right to enter the land without the landowner's consent,[[9]] and so does not confer property rights adversely affecting the title to any estate or charge.

The point about a defined area confuses the restrictive monopoly right to prevent others holding a market with the positive right to enter and hold it and may not be correct. It would therefore be prudent to lodge a caution or notice. In addition to being a franchise under para 10 of Schs 1 and 3, as markets and fairs are listed in the Law of Property Act 1922, Sch 12, para (5) they may also be manorial rights within para 10. That corresponds to the view of the Land Registry.[10] If so they may need to be protected on that ground as well as being franchises.

If the place is not fixed then, as the Registry says, there will be no defined land bound by the lord's rights and therefore no need to register to protect the positive right. However, to the extent that the market constitutes a restrictive right to prevent others from holding a concourse of buyers and sellers, it is possible that a proprietor of land within the franchise limits may argue that if the rights are not entered on his title he will take free of them.

Schedule 12, para (5) to the 1922 Act primarily relates to rights over copyhold land. It may have included fairs and markets because when the lord had the fee simple there was no need for a distinct right to prevent others holding them on copyhold land as it was not possible to have a right over his own land. Once the copyhold was enfranchised, the former tenant might have been able to argue that he acquired the fee in the same condition, that is free of the monopoly, and therefore it was necessary to confirm that the lord's rights continued. Alternatively, the expression 'manorial rights', which mainly comprised various revenues, may have been regarded as including market tolls.

Apart from registering a caution or notice, the market owner will be able voluntarily to register the market right itself as a relating franchise under s 3(1)(c) with its own title, whether or not he has a right of entry.

---

[8] Land Registry Practice Guide 18, *Franchises*.

[9] *Attorney-General v Horner* (1884) 14 QBD 245 at 254–5, 260; affd (1885) 11 App Cas 66 HL.

[10] Land Registry Practice Guide 66, *Overriding interests losing automatic protection in 2013*, par 4.6.3.2; see 9.5.

Market rights are normally regarded as appurtenances of the manor so that, unlike some franchises such as free warren,[11] it appears they will pass under general words which include franchises. This would be on the basis that they are frequent annexures to manors, their revenues are regarded as manorial rights and they would pass with a manor. They can, however, easily be severed to become rights in gross.

21.3   OPEN PLACES AND STREETS

Many open spaces in towns have no obvious owner. Some are registered as common land or town greens. Often such land is waste of the manor and is vested in the lord.

In practice, it was common to hold a market in one particular place even if there was no obligation to do so. The market place normally belonged to the owner of the franchise. In *Gloucestershire County Council v Farrow*[12] (16.8) Mr Farrow was assumed, for the purpose of argument, to be the owner of the market place and even though he had lost the right to hold a market he still had the other rights of an owner. Although the surface of a public highway is vested in the highway authority, the owner still has the subsoil and airspace. If a council wished to construct a pedestrian underpass or an electricity company wished to put a substation beneath the market place they would need to obtain the rights from the owner of the soil, usually the lord of the manor. Indeed, the same is true of any street or area within a town. Although the owner of the land beside the road may apply the presumption that he has title to the subsoil up to the middle (6.6), that does not always apply, particularly in towns which were deliberately laid out. House owners simply acquired title to their plots and the roads were left as manorial waste. There are many other areas such as racking lands where weavers spread out their cloth, mills and millpools (17.3).

In a few instances the lord owned the town walls and ditches and may still own the space left by their levelling or infilling. Many town defences were taken down in the seventeenth or eighteenth centuries and the resulting space laid out as gardens or public walks. Such amenities are usually maintained by the borough council but that is not conclusive of ownership. If a new street or car park is to be built across the area the lord may be able to claim compensation, although if there was a specific grant of murage to the borough corporation, that could have carried the freehold in the defences.

---

[11]   *Morris v Dimes* (1834) 1 Add & E 654, 110 ER 1357.

[12]   [1985] 1 WLR 741, [1982] 2 All ER 1031, (1984) 48 P&CR 85.

21.4   HOUSES

The lord may have rights over houses, shops and other buildings in the town. At the time of *Domesday Book* some town houses were held as outliers of manors (1.4). However, most houses ceased to be treated as parts of distant manors within a few years. Where the lord laid out a new town, the soil originally belonged to him. He might dispose of the land freehold or on lease.

Early houses in towns were held by a special form of freehold tenure called burgage. By the time Littleton wrote his book in or soon after 1474 this had become a form of socage but originally it was more like a lease. It had two special features: that a money rent was paid to the lord, and that burgage tenements could be left by will. The reason may have been that townsmen had commercial interests such as a workshop or shop and it would not necessarily be right for such properties to pass to an eldest son on the owner's death. Most burgage was held of the king especially in the older towns that had no lord. Rents were small and have not been collected for centuries. Where the burgesses obtained a charter and became a corporation they often commuted the burgage rents for a lump sum at the same time.

When Parliament came into existence the House of Commons comprised knights of the shire and burgesses. The knights came to be chosen at the county court by freeholders with lands worth 40 shillings a year or more. Two burgesses were chosen for each borough. Initially it was up to the sheriff to decide which of the boroughs in his shire should send members to Parliament[13] but soon certain towns sent representatives to Westminster. This was at first seen as an unwelcome burden as it involved expense, absence for a long period and the risk of getting caught up in dangerous national politics. Later it became a valued privilege.

The method of selecting members varied within the boroughs. Generally, a small group, perhaps the freemen or the mayor and council, chose the two members, although very occasionally election was made by all the inhabitants. The system was open to abuse whereby a dominant landowner could control the election of a rotten borough. In some boroughs, election was by burgage, so that the occupiers of particular houses chose the members. If the landowner controlled the house (since it was freehold he would not own it) he could ensure that the occupiers voted as he wished or risk eviction or loss of employment.

In the eighteenth century great landowners came to hold substantial interests in certain towns. The manor comprising a rotten borough could be bought and sold

---

[13]   Butt, R, *A History of Parliament, the Middle Ages* (Constable, 1989) 123.

for a large sum. In 1832 Parliament passed the great Reform Bill. The
Representation of the People Act 1832 changed the nature of elections and,
although a prominent local family might still have influence to select their own
candidate, they no longer had control. They might however still continue to own
the former town estate as an investment; and some country families still have
properties in the local borough.

As towns expanded in the nineteenth century it was the local landowners who
provided the land. Freehold land was sold for building but many freehold plots
were small. Although copyholds could be freely sold, by general custom the
copyholder could not, without the lord's consent, build or pull down a house to
redevelop the site. As a result, lords controlled the growth of towns. Some
demesne land was sold outright for a lump sum but other methods of sale
existed and still affect property rights.

One method was to sell the freehold but impose a restrictive covenant for the
benefit of the land which the seller retained.[14] This was an early form of private
town planning. The restrictions provided that any house should be erected at no
less than a minimum cost to ensure that it was of a standard sufficient for the
proposed neighbourhood, and the terms of sale prescribed a building line to
ensure that the houses were built behind open front gardens. Typical covenants
prevented unsocial uses such as a fried fish shop or tripe shop. They might
prohibit auction sales at the house or the holding of dissenters' meetings. All
sorts of extraordinary restrictions could be imposed depending on the personal
views of the landowner or developer and what the market would accept. For
modern purposes the most important were those which restrict alterations to a
house, either at all or without the plans being approved by the seller or his
successors, or which prevent additional houses from being built in the often
substantial garden. Where rights to give consent still exist they can be valuable.
Under s 84 of the Law of Property Act 1925 the owner of a house may be able
to apply to the Upper Tribunal (Lands Chamber) for a covenant to be lifted or
varied if it is obsolete or serves no useful purpose. However, since that course
may be expensive or the application refused, it is often cheaper and quicker to
buy consent from the descendant of the original landowner.

Another method of sale was to sell the freehold for a rentcharge. If building land
was worth £200 an acre and 10 houses could be fitted on the acre, and if the
£200 when invested in government stock might produce £10 per year, then the
landowner might agree with the builder to sell him the acre for a rentcharge of
£10. The builder put up the houses, sold them for a lump sum and divided the

---

[14]   See generally Newsom, GL, *Preston & Newsom's Restrictive Covenants affecting Freehold
       Land* (Sweet & Maxwell, 9th edn, 1998).

rentcharge among them. Rentcharges can now be redeemed under the Rentcharges Act 1977 (14.5) but many still exist.

The third method of sale was a combination of the above but using a long lease for 99 or 999 years. The landowner agreed with the builder to erect the houses. The builder did so and called on the landowner to grant a lease either to himself or to the purchaser and the landlord received his £1 per year per house as rentservice not rentcharge. Hundreds of thousands of houses were built using this method and the leases are still running. The landowner not only got his annual return but also had the benefit of covenants in the lease.

Where the lease was for 99 years the landlord's heirs expected to get the house back at the end of the term. By the 1960s this was a problem, especially in South Wales. Although householders had the right to stay in occupation under Part I of the Landlord and Tenant Act 1954 they had to pay a full rent, not just a ground rent. Parliament passed the Leasehold Reform Act 1967 (subsequently much amended) which applied to the whole of England and which allows long leaseholders to purchase the freehold as a modern form of enfranchisement. As a result, the great Victorian housing estates have been broken up. Nowadays, many landowners see no point in retaining fragments of the estates commanding rents not worth the cost of collection and ground rents are going the way of quitrents. Although the rules affecting these housing estates are not strictly part of the law of the manor, many were administered in manorial units. The (often hundreds of) counterpart leases in estate offices are frequently contained in deed boxes labelled by manor or the counterpart lease themselves are headed 'Manor of ...' indicating how those who drew them up saw the situation.

Even though these houses themselves are now of little value to the heirs of the former landowner, most estates had open spaces, common gardens, roadside verges and other similar features. Just as they create incidental value in villages for the lord so likewise when they are found in old housing estates they may also be worth something. It would be unusual for such rights to be annexed to a manor as such. The houses would normally have been built on demesne land, or on former waste, and title to the land would devolve in its own way; but occasionally it and a manor may pass together.

21.5   CORPORATIONS, TRUSTS AND CHARITY

The inhabitants of a town or village might seek to claim collective enjoyment of rights such as grazing or fishing. These are profits and therefore cannot be enjoyed as customary rights by an undefined and fluctuating class of people

(4.4) but sometimes the inhabitants were able to establish them through a device such as a trust.

In *Goodman v Mayor of Saltash*[15] (12.7) in 1882 the House of Lords got round the problem of ascribing a legal origin to the right of an undefined class of local people to take oysters from the River Tamar by presuming the existence of a local trust of which the Saltash Corporation were trustees for the benefit of the inhabitants. The corporation was a legal person capable of holding a profit in gross and on trust. The solution was ingenious and may have derived from the well-established practice of the homage acquiring the manor through trustees. However, it has not been much applied in other cases and in *Lord Fitzhardinge v Purcell*[16] an attempt to develop the idea was rejected.

A corporation would of course primarily hold rights on behalf of its own freemen. Sections 87 to 89 of the Inclosure Act 1845 provided that where the freemen, burgesses or householders as a class had rights of common then the valuer could allot land to two or more trustees nominated by them and the trustees would hold that land on behalf of the freemen or others. The allotment could then be leased and the rents divided among them. If the land was sold the trustees had to invest the proceeds and divide the income. Under the rule against perpetuities it is possible to bring most trusts to an end after a limited period of time, although in this case the trustees are better regarded as nominees on behalf of the corporation rather than a trust in the normal sense.

However, one type of trust can exist in perpetuity and that is a charitable trust. It followed that where such a communal trust existed the law often regarded it as set-up for charitable purposes. An example of land or rights held originally for freemen relates to the Huntingdon charities in *Peggs v Lamb*.[17] In 1205 King John confirmed certain privileges to the burgesses of Huntingdon, who must have been incorporated by then. The freemen had certain rights over lands nearby. When the borough was reorganised under the Municipal Corporations Act 1835 there were two separate sets of properties and in 1910 both of these were recognised as charities. One was the Huntingdon Commons for the Benefit of Freemen and the Widows of Freemen in the Ancient Borough of Huntingdon and the other was the Lammas Rights in the Ancient Borough of Huntingdon. The number of freemen and widows diminished over the years. In 1900 there were 34 but by 1990 there were only 15. The income, partly from land but more from the proceeds of sale of land, was by then considerable.

---

[15] (1882) 7 App Cas 633.

[16] [1908] 2 Ch 139.

[17] [1994] Ch 172, [1994] 2 All ER 15. See also *Hitchin Cow Commoners Trust v Hyde* [2001] EWHC 464 (Ch).

In the case in 1993 the court rejected the argument put forward on behalf of the freemen that they were entitled to the exclusive benefit of the charities. It is not clear if the freemen actually wanted the money or whether the court directed that arguments be put forward on their behalf so that all aspects should be considered. In the event it was decided that the class of beneficiaries of the charities be extended from just the freemen to the inhabitants of Huntingdon as a whole. This is consistent with a trend that ancient rights of no current value should be converted to modern ideas of public benefit.

Chapter 22

Fees, Honours and Estates

22.1   FEUDALISM

The manor existed in the context of the country as a whole, not just alongside the vill, parish and town. This chapter considers a legal structure that was so closely bound in with the manor that it cannot be separated. It must, however, be distinguished. It is the fee, and what is traditionally called the feudal system of which it formed part.[1] The word 'fee' has several legal meanings; in this context it relates to tenure. Tenures were described in 5.2 and could be of three different types: military, ecclesiastical or base. The special feature of the feudal structure was military. It is necessary to consider the origin of fees, how they were combined in a hierarchy of honours and how they now exist. If the lord was at the summit of the little society within the manor, he was at the base of a greater system which extended up to the king.

The ramifications of lordship, homage and allegiance governed what we would call foreign policy, the relations between the rulers, great and small, of Western Europe, their alliances in war and their support in peace. That is beyond the scope of a book about manors, but it should be borne in mind that the lord in his manor house knew himself to be part of a legal structure that bound kings and emperors. The King of Scotland owed homage to the King of England for Huntingdon, the King of England owed it to the King of France for Normandy or Aquitaine, and the status of Brittany or Burgundy was unfathomable.

The word 'feudal' is a late coinage and was not used at the time the feudal system is supposed to have existed in the eleventh and twelfth centuries. The Latin word was *feudum* anglicised as feu, fee or fief. It was used to describe

---

[1]   There is substantial literature on the feudal system: Bloch, M, *Feudal Society* (English translation by LA Manyon) (Routledge Kegan Paul, 1961) is much cited and is clear and readable; Poly, J-P and Bournazel, E, *The Feudal Transformation 900–1200* (Holmes and Meier, 1991) covers developments in France from a traditional viewpoint. For a contrary interpretation, see Reynolds, S, *Fiefs and Vassals* (Oxford University Press, 1994).

something granted in return for services, the fee as we would say. It usually took the form of land but could be money or other rights. Fiefs developed as part of a way of government, incorporated by the relationships of homage and fealty (discussed in 18.1), but this was simply part of the law of the land. In England it was far from being any sort of separate system. On the Continent the perception was different. In the middle of the twelfth centuries a number of treatises, later collectively known as the *Libri Feudorum*, were written in northern Italy,[2] setting out rules of tenure; these eventually led over much of Europe to a distinct set of legal rules known as feudal law, but this did not extend to England which by then already had its own legal system.

The word 'feudal' in English is encountered in the sixteenth century; and in the seventeenth century appears in the Tenures Abolition Act 1660 as 'feodal' (referring to the right of peers to sit in the House of Lords). An instance of the use of the word by a judge occurs in 1695 in *The Lord Gerard v The Lady Gerard*[3] where Holt CJ said: 'Feudal baronies were when the King, in the creation of the baronies, gave lands and rents to hold of him for the defence of the realm.' Later cases have used it in a wider and often undefined sense. It is therefore a word in current legal use but it can hardly be a term of art. In contrast to Scotland, where the expression had a clear meaning until the enactment of the Abolition of Feudal Tenure etc (Scotland) Act 2000 (23.5), there were no specific feudal rights in England. The coinages 'feudalism' and 'feudal system' are nineteenth century and their general use may owe much to the influence of the theories of Marx and Engels.

It should be appreciated that the words are employed in a variety of very loose senses. For instance, politicians often describe the nineteenth-century system of landlord and tenant as feudal. Thus, in October 1995 the Labour Party issued a paper entitled *An end to feudalism* proposing leasehold reform in blocks of flats.[4] The expression is used there rhetorically but incorrectly since the commercial relationship between the landlord of a building and the lessee of a flat is based on contractual arrangements which, however unfair they may be perceived to be, are far removed from the arrangements of homage and fealty between a baron and his knights.

After the election of the Labour Government, the proposals led to the Commonhold and Leasehold Reform Act 2002. That Act also created a new form of freehold ownership and the relationship between the owner of a unit in a commonhold and the commonhold association in some respects corresponds to

---

[2]   See generally Reynolds *op cit* 215 ff.

[3]   (1695) 1 Salk 253, 91 ER 222.

[4]   Dobson, F and Rainsford, N, *An End to Feudalism – Labour's new leasehold reform programme*, Labour Party, October 1995.

a form of tenure, including, in s 49(3), an equivalent to a right of escheat if the commonhold is redeveloped. It therefore created a new type of fee rather than ending such arrangements. That can hardly be what the authors of the paper had in mind.

Having said that, the words 'feudal' and 'feudalism' and the expression 'the feudal system' are widely used, including by some judges, and it will be convenient to do so here. The law has, over the years, developed and been interpreted in the light of what lawyers believed had happened and the way they thought previous generations had understood their rights at earlier times. It is therefore necessary to recognise the accepted account, however mistaken it may have been. It should not be taken as describing what modern historians think happened, or how people who lived in the eleventh century saw matters, but as a legal description of how later generations understood the past in order to justify their later rights (se 27.4). It was developed in periods up to the eighteenth century by lawyers who had little understanding of history in the modern sense and who based their explanation of then contemporary systems of landholding on what they understood or misunderstood of ideas worked out in the Middle Ages.

22.2 DEVELOPMENT AND INTRODUCTION OF FEUDALISM

The feudal system is said to have emerged out of the collapse of the Carolingian Empire. Carolingian ideas were themselves derived from those of the late Roman Empire. Emperors had as their senior assistants men with the title *comes* or companion. The companions of the emperor were available for any important task – to command an army, govern a province or run a department of state. The title survived and when Charlemagne revived the empire he used such men, called *comte* in French or *Graf* in German, to govern his realms. Charlemagne gave a count jurisdiction over an area known as a county and made him responsible for justice and local defence. Originally counts were men from another part of the empire and were moved on every few years; but later the office became hereditary in local aristocratic families. To support the costs of his administration a count received the revenues from royal lands in the county. This was known as a benefice. The concept seems to have originated in a grant of Church lands at the request of the king to a secular lord for a limited time, but later it came to have a wider meaning. The benefice was held as a fief from the emperor (or later a king or another lord) in return for performing these governmental services. Lands in benefice were distinguished from his inherited family lands which the count owned outright or allodially (24.3).

Thus, a count had two types of land: his allodial property and his benefice held from the king by service. He would need little of either for his own direct exploitation and both were occupied by tenants who paid rents or gave services in labour and produce. Around his lands, but within the county, were other allods, some being the estates of other aristocrats, others being the farms of smallholders. The count ran his county on the same model as the empire. He granted land as fiefs to his followers or vassals as benefices to be held in fee in return for services. Some of the land was granted out of his allod, some out of his benefice. He held courts for his tenants to take their advice and decide disputes between them. As royal or imperial representative he held courts for people generally. As lord he held separate courts for his vassals. In much of the Continent these two originally distinct jurisdictions tended to become confused, much as the court leet and court baron did in English manors.

In the ninth century Europe suffered invasions by Saracens, Vikings and Magyars. Any might strike without warning. There was not the wealth or the administrative structure to organise a common defence on the lines of the Roman legions which had guarded the frontiers. Instead, defence was in depth and every valley and settlement had its strong point, which became a castle. No region was exempt from attack – some were vulnerable to two or all three of the invaders. Furthermore, in uncertain times counts and other lords became effectively independent rulers and fought their neighbours. When an attack came the count would gather his vassals who held from him and owed him services and protect and defend them and their lands. Each of them likewise called on their own subtenants. Allodial holders were protected, if at all, secondarily. A man without a lord was without help. So long as royal courts continued to function he could appeal to them, but where a count established his own courts for his followers an allodial landholder might find it difficult to get justice. Consequently, he was under pressure to commend himself to a more powerful lord, to accept that lord's protection, and to acknowledge that his own lands had become held as a fief. As a result much land became held by tenure but the process was piecemeal, far from universal and the terms of each tenure might vary.

England had a different history and this led to different institutions. The numerous small Anglo-Saxon kingdoms were destroyed by the Vikings in 874. When King Alfred and his son Edward and grandson Athelstan beat the Vikings back the result was to form a single kingdom of the English. Under Edward the Confessor it was divided into large earldoms which might have developed into the equivalent of counties. However, the earls did not try to become independent but instead competed to dominate the whole kingdom. When the Confessor died in 1066 the most powerful earl was Harold.

When William defeated Harold at Hastings he took over a single realm which, by contemporary standards, was centrally controlled, and he strengthened that control. The experiences of his youth (5.4) encouraged him in that. To run and hold down a conquered country he introduced the familiar structure of fiefs. Although many historians consider that there were institutions in England which resembled those on the Continent, the words used (in English rather than French or Latin) were not the same and it seems unlikely that such underlying theories as existed were as complete. The Normans were therefore able to introduce a developed system and apply it with a thoroughness unknown in the lands where it had evolved. It was possible to establish more-or-less standard terms of tenure for all fiefs and to order them in a recognised hierarchy headed by the king, with no allodial land and a common system of law, at least as applied to the greater tenants.

All the lands of King Edward were now William's, and all the lands of Harold and his followers who had fought at Hastings were forfeit to him. During William's reign Saxon lords rebelled and he forfeited their lands too. By the time of *Domesday Book* there were few Saxon landowners left, and none of any power. William was careful in how he granted out the lands, and this is set down in *Domesday*. The book was compiled in 1086 at the end of his reign, but it claims to record conditions not only at that time but also *tempore Regni Edwardi* on the day in 1066 'when King Edward was alive and dead'. It assumed that England was then already divided into manors and that those manors had later been granted to William's followers.

22.3   NATURE OF CROWN GRANTS

The underlying rules concerning Crown grants were examined in 1992 in the Australian case of *Mabo v Queensland*.[5] That case concerned the Murray Islands off the coast of Queensland. They are occupied by native people who have their own ancestral (customary or allodial) garden land handed down the generations. In 1879 the islands were annexed by the Crown to Queensland. The government of Queensland argued that the 1879 annexation extinguished all native titles so that it, as exercising Crown rights, was free to dispose of the land. If it did so, it could grant that land to be held by tenure under common law. The High Court of Australia did not agree. It considered that the passing of sovereignty to the Crown did not of itself extinguish customary native titles. The Crown could grant the land to others, and in large parts of Australia that had happened, but if it did not do so the native titles persisted under the Crown's radical title.

---

[5]   (1992) 66 ALJR 408.

The High Court considered that in England the doctrine of tenure stems from the premise – perhaps a fiction – that after 1066 William the Conqueror granted all the land to his tenants in chief, but in Australia that did not happen. The High Court's analysis of the Australian position most likely reflects English experience although the concepts may be older. By 1066 most, perhaps all, land of the greater subjects was bookland which derived from a grant or confirmation in a royal charter or *bok* (2.2–2.3). This applied equally to Church lands as to lay lords. After 1066 much land continued to be held by ancient title and the monasteries carefully preserved and copied their charters until the Dissolution. Most customary lands occupied by peasants (both those that became villein and later copyhold tenements and socage) were undisturbed. It was principally the lands of leading laymen that were redistributed.

Lawyers in later generations came to presume that all lands lay ultimately in royal grant, and under the law as it developed that was the main basis for the jurisdiction of the royal courts. William granted the lands as fiefs in benefice and it came to be accepted that all titles, including those of the Church and of free socmen, had a similar origin. All land in England (save for Crown land) is now held in fee. The word 'benefice' was therefore not needed in its Continental sense and came to refer only to the special type of holding of a clergyman. Although *Domesday Book* records a few private allods, none survived. Crown land was not subject to tenure. If it has been retained since the time of William I, such as Windsor or the Tower of London or foreshore, it is referred to as allodial land, although most Crown land is now held in fee (24.3).

22.4   HONOURS

Instead of working out new arrangements after the Conquest, it was simpler for William to grant the lands of a single Saxon lord, known as the *antecessor*, to one of his followers, who took over the whole estates, often scattered throughout England, as a block. For example, *Domesday Book* shows Geoffrey de Mandeville as holding numerous manors in 1086. Many of those in 1066 had belonged to a Saxon theign, Asgar the Marshall, who had held lands dotted through 10 shires. Asgar was therefore Geoffrey's *antecessor* or predecessor, even though Geoffrey, as a follower of William, was in no sense his heir. This succession was so important that when, for example, Geoffrey claimed the manor of Clapham,[6] then in Surrey, his title was disputed because the manor had not previously belonged to Asgar. The lands were held on the same terms as before Hastings so that, for example, if under *trinoda necessitas* the *antecessor*

---

6   *Domesday Book*: Surrey 36b.

was responsible for repairing a bridge, then the Norman successor was also responsible.

Groups of manors were known as honours or baronies. The lands held by one vassal did not usually lie together in one place but were scattered over the country. Partly this was because of the preceding pattern of Saxon landholding, but it seems also to have been royal policy. Barons may even have chosen to have their manors scattered for insurance reasons, to spread the risks. Just as a modern stockbroker will recommend a balanced portfolio, so that if, for example, banking shares do badly an investment in chemicals may do well, the same principles applied in the Middle Ages, when land was the best investment. If it was a wet year the West might be flooded out but the East have a good harvest. If it was cold the North might suffer but the South be spared. Equally, it was unlikely that both Welsh and Vikings would raid in the same year. Using the same principle the lands of tenants within a manor were spread out in valleys and on heights, on north-facing and south-facing hills, on clay and sand.

An honour is a number of manors that devolve together. The word 'honour' (apart from its connection with honourable conduct) is nowadays more often associated with public recognition through the grant, in the Honours List, of public dignities, the Order of the British Empire or of the Bath, or of titles of nobility; but in the present context it has a different meaning.

Honours are also called baronies. A barony now has no connection with a baron and owning a barony does not confer any personal title let alone any rights associated with hereditary peers (23.3). However, it reflects the origins of many honours. In legal theory the king made a grant of manors to a baron who undertook to provide, say, five knights for the king's wars. The honour might be able to support more than that and, if so, the surplus was at the baron's disposal. He could keep the whole honour in hand and supply the knights from his own household if he wished or, as explained below, he might subinfeudate part to his knights who would hold their lands from him and retain the rest as demesne manors (which themselves contained demesne, freehold, villein and waste land). The initial significance of honour was tenurial, so that lesser lords held their manors from the baron but, over the years, freehold tenure ceased to be significant. Now the meaning of the word applies to demesne manors.

The honour was therefore originally, in theory, a strictly feudal arrangement for the provision of military service to the king based on the Continental model of benefices, but it soon became involved with the laws relating to holding, buying and selling land. After *Quia Emptores* it was no longer possible to subinfeudate in fee simple so that no new honours could come into existence save by statute; and with escheats, forfeitures and mere forgetfulness, tenure became simpler.

For many purposes it ceased to matter if a lord of a manor held from a baron or earl or direct from the king. In particular he ceased to be bound to attend or take his disputes to his lord's court. The honour court also lost its functions as cases could be transferred to the shire court or the royal court. The tenurial aspect ceased to be important. Instead, the meaning shifted so that a wealthy and often noble lord who had a number of demesne manors in hand regarded them as comprising an honour.

At the end of the Middle Ages the great noble families were able to concentrate power, wealth and honours in a very few hands. Many of these families were killed off or forfeited their lands in the Wars of the Roses and the process was completed by Henry VII and Henry VIII, who also took the monastic lands on the Dissolution. The result was that most functioning honours passed to the Crown. Henry VIII did establish the Honour of Ampthill by an Act of 1542, which was an exception. Although in principle there would seem no objection to the Crown combining manors in an honour at common law and infeudating the honour, this does not seem to have occurred. While this may have been because it was uncertain how far new freehold tenures could be created, it is more likely that the Crown wished to preserve seigniorial revenues such as wardship, rather than grant the potential right to a favoured baronial courtier.

Seen as a superior interest an honour may not have had any direct assets. *Crown Estate Commissioners v Roberts*[7] concerned a claim by Mr Roberts to have acquired the lordship marcher of St David's in Wales. Such a dignity was similar in some ways to that of an honour. Lewison J concluded that the effect of the Tenures Abolition Act 1660 in converting all freehold tenures (except frankalmoign) to free and common socage was to remove all the fruits of tenure *in capite* of the Crown. The consequence for the claimed right of lord marcher (which in the case was found to have been abolished) was that even if it had existed it would not carry any rights with it. Of course, an honour might not be held *in capite*; it could in principle be held of another honour but such cases must be rare. In *The Countess Dowager of Pembroke v The Earl of Burlington*[8] where there was a claim for certain jurisdictional rights for a manor court, the right was compared with that of a honour and it was said 'honours have more large incidents, than manors have', presumably on the basis that an honour court had originally had a superior jurisdiction to that of the courts of the manors comprised in it.

There were also ecclesiastical honours including abbeys and bishoprics. Most were endowed with estates to provide an income. Sometimes a bishop held a

---

[7]   [2008] EWHC 1302 (Ch), [2008] All ER (D) 175 (Jun).

[8]   (1676) Hardres 423, 145 ER 529.

manor in right of a particular office, such as a prebend,[9] in which case the bishop for the time being as corporation sole was the lord.[10] The same may not have been true of abbeys where the manors were held by a corporation aggregate comprising the abbot and chapter. At the Dissolution lands of abbeys passed to the Crown. As discussed in 20.10 bishops had the status of barons and their estates were baronies or honours. The manors forming the episcopal endowment passed automatically from one bishop to his successor.[11] In general bishops retained their estates until the nineteenth century and they are now held by the Church Commissioners. Bishops sit as the equals of barons in the House of Lords. However, now that episcopal lands have passed to the Church Commissioners, those honours have dissolved (20.10).

A few lay honours appear still to subsist. One was the Barony of Gilsland in Cumberland (which included the manors of Irthington and Brampton and 500 tenants). In 1881 it was found in the case of *Doe d Earl of Carlisle v Towns*[12] that a custom existed that copyhold land passed by conveyance not surrender and admission, and the custom applied throughout the honour. A notable survivor was the Honour of Clitheroe in Lancashire, once a possession of the Duchy of Lancaster but given in 1660 by Charles II to George Monck, first Duke of Albemarle and held in the early part of this century by the Clitheroe Estate Company[13] (14.8). Clitheroe was said originally to comprise some 28 manors as well as other land. Some of the manors which had been sold in the seventeenth and nineteenth centuries were repurchased in the twentieth. Although on the principles in *R v Duchess of Buccleugh*[14] they could not have been reinstated as part of a legal honour in the sense of being subject to a superior tenure, they were apparently administered along with and formed part of the honour in the sense of devolving with the other manors.

Finally the Crown itself has some honours. The two Royal Duchies of Lancaster and Cornwall are honours and include within them subsidiary honours such as the honour of Pickering and the honour of Launceston, as well as manors.

---

[9] *Doe d North v Webber* (1837) 3 Bing New Cas 922, 132 ER 666.

[10] *Dyke v Bishop of Bath and Wells* (1715) VI Bro Parl Cas 365, 2 ER 1136.

[11] Scriven, J, *A Treatise on the Law of Copyholds* (Butterworth & Co, 7th edn by Archibald Brown, 1896) 2.

[12] (1831) 2 Barn & Adol 585, 109 ER 1260.

[13] *Encyclopaedia Britannica* (Cambridge University Press, 11th edn, 1911): Clitheroe.

[14] (1704) 6 Mod 150, 87 ER 909; 1 Salk 358, 91 ER 312.

22.5   KNIGHTS' FEES AND FEUDAL INCIDENTS

Part of the reason for William's victory at Hastings was the quality of his fighters. Military techniques and the breeding of strong horses led to the employment of mounted soldiers, who in English came to be called knights. They were most effectively used in battle in the heavy charge of cavalry (or chivalry) whose massive impact could bowl over any lesser army in their way. If the manor is the product of the eight-ox plough then the fee is the consequence of the stirrup.[15] The invention of the stirrup allowed an armoured rider to stay on his horse while fighting and charging. To be effective he needed heavy armour and for that he needed a strong mount and replacement horses. He also needed a squire to hold his spare weapons, protect his spare horses and help him put on his heavy armour. Further, he needed sophisticated weapons – a steel sword, lance and mace. All this involved a lifetime of training as a professional soldier.

A knight's lifestyle was expensive. A knight could earn his income by serving a baron, which enabled the knight to live in the baron's castle and dine at his table, all at the baron's expense. However, as he grew older and raised a family, the knight would have wanted his own estate. The solution was for the baron to subinfeudate sufficient land to support the knight. Manors varied in the revenues they produced, so a knight's fee did not always correspond to one manor. It might be necessary to combine two or more small manors in a single fee. Alternatively, the baron might grant out a larger manor with good revenues to one knight who might in turn himself subinfeudate part of his manor as a sub-manor to another knight.

Knights' fees were initially intended to provide an income for a fighter and many were granted for life only. A grant of land 'to John' would only give John a life estate; in order to give him a fee simple it was necessary to grant the land 'to John and his heirs'. However, many fees quickly became, and indeed may have been from the beginning, heritable. They became capable of subdivision on sale or inheritance although until *Quia Emptores* any sale by substitution needed the consent of the chief lord (7.3). Early in the twelfth century references to a half or a sixth of a knight's fee appear and later fees could be divided even into fortieths.[16] The importance of this was economic. One source of royal revenue became scutage or shield money which was charged on knights who could not or would not serve in person when summoned to the host. If the fee was held by a widow or a child, scutage enabled an absent knight to be replaced. Eventually scutage became distinct from military service. The tenant of a half fee owed half

---

[15]   See White, L, *Medieval Technology and Social Change* (Oxford University Press, 1962).

[16]   Pollock, Sir Frederick and Maitland, FW, *The History of English Law before the time of Edward I* (Cambridge University Press, 2nd edn, 1898) 273.

the full payment. Long before knight's fees were abolished in 1660 the idea of knightly service in person had become obsolete. The last mustering of the feudal host was in 1385, and then it was purely ceremonial.

Feudalism therefore ceased to have much social or military function. Instead, it became a major source of revenue for the king and, so long as mesne tenancies remained important, for lesser chief lords. The value of scutage as such was eroded by inflation but there were many other aids and incidents. The Tenures Abolition Act 1660, s 1 lists 'wardships, liveries, primer-seizins and ouster-le-mains values and forfeitures of marriages' as well as 'aide pur file marrier and pur faier fitz chevalier'. Of these, wardship was the most resented, enforced by the Court of Wards and Liveries. This was the right of a lord to have the guardianship of a young heir while under age, and therefore to have possession of his lands. There was no concept of trusteeship, and in the hands of the royal exchequer this was a licence to exploit the lands and even commit waste so that when he came of age the heir took on a depreciated inheritance. The wardship was not normally exercised by royal officials directly but was sold to the highest bidder. Livery followed wardship as when the heir came of age he had to pay to take over his estates. Ouster-le-main was similar but for tenants *ut de honore* instead of tenants *in capite* (8.1). Marriage was the right of the lord to compel the heir or heiress to marry a person chosen by him. Primer seizin was due when wardship and livery were not and was the right of the lord when an heir of full age inherited to receive a year's profits of the lands. The two aids were sums of money due when the lord's daughter was married (pur file marrier) or his son was knighted (pur faier fitz chevalier). The Act of 1660 abolished all of these.

The size and content of a knight's fee was considered in *Anthony Lowe's Case*[17] in 1610 which concerned the sub-manor of Alderwasley. Anthony Lowe senior held some 59 acres of the manor by knight service. The manor was itself parcel of the manor of Bewraper. Both manors were held by the Crown as Duke of Lancaster. In 1524 Henry VIII as lord of Alderwasley released the 59 acres from the burdens of knight service such as wardship. In 1528 the king granted to Lowe the manor of Alderwasley, itself to be held of the manor of Bewraper at a rent of £26-10-0d and fealty, but again free of the burdens of knight service. By 1610 his descendant, Anthony Lowe the younger, had inherited the manor and its lands. The case strictly concerned his tenure and whether he held by knight service or socage.

The report does not make it clear why it mattered but the case was in the Court of Wards and it must therefore have involved a royal claim to some incident for land held by military tenure. The argument against Lowe was that when the king granted land it was automatically held by knight service. The court held that that

---

[17]   (1610) 9 Co Rep 122b, 77 ER 909.

would indeed be implied in the normal case, but here the grant by Henry VIII expressly provided that the land and manor should be held by fealty and rent service only, so that the feudal burdens did not apply and the land was therefore held in socage.

In a note on the case Coke also discussed the content of a knight's fee. This may be a general comment or it may have come up in argument. He says that some take the view that a knight's fee comprised eight hides of 100 acres each, but in his view it was a question of value, not of area. A knight's fee had to provide sufficient income to maintain the dignity of a knight. Coke's view appears right. Historically the required income had been £20 a year.[18] The relief (payable by an heir on succession) for such a fee was £5 and the relief for a barony was 100 marks or £66-13-4d (six marks made one pound), so it was said that a barony comprised 13⅓ knights' fees. That is an accident: £5 is 100 shillings and this was a simple increase of figures from shillings to pounds as from knight to baron. An earldom was put at 20 knights' fees, a marquisate at two baronies and a dukedom at two earldoms but these seem artificial since (23.2) dukes and marquesses were late introductions in England when the feudal system was in decline. The Act of 1660 mention reliefs in s 5 which preserves them when already payable for land in socage specifically, but the effect of converting other tenures to socage was to abolish them for land formerly held in knight service. This remained important in relation to copyholds until extinguished under the Law of Property Act 1922.

22.6   COMPLICATIONS OF TENURE

The main purpose of *Quia Emptores* was to prohibit subinfeudation as a means to avoid feudal incidents. One avoidance device was for a father to grant his son a subordinate freehold at a rent of a rose at midsummer. When the father died the chief lord was entitled to his primer seisin of one year's profits, namely one rose. A principal reason for subinfeudation was that it did not need the consent of the chief lord and therefore he could not charge money for giving consent. Another was that if the new tenant died without heirs the seller or his heirs could claim back the land sold by escheat. As a result tenures became ever more complicated. In their book on *Medieval England*[19] Edward Miller and John Hatcher quote the instance of John de Burdeleys who died in 1283:

---

[18]   Pollock and Maitland *op cit* 273; Bracton, Sir Henry (ed), *De legibus et consuetudinibus angliae* (c 1257) (SE Thorne (ed)) (Belknap Press of Harvard University Press, 1977) f 84.

[19]   Miller, E and Hatcher, J, *Medieval England: Rural Society and Economic Change 1086–1348* (Longman, 1978) 174; quoted by permission.

John held Sculton in Norfolk by sergeanty of being the King's larderer. In Cambridgeshire he held at Madingley, Rampton and Cottenham of Gilbert Pecche, who in turn held of the Bishop of Ely; and also in Comberton where he held of Saer of St Andrew who held of the Earl of Wichester and he of the Earl of Gloucester, and in Oakington where he held of Robert Bruce of the honour of Huntingdon. Finally, in Bedfordshirehe held Stagsden of the Abbot of Wardon, Sir William de Mountchesney and the Prior of Newnham, and some of the lands he held of Wardon were held by the abbey from the Beauchamps.

Another example from the time of Edward I is given by Maitland in *The History of English Law*:[20]

Roger of St German holds land at Paxton in Huntingdonshire of Robert of Bedford, who holds of Richard of Ilchester, who holds of Alan of Chartres, who holds of William le Boteler, who holds of Gilbert Neville, who holds of Dervorguil Balliol, who holds of the king of Scotland, who holds of the king of England

The honour of Huntingdon features in both these examples. The King of Scotland held that honour as a fief of the King of England annexed to the Scottish Crown. He owed homage for it and it was partly on that basis that Edward I claimed suzerainty over Scotland.[21] Similar relations between monarchs complicated the diplomacy of Europe.

As discussed in 24.5, the Crown sold lands to be held of the manor of East Greenwich. Although one manor could be held of another, most sub-manors must have arisen by subinfeudation before 1290. It would have been unusual for an existing manor to be granted as held of another and, after *Quia Emptores*, it would not have been possible for a subject to do this although the statute did not bind the Crown. So long as the law was understood and had a real significance that seems to have been Crown practice, at least up to around 1600, but it appears to have changed thereafter. It appears that in 1608 James I granted the manor of Nevilhall in Ulveston in Lancashire known by the name of Newhale to hold of his Majesty's manor of East Greenwich, in the county of Kent but it is possible this was land and not a manor.[22] On 22 March 1648, Parliament, in the absence of the king with whom they had just fought the Civil War, ordered that the manor or Lordship of Flawborowe, in the county of Nottingham, forfeited from the royalist Earl of Newcastle, should be sold to Colonel Edward Whaley

---

[20] Pollock and Maitland *op cit* 233.

[21] Powicke, Sir Maurice, *The Thirteenth Century 1216, 1307* (1991) 594.

[22] See www.myjacobfamily.com; available from Lancashire Record Office.

in satisfaction of money owned to him, 'to be held of the King, as of the Manor of East Greenwich, in the County of Kent'.[23]

A late example concerns Greenwich Hospital which was established in 1694 as a charity for those who had served in the navy. Its affairs were later governed by an Act of 1829.[24] Under an earlier Act various properties were vested in the commissioners of the Hospital and the Act of 1829 provided in s 22 that:

> the said Commissioners of Greenwich Hospital, and their successors, shall hold and enjoy all and singular the said baronies, manors, messuages, lands, tenements, tithes, and hereditaments, and the same shall for ever hereafter be and be deemed to be held of the King's Majesty, his heirs and successors, as of His Majesty's manor of East Greenwich in the county of Kent, by free and common socage tenure.

In the Middle Ages it would have been unusual, if not impossible, for a barony to be held of manor. However, special features may be relevant here. The commissioners were for many purposes regarded as an aspect of the Crown and their estates are now vested in the Secretary of State for Defence on behalf of Her Majesty. Furthermore, it is not too surprising that land relating to Greenwich Hospital should be held of the manor of East Greenwich.

22.7   LEGAL ESTATES

The modern successors to fees and honours are estates. The fee is now represented by the legal estate and the honour by the landed estate. The word 'estate' has many meanings. Its primary meaning is status, as in man's estate. It can mean an area of land owned by one family. It can also mean the property left by an individual on his death, as in free estate. It includes a housing or industrial estate and the business of an estate agent. But its primary meaning in law is the nature of an interest in land. Since 1925 there have been only two legal estates, the fee simple and the term of years or lease.[25]

The details of the law of estates belong to land law and are beyond the scope of this book.[26] In brief, the fee simple is the nearest English law has to absolute ownership – it can be sold, given away, left by will, mortgaged, leased or dealt with in any way. Although *Quia Emptores* prevented subinfeudation in fee

---

[23]   *House of Lords Journal*, Vol 10, 22 March 1648.

[24]   10 Geo IV (c 25).

[25]   Law of Property Act 1925, s 1.

[26]   The most respected textbook is Megarry, Sir R and Wade, H, *The Law of Real Property* (7th edn by Charles Harpum et al, 2008). For material relevant to manors, reference should be made to earlier editions Megarry and Wade.

simple, until 1925 lesser freehold estates could be created out of it. The two principal freehold estates were the life estate (which was not a fee) and the entail or fee tail, which passed automatically to a particular class of descendants, usually the direct male line. It was called tail because it was a *tailli* or cut down fee. *Quia Emptores* only affected fees simple and so life estates and fees tail were held by tenure from the holder of the fee simple. Subsequently, other estates developed, such as conditional fees.

Under the Settled Land Act 1925 life estates and entails have ceased to be legal estates at common law and subsist instead in equity. The tenant for life or tenant in tail in possession held the fee simple but as trustee for himself and others interested under the settlement. The Trusts of Land and Appointment of Trustees Act 1996 provided that new life estates or entails could not be created even in equity. New entails were prohibited altogether and lifetime rights exist only as beneficial interests under a trust of land, where the trustees hold the fee simple in the land.

There is an important distinction between a fee simple in land and a fee simple estate, and confusion between them has led to unnecessary problems. A common freeholder of land or a manor held the fee simple of it. In that sense the copyholder (whether pure copyholder or customary freeholder) did not have the fee simple of the land, which was in the lord. All land (except allodial Crown land) has a fee simple somewhere even though it may be a remote interest of little value. In the case of ancient parish consecrated land, the fee simple is said to be in abeyance (20.6).

As discussed in 5.4 some copyholders held a customary freehold, sometimes described as a fee simple. Even a pure copyholder who held at the will of the lord could, however, have a fee simple interest in his copyhold and this concept seems to date back to 1482.[27] If he did (and it was not a copyhold for years or for life) he could sell, mortgage or deal with the copyhold as owner. This may have had to be done by surrender and admittance but he could compel the lord to admit. Similarly, he could settle the copyhold on terms that his widow had a life interest and his son after her. In that case the widow had a life interest in the copyhold. That was different from the widow having freebench according to the custom of the manor or a copyhold for life. Where the copyholder made no special provision the customary rights may have taken effect, but if provision were made the widow had a life interest derived out of a fee simple interest in the copyhold even though her husband had not had a fee in the land. The words 'fee simple' used in this sense are known as words of limitation.

---

[27] See YB Hil 21 Edward 4; cited in Gray, CM, *Copyhold, Equity, and the Common Law* (Harvard University Press, 1963) 56.

This issue confused even the greatest lawyers. One of the longest disputes was whether an entailed interest could subsist in a copyhold. The question arose because entails were created under the statute *De Donis* 1285 which was long after 1189. How, it was asked, could a customary tenant hold land under a post-1189 Act? Even Coke saw problems, for the question was whether an entail 'may by any particular Custome be allowed that I may dispute, but cannot determine; for it is *vexata quaestio*, much controverted, but nothing concluded'.[28] But this misses the point. By Coke's time, copyholds (other than those for life or for years) had become tenements of inheritance. The custom of the manor might, of course, prescribe that on death, and disregarding any former surrender to the uses of the copyholder's will, the copyhold had to descend in a particular way. But the copyholder could dispose of his copyhold in his lifetime as he wished and so could provide that his property would descend as an entail, and the lord would be bound to admit accordingly.

Similarly, some writers were puzzled by the fact that the lord of the manor, even if he only had a life interest, could admit a copyholder.[29] The question arose because someone with a life estate could voluntarily only grant an interest for his life. He could sell the land but the purchaser's title would end when he died. If he leased the land the lease would expire when he died. Why then, it was asked, could a lord with a limited interest nevertheless validly admit a copyholder whose rights would survive him? The reason is that the copyholder had a customary right which did not derive from the lord. His right was not affected by the fact that the lord for the time being might only have a life interest or be an interloper or a child.

The distinction between, on the one hand, manorial rights and, on the other, fees and legal estates is illustrated further by *Sir Henry Nevill's Case* (*Goodchrome v Moor*)[30] in 1613, which held that a manor did not need to be held by feudal tenure nor to be freehold but could be held by copy. Sir Henry was lord of the manor of Wargrave which extended into several townships including Warfield. It was claimed there was a sub-manor of Warfield comprising 18 acres held by customary tenure by copy of the roll of the court of Wargrave. In 1586 Sir Henry admitted Robert Albany to the manor of Warfield, who then held it by copy. Alexander Goodchrome claimed to be customary tenant of two acres within Warfield. The question was whether he had a good title because if Warfield was not a manor he could not hold his two acres by copy of court roll of a non-existent manor. The court found in favour of the grant. Although it was

---

[28]   Coke, Sir Edward, *Complete Copyholder* (1630) s 47. See Scriven *op cit* 44; Gray *op cit* 109; Holdsworth, Sir William, *A History of English Law* (Sweet & Maxwell, 3rd edn, 1952) 13 vols 1926–1952, VII.202.

[29]   Watkins, C, *A Treatise on Copyholds* (James Bullock, 4th edn by Thomas Coventry, 1825) 1.31.

[30]   (1613) 11 Co Rep 17a, 77 ER 1166.

unusual, there was no reason why a manor could not itself be copyhold so that the lord could hold courts and do all necessary things. Presumably, although the report does not say so, the free suitors at the court baron would have been customary freeholders. This clarifies the position that manors were not, as such, part of the feudal system or necessarily held in fee. They could be held by any form of common tenure, knightly, ecclesiastical or in socage, and as the case shows, by customary tenure as well. Indeed, on the Continent their counterparts could be held allodially. A manor, fundamentally, is part of an economic system; a fee was part of a military or governmental system.

Manors are now held in fee simple, although it is possible to grant a lease of one. The Law of Property Act 1922, s 128(1), which enfranchised copyholds, refers to 'every parcel of copyhold land' which, on the face of it, does not include a copyhold manor. However, the definition of land in s 188 includes a manor and as the 1922 Act effectively abolished the status of copyhold and Sch 12, para (1)(a) says the land shall be freehold land[31] the effect is that a copyhold manor became freehold.

22.8   LANDED ESTATES

Most groups of manors are now held within landed estates. That term has no defined legal meaning although it is used in innumerable documents. It is often taken to be an area of land with a mansion house, a home farm, tenanted farms, cottages, woods and wastes. It can be any size. In *Greaves v Mitchell*[32] in 1971 the court held that the term could include a farm of 26 acres and some estate agents use it for as little as 10. The great estates can comprise 20,000 acres and in Scotland far more. In London the Grosvenor, Cadogan and other estates are small in acreage but immensely valuable.

Estates became important after honours declined. While an honour might comprise manors scattered over many parts of the country, an estate is more compact. It is not necessarily a continuous stretch of land (although that was the ideal) but is usually within a locality, and within one county or on the edges of adjoining counties. It tends to be held within one family, although not necessarily by one individual, or by an institution. Estates are generally freehold but can include leaseholds and, before 1926, often had copyholds as well. Most ancient estates include the lordships of several manors and, especially in the west of England, the estate was, until recently, administered in manorial units although these were not strictly observed and non-manorial freeholds belonging

---

[31]   Section 133 provides an exception for copyholds for life or for years.
[32]   (1971) 222 EG 1395.

to the family would be administered along with demesne. Their boundaries tend
not to be fixed. Where the estate is on the edge of an expanding town it may
move over the years as land is sold for building and the proceeds invested in
buying new farms on the far edge of the former holding.

In the eighteenth century landed estates were the basis of wealth and power.[33]
By the beginning of the twentieth they began to disintegrate. Reasons included
the agricultural depression, heavy death duties and the desire of landowners to
distribute their property among all their children instead of giving it all to the
eldest son. Often the final stroke was the death of an heir in the Great War. It is
said that a quarter of the farmland of England changed hands in the years
between 1918 and 1922.[34]

Those that survive still perform some of the old functions of the manor,
especially in relation to tenure. The modern estate is organised to rent. Many
have all their land in hand and the farm will sometimes still be called Manor
Farm, but such are better seen as large farms with amenity land rather than as
estates. It is still the case that if land or cottages can be rented it is likely to be
from an estate. So also will quarries, fishing and sporting. If there is a squire he
may have provided the cricket field, sometimes free but often rented to the local
club. He too will still own the waste, the common land and the odd bits and
pieces that do not belong to anyone else, but these will nowadays not be
associated with any particular manor. They will belong instead to the estate and
the squire will not consider himself lord of the manor.

Many estates are still owned by institutions. The Crown Estate and the Royal
Duchies include some estates. The Church Commissioners own others as do
universities and colleges. Modern charities such as the National Trust hold
estates, as do water companies and insurance funds. There are also so-called
land trusts, many of which have been set up to take on family estates. These are
established as charities to benefit from tax exemption and exist to provide rural
education. They tend not to make much profit as estates are expensive to run.
Finally, individuals who have made money in the City, sport or the arts have
bought estates. Estates are therefore far from being extinct but they are no
longer the dominant feature of the countryside they were as little as a century
ago. Few modern estates include lordships and traditional families and
institutions have sold titles to raise money.

---

[33]   Williamson, T and Bellamy, L, *Property and Landscape* (George Philip, 1987) 130.

[34]   Ibid 209. See also the discussions in (2007) 55 *Agricultural History Review*: Rothery, M, 'The
       wealth of the English landed gentry, 1870–1935' 251; Beckett J and Turner, M, 'End of the Old
       Order? 269; Thompson, FML, 'The Land Question, and the burden of ownership in England,
       c.1880–c.1925' 269; Thompson, M, 'The land market, 1880–1925: A reappraisal reappraised'
       289.

Chapter 23

Lords and Titles

23.1   LORD

The expression 'lord of the manor' is used to describe the holder of a right of property in an incorporeal hereditament known as a lordship. A lord of a manor may also be a landlord, that is a person who grants a lease of land to another, usually called a tenant or lessee. The word 'lord' is also used in a different sense to describe a peer of the realm, a person who before the House of Lords Act 1999 was entitled to a writ of summons to advise the sovereign in Parliament.[1] This is in a sense a dignity, that is itself an incorporeal hereditament, in that, until the emergence of life peerages, it descended to the holder's heir, but it is now no longer regarded as a property right.

The word 'lord' derives from Anglo-Saxon *hlaford* formerly *hlaf-weard* or loaf-ward, the keeper of loaves and therefore loaf-giver. The lord kept supplies of bread and gave them to his family and followers. Ultimately, the word may have a simple domestic origin. It was used as the translation of the Latin *dominus*. That also had a domestic origin from *domus* – a house. The *dominus* was master of the house, head of the family, owner of the slaves and farmer of the family land. *Dominus* was also the usual word for 'sir', for instance as used by soldiers to their officers in the army.

In the late Roman Empire it acquired new shades of meaning. The early emperors used various titles including *princeps* (see prince below) and *imperator* which initially meant general but from Domitian onwards to emphasise their power and majesty they called themselves *dominus*, lord of the Empire. This sense of *dominus* passed to the kingdoms that succeeded the empire and when the Carolingian Empire disintegrated in its turn and the powers of the emperor were, under the feudal system, taken over by the nobility,

---

[1]   Blackstone, Sir William, *Commentaries on the Laws of England* I.12.

they too called themselves *dominus*. The feudal relationship, at every level from king and count at the top to knight and sergeant, was between lord and vassal, *dominus* and *vassus* or *vassalus*.

Meanwhile, it retained its old meaning of master or owner. The demesne, *dominicum*, is the land held directly by the lord which he can deal with as he wishes. His lordship over bondsmen was more like the ownership of a slave-master than the protection of a superior. However, as the word was used in various shades of meaning, it became possible by use of the word *dominus* for a serf subject to a master to become a tenant holding from one who was himself a tenant either of a greater lord or of the king.

23.2   HEREDITARY PEERS

In England the word 'lord' acquired the technical meaning of a person who had a hereditary right and duty to be summoned to advise the king in his council. After the formation of Parliament in the thirteenth century the greater landowners (along with the bishops and abbots who were celibate) came to be seen as the House of Lords in contrast to the representatives of the shires and boroughs who made up the House of Commons. For that purpose, the lords were distinct from other free inhabitants of the realm. At times special rules applied to lords; for example, they could be taxed more heavily because they were assumed to be wealthier, they were allowed to wear special clothes or types of material and, because they sat in Parliament in their own right, they could not vote in general elections. However, in general the English aristocracy have, as such, no special powers or duties. Some titles are hereditary; others, increasingly, are not. Lords are known as peers from the Latin *par* or equal since they were equal to one another before the king. There were formerly various types of lords in Parliament comprising earls, barons, dukes, marquesses and viscounts. There are also princes and life peers.

The word 'earl' is Saxon. In early Saxon times freemen were either *eorls* or *ceorls*. The *eorls* were aristocrats and having special privileges. The *ceorls* or churls were the common people. The greater *eorls* were ealdormen, powerful nobles governing shires or great regions, accountable only to the kings. In the tenth century, when the Danes under King Cnut ruled England, the king governed through officials called *jarls*. By around 1050 *jarls* and ealdormen had fused in earls. Earls were seen as the English counterpart of the Continental count, *comte* or *Graf*. These were officials whose origin goes back to the late Roman Empire and who had responsibility for large territories (22.2). William the Conqueror as Duke of Normandy had counts under him and did not want to introduce them into England, although some of his followers who were already counts kept their titles. He gave his leading men the title of earl for their English holdings but as the French title was thought more polite an earl's wife became known as countess. Most earls, even when they took their title from a shire (or county), did not control all of it and had scattered honours.

Both earls and the king granted fiefs to lesser lords called barons. The word 'baron' simply means man: until late in the Middle Ages the normal legal phrase for husband and wife was *baron et feme*. A baron came to mean a man who had done homage for a substantial fief. As discussed in 22.4 a barony or honour refers to a group of manors and the owner of a barony need not be a baron.

The word 'duke' comes from Latin *dux* meaning leader, specifically war-leader or general. In the late Roman Empire dukes were given command of specific areas under threat from external attack. The military commander responsible for the defence of the four provinces of Britain was the *Dux Britanniarum* – the Duke of the Britains. In early Anglo-Saxon times the word was applied to former kings. When a great king (particularly the king of Mercia) gained ascendancy over a formerly independent people the former king, *rex*, became called little king, *regulus*, or even *subregulus*. This happened for example to the Hwicce,[2] once an independent kingdom in the West Midlands. When the sub-king opposed the king of Mercia or rebelled against him or when he died and his son succeeded, his title would be downgraded further to *dux*. On the Continent dukes might be independent rulers owing nominal allegiance to a king or emperor. Normandy was a duchy of this sort and there were others in Italy. Modern surviving independent duchies are Luxemburg and Liechtenstein. William did not establish any dukes in England. The title was recreated in 1377 when Edward III made his son Edward the Black Prince Duke of Cornwall. Since then most dukes have been of royal blood (sometimes, as with the children of Charles II, of the king but not the queen) although some great subjects, such as the Dukes of Marlborough and Wellington, have been raised for special reasons.

'Marquess' is the equivalent of the French *marquis* and the German margrave and means count of the march. Marches were frontier territories. The most important under the Carolingian Empire were on the eastern bounds of Germany, but there were also marches against the Bretons, in Navarre and in Italy. Marches were under the control of a march-lord, who had counts under him. In England there were two marches, with Wales and with Scotland. These were under the lordship of earls palatine, earldoms with special privileges,

---

[2]   Kirby, DP, *The Earliest English Kings* (Routledge, 1991) 12.

of Chester and Durham. This was dangerous since if the marcher lord was powerful enough to defend the frontier he was militarily strong enough to rebel.

Durham became attached to the bishop who had to be celibate and could not found a dynasty. Chester was eventually annexed to the Royal Family and the Prince of Wales is now also Earl of Chester. On the Welsh side of the border several lordships marcher were established – see below. The title of marquess was unknown in England until Richard II created Robert de Vere to be Marquess of Dublin in 1385. The office had no function and has always been ceremonial.

'Viscount' comes from the Latin *vicecomes* and has two meanings. On the Continent the viscount was an assistant to and vassal of the count. In Normandy, William had almost as much trouble with viscounts as with counts and therefore did not want to introduce them into England. However, the Latin word was used to translate the English sheriff or shire-reeve, a royal official in charge of a shire (19.3). Some sheriffs tried to make their post hereditary but did not succeed. The title of viscount was introduced in 1440 when John Lord Beaumont was created Viscount Beaumont in order to give him precedence over barons. Like marquess, it is purely ceremonial and has no function.

In England the title of prince is restricted to close members of the Royal Family and is not hereditary. On the Continent it occurs more widely. It comes from Latin *princeps*. When Augustus founded the Roman Empire he needed a title that would not upset traditionalists and republicans, and *princeps* means simply first (principal) citizen. Prince and princess came to apply to the children of the monarch.

Traditionally, most hereditary titles were entailed in the male line and could not be held by or pass through women, although there were always a few exceptions which passed by tail general. Now there are moves to provide that any title will pass to the eldest child of either sex. The precise way of descent is set out in the original patent which grants the title.

The right was held personally and not attached to land. In the *Berkeley Peerage Case*[3] Lord St Leonards said of the Tenures Abolition Act 1660:

> Not only were all tenures in capite ... taken away, but the lands were for ever turned into free and common socage. How can the Castle and Estate of Berkeley, holden as it now is by free and common socage, and not in capite or in chief, carry

---

[3]   (1861) 8 HLC 21, 11 ER 333.

with it a right in its possessor to sit in this House? It confers upon him just the same right, but no higher than the humblest cottage confers on its owner. The feudal tenure being abolished, of course the privileges annexed or flowing from it have ceased.

and specifically as to the righ to sit in the House:

The right to sit is saved, but it no longer depends upon the tenure which is extinguished. The title of Honor was left as a substantive personal right. The tenure was not saved in the particular instance in order to save the title of Honor, but the title of Honor was itself saved although the tenure was destroyed

In that case Admiral Berkeley was seised of the castle and other hereditaments including the Barony of Berkeley under the will of the late Earl Berkeley, but he had not succeeded to the earldom. There had been a hereditary mediaeval peerage but the line had either become extinct or, as was suggested in the case, had passed to someone unknown. However, the admiral claimed that the right to a writ of summons to the House of Lords passed with the castle and barony. The House held that it was not possible for such a dignity to be annexed to property, not least because the land might be sold, mortgaged or leased and an unsuitable person might thereby be able to purchase the right to sit in the House. Legal authorities made it clear that the right could not be sold. Furthermore, if someone were able to substitute a claim to the hereditary title there might be two persons, one sitting in hereditary right and the other by virtue of holding the castle. That was not acceptable. As indicated below, the law may be different in Scotland or Ireland.

23.3 LIFE PEERS

It had always been the case that some members of the House of Lords only had the right to be there for their life. Originally this applied to bishops and, before the Reformation, to abbots. In a sense this was not a life peerage as such but the grant to a corporation sole to be exercised by the holder for the time being.

Part of the function of the High Court of Parliament used to be as the highest tribunal in the land, exercised through the Judicial Committee of the House of Lords whose members had, of course, to be eminent judges. At one time there were enough judges who were either themselves hereditary peers or who were wealthy enough (perhaps from legal practice) to be raised to the peerage, but during the nineteenth century there were insufficient experienced lawyers among the members or potential members of the House. The Appellate Jurisdiction Act 1876 provided for a small number of eminent judges to be made life peers to carry out the judicial functions of the House. The Constitutional

Reform Act 2005 transferred this jurisdiction from the House to a newly established Supreme Court.

Since the Life Peerages Act 1958, Her Majesty, on the advice of the government, has been able to create life peers, such as retired politicians, or people eminent in public life, business, the arts, religion or simply members of the government or opposition, and all new creations are now for life only.[4] The right of hereditary peers to sit and vote in Parliament has long been considered an anachronism, and in 1999 Parliament passed the House of Lords Act which removed the right of most peers to be a member of the House and therefore to receive a writ of summons. There was a provision, intended to be temporary, that the hereditary peers could elect 92 of their number to represent them. Thus a number of former members who had played an active part in the business of the House continued to do so, but most were excluded.[5]

In *Baron Mereworth v Ministry of Justice*[6] this exclusion was challenged. Lord Mereworth inherited his title in 2002 and in 2010 claimed he had the right to receive a writ of summons. The matter came before a judge on an application to strike out the claim and the judge granted it on the basis that the matter was one for the exclusive jurisdiction of the House Committee for Privileges. However, on the basis that he might be wrong, he considered the substantive claim. Lord Mereworth argued on the basis of his human rights but the argument was not accepted. In particular the judge held that there was no interference with his right to enjoy his possessions because a right to be a member of a national legislature was not protected as such by the Convention. He applied the decision of the European Court of Human Rights in *De la Cierva Osorio de Moscoso v Spain*[7] that a nobiliary title is not a possession for the purposes of the First Protocol to the Convention. That case concerned a claim by the daughters of a Spanish nobleman to succeed in circumstances where the title went under Spanish law to a younger brother and the Court decided that the case was not admissible for hearing. Lord Mereworth also asked for a declaration that his letters patent of nobility were not affected. The judge saw no reason why they might be, but also saw no practical consequence save that the baron was entitled to call himself lord.

The judge did not need to consider the nature of a peerage which presumably still subsists as an incorporeal hereditament, namely a dignity. It is hardly a right

---

[4]	William Whitelaw was created first Viscount Whitelaw in 1983 but as he had only daughters the title ceased on his death in 1999.

[5]	See House of Lords Reform Bill introduced in 2012 session.

[6]	[2011] EWHC 1589 (Ch).

[7]	App Nos 41127/98, 41503/98, 41717/98, 45726/99, 28 October 1999.

of property since it cannot be sold[8] or given away and can only descend to an heir within the letters patent which created it, and even then the recipient can disclaim it. In the Spanish case the Court considered that the fact that the holder of a title might be able to exploit it commercially, for instance by licencing its use as a trade mark, did not make it a possession. In some English family settlements land or other property devolves with a title, but that is a matter of private arrangement save for the few estates settled by Parliament such as Stratfield Saye for the Dukes of Wellington or Blenheim for the Dukes of Marlborough; and even they have power to sell land.[9]

23.4   KNIGHTS, GENTLEMEN AND HONOURABLE

The aristocracy is not limited to peers, but the edges become blurred outside their ranks. The status of esquire and gentleman is now applied generally. Most knighthoods are individually created, although baronetcies are hereditary. Baronets were created in 1611 by James I openly to raise money. They comprise a hereditary knighthood and originally the title was bought for cash, although this was not as corrupt as it might at first sight appear. In 1242 it was established that any man wealthy enough to become a knight must either accept knighthood (and pay for the privilege) or pay to be excused. Independently, but shortly thereafter, certain leading military knights who had their own following became known as bannerets because they had their own small banner on the battlefield to rally their immediate followers. The idea of the leading knight and the wealthy knight therefore come together in the baronet, or little baron. Again this had no function except to raise money for the exchequer. Baronets do not as such sit in the House of Lords, although many peers are also baronets. It entitles the holder to be called sir and his son will inherit it after him. New creations are rare but still occur, although now as a mark of honour, and cannot be purchased.[10]

The simple knight or knight bachelor is the pillar of the system.[11] The name comes from Anglo-Saxon *cnicht* or boy, thus a young man following an established warrior. It translates the Latin *miles*, soldier. In 1066 this meant, on the Norman side, a heavy armoured mounted warrior with a horse, lance, sword and a few followers. He had to have wealth or be paid for by a wealthy lord (22.5). Gradually it became a social rather than a military term, meaning a man of standing in the community with an income of at least £20 a year and holding

---

[8]   *Berkeley Peerage Case* (1861) 8 HLC 21, 11 ER 333.

[9]   See *Hambro v Duke of Marlborough* [1994] Ch 158.

[10]   Denis Thatcher was created baronet in 1990 and, on his death in 2003, his son succeeded.

[11]   See Coss, P, *The Knight in Medieval England 1000–1400* (Alan Sutton, 1993).

a knight's fee. By the late Middle Ages the fee had become an established unit irrespective of its actual holder. There are now many knighthoods. They include knights bachelor (or ordinary knights) and members of the various orders such as the British Empire, the Royal Victorian Order, the Bath and, most exclusive of all, the Garter. Knighthoods cannot be inherited.

The squire or esquire was originally, like the *cnicht*, a young man following, in this case, a knight. Chaucer describes a typical carefree squire in his *Canterbury Tales*. He served meat before his knight (in this case his father) and attended him. In war a squire would arm his knight and follow him in battle with a spare horse and weapons. As the numbers of knights diminished in the late Middle Ages the word 'squire' came to refer to substantial landowners and, by the eighteenth century, the squire was the owner of an estate and the term included noblemen. Esquire is now a term applied to all adult males, usually on the envelopes of letters as 'Esq'.

Gentleman once meant a man of gentle birth or good family. In Tudor times attempts were made to limit the description to the head of a family which was entitled to a coat of arms regulated by the College of Heralds. The Latin equivalent is *armiger* or arms-bearer. It now refers to any good man, usually of some maturity, who has good manners and dresses well.

'Honourable' is a title. Marquesses are 'Most Honourable', earls, barons and members of the Privy Council are 'Right Honourable' and the children of peers are 'Honourable'. Like 'Esq', the term is most often used on the envelopes of letters. The eldest son and heir of a senior nobleman usually has a courtesy title. A duke's son may be called a marquess, the son of a marquess may be called an earl, and the son of an earl a viscount. The holder of a courtesy title has always been able to vote and to sit in the House of Commons, and many have done so. A courtesy title has no legal significance.

There are also memberships of various orders such as the Order of the British Empire, the Order of Merit and the Royal Victorian Order. The award of knighthoods and memberships of the orders are now known as honours. Neither honourable nor the honours system have any connection with honours as a group of manors described in 22.4.

Finally, lord of the manor is not a title in any of the senses given in this chapter. It refers only to the person who owns the lordship. He is not entitled to be called lord or my lord or to sit in the House of Lords: he is not necessarily a gentleman or indeed a human at all since a lordship can be owned by a company and many are owned by institutions. The Passport Office will allow the expression to appear on passports. The lord of the manor is not, as such, a lord in the sense of peer, although in the past most peers were squires who owned estates and as such were lords of manors.

23.5   WALES, SCOTLAND AND NORTHERN IRELAND

Wales was conquered by barons of the English kings and in order to settle the country they were granted special privileges including wide jurisdiction over large areas. These were initially along the frontiers and marches and the holder was known as a lord marcher. Their nature and significance was investigated in the case of *Crown Estate Commissioners v Roberts*.[12] Mr Roberts claimed to have purchased the lordship marcher of St David's at auction and further claimed that in right of his title he owned substantial areas of the seabed and foreshore in Pembrokeshire. The Commissioners disputed this in right of the Crown Estate. The judge held that Roberts had not in fact acquired the title of lord marcher, first because his interpretation of what he had bought was incorrect – he had simply acquired the manor of the City and Suburbs of St David's – but secondly because the status of lordship marcher had ceased to exist at the latest by the Laws in Wales Act 1535 when Welsh law was integrated into that of England. The marcher lordship is unique to Wales although to some extent it corresponded to palatinates and, because it comprised a number of manors, also to an honour.

Although this book is about the law of England and Wales, it is worth mentioning a feature which sometimes causes confusion. In England someone who acquires a lordship, whether it is a manor, barony or honour, does not thereby have the right to call himself 'Lord X'. The situation may be different in Ireland and Scotland.

This issue became important in the preparation of one of the first Acts to be passed by the Scottish Parliament after the Scotland Act 1998. The Abolition of Feudal Tenure etc (Scotland) Act 2000 was intended to remove certain archaic burdens on owners of land owed to feudal superiors. By s 1 of the Act 'The feudal system of land tenure, that is to say the entire system whereby land is held by a vassal on perpetual tenure from a superior is, on the appointed day, abolished'. It was not quite as simple as that: the Act required 77 sections and 13 Schedules. One effect of the abolition would have been to abolish baronies which in Scotland did carry the right to call someone 'Lord X' and which usually attached to a small piece of land such as a castle. Such titles were saleable for substantial sums and if they were simply abolished, those who had bought them would find that something that had cost them a lot of money was

---

[12]   [2008] EWHC 1302 (Ch), [2008] 4 All ER 828.

suddenly rendered valueless. Section 63 therefore, while abolishing any special privileges attached to a barony, stated that nothing in the Act would affect the dignity of baron as such. It ceased to be attached to land and became, and could be transferred as, incorporeal heritable property.

The position in Ireland is more obscure. The description 'barony' applies to an obsolete unit of local government which has no significance as a personal dignity. However, there appears to be an active market in the title to Irish baronies. Experts differ as to the legitimacy of sales and therefore as to whether someone can lawfully buy the right to call himself Lord X in Ireland. Although many laws are different north and south of the Border, the legal issues involved long predate the establishment of the Irish Republic and presumably the same rules would apply throughout.

Chapter 24

Royal Demesne

24.1 CROWN ESTATE

Special rules applied to Crown manors and related issues, including allodial land. All England can be compared to a manor. The Queen is lord, and all who hold of her, from the greatest earls and barons to the least Crown freeholder, are her tenants. They owe suit of court and are entitled to royal justice. The common law is sometimes described as the custom of the realm.[1] The king once had special sporting rights (12.2–12.3) and the Crown still has rights to the royal minerals of gold and silver (11.5). The Royal Forests, including areas (such as the Forest of Dartmoor) with no trees, were waste and used for grazing like a great common. Some forests were wooded and the timber could be taken for ships for the Navy or to build a palace or for sale. Around the coasts, the seabed, foreshore and marshland belonged to the Crown.

Crown manors derive from two sources. First, the theory in law (whatever its historical merit) is that all land in the country was initially at the disposal of the king and was granted out by him to be held in tenure (22.3). He retained some lands (perhaps amounting to as much as a third of England under William I) from which he took rents to finance his own expenses as king. The second source is acquisitions over the centuries by purchase, escheat or forfeiture, or by Henry VIII on the Dissolution. The king was expected to 'live of his own', that is to cover the normal expenses of peacetime government out of his regular revenues without raising taxes.

Royal estates diminished as lands and manors were granted to the Church or to favoured courtiers or were sold. This reduced royal revenues to such an extent that they did not cover the cost of government. In the Civil List Act 1760, George III agreed that instead of seeking to administer the country out of his own revenues, with some assistance from taxes, he would leave it to Parliament to find the money to run the administration. He surrendered his 'rents of lands',

---

[1]   *Veley v Burder* (1841) 12 Ad & E 265 at 302, 113 ER 812 at 828, per Tindal CJ.

that is the revenue from his income-producing estates, and in return received a civil list to cover his own immediate expenses. William IV added various assets by the Civil List Act 1831, notably the casual revenues which appear to have included escheats expressly preserved by s 12 of the Act, albeit for the benefit of the Treasury not for the king.

This system has been repeated by each successive sovereign on succession.[2] Management of Crown lands, including manors, was therefore taken on by officials accountable to Parliament. The administration has been revised from time to time, notably in the Crown Lands Act 1851, and is now carried out by the Crown Estate Commissioners under the Crown Estate Act 1961. However, as indicated below, that does not extend to the royal parks and palaces, and there are also numerous other Crown entities, notably various Secretaries of State, that administer different properties, such as lands held for training defence forces, woodlands, and office blocks for the Civil Service.

Royal mines are considered in 11.5. The interest of the Crown is best seen not as holding the strata in which gold and silver occur but as more like a profit, that is the right to take precious metals from the land of a subject, perhaps most analogous to the Crown interest in wild animals before the abolition of chase and warren. The statutory right to petroleum and natural gas is similar.[3]

24.2   ROYAL RESIDENCES AND PARKS

Some palaces and other residences were comprised within manors. The most important still remaining is Windsor, which belonged to the Saxon kings. Shortly before his death Edward the Confessor endowed the Abbey of Westminster, with the estate but soon after the Conquest William I reclaimed Windsor and the manor has been in royal hands ever since. Hampton belonged to the Knights Hospitallers of St John of Jerusalem. In 1514 they leased it to Cardinal Wolsey and he built Hampton Court. In 1531 the Hospitallers by way of exchange conveyed the freehold to the king. On Wolsey's disgrace Henry VIII took it in hand and it has remained royal property. Richmond Park is parcel of the manor of Shene. Hyde Park was part of the manor of Hyde acquired by Henry VIII from Westminster Abbey.

However, many palaces and parks in London are not comprised within manors. The Tower of London on the edge of the City was a fortress in its own right. The manor of Westminster belonged to the Abbey in the Middle Ages and

---

2   See now the Sovereign Grant Act 2011.

3   *Star Energy Weald Basin Limited v Bocardo SA* [2011] 1 AC 380.

although it is said that Cardinal Wolsey granted it to Henry VIII, Parliament had been meeting at the Palace of Westminster long before that. *Hall v Mayor of London*[4] concerned the status of Parliament Square Garden which, by the Greater London Authority Act 1999, s 384, was transferred from the Secretary of State for Culture, Media and Sport to be part of the hereditary possessions of Her Majesty, presumably as allodial land, although the court indicated obiter[5] that the freehold was vested in the Crown. The Court of Appeal held that under the Act the correct person to take possession proceedings was the Mayor of London.

The Crown Estate Commissioners manage Windsor Great Park. Most royal parks are administered by the Royal Parks, which is an agency of the Department for Culture, Media and Sport. That Department has contracted out the management of the historic royal palaces including the Tower of London, Hampton Court, part of Kensington Palace and Kew Palace to a charity called Historic Royal Palaces. However, where land within the boundaries of a park or palace was let or capable of being let in 1760 it fell to be managed (as rents of land) by the predecessors of the Crown Estate Commissioners so that for instance, they have certain detached properties within Hampton Court Park.

Those palaces still used by the Queen or the Royal Family, including Buckingham Palace, Buckingham Palace Mews and Gardens, St James's Palace (with Clarence House), Windsor Castle and Windsor Castle Royal Mews, buildings in Windsor Home Park, Hampton Court Mews and Paddocks, and residential areas of Kensington Palace, are known as occupied royal palaces. They are run on a day-to-day basis by the Royal Household, although the Department has overall responsibility for the buildings. Somerset House appears to be allodial land with its own constitution under the Somerset House Act 1984. The Palace of Westminster is under the management of the Parliamentary authorities.

The Queen also has certain properties which are her own personal belongings held as freeholds. These are governed by the Crown Private Estates Act 1862. The most important in England is the Sandringham Estate in Norfolk and any manors comprised in that estate would be the personal property of the Queen and not part of the assets of the government. The Queen is free to dispose of the private estates by gift or will.

---

4   [2010] EWCA Civ 817, [2011] 1 WLR 504.

5   Ibid at [25].

24.3   ALLODIAL LAND

Most Crown properties are freehold, resulting from purchases over the centuries. Some are leasehold but, as the sovereign cannot be the tenant of any person or be liable on covenants, such leases are taken in the name of a nominee, such as the Crown Estate Commissioners or a Secretary of State. Others remain allodial. They stand in the name of the Queen so that any dealing with them will need to name her, although any legal proceedings would be instituted in the name of an agent such as the Crown Estate Commissioners or the Attorney-General.

The expression 'allodial land' derives from the distinction found on the Continent between land held in benefice and land held without a seignior (8.1, 22.2). Since in England all land of subjects is held by tenure[6] the term 'allodial land' (or 'demesne land' for the purposes of the Land Registration Act 2002, ss 79–81: see s 132(1)) is land in which no freehold exists, that is Crown land which is not held in fee simple. It may include Crown manors held since the Conquest. Manors purchased by the Crown will normally be retained in fee.[7] If the manor itself is allodial then demesne land within the manor will also be allodial. Registered land can only be freehold or leasehold. Strictly escheated land is allodial; in practice the Land Registry keeps the freehold title open until it is disposed of by the Commissioners which they usually do as soon as possible, by sale if possible or, if not, by gift to a body, such as a local authority capable of dealing with it. However, if the Crown enters on the land it will be held allodially until a registered title is issued. Where a manor escheated in the past and has been retained it will be allodial.

Some of the royal parks and palaces are allodial, such as Windsor and the Tower of London, but not all. The Law Commission, in its report *Land Registration for the Twenty-First Century*, stated that 'we have had some interesting correspondence as to whether Buckingham Palace is held by the Crown in demesne or (as we think) in fee simple'.[8] Demesne is the Commission's term for allodial land. Land allocated to the Crown by statute without a fee simple, including Parliament Square,[9] may be allodial. Under the Trafalgar Square Act 1844, the care, control, management and regulation of the Square was vested in the Commissioners of Woods, subsequently the Office of Works, now the Secretary of State for Culture, Media and Sport. Regulation was passed to the

---

6   Coke, Sir Edward, *A commentary on Littleton being the first part of the Institutes of the Laws of England* (1628) 65a.

7   Ibid 15b.

8   Law Commission No 271, *Land Registration for the Twenty-First Century: a Conveyancing Revolution* para 119, n 22.

9   Greater London Authority Act 1999, s 384(1).

Mayor of London by the Greater London Authority Act 1999, s 383, but title presumably remains allodial.[10] Somerset House is also allodial by statute.[11]

24.4   FORESHORE AND PURPRESTURES

Most Crown foreshore was allodial, although the Commissioners now have a policy of registering title to foreshore so it becomes Crown freehold. The seabed remains allodial. There is a rebuttable presumption that foreshore around England and Wales is Crown property and is under the management of the Crown Estate Commissioners (or in Lancashire and Cornwall of the Royal Duchies). In the past many lords of coastal manors claimed to own the foreshore on the basis that they had the right to wreck, and their control of the foreshore to recover materials from vessels in distress conferred a title. Following full investigations in the nineteenth century in which the authorities conceded many claims, the principle of Crown ownership was established. Where the position was uncertain the Crown or the Duchies could sell the foreshore to the coastal lord for a reduced sum to compromise the dispute. Many lords accepted this as a way of establishing a good documentary title but it can confuse the issue. If the foreshore had been held with the manor since 1189 it was manorial waste and parcel of the manor. If it was acquired as a result of a conveyance from the Crown it was not parcel of the manor. The effect of such compromises was to sever the foreshore from the manor.

The upper and lower limits of foreshore are ascertained in different ways. The upper limit is the median high water mark of ordinary tides. Usually this is measured by finding the high and low water mark of spring and neap tides and taking a limit midway between them.[12] Low water mark was for many years undefined, but *Anderson v Alnwick District Council*[13] held for the purposes of interpreting a local authority byelaw that foreshore should be taken to extend down to the lowest limit of astronomical tides, so that the rights of the owner extended to the maximum extent revealed by any tide. The case is strictly authority for its own facts and does not necessarily define the extent of private ownership, but in practice it is accepted as a general guide. In general the rights do not extend into the deep sea, all of which is Crown land. The position may be different in estuaries. Where a lord or other owner has had a grant of a several

---

[10]   House of Commons Debates, Vol 415, c 428W (27 November 2003).

[11]   The Duchy of Cornwall Office Act 1854 provides that the new office of the Duchy would vest in Her Majesty in fee simple but that the former offices at Somerset House will simply vest in Her Majesty.

[12]   *Attorney-General v Chambers* (1854) 4 De GM&G 206. See also *Mellor v Walmsley* [1905] 2 Ch 164.

[13]   [1993] 1 WLR 1156.

fishery he may also own the river bed even if it is always under water. Likewise, some corporations own the beds of harbours[14] (15.5).

The limits of foreshore will change if the land or the shore is eroded (dereliction or diluvion) or extended (accretion). If material is slowly and imperceptibly added to land over a period of time the owner of the land is treated as having his property increased, in much the same way as when a river alters its course.[15] Similarly, if the limits of foreshore change the rights of the owner will be adjusted accordingly. Foreshore is therefore a movable freehold, like lot meadows considered in 10.6.

The sea shore was protected by laws which prohibited purprestures, that is encroachments on public assets such as the sea shore or navigable rivers or highways. These were seen as actionable as being infringements on matters for which the king was responsible. At one time there was a theory that highways were vested in the king[16] although, as indicated in 6.6, that was not the prevailing view in English law. The sea shore generally was so vested. It appears that the law may have been used to protect other royal properties, such as forests and the Duchy estates.[17] In general the king could either remove the encroachment or (which often happened in forests) allow it to continue as an assart but charge a rent for it. The law may have fallen into disuse if the better view came to be that the royal estates could adequately be protected by civil rather than criminal procedures.

The word 'purprestures' also seems at an early time to have been used to describe particular lands in other manors. *Vaughan d Atkins v Atkins*[18] involved lands in the manor of Bitterne belonging to the Bishop of Winchester known as purprestures which passed on the death of the tenant to his eldest son, while other land called bond land passed to the youngest. The law of purprestures is now rarely invoked in England. It appears it was an equitable jurisdiction[19] and was largely replaced by common law proceedings in public nuisance.[20]

---

14 *Ipswich Borough Council v Moore* [2001] EWCA Civ 1273.

15 *Southern Centre of Theosophy Inc v South Australia* [1982] AC 706.

16 Bracton, Sir Henry, *De legibus et consuetudinibus angliae* (c 1257) f 180b.

17 *Attorney-General to the Prince of Wales v St Aubyn* (1811) Wight 167, 145 ER 1215.

18 (1771) 5 Burr 2764, 98 ER 451.

19 *Attorney-General v Richards* (1794) 2 Anst 603, 145 ER 980.

20 See *Attorney-General v Parmeter* (1811) 10 Price 378, 147 ER 345; *London Corporation v Attorney-General* (1848) I HL Cas 440, 9 ER 829 which also defined purpresture as 'a wrongful inclosure of a part of the freehold of the Crown'; *In re Corby Group Litigation* [2009] QB 335 at [15].

However, it is the subject of a considerable amount of law in various jurisdictions of the United States.[21]

24.5   EAST GREENWICH AND OTHER LORDSHIPS OF SOLD LANDS

East Greenwich was a royal manor of particular importance. This was mentioned in 22.6 in relation to tenure and in 3.6 as the principal manor from which lands in America were granted to be held (Windsor and Hampton Court were also so used, but less often). However, it was more important in England where it was reckoned that there were more than 10,000 freeholds held of East Greenwich. Other Crown manors seem to have been employed, including Bardney, Swynshedd, Louth, Shenstone and the honours of Bolingbroke and Hampton Court, but from the mid-sixteenth century most lands sold by the Crown were granted to be held of East Greenwich. The lands so granted were often those of dissolved monasteries but they could be any lands which had come in by escheat or forfeiture or were simply ancient Crown lands held for centuries.

The reason related to tenure and feudal incidents (8.1, 22.6). Lands held *ut de corona* and *in capite* were subject to greater burdens than those held *ut de honore*. American lands had no previous tenure and had to be held of some lord. In England it may have been a matter of bargain. A buyer might be prepared to pay for lands from the Crown but not if they were subject to heavy liabilities. It is also possible that there was a concern on the part of the Crown that a tenant *in capite* might claim a seat in the House of Lords, although that seems unlikely.

Magna Carta 1215 c43 provided that if anyone held of a barony or honour which had escheated to the Crown and died his heir would owe only the same service which would have been due to the baron, not those greater services owned by a tenant in chief. This was confirmed by *Gilbert's Case*[22] where it was held that lands held of an honour or manor could never be held of the king *in capite*, even though the honour or manor had escheated to him for treason (this would later be regarded as forfeiture, not escheat). *Estwick's Case*[23] concerned a farm called Milton Grange in Bedfordshire, formerly part of the possessions of the Monastery of Wooborne which King Philip and Queen Mary had granted to Aringal Wade to be held in chief of their manor of East Greenwich in the

---

[21] See eg *Revell v People* (1898) 177 Ill 468, 52 NE 1052; *Cobb v Commissioners of Lincoln Park* (1903) 202 Ill 427, 67 NE 5; *Hawaii v Kerr* (1905) 16 Haw 363; *Sullivan v Leaf River Forest Products Inc* 791 F Supp 627 (SD Miss 1991).

[22] (1538) 1 Dy 44a, 73 ER 96.

[23] (1612) 12 Co Rep 135, 77 ER 1410.

County of Kent at the service of one-twentieth part of a knight's fee, that is in knight service. The farm came to Christopher Estwick and on his death the question arose of the seigniorial dues. The Court of Wards held that as the land was granted to be held of the manor it was *ut de honore* and not in chief.

Where land was granted by the Crown to be held of the manor of East Greenwich at a rent, that did not make the rent parcel of the manor.[24] It might follow that the land was also not parcel of the manor so that it would escheat to the Crown in chief, but the position is not clear. The Tenures Abolition Act 1660, s 1 converted tenures by knight service *in capite* or in socage *in capite* into free and common socage and s 4 provided that new tenures should not be *in capite*.

24.6   REGISTRATION OF TITLE TO ROYAL DEMESNE

The way the system of land registration applies to manors is explained in 25.7. Special rules apply to the Crown. The Crown has wider rights than private parties to lodge cautions against first registration to protect its interests under the joint effect of the Land Registration Act 2002, s 15, s 81 and Sch 12, paras 14 and 15. These will cease on 12 October 2013 unless extended. This applies to any land belonging to the Crown. Special rules also relate to what is discussed above as allodial land but which the Act calls demesne land, defined by s 132(1) as 'land belonging to Her Majesty in right of the Crown which is not held for an estate in fee simple absolute in possession'. Under the Act only freehold and leasehold land can be registered and so s 79 allows the Crown to create a fee simple in demesne land in order to apply for first registration. Section 80 provides that when demesne land is granted by the Crown to a subject either by infeudation of a freehold or by lease, it will be compulsorily registrable in the same circumstances as apply to a transfer or conveyance of an existing freehold or a grant of a new lease or assignment of an existing one.

Under the Land Registration Act 2002, Schs 1 and 3, para 12 a right to rent which was reserved to the Crown on the granting of any freehold estate (whether or not the right is still vested in the Crown) qualifies as a temporary overriding interest. This may arise from a grant in fee farm.[25] In *Land Registration for the Twenty-First Century* (8.43) the Law Commission indicated that the Crown may have reserved such rents and then sold the right to collect them. It did not indicate how this was done but rent may have been payable to a manor which was sold. In such a case the current lord may be entitled to them.

---

[24]   *Morris v Smith and Paget* (1582) Cro, Eliz 38, 78 ER 303.
[25]   See Law of Property Act 1925, s 146(5)(a).

Most will be small and possibly not worth collecting, but if he wishes to retain them it would be sensible to register a caution or notice against the burdened land before the first registration or disposition of land after 12 October 2013.

24.7   THE ROYAL DUCHIES

Many of the same rules and practices that apply to manors held in right of the Crown apply also to the Duchies of Lancaster and Cornwall. Duchy lands are not allodial as they are held from the Crown by freehold tenure (even though the sovereign is Duke of Lancaster and may, if there is no Duke of Cornwall, also be entitled to that Duchy). The Duchy of Lancaster represents the remains of the family lands of Henry Bolingbroke, Duke of Lancaster, who became king in 1399 and decided to keep them separate. The Duchy of Cornwall derives from the estates of the Earls of Cornwall. In 1377 the Duchy was granted by Edward III to his son, the Black Prince. It is held by the eldest son of the monarch who is heir apparent; if there is no such person it reverts to the Crown. Each of the Duchies forms a great honour and has several lesser honours within it.

One curiosity relates to conventionary tenements of the Duchy of Cornwall. As mentioned in 24.9 Bracton refers to these in connection with ancient demesne. The Cornish version may have similar origins. In Cornwall there are 17 manors known as Assessionable Manors. At one time all were held by the Duchy but some have been sold. They did not include copyhold land but instead there were so-called conventionary tenants who held their land by virtue of coming every seven years to a special manorial assession court and paying a fee fixed from ancient times to renew their holding.

The nature of these holdings came up for consideration in *Rowe v Brenton*.[26] Mr Brenton was captain or leader of a company of miners operating in the manor of Tewington under a licence from Messrs Williams and Smith who, in turn, held a mineral licence from the Duchy of Cornwall. The Duchy had earlier sold the surface lands but reserved the minerals. Captain Brenton (as he was known) wished to work the mines in lands called Nansmellyn which were held by Mr Rowe as Conventionary Tenant. Rowe claimed that conventionary tenements were copyhold and that, in accordance with the ordinary rules of copyhold land (11.7), Captain Brenton had no right to enter and work the mines without his consent. After an exhaustive investigation the court decided that conventionary tenements were really leaseholds, originally granted for seven years, and that over the centuries the tenants had acquired a right to renew on tendering a fixed

---

[26]   (1828) 8 B&C 737, 108 ER 1217.

premium. Unlike copyholds the landlord of leaseholds did at that time have the right to enter and work the minerals without the tenant's consent.

The outcome of the case was that under the Duchy of Cornwall (No 2) Act 1844 the conventionary tenements were enfranchised to freeholds and the mineral rights became governed by a code set out in the Act which still applies, and adds to the complexities of Cornish mineral law. If conventionary tenancies are similar to the ones mentioned by Bracton it suggests that already in his time, well before 1290, new perpetual types of landholding could no longer be easily created and resembled leaseholds more than copyholds.

24.8   PARLIAMENTARY MANORS

This is a convenient term to apply to manors relevant to government and Parliament.[27] Originally, membership of the House of Commons was a duty, usually burdensome and unwelcome. If a member was elected he was not allowed to resign. Following the Civil War membership was considered a privilege. Circumstances can arise when a member needs to resign, if he is in disgrace, or for family or business reasons, or if he leaves his party and wants to fight his seat again. In such circumstances the member must apply for an office of profit under the Crown. Some paid offices are thought to be incompatible with membership of the House because of a conflict of duties. These are set out at length in the House of Commons Disqualification Act 1975. One way of resigning could be to take such an employment but that may not be suitable and there is a traditional alternative.

The member must apply to the Chancellor of the Exchequer to be appointed to one of two stewardships. One is the steward or bailiff of the manor of Northstead and the other is steward or bailiff of the three Chiltern Hundreds of Stoke, Desborough and Burnham. These are usually appointed alternately. Previously there were also the stewards of the manors of East Hendred (until 1840) and Hempholme (until 1865), but these were sold by the Crown and can no longer be used. Under the Law of Property Act 1922, s 142A (added by the Law of Property (Amendment) Act 1924, Sch 2) even though all manorial incidents became extinguished in Crown manors, and therefore the steward could not derive any actual profits from the manor, the acceptance of the office of steward or other principal officer was deemed to be an acceptance of an office of profit from the Crown for the purposes of s 25 of the Succession to the Crown Act 1707, which allowed the holder of an office of profit to continue to hold it if he submitted to re-election and was elected. Thus holding the office of

---

[27]   Erskine May, *Treatise on the Law, Privileges, Proceedings and Usage of Parliament* (LexisNexis Butterworths, frequent editions).

steward can be one way of a member making a point by resigning and getting his constituents to send him back.

Another group of Parliamentary manors relates to the Chequers Estate. In the nineteenth century much political discussion took place in the great country houses. At the beginning of the twentieth century Sir Arthur Lee took the view that a man might become Prime Minister who did not have enough private wealth to own a country estate. He gave his own estate, with the manors of Ellesborough, Chequers and Mordaunts and of Great Kimble and Little Kimble in Buckinghamshire as a residence for the Prime Minister of the day. This was confirmed in the Chequers Estate Act 1917.

24.9   ANCIENT DEMESNE

A manor of ancient demesne is one mentioned in *Domesday Book* as having been held by the king, either Edward the Confessor at his death in 1066 or William I in 1086.[28] Normally the manor is described as *terra regis* – land of the king. The term should not be confused with demesne land in the Land Registration Act 2002, as discussed above.

Where a manor was in the hands of the king, then its court was the royal court. In practice, of course, the area of a royal estate the size of a manor became treated and administered as a manor like any other because that was the most efficient way of running it. However, since the tenants of the manor had the right to go to the royal court, they were in some sense regarded as holding by a common law tenure, not a customary one, and the terms of their holding could be recognised by the common law courts. There were two special features of tenure in ancient demesne, first a type of tenure and secondly a freedom from toll.

Bracton[29] suggests that there were four types of tenure in these manors. First, there were common freeholds in knight service or common socage. Secondly, there were ordinary villeins holding by customary tenure. Thirdly, there were *adventiti*, men who had come to the land in recent times who held (presumably demesne land on lease) under the terms of an agreement *per conventionem*. These were like those in any manor. Fourthly, there were tenants in ancient demesne known as villein socmen or (in a phrase he took from the law of the

---

[28]   Hallam, E, *Domesday Book through Nine Centuries* (Thames & Hudson, 1986) Ch IV, especially maps on pp 78–94; Pollock, Sir Frederick and Maitland, FW, *The History of English Law before the time of Edward I* (Cambridge University Press, 2nd edn, 1898) 383; Hoyt, RS, 'The Nature and Origins of the Ancient Demesne' (1950) 255 *English Historical Review* 145.

[29]   Bracton *op cit* f 7, 209.

late Roman Empire) *ascripticii glebae*. Bracton also says[30] that there are no freeholds in manors of ancient demesne, but that contradicts his earlier statement and is incorrect. In the case of *Merttens v Hill*[31] in 1901 the court held that the freehold in socage of a villein socman is in the tenant. Such tenants had two special privileges.

First, if they were dispossessed they could use a royal writ of right to recover possession. This 'little writ of right close' gave them a royal remedy and hence a free standing, and could be taken out even against their lord if the king had granted the manor to a subject. Secondly, their customary obligations were limited and if their lord tried to impose new burdens on them they could claim the benefit of a writ of *monstraverunt*. In this they were more like freeholders whose services were certain, rather than villains, whose duties were uncertain.

Tenure by ancient demesne still exists. Some of its main features were clarified in *Merttens v Hill*. Mr Merttens was lord of the manor and soke of Rothley in Leicestershire, a manor of ancient demesne. The manor included an outlier at Grimston, several miles away. Mr Hill had bought a piece of land comprising 21 acres at Grimston known as The Wongs. Merttens claimed that there was a custom that when any parcel of the manor was sold, the lord was entitled to a payment of one shilling for every pound of the purchase price. Mr Hill disputed his claim. The judge, Cozens-Hardy J, found that Hill was a tenant in ancient demesne, that he held in common (not customary) socage, that under *Quia Emptores* it was unlawful for the lord to charge money on the transfer of a fee simple and therefore that the claimed right was bad.

Although the tenure is common (because recognised at common law) it is not free (because formerly held by villeins). It is easy for tenure in ancient demesne to be converted into frank-free tenure but if that has not occurred it still subsists. The Law of Property Act 1922 did nothing to affect this status, although the incidents were abolished, like those of other freeholds.

An important right of tenants in ancient demesne was that they were free of tolls throughout England. This extended to many of the tolls discussed in 15.1–15.3 and 21.2 including stallage, cheminage, pontage, pavage, picage, murage, lastage and passage.[32] The exemption applied for agricultural purposes, such as crops and manure. In some cases it could also apply to towns under royal

---

[30]   Ibid f 272.

[31]   [1901] 1 Ch 842.

[32]   Hallam *op cit* 106.

protection whose citizens held their houses by burgage tenure, but again only for agricultural purposes. Coke[33] says:

> Tenants in ancient demesne, for things coming of those lands shall pay no toll, because at the beginning of their tenure they applied themselves to the manurance and husbandry of the King's demesnes and therefore for those lands so holden, and for all that came or renewed thereupon, they had the privilege: but if such tenant be a common merchant for buying and selling of wares or merchandises, that arise not upon the manurance or husbandry of those lands, he shall not have the privilege for them, because they are out of the reason for the privilege of ancient demesne, and the tenant in ancient demesne ought to be a husbandman than a merchant by his tenure and so the books do be intended

It appears[34] that townsmen claimed a wider exemption and it is possible that the law was never settled. The reason for this could have been that the king himself was exempted from tolls and therefore the tenants on royal manors and in royal towns were treated as representing him, especially if they travelled in the course of their tenurial duties.

The modern successor to a tenant in ancient demesne could still claim exemption from any ancient toll. In *Iveagh v Martin*[35] Paull J said:

> I have not got to decide how far any right may extend today throughout the kingdom, although where any such right comes into conflict with the right granted by an Act of Parliament the right given by the Act may well prevail over any ancient right not to pay dues.

That must be right. A tenant in ancient demesne could not, for example, claim freedom from motorway tolls but the point remains to be tested in court.

24.10 CHANGES AFFECTING ROYAL MANORS

A manor of ancient demesne kept that status even after the king granted it to a subject or to the Church. Indeed, most of the disputes about such manors concerned those where the king was no longer lord and the lord tried to establish new rights over the tenants. The manor court was known as a Court of Ancient Demesne. These courts did not lose their jurisdiction under the Administration of Justice Act 1977 and so may still have functions. At least one, Portland, was

---

[33] Coke, Sir Edward, *The second part of the Institutes of the Law of England*; cited in *Iveagh v Martin* [1961] 1 QB 232 at 264.

[34] *Ward v Knight* (1588) 1 Leo 231, 74 ER 212; Cro Eliz 227, 78 ER 483; *Truro Corporation v Reynalds* (1832) 8 Bing 275, 131 ER 407.

[35] [1961] 1 QB 232, [1960] 2 All ER 668.

expressly preserved. Correspondingly, where the Crown acquired a manor that was not ancient demesne it would not change its nature and the rights and duties of the lord would remain. Although, until the Crown Proceedings Act 1947, the Crown could in general not be sued in the royal courts, there were procedures for tenants to assert their rights. When the manor was resold the normal remedies revived.

Thus, despite the fact that after 1290 private lords could not refuse consent to an assurance of freehold land as *Quia Emptores* did not bind the king, he could control sales of freeholds held in chief. Where a manor came to the Crown, that rule did not apply to a sale of a manorial freehold because the accident of a new lord, even a royal one, could not change existing rights. Such manors were held *ut de honore*.

Manors continued to exist even when they came into royal hands. Normally when a lesser interest becomes held by the owner of a greater one it will cease to exist. Thus if a freeholder acquires a lease of the same land it is said to merge. There are exceptions to this, for example if the two interests are owned in different capacities as if one is a trust holding[36] or special rights affect the lease, such as a mortgage or right of way. It may be possible to keep a lease outstanding for good reason. Similarly, when a copyhold became held by the lord it was normally extinguished except in limited cases where the lord regranted it without having leased it first,[37] although this rule does not seem to have applied to the Crown.[38] When the lord of a head manor acquired the sub-manor the latter disappeared. However, a manor, as a lesser interest, did not merge in the Crown rights. The reason is that a manor is a unit of custom and, as the king could not abolish customary rights, there had to be a manor to support them.

In the same way, if a manor was subject to special services these would not be abolished if the manor passed to the Crown. This was specifically decided in *R v Duchess of Buccleugh*[39] where the manor was said to be subject to a duty to repair a bridge. The manor had at one time belonged to the Royal Duchy of Lancaster but the court held that even though the manor had passed through royal hands that did not abolish the duty. It may have been unenforceable while the Crown held the manor but it could (if the duty existed) be enforced again against a later private lord. Thus the manor of Newark was subject to the duty to repair the Trent Bridge and the Markham Bridge; and when part of the

---

[36]   Law of Property Act 1925, s 185.

[37]   *French's Case* (1576) 4 CoRep 31a, 77 ER 960.

[38]   *Pemble v Stern* (1668) 2 Keb 213, 84 ER 133.

[39]   (1704) 6 Mod 150, 87 ER 909, 1 Salk 358.

demesnes were sold it was necessary to pass the Newark Bridges Act 1837[40] to abolish the duty. Where a franchise is an appurtenance of the manor it will be extinguished on coming into royal hands only if it is a flower franchise but not if it is a produce franchise (16.7).

One point that is uncertain is whether the boundaries of a Crown manor can increase if the Crown acquires land in the vicinity that was not parcel of the manor. Additions to manors are considered in 7.4. For private lords the position is clear under *R v Duchess of Buccleugh* that manors cannot be enlarged. There are two reasons for this. One is that since *Quia Emptores* no land can be granted to be held of a lordship. If it is ever outside the bounds of a manor (whether because it was never in it or because it once was but has been assured out by substitution) it can never again be brought within the lordship of a subject (save by statute). That rule as it stands cannot apply to the Crown since all land is so held.

The second reason is that the area governed by custom cannot be extended. Clearly for the reasons given by Coke and set out in 4.3 the king cannot make a new manor, but it is not so clear that he may not ascribe land to an existing manor. In his discussion Coke is clear that a common person cannot do this but the implication is that the king might.[41]. However, there seems no reason in principle why existing customs cannot be taken to apply to additional land if that addition is held directly from the Crown. Although customs must pre-date the limit of legal memory, and since the customs of all manors are distinct, it is arguable that if the customs of the manor of Dale did not apply to Blackacre in 1189, it is not possible for those customs to be introduced to it at a later date. Nevertheless, as described in 24.5, much land across England and indeed overseas was granted to be held of the manor of East Greenwich. Even though if it escheats it may do in chief and not to that manor, it would seem that as land can be granted to be so held then it is possible for a Crown manor to be extended to include additional land. That being so it appears that there was no objection to the addition of land to a royal manor. Although lands granted to be held of East Greenwich were not administered with that manor it may be possible for the Crown in another case to manage land in the locality of an existing manor as part of it.

In the seventeenth and eighteenth centuries when the English or British Crown acquired new territories in America, Australia and elsewhere the common law (which is the custom of the realm) was extended to them (3.6).[42] Similarly, when (as happened under the Territorial Sea Act 1987) the Crown annexed large areas

---

[40] 7 Will 4 (c 15).

[41] See Coke, Sir Edward, *Complete Copyholder* (E Flesher et al, 1630) s 31.

[42] See generally *Mabo v Queensland* (1992) 66 AJLR 408.

of the seabed around the coast of England the common law was also applied.[43]
That was by virtue of statute but it could have been done under the prerogative.
It is managed by the Crown Estate Commissioners. If such can happen outside
or around the bounds of England it can likewise happen to royal manors within
the realm.

---

[43]   *Post Office v Estuary Radio Ltd* [1968] 2 QB 740.

PART V

CONCLUSION

Chapter 25

Rolls and Registration

25.1 EVIDENCE OF RIGHTS

The rights discussed in this book can be enforced only if there is evidence to substantiate them. The rules of law derive from Acts of Parliament, from decided cases and from custom, but the rights of individuals depend on documents. For example, if there is a question as to respective rights to the value of minerals, this may give rise to the issue of whether particular land was once copyhold. Likewise, if a lord wishes to claim a share of the mineral value, he will need to establish title. If the land was once waste the rights may depend on the terms of inclosure.

For present purposes the documents are of two main types – manorial documents and title deeds.[1] The distinction is made in s 144A of the Law of Property Act 1922. 'Manorial documents' are defined as 'court rolls, maps, surveys, terriers, documents and books of every description relating to the boundaries, franchises, wastes, customs or courts of a manor' but do not include deeds or other documents which evidence the title to the manor itself.

It will be rare in modern conditions for oral evidence of a custom to be available, although a few local people whose families have lived in the locality for generations may speak to practices they have known all their lives and what their parents may have told them. This of course will only take the evidence back a century at most, but once a court is satisfied that a practice has been carried on for many years it may be able to presume that this has been the case since 1189, thus throwing the burden of disproof on to the party resisting the custom. This is unlikely to be of much practical relevance in modern conditions save exceptionally for instance on a claim to a customary way (4.8) or for men of a manor to use a quay (15.5).

---

[1] Stuart, D, *Manorial Records* (Phillimore, 1992); and Ellis, M, *Using Manorial Records* (Public Record Office Publications, 1994) are both elementary and helpful.

Evidence may also be available from local histories, published recollections of people who knew the locality in earlier years or records of magistrates' courts where a matter came up for consideration. Old maps, particular tithe maps, are often relevant. In addition to inclosure Acts and awards (25.3), local acts, reports of cases decided in the royal courts, minutes of local council meetings and other official sources may exist. Claims to rights of common now depend on the registers completed in the years up to 1970. In general the register is conclusive but it may be necessary to have recourse to other evidence to substantiate such details as when the rights can be exercised or whether the registered number is accurate (10.1).

25.2   MANORIAL ROLLS

The most important manorial documents are rolls. The earliest rolls date from the mid-thirteenth century[2] but many series of manorial rolls begin in the time of Edward II. The oldest are literally rolls, written in Latin on membranes which are attached to one another and kept rolled up, so that to see the earliest entries it is necessary to unroll a long strip. Books (or codices) are known from Roman times but rolls could be kept conveniently in bespoke canisters. These can only be read and understood by experts. They make much use of abbreviations and are often written in a handwriting that cannot now be easily understood by laymen. Subsequently, they came to be kept in book form, sometimes in specially made court books or merely in exercise books bought from the local stationer. They were written in English in the script known as the fair legal hand, or conversely in a scrawl by the clerk to the local solicitor who was steward. Many series of court rolls have been printed and published by local history societies, often edited with more enthusiasm than legal (or even historical) knowledge, but they are still useful and interesting.

The series of rolls generally stops in 1925 although where it took time for manorial incidents to be extinguished they could extend past this date. The final documents, not part of the roll itself but kept with it, are the receipts for the sums paid for the redemption of incidents (14.8). These are usually on mass-produced printed slips of paper, completed by hand or by typing. Such documents can be important evidence, for instance that on composition of incidents the mineral rights were excepted to the lord.

In *Heath v Deane*[3] Joyce J said: 'The rolls of a court baron or of a customary court are evidence between the lord and his copyholders or free tenants. They

---

2   Razi, Z and Smith, R (eds), *Medieval Society and the Manor Court* (1996).

3   [1905] 2 Ch 86.

are the public documents by which the inheritance of every tenant is preserved and the records of the manor court, which was anciently a court of justice, relating to all property within the manor.' In *Burgess and Fosters Case*[4] it was held that rolls were not documents of record: if they are incorrect, evidence can be brought to show that, and if they are lost, evidence can be brought to show their contents.[5] The Law of Property Act 1922, s 144 provides that:

> Court Rolls shall (whether before or after the manorial incidents have been extinguished), for the purposes of section fourteen of the Evidence Act, 1851, be deemed to be documents of such a public nature as to be admissible in evidence on their mere production from the proper custody.

In addition, there may be other grounds for requiring their production. This can apply to any document in private custody. For example, a claim may be made under the Wildlife and Countryside Act 1981, s 53(3)(c)(i) that evidence has been discovered that a particular route is a public footpath. This could give rise to an inquiry under the Rights of Way (Hearings and Inquiries) Procedure Rules 2007.[6] Paragraph 3(1)(b) of those Rules incorporates para 9 of Sch 15 to the Wildlife and Countryside Act 1981, which in turn incorporates s 250(2) of the Local Government Act 1972, which gives power to order any person to produce any documents in his custody or under his control.

25.3   OTHER MANORIAL DOCUMENTS

Maps and surveys are self-evident. Written surveys go back to the Middle Ages: maps date from the sixteenth century. Both need to be interpreted with care. Some are beautifully produced, fine examples of a surveyor's art, setting out precise boundaries, whilst others may be only sketch maps or diagrams. Generally, such documents relate only to the manor under consideration, and if it comprises part of a village the rest of the settlement is ignored. They usually refer to particular legal rights, to holdings rather than physical strips, and to head holdings rather than actual occupation. In addition these documents were often produced for a special purpose, such as a lawsuit, and when looking at a survey it is essential to ask why it was made and who paid for it.

Terriers are lists of tenements, from terra – land or territory. They contain the name of the tenant, the name of the tenement, the area, the quitrent and other services and were used for administration. Modern landlords use similar

---

[4]   (1583) 4 Leo 215, 289; 74 ER 830.

[5]   *Snow v Cutler and Stanly* (1662) 1 Keb 567; 83 ER 1115, *Doe d Priestley v Calloway* (1827) 6 B and C 484; 108 ER 530.

[6]   SI 2007/2008.

documents to run leasehold estates. Custumals are lists of rents payable by customary tenants but may include descriptions of local customs, often sworn to by a jury of copyholders following a dispute. They may specify two or three customs or stretch to many pages. Customs are generally those of inheritance which are no longer in force, but they can also include details of rights of common or special customs, for instance in relation to minerals. Other documents include extents, setting out the limits of the manor, and various types of report.

Other documents may also be relevant to inclosure. These are not strictly manorial documents, but may relate to manorial rights. There may be information in the preliminary work such as records of meetings and occasionally reports of proceedings in Parliament, but the first important document will be the Act itself. A remarkably complete collection of inclosure Acts is in the Law Society's library. Following the passing of an Act an award was produced. This comprised a map and an accompanying statement, usually with a schedule of allotments. Many county record offices hold copies and a few, such as those of Berkshire, are available on the internet. Others are held in private collections. Occasionally other surveys and maps are made during the inclosure process, which show matters relevant to the Act. Even where they set out allotments the parties might make other arrangements before reorganising their affairs on the ground.

The rolls of the court leet have a special status as coming from a court of record (13.1) but, apart from that, these documents are simply evidence to be weighed and accepted or not as the court decides. The court will normally pay respect to these rolls since most were prepared with care by responsible people.

25.4   OWNERSHIP AND CUSTODY

Because of their importance as evidence of title most of the older cases concerning rolls relate to who is entitled to have them produced to support his argument in court. In an appropriate case the Court of King's Bench (now the Administrative Court) would grant an order of mandamus (now judicial review) for the production of court rolls.[7] Most of that law is now obsolete because there is a wide jurisdiction under disclosure to have documents relevant to an action produced in court. In this century, however, two issues have dominated discussion of court rolls, namely who owns them (and can sell them) and in whose or what custody they should remain.

---

[7]   Scriven, J, *A Treatise on the Law of Copyholds* (Butterworth & Co, 7th edn by Archibald Brown, 1896) 453.

There is no doubt that ownership as such originally belonged to the lord, but this is a restricted form of ownership because it does not necessarily include the right to possession and enjoyment. The leading case is *Beaumont v Jeffery*[8] which concerned the ancient rolls of the manor of Great Tey in Essex. In or before 1902 the then lord of the manor wanted to clear out his office. The manor comprised five freehold and 12 copyhold tenements. The lord sold all the old pre-1659 rolls to Mr Poole, a waste paper dealer in Portugal Street, Lincoln's Inn Fields. Poole recognised that they were more than just waste paper and resold them in 1902 to Mr Jeffery, a bookseller and dealer in old manuscripts. Jeffrey advertised them for sale at various times but in 1923 sent them to an auction to be held on 22 June. Mr Beaumont was a solicitor interested in manors. He was lord of between 20 and 30 manors and was steward of about 120. On 19 June 1923 he acquired Great Tey and the following day wrote to Jeffery and contacted the auctioneers claiming ownership of the rolls. They were withdrawn from auction and Beaumont sued for possession of the rolls. The court held that it was lawful to sell manorial documents. While copyholders had the right in appropriate cases to inspect the rolls and have them produced in court, their claim could be made just as well against a purchaser as against the lord or his steward. In this case the pre-1659 rolls were of historical interest only. Beaumont lost his case.

The case seems to have produced something of a stir, and in the Law of Property (Amendment) Act 1924 the 1922 Act was amended by introducing a new s 144A which is now the governing law. This section relates primarily to custody of the rolls. It has been argued that it reverses *Beaumont v Jeffery* but that is not quite right. It does indeed say that (save for transfer to a repository as mentioned below) manorial documents 'shall remain in the possession or under the control of the lord for the time being of the manor' to which they relate, but it goes on to define 'lord of the manor' as including any person entitled to manorial documents. It follows that if the lord were to sell the documents the buyer would then be the person entitled and there is nothing to prevent a sale as such.

However, the rules of control are strict and take away much of the benefit of ownership. The old law of custody was laid down in *R v Tower*.[9] That case concerned whether the lord's consent was needed for tenants to cut timber. In the course of proceedings a claim was made to inspect the rolls. Lord Ellenborough said that the lord is a trustee and guardian of the tenants' rights. This must not be taken literally, but the court would compel him to take some care of the rolls. This was not limited to lords who, in any case, did not usually

---

[8]   [1925] 1 Ch 1.

[9]   (1815) 4 M&S 162, 105 ER 795, 16 RR 428.

keep the rolls themselves. Coke[10] says that if the steward shows a court roll to a tenant to prove that the land is copyhold and the tenant tears the court roll in pieces to deny the evidence, that will give rise to a forfeiture. Coke's example appears to be based on an actual case. The steward normally had custody of the rolls and Coke argues[11] that if he burns the rolls he forfeits his office.

Re Jennings[12] concerned a dispute between lord and steward as to who had custody of the rolls. John Dickson was lord of the manor of Beverley Water Towns in Yorkshire. In 1898 he granted to Mr Jennings the office of steward for life. Jennings seems to have been his personal solicitor. Dickson's heir was Mr Wise. Dickson died in 1899 appointing Jennings and Wise as his executors and left the manor to Wise. Wise was also a solicitor and did not get on with Jennings. He could not deprive him of the stewardship but he tried to make life difficult and claimed custody of the court rolls. It was clear that Jennings would need them when he held court but Wise wanted to have them at other times. Jennings refused. The case appears to have been fought out of animosity since no money or property was at stake. Jennings won. The court decided that although the lord was owner of the rolls, and could demand them if the steward misbehaved or was deprived of his office, so long as the steward was of good conduct he was entitled to retain them.

Since 1925 few stewards have been appointed and the law is governed by s 144A. The basic rule is that the lord is entitled to possession or control of the manorial documents but he may transfer them to any public library, museum or historical or antiquarian society (which the Manorial Documents Rules call a 'repository'). If the Master of the Rolls is of the opinion that the documents are not being properly preserved or if the lord so requests, then the Master of the Rolls may direct that they be transferred to a repository, in which case the repository shall have custody of them and is responsible for preserving and indexing them.

At common law freehold tenants of the manor are entitle to inspect the court rolls.[13] So may a copyholder.[14] Under s 144 any person interested in former copyhold land which has been enfranchised has the right to inspect the rolls. The word 'interested' here means legally interested as owner or having a right in the land, and does not mean curious or even wishing to carry out historical research. In *R v Earl of Cadogan*[15] it was claimed that the earl, as lord of the

---

10   Coke, Sir Edward, *Complete Copyholder* (E Flesher et al, 1673) s 57.

11   Ibid s 45.

12   [1903] 1 Ch 906.

13   *Warrick v Queen's College, Oxford* (1866–67) LR 3 Eq 683.

14   *R v Shelley* (1789) 3 TR 141, 100 ER 498.

15   (1822) 5 B and A 902, 106 ER 1421.

manor of Chelsea, was liable to repair a river wall and the banks of the Thames. The prosecutor wished to inspect the court rolls to investigate the position. If the action had been purely civil the court might have ordered inspection, but as it was in the form of a criminal case for public nuisance it did not so order on the principle against self-incrimination.

If the documents are in a repository the lord can require them to be produced to him without charge, but under rules made in 1967 he must give three months' notice to the Historical Manuscripts Commission before removing documents from any repository. In practice most repositories are open to the public, or at least to scholars, but that does not apply where the rolls are still in the private custody of the lord.

The documents have to be properly preserved and the Master of the Rolls can make enquiries about that. High standards are applied relating to temperature, humidity and other factors and a lord who is careless about his rolls may lose the right to keep them. This was formerly supervised by the Historical Manuscripts Commission which, in April 2003, was incorporated into The National Archives. Detailed provisions are laid down in the Manorial Documents Rules 1959, as amended in 1963 and 1967.[16] These fill in certain details in the Act and extend the meaning of repository to include any local authority, following s 7 of the Local Government (Records) Act 1962. Under the Parochial Registers and Records Measure 1978, s 8, 'repository' also includes a diocesan record office. Under r 11 of the 1959 Rules no manorial documents may be removed outside England and Wales without the consent of the Master of the Rolls, so that if, say, a US citizen purchased a manor, he could not take the rolls home with him.

25.5   TITLE DEEDS

The definition of manorial documents specifically excludes title deeds to the manor itself and, by implication, excludes post-enfranchisement title deeds to former copyhold land. These can also be of some historical interest and value.

In England, there are now two types of evidence of title to land and manors: unregistered and registered. Registered titles are considered below. Unregistered titles are the traditional type and in principle go back many centuries. They depend on the legal presumption that a person who can demonstrate the oldest seisin in the property has a better title (or right: 9.3) than anyone else. Therefore, the object of an unregistered title is to produce a chain of deeds and events

---

[16]   SI 1959/1399, SI 1963/976, SI 1967/963.

which give a complete picture of successive owners as far back as necessary to show that the chain is better than any other. Each successive owner's title therefore depends on that of his predecessor. In practice, conveyancers will accept relatively short titles. Under the Law of Property Act 1969, s 23, amending the Law of Property Act 1925, s 44(1), a title beginning with a good root not less than 15 years old is normally acceptable. A good root is one on which a solicitor would have been expected to investigate the title for a similar earlier period (before 1969 it was 30 years and before 1926 it was 40 years[17]), namely a dealing for money that is a sale or mortgage. It may, in theory, be necessary to produce chains of documents going back over 100 years. In practice, many manors derive from family or institutional estates which have not been the subject of such a transaction for a long time and buyers will accept other evidence.

Unregistered title is proved by producing documents and deeds, or formal copies or extracts known as abstracts and epitomes. Title can be shown by various documents, particularly conveyances and mortgages, but also family settlements, wills and transfers following death, deeds of gift. This is not the place to describe the process in detail, which is covered in books on conveyancing. As a result of the spread of registered titles unregistered land is becoming less common (25.6). The skills to handle unregistered titles are therefore becoming scarce.

In the case of former copyhold land the title will consist of a copy of the relevant extract from the court roll showing the surrender of a former owner and admission of a new tenant, followed by enfranchisement either by a deed or by an award or agreement or receipt under the 1922 Act or one of its predecessors, after which the land passed in the same way as other freehold land. It is not necessary to provide the title of the freeholder making the enfranchisement.[18] Title deeds to such land often include old extracts from court rolls, usually in a standard form. When the land is registered and the Land Registry is aware that it was formerly copyhold it makes a note that the land is subject to the rights of the lord of the manor.[19] As all remaining copyhold land was enfranchised in 1926 it is now rare to find a title which includes a surrender and admittance, but this can still arise in relation to institutional or corporate landholders. Thus, when the titles to the London railway stations were registered at the beginning of the twenty-first century, many proved to have been acquired as copyhold.

The titles to manors themselves may be different. In 1925 many manors were subject to family settlements. It was common in 1926 for a document called a

---

[17]   Vendor and Purchaser Act 1874, s 1.

[18]   Law of Property Act 1925, s 44 (6).

[19]   Land Registration Rules 2003, r 5(b)(iii).

vesting deed to be prepared describing the family estates. A standard form was prescribed in Form 1 of Sch 1 to the Settled Land Act 1925 which suggested that the description of the estates be put in a schedule. The first part of the schedule was to contain particulars of the manors, advowsons and other incorporeal hereditaments. The freehold land was referred to in the second part. It is possible that the effect of drawing a deed in this way was that if waste of the manor was referred to in the second part, then that separated it from the manor as such. *Hampshire County Council v Milburn*[20] suggests the contrary; but it is the case that since 1925 many landed estates have administered waste land as a separate asset distinct from the manor.

Many lawyers assumed that manors were no longer of any importance and stopped mentioning them in title deeds. That can now cause problems if the present owner of the estate wishes to sell the manor. However, the deeds should have transferred title to the waste down the generations, although sometimes the contrary applied, and the title deeds mentioned the manor but not the waste. In such a case, where the waste is to be sold it may be necessary to provide evidence that the land was once waste of the manor.

Where property is sold the buyer normally becomes entitled to custody of the title deeds which relate exclusively to it. Where the deeds also comprise other property the buyer will not be so entitled, but the seller can give a statutory acknowledgment that if necessary (for instance to prove a disputed title) he will produce them in court. Often the seller will also give an undertaking that he will keep the deeds in safe custody. Ancient title deeds can be of some value, leading to disputes about ownership. It is therefore best to identify on sale which, if any, deeds will be handed to the buyer. For instance, if all the land of a manor has been sold and the title is all that is left the buyer may otherwise become entitled to take the deeds, which may go back many years and contain information of family interest to the seller.

25.6   LAND REGISTRATION ACT 2002

The Land Registration Act 2002 has made several important changes affecting manors. Although the Act is in principle concerned with procedure, the effect will be to alter the substantive law of rights and duties. As its title indicates, the Act governs the registration of title to land. On the face of it the result is that information formerly contained in title deeds or ascertainable from other evidence is now to be found on the register of title. However, the effect of the Act is that lords may need to take steps to secure their rights before 13 October

---

[20]   [1991] AC 235, [1990] 2 All ER 257, (1990) 61 P&CR 135.

2013, although in some cases it may be possible to risk a short delay. The consequences of the Act affect the titles to manors themselves, as well as mineral rights (11.9), sporting rights (12.4) and franchises (16.9), including markets rights (21.2) and tolls (15.1). Issues affecting those types of property may also turn on the meaning of 'manorial rights' (9.5). The present context considers the broader principles and effect of the Act.

In the nineteenth century Parliament began to provide for government guaranteed registers of title to land giving the name of the owner, a description of the land and the rights affecting it. Initially this was voluntary and few titles were registered. The Land Registration Act 1925 consolidated and replaced earlier legislation (notably the Land Registry Act 1862) and the Land Registration Rules 1925[21] were made under the 1925 Act. The Act and Rules were supplemented and replaced by numerous provisions over the years and then repealed and replaced by the 2002 Act and the Land Registration Rules 2003,[22] which both came into force on 13 October 2003.

It is now compulsory to register title to unregistered land on any change in legal or nominal ownership. This first applied to land sold in central London in 1900. By December 1990 this was extended to the whole of England and Wales. It has since become compulsory to register title not only on any sale but also on most dealings with unregistered titles. The triggers for compulsory registration of title comprise almost every change in legal title, such as a gift or transfer to a beneficiary on inheritance, an appointment of new trustees and most mortgages. There is also an active programme of voluntarily registering title even where the land is not expected to change hands for years to come. Well over half the individual titles to land in England have now been registered, the majority being houses. In addition, over half the area of land, much of it in farms, woods and open country, has also been registered. This means that the proof of ownership is contained not in title deeds but on the database administered by the Land Registry, whose work is guaranteed by the government.

Although it is government policy to complete the register by including every piece of land, this is unlikely to be realised for many years. As compulsory registration is triggered by a change, no occasion will arise for many properties. This includes some which are or once were parcel of manors and which either have been inherited before registration became compulsory or belong to long-established institutions such as an ancient charity or a company. Furthermore, there are areas to which it is often difficult to show title or which may have no known owner (such as some common land: 10.1) and land where the title is doubtful. The official plan incorporated in a registered title may not include an

---

[21]   SR&O 1925/1093.

[22]   SI 2003/1417, as subsequently amended.

adjacent road or verge (6.5–6.6) or river (6.8), but where the *medium filum* presumption applies, half the width may nevertheless be included in the title by virtue of the general boundaries rule in the Land Registration Act 2002, s 60(1).

The register of title itself consists of four principal parts, namely a property register which describes the land and sets out certain rights affecting it, the proprietorship register which names the proprietor, the charges register which sets out certain adverse rights affecting the land and an official plan of the land. In the case of property other than land, including a manor, a franchise, a rentcharge or a profit, these have to be modified to suit the circumstances. Copies of other documents creating rights may also be filed in the Registry and referred to in title entries.

It is possible to register certain adverse interests against a property. Rights which are established to the satisfaction of the Land Registry will be entered in the title as such. In addition someone claiming a right which has not been proved may register a notice on the charges register. Notice is not itself conclusive that the claimed right exists but it constitutes notice of the claim and the date of registration can be relevant to priority, that is in some instances whether it is binding on someone who acquires the property. If title is not registered there is no register on which to enter a notice and instead a claimant can lodge a caution against first registration. When someone applies to register the land for the first time both he and the cautioner will be notified. Either a caution or a notice may be challenged by a proprietor of the land and, if the parties cannot agree, the issue is referred to adjudication under the Adjudicator to Her Majesty's Land Registry (Practice and Procedure) Rules 2003,[23] as amended.

25.7 REGISTERED TITLE TO MANORS

Until 2003 it was possible to register title to a manor under the Land Registration Act 1925 and its Rules. Manors registered before that date can remain on the register. Under s 3(viii) of the Land Registration Act 1925 land was defined as including a manor for the purposes of the Act. Rule 50 of the 1925 Rules dealt with the registration of 'manors, advowsons, rents, tithe rentcharges or other incorporeal hereditaments' and provided that they might be registered in a similar way to land. Rule 51 provided that on the registration of a manor the person applying had to provide the Land Registry with 'a plan of the lands (if any) alleged to be the demesne lands of the manor' or to refer to the areas of the General Map already in the Registry which comprise the demesnes.

---

[23]   SI 2003/2171.

In the years after 1925 few manors were registered with their demesnes in this way as most lords did not see any need to do so. Until the extension of compulsory registration in the years up to 1990 most rural areas were not compulsorily registrable so the land did not need to be registered on a purchase. The expression 'demesne lands' in this context excluded former copyhold[24] as well as waste, even though waste can easily be converted into demesne. Strictly speaking, demesne meant land in the occupation of the lord or his lessees which had passed with the manor continuously since 1290; accordingly r 51 ought to have excluded land subsequently purchased and held with the manor[25] and it must be doubtful how many such maps are accurate. The purpose of this requirement in the Rules is not clear but in most cases where demesnes remained parcel of the manor it may have been thought that an applicant for registration would wish to register the demesne in any case, and if the purchase was in a compulsory area he was bound to do so.

When the market for manors took off in the 1980s some buyers sought to register the title they had acquired, and in the run-up to October 2003 many lords who did not have registered titles applied for them. When they sent their plans into the Registry many lords did not appreciate the distinction between the bounds of the manor (7.1) and the demesne land (which a buyer of the title hardly ever acquired) and sent in a plan of what they believed were the manorial limits. It appears that some members of the Registry staff were equally confused and the practice developed of including with the title to the manor a copy of the plan submitted even though the area covered might extend to several square miles and therefore would include areas of land which had their own registered titles. Many of the submitted plans were inaccurate even as showing the bounds. One applicant might have included land which a later applicant for a neighbouring manor thought was within the bounds of his own, leading to unnecessary and time-consuming disputes.

It is not possible after 12 October 2003 to register title to a manor. This was a deliberate decision taken when the 2002 Act replaced the 1925 Act.[26] In the drafting of the Act effect was given by a roundabout route. Section 3(1) provides that a legal estate may be registered in an estate in land, a rentcharge, a franchise or a profit a prendre in gross. The issue is whether land includes a manor for the purposes of the Act. Section 132 of the 2002 Act has its own definition of land, different from that in the 1925 Act, which therefore overrides any other under the Interpretation Act or under the common law (27.6). It is not comprehensive but says that land includes buildings, land covered with water

---

[24]   Coke *Copyholder op cit* s 14.

[25]   Ibid s 31; *Baxendale v Instow Parish Council* [1982] 1 Ch 14, [1981] 2 All ER 620.

[26]   Law Commission No 271, *Land Registration for the Twenty-First Century: a Conveyancing Revolution* para 3.21.

and mines and minerals. It is evident from s 3 that land does not include rentcharges, franchise or profits. Section 88 provides that in its application to rentcharges, franchises, profits and manors, the Act can be modified by rules and it follows that manors are not land either. As they are not included in s 3 they cannot be the subject of an application for first registration. This is borne out by r 2(2) which distinguishes between an estate in land, on the one hand, and a rentcharge, franchise, manor or profit a prendre in gross, on the other.

Manors registered before 13 October 2003 remain on the register and will be administered by the Registry. Rule 2(2)(b) of the 1925 Rules provides that the register of title must include an individual register for each registered estate which is a rentcharge, franchise, manor or profit a prendre in gross, vested in a proprietor. There is also a separate index of manors under r 10(1)(b)(iv) listed by name. This may be difficult to search as many manors have several names or their spellings vary. A transfer of a manor will be in the normal form, usually TR1. A lease of a registered manor or franchise for more than seven years will itself be registrable under Sch 2, para 4 to the Act. Under Sch 2, para 5, those up to seven years must be protected by notice. It follows that although a lease of land for up to seven years is normally an overriding interest under Schs 1 and 3, para 1, such a lease of a registered manor is not.[27]

The proprietor of a registered manor may apply for the title to be removed under s 119. In that case title on a subsequent sale will comprise an official copy of the registered entries up to cancellation and a chain of deeds or other documents thereafter. Although most owners of registered manors may wish to keep them on the register there may be reasons to request their removal. One feature of manors is their historic interest and the chain of owners over the centuries. With registration, much of that information may be lost. Instead of a collection of title deeds, the owner simply has a copy of a computerised register. When a manor is sold the name of the new proprietor is substituted for the former one and there is no indication of the historic chain. Some owners may consider that the succession of owners is an important part of what they have bought. Furthermore, many manors now belong to people who do not live in England. If, say, an American citizen sells an English manor to a Japanese citizen the parties may prefer that their dealings are not notified to an English government body, nor that the transaction is dealt with by lawyers based in England with knowledge of English law.

Land Registry Practice Guide 1 on First Registration states:

> Many manorial titles include no physical land. Sometimes, however, land may still be attached to a manor and title to it may pass on a transfer of the manor. The

---

[27] See also 27.6.

compulsory registration provisions of the LRA 1925 did not apply to land that was part of a manor and included in the sale of a manor as such (s.123(3)(c), LRA 1925 (repealed)). There is no such exception in the LRA 2002. Therefore, if a manor includes physical parcels of land, the title to the land concerned must be registered following a transfer, mortgage or lease of a kind that triggers first registration. The lordship of the manor itself cannot be registered.

The reference here is to unregistered titles. Where a manor is already registered together with demesne land in the same title then, if the manor is deregistered, either the title will continue for the land or a new title may be opened.

The consequence of failure to apply for first registration is that legal title reverts to the transferor although he holds it in trust for the transferee. Under the Law of Property Act 1925, s 62(3) waste can be included in a conveyance or transfer of a manor by operation of law (9.2). The parties may not be aware of it and, even if they are, it can be difficult to identify or to satisfy the Registry as to title. Under the 1925 Act, s 123(3)(c)[28] special exemption was made for 'corporeal hereditaments which are part of a manor and included in the sale of a manor as such' so that where a manor in a compulsory area was sold with waste it was not compulsory to register the waste. This exemption has been removed by the 2002 Act.[29] This presents a problem in that the transferee is obliged to register title to land which he may not know he has acquired or, if he believes he has, he cannot persuade the Registry that he has. In practice this rarely matters since the land is unlikely to be of significant value. If subsequent evidence of title comes to light the Registry will normally accept an application to register out of time.[30]

25.8 RENTCHARGES, FRANCHISES AND PROFITS

Rights associated with manors may be registrable with their own titles. As indicated in 11.7–11.8, 12.4–12.5, 14.5 and 16.9, a lord may be entitled to a manorial rentcharge, franchise or profit. Rule 7 provides that where practicable, the property register of a registered estate in a rentcharge, franchise or profit a prendre in gross must, if the estate was created by an instrument, also contain sufficient particulars of the instrument to enable it to be identified. Where it is not practicable to produce the instrument, other evidence, such as exercise of rights over the centuries, should be provided. Most rentcharges will have been created by a deed but manorial rentcharges arising on enfranchisement may have arisen by simple agreement (14.5) and a few may have ancient

---

[28]   Substituted by Land Registration Act 1997, s 1 and using the same wording as in the proviso to the 1925 Act, s 120(1).

[29]   See Law Commission 271, *op cit* para 3.23.

[30]   Land Registration Act 2002, s 6(5).

undocumented origins. Franchises have either subsisted since before 1189, in which case there is unlikely to be any instrument, or have been created since then by a royal charter, which can be produced or a copy obtained from the Privy Council Office or some other source. Profits in gross are normally only created expressly by deed. Some important profits depend on inclosure Acts whilst others derive from the enfranchisement of copyholds and will be referred to in the enfranchisement documents. Profits may in principle have arisen by prescription at common law since before 1189, by lost modern grant or under the Prescription Act 1832, s 1.

Rule 10 requires the Registry to keep an index which can be searched. For land and affecting franchises this is by reference to maps, but for incorporeal rights it is by verbal description. It includes provisions for relating franchises.

Land Registry Practice Guide (PG) 16 deals with profits, PG 18 with franchises and PG 22 with manors. PG 13 deals with searches in the register on such matters. As explained in 10.1, a right of common cannot be registered as a profit under the Commons Act 2006, ss 3(7) and 61(1). It will nevertheless be a profit for the purposes of binding the land under s 28 of the 2002 Act. Although it will not be registered against the title, it will be registered under the 1965 or 2006 Acts and on a disposition will therefore bind a proprietor under Sch 3, para 3 to the 2002 Act.

On first registration of land covered by Sch 1, para 3 the proprietor is bound by all legal profits. If a profit is not entered on the register it may nevertheless be able to take effect as an overriding interest (25.9). Subsequently, a person acquiring a registered title under a disposition for value (or taking a lease, charge or other interest) is not bound by an unregistered profit (other than those registrable under the Commons Registration Act 1965 or the Commons Act 2006) unless he knows about it, it would be obvious on inspection or it has been exercised in the year preceding the disposition under Sch 3, para 3. Thus, if the lord has sporting rights under an inclosure award or the right to enter and take minerals (falling short of an estate in the mineral strata themselves) they may not be enforceable against such a person.

25.9 TRANSITIONAL PROVISIONS AFFECTING OVERRIDING INTERESTS

The general rule is that a proprietor of a registered title holds it free of all rights except those mentioned on the register. This is subject to certain defined exceptions, the most important of which are rights known as overriding interests. The concept of these (although not the name) goes back to the Land

Registry Act 1862, which referred, in s 27, to various rights including tithe rentcharges, rents payable to the Crown, liability to repair highways by reason of tenure, rights of common, manorial rights and franchises. This was amplified by the Land Registration Act 1925, s 70(1) which included rights of common, customary rights (until extinguished), profits a prendre, rights of sheepwalk, liability to repair highways by reason of tenure, quitrents, Crown rents, heriots, and other rents and charges (until extinguished) having their origin in tenure, liability to repair the chancel of any church, liability in respect of embankments and sea and river walls, tithe rentcharges, payments in lieu of tithe, charges or annuities payable for the redemption of tithe rentcharge, rights of fishing and sporting, seignorial and manorial rights of all descriptions (until extinguished), and franchises.

The 2002 Act radically reduced this list. Some rights, such as certain profits a prendre as described in 25.8, will still be overriding for the indefinite future, but several of the other categories listed above will, to the extent that they are listed at all, be temporary. In its report leading to the Bill that became the 2002 Act the Law Commission reached the view that there were certain ancient rights which were treated by the 1925 Act as overriding for reasons which were good at the time but which should no longer be so regarded.[31] As some of them are valuable it would not be right to abolish them at once, but those entitled to them were given 10 years in which to have their rights noted on the title to the burdened land. If the beneficiary does not do so before the first registration or disposition of land after 12 October 2013 then under s 117 they become vulnerable to loss.[32]

The rights are set out in Schs 1 and 3, paras 10 to 16. Schedule 1 deals with the position on first registration and Sch 3 on a disposition. The two schedules are almost, but not quite, identical, but the paragraph numbers correspond. The rights subject to the transitional provisions are:

10   A franchise

11   A manorial right

12   A right to rent which was reserved to the Crown on the granting of any freehold estate (whether or not the right is still vested in the Crown

13   A non-statutory right in respect of an embankment or sea or river wall[33]

---

[31]   Law Commission No 271 *op cit* paras 8.35 ff.

[32]   See Land Registry Practice Guide 66, *Overriding interests losing automatic protection in 2013.*

[33]   See *London and North-Western Railway Company v Fobbing Levels Sewer Commissioners* (1897) 75 LT 629.

14   A right to payment in lieu of tithe

16   A right in respect of the repair of a church chancel[34]

In addition, rights which remain overriding for the indefinite future include:

3   A legal easement or profit a prendre, except for an easement, or a profit a prendre which is not registered under the Commons Registration Act 1965 [and subject to certain conditions]

4   A customary right

5   A public right

The 2002 Act did not as such extinguish the rights in paras 10 to 16. Under s 11 on first registration the estate in the property is vested in the proprietor subject only to interests which are entered on the register or which are overriding, or certain rights under the Limitation Act 1980. Once the property is registered the basic rule in s 28 is that the priority of an interest such as those listed above affecting a registered estate is not affected by a disposition of the estate and it makes no difference whether the interest is registered. However, s 29 provides that if a registrable disposition of a registered estate (such as a transfer of the freehold or a lease for more than seven years) is made for valuable consideration (generally money or by exchange) then the interest is postponed to the rights of the person taking under the disposition. The effect of this is that until the first registration or disposition of land after 12 October 2013 the rights will bind the land and any proprietor. If the land is first registered after that date and there is no entry or notice on the title then the first proprietor (whether or not he acquired for value) and any later proprietor who acquired for value takes free of the interest. If the land was already registered by that date and the interest is not entered or noted then it will continue to bind the proprietor who held the estate on that date and any subsequent proprietor except one who acquires under a disposition for value. The right is therefore vulnerable to a first registration or disposition for value after 12 October 2013.

Paragraph 10 refers to a franchise. This will only be relevant to land registration if the burden is attached to a particular area of land and an issue arises between the lord and the registered proprietor (16.9).

---

34   Paragraph 15 concerned transitional rights involving adverse possession. Paragraph 16 was added by Land Registration Act 2002 (Transitional Provisions) (No 2) Order 2003 (SI 2003/1953).

Under para 11, the meaning of 'a manorial right' is obscure as the 2002 Act does not itself define it. The view of the Land Registry, based on the Law Commission report,[35] is that it refers to a right of the type preserved by the Law of Property Act 1922, Sch 12, paras (5) and (6), namely mineral rights in copyhold land, franchises, privileges of the lord in respect of fairs and markets, and sporting rights, as well as liabilities for works required for the protection or general benefit of any land within a manor or for abating nuisances therein[36] (which might benefit a tenant as well as a lord). The specific rules relating to minerals are considered in 11.9, fairs and markets in 21.2 and sporting rights in 12.4.

For the reasons set out in 9.5 this appears to be the better view but it is not beyond challenge. If it is not correct then manorial right may have a much wider meaning. The expression could include rights of any sort and adjuncts, appurtenances, annexures and appendices held or enjoyed with a manor. Clearly it does not include surface land, whether demesne or waste, which is in any case compulsorily registrable on a change of ownership as described above; but it might include excepted manorial minerals even where they are land. It could include any rights of the type referred to in the Law of Property Act 1925, s 62(3). It might also include ceremonial rights, such as the right to receive a pair of gloves when visiting the manor and, if that was due from the tenant of particular farm (17.7), the right could be noted on the register. Although that would best be seen as rent having its origin in tenure and so qualifying as an overriding interest under the 1925 Act, and not a manorial right, even if due to the lord of the manor, it cannot be an overriding interest under the 2002 Act and therefore would not bind the land unless entered. If the land has been first registered or passed on a disposition for value since 12 October 2003 it may now be too late to have it noted. If any land was held by Grand Sergeanty (18.4) before 1660, so that the honourable service was preserved by the Tenures Abolition Act, this would best be seen as a right benefiting the land and would not be affected. Any benefiting rights continue to subsist whether or not mentioned on the register under s 11(3), provided they are not also an unregistered burden on other registered land. In view of the complications of giving a wide meaning to the expression 'manorial right', the better view, and one consistent with the law that developed out of cases on inclosure Acts, is to prefer the narrower meaning.

It is possible that if a lord is able to claim escheat, that is a manorial right (7.7). However, ss 11 and 29 of the 2002 Act refer to rights binding estates, not land. On escheat the estate is extinguished and there is nothing to bind. Accordingly, there is no need to protect a potential right to escheat on the register. If it occurs

---

[35]   Law Commission 271 *op cit* para 8.41.

[36]   Land Registry, Landnet (June 2011).

and a lord can (and wishes to) demonstrate a claim he may wish to apply for his interest to be noted on the title. Escheat is referred to in s 82 of the Act and in more detail in r 173 in a section headed 'the Crown'. The rule itself is headed 'Escheat etc' and deals with the situation where a registered freehold estate in land has determined. The wording of the rule is not limited either to escheat or to the Crown and presumably if a lord was able to establish a right to escheat it would apply.

The terms of some inclosure Acts and awards conferred mineral, sporting and possibly other rights in the land which had once been common waste and occasionally copyhold land (and therefore vested in the lord) on the lord after inclosure. Although the courts tended to lean against such rights there were instances where they existed and such rights will still be in force. The issue is whether they are manorial rights for the purposes of Schs 1 and 3 to the 2002 Act. If the Land Registry interpretation, that 'manorial rights' means only those rights referred to in Sch 12 to the 1922 Act, is correct, then they are not. While they may once have had reference to copyhold land, that status was normally lost on inclosure save in the few cases where the inclosure Act allotted new copyhold. In that case the right of the lord to minerals may either be a corporeal right or a profit and the right to sporting would be a profit. Although annexed to the manor, they were not inseparable and would not be manorial rights as such.

Under para 4, customary rights (4.4, 4.8) are not subject to the time limit, but where any particular right is both customary and also falls within paras 10 to 16 it is likely that a court would construe 'customary' restrictively (4.1). Although manorial rights originally subsisted by custom, the Law Commission view[37] is that customary rights referred either to rights abolished by the 1925 reforms or to local customary rights. If the effect of Sch 12, para (5) to the 1922 Act was to convert what had been customary rights to statutory rights that would be correct, but it is not necessarily clear that the meaning in para (5) of 'shall not affect' was to do that. However, it is likely that a court would so interpret the 2002 Act to avoid any particular right being both a customary right (which continues to be overriding after 12 October 2013 under para 4) and a manorial right (under para 11) at the same time.[38]

Under para 5 'public right' includes highways and probably town or village greens (19.7). These are not subject to the time limit.

The remaining interests have been discussed elsewhere and must be protected or lost. Crown rents (para 12: see 14.6) are rare and usually too small to be worth protecting. Flood defences (para 13: see 9.5) may also be manorial rights if that

---

[37] Law Commission 271 *op cit* para 8.27.

[38] Under r 80(e)(ii) it is possible to apply for a notice in respect of a customary right.

expression includes liabilities not affected under the Law of Property Act 1922, Sch 12, para (6). Tithe (para 14: see 20.9) is mostly obsolete but some payments in lieu of tithe have become rentcharges and may still be protected as such. Many parochial church councils have carried out research to identify land subject to chancel repair liabilities (para 16: see 20.8).

25.10 PROTECTION OF MANORIAL RIGHTS

In many cases the lord's right will have been protected automatically by the Registry. If, on first registration, it appears that the land was former copyhold, the Registry enters a note. A typical entry[39] is:

> The land was formerly copyhold of the Manor of Pinechester. This registration takes effect subject to the reservation of any rights of the lord referred to in the 12th Schedule of the Law of Property Act 1922.

A lord who is entitled to an affecting franchise, a manorial right, Crown rent, tithe modus or corn rent or who wishes to protect rights to an embankment or a parochial church council which wishes to retain rights to chancel repair payments will need to protect them. In practice the most significant is the property right in minerals which can be worth substantial sums. If an application is made by 12 October 2013 to register a caution or notice there will be no fee. Even after that date it may still be possible to protect the interest, but a fee will be payable.

So long as title to the land is unregistered the manorial rights continue to subsist as the rights bind unregistered land in any case as legal interests under the Law of Property Act 1925, s 1(2). The lord can at any time lodge a caution against first registration. That step does not by itself give any legal protection but none is needed. If an application is made for first registration of the land protected the Registry will serve notice on the person lodging the caution who can then apply for a note of his manorial rights to be entered on the register. The applicant for first registration may not object, in which case a notice will be entered to protect the lord's rights, or he may object, in which case the matter will be referred to adjudication.

If the title is already registered the lord may apply at any time until the first disposition for value after 12 October 2013 to have a notice of his rights entered on the register.[40] A notice may be unilateral, in which case it does not need to be supported by evidence, or it may be agreed. An agreed notice either has the

---

[39] Land Registry PG 66 *op cit* para 3.

[40] Land Registry PG 66 *op cit* para 6.2.

consent of the proprietor or must be supported by evidence to satisfy the Registry, such as an enfranchisement agreement. The Registry will normally notify the proprietor after a unilateral notice has been entered, and if he objects the matter will be referred to adjudication.

Entry of a caution or notice is not itself evidence that the lord has any rights: it is simply notice that he claims them. As such, the extent of any rights may have to be decided at another time. However, if a proprietor does not challenge the entry or notice that may be taken as evidence that the right protected is accepted as valid. Care must be taken in applying for a caution or notice as if this is done without good cause and the proprietor suffers loss, he may claim for compensation under s 77 of the 2002 Act against the applicant.

Standard Land Registry entries also refer to the exception of minerals on enfranchisement, although strictly that may not be necessary under the rules relating to excepted minerals. This depends on whether the exception continues to be a manorial right. It would seem that once it has been converted from a customary right of property by the creation of a legal estate in the excepted minerals to a fee simple in them, it stands alone and its manorial origin ceases to be relevant. Having said that, where lords are aware of exceptions it would be sensible to protect them, although an applicant for a caution or notice may find that the Registry requires a fee to be paid. Indeed, where undoubted mineral rights exist, even unconnected to a manor or excepted out of a sale of demesne land, it is sensible to have a note made on the surface title in order to bring this to the attention of the surface owner and any intending mineral operator at any time when working the minerals is proposed, to ensure that the claims of the mineral owner are recognised at an early date.

A person seeking to be registered as proprietor of land may have a duty to disclose manorial and other rights affecting the land of which he (or his conveyancer) is aware. On first registration rr 23(1) and 28(1) require the use of form FR1 in which panel 11 requires the use of form D1, which obliges the applicant to disclose known overriding interests. If this is before 13 October 2013, when manorial rights continue to be overriding, the right must, if known, be disclosed. (Strictly, a right cannot be overriding until the first edition of the register has been issued, but the Registry uses the expression for convenience.) In addition panel 12 of form FR1 is a certificate that the applicant for first registration has disclosed all known rights. If they are shown up in the documents of title, Land Registry staff should pick them up.[41] Even after 12 October 2013 manorial rights are still rights, even if not overriding. Overriding status is relevant to priority under the Land Registration Act but

---

[41] Rule 28(2)(b).

does not affect their status as legal interests under the Law of Property Act 1925, s 1(2). The applicant therefore has a duty to disclose them.

On a disposition, r 57(1) requires disclosure in form AP1, panel 11 of which requires the use of form D1. There is no equivalent in form AP1 to panel 12 of FR1 so the duty extends only to overriding interests and, as after 12 October 2013 manorial rights are no longer overriding, there is no duty to disclose them even if known. Before that date there is a duty to disclose even on a disposition. If there is a duty to disclose and if an applicant knows that another person claims an unregistered disclosable manorial right but does not admit that the right exists, care must be taken in giving a statement that there are no interests as failure to disclose will be a breach of duty (Land Registration Act 2002, s 71) and may constitute an offence (s 123).

If the rights are not disclosed on first registration they will not bind. If the applicant deliberately conceals a known right he will be liable to the lord and the lord will probably be entitled to rectification, although if there is a third party interest such as a mortgage this may be resisted. If the land is registered before 13 October 2013 the right will bind until the first disposition. If that is not a transfer it may still bind interests other than those created. For instance, if the disposition is a lease or mortgage, and the lease expires or the mortgage is redeemed, the right will still bind the freeholder. Once again there is a duty to disclose overriding interests, for instance on form AP1 box 11 when applying to close a leasehold title.

Prior to the coming into force of the 2002 Act it was possible for a landowner to protect his land against the risk of someone else registering as proprietor (for example on the basis of incorrect or disputed title deeds, or by claimed adverse possession or fraud) by registering a caution against first registration. Many therefore used this as a substitute for actually registering their land. No evidence ws required to be produced, although if someone lodged a caution without good cause and another person suffered loss there might be a claim for damages against the cautioner.

Some lords of manors lodged cautions over roadside verges and similar isolated pieces of land on an unsupported allegation that they were manorial waste. Thus, the owner of a cottage next to a highway who needed to cross the verge could, on selling the cottage, find that the lord of the manor disputed his claim to a right of way. A fight against a determined lord would be expensive even if the cottage owner won in the end. In such case, the owner would have little option but to pay the ransom demanded by the lord even though, if the matter had gone to court, it would have been found that the house owner owned up to the *medium filum* and therefore the verge. Section 15 of the 2002 Act now provides that a caution may not be used to protect a freehold or a lease over seven years.[42] However, it may still be used to protect other interests, such as a franchise, rentcharge or rights of way.

25.11 HUMAN RIGHTS AND THE TRANSITIONAL PROVISIONS

The issue arises whether the provisions depriving manorial and other rights of overriding status could constitute a breach of Art 1 of the First Protocol to the European Convention on Human Rights, now incorporated in the Human Rights Act 1998, which protects a person in the enjoyment of his possessions. This was considered in some detail by the Law Commission.[43] First, it concluded that the provisions constituted a control, not a deprivation. The rights were not abolished as such but merely became unenforceable. Secondly, it was a legitimate aim for a state to pursue the object of having rights of such an unusual nature registered. Thirdly, the period of 10 years for protection without fee was proportionate.

Article 1 of the First Protocol protects many different sorts of right. In *Parochial Church Council of the Parish of Aston Cantlow v Wallbank*[44] Lord Hobhouse observed that 'possessions applies to all forms of property and is the equivalent of assets'. The term 'possessions' has been widely interpreted by the European Court of Human Rights to include many intangible rights including a landlord's entitlement to rent and other contractual rights.[45] In *Posti and Rahko v Finland*[46] the European Court held that the applicants' right under a lease granted by the state to engage in fishing on state-owned waters constituted a possession within the scope of Art 1. Thus, manorial rights are clearly property for the purposes of the Convention.[47]

In *JA Pye (Oxford) Ltd v UK*[48] concerning the loss of beneficial legal title to property through the operation of the doctrine of adverse possession, the UK Government argued that the risk of loss of the applicants' property through adverse possession should be viewed as an incident of property. The Grand

---

[42] Or certain other registrable leases.

[43] Law Commission 271 *op cit* para 8.89 ff and elsewhere. See also 29.1 for the view of the then government.

[44] [2004] 1 AC 546 at [91].

[45] See *Mellacher v Austria* (1989) 12 EHRR 391 at [43]–[44]; and Application No 10741/84 *S v United Kingdom* (1984) 41 DR 226 (concerning the benefit of a restrictive covenant and entitlement to annual rent).

[46] (2003) 37 EHRR 6.

[47] See also *Baron Mereworth v Ministry of Justice* [2011] EWHC 1589 (Ch): see 23.3.

[48] (2008) 46 EHRR 45.

Chamber of the European Court rejected that suggestion as such but took the argument into account.

The Court will look at the reality of the situation so that if a state legislates in such a way that a proprietor is effectively deprived of his rights that will be regarded as a violation.

However, the cases show that states may, under Art 1 of the First Protocol, lawfully control the use of property in accordance with the public interest and make and enforce laws for that purpose. Thus, in *Pye* the Grand Chamber held that it was legitimate for English law to establish a limitation period for the occupation of land, although the Court noted with approval that changes had been made in the 2002 Act to the rules for adverse possession by the time the case reached the Grand Chamber. It is therefore possible that the effect of the 10-year period is analogous to a legitimate limitation period.

There is, however, a difference. In *Pye* the Grand Chamber, following the representations of the UK Government, considered it relevant that the company had originally acquired the land subject to the possibility that it might be lost by the operation of adverse possession. That would not apply to manorial rights. The limitation rules were seen as part of a regulatory system rather than as expropriation. The Court accepts that limitation rules are proper in principle. This is a matter for the domestic rules of each state. However, in Pye the dispute was between two private parties. In the case of manorial rights the effective loss of rights on the first registration or disposition of land after 13 October 2013 is the result of direct state intervention which, by s 117 of the 2002 Act, has deprived lords of their rights. Similar principles may apply to chancel repair liabilities in view of *Aston Cantlow v Wallbank*.

On balance it is likely that any challenge to the loss of overriding status would be unsuccessful. The 10-year period has been well publicised and would probably be seen as a sufficient time in which those having rights could take steps to protect them. Such steps involve research and some expense, especially if the claimant needs to employ experts such as archivists or researchers, but this may be seen as proportional in order to establish a modern registration system free of what may be regarded as archaic rights.

Chapter 26

Buying and Selling

26.1   THE MARKET IN MANORS

In the 1980s a market developed in lordships. Manors (as distinct from their lands and revenues) had been bought and sold for years. It seems from *Beaumont v Jeffery*[1] (25.4) that in the early 1920s Mr Beaumont collected manors: there is no suggestion, however, that he was the squire of vast estates. By 1980 many people with spare money were looking for something interesting to invest in. Lordships had no revenues, usually no land, and were of curiosity or status value only, but they were scarce (for no new manors could be created) and of historic interest. In 1981 a typical manor could be purchased for around £2,000. By 1984 this had risen to around £4,000 and by 1987 to £10,000. Unusual manors were much more expensive. Henley-in-Arden was sold for £87,000 (£95,000 including the buyer's premium) in 1988.[2]

Most property is valued by reference to its income yield or, if it is a building, to its construction cost. If a manor has any income at all it will be, at most, a few pence from rents of assize and have no buildings. Its only basis for value is demand, and that depends on the number of buyers and the money available to them. After 1990 a decline in the economy was reflected in property values. Prices of houses, offices and farmland fell and manors could not be sold at any price. Although the market in real property revived, manors did not boom to the same extent. By 1994 a West Country manor in a small village might cost £4,000. A well-known manor in a commuter town near London could be £10,000 and in 1996 Wimbledon was sold for £171,000.[3] In 1994 the manor of Worksop, which carries rights in grand sergeanty at the coronation, was said to have been sold to a resident of Worksop for £40,000. Such manors have special features. The market for less distinguished manors largely settled down. A typical lordship for a village might change hands for between £5,000 and

---

[1]   [1925] 1 Ch 1.

[2]   *The Times*, 10 December 1988, p 26.

[3]   *The Times*, 30 November 1996, Supp, p 11.

£10,000. If there is historic interest or competition between two or more buyers, that could raise the price. If it is one of several manors within a village it might be less valuable. A local council may be prepared to pay something to acquire the manor of a town, although with constraints on spending this could be seen as a waste of council taxpayers' money. Sales of honours, comprising several manors, are rare and can also attract a premium.

Some manors may have negative value. For example, some may be subject to a liability to chancel repairs – although this would be unusual since the liability normally attaches either to land or to the lay rectory. If a manor includes waste which attracts travellers whom the lord has the responsibility to evict, or is used as an unlawful tip which the lord is responsible for clearing, this would incur expense without any return.

Some manors may have been bought under a misapprehension. A buyer should be aware that an English manor is simply a right of property; it does not confer a title or the right to be called 'Lord X' or 'Lady Y'. The Home Office authorises the owner of a lordship to include on his passport the words 'The holder is also known as lord of the manor of ...'.[4] Different issues can affect Scottish baronies and, it is alleged, some Irish baronies (if they exist as titles), which may carry the right to be called Lord X (23.5).

The process of selling and buying a manor is based on that of land. The following account assumes familiarity with that process and considers the special issues which apply to manors. What follows is an ideal. The research and careful consideration of documents takes time and expertise and is therefore expensive. If a manor is to be sold for as little as £4000 neither seller nor buyer will wish to spend half that again on professional fees. In practice therefore there is a tendency to reduce the formalities to a minimum and use standard forms and procedures. This may be risky in that each manor is unique and has its own appurtenances and burdens. The risks can be potentially serious for a seller who believes that he has simply disposed of a title of historic interest but no other value, only to find that the buyer claims to have bought roadside verges controlling access to homes and fields, or even whole fields or houses, in addition to common land, ponds or copyhold minerals. Much depend on the precise wording of the conveyance and of any preceding contract or sale catalogue.

---

[4]   Home Office Guidance on *Observations in passports* (7 February 2012).

26.2   AGENTS

Manors are unusual items and it is best to seek advice from a specialist, such as a surveyor who is familiar with the problems and the market. Such a specialist will approach known owners of manors, investigate the history, advise on whether to sell at auction or advertise the manor like a house, and generally do all that a selling agent of land will do. Other surveyors may principally handle country estates but may also have expertise in associated rights such as lordships. Regrettably there are also some in the business who hold themselves out as having skills they do not possess, which can lead to problems, notably selling titles the purported seller does not own or even non-existent manors.

An agent who deals in land has to comply with the rules laid down in the Estates Agents Act 1979 and the Property Misdescriptions Act 1991. Section 1 of the 1979 Act applies to things done in the course of a business on behalf of clients who wish to dispose of or acquire an interest in land. The issue whether a manor is land for the general purposes of the law is considered in 27.6 but whether or not that is so, if a statute provides a special definition then then those provisions will override the general law for the purposes of that Act. Section 2 of the 1979 Act defines land as a legal estate in fee simple or a lease which has a capital value. As explained in 22.7 a manor is held for a legal estate in fee simple. It may also be held on lease, although that is unusual. It follows that even though a manor may not be land for general purposes it would be land within the meaning of the 1979 Act. If the matter came up for decision in court the judge would consider the purpose of the Act, which is to protect members of the public from being exploited by unscrupulous dealers in property. The buyer of a manor is entitled to protection in the same way as the buyer of a house.

The Act requires an agent to comply with certain standards concerning information, terms of sale, deposits and so forth. Even if a court were to conclude that a manor is not 'land', the Act represents good practice and an agent advising on such a sale will observe its terms just as much as if he was selling a field or a wood. The 1979 Act is supplemented by the Property Misdescriptions Act 1991 which prohibits false or misleading statements in relation to 'prescribed matters'. By s 1(5)(d) and (6) these in effect relate to the same sorts of property as covered by the 1979 Act. The specific topics are prescribed in the Property Misdescriptions (Specified Matters) Order 1992.[5] The Schedule to the Order specifies a number of matters concerning the subject of a sale, mostly affecting physical land but also including (in para 13) its history and (para 17) its tenure or estate.

---

[5]   SI 1992/2834.

The agent will therefore try to find out as much as he can about the history of the manor. A manor with an interesting history or one which belonged to prominent historical figures may have an enhanced value. Was it in *Domesday Book*? Does it have any special rights, such as a market, a port or fishing rights? If there is an auction catalogue it may be illustrated with the arms of the present or a former lord, a picture of the manor house, a reproduction of an inclosure map or a sixteenth-century survey.

The agent will seek to introduce buyer to seller, negotiate a price (or arrange an auction) and do what he can to help the parties reach an agreement, just as he would on the sale of land. In the 1980s there was little information about what buyers were prepared to pay and many early sales were by auction, often accompanied by publicity as such a sale was a good story for the newspapers. More recently, as the market has settled down, private treaty sales have been the rule.

Auctions and sales are usually accompanied by a brochure. This may be illustrated with pictures of title deeds, coats of arms, portraits of former lords and other material but consists mainly of a verbal account. Care must be taken to ensure that nothing misleading is said. For instance there may be a good set of manorial documents but if it is not intended to include them in the sale this should be made clear and the buyer given the right to inspect them.

26.3   LAWYERS

Once the agent has introduced buyer and seller and the price is agreed the parties will ask their lawyers to deal with the documents. It is best for the seller's lawyer to be involved from the outset in approving the sale brochure and in preparing a draft contract ahead of marketing.

Anyone has the right to do their own conveyancing, but in relation to manors this can be complicated and most people employ a professional to do it for them. Under the Legal Services Act 2007, s 12 certain types of legal service are reserved activities which, under s 13, can only be carried out for a fee or reward by a person who is either authorised or exempt or, under s 15, is employed by such a person. Authorised persons include solicitors, barristers and licensed conveyancers. A person is exempt if he is doing his own conveyancing or is helping another for no fee or reward. A number of other exempt categories exist but these are unlikely to be relevant to the sale of a manor.

Because a freehold manor is real property, a distinction is made between the contract, which may be a relatively informal document, and a conveyance or transfer, which must be a deed. Under Sch 2, para 5 to the 2007 Act certain activities are reserved instrument activities. These include preparing a transfer for the purposes of the Land Registration Act 2002 (which would apply where the title to the manor is already registered), making an application or lodging a document for registration under that Act, and preparing any other instrument relating to real or personal estate for the purposes of the law of England and Wales. 'Real estate' is an American term but the words would probably be construed in an English sense as real property. A manor is undoubtedly real property and therefore it is an offence for an unauthorised person to prepare a transfer or conveyance of a manor for reward. 'Instrument' is not exclusively defined but it is clear from the context that it includes a conveyance. A manor can change hands only by a deed because the Law of Property Act 1925, s 52 requires a deed for a conveyance of land. 'Conveyance' includes Land Registry transfer and, under s 205(1)(ix), 'land' includes a manor.

Preparing a contract raises a more difficult issue. Many manors are sold at auction and the particulars are often prepared by the auctioneers, sometimes without the assistance of a qualified lawyer, as if so, preparing a contract for a fee will be an offence. Under Sch 2, para 5(3) to the 2007 Act 'instrument' includes a contract for the sale or other disposition of land (except a contract to grant a short lease, broadly one up to three years – see 27.6) so it is relevant whether a manor is land for this purpose. The Legal Services Act does not contain its own definition of land and therefore the Interpretation Act 1978 applies. This defines land as including 'buildings and other structures, land covered with water, and any estate, interest, easement, servitude or right in or over land'.

Thus, Sch 2, para 5(1) to the 2007 Act (substituting for the word 'instrument' the definition in para 5(3)) prohibits preparing a contract for the sale of land relating to real estate. The key word is 'land'. It must 'relate' to real estate but the question as to whether it actually 'is' real estate is not relevant. This wording may have been included because, although leases comprise land, the term of years granted by the lease is a chattel, that is personal property not real property. Certain adjuncts, such as manorial waste, are land; copyhold minerals are an interest in land or a right in land and so within the Interpretation Act definition. As such, if they are included the sale is a reserved instrument activity. A manor is real property and therefore real estate but if a manorial title is sold on its own without anything else then, as discussed in 27.6, it is probably not land at common law. It may 'relate' to real estate, in that a manor may have boundaries which can be traced on a map, but if the sale is not actually of land then it does not matter if it relates. A local history or ancient map may relate to land but they are not covered by the provision because they are not land.

Accordingly, a contract to sell a manor on its own, without waste or mineral rights or other rights in or over land, is not a reserved instrument activity and an auctioneer who is not authorised under the 2007 Act may, for a fee, lawfully prepare such a contract. However, such transactions are rare and it may be difficult for someone who is not a trained lawyer to know the precise effect, particularly having regard to the Law of Property Act 1925, s 62(3). In practice most auctioneers and agents will wish the contract to be prepared by a professional lawyer. As considered in 27.6 the contract itself will need to be in writing.

26.4   TERMS AND CONDITIONS OF SALE

The first task for a lawyer, whether acting for seller or buyer, is to check the title. This may be unclear or incomplete. The manor may have a registered title which will be proved by official copies of the register. If an unregistered title is offered, the buyer's solicitor should carry out a search in the Index of Manors (25.7) to ensure that it is not registered, bearing in mind that manors may be known by several different names or spellings. If it is not registered, there may be a good chain of title deeds, but that is often not the case. If it has not been mentioned in title deeds since 1925 it may be difficult to establish whether it is included in a general description of property. The person who is beneficially entitled to the manor, as a descendant of the former owner, may not have the legal title, which may therefore have to be traced through a chain of executorships (6.9). In such a case the theoretical and strict legal solution may be to take out a special grant of letters of administration; but the cost of doing so may be out of all proportion to the value of the manor. If the title is incomplete the seller's conveyancer must include a special provision in the conditions of sale. The buyer's conveyancer may have no choice but to accept that but his client will run the risk that someone else may later be able to put forward a better title.

The second task is to decide or agree what is to be included in the sale. If the lord is selling a manor where he still has demesne land he needs to be especially careful since at common law a conveyance of a manor in the past included the demesnes. In practice such a sale is unusual because if a squire still owns the village or farmland he will probably want to continue to be lord of the manor. Historically, the demesne was such an integral part of the manor that a conveyance or devise of 'the manor of Dale' automatically included the demesnes. It is not clear that a court would necessarily so interpret such words now. Suppose a buyer made a successful bid of £5,000 at a manorial auction for the manor and could show on a balance of probabilities that 100 acres of farmland or indeed a manor house had been held with it for centuries. A court might construe the auction particulars and the conveyance in light of the circumstances as applying to the title lord of the manor excluding the land. However, the point has not been determined and it would be unwise for a seller to take the risk.

The Law of Property Act 1925, s 62(3) does not refer specifically to demesne land but provides that a conveyance of a manor 'includes' the matters mentioned. The list of items included is therefore not exclusive. Its terms include the words 'hereditaments whatsoever, to the manor appertaining or reputed to appertain, or, at the time of conveyance, demised, occupied, or enjoyed with the same'. In modern conditions it would be rare for any cultivated land to be reputed to appertain to the manor or indeed to be enjoyed with it, in so far as a manor is generally seen as a title not a substantial property.

In *Crown Estate Commissioners v Roberts*[6] the University of Wales (which had succeeded to the estates of the former bishop of St David's) put up for sale 'the Manor of the City and Suburbs of St David's'. The conveyance did not exclude s 62(3) of the Law of Property Act 1925, which was therefore implied, but it did, as quoted by the judge, expressly exclude any corporeal demesne land appurtenant to the manor, as well as minerals.

Mr Roberts was the successful bidder. He claimed thereby to have acquired a lordship marcher in addition, although that claim failed. He did, however, acquire the manor for what appears to have been a modest sum. He claimed to have acquired with the title a potentially valuable extent of foreshore adjacent to a harbour intended for expansion, principally on the ground that it was appurtenant to the lordship marcher. He also claimed the foreshore as appurtenant to the manor as waste, but the judge found that it was not parcel of the manor. The judge accepted that the sale included a moiety of a franchise of wreck. As Roberts was not claiming any other land it was not necessary to consider how far land held with a manor, but not strictly demesne might have been included under s 62(3).

In *Eastwood v Ashton*[7] Earl Loreburn said: 'We must look at the conveyance in the light of the circumstances which surrounded it in order to ascertain what was therein expressed as the intention of the parties.' Where the words of the conveyance are clear the court will apply them without inquiring into the background. Furthermore, s 62(4) states that s 62 applies only in and so far as a contrary intention is not expressed in the conveyance. It may be possible to apply equitable principles to rectify the conveyance if it can clearly be shown that it was not intended to include valuable land. The problem is that

---

[6] [2008] EWHC 1302 (Ch), [2008] 4 All ER 828.

[7] [1915] AC 900 at 906.

rectification normally only applies where there is a common but unexpressed intention, while in cases such as this the buyer may be intending to take advantage of poor drafting on the part of the seller's advisers. Provided, therefore, that this is a commercial decision not amounting to fraud there may be no remedy.

Waste will be included in the sale under s 62(3) unless it is varied by the terms of sale. Some lords like to retain any waste in case it has a value for a ransom strip or can be sold for an extension to a garden in the future. Others wish to be rid of any possible responsibility for open waste land of uncertain area or use. Likewise, if the manor has rights to minerals in enfranchised copyhold land, or if minerals were excepted under an inclosure Act, the lord will need to decide whether to seek to reserve them or to include them in the sale.

The right to certain documents (25.2–25.4) may be expressly mentioned in the conveyance. These generally have little market value, but their existence may increase the price. Occasionally manorial documents such as ancient maps may be of interest to a collector, but provided they are subject to the Manorial Documents Rules they cannot be exported and must be kept in proper conditions.

Franchises can often be important. A market is now usually seen as a separate right, but where a market was created, for example in the thirteenth century, it may be capable of being revived and have potential commercial value, as may a claim to port rights. Sporting rights may be held under an inclosure Act. There may be mineral rights. All of these should be considered and the terms of sale drafted so as to include or exclude them as appropriate. Most other matters under s 62(3) do not present problems. Either the lord knows about them, and whether they have value, or he does not, in which case they are unlikely to exist.

An uncertain point is whether it is possible in law to strip the manor of all attributes so that the bare lordship is conveyed and nothing with it. In *Gloucestershire County Council v Farrow*[8] Goulding J at first instance considered the effect of certain words in a conveyance in 1945 which passed:

> ALL THOSE the Manors or Lordships of Stow-on-the-Wold and Maugersbury in the County of Gloucester but not including in the Conveyance hereby made any land hereditaments and premises comprised in [a previous] Conveyance other than the said Manors or Lordships

He found the wording difficult to follow. In that case it was agreed that the effect was to convey 'more than the bare feudal superiority of freehold estates,

---

[8]   [1985] 1 All ER 878, CA; [1983] 2 All ER 1031.

and it is highly unlikely that anyone would have thought of so limited a transaction in 1945'. He accepted therefore for the purposes of the case that it could have passed title to the waste, including the town square of Stow-on-the-Wold. However, it is not clear that such a transaction would have been considered 'highly unlikely' in 1945. In principle there seems to be no reason why what Bracton[9] calls a *nudum dominicum* or bare lordship could not be passed, and if it was possible in the thirteenth century it should be so now.

If title to the manor is unregistered the conveyancing documents will be in the same form as deeds for the conveyance of unregistered land. In the nineteenth century these were lengthy, elaborately worded and written on legal parchment in impressive-looking indentures. Nowadays the conveyance will be as short and stylised as possible and produced on a computer. If title is registered the buyer has a choice. He may continue the registration, in which case title will pass by a transfer in normal form and the buyer will apply to be registered in place of the seller in the same way as for land. Alternatively, he may apply under s 119 of the Land Registration Act 2002 for title to be removed from the register. On a future sale title will be shown by producing an official copy of the registered title, evidence of deregistration and a chain of deeds in the normal way after that. It is no longer possible to register title to a manor (25.7).

Another issue is the title guarantee (18.3). Most land clearly belongs to the seller, has a good title and can be sold with full title guarantee. This is not true of manors. If the seller has an absolute registered title he can sell the manor safely. The same may apply where there is a clear title derived from a landed estate, particularly one belonging to an established family or an ancient institution. However, many titles traded in recent years have not been clearly established. The original seller may be entitled to the manor but the succession of deeds may be incomplete or doubtful. The manor itself may be of doubtful authenticity. It is possible that a manor may have been sold at some earlier time without any record. In many cases, therefore, the seller will wish to give only limited title guarantee or none at all.

26.5   TAXATION

The holder or buyer of a manor may be subject to tax in respect of it. A manor and its attributes are taxable in the same way as anything else. Manors as such have not been units of taxation in the past. In Anglo-Saxon times tax known as

---

[9]   Bracton, Sir Henry, *De legibus et consuetudinibus angliae* (c 1257) (SE Thorne (ed)) (Belknap Press of Harvard University Press, 1977) f 264b.

the geld or Danegeld was levied on the hide. Maitland[10] argued that the origin of the manor was a house where or through which geld was paid. Certainly in *Domesday Book* manors are said to 'answer for' so many hides, but his theory is not now accepted by historians. Later, taxes were levied on the vill or by reference to the annual value of land, and rates were charged through the parish. Royal revenues were also raised through knights' fees by scutage and feudal incidents (22.5). Manors varied too much in size and wealth to be a sensible basis of taxation.

The main modern taxes to consider are income tax, capital gains tax, inheritance tax and value added tax. A company which owns a manor may be subject to corporation tax calculated in a similar way to income or capital gains tax. Aggregates levy and landfill tax may be relevant to a lord with rights to minerals or to the void left by their removal. The details of all these taxes are specialist topics and the following are general remarks which may not apply in all cases. The tax laws applicable in England and Wales are complex and change constantly. As such, anyone concerned with them will need to take specialist advice.

Income tax is payable under the Income Tax (Trading and Other Income) Act 2005, s 264(a) on income generated from land in the United Kingdom. This is explained in s 266(1) as including 'exploiting an estate, interest or right in or over land as a source of rents or other receipts' and 'other receipts' is widely defined to include rentcharges or the exercise of any other right over land. This would include rents of assize (save that the expenses such as postage would wipe out any taxable profit). It could also include revenue from sporting rights. Land itself is not defined but exploiting does not include mines and quarries since s 267(c) treats these as not generating income from land for this purpose. Under s 12 profits from mines and quarries, rights of fishing, rights of markets and fairs, tolls, bridges and ferries are taxed as a trade rather than as income from land. Some aspects are dealt with in more detail so that s 315 deals with sea walls, ss 319 and 339 and following with mineral royalties and s 344 with wayleaves, for example a right to run cables in manorial waste. Apart from such special provisions, and on the basis that a manor is not land for tax purposes, the special rules will not apply, for example, to a lease of a manor but any revenue generated would still be caught under the residual rules for taxing profits.

Where someone acquires and sells property such as a manor any gain is normally subject to capital gains tax. The definition of 'land' in s 288 of the Taxation of Chargeable Gains Act 1992 includes hereditaments of any tenure but in any case a manor would be an asset for the purposes of the tax under s 21.

---

[10]   Maitland, FW, *Domesday Book and Beyond* (Cambridge University Press, 1987; first published 1897) 120.

If someone bought and sold manors on a regular basis by way of trade he would be subject to income tax, but this is unusual.

Inheritance tax is payable on death and on some lifetime transfers. It is levied on all assets, and lordships are frequently assessed. The value is agreed with the local district valuer, who has access to information about the prices paid in recent deals. HM Revenue and Customs publishes on the internet various internal documents relating to the interpretation of difficult issues, policy valuation and other matters. One document relates specifically to lordships and baronial titles.[11] It states correctly that these may be valuable and, where appropriate, those concerned with the valuation of the estates of deceased persons should enquire whether such titles attach to the estate. Unfortunately the published text is seriously incomplete, most of it being withheld from public access because of exemptions in the Freedom of Information Act 2000. It is therefore difficult to assess how the Revenue approaches such matters.

Two points of interest arise, however. The first is that tax on 'land of any description' can be paid by instalments over 10 years, while tax on other assets must be paid within six months of death. Is a 'lordship' land for this purpose? In practice it is sometimes treated so, although the definition in the Inheritance Tax Act 1984 does not provide much assistance. The second relates to heritage exemption. The Treasury can (if it thinks fit) exempt some assets from death duties subject to certain conditions. There are two relevant categories. One, in s 31(1)(b) of the Inheritance Tax Act, is 'any land which in the opinion of the Treasury is of outstanding scenic or historic or scientific interest'. If a manor is land it might qualify as being of historic interest, but it is understood that the Treasury does not consider a manor to be land. The other, in s 31(1)(a), is 'any ... thing not yielding income' of similar interest. Again, it is thought the Treasury does not consider a manor to be a thing for this purpose.

Value added tax is a European tax governed by rules which apply throughout the European Union. It is charged on supplies of goods and services, which means virtually everything. Land is normally treated as goods. However, certain things, including land, are exempt under the Value Added Tax Act 1994, Sch 9, group 1, unless brought within the tax under certain rules. Does this exemption extend to manors? At one time the view of Customs and Excise which used to manage the tax was that manors were exempt. In 1990 it issued a formal guide[12] which stated that a transfer of title to a lordship of a manor was a supply of an interest in or right over land. Under European law this may well be correct. The

---

[11]   HM Revenue and Customs, Inheritance Tax Manual 23194: 'Special valuation matters: Lordships of the Manor and Baronial Titles'.

[12]   Customs and Excise, VAT Notice 742B (January 1990) on Property Ownership.

Petite Larousse Dictionary,[13] for example, defines '*Seigneurie*' as '*Autorité d'un seigneur, Territoire sur lequel s'étendait cette autorité*', and '*Manoir*' as '*Habitation d'une certaine importance, entourée de terres*'. However, it appears that Customs and Excise may have changed its view. It has been suggested that if a taxpayer is subject to VAT in respect of his general turnover and sells some manorial titles there may be a claim to VAT on the proceeds. Furthermore, while a manor itself may be exempt, the rights that go with it, such as sporting rights or a franchise, may not be exempt, although they may be treated as within the scope of the exemption for land if that exemption has not been waived.

Stamp duty land tax (SDLT) is charged on transactions in land worth above (normally) £150,000. Under the Finance Act 2003, s 48(2)(c)(ii) an advowson, franchise or manor are exempt from SDLT. The way s 48 is drafted suggests that if the exemption were not conferred these would be within the charge and treated as land, but that may not have been intended. Under the former stamp duty under the Stamp Act 1891 which SDLT replaced, a conveyance of a manor was chargeable. The reason for the change is partly because such things are not now in general regarded as land, partly because it is rare for them to change hands for more than £150,000 (indeed an advowson cannot be sold) and partly because it is virtually impossible to police. The principal means of checking that SDLT is paid is that a transaction affecting it can only be registered at the Land Registry if there is evidence of payment. While some franchises and manors are registered, registration is not compulsory and most are not. Suppose a lord resident in Delaware sells a manor to a buyer resident in Tokyo (a not uncommon sort of deal). The conveyance will never need to come into the United Kingdom or be notified officially here and it would be impractical to enforce any charge to tax. Section 48(3)(b) defines 'franchise' as meaning a grant from the Crown such as the right to hold a market or fair, or the right to take tolls. The value of the right to take tolls simply by virtue of ownership of land, such as a private road or bridge, and not under a Crown grant is not exempt. Although some franchises existing prior to 1189 may be unable to show a Crown grant, this will be presumed by virtue of *Quo Warranto* 1290. If a manor is sold together with land, such as manorial waste, then, under the Finance Act 2003, Sch 4, para 4, the price needs to be apportioned. However, as the tax is not due on sales whose value (taking into account any related taxable transaction) does not exceed £150,000 in practice most such sales will not be subject to it.

---

[13]   *Petit Larousse* (1963) 'Seignurie'.

Chapter 27

What is a Manor?

27.1 JURISPRUDENCE OF THE MANOR

This chapter aims at a jurisprudential assessment of the legal nature of the manor. This is particularly concerned with the essence of a manor. What really makes it? To answer that question it is necessary to look at the underlying ideas, to see how they have been applied in the past, and to attempt a definition. There are broadly three approaches to the manor. One is to see it as a community and a form of local economic organisation. The second is to regard it as a unit of custom, an area where local law modifies the common law of the realm. The third is to consider it as a piece of property, as a bundle of rights of the lord and of obligations on him.

Despite the historical detail of some chapters, this book has described what the manor is in the twenty-first century, but that carries with it what it was, or at least what it was thought to be. Manors developed 1000 years ago. In some sense the manor transferred by a conveyance drafted by a solicitor today is identical to the manor of the same name described in *Domesday Book*. There is continuity. A historian may discover the names of a succession of lords since 1066, and that what was handed on from one generation to the next has hardly changed. What will be referred to below as the substance may not have changed. But the appearance, the function and what will be described as the accidents of the manor have changed a great deal. The manor of 1086 was not the same as that of 1290, 1348, 1600, 1845, 1925 or today.

Until the Black Death the manor was primarily a means of organising farmers and farm production for the support of lords and for local co-operation among farmers. Its other functions were incidental. Although practice and the terms of occupation varied a great deal over time and across the country the impression is of the manor as a means for lords, whether individuals or institutions such as abbeys or the Crown, to control farmers and labourers, partly to provide an income and partly to govern the countryside. After 1348 conditions changed

with the gradual disappearance of serfdom and the shift to a more commercial
outlook, but the old ways of thinking about and understanding manors remained
until about 1600.

Modern ideas of manors derive largely from Sir Edward Coke.[1] As judge, law
reporter and writer of textbooks no one has had a greater influence on the shape
of the common law. Coke's book on copyhold has been the most influential text
on the subject. Coke's knowledge was not only academic or seen from the
bench. He made a fortune from the law and at various times was lord of over 60
manors, together with their lands and services.[2]

Coke was born in 1552 and died in 1634. He lived at a time when villeinage
disappeared. He was a contemporary and rival of Francis Bacon and his life
overlapped those of Shakespeare and Hobbes. His writings had a great influence
on the development of English (and American) liberties and therefore on
democracy. His mind was trained in learning and ideas derived from what we
call the Middle Ages: to him these were simply the years before his time and the
concepts he used were those familiar to preceding generations of lawyers.
However, at this time new ideas were replacing those which had prevailed for
centuries. Coke thought and wrote in a traditional way but he was practical
lawyer in the forefront of new developments and his ideas about the manor were
such as to suit the world of his time. His work provided the basis for all later
decisions and discussion. Therefore, although the manor may be seen
historically as a mediaeval institution, the legal analysis depends on the work of
Coke and for most purposes can disregard what has gone before. There are three
relevant aspects of Coke's thought: his philosophy, his politics and his history,
all of which have affected the idea of the manor.

27.2   COKE'S PHILOSOPHY

Coke begins his discussion with a brief historical account. He speculates as to
whether the Saxons knew the idea of a manor and does not reach a conclusion,
but he then refers[3] to:

---

[1]   For an account of Coke's life, see Bowen, CD, *The Lion and the Throne. The Life and Times of
Sir Edward Coke* (Little Brown & Co, 1985). For the general philosophical background, see
Copenhaver, BP and Schmitt, CB, *Renaissance Philosophy* (Oxford University Press, 1992).
For his political/legal approach, see Burgess, G, *The Politics of the Ancient Constitution* (The
Macmillan Press Ltd, 1992).

[2]   Bowen *op cit* 527.

[3]   Coke, Sir Edward, *Complete Copyholder* (1630) ss 10, 11.

the Normans, from whom we had the very form of Manors which is observed amongst us at this present hour. I confess, indeed, that sithence the original Creation of manors, Time hath brought in some Innovations and Alterations, as in giving a large Freedom until Copy-holders both in the nature of their Service, and in the manner of their Tenure. Yet I may boldly say, that the self-same form of Manors remains unaltered in substance, though something altered in circumstance.

He discusses at length the services owed by tenants of the manor and it is evident that what he describes is a shift from the original concept of cultivators owing duties to the lord to a newer one under which they hold their lands, whether freehold or copyhold, as property subject to conditions but otherwise at their disposal. Correspondingly, the right of the lord is one of property, and ownership of rights, rather than a position of superiority and control. Lord and tenant alike have rights and duties. As he says:[4]

> No marvel then that many able men turn Copy-holders, and many Peasants turn Free-holders: no marvell, I say, that men of all sorts and conditions, promiscuously, turn both Free-holders and Copy-holders, sithence there is such small respect had unto the quality of the Land in the reservation of our Services.

Nevertheless, he was imbued with the ideas of his time, which emphasised the concept of status or, as it was then put, degree. Degree, the relationship of superior to inferior, was understood to run through all creation from God to the lowliest worm and among humans from the king or queen to the humble farm worker. The manor was seen as a part of that structure, headed by the lord, and within which copyholders and freeholders had their place.

Degree was only part of the analysis. Coke needed to examine two other concepts, expressed in the terms of traditional thought. The first is the concept of substance which derives from the philosophy of Aristotle[5] who taught in Greece in the fourth century BC, although the way his concepts influenced the thought and work of mediaeval lawyers and administrators was far removed from the reflective philosophy of its origin. The idea of substance, that which stands below something, from Latin *sub stare*, can be considered with reference to an object such as a table. The substance is what makes it a table as such, rather than a bench or a desk. It also has certain special features: it is made of wood; it is square; it is three feet high; it is brown. These do not affect its 'tableness' as such and are called accidents. Other things may be square and brown and wooden. Substance and accidents together make a particular thing.

---

4 Ibid s 7.

5 Aristotle, *Metaphysics* (c 330 BC) *Z.28a*.

In the case of tables this is not much practical use. A prospective buyer who goes into a shop does not want to buy tableness, but something of the right size, shape and material on which to put food. In the case of legal concepts, by contrast, it is important. This sort of analysis enabled lawyers and civil servants to associate an enormous variety of different units of every shape and size that operated across the country by analysing the underlying idea and establishing general rules which could be applied to what appeared to be different circumstances. Even though each manor was different, with its own customs and peculiarities, they were subject to general laws, they could be dealt with as property and there could be rules about courts and legal proceedings. Classifying something as a manor enabled people to deal with it as an idea. Of course this existed before the twelfth century. *Domesday Book* regards almost every piece of land in the country as being within a manor even though they vary in size, population, equipment and revenue. Aristotelian philosophy sharpened notions of law and government considerably. To some extent these ideas also came from the rediscovery of Roman law in the thirteenth century; which in turn had been affected by philosophical ideas current during the late empire.

Coke does not directly discuss the substance of the manor, but the concept of accidents occurs in his discussion of services (s 22). He first distinguishes between services of profit and others:

> Services of Profits are of two sorts. 1. Tending to the publick Profit of the Commonweal; as when the Lord injoyneth his Tenant to amend High-ways, to repair decayed Bridges, or similia. 2. Tending to the private Profit of the Lord; as where the Tenant is injoyned to be the Lord's Carver, Butler, or Brewer, or is tied to pale the Lord's Parks, to tile the Lord's Houses, to thatch the Lord's Barns, and similia. And thus much for Corporal Services.

In treating of other services he distinguishes annual services from those which are accidental:

> Annual services are in number infinite, in nature all one, for they tend to the increase of the Lord's Coffers, and are reserved in their Duties, as well for Copy-hold-Land as Free-hold-Land: though in the Saxons time, and long after the Conquest, they were never or seldome reserved for Copy-hold-Land but only for Free-hold-land. I will not enumerate many particulars of Annual Services, for that were as endless as numbering the sands of the Sea.

He indicates that they are all in render, that is in money payments. These are of the type discussed in Chapter 14. Accidental services are also discussed in Chapter 14 or elsewhere, namely wardships (22.5), heriots and reliefs (14.3), amerciaments (14.2) and forfeitures and escheats (7.6). Annual services arise regularly while accidental services only when there is an event such as a death or default. Thus, accidental revenues are not of the essence, while annual revenues are those which gave an inherent value to the manor. In the eighteenth century, regular revenues were known as manorial rights and gave a saleable value to the manor (9.5).

Other accidents or attributes of the manor were its special customs as well as the adjuncts, annexures and appurtenances which varied from one manor to the next. While manors were still functioning institutions, no one would have tried to separate bare lordship from its additions. However, today that is precisely what some lawyers try to do (26.4). To sell the manor without anything else is like trying to sell the substance without selling the accidents – it is both philosophically and legally dubious, although a lawyer instructed to achieve that result will have to find a way of producing a legal arrangement that has that effect.

A third concept, after degree and substance and accident, is cause. The Aristotelian[6] and mediaeval ideas of cause were not the same as ours and the 'causes' of the manor are more like a series of definitions than explanations of how it arose. Aristotle describes four types of cause: material, formal, final and efficient. To go back to the example of the table, these are as follows. The material cause is the material of which it is made, namely wood. The formal cause is its structure – it is square and has four legs. The final cause is its purpose – to support plates of food. The efficient cause is closer to what would now be considered the 'cause', namely how the table came into existence, in this case the work of a carpenter. There are also other types of cause. The *causa causans* is the thing that gives rise to it, similar to the efficient cause, often contrasted with the *causa sine qua non*, the thing without which it could not have come into existence. These are sometimes called sufficient cause and necessary cause.

Coke seeks to define a manor in s 31 of his treatise on copyhold in Aristotelian terms. He says that there are two material causes, namely the demesnes and services, for the manor is comprised of those. He discusses the procedure to enforce accidental services. This leads to a consideration of the remedies where strangers or outsiders interfere in the running of the manor:

> But to meddle with Strangers were to wander out of the little Commonweal; and therefore to keep my selfe within my bounds and limits, I will here conclude touching the two Material Causes of a Manor, viz. Demesnes and Services. A word touching the Efficiant Cause of a Manor, and then I will end the Definition of a Manor.

---

[6]   Aristotle, *Physics* (c 330 BC) 194b.

He then determines the efficient cause of a manor as long continuance or time, as discussed below. He does not give a formal cause but states that the *causa sine qua non* is the court baron. Historians consider that that is not correct as a matter of fact, but later lawyers have accepted Coke's authority on this and, as a result, since there can now be few courts baron (because few freehold tenants), most manors are reputed (8.5). Coke does not suggest a final cause in s 31, but from s 62 of his book it appears he considers this to enable people to live together in community in amity (29.3).

27.3   COKE'S POLITICS

Even as Coke was writing, setting out the ideas developed through the Middle Ages, the system of degree that had ordered life in those centuries was changing. Within a generation there was the Civil War, the execution of the king and the enactment of the Tenures Abolition Act 1660. During the Middle Ages, despite (or through) rebellions, civil wars, forfeitures and executions, there had existed in England a rough balance of power between the king and the landholders. By Coke's time, travel was easier, wealth was greater and more diverse, commerce and trade increased and the balance broke down. This occurred nationally, but similar causes – trade, sheep farming, population growth – led to a similar breakdown locally in the manors.

Nationally, the response of the monarchy was to try to strengthen royal power. James I held and taught the divine right of kings, sought by use of the Court of Star Chamber to control the powers and abuses of local landowners, and tried to do all this using revenues from royal estates and feudal incidents without calling on Parliament to vote taxes. In this he was supported by (among others) Francis Bacon, essayist, philosopher (who attacked and discredited Aristotelianism) and one of the founders of modern science and as lawyer, Attorney-General (seven years after Coke) and later Lord Chancellor.

Coke was not opposed to royal power as such. He served the king loyally for many years on the Privy Council. But he did oppose what he considered to be the abuse of the prerogative, the exercise of irresponsible, unaccountable or arbitrary power. He was concerned lest the prerogative courts and the Court of Chancery should usurp the authority of the common law courts and, as Chief Justice, he supported the rules of the common law against the equity promulgated by the Chancellor. To do this he needed a source of authority to oppose the ideas of divine right. Since Bracton,[7] English lawyers had held that the king was under God and the law. But what law? Coke found it in the

---

[7]   Bracton, Sir Henry, *De legibus et consuetudinibus angliae* (c 1257) (SE Thorne (ed)) (Belknap Press of Harvard University Press, 1977) f 5b.

common law, from time immemorial, originating in Saxon times, enhanced by Magna Carta, and handed down by generations of judges. But it was not sufficient to base it on the decisions of judges alone for in Coke's day they were appointed by the king and could be dismissed by him (as Coke was in 1616) and were prone to decide in accordance with royal wishes. So Coke looked to the basis of common law in custom, and saw it as the custom of the realm.

By his time custom had largely lost its importance as a source of law for the nation but, it was still strong in the manors. This was the other side of the problem because the very men – the free landowners, whose liberties Coke was defending against the king – when they went home to their manors, might turn into local tyrants. Inclosures and dispossessions were frequent, though less common than some propagandists made out. One of the main functions of the Star Chamber was to punish such acts. Coke was no friend of inclosure, as he makes clear in his note to the report of *Tyrringham's Case*,[8] but he needed a different and better solution. This he found in custom, the custom that protects the copyholder. The law already protected copyholds, but under his guidance it came to protect and regulate custom against a lord who sought to abuse it, and so help protect the copyholder against eviction. This perhaps underlies his insistence that a court is a *sine qua non* of a manor, since if a landowner seeks to claim to be lord of a manor, Coke stated that he must hold a court and listen to the suitors. Although they were freeholders not copyholders, it was hoped that they would stand up to the lord as the House of Commons stood up to the king. He wrote his *Complete Copyholder* in the hope that it would bring harmony into the countryside.

27.4   LAW AND TIME

Deriving law and custom from time immemorial is problematic. It must be related to particular conditions; accordingly Coke had to develop a view of history and time. Originally, he took the view that the protection of copyholds derived from time immemorial. Bacon, on the contrary, held the view that this came from a change in the law. When Coke wrote his *Copyholder* at the end of his life he had also come round to this view.[9] To a lawyer, time is a commodity to be bought and sold. Much of land law is concerned with 'future interests', which arise after someone now living has died or a lease now running has

---

[8] (1584) 6 Co Rep 36b, 76 ER 973.

[9] See Coke's first view in Coke, Sir Edward, *A commentary on Littleton being the first part of the Institutes of the Laws of England* (1628) 73, 74, 77 and his later view in Coke *Copyholder op cit* s 7. Bacon's view can be seen in Bacon, F, *Works* xiv, 302–3, cited in Gray, CM, *Copyhold, Equity, and the Common Law* (Harvard University Press, 1963) 88.

expired. A good example is *Sir Moyle Finch's Case*[10] (8.4). All the relevant events – the lease and the various resettlements – took place while Lady Moyle was alive. None had any effect at the time, and all dealt with future interests. Such interests can be bought, sold, given away, resettled or leased out. They have a present value.

Correspondingly, lawyers tend to treat the past in the same way as the present and future. Past property rights in land are themselves of little worth but can form the basis of a future claim. The legal attitude to the past is of practical importance and is shown in two ways. The first is the rule of precedent. This book contains numerous references to old decisions of the courts, not just as historical illustrations. The law provides that a decision of a competent court creates a binding precedent that is itself a source of law. However, precedents are not always suitable. Many legal arguments – and the decisions of judges – are concerned to weigh up precedents, distinguish between them and, while respecting old law, to put it aside if justice requires and if the legal reasoning can be devised to do so.

The second factor is the nature of legal argument. Many rights of property depend on historical research. A lawyer, acting for a client, is not engaged in a disinterested search for truth. He is looking for truth, but a truth that will support his client's case. The nature of the English adversarial system is that his client's opponent will also engage a lawyer who will also search for a truth that supports his case. The result (and this applies in particular to cases concerning manors) is that the judge is involved in a balancing exercise, of historic facts and legal precedents produced by one side against those produced by the other, and out of that he must come up with a just result, or at least a just result according to law. There are two consequences of this.

The first is that the past is brought into the present. An example is *Attorney-General for the Duchy of Lancaster v G E Overton Farms Ltd.*[11] The case involved a claim by the Duchy to treasure trove in coins discovered in 1975 on land belonging to Overton Farms. They had been minted in the late Roman Empire but they were so debased that they had virtually no metal content. (As it happens one result of this was that coinage became worthless so that there was no point in free men paying money rent for their land and, in consequence, they had to pay in kind or services, so leading to the spread of the status of *colonus*.) If the minute fraction of silver the coins did contain was enough to make them treasure trove they belonged to the Duchy, which could give them to the British Museum. If not, they belonged to the landowner, Overton Farms, which could sell them. The court considered various authorities including Coke (with whom

---

[10]   (1610) 6 Co Rep 63a, 77 ER 310.

[11]   [1981] Ch 333; [1982] Ch 277, [1982] 1 All ER 524.

the judge, Lord Denning MR, agreed), Bracton and Blackstone (with whom he disagreed) before finding in favour of the landowner and against the Duchy. In the argument of counsel various cases were relied on including *Attorney-General v Trustees of the British Museum*[12] in 1903. That case in turn relied on the *Case of the Abbot of Strata Mercella*[13] in 1591, which itself relied on earlier cases dating back to Edward III. The fourteenth-century cases were not expressly referred to in the 1981 case, but they were in a sense present.

The second consequence is that the present is taken into the past. Whether considering the words of Best CJ in *Garland v Jekyll*[14] about the efforts of lawyers in Westminster Hall to free villeins (8.5), or the speech of Lord Templeman in *Hampshire County Council v Milburn*[15] (6.3) about the history of the manor ('The manorial system which the Normans partly inherited and partly established displayed a variety of local laws and customs...'), the attitudes of one age are applied to and interpret the institutions of an earlier one. This needs to be approached cautiously. The question of reasonableness of custom arose in *Hilton v Granville*[16] in 1861 where Lord Wensleydale referred (in the light of knowledge of the time) to the idea that the rights of copyhold tenants originated in grants by the lord. When the matter came up again in *Wolstanton Ltd and Attorney-General of the Duchy of Lancaster v Newcastle-Under-Lyme Corporation*[17] (4.3) in 1940 Viscount Maugham said:

> My lords, since the year 1861 a good deal has been discovered by the researches of some very able legal historians in relation to the status and nature of villeins and villeinage and to the origin of the legal interest or estate called copyhold; and I do not think we are called upon to accept the historical views of noble Lords in that year.

The effect of centuries of judges interpreting and applying the decisions of earlier ages has been to build up a changing view of the past, which has adapted to each century the inheritance of earlier ages. Manors have been especially prone to this. The year 1189, so emphasised by Coke and his successors, was (save for the coronation of a new king) not itself of any particular significance in law-making or interpretation. Where possible the courts have tried to escape the strict consequences of testing easements or customs by that year. But the very existence of the rule about time immemorial has meant that the courts have

---

[12] [1903] 2 Ch 598.

[13] (1591) 9 Co Rep 24a, 77 ER 765.

[14] (1824) 2 Bing 273 at 330.

[15] [1991] AC 235, [1990] 2 All ER 257, (1990) 61 P&CR 135.

[16] (1844) 5 QB 701, 114 ER 1414, 5 Ad & El NS 701; 4 Beav 130, 49 ER 288; 5 Beav 263, 49 ER 579; Cr & Ph 283, 41 ER 498; 10 LJ Ch 398, D & Mer 614.

[17] [1940] AC 860.

had to devise ingenious means of doing justice where the rule would have caused unfairness, and the effect of that has been to complicate the law.

It remains true, in Coke's words,[18] that:

> Time is the Mother, or rather the Nurse, of Manors; Time is the Soul that giveth life unto every Manor, without which a Manor decayeth and dieth: for 'tis not the two Material Causes of a Manor, but the Efficient Cause, (knitting and uniting together those two Material Causes) that maketh a Manor. Hence it is that the King himself cannot create a perfect Manor at this day; for such things as receive their perfection by the continuance of time come not within the compass of a King's Prerogative:

This was not just an account of the legal origin of manors. It was also a political statement.

Thus, by the mid-seventeenth century and under Coke's influence the idea of the manor as it is now understood had become established. It was a society, organised by degree, with lord, freemen and copyholders. It consisted of a basic fundamental idea with its essential components (demesne and services) but each had its own special features, customs and appurtenances. It existed from ancient times as a balanced community focussed on the manor court. So it stayed. By the time of Coke's death in 1634 manors were becoming outdated, and later they were replaced by estates, their common fields and pastures were inclosed, customs were increasingly obsolete or declared unreasonable and in 1926 the remaining copyholds were enfranchised.

Ideas also changed. Coke was a lawyer through and through. His contemporary and rival, Francis Bacon, although serving as Attorney-General and Lord Chancellor, was also an essayist and philosopher who set out the ideas that underlie modern science. Younger men, such as Hobbes and, later, Locke, developed further ideas that support modern politics and law. States, local government, companies, freedom of contract and freedom of expression all developed from what they taught. So how does the manor, worked out in the Middle Ages, given classic expression by Coke, fit into this new world?

27.5   OWNERSHIP AND PUBLIC LAW

Since the time of Coke there have been great changes in philosophy, politics, history, society and law, but until the twentieth century the legal idea of the manor changed little. Its economic basis was gone and its social fabric unravelled; there was therefore no need to rethink manors, as contract, property

---

[18]   Coke *Copyholder op cit* s 31.

or constitutional law were rethought, and the powerful impress of Coke's ideas discouraged any new ones. However, legal ideas have developed and are no longer expressed in the terms that were already going out of fashion in Coke's time.

There are many theories of law or jurisprudence. In England two of the best known are those of John Austin in his Lectures on Jurisprudence and HLA Hart in *The Concept of Law*.[19] Austin saw law as a command by a superior to an inferior which the superior was able to enforce. This view corresponds well to those aspects of the manor which emphasise the role of the lord and his court and the idea that all rights depend on grant. Hart criticised Austin's ideas and put forward his own, which saw law as a set of generally accepted rules. This fits better with the communal aspect of the manor and the importance of custom. Indeed, the nature of custom is one of their main points of difference. Austin did not consider customs to be law until they had been recognised and enforced by the courts. Hart (in the tradition of Bracton and Coke) gave custom the force of law once it was accepted.

These two theories of law, as well as the many other ones worked out in other countries, are themselves of little direct use to a practicing lawyer. A different approach is needed, to examine the nature of concepts such as ownership or property. They are best seen as comprising bundles of legal rights. That approach is especially suitable for a manor – for it is not just one thing but a collection, miscellaneous, even ramshackle.

Under English law no one can own land or other real property as such. They can only own an estate or interest in, or right over, the land or property. They can own a fee simple or a lease or may have rights under a trust. They may have an easement or a profit à prendre. The effect of this rule is that it allows the creation of varieties of different rights and powers. The justification for the rule in the case of land is that in law no one can own the land itself – its minerals, plants, rocks or the animals that live on it or fly through the air over it. Rights over each of these can, as discussed, belong to different persons. One person can have the right to plant and harvest crops for a period of time, another to exploit the tin or iron, another to take sand, another to put out his animals to graze, another to hunt or fish, and so on. Many of these distinctions first emerged in the context of manors and were only later applied to land of any sort. At a time when a manor involved the greater part of a local society – both free tenants and bondsmen – it would not have been right to regard the lord as owning people, but only as owning something that gave him a right to certain services from them.

---

[19] Austin, J, *Lectures on Jurisprudence* (Campbell (ed), John Murray, 1885); Hart, HLA, *The Concept of Law* (Oxford University Press, 1961).

Manors therefore were more than just properties. They were also communities, with the common wastes, meetings in court baron, customary rules of inheritance, services and the differing status of tenants. Most of these aspects have disappeared with time.[20] This communal aspect of manors raises another issue. If a manor is not just land, is it private property? The modern view, indeed the view since the thirteenth century, is that it is private, but with a difference. It is not quite like a piece of land or a chattel.

Whatever the understanding of the Saxons, one of the consequences of the Norman Conquest and feudalism was to combine together what we call private and public law; and the distinction has emerged slowly since then (5.1). The king granted portions of the realm in tenure and each lord had his own court. Often he also held franchises which were a grant of royal authority. In theory, there was a distinction between the private system of honorial and manorial courts for tenants and subtenants, and the public system of shire, hundred and leet or frankpledge, but especially at the local level these were more often combined than not. Coke, as quoted above (27.2), saw manors as including public profits, such as an obligation on tenants to repair highways and bridges (15.3).

In modern times the distinction has been clarified. Criminal law and taxation were separated from private law, although until the mid-seventeenth century much royal revenue came from seigniorial dues, and private criminal jurisdictions continued in theory until the nineteenth century. The courts became seen as public institutions to such an extent that the Administration of Justice Act 1977 abolished ancient private jurisdictions (13.4). Now, such matters as charity law and pensions, which only a few years ago were seen as private law, are considered public. It took time for the distinction between public and private law to be accepted. Indeed, when the idea that there was such a thing as public law started to be circulated in England it was opposed by many lawyers, as exemplified in AV Dicey's Introduction to the *Study of the Law of the Constitution* first published in 1885. The concept of public law was not fully incorporated until the decision of the House of Lords in *O'Reilly v Mackman*,[21] although now it is recognised that the two aspects of law are separate but related.

The modern legal test is jurisdictional. If something is public then judicial review will lie from the courts to correct improper actions. Thus, local authorities, magistrates, even the City Panel on Takeovers, are public in this way. On the other hand, trades unions and the Jockey Club, however influential

---

[20]   Bracton *op cit* f 76, 78.

[21]   [1983] 2 AC 237.

they may be, are not.[22] Under this test a manor was public. If a steward did not hold a court to admit a copyholder or if he did not make the manorial rolls available to prove title, an aggrieved person could issue a writ of mandamus, the predecessor of judicial review, to require him to do so.[23] This applied not only to the court leet (which was a court of record) but also to the court baron (which was not). However, this may have been[24] because the royal courts were not only the highest 'public' courts. They also had a feudal jurisdiction over the courts of lords who held their manors directly or indirectly from the king.

The manor today is regarded as private. This may derive from the struggles of the seventeenth century when landowners, using concepts developed by Coke, asserted their rights of property against the king. They regarded their manors as their private business and indeed the steady royal opposition to inclosure came to be seen as an interference with their affairs. After 1660 government opposition ceased.

27.6   WHETHER THE MANOR IS LAND

The issue as to whether a manor is land has important consequences. If it is land then an agent who advises on selling it is subject to the Estate Agents Act 1979. Therefore if he does not give written information about his terms, keep client's money in a special account or do other specified things, he commits an offence and can be fined (26.2). If it is not land then those conditions do not apply. If a manor is land then VAT is not payable on sale, and if someone dies owning the manor death duties are payable over 10 years (26.5).

The question as to whether a manor is a corporeal hereditament or incorporeal was considered in 9.2. It is clear that at one time it was corporeal. In the early Middle Ages it would pass by the ceremony of feoffment with livery of seisin which was the means of granting corporealities. In *Tyrringham's Case*[25] the court specifically considered a manor to be land: 'a thing incorporate, as an advowson, may be [appendant] to a thing corporate as to a manor'. Coke would have agreed, since to him the demesnes were an essential feature. Bracton might

---

22   *Hamlet v General Municipal Boilermakers and Allied Trades Union* [1987] 1 WLR 449, [1987] 1 All ER 631; *R v Panel on Takeovers and Mergers, Ex p Datafin plc* [1987] QB 815, [1987] 1 All ER 564; *R v Disciplinary Committee of the Jockey Club, Ex p Aga Khan* [1993] 1 WLR 909, [1993] 2 All ER 853.

23   Scriven, J, *A Treatise on the Law of Copyholds* (Butterworth & Co, 7th edn by Archibald Brown, 1896) 449ff.

24   Custom was tested by the idea of reasonableness (4.4), which is now a public law concept.

25   (1584) 4 Co Rep 36b, 76 ER 973.

not have agreed.[26] He distinguished lordship in possession where it carries a right to occupation (directly or through villeins) from lordship in service – bare lordship – where all the lord is entitled to is the services (military or agricultural or in money) and not the land itself. This corresponds to the distinction between *dominium utile* and *dominium directum* (5.7). Blackstone[27] probably still thought of a manor as corporeal, at least he did not include lordships in his list of incorporeal hereditaments. However, a change took place after his time.[28]

The 1925 legislation can be misleading. The definitions of land in the Settled Land Act 1925, s 117(1)(ix), the Trustee Act 1925, s 68(6), the Law of Property Act 1925, s 205(1)(ix) and the Land Registration Act 1925, s 3(viii) all include manors, but that is simply a shorthand way of using language. If legislation makes provision for the methods of conveying land, for the number of trustees of land, or for what happens to land on death, then if the same rules apply to manors it is simplest to include them in 'land' to avoid surplus verbiage. That does not mean, however, that manors are land. A better view comes from the Settled Land Act 1925, Sch 1, form 1 of which provides a suggested form of vesting deed. The note says, 'In the first part of the First Schedule give particulars of the manors, advowsons and other incorporeal hereditaments'. The Law of Property Act 1925, s 201 is headed 'Provisions of this Act to apply to incorporeal hereditaments'. Originally this stated, 'The provisions of this Act relating to freehold land apply to manors, reputed manors, lordships, advowsons, tithe and perpetual rentcharges, and other incorporeal hereditaments, subject only to the qualifications necessarily arising by reason of the inherent nature of the hereditament affected'. The Land Registration Rules 1925, r 50 also treated manors as incorporeal.

That is in general the modern view. A manor may – indeed usually will – include land, especially waste, but the manor itself is not land. It is localised. It subsists in a particular county, usually within one parish, with ascertainable boundaries, but that does not make it land. As discussed in 25.7 the Land Registration Act 2002 so defines its subject matter as to make it clear that a manor is not land for its purposes and manors could not be registered after the Act became law.

One curiosity relates to short leases of manors. In general all conveyances (defined to include leases) must be by deed.[29] An important exception[30] allows the creation of leases of corporeal property taking effect in possession for not

---

[26] Bracton *op cit* f 264b.

[27] Blackstone, Sir William, *Commentaries on the Laws of England* II.3.i.

[28] See *Earl of Carysfort v Wells* (1825) M'Cle & Yo 600 at 610, 148 ER 551 at 555.

[29] Law of Property Act 1925, ss 52 and 205(1)(ii).

[30] Ibid, s 54(2).

more than three years at the best rent. Thus, a monthly tenancy of a room or an annual tenancy of a farm need not be by deed. The need for a deed for corporeal hereditaments dates from the Statute of Frauds 1677. Before that, freeholds were assured by livery and seisin and leases could be granted informally or, as it was said, 'by parol'. Even before 1677 the common law required any disposition of an incorporeal hereditament to be by deed[31] and that included, for instance, even a short lease of a right of way. Coke[32] therefore distinguishes between corporeal things 'as lands and tenements, which lie in livery and pass by livery either with or without deed, and incorporeal, which lie in grant, and cannot pass by livery, but by deed only, as advowsons, commons &c'. Commenting on this passage in *Hewlins v Shippam*[33] Bayley J said, 'it seems to be his [Coke's] opinion, that (except in certain specified cases), where livery is necessary as to the one, a deed is necessary as to the other'.

The re-enactment of the 1677 Act in the Law of Property Act 1925 refers to land. As indicated the Act defines land as including a manor, but s 54(2), which contains the exception, says that 'Nothing ... shall affect' the creation by parol of short leases, suggesting that the rules of the common law still apply. If a manor was once corporeal but the law has changed so that it is now incorporeal, will this apply to a short lease of a manor? In the Middle Ages manors could pass by livery, so presumably, in the absence of any express change, the rules are the same so far as the exception is concerned, and in the unlikely event of a lease of a manor for up to three years this could be done by parol notwithstanding that such a lease is now incorporeal. However, in view of the uncertainty surrounding this issue, the safe course would be to use a deed. The Land Registration Act 2002 has special rules for leases of registered manors (25.7).

Likewise, it is unclear whether a contract for a sale of a manor has to satisfy the Law of Property (Miscellaneous) Provisions Act 1989, s 2. This requires a contract for the sale of an interest in land to be in writing, but land itself is not defined in the Act. The section replaces the Law of Property Act 1925, s 40, which incorporated the definition in s 205(1)(ix). It is therefore likely that a court would apply the same definition, so that a contract for a manor would have to satisfy the 1989 Act.

---

[31] *Wood v Leadbitter* (1845) 13 M& W 838, 153 ER 351.

[32] Coke on *Littleton op cit* 9a.

[33] (1826) 5 B& C 22, 108 ER 82.

27.7   DEFINITION

A manor, as this book has shown, is a bundle of rights, a collection of miscellaneous legal things. In the past there was no need to define a manor. People knew what it was even if they could not define it accurately. Although Coke indicates that he is providing a definition, it is not one in the modern sense. However, since the law relating to manors is less familiar, there is a risk that people, even lawyers, may misunderstand what is involved. Failure to appreciate some of the rules about manors led to problems under the Commons Registration Act 1965.

A definition is only useful or relevant for a specific purpose, in this context to determine property rights, including the practical consequences of a conveyance of a manor or to determine what rights people may have in specific situations. The first function is to decide what a buyer of a manor may expect to get. The Law of Property Act 1925, s 62(3) is a starting point, but in practice may be modified or excluded. It implies a variety of rights as well as corporeal properties such as waste, assuming that the seller was in a position to pass them on.

Perhaps more important is what s 62(3) does not mention. It does not refer to demesne land, and it is possible that the former rule that a conveyance of a manor carried the demesne no longer applies (26.4). Apart from proof that specified land has at all times since 1290 been held with what has at all times been a legal manor, it is probable that a judge would be prepared to say that someone who had paid, say, £5,000 for a manor would not expect to obtain thereby its fields or houses, and the conveyance should be construed accordingly. It is not so clear that the same would apply to waste (especially as it is mentioned in s 62(3)) since waste has little value and may be a liability.

Another issue is escheat. This is unlikely to become a practical problem since the issue of escheat normally arises in the context of onerous property which no one wants. It would also be rare for a lord to be able to prove that any specific piece of land was held from him. If he was keen to acquire escheated land (perhaps because it adjoined some land he already owned) in practice the simplest course would be to buy it from the Crown Estate Commissioners, as that would be a great deal cheaper than fighting the Commissioners for it in court. It is therefore unlikely that there will be occasion for any decision on this.

Nevertheless, it may be useful to attempt a general definition. It needs to be evident that a manor is now incorporeal. For the purposes of the Trusts of Land and Appointment of Trustees Act 1996 (8.3), it should be clear that a manor cannot be divided. The essential feature is still that for a legal manor to exist there must be at least two free tenants (8.4). A manor, as Coke indicates, is a unit of custom (4.1). A suggested definition is as follows:

> A legal manor is an incorporeal hereditament comprised in one lordship over defined areas of land held in more than one parcel sharing a set of customs and having more than one dependent freeholder owing suit of court. A reputed manor is a former legal manor having fewer than two dependent freeholders.

Chapter 28

What Remains

28.1   LORDSHIP, LAND AND BENEFITS

Over the centuries most attributes have been stripped from the manor until little is left. The following is a summary of what may remain to be held by a lord who has inherited a title or by an ancient institution and what might be available for the buyer of a manor.

First, there is the lordship – of the manor, the honour or barony, or hundred or borough. That is a title, a distinction of little importance in itself but part of the heritage of a small portion of England. It carries the right to be known as owner of a lordship even though there is no right to be called my 'lord'. Many people value the title for its historic interest or for its association with a village or a town.

Secondly, there is land. If the lord still holds demesne he probably does not think of it as belonging to a manor. He does not distinguish his type of ownership from that of his neighbours who are not lords of manors, nor the demesne lands of the manor from the other lands he owns. But if he sells 'the manor' without reserving the land the buyer could argue that he has acquired valuable interests. In practice, as discussed in 26.4, it is unlikely that a court today would so construe the sale of a manor, but the risk of an argument arising from a poorly drawn sale contract remains. The outcome might be different under a will. If a lord left 'my Manor of Dale' to his son and the rest of his property to his daughter and the manor had (or was even reputed to have) demesne land, a family dispute could arise over the meaning of the will.

The waste (6.3) is still often associated with the manor. It is not unusual to refer to the lord of the manor as such when considering ownership of common land (10.1) and the Commons Registration Act 1965 has given rise to many recent cases to distinguish waste not subject to rights of common which is of the manor from that which is not of the manor. Waste includes numerous scraps and pieces of land. Roadside verges (6.5), the soil of roadways laid out under inclosure awards (6.6), odd corners of uncultivated land and stream beds (6.7) may all be waste and so belong to the lord. Other land, such as village greens (19.6), millponds and mill leats (17.3) and even marketplaces (21.3) are the lord's unless someone can claim a better title.

Thirdly, there are various rights. The most important rights are rights to minerals. In former copyhold land and in the absence of special custom or an exception on enfranchisement this merely gives mutual rights of veto to lord and landholder so that each can prevent the other from exploiting the minerals (11.7), but even a half share in minerals may be worth something. Such rights are vulnerable if they are not protected by notice on the register or caution against first registration before the first registration or disposition of land after 12 October 2013 (11.9). The lord may also have the freehold of mineral rights in former waste preserved under an inclosure Act (11.6) or in former copyhold where they were excepted on enfranchisement (11.8).

Sporting rights may still exist, depending on custom and local conditions. Some may have been lost by the abolition of free warren in 1971 (12.3) but others may remain, especially several fisheries (12.7). Occasionally, the lord may have such rights by virtue of an inclosure award (12.5). These rights take effect as profits and again need to be protected unless they are regularly exercised.

28.2   ANCIENT RIGHTS

The lord may still have the right to markets and fairs (21.2). While most functioning markets have been sold, there may be ancient markets capable of being revived. Again if these apply to specific pieces of land they may rank either as manorial rights or as affecting franchises and, if so, they will need to be protected before the first registration or disposition of land after October 2013 (16.9). Most port rights and tolls are now obsolete, but the lord may still own the bed of the harbour and be able to claim mooring fees (15.4). The lord may have other franchises, such as wreck (16.6), which is common but nowadays is seen more as a burden than a privilege as it may carry an obligation to clear up any debris that comes ashore from a wrecked vessel.

Fourthly, there are the courts (13.1). The 1977 Act removed their jurisdiction but did not abolish them as such. Courts customary are no longer held because no customary tenants have existed since 1925, but if the lord can locate two free tenants then he can hold a court baron, and any local resident can come to a court leet (19.5).

If the manor comprises free tenants the lord may have the right to escheat (7.7) if a tenant is made bankrupt or if a company goes into liquidation and the trustee in bankruptcy or liquidator disclaims the freehold. As disclaimed property must be onerous such a scenario is unlikely if the freehold still has value. On escheat the lord will probably only be left, for example, with a dangerous worked-out quarry, a contaminated factory site, a listed building in ruinous condition or a similar problem. Free tenancies are rare (5.7). Apart from possible creation by statutory enfranchisement between 1841 and 1925 (or perhaps under an inclosure Act) they must have been granted before 1290 and will only rarely be recognised. The existence of a rent of assize or the land being former glebe may point to that.

Manorial rents are even more rare and usually not worth the cost of collecting (14.1). A few pence may be payable as a rent of assize or for a lease of 1000 years payable at the manor court. A few manorial rentcharges granted on enfranchisement instead of compensation being paid in full remain, but these will expire in 2037 (14.5).

Church rights can be of interest. Since 1 January 1989 advowsons cannot be appendant to a manor but the lord will often still be the patron (20.2). Corn rents, which will need to be protected under Land Registration Act 2002 before the first registration or disposition of land after 12 October 2013, are unlikely to be worth the cost of doing so. Rights to a particular pew, the use of a side chapel or a special burial vault, or liability to repair the chancel are more likely to be attached to land than to a lordship. If the lord is lay rector he may have the freehold in the churchyard although this will carry little benefit (20.6).

The lord may own the rolls (25.2) and other manorial documents (25.3), although he cannot take them out of the country and they must be kept safe and accessible to people with a right to inspect (25.4).

Ceremonially, a few manors owe the services of grand sergeanty at the coronation (18.4). Equally, there may be freehold tenements within the manor which still owe ceremonial duties, such as rendering a pair of gloves on a visit by the lord (17.7).

Finally, there are a variety of miscellaneous rights. The lord may have the power to appoint a gamekeeper with special powers to seize items under the Game Act 1831 (12.8). He may approve commons regulations under the Commons Act 1876 or consent to the exercise of powers by a commoners council under the Commons Act 2006 (10.8). Other special rights may also exist under local Acts. In addition, there may be special annexures comparable to the appointment of a Master of Ewelme Hospital (17.5).

28.3   THE HERITAGE

Any particular manor is likely to have only a few of these things and most are obsolete or valueless. If they had any value they would probably have been sold long ago to pay debts or raise money to buy land. But here and there in villages and indeed in towns up and down the country many strange and unexpected rights associated with manors still survive.

The chief interest is historical. Many lords are interested in the history of their manor, the previous holders, the contents of the rolls and the life of the community. Someone who has bought a title will rarely be accepted as a local leader but, nevertheless, he may give money to local projects, write to local papers on local issues and help with employment. Even holding a court may provide a forum for people to discuss matters of local interest.

Other rights survive under inclosure Acts. Many Acts laid out paths and roads which still survive as public paths protected under the Highways Act 1980 and the Wildlife and Countryside Act 1981.

In England there is a full if illogical system of protecting antiquities. The manor house itself may be a listed building subject to the Planning (Listed Buildings and Conservation Areas) Act 1990. The ridge and furrow pattern of the fragments of open field, the fishponds and the ruins of an old Norman motte will be ancient monuments within the Ancient Monuments and Archaeological Areas Act 1979. Manorial rolls are governed by s 144A of the Law of Property Act 1922. The shape of hedges planted on a reverse 'S' line to follow the boundaries of old strips may be protected under the Hedgerow Regulations 1997 (7.13). The waste is subject to the Commons Registration Act 1965 or the Commons Act 2006 or to public access under the Countryside and Rights of Way Act 2000. It may also be subject to a management agreement with English Heritage under the Wildlife and Countryside Act 1981. Other protections, such as local plans, charitable ownership, National Trust covenants, European Regulations and others protect the physical remains of the past. But although they were part of the manor, the manor itself is not physical or corporeal.

Institutions also survive, although to a lesser degree. A few manor courts still function. Some parishes occasionally beat their bounds although that is hardly an activity of the manor. The village green may even host an annual maypole (19.8). Few institutions are protected because it is hard to make laws to encourage people to support them. The manor is hardly even an institution.

The manor is a concept, a legal idea. It exists in the human mind and in legal and historical texts. It follows that it cannot be destroyed by neglect or vandalism, though manors may be forgotten and abolished by Parliament or other legal processes. Parliament has certainly weakened the manor for the best of motives. The Commons Registration Act 1965, the Wild Creatures and Forest Laws Act 1971, the Administration of Justice Act 1977 and the Rentcharges Act 1977 have, in their own way, contributed to this. The Land Registration Act 2002 contained provisions designed to prevent certain abuses. Those laws were inspired by the wish to improve the law and some of the Law Commission work was intended to remove anomalies in the interests of efficiency. There can be no objection to that. If the manor serves no good purpose and its existence is an obstacle to prosperity then it should go. Most of these laws were not deliberately intended to attack the manor – there was no equivalent to the work of the French National Assembly 200 years before – but the philosophy of law that underlay them is not compatible with the continued existence of ancient institutions of no contemporary value.

Chapter 29

The Future

29.1 OFFICIAL PROPOSALS FOR REFORM

Much of this account has described how the system of holding and organising land in the manor, which reached its height some time about 1189, has been steadily dismantled over the centuries. Certain rights or obligations once existed but have been reduced or varied, and this book has described the fragments which are left. In 1925, many thought that manors would cease to exist, but they have been resilient and survive today. For the most part they now make up a harmless antiquarian interest but from time to time ancient rights survive, or are claimed to survive, in a way that can threaten established interests. A number of the more recent cases mentioned in this book arose because someone had acquired the lordship of a manor and sought to use that to assert unexpected rights. In general judges have been able to restrain such abuses but often it has involved landowners and others in substantial expense, time and trouble.

For that reason manorial law has attracted the attention of members of Parliament and others. In 2004 Paul Flynn MP instituted a debate. In response David Lammy the Parliamentary Under-Secretary of State for Constitutional Affairs, said, in referring to the Land Registration Act 2002:[1]

> The Government have introduced specific reforms that should address the worst of the problems highlighted by my hon. Friend, but fundamental reform of this difficult and complex area of law may be needed. That would be a significant undertaking requiring considerable expertise.

In the particular context of escheat he quoted Charles Harpum, the former Law Commissioner, who, he said:

> in something of an understatement, commented: 'The present state of the law can be described rather charitably as nonsensical.' Following discussions with my

---

[1] *Hansard*, House of Commons, col 202WH (3 February 2004).

Department, the Law Commission is considering whether the proposed reviews should form part of its ninth programme of law reform. I have no doubt that it will pay much heed to what Charles Harpum said. The draft programme will be sent to my noble Friend the Secretary of State for Constitutional Affairs for approval later this year. Whether the reviews of the feudal and manorial systems will be included in the programme depends on their relative priority compared with other proposed reforms. The proposals have no special priority in the assessment process; there are always several worthy contenders for each place on the programme. Any further reform that results from the process will, of course, have to comply with the European convention on human rights.

The Law Commission had already indicated that this subject needs reform. In *Land Registration for the Twenty-First Century* it said:[2]

We cannot immediately see any good reason for the retention of the remaining aspects of feudalism in England and Wales. We note that the Scottish Parliament recently abolished the admittedly more pervasive feudal system that applied in Scotland.

In relation to escheat it said (para 11.27):

We had extended discussions with both the Crown Estate and the then Treasury Solicitor to see if a more rational system could be constructed, at least for registered land (we were constrained by the scope of the Bill). We explored a possible solution, but in the end it foundered because of the uncertainty of the present law. Given that uncertainty there was a risk that in solving one set of problems, we might have created new ones. What is needed is a fundamental reform of the law governing both ownerless property, and the Crown's responsibilities in relation to it.

The Commission stated in the past that:

There are several residual but significant feudal elements that remain part of the law of England and Wales. The Commission's 9th Programme included a review of feudal land law. The Commission was not able to carry out work in this area during the 9th Programme because of the demands of other projects. The feudal land law project was automatically considered for inclusion in the 10th Programme, alongside proposals for new projects suggested by consultees.

However, in its eleventh programme of law reform[3] published on 19 July 2011 it said of the project on feudal land law:

---

[2]   Law Commission No 271, *Land Registration for the Twenty-First Century: a Conveyancing Revolution* para 2.37.

[3]   Law Commission No 330, *11th Programme of Law Reform* (2011).

3.2 This project formed part of the Law Commission's Ninth Programme. The project was to consider the residual feudal elements that remain part of the law of England and Wales. The project was left out of the Tenth Programme on the basis that, although Commissioners remained of the view that this is an important area of the law suitable for consideration by the Law Commission, the extent and nature of the problems presented by competing law reform work suggested that greater public benefit would flow from conducting those projects before a review of feudal land law. The project was therefore deferred for consideration as part of Eleventh Programme.

While reform is therefore not imminent it is on the horizon and a number of issues need to be examined.

29.2   SPECIFIC REFORMS

The following comments are listed by reference to the chapters in which the topics are discussed.

4   The law of custom needs to be examined. Since 1925 custom has concerned only a few local practices, either secular, dating back in theory to 1189, or religious, dating back to the Reformation. Customary rights are preserved as overriding interests under the Land Registration Act 2002 but there is no public record of what they are. It is possible that some practices have simply been carried on for centuries and are generally accepted in a locality, but there is nowhere that a prospective purchaser of land can find out authoritatively whether a custom applies. It would now seem reasonable to provide that any local custom must be published so that a comprehensive list can be drawn up.

5   The principle of tenure serves no modern function and can be abolished. Tenure in England does not carry the abuses which led to the Abolition of Feudal Tenure etc (Scotland) Act 2000 and the only practical consequences appear to be escheat (see 7 below) and payment of a few dues (see 14 below). At present virtually all tenure is in free and common socage except possibly for some land in frankalmoign, ancient demesne and ancient consecrated land where the fee simple is in abeyance. There is also some allodial land (see 24 below).

Likewise the concepts of seisin and (to the extent it may still exist) of right can be abolished.

6   Various miscellaneous pieces of land traditionally belong to the lord. With time title to most of these will be registered and should therefore be regarded as severed from the manor. Even now it is

virtually impossible to know whether any land is demesne as even where the lord is regarded as the owner the land may have been sold from the manor over the centuries and repurchased, or the manor itself may have become reputed.

Waste presents a different problem. Substantial areas of unclaimed common land must belong to someone. It may be sensible for such areas to be vested in the local authority. While on the face of it depriving someone of his property is a breach of the First Protocol to the European Convention on Human Rights, it appears from *JA Pye (Oxford) Ltd v UK*[4] that this can be justified for good cause. Where some unknown person or family has not claimed land for many years, perhaps centuries, there seems good reason to confer ownership on a responsible public body.

More difficult is the matter of odd pieces of land, notably roadside verges. It may be sensible to give statutory force to the presumption that the owner of adjacent land is also the owner of the verge but there are many cases where the distinction is deliberate, for instance where a developer laid out a building estate and intended that the roads and verges should remain in its ownership (perhaps as a ransom strip). Alternatively, the freehold should pass to the highway authority. This is likely only to be a problem with unregistered land, which is where the manor becomes relevant. The simplest course would seem to be for the owner of adjacent land to be able to apply to the Land Registry for title (perhaps initially as a qualified title) and in the application to say whether he is aware of any claim by any other person. The Registry should serve notice on such a person and possibly on any known lord of the manor. However, the lord should not be allowed simply to assert title but must provide a reasonable case and be bound to apply for first registration. After a period of, say, five years the adjacent owner should be registered with absolute title.

7   The law of escheat should be abolished, thereby completing a process intended to take place in 1925. Land disclaimed by a trustee in bankruptcy or liquidator should become bona vacantia (perhaps under a more modern name) and the Crown authorities should cease to be able to disclaim freehold land (it will still be important to be able to disclaim leaseholds). This should not adversely affect any lords still potentially entitled to escheat because disclaimed property must be onerous and in any case it is a matter of chance whether it arises – and indeed rights of mesne lords may no longer exist.

The status of fencing obligations in inclosure Acts needs to be clarified. The Law Commission has proposed a new system of

---

[4]   (2008) 46 EHRR 45.

positive obligations[5] and any relics of the old law should be assimilated to that.

9   There is a distinction between a situation where a landed family is selling off a manor for the first time and where a manor has been sold and bought in recent years. For the former, s 62(3) should be repealed and instead any conveyance of a manor should be presumed to include only the bare title to be called lord. If the parties wish to include other property it should be specified and not covered by general words. For the latter, a successor should take on whatever rights have lawfully been passed to the seller or testator.

If tenure is abolished so that all rights to land depend on possession the lord's rights to property (principally in minerals in enfranchised copyhold) which depended on either seisin or possibly on right will need to be preserved. In many cases these will already be protected on the register but they should be given an expression consistent with modern terminology. In this context the meaning of 'manorial right' in the Land Registration Act 2002 should be clarified.

10   The law of common land has been radically reformed in recent years and there can be little appetite for further change. Possibly the right of the lord to veto regulations under the Commons Act 1899 might be removed. For vesting of unclaimed land, see 6 above.

11   The law of mineral ownership is in poor condition. Once 12 October 2013 has passed there should be a reasonably complete register of rights to pure property interests in former copyhold land (although it is still open to lords to protect their interests until the first registration or disposition of land after that date) but that will not cover mineral exceptions (which are widespread and go beyond manorial rights) or mineral profits (although these will be subject to the conditions in the Land Registration Act 2002, Sch 3, para 3). Eventually it may be necessary to seek to register all mineral rights but that will be a lengthy and complex business and will incur owners in substantial expense.

12   Likewise there is little generally available information about sporting rights. These will mostly exist as profits. Although it is not now compulsory to register title to profits, that may become desirable. Even so, it will take a full generation before most profits owned by individuals are registered and longer for those owned by companies. There may be a few surviving manorial rights which may not confer a right of entry on former copyhold land and a few former rights of free warren may be impliedly converted to sporting rights after the Wild Creatures and Forest Laws Act 1971.

---

[5]   Law Commission No 327, *Making Land Work: Easements Covenants and Profits à Prendre.*

13   The manorial courts were reformed following the Administration of Justice Act 1977. It may be worth checking later experience to see whether any courts not mentioned in the Act have been revived and, if so, to what effect, but it seems unlikely that any reform is needed here.

14   Most surviving rentcharges will cease to be payable in 2037. Crown rents will either be protected on the register or will disappear after the first registration or disposition of land after 12 October 2013. If any other manorial payments for freeholds are still due, such as rents of assize or other chief rents, they should be abolished.

15   Many statutory tolls should continue but there can be few traditional tolls left. Some may still in theory be payable to a lord of the manor although they are probably rarely collected. In the same way as for ancient courts it may be sensible to provide for the abolition of any ancient tolls which may survive in theory to prevent them being revived, perhaps after a period giving time for those entitled to assert title. As tolls will often be due in respect of highways or harbours the land is not likely to be registered for some time to come, so the status of tolls under land registration is not relevant.

Although widely believed to have been settled, the issue of whether the owner of a river bed is entitled to charge owners of pleasure yachts for mooring is still a contentious issue in some quarters. The relationship between owners of the bed, harbour authorities with rights to regulate moorings and boat owners can lead to disputes and the law needs clarifying.

16   Franchises affecting defined areas of land will cease to be overriding after 12 October 2013 subject to subsequent disposition or first registration. Other franchises, except markets (see 21 below) and private ferries, are unlikely to be significant.

17   Other miscellaneous rights may be relevant. Where powers are reserved to a lord in local legislation it may be worth examining whether they still serve a proper function or if the power should be attached to something else, such as ownership of a particular piece of land.

18   The law of allegiance is a matter for state regulation and international law. It may be sensible to reshape the whole law and possibly abolish any remaining relics of homage and fealty. To the extent that they are still relevant to the coronation ceremony, see 23 below.

19   The law of village greens is under constant review and the subject of much litigation. It has developed in a way unexpected by the Royal Commission which led to the Commons Registration Act 1965, but it is politically contentious and if it is to be reformed this is more than a simple matter of 'lawyers' law'.

20 Much of the law of the Church of England is archaic and in need of reform but the initiative must come from the General Synod. The law of consecrated land needs to be rationalised and the status of lay rector abolished. As advowsons are now wholly in gross this may be possible. The fee simple of the church and churchyard should be vested in the parochial church council, which should have power to grant rights over it.

21 The law of markets is confused and unduly reliant on mediaeval origins. Markets serve an important function but need to be separated from reliance on grants of franchise. A register of legal markets and fairs should be created. This may need to be harmonised with domestic and European law on monopolies and competition. Clauses 21 to 23 of the Deregulation and Contracting Out Bill in 1994 proposed to remove rights of local authorities with market franchises to object to proposals to set up competing markets within 6⅔ miles of their own, but this was referred for further consideration and has not been pursued since.

22 If tenure is abolished it may also be sensible to abolish the fee simple and provide for a simple category of (allodial) freehold land.

23 House of Lords reform is the subject of constant political debate. Proposals for reform were introduced into Parliament shortly before this book was published. If that happens there will be no need for the House itself to keep a register of hereditary peers. This can be a problem as indicated by the experience of some Continental countries which have taken away any special rights attached to noble status without abolishing the status as such. It is easy for pretenders to claim bogus titles or even to make bogus claims to existing titles. So long as peers have standing at the coronation there will be some basis for an official register.

24 In general, Crown land should be subject to the same rules as that of subjects. Some functional distinctions will remain, particularly associated with government. Allodial land should become freehold.

25 Only a limited number of manors are registered at the Land Registry and that number is likely to diminish as some are deregistered. There is a need for a comprehensive and authoritative list of manors, honours and lordships. This could not be justified as public expenditure but there is scope for a private initiative. The rules on manorial documents may need to be reviewed in light of modern treatment of and public interest in historical documents.

26 It is not clear if the laws which govern agents and lawyers who work for a fee on the sale of land extend to manors and this should be clarified.

29.3   LEARNING FROM THE MANOR

For most purposes the manor is a historic curiosity, an institution which has lasted over 900 years and has left occasional relics behind. Even so its very survival has something to teach the modern world. It emerged – one cannot say was devised as no single individual was responsible – to enable small communities to live and work together. It was shaped by values different from those accepted today, but there was much which reflects modern needs. It balanced the needs and abilities of occupiers with few assets, those with a little more and those who had considerable power. In doing so it developed sophisticated legal rules in the form of local custom, tenure, different rights and local courts as means to resolve disputes.

The nearest modern parallels are in blocks of flats. Some are relatively superficial. When the Leasehold Reform Housing and Urban Development Act 1993 conferred on tenants the right to acquire the freehold (the homage taking the manor, so to speak) it is described as a right of collective enfranchisement. Section 1(6) allows the landlord in that case to reserve the mineral rights, but he must not deprive the land of support[6]). Likewise under the new system known, not as copyhold, but as commonhold, there is an equivalent to escheat. In addition to these obvious features there are deeper similarities such as the retention of common parts, the need for a system of raising money to meet common expenditure and in some cases a means of resolving disputes between flat owners. It has to be said that those faced with such problems had little conscious knowledge that similar issues had been resolved centuries before, but it is not surprising that they have come up with similar solutions.

The importance of the manor lies in this. It is not just an institution of historic interest. It was a sophisticated way of allowing people to live and work together. The fact that food is no longer grown in land broken up by a plough drawn by eight oxen is to that extent irrelevant. The ideas worked out in the manor are of enduring importance and as relevant today as a 1000 years ago.

This book can end with the words with which Coke ended his own treatise on copyhold:[7]

> And so I conclude with Copy-holders, wishing that there may ever be an perfect Union betwixt them and their Lords, that they may have a feeling of each others wrongs and injuries; that their so little Commonwealth, having all its Members knit together in compleat order, may flourish to the end.

---

[6]   Compare *Wolstanton Ltd and Attorney-General of the Duchy of Lancaster v Newcastle-under-Lyme Corporation* [1940] AC 860.

[7]   Coke, Sir Edward, *Complete Copyholder* (E Flesher et al, 1630) s 62.

Appendix 1

Precedents (note 1)

1   **CONTRACT FOR SALE BY PRIVATE
TREATY INCORPORATING TEXT OF
CONVEYANCE (NOTE 2)**

THIS AGREEMENT is made the [day] of [month] 20[ ]

BETWEEN

(1)   [Seller] of [Address] ('the Seller') and

(2)   [Buyer] of [Address] ('the Buyer')

WHEREBY IT IS AGREED as follows:

1   The Seller will sell and the Buyer will buy at the price of [ ] pounds (£) ALL THAT Manor or Lordship or Reputed Manor or Lordship of Dale in the County of Barset (note 3) ('the Manor') as the same is more particularly described in the annexed form of conveyance ('the Conveyance')

2.1   The Seller sells [with limited] [without any] title guarantee (note 4)

2.2   The Seller's title having been produced to the Buyer or his solicitor before the date of this agreement he buys with full knowledge of it and shall not raise any objection or requisition relating to matters before this agreement (note 5)

2.3   The Seller will retain all title deeds relating to the legal estate in the Manor and will give the Buyer an acknowledgment for production [and an undertaking for safe custody]

3.1   The Manor is sold together with and subject to the exceptions reservations and existing rights contained or referred to in the Conveyance

3.2   The Manor is also sold subject to [complete as applicable, for example rights of common, repair of highways or sea walls, chancel repairs] and to any other incumbrances which may exist

4   [Manorial document – see below]

5   [Waste and minerals – see below]

6.1   The Seller shall not be required to define the boundaries, extent, nature or constituents of the Manor or of any [demesne] waste or former copyhold or dependent freehold or any incumbrances [other that those specified in this agreement] or to provide any information other that disclosed in written replies to written enquiries by the Buyer or his solicitor before this agreement or mentioned in this agreement

6.2   The Buyer having had the opportunity of investigating any matters relevant to the sale takes with full knowledge of them and shall not make any requisition relating to the state of affairs existing at the date of this agreement or to any past acts or events

7   The assurance to the Buyer shall contain the provisions set out in the Conveyance

8   [Other standard provisions, such as deposit, completion formalities, interest on late completion, duplicate conveyance, incorporation of standard conditions of sale so far as applicable to sale of an incorporeal hereditament (note 6)]

Note 1   As explained in 26.3 most contracts and conveyances of manors will be prepared by qualified lawyers and these forms are designed to help them. They will need to be adapted to the circumstances of each case. These precedents are designed for an original sale out of an estate or family holding. Once the manor has been sold on its own, either a conveyance, usually by reference to the initial sale document, or, if title has been registered, a transfer will be used and the contract will simply refer to whatever the seller has.

Note 2   The traditional form of contract outlined the contents of the conveyance but left it to the buyer's solicitor to draw the document. It is often simpler to prepare the end document at the outset and then incorporate it in a contract, especially where the buyer may be acting in person and not wish to incur the expense of a solicitor, and where even practicing conveyancers are increasingly unfamiliar with unregistered conveyancing. This needs to be read with s 48(1) of the Law of Property Act 1925 if the seller's solicitor wishes to charge for preparing the deed.

Note 3   The wording should be taken from the title deeds but this is the usual form.

Note 4   Although it is possible to give the covenants implied by a full title guarantee, the difficulties of most manorial titles are such that it should only be done after careful thought. Often no title guarantee will be appropriate. Many manors are sold by limited owners, such as private trustees, charities and other institutions and the necessary modifications should be made.

Note 5   Normal modern practice on the sale of unregistered land by private treaty is to deduce title before contract. Manorial titles are especially likely to have problems and the buyer's solicitor should normally insist on seeing it even if not offered.

Note 6   Most of the standard provisions are not applicable but they cover notices to complete and other matters which may be needed.

2 PARTICULARS AND CONDITIONS FOR SALE BY AUCTION

Particulars of Lot X

The Manor or Lordship or Reputed Manor or Lordship of Dale in the County of Barset Together with [specify] Except and Reserving [specify] (note 7)

Special conditions

1   The Seller [as to lot X] is [Seller] (note 8)

2   The Seller sells [with limited] [without any] title guarantee (note 4)

3.1 Title [to Lot X] will commence with a Vesting Deed executed to give effect to the Settled Land Act 1925 dated 1926 and made between [Parties] and the Buyer will, notwithstanding any statutory provision to the contrary, accept without requisition that the statements in that deed were correct and that it was effective to vest [lot X] in the person in whom it ought to be vested and that the persons named as trustees were correctly named (note 9)

3.2 [Lot X] passed under the Will of [Testator] who died on [date] and which was proved in the [Principal] Probate Registry on [date] by [executors] and the Buyer will accept without requisition or enquiry that it was comprised in the free estate of the testator and in the general words of an Assent dated [date] and made between [parties]

4.1 [Lot X] is sold subject to [specify] (note 10)

[4.2 The Seller is not aware of any incumbrances affecting this lot other than as disclosed in the Particulars or these conditions [or any statement made by the Auctioneer at the beginning of bidding] but the sale is subject to any which may exist]

[5   The Seller shall not be required to define the boundaries, extent, nature or constituents of the Manor or of any demesne waste or former copyhold or dependent freehold or to provide any information other that disclosed in the information available prior to the Auction at the offices of the Seller's solicitors and of the Auctioneers or mentioned in the Particulars or these Conditions]

6   [Other clauses as required]

Note 7   The auction particulars should describe the manor and its rights as fully as possible, and not normally by reference to a draft document referred to. However, a bidder at an auction of manors will frequently not previously have consulted a lawyer, so the provision of a standard form conveyance may be useful.

Note 8   Most auctions of manors include a number of lots put up on behalf of different sellers. The auctioneers will want to keep the legal parts of the auction brochure as short as possible and the special conditions of each lot to a minimum. The auctioneers will have its own standard general conditions which should cover many matters arising on manorial sales.

Note 9   In contrast to note 5 it will be necessary to give a root of title at auction because many bidders will not have investigated anything before coming into the auction room (if they do not bid by telephone or electronically). The condition should give an indication of any likely problems, without being so cautious as to put bidders off, and may need careful drafting.

Note 10   For the same reason as note 9 a general outline of all incumbrances should be given in the particulars or conditions. Reference to other documents by itself is not enough. Equally, any summary must be accurate.

3   CONVEYANCE

THIS CONVEYANCE is made the [day] of [month] 20[ ]

BETWEEN

(1)   [Seller] of [Address] ('the Seller') and

(2)   [Buyer] of [Address] ('the Buyer')

WHEREAS the Seller is seised of the hereditament[s] conveyed by this deed for a legal estate in fee simple [subject as mentioned below but otherwise] free from incumbrances and has agreed with the Buyer for the sale of it [them] to him at the price of [ ] pounds (£)

NOW THIS DEED WITNESSES as follows:

1   In pursuance of the recited agreement and in consideration of the sum of [ ] pounds (£) by the Buyer paid to the Seller (receipt of which the Seller acknowledges) the Seller [with limited title guarantee] HEREBY CONVEYS to the Buyer ALL THAT Manor or Lordship or Reputed Manor or Lordship of Dale in the County of Barset [TOGETHER WITH – see below – EXCEPT AND RESERVING – see below] TO HOLD the same unto the Buyer in fee simple [SUBJECT – see below] (note 11)

2   [Agreements and Declarations if required]

3   THE Seller acknowledges the right of the Buyer to production of the deeds [and documents] specified in the Schedule and to delivery of copies thereof [and undertakes with him for the safe custody of them] (note 12)

IN WITNESS whereof the Seller has executed this Conveyance as a deed the day and year first above written

SIGNED as a Deed by the above named Seller

....

in the presence of:

....

Witness signature

Witness name ....

Address ....

Occupation ....

Note 11   The rights granted with the manor, or excepted or reserved, and existing incumbrances may conveniently be set out in schedules if they are long or complicated.

Note 12   The acknowledgement relates to title deeds necessary to show title to the property sold, not strictly to manorial documents, but s 64 of the Law of Property Act 1925 refers in general terms to 'documents' and could be used for that purpose where they are excluded from the sale.

4   SPECIAL CLAUSES TO BE INCORPORATED IN CONTRACTS AND CONVEYANCES

4.1   Sale of bare lordship

1   EXCEPT AND RESERVING to the Seller all demesne (note 13) and waste of the Manor and mineral and sporting rights in former copyhold land and all corporeal and incorporeal hereditaments belonging or reputed to belong to the Manor and all such [rights of property] [hereditaments] as are referred to in section 62(3) of the Law of Property Act 1925 and all other rights held or enjoyed or which (apart from this exception) would pass with the Manor save only the Manor itself and courts and inseparable services

2   IT IS AGREED AND DECLARED that this Conveyance is intended to and shall pass only the bare lordship or seigniory or feudal superiority of the Manor and such adjuncts as are necessarily and inseparably incident to it

Note 13   At common law a conveyance of a manor included demesne land. In modern conditions much depends on the true construction of the conveyance. In practice if the demesnes are being sold they will be described as such and title will be registered after sale. The same will be true of identifiable waste. It will be unusual for the parties to wish to include demesne although they will often want to carry unknown waste in the conveyance.

4.2   Market

1   TOGETHER WITH/EXCEPT AND RESERVING the (Tuesday) Market of the Town of Dale and all franchises and rights appertaining to that Market [OR and all tolls liberties and free customs belonging to it and all other franchises and rights of market and market tolls had and enjoyed and exercised by the Seller in the Town of Dale or any part of it] (note 14)

Note 14   If a functioning market has been one of the appurtenances of the manor the title deeds will usually refer to it and the same words should be used in the sale deed.

4.3   Wreck

TOGETHER WITH/EXCEPT AND RESERVING the right of wreck with jetsam flotsam and lagan (and derelict) on the foreshore of the parish of Dale [with all necessary rights of access as hitherto exercised by the Seller for the purpose of exercising that right]

4.4   Waste

1   EXCEPT AND RESERVING to the Seller in fee simple all wastes and commons of the Manor

2   TOGETHER WITH all waste and common land of the Manor subject to all rights exercisable over it

3   The sale includes the manorial waste known as Dale Common registered under the Commons Registration Act 1965 as Barsetshire Unit CL 999

4   The sale includes such manorial waste as is parcel of the Manor but the Seller shall not be required to define or specify or identify it

5   The waste is sold subject to all rights of common and other rights of third parties whether registered or not and whether or not known to the Seller and whether or not discoverable on inspection

4.5   Minerals

1   The sale includes such rights as the Seller is able to convey in the minerals within and under the former copyhold lands of the Manor but the Seller shall not be required to define or identify them

2   There will be excepted and reserved to the Seller in fee simple

2.1   all mines minerals stone and substrata within and under the manorial waste and other lands conveyed with the Manor [continue with usual form of mineral reservation with or without right of surface entry, right to let down the surface, compensation provisions and other common form provisions]

2.2   all property in minerals within and under the former copyhold lands of the Manor with all such rights of working and exploitation and all royalties and other rights as belong to them

2.3   all mines minerals and stone and substrata or rights to take or work them excepted or reserved out of any enfranchisement of copyhold whether by statute or at law and whether or not subject to agreement with the holder of the enfranchised land

2.4   all mines and mineral rights excepted or reserved to the lord of the Manor under [the Dale Inclosure Act 17 (George III c) and the Award dated 17 made under it] OR [any inclosure Act or award affecting the Manor]

4.6   Manorial documents

1   The sale includes such rights as the Seller is able to assign in the manorial documents of the Manor subject to the Manorial Documents Rules 1959 to 1967. The documents are in the custody of the Barsetshire County Record Office and the Seller will on completion hand over a notice informing it of the sale

2   The Seller excepts and reserves to himself the manorial documents of the Manor and all rights in them save that the Buyer will have the right to inspect such of them as are in the custody of the Seller or his successors as owners of the documents on giving reasonable notice

3   TOGETHER WITH/EXCEPT AND RESERVING all court rolls records and other documents of the Manor of Dale provided that the [Seller/ Buyer] shall be at liberty (on giving reasonable notice) to inspect them and to take copies of them (note 15)

Note 15   If the manorial documents are handed over but the seller keeps the mineral rights he should keep a right to inspect the documents in case of any problems concerning the extent of copyhold lands. The person who has them can give the other an acknowledgment for production unless they are in the custody of a repository.

Appendix 2

Extracts from Statutes

QUIA EMPTORES 1290

Freeholders may sell their Lands; so that the Feoffee do hold of the Chief Lord.

FORASMUCH as Purchasers of Lands and Tenements of the Fees of great men and other Lords, have many times heretofore entered into their Fees, to the prejudice of the Lords, to whom the Freeholders of such great men have sold their Lands and Tenements to be holden in Fee of their Feoffors, and not of the Chief Lords of the Fees, whereby the same Chief Lords have many times lost their Escheats, Marriages, and Wardships of Lands and Tenements belonging to their Fees; which thing seemed very hard and extream unto those Lords and other great men, and moreover in this case manifest Disheritance: Our Lord the King, in his Parliament at Westminster after Easter, the eighteenth year of his Reign, that is to wit, in the Quinzime of Saint John Baptist, at the instance of the great Men of the Realm, granted, provided, and ordained, That from henceforth it shall be lawful to every Freeman to sell at his own pleasure his Lands and Tenements, or part of them; so that the Feoffee shall hold the same Lands or Tenements of the Chief Lord of the same Fee, by such Service and Customs as his Feoffor held before

TENURES ABOLITION ACT 1660

Whereas it hath been found by former experience that the courts of Wards and Liveries and tenures by knights service, either of the King or others, or by knights service in capite, or soccage in capite of the King and the consequents upon the same have been much more burthensome, grievous and prejudiciall to the kingdom than they have beene beneficiall to the King, And whereas since the intermission of the said court which hath beene from the fower and twentyeth day of February which was in the yeare of our Lord one thousand six hundred forty and five many persons have by will and otherwise made disposall of their lands held by knights service, whereupon diverse questions might possibly arise, unless some seasonable remedy be taken to prevent the same:

1.   The court of Wards and Liveries, and all wardships, liveries, primer-seizins and ouster-le-mains values and forfeitures of marriages by reason of any tenure of the Kings Majesty or of any other by knights service and all meane rates, and all other gifts grants charges incident or ariseing for or by reason of wardships liveries primer seisins or ouster-le-main, be taken away and discharged and are hereby enacted to be taken away and discharged from the said twenty-fourth day of February one thousand six hundred forty-five, any law, statute, custome, or usage to the contrary hereof in any wise notwithstanding, and that all fines for alienation seizures and pardons for alienations tenure by homage, and all charges incident or ariseing for or by reason of wardship, livery, primer-seizin, or ouster-le-main or tenure by knights service escuage and also aide pur file marrier and pur faier fitz chevalier and all other charges incident thereunto be likewise taken away and discharged from the said twenty-fourth day of February one thousand six hundred forty and five, any law statute custome or usage to the contrary hereof in any wise notwithstanding, and that all tenures by knights service of the King, or of any other person, and by knights service in capite, and by socage in capite of the King, and the fruits and consequents thereof happened or which shall or may hereafter happen or arise thereupon or thereby be taken away and discharged any law statute custome or usage to the contrary hereof in any wise notwithstanding, and all tenures of any honours mannours lands tenements or hereditaments of any estate of inheritance at the common law held either of the king or of any other person or persons bodyes pollitique or corporate are hereby enacted to be turned into free and common soccage, to all intents and purposes, from the said twenty fourth day of February one thousand six hundred forty-five, and shall be soe construed adjudged and deemed to be from the said twenty-fourth day of February one thousand six hundred forty five, and for ever thereafter turned into free and common soccage, any law statute custome or usage to the contrary hereof in any wise notwithstanding.

2.   And that the same shall for ever hereafter stand and be discharged of all tenure by homage escuage voyages discharged royall and charges for the same wardships incident to tenure by knights service and values and forfeitures of marriage and all other charges incident to tenure by knights service and of and from aide pur file marrier & aide pur faier fitz chivalier any law statute custome or usage to the contrary in any wise notwithstanding. And that all conveyances and devises of any mannours lands tenements and hereditaments made since the said twenty fourth of February shall be expounded to be of such effect as if the same mannours lands tenements and hereditaments had beene then held and continued to be holden in free and common soccage onely any law statute custome or usage to the contrary hereof any wise notwithstanding.

...

4. And be it further enacted by the authority aforesaid that all tenures hereafter to be created by the Kings Majestie, his heires or successors upon any gifts or grants of any mannours lands tenements or hereditaments of any estate of inheritance at the common law shall be in free and common soccage, and shall be adjudged to be in free and common soccage onely, and not by knight service or in capite, and shall be discharged of all wardship value and forfeiture of marriage livery primer-seisin ouster le main aide pur faier fitz chivalier & pur file marrier any law statute or reservation to the contrary thereof any wise notwithstanding.

5. Provided neverthelesse and be it enacted, that this Act or any thing herein contayned shall not take away nor be construed to take away any rents certaine herriots, or suites of court belonging or incident to any former tenure now taken away or altered by vertue of this Act, or other services incident or belonging to tenure in common soccage due, or to grow due to the Kings Majestie or meane lords, or other private person, or the fealty and distresses incident thereunto, and that such reliefe shall be paid in respect of such rents as is paid in case of a death of a tennant in common soccage.

6. Provided always and be it enacted that anything herein contayned shall not take away nor be construed to take away any fines for alineation due by perticular customes of perticular mannours and places, other then fines for alienations of lands or tenements holden immediately of the King in capite.

7. Provided alsoe and be it enacted that this Act or anything therin contained shall not take away or be construed to take away tenures in frank almoigne or to subject them to any greater or other services then they now are, nor to alter or change any tenure by copy of court roll or any services incident thereto not to take away the honorary services of grand sergeantie other then wardship marriage and value of forfeiture of marriage escuage voyages roayll and other charges incident to tenure by knights service and other then aide pur faier fitz chevalier and aide pur file marrier.

...

10. Provided alsoe that neither this Act nor any thing therein contained shall infringe or hurt any title of honour feodall or other by which any person hath or may have right to sit in the lords house of Parliament as to his or their title of honour or sitting in Parliament, and the privilegdge belonging to them as peeres. This Act or any thing therein contained to the contrary in any wise notwithstanding.

LAW OF PROPERTY ACT 1922

144 Power to inspect Court Rolls

Any person interested in enfranchised land may on payment of the fee prescribed by the Lord Chancellor, inspect at any reasonable hour any Court Rolls of the manor of which the land was held; and Court Rolls shall (whether before or after the manorial incidents have been extinguished), for the purposes of section fourteen of the Evidence Act, 1851, be deemed to be documents of such a public nature as to be admissible in evidence on their mere production from the proper custody.

144A Manorial documents

(1) All manorial documents shall be under the charge and superintendence of the Master of the Rolls.

(2) Save as hereinafter provided, manorial documents shall remain in the possession or under the control of the lord for the time being of the manor to which the same relate and he shall not be entitled to destroy or damage wilfully such documents.

(3) The Master of the Rolls may from time to time make such enquiries as he shall think fit for the purpose of ascertaining that any manorial documents are in the proper custody, and are being properly preserved, and the lord of the manor to which such documents relate, or the governing body of any public library, or museum or historical or antiquarian society, to which the same may have been transferred, as hereinafter provided, shall furnish the Master of the Rolls with all such information with respect thereto as he may require.

(4) The Master of the Rolls may direct that any manorial documents which, in his opinion, are not being properly preserved, or which he is requested by the lord of a manor to deal with under this subsection, shall be transferred to the Public Record Office, or to any public library, or museum or historical or antiquarian society, which may be willing to receive the same, and if the same shall be transferred to any public library, or museum or historical or antiquarian society, the governing body thereof shall thereafter have the custody thereof and shall be responsible for the proper preservation and indexing thereof.

(5) Nothing contained in this section shall prejudice or affect the right of any person to the production and delivery of copies of any manorial documents or to have the same kept in a proper state of preservation; in particular the lord of the manor shall remain entitled to require the same to be produced to him, or in accordance with his directions, free of any cost.

(6) In this section 'manorial documents' mean court rolls, surveys, maps, terriers, documents and books of every description relating to the boundaries, franchises, wastes, customs or courts of a manor, but do not include the deeds and other instruments required for evidencing the title to a manor; 'manor' includes a lordship and a reputed lordship; and 'lord of the manor' includes any person entitled to manorial documents..

(7) The Master of the Rolls may make rules for giving effect to this section, and may revoke or vary any such rules.

TWELFTH SCHEDULE

Effect of Enfranchisement

(4) An enfranchisement by virtue of this Act shall not deprive a tenant of any commonable right to which he is entitled in respect of the enfranchised land, but where any such right exists in respect of any land at the commencement of this Act it shall continue attached to the land notwithstanding that the land has become freehold.

(5) An enfranchisement by virtue of this Act of any land (including any mines and minerals hereinafter mentioned) shall not affect any right of the lord or tenant in or to any mines, minerals, limestone, lime, clay, stone, gravel, pits, or quarries, whether in or under the enfranchised land or not, or any right of entry, right of way and search, or other easement or privilege of the lord or tenant in, on, through, over, or under any land, or any powers which in respect of property in the soil might but for the enfranchisement have been exercised for the purpose of enabling the lord or tenant, their or his agents, workmen, or assigns, more effectually to search for, win, and work any mines, minerals, pits, or quarries, or to remove and carry away any minerals, limestone, lime, stones, clay, gravel, or other substances had or gotten therefrom, or the rights, franchises, royalties, or privileges of the lord in respect of any fairs, markets, rights of chase or warren, piscaries, or other rights of hunting, shooting, fishing, fowling, or otherwise taking game, fish, or fowl.

Provided that the owner of the enfranchised land shall, notwithstanding any reservation of mines or minerals in this Act (but without prejudice to the rights to any mines or minerals, or the right to work or carry away the same), have full power to disturb or remove the soil so far as is necessary or convenient for the purpose of making roads or drains or erecting buildings or obtaining water on the land

(6) An enfranchisement by virtue of this Act shall not affect any liability subsisting at the commencement of this Act (whether arising by virtue of a court leet regulation or otherwise) for the construction maintenance cleansing or repair of any dykes, ditches, canals, sea or river walls, piles, bridges,

levels, ways and other works required for the protection or general benefit of
any land within a manor or for abating nuisances therein; and any person
interested in enforcing the liability may apply to the court to ascertain or
apportion the liability and to charge the same upon or against the land or any
interest therein; and the court may make such order as it thinks fit; and the
charge when made by the order shall, be deemed to be a land charge within
the meaning of the Land Charges Registration and Searches Act, 1888 (as
amended by any subsequent enactment), and may be registered accordingly;
and, in addition, the jurisdiction of any court leet, customary or other court, in
reference to the matter is hereby transferred to the court.

(7)   A right preserved to the lord by virtue of this schedule shall not for the
       purposes of Part VI of this Act be deemed to be a manorial incident unless it
       is otherwise agreed.

LAW OF PROPERTY ACT 1925

62 General words implied in conveyances

...

(3)   A conveyance of a manor shall be deemed to include and shall by virtue of
       this Act operate to convey, with the manor, all pastures, feedings, wastes,
       warrens, commons, mines, minerals, quarries, furzes, trees, woods,
       underwoods, coppices, and the ground and soil thereof, fishings, fisheries,
       fowlings, courts leet, courts baron, and other courts, view of frankpledge and
       all that to view of frankpledge doth belong, mills, mulctures, customs, tolls,
       duties, reliefs, heriots, fines, sums of money, amerciaments, waifs, estrays,
       chief-rents, quitrents, rentscharge, rents seck, rents of assize, fee farm rents,
       services, royalties jurisdictions, franchises, liberties, privileges, easements,
       profits, advantages, rights, emoluments, and hereditaments whatsoever, to the
       manor appertaining or reputed to appertain, or, at the time of conveyance,
       demised, occupied, or enjoyed with the same, or reputed or known as part,
       parcel, or member thereof.

       For the purposes of this subsection the right to compensation for manorial
       incidents on the extinguishment thereof shall be deemed to be a right
       appertaining to the manor.

205 General definitions

(1)   In this Act unless the context otherwise requires, the following expressions
       have the meanings hereby assigned to them respectively, that is to say:

(ix) 'Land' includes land of any tenure, and mines and minerals, whether or not held apart from the surface, buildings or parts of buildings (whether the division is horizontal, vertical or made in any other way) and other corporeal hereditaments; also a manor, an advowson, and a rent and other incorporeal hereditaments, and an easement, right, privilege, or benefit in, over, or derived from land; but not an undivided share in land; and 'mines and minerals' include any strata or seam of minerals or substances in or under any land, and powers of working and getting the same but not an undivided share thereof; and 'manor' includes a lordship, and reputed manor or lordship; and 'hereditament' means any real property which on an intestacy occurring before the commencement of this Act might have devolved upon an heir;

ADMINISTRATION OF JUSTICE ACT 1977

23 Jurisdiction of ancient courts

(1)   The following courts, namely –

(a)   any court of a description specified in Part I of Schedule 4 to this Act except –

(i)   the Estray Court for the Lordship of Denbigh, and

(ii)   the court leet for the Manor of Laxton, and

(b)   the courts specified in Part II of that Schedule,

being the courts which appear to the Lord Chancellor to have, but not to exercise, jurisdiction to hear and determine legal proceedings, shall cease to have any jurisdiction to hear and determine legal proceedings; but any such court may continue to sit and transact such other business, if any, as was customary for it immediately before the coming into force of this section, and in the case of the courts specified in Part III of Schedule 4 to this Act the business that is to be treated as having been customary shall (apart from business relating to the appointment of officers of the court) be the business specified in relation to that court in column 2 of that Part.

(2)   The descriptions of courts in Part I of Schedule 4 to this Act include courts held for manors of which the Queen or the Duke of Cornwall is the lord.

(3)   Any jurisdiction –

(a)   of the Court of the Chancellor or Vice-Chancellor of Oxford University, and

(b)   of the Cambridge University Chancellor's Court,

other than that which presently exists under the statutes of those universities, is hereby abolished.

(4)   The Lord Chancellor may by order make any incidental or transitional provision which he considers expedient in consequence of this section and may by such order provide –

    (a)   for enabling any jurisdiction appearing to him to have been formerly exercised by a court specified in Part I or II of Schedule 4 to this Act to be exercised instead by the High Court, the Crown Court, a county court or a magistrates' court; and

    (b)   for such amendments or repeals of provisions of any local Act as appear to him to be required in consequence of this section.

(5)   The power to make orders under this section shall be exercisable by statutory instrument subject to annulment in pursuance of a resolution of either House of Parliament; and any such order may be varied or revoked by a subsequent order made under the power.

Glossary

These are not formal definitions but a guide to general meaning. Most of the words are discussed in the text.

Accidental services: occasional payments to lord, such as due on death of tenant
Acre: an area that could be ploughed in a day. The modern statute acre is 4840 square yards or about 0.4 of a hectare
Adscriptus (adscripticus) glebae: registered with the soil. The status of a *colonus* who could not leave his holding
Adjunct: a right automatically adjoined to a manor
Admission: see admittance
Admittance: procedure for a new copyholder to take a holding
Advowson: right to present an incumbent to a benefice
Anchorage: right to put down anchor overnight in a port, right for the port owner to charge for that
Allod, allodial land: land held without a superior in tenure
Amercement: penalty fixed by a court
Annexure: right that becomes attached to a manor
Annual services: regular payments to lord such as rent
Appendant right: right which may become held with a manor, eg common appendant, advowson appendant
Appropriate (rectory): rectory appropriated by a monastery which put in a vicar as incumbent
Appurtenance: right that appertains to a manor or to land, such as right of way
Assize: sitting, usually of a court
Assoin: see essoin
Assurance: transfer of property by substitution

Bailiff: deputy of a steward
Balk (baulk, meer, slade): space between two strips
Ballastage (ballatage, lastage, lestage): toll for providing ballast
Bare lordship: seigniory which carried no other rights
Baron (court): assembly of the free suitors or freeholders
Baron (dignity): lowest rank in the peerage
Baronet: hereditary knighthood

Barony: sometimes synonym for honour

Beastgate: holding of grazing land in common

Benefice: position of a clergyman in a parish (or other post) understood as property. On Continent, type of tenure

Black rent: rent payable in pepper

Bookland: Anglo-Saxon tenure by charter

Bondsman: unfree tenant bound usually to the soil, sometimes to a lord

Bordar: type of bondsman

Bote: a profit, usually of wood

Burgage: form of socage found in towns

Bushelage: a toll by reference to corn weighed by the bushel

Canon law: law of the Church

Carriage: a toll for carrying

Castle guard: a type of military tenure

Cattlegate: holding of grazing land in common

Ceorl (churl): Anglo-Saxon free commoner

Champion (coronation): duty performed at the coronation; formerly a service in grand sergeanty

Champion (landscape): region comprising open field systems

Charter: documentary grant now issued by the Privy Council

Chase: rights analogous to forest held by a subject and without forest court

Chattel: personal property. Includes goods, debts, leases

Cheminage: toll of way

Chief Lord: the lord above the holder of the land or manor

Chief rent: rent due to a tenurial superior

Civil law: Roman law as understood in England

Close: cultivated enclosed piece of land usually held in severalty

Closed manor or village: under tight landowner control

Colibert: type of bondsman

Colonus: Roman tenant farmer bound to the land

Commendation: surrender of allod to new lord and taking it back in fee

Common: the word indicates sharing but is used in different meanings

Common, in: land or rights shared among several owners who each have a separately owned interest without being divided

Common calling: services to be provided (if available) to anyone who could pay

Common calling: trade whose benefits must be made available to anyone able and willing to pay

Common field: area of agricultural system of strips

Common land: land subject to rights of common (for the purposes of the Commons Registration Act 1965 also includes waste of the manor)

Common law: law of whole community of England, system practised in the English courts, as contrasted with custom, equity, statute, canon law and civil law

Common right: right automatically attached to a holding, such as common appendant

Common, right of: a profit held in common with others

Commonable: land subject to mutual arrangements similar to rights of common but terminable on any strip at the will of the owner of that strip. Also right held by copyholder over lord's land. Also beast through which right of pasture may be exercised. Sometimes incorrectly used as synonym for common

Commons, House of: assembly of representatives of communities of the realm

Commutation: settlement of rights for a fixed money payment

Constable: officer appointed to keep the peace

Conversion: turning of one right or status into another, as of allod into fee or copyhold into leasehold

Conveyance: assurance of land (usually freehold) or other rights

Copyhold: manorial land held by copy of court roll.

Copyhold, pure: land held at the will of the lord according to the custom of the manor

Corn rent: type of payment to a church

Corporeal hereditament: land

Corporal services: service due to lord by work in person

Corporation: individual or body of persons with existence either perpetual or outlasting any specific individual

Corporeal: tangible

Cottar: type of bondsman, cottager

Count: official of Roman Empire, companion of the emperor, later often an independent feudal aristocrat

County: on Continent, area of jurisdiction of count. In England, a shire

Court: assembly to advise a lord, make regulations and determine disputes

Covenant: formal legal agreement usually by deed

Custom: law of uncertain and usually ancient origin; a payment of like origin

Customary freehold: land held according to the custom of the manor but not at the will of the lord

Customary land: land held by customary right, includes pure copyhold and customary freehold

Custumal: record of customary payments and services (may incidentally record customary rights)

Deed: formal legal document (formerly sealed)

Demesne: land under direct control of lord

Demise: grant of lease

Deodand: prerogative or franchise right to chattel which has caused an unlawful human death

Derelict: items (often part of a wrecked vessel) which come to shore

Dignity: incorporeal hereditament of status, as peerage

Dissolution: of the monasteries under Henry VIII

Distrain: right of tenurial superior to take and sell chattels on a holding to recover sums due

Dominium directum: ownership by superior lord

Dominium utile: ownership by person in possession (actual or notional)

Due: a money payment owed to a person

Earl: prominent nobleman, English counterpart to count

Easement: servitude which does not involve taking produce of servient tenement

Ejectment: procedure based on law of trespass and lease (often fictional) for recovery of land

Enclosure: land surrounded by a physical limit such as hedge

Enfranchise: to free. Used originally of slaves, later of bondsmen, then of copyholds, now of long leases

Enfranchisement: process of copyhold land becoming freehold

Enjoyment: right to occupy land or take its fruits or revenues

Entail: means of restricting ownership of land to members of a family, usually in the senior male line

Entry fine: payment by copyholder (or lessee) on taking over a holding

Eorl: Anglo-Saxon aristocrat

Equity: system of law developed by the chancellors to supplement the common law

Escheat: land coming back to chief lord

Essoin: excuse for not attending court

Estate (landed): collection of lands, usually geographically contiguous though not necessarily tenurially associated

Estate (legal): quantum of ownership of real property, now restricted to fee simple and lease

Estover: type of right of common

Estray: franchise of right to unclaimed straying beasts

Exception: right or land not included in grant

Extent: survey of manor

Fair: occasional gatherings, often once a year, for buying and selling

Farm: a lease, hence the land comprised in it, hence agricultural land

Fealty: duty of being faithful owed to a tenurial superior

Fee: return for services, once in land, now in money. Type of legal estate

Fee farm: fee granted for service of a substantial money rent

Feoffment: grant of land in fee

Feorm: Anglo-Saxon rent, usually as food

Ferry: franchise of monopoly of carrying passengers across a waterway

Feudum: fief or fee

Feudal (feodal): seventeenth-century term for the system of grant of land for service and fealty which had been current in previous centuries

Feudalism, feudal system: nineteenth-century term for the alleged mediaeval system of tenure

Fief: fee, land held in return for service of fealty

Field: open area used for growing crops, later any agricultural enclosure

Fine (penalty): fixed sum payable to put an end to an offence

Fine (premium): fixed sum payable on entry to inferior tenement

Fine (proceeding): action of covenant, usually collusive as in breaking an entail or recording exchange or compromise

Flotsam: items of wreck which float ashore

Folkland: Anglo-Saxon tenure for various ancient dues to the king

Foreshore: land between high and low watermark of the tide

Forest: area under jurisdiction of forest court which limited hunting and certain other exploitation to the Crown

Franchise: grant of prerogative in hands of subject

Frankalmoign: tenure of Church lands for uncertain ecclesiastical services

Frankpledge: system of mutual responsibility of members of a tithing

Free: exempt

Freebench: right of copyholder's widow to enjoy part of the holding

Freehold: legal estate held by a free man, hence free tenement

Free fishery: several fishery, free from rights of the public

Free warren: franchise of right to take beasts of warren on a holder's own land without royal consent

Fundus (Roman): landed estate under Roman Empire

Fundus (sea): bed below low watermark of tides

Grand sergeanty: form of military tenure for highly honourable service to the king, typically at the coronation

Grant: creation of new estate or interest in land

Gross, in: right separate from land or manor

Hall: place of residence of Anglo-Saxon lord

Hayward: officer responsible for hedges

Heir: person ascertained on death of a holder of real property as entitled to succeed

Hereditament: property which passed to an heir, real property

Heriot: item (usually the best beast) due on death (usually of copyholder) to lord, either heriot service or heriot custom

Hide: area of arable land with associated pasture sufficient for a substantial
    Anglo-Saxon family, typically 120 acres
Highway: public right of way for all subjects of the Queen
Holding: land occupied as a unit usually from one lord
Homage (ceremony): placing of hands between those of the lord and agreeing to
    be his 'man'
Homage (tenants): unfree tenants, subsequently copyholders, collectively
Honour: group of manors which devolve together
Hundred: 100 hides, a subdivision of a shire

Impropriate: an appropriated rectory which after the Dissolution passed into lay
    hands
Incident: manorial rights or dues
Inclosure: land (usually formerly common or commonable) held severally and
    able to be enclosed
Incorporeal hereditaments: intangible property including manors, franchises,
    servitudes, etc
Incumbent: clergyman admitted to a benefice
Incumbrance: burden on property, such as charge or easement

Jetsam: items thrown from a vessel in danger of sinking which come to land
Jurisdiction: legal power, typically exercised through a court

Keyage (Quayage): toll for using a quay
Knight service: simplest form of uncertain military tenure
Knight's fee: holding of one knight in fee

Lagan (ligan, ligam): items thrown out of a vessel to lighten it
Land: in general this is self-explanatory but the term is often widened to include
    rights associated with land or incorporeal hereditaments
Land (Anglo-Saxon): the English precursor to manors or landed estates
Lease: contract for possession of a holding for a defined period of time, now a
    legal estate
Leat: artificial watercourse to take water to the top of a mill-wheel
Leaze: undefined area of or rights of property in or common rights over a field
Leet: local public court for a vill or tithing
Legal manor: manor which retains full legal status including two dependent
    freeholders to serve as suitors at the court baron
Legal memory: the origin of rights arising since 1189 usually had to be
    specifically proven by grant. A lawful origin was presumed for those shown
    to be older
Liberty: private jurisdiction, free from supervision by sheriff

Livery and maintenance: arrangement in late Middle Ages for a powerful man
   to protect from the law those who served him and wore his uniform
Livery of seisin: ceremony whereby seisin was handed over on grant
Loadage: toll for loading
Lord: superior
Lordship: collection of rights belonging to a lord, often a synonym for manor

Manorial right: right connected with manor by custom, such as revenues or
   minerals
Mansion: great house, typically focus of a landed estate
March: county or military district on border of a royal territory with defence
   needs
Margrave: count with responsibility for a march, often with jurisdiction over
   other border counts
Market: concourse of buyers and sellers typically on defined days of the week.
   Franchise of exclusive right to authorise it
Marquess: English peerage introduced as equivalent to margrave but without
   functional responsibilities
Meer: balk
Merchet: sum payable to lord for permission to marry, usually by villeins for
   daughters to marry out of the manor
Metage: toll by reference to items measured
Mill: building designed to grind corn
Mineral: substance naturally in the soil which can be taken out for profit
Modus rent: church payment originated as substitute for another
Murage: toll for cost of repairing walls

Native: peasant, hence bondsman
Nudum dominium (dominicum): bare lordship without direct rights over the land
   itself

Open field: area of strips, usually commonable but sometimes common
Open manor or village: where control was weak because the tenants had free
   rights or there were many lords and no central control

Palatine: territory or honour of special liberties; English type of march
Pannage: right of common of grazing pigs in wood
Parcel: defined tenement or portion of tenement, hence land comprised in a
   grant or assurance
Parish: area of local church jurisdiction, adapted in the nineteenth century to
   secular local government
Park: franchise with enclosed area of land held by lord for private hunting of
   deer

Particulars: legal description of property, usually in sale contract

Passage (peage, payage): toll of charging persons passing over land

Pasture: profit of taking grass through the mouths of beasts

Pavage: toll to recover cost of paving a way

Pedage: toll of charging persons passing on foot

Personal: right which can be enforced against identifiable persons

Personal property: chattels and some intangible assets

Petty sergeanty: form of tenure, usually military, for personal services

Piccage: toll for right to put posts in the ground to erect a market booth

Pilotage: toll for services of a pilot

Pinder: official responsible for village pound

Piscary: right of common to take fish

Pontage: toll for use of bridge

Portage: toll for carriage of goods

Porterage: toll for employment of porter

Possession: originally a simple idea (as seisin). Later a right to immediate occupation or use of or income from land (or other right)

Pound: enclosure for keeping animals found straying

Prerogative: residue of royal rights

Prescriptive right: right originating in exercise over many years, strictly since before legal memory, as distinct from grant

Profit: servitude of taking a substance from the land of another

Property: ownership

Quitrent: rent payable for being quit of obligation to pay or perform former rents or services

Real: right that can be enforced against anyone

Real estate: US term for real property

Real property: freehold land and certain incorporeal hereditaments

Reasonable: standard by which behaviour or claimed rights is tested. The law will not authorise something held to be unreasonable

Record: legally recognised account admitted without special proof

Rector: incumbent of benefice that was not appropriated

Rectorial manor: either appropriated or impropriate manor held with rectory or manor held by rector

Reeve: official responsible for administration: village reeve or shire reeve (sheriff)

Regardant (villein): villein appendant and therefore his services could not be transferred in gross

Regulated pasture: pasture subject to scheme of management, where soil belongs to stintholders but minerals belong to lord

Relief: sum payable by an heir on entry

Rent: sum certain payable out of a tenement, normally land. Including rent of assize, rentcharge, chief rent, fee farm rent, quitrent, rent seck

Reputed manor: manor which has ceased to be a legal manor and is one by reputation only

Reservation: right (usually servitude) regranted to grantor of tenement

Roll: minutes of proceedings in court. Originally kept literally on a rolled-up membrane, the term later applied to bound volumes

Roman law: law developed under the Roman Empire and later becoming the principal type of system on the Continent, contrasted with common law

Royal court: court held under royal authority, particularly the three common law courts in Westminster Hall of Common Pleas, King's Bench and Exchequer

Royal demesne: lands held by the Crown, either allodially or as freehold

Royal mine: gold and silver ores

Royalty: sum payable for exploitation of a right, as minerals, copyright

Rustic: native

Scavage (shewage): toll for displaying goods as at a market

Seal: an individual or corporation's impression on a document instead of a signature

Seigniory: lordship

Seigniorial right: see manorial right

Seisin: originally like possession, this was a statement of fact. Later refined into a legal status which defined who could take certain types of proceedings to recover land

Serf: bondsman

Sergeanty: tenure for services

Services: duties performed in return for grant of land, including rentservice

Servitude: right to do (or restrain doing of) something on land of another, comprising easements and profits

Servitude: slavery

Settlement (trust): arrangement for land to be passed down within a family

Settlement (village): locality occupied by permanent inhabitants under a grant

Several: private, often contrasted with common.

Several fishery: private fishery in a tidal estuary

Sheriff: royal officer responsible for shire, shire-reeve

Sheriff's tourn: view of frankpledge

Shewage: see scavage

Shire: division of England, the share allotted to a town

Slade: balk

Slave: human being as a chattel

Socage: tenure for base or agricultural services

Soil, right in: right of common to take minerals

Soscet: type of bondsman

Stallage: toll for right to keep a stall
Statute: law made by Parliament or some privileged corporation
Steward: official appointed by lord over manor, president of manor court
Stint: defined proportion of common, a stinted and gated pasture was regulated
Strip: length within open field belonging to one tenant
Subinfeudation: grant of inferior common freehold before 1290
Sub-manor: unit granted before 1290 out of manor carrying right to hold court
    baron
Substitution: assurance of freehold land whereby new tenant replaced old
    subtenant as holder of inferior tenement
Suit: obligation to attend, as suit of court, of mill
Suitors: manorial freeholders attending court baron
Surrender: release by copyholder to lord, normally subject to conditions
    including that the holding be regranted by admission, now used of transfer of
    leasehold to landlord which extinguishes it

Tenancy: legal description of holding
Tenant: holder of land under some lord
Tenement: land or other hereditament
Tenure: manner in which a tenement was held
Term: lease, period for which a lease endured
Terrier: list of tenements
Timber: wood of a specified minimum size and species
Time immemorial: 1189
Tithe: literally a tenth. Church due charged on land
Tithing: subdivision of a hundred, 10 hides, a vill
Title: legal evidence of right of property
Toll: franchise of right to charge members of the public in return for provision
    of a common service
Toll thorough and toll traverse: types of toll of way
Tributarius: Roman term meaning taxpayer, used of farmers bound to the land
    they owned
Trinoda necessitas: minimum services for bookland, comprising service in the
    royal army, repair of bridges and contribution to town defences
Tronage: toll by reference to weighing
Trust: arrangement whereby one person holds or administers land or other
    property on behalf of others
Turbary: right of common to take turf

Verge: strip of land along side of road
Vicar: substitute for rector in appropriated benefice
Vicinage: permission for beasts to stray from one common to another
View of frankpledge: supervision of vill, court leet

Vill: settlement

Villa: substantial Roman country house, later landed estate

Village green: piece of land within village where customary activities could be carried on

Villein: superior type of bondsman

Viscount: deputy for count

Waif: franchise of right to unclaimed property dropped by a thief in flight

Warren: franchise of right to take certain types of game

Warren: mound or place for keeping beasts of warren, especially rabbits

Waste: uncultivated, unoccupied land often subject to rights of common

Way: route over land used to get from one place to another

White rent: rent payable in silver

Will: legally expressed intention during life or after death

Woodland landscape: parts of England where land is divided into closes by hedges

Bibliography

LAW

Legal texts about manors have traditionally been entitled *Copyhold* and the text refers frequently to the books by Coke, Watkins and Scriven. Others of less authority are by Rouse (1837 and 1866), Shelford (1853), GW Cooke (1853) and Elton (1893). Most such books intended for lawyers are technical and difficult to follow but a clear readable text is by Benaiah Adkin published in 1919 and intended for surveyors with little legal background

A modern work which was indispensable is the comprehensive *Halsbury's Laws of England* which runs to over 100 volumes, particularly the titles on Copyhold, Commons, Custom, Ecclesiastical Law and Franchises. Legal dictionaries are also helpful, particularly *Stroud's Judicial Dictionary*. Some works on special subjects are referred to in the notes to the relevant chapters

The Law Commission is engaged in reform of the law and bringing it up to date. It operates by publishing summaries of the existing law based on considerable research with proposals for reform. As many of the topics covered in this book have been the subject of the Commission's attention its conclusions carry weight.

Much of the modern law is affected by land registration and the Land Registry publishes practice guides aimed at professional advisers which give their view on some aspects of the law.

HISTORY

A great many historical texts and articles touch on the manor in some way. A good general guide is Bennett, *Life on the English Manor*, although this is now somewhat outdated. The legal rules applied by the royal courts are set in historical context in AWB Simpson's *Introduction to the History of the Land Law*, although he has little to say on manors as such. Holdsworth's *History of*

English Law deals only incidentally with manors. That is now being replaced by the multi-author *Oxford History of the Laws of England*. The leading historian in the early history of manors was FW Maitland, especially *Domesday Book and Beyond*, and *The History of English Law* (known as *Pollock and Maitland*, although Sir Frederick Pollock contributed virtually nothing but his name). Maitland inherited a manor, trained as a barrister and lived when the manorial system was still (just) operating and even when he is writing about the eleventh century his side comments on later developments are illuminating. Some of his conclusions are now dated, but his understanding of the subject is unequalled. A standard source book which extracts several legal documents is Stubbs' *Select Charters* and a later work along the same lines, *Sources of English Constitutional History* by Stephenson and Marcham. There is also a good deal of general discussion in periodicals published by learned societies. Nearly all local history depends on manorial sources; indeed, many are simply histories of particular manors.

WORKS REFERRED TO

Abels, Richard P, *Lordship and Military Obligation in Anglo-Saxon England* (University of California Press, 1988)

Adkin, Benaiah W, *Copyhold and other Land Tenures of England* (Sweet & Maxwell, 1919)

Anglo-Saxon Chronicle (translation by GN Garmondsway) (JM Dent & Sons Ltd, 1972)

Aristotle, *Metaphysics* (c 330 BC)

Aristotle, *Physics* (c 330 BC)

Austin, J, *Lectures on Jurisprudence* (Campbell (ed)) (John Murray, 1885)

Bacon, Francis, *Works*

Beckett, John and Turner, Michael, 'End of the Old Order? FMLThompson, The Land Question, and the burden of ownership in England, c1880–c1925' (2007) 55 *Agricultural History Review* 269

Bennett, HS, *Life on the English Manor 1150–1400* (Alan Sutton, 1987)

Beresford, MW, 'Mapping the Medieval Landscape, forty years in the field', in SJR Woodell (ed), *The English Landscape, Past, present and future* (Oxford University Press, 1985)

Bettey, JH, *Manorial Custom and Widows' Estate*, Archives XX No 88 (October 1992)

Bettey, JH, *Wessex from AD 1000* (Longman, 1986)

Blackstone, Sir William, *Commentaries on the Laws of England* (http://avalon.law.yale.edu/subject_menus/blackstone.asp)

Blair, John, *Early Medieval Surrey: Landholding, Church and Settlement before 1300* (Surrey Archaeological Society, 1991)

Bloch, Marc, *Feudal Society* (English translation by LA Manyon) (Routledge Kegan Paul, 1961)

Bois, Guy, *The transformation of the year one thousand* (French edn, 1989) (English translation by J Birrell) (Manchester University Press, 1992)

Bowen, Catherine Drinkwater, *The Lion and the Throne. The Life and Times of Sir Edward Coke* (Little Brown & Co, 1985)

Bracton, Sir Henry (ed), *De legibus et consuetudinibus angliae* (c 1257) (SE Thorne (ed)) (Belknap Press of Harvard University Press, 1977)

Brandon, Peter and Short, Brian, *The South-East from AD 1000* (Longman, 1990)

Britton, *Containing the Antient Pleas of the Crown* (http://books.google.co.uk)

Burgess, Glenn, *The Politics of the Ancient Constitution* (The Macmillan Press Ltd, 1992)

Burnett, David, *A Royal Duchy* (Dovecot Press, 1996)

Butt, Ronald, *A History of Parliament, the Middle Ages* (Constable, 1989)

Carty, Peter, 'The ownership of fish', *Water Law*, July–August 1995

Cheyney, Edward P, 'The Manor of East Greenwich in the County of Kent' (1905) 11(1) *American Historical Review* 29–35

Chibnall, Marjorie, *Anglo-Norman England 1066–1166* (Basil Blackwell, 1986)

Chitty, Joseph, *A Treatise on the Law of the Prerogatives of the Crown and the Relative Rights and Duties of the Subject* (1820) (http://books.google.co.uk)

Clarke, HB, 'The Domesday Satellites', in Peter Sawyer (ed), *Domesday Book: A Reassessment* (Edward Arnold, 1986)

Coke, Sir Edward, *A commentary on Littleton being the first part of the Institutes of the Laws of England* (http://books.google.co.uk)

Coke, Sir Edward, *Complete Copyholder* (E Flesher et al, 1673)

Coke, Sir Edward, *The second part of the Institutes of the Law of England* (http://books.google.com)

Copenhaver, Brian P and Schmitt, Charles B, *Renaissance Philosophy* (Oxford University Press, 1992)

Coss, Peter, *The Knight in Medieval England 1000–1400* (Alan Sutton, 1993)

Customs and Excise, *VAT Notice 742B (January 1990) on Property Ownership*

Department for Culture, Media and Sport, *The Treasure Act 1996 Code of Practice* (2nd Revision 2007)

Department of the Environment, Food and Rural Affairs, *Common Land Policy Statement* (July 2002)

Dictionary of National Biography (Oxford University Press, 1975)

Dobson, Frank and Rainsford, Nick, 'An End to Feudalism – Labour's new
    leasehold reform programme' (Labour Party, October 1995)
Domesday Book (A Williams and GH Martin (eds)) (Penguin, 2002)
Donne, J, *Devotions upon Emergent Occasions* (1624)

Ellis, Mary, *Using Manorial Records* (Public Record Office Publications, 1994)
Encyclopaedia Britannica (Cambridge University Press, 11th edn, 1911)
Erskine May, *Treatise on the Law, Privileges, Proceedings and Usage of
    Parliament* (LexisNexis Butterworths, frequent editions)

Faith, R, *The English Peasantry and the Growth of Lordship* (Leicester
    University Press, 1997)
Fenwick, John, *Treasure Trove in Northumberland* (1851)
    (http://books.google.co.uk)
Fletcher, John, *Gardens of Earthly Delight: The History of Deer Parks*
    (Windgather Press, 2011)

Gadsden, GD, *The Law of Commons* (Sweet & Maxwell, 1988)
Galbraith, VH, *The Making of Domesday Book* (Oxford University Press, 1961)
Ganshof, Francois Louis and Verhulst, Adriaan, 'Medieval Agrarian Society in
    its Prime, France, the Low Countries and Western Germany', in MM Postan
    (ed), *The Cambridge Economic History of Europe Vol 1* (Cambridge
    University Press, 2nd edn, 1966)
Gelling, Margaret, *Signposts to the Past* (Phillimore, 2nd edn, 1988)
Gray, Charles Montgomery, *Copyhold, Equity, and the Common Law* (Harvard
    University Press, 1963)
Greven Jr, Philip J, 'Family Structure in Seventeenth-Century Andover,
    Massachusetts' (1966) 23(2) *The William and Mary Quarterly*, Third Series
    234

Hale, Sir Matthew, *The Prerogatives of the King* (Selden Society, 1976)
Hallam, Elizabeth, *Domesday Book through Nine Centuries* (Thames &
    Hudson, 1986)
Halsbury's Laws of England (Butterworths Lexis Nexis, 4th and 5th edns,
    various dates)
Hart, HLA, *The Concept of Law* (Oxford University Press, 1961)
Harvey, Sally PJ, 'Taxation and the Ploughland in Domesday Book', in Peter
    Sawyer (ed), *Domesday Book A Reassessment* (Edward Arnold, 1985)
Hemeon, M de W, *Burgage Tenure in Mediaeval England* (Harvard University
    Press, 1914)
Hey, David, 'Kinder Scout and the legend of the Mass Trespass' (2011) 59(2)
    Agricultural History Review 199

Hildebrandt, Helmut, 'Systems of Agriculture in Central Europe up to the Tenth and Eleventh Centuries', in D Hooke (ed), *Anglo-Saxon Settlements* (Basil Blackwell, 1988)

Hill, Sir George, *Treasure Trove in Law and Practice from the Earliest Time to the Present Day* (Oxford University Press, 1936)

Hill and Redman's Law of Landlord and Tenant (Butterworth Lexis Nexis, looseleaf, various dates)

Hilton, RH, *The English Peasantry in the Later Middle Ages* (Clarendon Press, 1975)

HM Revenue and Customs, *Inheritance Tax Manual 23194, Special valuation matters: Lordships of the Manor and Baronial Titles*

Hohfeld, WN, *Fundamental Legal Conceptions as applied in judicial reasoning* (Yale University Press, 1919)

Holdsworth, Sir William, *A History of English Law* (Sweet & Maxwell, 3rd edn, 1952)

Hoskins, WG, *The Making of the English Landscape* (Penguin Books, 1970)

Hoyt, Robert S, 'The Nature and Origins of the Ancient Demesne' (1950) 255 *English Historical Review* 145

Hutchinson, Lincoln, 'Roman and Anglo-Saxon Agrarian Conditions' (1983) 7(2) *The Quarterly Journal of Economics* 205

Hyams, Paul R, *King, Lord and Peasants in Medieval England* (Oxford University Press, 1980)

Jessel, Christopher, 'Customary Ways' (2009) *Rights of Way Law Review* 119

Jones, Philip, 'Medieval Society in its Prime: Italy', in MM Postan (ed), *The Cambridge Economic History of Europe Vol 1* (Cambridge University Press, 2nd edn, 1966)

Justinian, *Imperatoris Iustitiani Institutionum* (Oxford University Press, 1906)

Kirby, DP, *The Earliest English Kings* (Routledge, 1991)

Land Registry, *Landnet 25* (www.landregistry.gov.uk/professional/guides)

Land Registry Practice Guide 1, *First registrations* (www.landregistry.gov.uk/professional/guides)

Land Registry Practice Guide 18, *Franchises* (www.landregistry.gov.uk/professional/guides)

Land Registry Practice Guide 65, *Registration of mines and minerals* (www.landregistry.gov.uk/professional/guides)

Land Registry Practice Guide 66, *Overriding interests losing automatic protection in 2013* (www.landregistry.gov.uk/professional/guides)

Langdon, John, Horses, *Oxen and Technological Innovation* (Cambridge University Press, 1986)

Law Commission No 72, *Jurisdiction of Certain Ancient Courts*

Law Commission No 194, *Landlord and Tenant: Distress for Rent*
Law Commission No 199, *Transfer of land: Implied covenants for title*
Law Commission 254, *Land Registration for the twenty-first century: a consultative document*
Law Commission No 271, *Land Registration for the Twenty-First Century: a Conveyancing Revolution*
Law Commission No 327, *Making Land Work: Easements Covenants and Profits à Prendre*
Law Commission No 330, *11th Programme of Law Reform* (2011)
Law Commission, *16th Statute Law (Repeals) Report* (20 May 1998)
Law Commission, *Statute Law Repeals: Consultation Paper: Repeal of Turnpike Laws* (February 2010)
Loyn, HR, *Anglo-Saxon England and the Norman Conquest* (Longman, 2nd edn, 1991)

Maer, Lucinda and Gay, Oonagh, *The Royal Prerogative* (House of Commons Library SN/PC/03861 2009)
Maitland, FW, *Domesday Book and Beyond* (Cambridge University Press, 1987; first published 1897)
Mattingly, David, *An Imperial Possession: Britain in the Roman Empire* (Penguin, 2006)
McKitterick, Rosamond, *The Frankish Kingdoms under the Carolingians* (Longman, 1983)
McPherson, CBE, The Hon Judge BH, Judge of Appeal, Queensland, 'Revisiting the Manor of East Greenwich' (1998) 42(1) *American Journal of Legal History* 35–56
Megary, Sir R and Wade, H, *The Law of Real Property* (7th edn by Charles Harpum et al, 2008)
Miller, Edward and Hatcher, John, *Medieval England: Rural Society and Economic Change 1086–1348* (Longman, 1978)
Mills, Dennis R, *Lord and Peasant in Nineteenth Century Britain* (Croom Helm Rowman & Littlefield, 1980)
Ministry of Justice, *The Governance of Britain: Review of the Executive Royal Prerogative Powers: Final Report* (HMSO, 2009)
More, Sir Thomas, *Utopia* (various eds)
Muir, Richard, *The Lost Villages of Britain* (Michael Joseph Ltd, 1982)

Newsom, GH and Newsom, GL, *Faculty Jurisdiction of the Church of England* (Sweet & Maxwell, 2nd edn, 1993)
Newsom, GL, *Preston & Newsom's Restrictive Covenants affecting Freehold Land* (Sweet & Maxwell, 1998)
Nugee, EG (2008), 'The Feudal System and the Land Registration Acts' (2008) 124(4) *Law Quarterly Review* 586

Orlik, Michael, 'Roadside Waste and Manorial Waste', (2002) *Rights of Way Law Review* 2.2.35

Oxford English Dictionary (Oxford University Press)

Parain, C, 'The Evolution of Agricultural Technique', in MM Postan (ed), *The Cambridge Economic History of Europe Vol 1* (Cambridge University Press, 2nd edn, 1966)

Pease, JG and Chitty, H, *Law of Markets and Fairs* (Edward F Cousins and Robert Anthony (eds)) (Butterworths Lexis Nexis, 1984)

Pennington, Robert R, *Stannary Law* (MW Books, 1973)

Percival, John, *The Roman Villa* (Batsford, 1988)

Petit Larousse (Librairie Larousse, 1963)

Pitt Review, *Lessons learned from the 2007 floods* (National Archives website)

Poly, Jean-Pierre and Bournazel, Eric, *The Feudal Transformation 900–1200* (Holmes and Meier, 1991)

Pollock, Sir Frederick and Maitland, Frederic William, *The History of English Law before the time of Edward I* (Cambridge University Press 1898)

Powicke, Sir Maurice, *The Thirteenth Century 1216, 1307* (Oxford University Press, 1991)

Rackham, Oliver, 'Ancient Woodland and Hedges in England', in SJR Woodell (ed), *The English Landscape, Past, present and future* (Oxford University Press, 1985)

Rackham, Oliver, *Trees and Woodlands in the British Landscape* (JM Ltd, 1990)

Rackham, Oliver, *The Illustrated History of the Countryside* (George Weidenfeld & Nicolson Ltd, 1994)

Razi, Z and Smith, R (eds), *Medieval Society and the Manor Court* (Oxford University Press, 1996)

Reed, Michael, *The Age of Exuberance 1550–1700* (Paladin Grafton Books, 1986)

Reynolds, Susan, *Fiefs and Vassals* (Oxford University Press, 1994)

Roberts, Brian K, *The Making of the English Village* (Longmans, 1987)

Rothery, Mark, 'The wealth of the English landed gentry, 1870–1935' (2007) 55 *Agricultural History Review* 251

Round, JH, *Feudal England* (Longmans Green & Co, 1895)

Rowlands, Marie B, *The West Midlands from AD 1000* (Longmans, 1978)

Rowley, Trevor, *Villages in the Landscape* (JM Dent & Sons Ltd, 1978)

Rowley, Trevor, *The High Middle Ages* (Paladin Grafton Books, 1988)

Royal Commission on Common Land, Cmnd 462 (1958)

Sawyer, Peter, '1066–1086: A Tenurial Revolution?', in Peter Sawyer (ed), *Domesday Book: A Reassessment* (Edward Arnold, 1985)

Scriven, John, *A Treatise on the Law of Copyholds* (Butterworth & Co, 7th edn by Archibald Brown, 1896)

Select Committee on Environment, Food and Rural Affairs, Ninth Report, 14 July 2008

Shoard, M, *A Right to Roam: Should We Open Up Britain's Countryside* (Oxford University Press, 1999)

Simpson, AWB, *An Introduction to the History of the Land Law* (Oxford University Press, 1961)

Skyrme, Sir Thomas, *History of the Justices of the Peace* (Barry Rose Publishers, 1994)

Stephenson, Carl and Marcham, Frederick George, *Sources of English Constitutional History* (Harper & Row, 1937)

Stroud's Judicial Dictionary of Words and Phrases (Sweet & Maxwell, 5th edn by John S James, 1986)

Stuart, Denis, *Manorial Records* (Phillimore, 1992)

Stubbs, William, *Select Charters from the beginning to 1307* (Oxford University Press, 1942)

Tacitus, Cornelius, 'De origine et situ Germanorum' (c 98), in *Tacitus on Britain and Germany* (Penguin Books, 1948)

Taylor, Christopher, *Fields in the Landscape* (Alan Sutton Publishing, 1987)

Taylor, Christopher, *Village and Farmstead* (George Philip, 1983)

Thompson, EA, 'Zosimus 6 10 2 and the Letters of Honorius' (1982) 32(2) *The Classical Quarterly*, New Series, 445

Thompson, EP, *Customs in Common* (Merlin Press, 1991)

Thompson, FML, 'The Land Question, and the burden of ownership in England, c.1880–c.1925' (2007) 55 *Agricultural History Review* 269

Thompson, Michael, 'The land market, 1880–1925: A reappraisal reappraised' (2007) 55 *Agricultural History Review* 289

Tocqueville, Alexis de, *Ancien Regime* (English translation by John Bonner) (JM Dent & Sons Ltd, 1998)

Warman, Henry J, 'Population of the Manor Counties of Maryland' (1949) 25(1) *Economic Geography* 23

Warner, Peter, 'Shared churches, freemen church builders and the development of parishes in eleventh century East Anglia' (1986) 8 *Landscape History* 39

Watkins, Charles, *A Treatise on Copyholds* (James Bullock, 4th edn by Thomas Coventry, 1825)

Wheeler, George, 'Richard Penn's Manor of Andolhea' (1934) 58(3) *The Pennsylvania Magazine of History and Biography* 193–212

White, Lynn, *Medieval Technology and Social Change* (Oxford University Press, 1962)

Williamson, Tom, 'Explaining Regional Landscapes: Woodland and Champion in Southern and Eastern England' (1988) 10 *Landscape History* 5

Williamson, Tom and Bellamy, Liz, *Property and Landscape* (George Philip, 1987)

Yelling, JA, *Common Field and Enclosure in England 1450–1850* (MacMillan Press Ltd, 1977)

Index